LAND TENURE IN THE SOUTHWESTERN STATES

THIS STUDY WAS SPONSORED BY THE

SOUTHWESTERN LAND TENURE RESEARCH COMMITTEE

C. O. BRANNEN, *Chairman*

UNIVERSITY OF ARKANSAS

JOSEPH ACKERMAN, *Executive Secretary*

FARM FOUNDATION

O. D. DUNCAN

OKLAHOMA AGRICULTURAL AND MECHANICAL COLLEGE

LIPPERT S. ELLIS

BUREAU OF AGRICULTURAL ECONOMICS

L. P. GABBARD

TEXAS AGRICULTURAL AND MECHANICAL COLLEGE

B. M. GILE

LOUISIANA STATE UNIVERSITY

PETER NELSON

OKLAHOMA AGRICULTURAL AND MECHANICAL COLLEGE

FRANK J. WELCH

MISSISSIPPI STATE COLLEGE

The Social and Economic Significance of

LAND TENURE IN THE SOUTHWESTERN STATES

A Report of the

Regional Land Tenure Research Project

Edited by

HAROLD HOFFSOMMER, Director

The University of North Carolina Press

Chapel Hill

PRINTED IN THE UNITED STATES OF AMERICA
BY THE SEEMAN PRINTERY, INC., DURHAM, N. C.

Acknowledgments

To assign proper credit to those who contributed to the various phases of the following report is extremely difficult, if not impossible. As a thoroughgoing experiment in research cooperation, the written product of the Project represents a fusion of the work and thoughts of many people. In its beginning, the Project was envisioned by the Southwestern Land Tenure Research Committee[1] who conceived its general plan and subject matter content and continued throughout the Project in close touch with the work.

The Project was carried forward by the members of the Departments of Agricultural Economics and Rural Sociology in the Agricultural Colleges of the five cooperating states, representatives of the Bureau of Agricultural Economics, U. S. Department of Agriculture, and the special regional staff which gave full time to the effort.

The cooperating personnel functioned more or less in groups in accordance with the stage of Project development. Schedule committees, guided by the pattern developed by the Project as a whole, designed the schedules. Field workers collected the survey information, clerical and supervisory workers tabulated it, and six workers' conferences planned the type of tabulation and analysis to be made, and finally the materials were assembled into the following report. A number

[1] The following constituted the membership of the Committee at the time this report was written; C. O. Brannen, Chairman, University of Arkansas; Joseph Ackerman, Executive Secretary, Farm Foundation; O. D. Duncan, Oklahoma Agricultural and Mechanical College; Lippert S. Ellis, Bureau of Agricultural Economics; L. P. Gabbard, Texas Agricultural and Mechanical College; B. M. Gile, Louisiana State University; Peter Nelson, Oklahoma Agricultural and Mechanical College; and Frank J. Welch, Mississippi State College. Chris O. Henderson and E. R. Hensen successively represented the United States Bureau of Agricultural Economics, preceding Lippert S. Ellis. The Project Director was a member of the Committee from Louisiana State University until granted leave from that institution to become full-time director of the Project. Roscoe J. Saville also served on the Committee from Louisiana State University in the very early stages of the Project development.

of the regional staff members, since they were full-time Project employees, served in most or all of the above capacities. Those having major responsibility for writing specific chapters of this report are as follows:

Chapter I. The Problem and the Region
HAROLD HOFFSOMMER and HARALD PEDERSEN

Chapter II. Tenure and the Farm Organization
HOWARD J. STOVER

Chapter III. Tenure and Family Status
MERTON D. OYLER

Chapter IV. Factors Related to Changes in Tenure Status
RALPH J. RAMSEY

Chapter V. Leasing Arrangements and Landlord-Tenant Relationships
RALPH J. RAMSEY

Chapter VI. Land Tenure and Soil Conservation
O. HOYLE SOUTHERN

Chapter VII. Legal Aspects of Land Tenure and Farm Credit
ERLING D. SOLBERG

Chapter VIII. Use and Sources of Capital
RALEIGH BARLOWE

Chapter IX. Impacts of Federal Programs on Tenure
J. JOE REED

Chapter X. Community and Institutional Factors in Tenure
MERTON D. OYLER

Chapter XI. Summary and Conclusions
HAROLD HOFFSOMMER

The entire report was edited by the Project Director.

As indicated above, the data presented in this report result from the close cooperation of a great many people. The personnel of the committees who developed the farm and family field schedule was as follows: Joseph Ackerman, Desmond Anker, Roy A. Ballinger, Frank Barlow, Raleigh Barlowe, Alvin L. Bertrand, Robert Bowlus, C. A. Bonnen, M. S. Brooks, J. L. Charlton, Chris Henderson, E. L. Langsford, A. C. Magee, Don A. Marshall, Robert McMillan, T. J. McNeeley, Joe R. Motheral, W. G. O'Leary, Otis Osgood, Herbert Pryor, Ralph J. Ramsey, R. J. Saville, W. H. Sewell, T. J. Standing, Howard Stover, Frank J. Welch, Paul Williamson, W. T. Wilson, and Martin Woodin.

The following persons, apart from members of the regional staff, were members of one or more of the six workers' conferences: Joseph Ackerman, Oscar F. Allen, Desmond Anker, Robert Bowlus, P. N. Bragg, J. L. Charlton, K. C. Davis, Marshall Harris, T. R. Hedges, Steen C. Lemon, A. C. Magee, Don Marshall, Robert McMillan, D. Gray Miley, J. Lambert Molyneaux, Joe R. Motheral, W. G. O'Leary, Otis Osgood, Julien Tatum, and H. P. Todd.

The regional staff personnel resident at and working full time in the regional office for either a part of the Project or for its duration were as follows: Harold Hoffsommer, Director; Howard Stover, Statistician and Agricultural Economist; Merton Oyler, Rural Sociologist; Ralph Ramsey, Associate Rural Sociologist; Harald Pedersen, Assistant Rural Sociologist; J. Joe Reed, Agricultural Economist; I. W. Moomaw, Associate Agricultural Economist; Raleigh Barlowe, Assistant Agricultural Economist; Luther Bohanan, Assistant Agricultural Economist; Harold Scoggins, Assistant Agricultural Economist; and Betsy Castleberry, Junior Statistician.

In addition to the above, Hoyle Southern and Erling D. Solberg of the Bureau of Agricultural Economics, U. S. Department of Agriculture, were associated full time with the regional staff for a part of the Project's duration.

To the members of the regional staff special acknowledgment is due since, as full-time employees on the Project, they are largely responsible for the organization of the regional materials herewith presented. Incident to the period of its operation which began in the summer of 1942, the Project experienced an unusual personnel turnover because of World War II conditions. To Mr. Ramsey, who was connected with the Project from its early planning to its conclusion, special acknowledgment is due for competence on all phases of the Project work and particularly for his contribution in carrying forward the tabulations and statistical analysis when these tasks were relinquished midway by others because of military service. Although not a resident member of the regional staff, the Project wishes to express appreciation to Marshall Harris, of the United States Bureau of Agricultural Economics, for helpful counsel throughout the Project.

Special recognition is also due those who performed the arduous and exacting task of collecting the field data. Because of the length of the schedule and the intricacy of the questions, special emphasis was placed on this phase of the work. Apart from the regular members of the regional staff, the following persons contributed to this phase of the Project in one or more of the five states: William H. Alexander, Eugene Arrington, Mrs. Jeannette Barlowe, J. Allan Beegle, Walter H. Bennett, Robert E. Bowlus, Charles W. Bowman, Peter N. Bragg, M. S. Brooks, F. A. Buckley, Gordon E. Burks, K. C. Davis, R. K. Dupree, R. L. Fisher, Marvin Guin, T. R. Hedges, James F. Hudson, William Hudson, Lonette L. Jones, E. C. Jones, A. L. Johnson, Mrs. A. L. Johnson, Sandor B. Kovacs, A. C. Magee, Robert T. McMillan, Donald Marshall, Blanche Mears, Murphy Mears, Luis F. Moore, Joe Motheral, William McClung, S. E. McCoy, H. L. McCracken, W. E. McCullough, John U. Nelson, Mrs. Hazel O'Leary, W. G. O'Leary, Otis Osgood, Raymond E. Page, Herman J. Putman, Maurice Ray, Wendell Rollins, H. L. Slaughter, L. A. Sprain, Murray Thorn, H. P. Todd.

The Project is deeply grateful to the farm families of the region who so generously contributed the survey information, to the county and state officials, and to many other community and neighborhood leaders for facilitating the work.

The Project itself, in view of its cooperative nature, would of course have been impossible without the close collaboration and cooperation of the five state agricultural colleges in the survey states. Especial mention should be made of the University of Arkansas, which furnished office space for the regional staff during the first year of the Project and served as disbursing agency for the Project funds through its entire operation.

The Project was made possible through the generous grants of the General Education Board and the Farm Foundation. To the late A. R. Mann and other officials of the General Education Board, the Project is deeply grateful for wise counsel and encouragement throughout. Likewise to Joseph Ackerman and other officials of the Farm Foundation the Project is indebted for continuous encouragement, guidance, detailed work, the cooperation incident to the professional phases of the Project, and for making available the services of Agnes Lorentzen for work on the manuscript. Those who worked on this Project were drawn from several research institutions but this report is not presented as an official publication of those institutions. The participants in the Project are presenting this report as the product of the joint effort for which they are responsible as a group.

These acknowledgments cannot be closed without mention of appreciation for the painstaking work done by the regional clerical staff headed by Florence Bowman. Acknowledgment is also due Alberta Broyles, secretary and administrative assistant in the regional office, for her diligence in attending to the business detail of the Project and for her attention to the final closing out of the Project business following the disbanding of the regional staff.

To all of the above and to the many others contributing to this undertaking whose names have not been mentioned, the Project owes a debt of gratitude for the fine spirit of cooperation and workmanship without which a venture of this kind could not have attained success.

HAROLD HOFFSOMMER.

Contents

Figures

LAND TENURE IN THE SOUTHWESTERN STATES

CHAPTER I

The Problem and the Region

Land tenure, which pertains to the conditions under which landed property is held and used by individuals, groups of individuals, or governments, has been a subject of concern since the beginning of agriculture itself. Influenced by changing social, economic, and political situations its forms have undergone constant adjustment. Nevertheless its basic problems, revolving as they do around the rights in the use of land and in the instruments of agricultural production, remain surprisingly similar through historic changes and among varying cultures.

PROBLEMS OF LAND TENURE

Within the broad framework of tenure considerations, certain problems of especial significance have emerged in the United States during the past several decades. Notable among these is the rapid increase in tenancy and the decrease in equity of farm operators in the land they cultivate.[1]

An increasing number of farm families, though owners, have attained only a semblance of ownership and in many instances have even lost their equities and returned to a tenant status. At the same time the transition from tenant to owner appears to be increasingly difficult. Furthermore a considerable segment of the farm population has not reached a stage of economic and social advancement where it is even in a position to aspire to ownership.

On the other hand it has become increasingly evident that the farm groups whose current relationship to the land is unsatisfactory are not all tenants, any more than the relationship of all tenants to the land is unsatisfactory. In general, however, unsatisfactory tenancy

[1] For a general statement of tenancy problems, see *Farm Tenancy,* Report of the President's Committee, Prepared Under the Auspices of the National Resources Committee, Washington, D. C., February, 1937.

relationships touch such a great number of farm families that the security of the whole rural life structure is affected. Crucial concerns at the present time relate to tenants, croppers, farm laborers, families on submarginal land, families on farms of inadequate size, owner farmers greatly in debt, and farm young people unable to obtain farms. But with modern technological advancement, both as it applies to farming methods and to the industry of the country as a whole, radical adjustments are becoming mandatory for the entire agricultural population. This project was concerned particularly with the impact of these problems on cotton farming and the culture pattern surrounding it in the Southwestern Region.

NATURE OF THIS STUDY[2]

Purpose

Briefly stated, the purpose of the study herein presented is to determine and measure the relationships between the tenure status of the farm family and its economic and social performance.

The intent is neither to condone nor criticize what is found but simply to show the effect of tenure factors on the social and economic accomplishments of the farm family. On the basis of the relationships thus established it is planned that a separate policy statement will be developed translating into suggestions for social action those items which appear to need rectifying. The present report however is restricted to a statement of the incidence of these relationships without regard to their evaluation in terms of welfare.

ITEMS OF INQUIRY

It is readily evident that the performance of a farm family may be considered from many angles. The question immediately arises therefore as to which of these performances are related to tenure, and

[2] Additional reports developed from this study: (1) Harold Hoffsommer, *Regional Research Cooperation, A Statement of Regional Research Procedures as Developed by the Regional Land Tenure Research Project*, University of North Carolina Press, Chapel Hill, 1949. Among other items the following are treated in this report: objectives of regional research; the project working plan; the project organization methods of data collection; departmental background in cooperating institutions; formulation of schedule; schedule of committee meetings; schedule of instructions; schedule additions; plan of field work; editing and tabulation of data; problems of comparability between states; decisions on what and how to tabulate; difficulties of tabulation; workers' conferences; returning data to cooperating states; cooperation with Bureau of Agricultural Economics; state reports; regional reports; administrative arrangements; selection of headquarters; problems of handling finances; functions of project director, the regional staff, and the regional committee; and general suggestions from the experience of the project regarding regional research cooperation. (2) Report on Tenure Policy by the Southwestern Land Tenure Research Committee (in process). (3) For a list of the thirty-eight reports either published or in process by the cooperating states see *Regional Research Cooperation*, pp. 133-36, cited under (1) above.

if related, to what extent? In order to test these relationships, the study covers a wide variety of items, among others: attaining ownership, leasing arrangements, division of inventories, receipts and expenditures between landlord and tenant, land organization, crop production and disposal, livestock production and disposal, farm equipment, use of labor, receipts and losses, tenure history, labor organization, credit, household and family composition, housing, household equipment, levels of living, migration and mobility, various types of social and economic participation, and institutional and community relationships. In addition to the above fields of inquiry, specialized work was done on the legal aspects of tenure and the impacts of certain government programs.

A second type of inquiry concerns the problem of classifying tenures. Unless the various types of tenures can be classified into relatively homogeneous groups, they cannot be effectively related statistically to the various performance characteristics of the farm families. This has proved to be a particularly perplexing problem of which more will be said later.

SPECIAL CHARACTERISTICS

The present study differs from most other studies in several respects:

1. The research was carried on cooperatively by the tenure research workers of the region. That is to say, the actual work of formulating the project, collecting the data, and carrying forward the analysis was done cooperatively through regional workers' conferences with the coordination of a regional staff. The research workers in the five agricultural colleges of the region, that is, Arkansas, Louisiana, Mississippi, Oklahoma, and Texas, pursued the study themselves. This is in contrast to the type of regional study in which the work is all done from the central agency.

2. The essential phases of the subject matter inquiry and study procedure were uniform throughout the five states. After agreement as to the common regional tenure problems, uniform information was collected with the use of identical survey schedules, excepting for minor adjustments to fill the needs of the different subareas.

3. A further distinctive feature of the study inheres in its utilization in combination of several subject matter fields, principally land economics, farm management, and rural sociology, although specialists in law and government were also regular members of the regional staff. Realizing that the problems of tenure cut across all

these fields their subject matters have been fused. The principal problems of tenure were set up, after which the respective subject matter fields addressed themselves to those angles of the problems for which their training and subject matter tools made their work effective. Throughout the tabulation and interpretation of the data there was a relatively complete fusion of these several approaches, so that the conclusions of any one subject matter field were reached only after consultation and in the clear light of the findings of the other approaches. In fact, the tabulations for all of the data were carried on simultaneously and all subject matter fields were equally represented in determining the plans and procedures of analysis. The central focus of this approach was not that of land economics, farm management, or rural sociology but rather that of the tools of these several disciplines which were concentrated on the single subject of tenure. The effect of this was to break down compartmentalization and to view the problem as a whole rather than from a restricted angle which would inevitably have resulted had a single subject matter discipline approached so broad a problem.

TERRITORIAL SCOPE

The territorial scope of the study comprises the five-state area of Arkansas, Louisiana, Mississippi, Oklahoma, and Texas.[3] The term *region* as used in this study does not necessarily imply a homogeneous area although it is assumed that these five states have much in common by virtue of their cotton economy. Within the general framework of this economy the study emphasis is upon subregions rather than upon the region as a whole. These subregions transcend state lines but represent sufficient homogeneity to make comparisons desirable and at the same time sufficient diversity to make such comparison suggestive and stimulating.

There is no attempt to justify the region as a homogeneous area excepting in a very broad way. It should further be indicated that the cotton area of the South extends far beyond the bounds of the present study. Apart from the cotton economy which dominates the entire area under study, the chief bond of unification is a functional one, that is, a determination among the social science research workers of the area to pool their resources in a program of research cooperation in an effort to throw new light upon their common problems.

The chief subregions within the five-state area are shown in

[3] The Southwestern Land Tenure Research Committee did not include representatives from Mississippi until this project was formed.

Figure 1. It will be observed that they frequently transcend state lines. Since the limitations of the study made it physically impossible to sample all subregions within the region, certain selections were made based upon (1) availability of existing data in the subregion (2) importance of the subregion in the region as a whole and (3) number of states interested in the subregion in question. On this basis the following subregions were studied:

Western Coastal Plain (Arkansas, Louisiana)
Eastern Coastal Plain (Mississippi)
Rolling Plains (Oklahoma)
Blackland Prairie (Texas)

In addition to the above subregions which were covered by the regional intensive survey, the University of Arkansas did a follow-up study on labor and certain other tenure aspects in the Delta, Coastal Plain, and Ozark-Ouachita areas using an adapted form of the regional schedule.[4]

Several areas other than those actually studied were included in the original plan but later dropped because the task of collecting the data in the areas first studied proved to be more time consuming and expensive than had originally been anticipated.[5]

STUDY PROCEDURE

Sample counties within each of the subregions were selected for intensive survey. The counties selected were statistically typical, so far as could be ascertained from census information, of the subregion for the major items under consideration. However, since so many items of information involved in the survey were not available in the census it became impractical to attempt a complete statistical jus-

---

[4] Otis T. Osgood and John W. White, *Land Tenure in Arkansas, IV, Labor Used on Cotton Farms*, 1939-1944, University of Arkansas, Agricultural Experiment Station Bull. 459, August, 1945. This report is a follow-up of three previously published Arkansas Experiment Station bulletins on the subject of land tenure, Nos. 384, 397, and 438.

[5] These areas were:

Coast Prairie (Louisiana, Texas)
Loessial Uplands (Arkansas)
Cross Timbers (Oklahoma)
Delta (Arkansas, Louisiana, Mississippi)

The Coast Prairie and Loessial Uplands (Grand Prairie) represent the rice-areas in the states of Louisiana, Texas, and Arkansas. While the original study plan contemplated some work in the Delta—an obviously important area in the cotton economy of the South—this work was not to be stressed since it was thought that this area represents unique conditions, not applicable to other sections and in addition relatively more work had already been done here than in the other areas. The Delta work planned for both Arkansas and Mississippi represented follow-ups of previous studies. In Louisiana it concerned the small farm economy in the new ground sections.

tification of the county selections. Moreover, the sample was not selected with the intention of describing the universe of the sample area as a whole but rather to get sufficient numbers in the various tenure groups so that relationships could be established between tenure status and performance.

It cannot be overemphasized that the survey data herewith presented are not intended to convey a description of the area as a whole but rather to show the relationships between the particular factors under consideration. By way of illustration, regional tables showing numbers of sample cases by tenure groups in the area do not necessarily imply that the percentage of families in the given tenure groups represent the correct proportion of families in those groups for the area as a whole. What these data are intended to show is the relationship between the tenure groups with respect to the item in question. It would have been practically impossible to have selected the proper number of cases in each tenure group so that it would have been proportional to such cases in the area as a whole, since some of the new tenure classes into which the cases were divided in the analysis could not be anticipated in advance.

These comments with respect to sample representativeness and adequacy apply to the regional analysis but may or may not apply to reports worked out in the individual states on the basis of data collected for the Regional Project. In some of the states the samples are assumed to be representative of the subregion or farming area in question. In others by proper weighting the sample may become representative. These correction factors were not applied in the rather complex regional analysis partly because of the statistical difficulties involved but more especially because of the analysis, emphasis is on relationships rather than area description. Furthermore, the general descriptions of the areas are already available from census and other materials.

As already indicated, the sample areas within the states were determined on the basis of subregions within the region as a whole. Therefore, the sampling may be properly referred to as regional rather than state in scope. The detailed method of selecting the actual cases to be interviewed within the stipulated areas, however, was left to the discretion of the individual states, save for certain general guides.[6] Chief among these was the emphasis that the study is primarily one of relationships rather than the description of a universe, hence

[6] Harold Hoffsommer, "Organization and Objectives of the Regional Land Tenure Research Project," *Journal of Farm Economics*, XXV, No. 1 (February, 1943), 255.

the necessity of getting sufficient cases in the categories to be compared regardless of their numerical importance in the general population. A further suggestion concerned the use of some form of block sampling since a part of the study deals with the interactions of families associated with one another in neighborhoods and communities.

Within the broad framework of the regional plan, each state determined the particular methods which best suited its needs. For example, in Arkansas and Texas certain minor type tenure situations were omitted from the sampling in order to lay greater stress on the major situations. The state differences have not appreciably limited the regional usefulness of the materials. In fact, they have rather enhanced it since the uniformities are sufficient for regional use and at the same time bring out a wider range of data than would have been possible had the procedure as between the states been entirely uniform.

In all states the emphasis for sampling was the family, not the farm. This means that the tenure history is largely that of the family, not the farm. Several of the states limited the sample to farm families while others enumerated families with nonfarm occupations and owners who rented out the major part of their farms.

All of the questions as stated on the schedules were asked all cooperators in so far as they applied. Among other things this meant that the operations of croppers whose names fell within the sample were handled in the same manner as the operations of tenants and owners. This does not mean however that croppers were considered to be managing operators but rather that the same measures were applied to them as to renters with a view of determining the extent to which, if any, they have the qualities of operators.[7] On the other hand, where operators in the sample have croppers on their land, the croppers are considered to be a part of the larger operating unit. Where operators have renters on a part of their land however, the

[7] The tabulation of cropper and laborer data gave rise to considerable difficulty. Early in the Project it was decided, after some discussion, that croppers and laborers should be included in the study of tenure, since they are regarded as an integral part of agricultural operations. But both schedule taking and tabulation difficulties arose from the fact that most farm management measures have not been adjusted to cropper and laborer situations, since the concern of farm management heretofore has been with management and operation, which normally excluded croppers and laborers. Since the present study undertakes to include all farm families, regardless of management status, certain new problems are introduced. These consist basically of applying economic measures to non-managing tenant, cropper, and laborer families, rather than regarding such families simply as labor items in a larger farming operation. Such treatment demands a tenure history approach to all agricultural workers, whether managers or non-managers. Although the tenure workers of the region are in essential agreement on this point, awareness of the problem came too late to include certain items on the schedule which would have been helpful.

land operated by such renters is not considered a part of the larger operating unit. The final decision as to which acreages were included in the farm (cropped out) and which were not included (rented out) was left to the decision of the cooperator after the enumerator had explained the point of view and defined the terminology used in the study. This having been decided, all other schedule items applied to the acreage included in the farm.

SAMPLING METHODS

Arkansas. The Arkansas sample consists of a contiguous area of Coastal Plain type soil in Nevada, Columbia, and Union counties. Excluded from this were bottom land areas along the Missouri, Ouachita, and Dorcheat rivers, and the areas of concentrated oil development, mainly forest lands. Communities only partially within the sample area were also excluded. By the use of community and neighborhood maps alternate neighborhoods were selected for the primary sample.

By a stratified, purposeful type of sampling the object was to get one hundred cases in each of five major tenure groups: white owners, white renters, Negro owners, Negro renters, and Negro croppers. In addition, all white croppers, known to be few in the area, were interviewed but the resulting number of cases proved insufficient for extended statistical analysis.

From the 1940 census it was estimated that a coverage of one-sixth of the white owners and one-third of the other major tenure classes would approximate the 100 schedules desired for each type.

The first task in the field procedure was to identify all neighborhoods of the area. This was accomplished through the use of school and church records, county newspapers, directories, maps, and through the assistance of county officials and agents. In several instances it was necessary to make reconnaissance trips into the localities to identify particular neighborhoods. Schedule takers, with the assistance of long-time residents in the area, listed the names of the farmers by race and tenure for each neighborhood. From this list every sixth or third name was selected for interviewing.

Substitutions of alternate neighborhoods were made in several instances to meet the requirements of the sample. Also in one county several neighborhood substitutions were made in order to reduce the amount of travel. Of a total of 87 neighborhoods in the sample area of the three counties, schedules were taken in 46, of which 7 were alternate neighborhoods.

In order to compute representative averages and thereby describe the tenure universe in the sample area under consideration, the following weightings should be applied to the number of cases interviewed: white owners, 2; white renters, 1; white croppers, 1/3; Negro owners, 1; Negro renters, 1; Negro croppers, 1.

Louisiana. Following conferences with members of parish agricultural planning committeemen and other planning groups of the Extension Service the following community centers conventionally used for extension and other meetings were selected: Lincoln Parish, Hilly; Bienville Parish, Bryceland; Winn Parish, Gaar's Mill; Jackson Parish, Weston.

The selection of cases within these communities was based on complete enumeration of the rural population regardless of tenure status or occupation. Interviewing began at the community center and progressed outward. Approximately 100 schedules were taken in each area. The cases interviewed are identified with one or the other of the thirteen minor trade centers within the community areas in question.

Mississippi. Jefferson Davis and Marion counties in the Longleaf Pine Area of Mississippi were selected as sample areas. Using neighborhood and community maps prepared by the Agricultural Extension Service, 20 sample neighborhoods were selected by taking every fifth neighborhood in Marion County and every fourth one in Jefferson Davis. The neighborhoods were first numbered from left to right and several trials were made to get areas which were not contiguous and areas which represented different type situations of tenure, soils, type of farming, race combinations, and opportunity for off-farm employment. Some of the neighborhoods as delineated were relatively large in area and population. These were divided, by noting the clustering of houses on the map, into areas approximating 20 houses each. The selection of these sub-neighborhoods was based on chance.

This procedure resulted in eleven areas in Marion and nine in Jefferson Davis County with a calculated total sample of 400 cases. An attempt was made to interview every family,[8] regardless of tenure status, within the selected areas.

Oklahoma. The Oklahoma sample consisted of a quadrangle

[8] In several instances where the operations appeared to be separate, two schedules were taken on one household. In another instance, one schedule covered the activities of two households because the operations and finances were so closely related that they could not be separated.

shaped area approximately thirty miles wide by fifty-five miles long and comprised the total of Jackson County, Looney Township in Harmon County, Tilley and Quartz Townships in Greer County, Mountain Park Township in Kiowa County, and Hunter, Maguire, Hazel and Richmond Townships in Tillman County. The plan was to sample the entire rural population irrespective of occupation or tenure status. To this end a grid method of sampling was applied which utilized a series of diagonal and cross lines drawn across the map of the quadrangle shaped area at four-mile intervals. Schedules were to be taken on the two families living closest to each line intersection.

It was originally hoped that a sample of farm operators living in villages might be included by this method but as the plan worked out, none of the points fell within the town limits of a village and no substitutions in this regard were made. The general sampling plan, however, was modified within the area of the proposed Altus-Lugart Irrigation Project where three instead of two schedules were taken at each intersection.

Texas. The area chosen was that of Bell County which represents the Blackland Prairie. The Blacklands of Bell County are not contiguous and for this sample only that part located in the northeastern part of the county was selected. Although erosion varied somewhat, it was attempted to keep the variation in soils within the sample area at a minimum. The sample was further restricted by limiting it to certain size groups based on acres in cropland and selected tenures as indicated by Agricultural Adjustment Administration records. In addition, certain materials were available from a former study in the area.[9]

The selection of individual cases was done entirely from Agricultural Adjustment Administration records and considerable time and effort was spent in securing the sample. All 1941 Agricultural Adjustment Administration records for farms clearly within the Houston clay soil area and not on the outskirts of Temple were pulled from the files. Corrections were made for splits and combinations of work sheets. This resulted in 1222 work sheets from which data on specific crops and land uses as well as tenure, total acres in cropland, name, address, and location were listed on prepared forms. Farms which lay only partly within the sample area were discarded. Partnerships, nonresident operators, and clear cases of estate operatorship were elimi-

[9] B. H. Thibodeaux, C. H. Bates, and C. A. Bonnen, *Farm Business Report, Elm Creek Watershed, Black Prairie Area, Texas, 1933.* Division of Farm and Ranch Economics, Texas A. & M. College, April, 1937.

nated as being unusual type cases. Those farms of less than fifteen acres of cropland were eliminated as not being bona fide farming operations. Cash renters and "cropper operators" were eliminated as not being numerically significant. This left four tenure groups—full owners, part owners, share renters, and share-cash renters. All farms were then classified by acres in cropland into three groups—15-60, 60-120, and over 120 acres. Part owners with less than 60 acres and share-cash renters with over 120 acres were dropped because the group was not numerically significant. This process resulted in a ten category sample.

Within each category Tippett's Tables of Random Numbers was applied to determine the order of sampling. After the sample was selected, those farmers interviewed in the previous study referred to above were given preference at the top of each list. This method of sampling was intended to give an adequate sample of the major type situations in the sample area. The sampling was by farms rather than by farmers. For example, if an operator who was on a farm in 1941 as shown by the Agricultural Adjustment Administration records had moved and a new farmer was on the place in 1942, the new farmer was interviewed. The actual sample varies somewhat from the plan because of changes in size of farm and tenure of operator between the years 1941 and 1942.

The cropper and laborer sample included all croppers and laborers who were on the operating units selected by the above procedure.

Comparison Between States. Apart from the mechanical differences in sampling procedures among the states, they also differ, as may be noted above, in sampling objectives. Arkansas and Texas tended to concentrate on the usual type tenure cases with the view of building up statistically valid samples for these type situations. Unique cases were, therefore, sometimes excluded from the sample. On the other hand Louisiana, Mississippi, and Oklahoma tended to include all classes of tenures, some of which were unique and variant from the common types. To adequately describe some of these variant cases considerable information additional to that requested by the schedule is necessary. In some instances the interviewers obtained this extra-schedule information, in others they did not.

To this observation it should be added that the numerically less important tenure types of the present may be the emerging significant types of the future. Furthermore, it is from these variant cases that new clues for more satisfactory tenure arrangements are frequently obtained.

Therefore, although the sampling procedure of the states was not uniform, the variations probably enrich rather than limit the value of the data as viewed from the regional standpoint, particularly since the objective of the regional analysis was focused upon the study of relationships rather than upon area description. Thus groups of special types of cases, not now sufficiently numerous for valid statistical analysis, are useful either for case studies or for retention pending the addition of similar cases to the sample for future statistical analysis.

FIELD WORK, TABULATION, AND REPORTS

As previously indicated, a major objective of the study was that of devising a method of regional research cooperation which is the subject of a separate report. Since the study was regional in scope, combined several subject matter fields, and was carried forward on a cooperative basis between the five states by means of a regional office, the procedures were quite different in many respects than those conventionally used in studying subject matter of this kind.

In general the cooperative aspect of the study ramifies throughout the project procedure. The entire project was under the sponsorship of a regional committee. The general objectives of the study were drawn up by this committee after which a schedule committee from the five states was appointed to draw up a survey schedule. After three meetings covering a period of time a schedule was turned over to the regional committee which, with certain changes by the committee, was adopted as the regional schedule to be applied to the sample area in each of the fives states.

The collection of the schedule data was under the immediate jurisdiction of the states with the regional office acting as the coordinating agency. Following the collection of the data they were sent to the regional office for tabulation, these tabulations being outlined in general at a series of tenure workers' conferences. The tabulations were done in the regional office with the use of punch card machines. Duplicate copies of the data were sent to the states. The tenure workers in the states utilized these data for individual state reports and the workers in the regional office utilized the same materials for this regional report. The original project plan contemplated that the state reports would be available for reference and use in writing the regional report. However, due largely to the war emergency during the project period, the timing of the work was such that it was necessary to write the regional report before the completion of most of the state analyses.

PROBLEM OF ESTABLISHING TENURE RELATIONSHIPS

Classification of Tenure Types

It has already been indicated that the purpose of this study is to establish relationships between tenure status and performance factors. To accomplish this it becomes necessary to define the various types of tenure status with great care. A survey of the tenure literature of the region indicates that the tenure classifications used in the various studies, not to mention their definition of the specific types, vary greatly. Probably the chief conclusion that may be gathered in this regard from these studies is that tenure classification depends on the objective of the study and on the nature of the data utilized in the analysis. There is, therefore, no single classification which has been accepted by these studies as suitable for general use.

Apart, however, from arriving at a single over-all tenure classification, these studies all contribute to better understanding of the individual factors of importance in the tenure arrangement, which is the key to the classification approach of the present study. A brief summary, therefore, follows indicating the classifications used in the various studies within the region as well as those in the census.

Census Classifications. The study of land tenure may be approached from the standpoint of the land or from the standpoint of the people on the land. In the first instance, all land is classified according to the arrangements governing the use of the individual parcels of land. In the second instance, all people associated with the land are classified according to the arrangements governing their use of the land.

The census of agriculture follows the first approach. Historically, it was initiated to supplement the population census with data on the use and distribution of land. Though the terminology was changed to "owners" and "tenants" in the reports for 1900 and has so continued in each census report since, the operator's tract and not the operator is the unit of enumeration.

The major classification of farm operators into owners and tenants has been used, and defined consistently, by the census of agriculture since the first enumeration so that the changing importance of each group can be studied back to the first enumeration.[10] In 1900 owners were subdivided into four groups: (1) owners (2) owners and tenants (3) part owners and (4) managers. The second group included only

[10] *Cash Rent,* Agriculture Census of the United States, 1940, Washington, 1944, p. 133.

those farms that were "joint operated" by an owner and a tenant receiving a share of the produce—usually a father-son relationship. This group was recognized in the instructions for enumerators in 1910, but they were included with full owners in the tabulations for the reports of that year. From 1910 through 1940 the classification of owners into the three subgroups (full owners, part owners, and managers), all of which were classified as owner farms prior to 1900, has been consistently followed in each report.

The division between cash and share tenants which was established in 1880 was continued through 1900. In 1910 "share-cash" and "unspecified" tenants were reported separately. The tenant group was further subdivided in 1920 when standing renters and croppers were reported separately in the South. In the North and West standing renters were included with cash tenants. With these additions for 1920 the census reports showed four categories of tenants for the North and West and six categories for the South. In the 1930 census, classifications were consolidated and the reports for the North and West included only cash and "other" tenants and the reports for the South cash tenants, croppers, and other tenants. In 1940, however, tenants were again subdivided with reports for the North and West including cash, share-cash, share, and other tenants, and for the Southern states croppers were added to the above classification. A persistent difficulty in interpreting census data in the South has been that cropper tracts have been regarded by the census as farms. A primary objection to this procedure is that it obscures the plantation organization and gives an erroneous picture of agricultural practices in the South. The plantation is a unified agricultural organization of considerable size under one management, of practically a continuous tract of land, operated as a single unit with respect to the method of control of labor and products, all of which may be worked by wage hands, or all or a part of which may be subdivided and let to croppers. It is practically always devoted to the production of a staple crop.[11] The labor force available to operate a plantation may include wage hands, croppers, and tenants.

Tenure Studies in the Southwestern Region. At the beginning of this survey there had been made in the five states of the region 48 major studies[12] which either pertained to tenure outright or used

[11] C. O. Brannen, *Relation of Land Tenure to Plantation Organization*, U. S. Department of Agriculture Bull. 1269, Washington, 1924.

[12] See Appendix, p. 649, for a list of these studies.

tenure as a focal point of analysis. Nearly every study includes recommendations for the improvement of tenure conditions but six publications primarily enumerate problems and suggest possible remedies. The remaining 39 studies are primarily descriptive. Ten of these describe the states in terms of tenure, 5 study the credit facilities available to the various tenure groups, 12 analyze sociological factors in terms of tenure, 1 deals with leases, 5 pertain only to farm laborers, and 6 are farm management studies of labor organization on the farm (3 of this last group pertain exclusively to the plantation). Legal studies, analyses of the laws pertaining to agricultural land tenure, have been made in Arkansas, Oklahoma, and Texas.

The descriptive studies may be further subdivided on the basis of the tenure categories used in describing the area of study. Seventeen studies include laborers as a tenure category. In 20 studies croppers are isolated as a separate tenure category apart from other tenants. In one study croppers are grouped with laborers. Two studies use the tenure category "cropper-laborer," which is defined as "a member of the plantation labor force who cultivates some crop acres on a share basis the same as croppers, but who also works for day wages in the operator's crops for 50 percent or more of his annual income."[13]

In the pioneer study of land tenure in Arkansas, Nourse uses the two major categories of owners and tenants. He cautions against misinterpretation of the data due to the inclusion of sharecroppers in the figures for tenants, pointing out that "this is highly misleading when comparisons are made between northern and southern states . . . since the cropper is virtually a laborer hired by the landlord at a wage which consists of a guaranteed living plus a premium in case the crop yields a surplus." Nourse continues that "it is doubtful whether the cotton acreage on which one family can do the hand labor can be organized economically," concluding that five families constitute the smallest efficient economic unit for cotton farms, thus emphasizing the economic holding as more important to the welfare of the farmer than the manner in which the land is held. Likewise, it is pointed out that ownership is not always the most desirable tenure status since it frequently restricts the farmer to an enterprise too small for efficiency and frequently retards rather than stimulates his economic progress.[14]

---

[13] Frank J. Welch, *The Plantation Land Tenure System in Mississippi,* Mississippi Agricultural Experiment Station Bull. 385, June 1943, p. 7. See also Otis T. Osgood and John W. White, *Land Tenure in Arkansas, IV, Labor Used on Cotton Farms, 1933-1944,* Agricultural Experiment Station Bull. No. 459, August 1945, p. 5.

[14] E. G. Nourse, *A Preliminary Survey of Land Tenure in Arkansas,* University of Arkansas Bulletin, Vol. 13, No. 11, Fayetteville, 1919.

Size was also combined with tenure, as a control factor, in the credit studies in Arkansas. It was observed, "The costs of seasonal credit to the large plantation farmer compares favorably with similar costs in other regions of the country, but costs of seasonal credit to the small farmer (both owner and tenant) place him at a disadvantage in the sense that farmers in many competing sections are able to control the necessary capital at lower costs."[15]

Two social studies of land tenure in Arkansas use only the two way classification of owners and tenants in the general analysis of the data. Each arrives at a new grouping of farmers based on performance, age, and status. Metzler classifies farmers into four groups: (1) those who had always been owners (2) those who had always been tenants (3) those who had moved from tenancy to ownership and (4) those who had dropped from ownership to tenancy. However, after having set up the groupings he observes that the past performance of the individual has little effect on present practices. Farmers who had risen to ownership tended to adopt the farm practices of owners, and farmers who had dropped from ownership to tenancy tended to adopt the practices and business habits prevailing among tenants.[16]

A later Arkansas study also begins with the two tenure categories but arrives at the conclusion that both renting and owning have distinct meanings at different stages of the tenure cycle. In the early stages renting provides farming experience and the means by which some capital may be saved for the purchase of a farm. The young renter behaves as a prospective owner but the older renters have accepted renting as a permanent status. The families that remain in the renter status do not have the security of those in the owner status. There is no evidence that the families who remain renters, instead of investing income in farm ownership, use it to enhance the level of family living or the advancement of their children. The operation of the tenure process selects operators not only of the ability to accomplish the objective of farm ownership but to translate farm resources into higher level of living and performance in the community.[17]

In the analysis of the tenancy situation in Arkansas upon which

[15] B. M. Gile and A. N. Moore, *Farm Credit in a Plantation and an Upland Cotton District in Arkansas*, Arkansas Agricultural Experiment Station Bull. 228, June 1928, p. 43.

[16] Wm. H. Metzler, *Relationship of Tenure to Farming Practices, Family Life, and Community Participation of Farmers in Upland Areas of Arkansas*, Department of Rural Economics and Sociology, University of Arkansas, Preliminary Report, February 1940.

[17] J. L. Charlton, *Social Aspects of Farm Ownership and Tenancy in the Arkansas Ozarks*, Arkansas Agricultural Experiment Station Bull. 471, September 1947, pp. 78-80.

the delineation of tenancy areas was based, tenants were classified into two broad groups: (1) those whose major contribution to production is labor, commonly referred to as sharecroppers, and (2) all other tenants who provide their own workstock and equipment and are referred to as renters.[18] In subsequent studies in the same series, pertaining to labor organization and tenure change, the tenant categories of share renter, sharecropper, and wage laborers were used. The fourth study in the series concludes "present trends indicate that the most common type of share cropper in mechanized production will be a combination cropper and wage laborer who uses the same production methods on his own cotton as on the operator's crop. . . . It seems evident therefore that, as farmers gain more experience in the use of labor-saving equipment, and as this equipment is made more adaptable to cotton production and harvesting, hand labor and the usual forms of tenure of laborers will continue to decline in importance on an increasing number of cotton farms, both upland and lowland."[19]

In analysis of sugar cane farms in Louisiana the labor force on the farm is classified under two groups of laborers (1) the resident laborer residing in quarters on the farm and (2) the nonresident laborer who works on the farm largely during the harvest or cutting season. The analysis points out that "the position of the resident laborer on the sugar farm is analogous to that of the share cropper on the cotton farm, excepting that the former is paid wages rather than a share of the crop and works on the farm at large rather than on an acreage assigned particularly to him."[20]

Another study in Louisiana divides farm tenure into three major classes: ownership, tenancy, and labor. Tenants are further subdivided, on the basis of the amount of management performed, into independent, semi-independent, and dependent tenants. The seven indices used to measure the landlord's control over the tenant were: (1) the frequency of supervision (2) the landlord's part in marketing the tenant's

[18] J. A. Baker and J. G. McNeely, *Land Tenure in Arkansas, I. The Farm Tenancy Situation*, Arkansas Agricultural Experiment Station Bull. 384, January 1940.

[19] Otis T. Osgood and John W. White, *Land Tenure in Arkansas, IV. Labor Used on Cotton Farms*, 1939-1944, Arkansas Agricultural Experiment Station Bull. 459, August 1945, p. 31. See also J. G. McNeely and Glen T. Barton, *Land Tenure in Arkansas, II. Change in Labor Organization on Cotton Farms*, Bull. 397, June 1940, and J. G. McNeely, Glen T. Barton, and Trimble R. Hedges, *Land Tenure in Arkansas, III. Income and Changes in Tenure Status of Share Renter, Share Croppers and Wage Laborers on Cotton Farms*, Bull. 438, June 1943.

[20] Harold Hoffsommer, *The Sugar Cane Farm*, Louisiana Agricultural Experiment Station Bull. 320, June 1940, p. 63.

share of the crop (3) the tenant's freedom to work other than for the landlord (4) the presence of a commissary on the farm (5) proportion of production credit supplied by the landlord and the tenant (6) the landlord's part in supplying credit for the tenant's living expenses and (7) nearness of the landlord's residence to the tenant's farm.[21]

Variations in tenure categories utilized in the analysis of data, resulting from a difference in approach to the subject are illustrated in three plantation studies in Mississippi. The most extensive classification is used by Welch, who includes the planter or owner, the manager, the sharecropper, share tenant, cash or standing tenant, cropper-laborer, wage worker, and seasonal laborer.[22]

Langsford and Thibodeaux, discuss the plantation from the standpoint of labor organization and use of the land. Their primary interest is in labor force used and they group the members of the labor force under four groups: Sharecroppers, share tenants, cash tenants, and wage laborers.[23] In the third plantation study Boeger and Goldenweiser set out to analyze the tenant systems prevailing on the plantation. In the analysis they classify the tenant systems in three categories: Sharecropper, share renter, and cash renter.[24]

Several level of living studies made in Mississippi use tenure as a control in the analysis. In one study tenure is combined with the quality of soil. The comparisons between owners on poor soil and croppers on rich soil indicate that "owner (farm) families had on the whole somewhat higher incomes than did cropper families, but the greatest difference in these two groups was not in the amount of income but in the source of income. The croppers had a larger proportion of their income in the form of cash derived from the sale of crops; the owners had a larger part of theirs in the form of farm furnished goods and in cash from work off the farm."[25]

[21] Ralph J. Ramsey and Harold Hoffsommer, *Farm Tenancy in Louisiana,* U. S. Department of Agriculture, Bureau of Agricultural Economics, February 1941, also Ralph J. Ramsey, *Criteria for Classifying Louisiana Tenants,* Master's Thesis, Louisiana State University, June 1940.

[22] Frank J. Welch, *The Plantation Land Tenure System in Mississippi,* Mississippi Agricultural Experiment Station Bull. 385, June 1943, p. 7.

[23] E. L. Langsford and B. H. Thibodeaux, *Plantation Organization and Operation in the Yazoo-Mississippi Delta Area,* U. S. Department of Agriculture Technical Bulletin No. 682, May 1939.

[24] E. A. Boeger and E. A. Goldenweiser, *A Study of the Tenant Systems of Farming in the Yazzo-Mississippi Delta Area,* U. S. Department of Agriculture Bull. 337, January 1916.

[25] Dorothy Dickins, *Owner Farm Families in Poor Agricultural Areas and Cropper Farm Families in Rich Agricultural Areas,* Mississippi Agricultural Experiment Station Bull. 359, June 1941, p. 3.

An analysis of social factors related to farm ownership made in Oklahoma was initiated with the assumption that "agriculture and the nation are best served when a goodly proportion of those who till the land own the acres they work." The study concludes that "individual initiative and effort are the most important elements in the achievement of farm ownership at the present time. However, the study shows that farmers will need assistance at the hands of the public, particularly in the form of enlarged credit facilities, if farm ownership is to increase relatively in the future." Observing that the early social background of heads of families engaged in agriculture exerts a dominant influence in determining the tenure status, the classification of owner and nonowner is supplemented for purposes of analysis with a further subdivision based on the tenure of parents. On this basis the study reveals that farmers whose parents were landless only rarely become farm owners themselves and farmers whose parents were landowners achieve farm ownership in far greater than expected proportions.[26]

Where census data were used in the analysis of tenure groups in Oklahoma, sharecroppers and farm laborers were generally combined because it was observed that "legal, social, and economic distinctions do not justify separate treatment."[27]

In the general analysis of tenancy in Oklahoma and in description of tenancy areas in the state, the classification of tenants used by the census has been utilized. The owner groups and laborers are omitted from the discussion.[28]

In an analysis of farm ownership and tenancy in the Texas Blackland Prairie, Sanders observed in 1922 that on the basis of prevailing economic factors it would take the average share tenant 28 years to pay for the farm he was operating. Continuing he stated: "The different tenure stages function not only as stepping stones in tenure progress but they function also as selective agencies, tending to

---

[26] Robert T. McMillan and O. D. Duncan, *Social Factors of Farm Ownership in Oklahoma,* Oklahoma Agricultural Experiment Station Bull. B-289, November 1945, p. 3. See also Robert T. McMillan, "The Relationship of Selected Social Background Factors to Farm Tenure Status," *The Southwestern Social Science Quarterly,* March, 1943.

[27] Robert T. McMillan, *Migration and Status of Open-Country Families in Oklahoma,* Oklahoma Agricultural Experiment Station Technical Bull. T-19, September 1943, p. 7. and T. Lynn Smith, "The Agricultural Population: Realism vs. Nominalism in the Census of Agriculture," *Journal of Farm Economics,* Vol. XX, August 1938.

[28] John H. Southern, *Farm Tenancy in Oklahoma,* Oklahoma Agricultural Experiment Station Bull. 239, December 1939 and John H. Southern, *Farm Tenancy Areas in Oklahoma,* U. S. Department of Agriculture, Bureau of Agricultural Economics, October 1944.

keep the operators of least ability in the lower stages. . . . The group of operators who accumulated wealth most rapidly included those who had been most consistent in the application of their time to operating farms, had the most diversification of farm enterprises, raised the largest amount of family food on the farm, and moved least frequently from farm to farm." The analysis was based on four tenure groups—owners, owners additional, share tenants and sharecroppers—as defined by the census of agriculture.[29]

In delineating the tenancy areas for Texas an "Index of Nonownership" was used which was the ratio of nonowners to all farm workers. The category nonowners included sharecroppers, other tenants, and resident farm laborers. A subsequent analysis of tenure in Texas omits laborers from the tenure groups and discusses the tenure trends in terms of the census definition of farm operators. The data indicate that croppers and other marginal workers with the weakest attachments to the land were affected to a greater extent than other tenure groups by the reduction in number of operators between 1930 and 1940.[30]

TENURE CLASSIFICATIONS UTILIZED IN REGIONAL STUDY

It is evident that the studies mentioned above do not follow a consistent pattern of tenure classification. Each study classes tenure according to its particular purposes and according to the data available. What then are the guideposts of classification for a comprehensive study such as the present one which has as its object the statement of relationships between pure tenure factors and performance?

Several observations may be made. In the first place, generalizations based solely on a comparison of the performance of the conventional tenure groups can hardly yield significant results in terms of tenure relationships. It is not enough to compare the performance of owners and renters as groups. It is in addition necessary to know the factors which make for any difference in performance that may be noted. Such factors may or may not be casually related to either ownership or tenancy. That is to say, the observed performance might be achieved within the pattern of either tenure status.

It therefore becomes necessary to isolate the practices of operators

[29] J. T. Sanders, *Farm Ownership and Tenancy in the Black Prairie of Texas*, U. S. Department of Agriculture Bull. 1068, May 1922, p. 4.

[30] Joe R. Motheral, *Type of Farm Tenancy Areas in Texas*, U. S. Department of Agriculture, Bureau of Agricultural Economics, October 1941; and Joe R. Motheral, *Recent Trends in Land Tenure in Texas*, Texas Agricultural Experiment Station Bull. 641, June 1944.

regardless of their tenure status and to note the end result of such practices. A given type of performance yields given results regardless of the tenure status of the operator. By setting up the conventional tenure groups first and making them the basis of all further analysis it becomes impossible to discern the practices which are essentially tenure connected and those which would function much the same regardless of the tenure group in which they are employed. Without such knowledge of the cause and effect relations of individual factors, the results of the comparisons of broad tenure groups are largely without meaning, since in the final analysis all that can be said is that an owner, for example, performs as he does because he is an owner. Actually his owner status covers a variety of performances some of which are related to ownership and some of which could be practiced under another tenure status. Although establishing relationships between given types of tenure performance and their results has been a constant goal of the present analysis, it is a goal which has been only partially achieved.

As a second general observation it may be said that although it is desirable to relate individual factors as indicated above, it is also desirable, particularly because of terminology difficulties and because of the existing sources of data, that some general and broad tenure classification be utilized. It should of course always be borne in mind that when using such a classification great care should be exercised in drawing generalizations. Tables set up on such a basis need to be interpreted in the light of tabulations on related factors.

The procedure of the present study constitutes the use of a modified conventional tenure grouping together with a great variety of sorts and cross tabulations. The effect therefore is that of an individual factor analysis of some detail combined with a semi-conventional tenure classification for table presentation purposes. Because of its unusual scope and subject matter coverage, the study has exceptional opportunities in the utilization of such a method.

The general tenure classification used is as follows:[31]

Full Owners. Those having title to all the land included in their operating unit and operating such land under their direct supervision. Those owning land and renting it out with little control over its operation were classified as nonfarm (landlords).

Part Owners. Those who own part and rent part of their operating unit. Ownership of a farmstead only was not considered to consti-

[31] See statistical tables 1 and 2 in the Appendix.

tute part ownership. However, if the operator owned a farmstead with some cropland in a cash crop and rented additional acreage, he was classified as part owner. The renting of any land was sufficient to classify an owner as part owner. In the main, part owners are owners of sizable tracts, renting additional land in varying amounts. An exception occurs in Mississippi, however, where about one-half of the Negro part owners in the sample were croppers on their rent tract. They are essentially croppers who own their farmsteads and a small amount of cropland. The characteristics of these part owners in Mississippi were found to be more like Negro croppers than like Negro owners.

Share Renters. Those paying a share of the crop as rent, either one-third and one-fourth, straight one-third, or straight one-fourth. Shares on alfalfa and peanuts on these farms usually varied from the others.

Share-cash Renters. Those paying share rent *and* cash rent either at a rate per acre or a flat sum. Share-cash renters in the Texas sample paid combinations of share and cash on the same rent tract. This practice was followed to a lesser extent in the Oklahoma sample. Most of those so classified in the other samples paid cash rent on one tract and share rent on a second tract. In parts of the analysis that follows, straight cash and standing renters are included in this category.

Croppers. The usual definition is followed, comprising those receiving a share of the production and owning no equipment or workstock. The share received (and paid the landlord) is usually one-half. Croppers in the Coastal Plain samples were full-time croppers. In the Texas Blackland Prairie sample the croppers belong more in a cropper-laborer category since all did wage work for their landlord and received about as much income from that source as from their share in the crop. As stated above the Negro part owners in the Mississippi Coastal Plain sample were essentially croppers who owned a little land. Two of the Oklahoma Rolling Plain croppers sampled were operating croppers. The others were essentially farm laborers who were given a share in the production of designated acreages of cotton or a share in the income from the sale of dairy or poultry products. They commonly received one-half of the milk or eggs sold.

Other Tenants. Classed under this heading were those who paid no rent or had peculiar rental arrangements which did not permit their classification into one of the other categories. For example, one farmer paid one-half share on 5 acres of cotton for the use of workstock and equipment while on the remainder, which also included cotton, he paid the customary one-third and one-fourth share.

Indeterminate Tenure. This does not follow a census classification. It was used for those cases of farm operators who were owners in prospect on at least a part of the land they operated. Their rent, if any, was usually not paid in the conventional manner. Nearly all of them paid the taxes and upkeep on the land. Some of them took care of the person in whose name the deed was filed, usually a close relative. It was understood that the operator would eventually be given a full title to the land but the change had not been made at the time of the enumeration. One such case had paid off the other interested parties and had been given a deed which had a clause in it stating that he was to pay his mother one-third and one-fourth rent as long as she lived in addition to providing her with food and shelter. In another case, enumerated in the late summer of 1943, the titleholder (an uncle) had died intestate in the previous January. In settling the estate, it was found that there were closer heirs, and the nephew was not allowed the expected inheritance, yet he continued to operate the land. In Louisiana it is possible for the legal title in land to be held by a deceased person for a long period of time. Under such arrangements, the heirs may operate the land as owners but are restricted in selling and mortgaging. Such limitations to ownership called for a separate tenure category. In addition to these complications of title, some of these operators owned and rented additional land.

Nonfarm. This includes all persons enumerated who were employed full time at a nonfarm occupation but had varying amounts of farming activities. These varied from no farm operations to full time farms. Others were owners of farms but rented out all or nearly all of the acreage.

Other Tenure Classifications. While the tenure classifications, as defined, were used for the majority of tabulations, the groups have been combined also into the owner and nonowner categories. In three states, Arkansas, Louisiana, and Mississippi, these categories were made separately for the racial groups, white and Negro. In Texas, ethnic characteristics were combined for some tables with tenure as a major classification.

In addition to the over-all classification of tenure following the census definition, the families were classified according to amount of equity in the farm operation as expressed in terms of dollars and as a percentage of total valuation. Kinship to landlord was coded for all farmers who leased land, including part owners. Degree of dependence on the farm was measured in terms of labor used on the farm as a percentage of total family labor applied during the year and farm income as a percentage of total income. Also tabulated was the type of landlord as measured by occupation, color, sex, kinship, and age for individuals and distance to residence from farm and frequency of supervision for both the individual type and a limited number of corporate types of landlords. Sixteen items were combined to construct an index of division of management between landlord and tenant.

In the consideration of leasing arrangements, a division of management index was computed for each lease. For example, a share-cash tenant might have share-cash arrangements on each of two leases or might have a share on one and cash on the other. In addition part owners were classified by method of rental payment along with full renters and croppers. In the study of leasing arrangements the lease was considered to be the unit of measure rather than the operator.

TENURE BACKGROUND IN THE SOUTHWESTERN STATES

The purpose in this section is to describe the Southwestern Region in terms of the trends which resulted in the social and economic situation prevailing at the time this survey was made in 1942. The current situation is presented in terms of 1940 census data and, where pertinent, is related to the situation in other areas of the United States and to the general situation in the nation. Differences within the region are pointed out. The sample survey areas are emphasized in the description, though not to the exclusion of other areas. A brief survey of the physical characteristics and of the historical development of the area is included along with a statement of the general characteristics of farming and farm family living in the region.

Physical Divisions

The Southwestern Region includes the five states of Texas, Oklahoma, Arkansas, Louisiana, and Mississippi covering an area of 478,249 square miles, which is approximately one-sixth of the total land area of continental United States. The area lies in four major topographical divisions—the Gulf Coastal Plain, the Interior Plain, the Interior Highlands, and the Inter-Mountain Plateau. (Figure 1)[32]

Climate

The Southwestern Region is subject to a wide range of climatic conditions. The average annual precipitation for southwest Texas is less than 10 inches, and for southeastern Louisiana and Mississippi it

[32] See Frederic B. Loomis, *Physiography of the United States*, New York, 1947, for a complete discussion of the physical division and characteristics of the region.

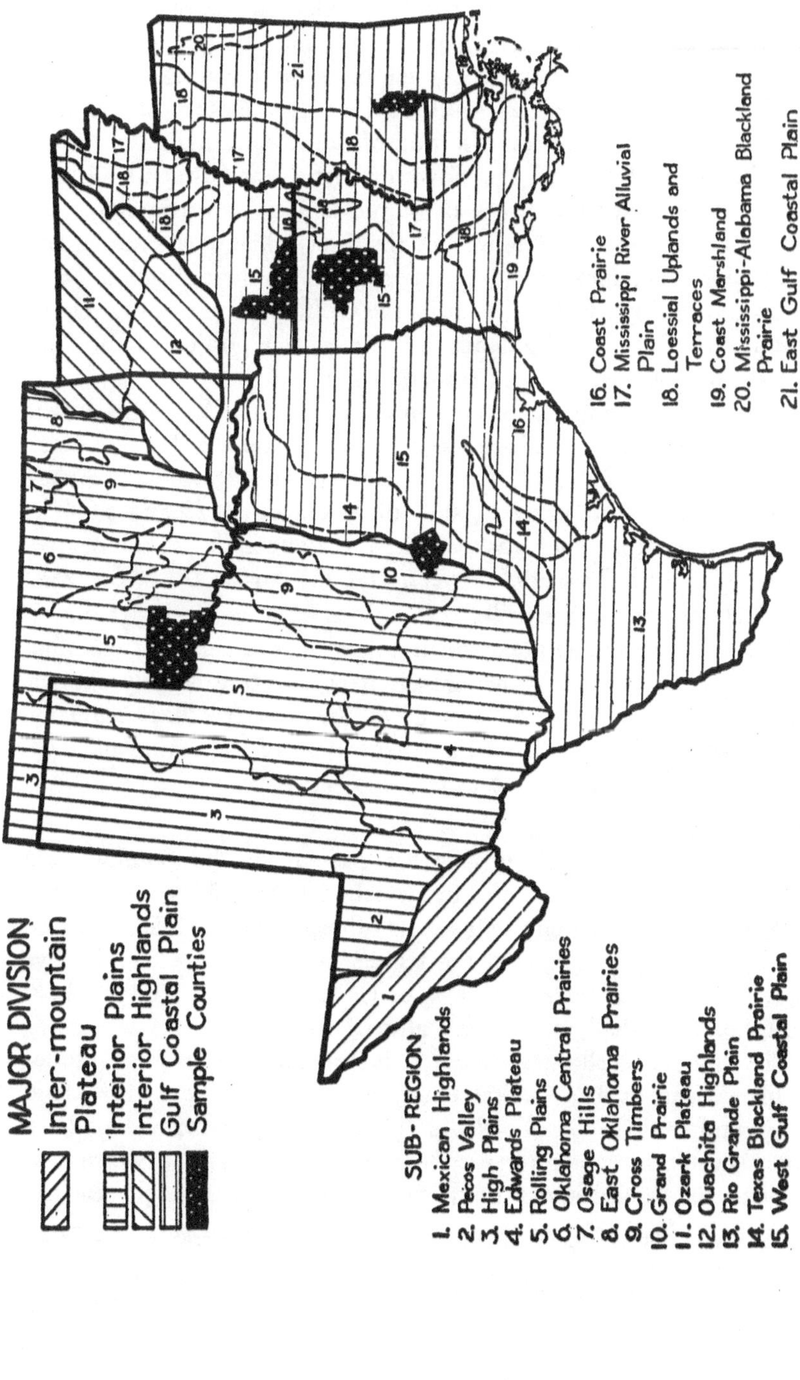

Source: Major physical divisions and subregions adapted from Fenneman and others.

FIGURE 1. Major physical divisions, subregions, and sample counties of the Southwestern Region.

is over 60 inches. Four of the five climatic zones utilized in describing the climate of the United States are found in the region.[33]

The Mexican Highlands and the Pecos Valley are in the arid zone. The semiarid zone is a band about 150 miles wide through the Texas and Oklahoma Panhandles southward to the mouth of the Rio Grande, including the western section of the Rolling Plains, all of the High Plains, and most of the Edwards Plateau and the Rio Grande Plain. The eastern edge of the subhumid zone is approximately on a line along the western extremity of the East Oklahoma Prairies and the Interior Highlands extending due south from there through Texas and swinging slightly east as it nears the Gulf. The rest of the region, including the Interior Highlands and the greater portion of the Gulf Coastal Plain, is in the humid climatic zone.

Temperatures range from an annual average of 55 degrees in the Texas and Oklahoma Panhandles to 70 degrees on the Texas, Louisiana, and Mississippi Gulf Coast. January averages for these areas are 35 and 55 degrees, respectively, and July averages are 85 and 80. The highest temperature ever observed in the Panhandle is 115 degrees and on the Gulf Coast 105 degrees, and the lowest, 20 below zero, and 10 above zero respectively.

Not only are the winters much colder in the inland areas than along the coast but the growing season is also considerably shorter. The coastal regions have an average of 300 frost free days annually. In contrast, the Panhandle and northern areas of the region have between 180 and 200 frost free days.

Soils

Several associated soil groups are present in the Southwestern Region. They range from the fertile alluvial soils of the Mississippi Delta to the shallow, stony soils of the lithosol group in the arid west. Broadly speaking, the soils of the region can be described under five major soil groups; red and yellow podzolic, rendzina, reddish chestnut, lithosols or shallow soils, and alluvial soils.[34]

The red and yellow podzolic soils predominate in the Interior Highlands and on the Coastal Plain, excluding the Texas Blackland Prairie and the Rio Grande Plain. These soils were formed under a native vegetation consisting predominantly of pines in a warm-temperate to subtropical and humid climate. They are strongly leached,

[33] The data on climate are taken from *Climate and Men Yearbook of Agriculture*, 1941, Washington.

[34] Information about the major soil groups has been drawn primarily from the section, "Soils of the United States," in the *Yearbook of Agriculture*, 1938, Washington.

acid in reaction, and low in organic matter and mineral plant nutrients. The surface soils are prevailingly light colored and sandy and the subsoils are heavier, tougher, and of red, yellow, or mottled color. Though low in inherent fertility they are easily tilled and respond readily to fertilization. Norfolk, Ruston, and associated soils are the most prevalent subgroup in the region.

Rendzina soils are prevalent in the Mississippi-Alabama Blackland Prairie, the Texas Blackland Prairie, the Grand Prairie, a large area of the Rio Grande Plain, and the southern portion of the Cross Timbers in Central Oklahoma. The surface soils are dark-gray, black overlying soft light-gray, or white highly calcareous subsoils. The parent materials are chalk, soft limestone, or marl and the soils may be regarded as immature. The dark color is derived from large amounts of black organic matter from a grass vegetation. Houston soils are dominant on the Texas Blackland Prairie and Austin, Denton, and associated soils are prevalent on the Grand Prairie in Central Oklahoma. Sumter, Vaiden, and associated soils prevail in the Mississippi-Alabama Blackland Prairie and the soils of the Victoria and Goliad varieties predominate on the Rio Grande Plain.

The reddish chestnut soils are developed on the grassy plains from southern Kansas south through Oklahoma and Texas to the Gulf of Mexico. In the region they are found primarily on the Rolling Plains and the High Plains with smaller areas on the Rio Grande Plain. The surface soils are typically dark reddish brown to red in the upper part and lighter or grayer in color and highly calcareous in the lower part. The soils have a relatively high inherent fertility, but the low rainfall and the high rate of evaporation tend to limit plant growth. Miles-Vernon and St. Paul-Abilene are the most prevalent associated soil groups on the Rolling Plains, while Duval-Webb soils prevail on the Rio Grande Plain, and Amarillo, Greensberg-Pullman-Richfield, and Zita-Pullman associated soil groups are found on the High Plains.

Lithosols and shallow soils are dominant on the Edwards Plateau and in the Mexican Highlands, and, though not dominant, they are present in numerous areas of the High Plains and Rolling Plains, particularly along the eroded transition border between these two subregions. This is a group of soils varying greatly in character and degree of soil development, nature, depth of soil and soil material, and in external features of relief, stoniness, and drainage. For the most part they are soils on rough hilly or mountainous terrain. They are stony in many places, and commonly have little soil development and no definite profile. In some areas there is practically no native vegetation, in others there is a sparse cover of grass, and in still others the vegetation consists largely of brush or thin open stands of small trees. The chief use of the land is for livestock range, though in some areas it has scenic and recreational value.

Alluvial soils, though they occur throughout the region, are most prevalent on the Coastal Plain. The largest area is along the Mississippi River in Arkansas, Louisiana, and Mississippi. In addition there are the rather broad plains along the Arkansas and Red rivers and along the Rio Grande, and numerous smaller areas on the flood plains and first bottoms of the smaller streams that dissect the Coastal Plain. These soils are for the most part inherently fertile and, where properly drained and protected from overflow, are highly productive.

TYPE OF FARMING

The farmer's adjustment to his physical environment results in a more or less uniform pattern of agricultural practices within a given area. Soil fertility and climatic conditions influence the selection of crops and general farm organization. Topography is a determining factor in mechanization. Distance to market, differential freight rates, trends in the world market for specific agricultural products, and government agricultural programs affect the general pattern of land utilization.

Agriculture in the Southwestern Region is widely diversified. It ranges from the commercialized fruit and vegetable enterprises and large cotton farms to the self-sufficing farm. There are highly mechanized farms where nearly all the work is done with machinery and there are farms where the cropper and his mule are the primary source of labor and power as they have been for nearly a century.

Agricultural specialists in the five states have delineated 66 types of farming areas for the region. These comprise 18 major types of farming areas in Texas, 16 in Oklahoma, 9 in Arkansas, 13 in Louisiana, and 10 in Mississippi. (Figure 2)[35]

Cotton is grown in nearly all parts of the region. (Figure 3) In over half of the areas delineated and described cotton is the dominant enterprise and in 53 of the 66 areas cotton is mentioned as a

[35] Discussion on type of farming is drawn from state maps, published by the state agricultural experiment stations for the separate states. Since the work of delineating and describing these areas was done independently in each state, the boundaries for similar and contiguous areas in adjoining states do not always meet at the state lines. This is due in part to the dissimilar weighting given the various items used in delimiting the areas in the several states. Furthermore, delineation followed county lines in some instances and minor civil divisions in others.

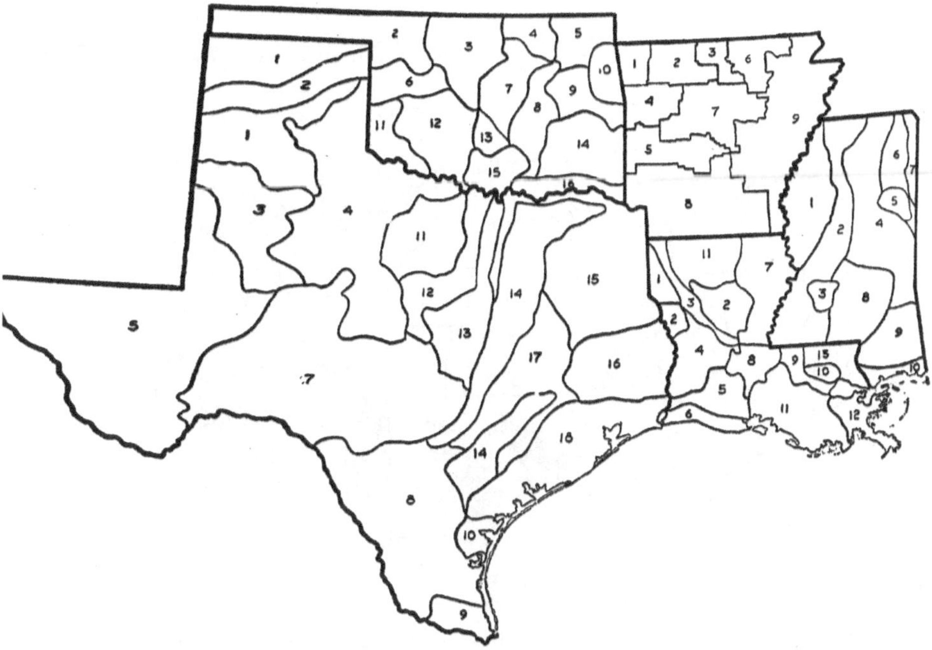

Source: Type of farming maps made by the State Agricultural Experiment Station Staffs in each state

FIGURE 2. Type of farming areas in the five states of the Southwestern Region.

ARKANSAS
1. Northwest Arkansas
2. Northwest Ozark
3. North-Central Ozark
4. Upper Arkansas Valley
5. Ouachita Mountain
6. Northeast Ozark
7. Central Arkansas
8. South Coastal Plain
9. Delta

LOUISIANA
1. North Louisiana Upland Cotton Area
2. Central Louisiana Cutover Pine Area
3. Red River Delta Area
4. Cutover Flat Woods Area
5. Louisiana Rice Area
6. Cameron Parish Cotton Area
7. Mississippi Delta Cotton Area
8. Central Louisiana Mixed Farming Area
9. Brown Loam Mixed Farming Area
10. Louisiana Strawberry Area
11. Sugarcane Area
12. New Orleans Dairy, Trucking, and Fruit Area
13. East Louisiana Cotton and Dairy Area

MISSISSIPPI
1. Yazoo-Mississippi Delta
2. Brown Loam Area
3. Copiah Truck Area
4. Clay Hills or Shortleaf Pine Area
5. Oktibbeha Dairy Area
6. Mississippi-Alabama Black Prairie
7. Upper Coastal Plains
8. Longleaf Pine Area
9. Lower Coastal Plains
10. Gulf Coast Area

OKLAHOMA
1. Cash Grain and Livestock
2. Livestock and Cash Wheat
3. Cash Grain and General Farming
4. Range Livestock
5. General Farming
6. Cotton, Cash Grain, and General Farming
7. General Farming
8. Cotton General Farming
9. Cotton and Dairying
10. Fruit and General Farming
11. Cotton
12. Cotton and Grain
13. Cotton and Livestock
14. Cotton and Self-sufficing
15. Range Livestock
16. Cotton and General Farming

TEXAS
1. Panhandle Wheat Area
2. Canadian River Grazing Area
3. High Plains Cotton Area
4. Rolling Plains
5. High Plains and Trans-Pecos Cattle Grazing Area
6. Upper Rio Grande Valley Area
7. Edwards Plateau Grazing Area
8. Rio Grande Plains Area
9. Lower Rio Grande Valley Area
10. Corpus Christi Cotton Area
11. North-Central Grazing Area
12. Western Cross Timbers Farming Area
13. Grand Prairie Area
14. Black Prairie Area
15. Northeast Sandy Lands Area
16. Piney Woods Lumbering Area
17. Post-Oak Area
18. Coast Prairie Area

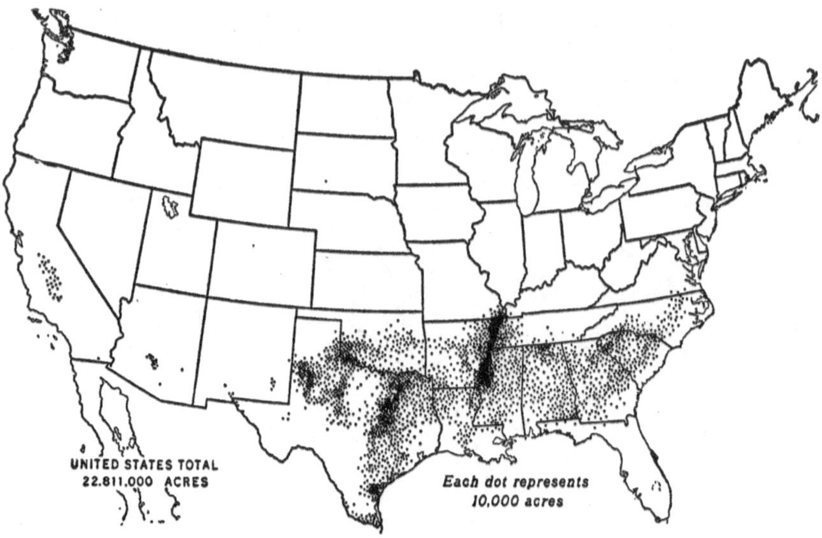

Base figures from the Bureau of the Census. U. S. Dept. of Agriculture, Bureau of Agricultural Economics.

FIGURE 3. Distribution of cotton acreage in the United States, 1939.

major crop. The Panhandle wheat areas of Texas and Oklahoma, the grazing areas in west and south Texas, and the rice and sugar areas of Louisiana are the only major areas in which cotton does not make a significant contribution to the farm economy. There are in addition a few small islands within the area where cotton has been replaced by other crop specialties, such as the vegetable area in Copiah County, Mississippi, the Oktibbeha dairy area also in Mississippi and the rice area in Arkansas.

Two of the most intensive cotton producing areas in the United States lie within the region—the Mississippi Alluvial Plain and the Texas Blackland Prairie. (Figure 4) Cotton acreage in the United States begins on the Atlantic seaboard and moves around along the gulf coast into central and west Texas. It is fairly evenly distributed throughout the region.

Four major cotton producing areas can be differentiated on the basis of the prevailing farming systems. The delta cotton is primarily confined to the Mississippi Alluvial Plain; upland cotton to the Coastal Plain; blackland cotton to the Texas Blackland Prairies; and dryland cotton to the southern half or two-thirds of the High Plains and Rolling Plains.

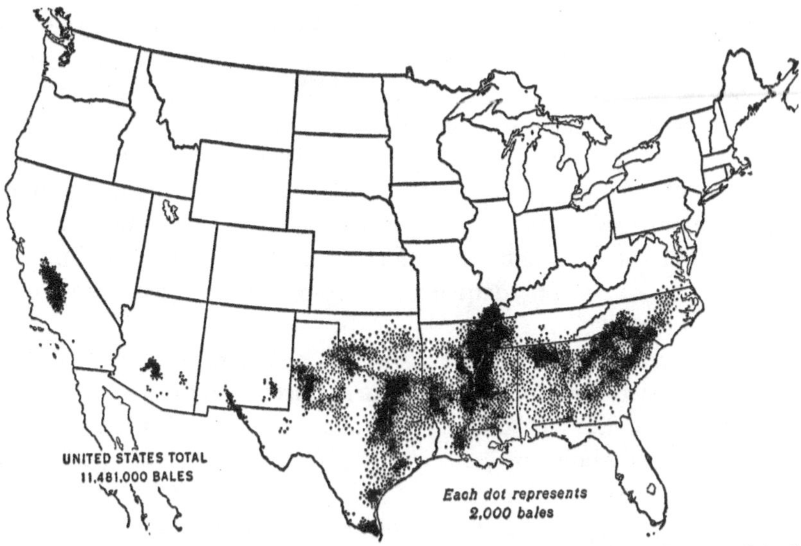

Base figures from the Bureau of the Census. U. S. Dept. of Agriculture, Bureau of Agricultural Economics.

FIGURE 4. Distribution of cotton production in the United States, 1939.

The delta cotton area is characterized by the plantation economy. The large farms are subdivided into small cropper tracts. These small tracts are tilled by cropper families who supply the labor necessary to produce the crop. Even though the land is level and well-suited to cultivation with power-driven equipment, this area has lagged behind western areas in mechanization. The cropper tracts usually are devoted entirely to cotton. Surplus land on the plantation, land not planted to cotton, is generally operated by the owner or manager with wage laborers and planted to corn or grain sorghums or converted to pasture. The proportion of tenancy is high, over 60 per cent for nearly all counties in the area with 90 per cent of the farms operated by tenants or sharecroppers in one-third of the counties.

The gently rolling topography of the upland cotton areas and the numerous streams result in small irregular fields poorly adapted to cultivation with mechanized equipment. Though lacking in inherent fertility, the soils respond readily to commercial fertilizers and these are used extensively throughout the area. The basic cropping system of cotton and corn is supplemented with numerous other crops, including peanuts, sweet potatoes, and watermelons. Tenancy, though higher than the national average, is considerably lower than for the delta cotton areas.

The cotton-corn cropping system is supplemented in the blackland cotton area with small grains, hay, and other forage crops. Cotton acreage in the area reached a peak in 1925 and has declined steadily since that time. During this time the yield per acre has fluctuated considerably, though the general trend has been to maintain a stable yield, which when combined with the decreasing acreage has resulted in a marked decline in total production. The general impression is that though cotton is still a major crop in the area it is declining in importance. As yet no adequate cash crop substitute has been found to take its place.

The chief distinguishing characteristic of the dryland cotton areas is the extensive mechanization. Where mechanization in the other areas has been limited to the preparation of the soil, planting, and cultivating, the whole process, including harvesting, is being performed with power-driven equipment on the High Plains and Rolling Plains. The level topography of the area and the large farms are well adapted to the utilization of mechanized equipment.

Early History and Settlement

For two and a half centuries, following the discovery of America by Columbus, Spain, France, and England at various times claimed all or part of the territory which now constitutes the Southwestern Region. Each of these governments, through its colonization or exploitation policy and through the laws enforced in the territory, contributed to the present settlement pattern in the region.[36]

Population Growth and Development

The first federal census for Mississippi was taken in 1800 and returned a population of 7,600.[37] During the next decade the population increased by more than 300 per cent. In 1817 the territory was organized as a state and admitted to the Union. At the time the territory became a state sixteen counties had been organized, all of them lying in the southern quarter of the state. The remaining area in the state was still Indian territory. In a series of treaties, the first in 1801 and the last in 1832, the Choctaw and Chickasaw Indians ceded all their territory east of the Mississippi to the United States government and agreed to move west of the river as early as practicable.

---

[36] An excellent source of detailed information in this regard may be found in the state guide series of the *Federal Writers Project.*

[37] Data on population growth and composition were compiled from United States Census volumes and from special studies by the United States Bureau of Census and by the state agricultural experiment stations. The special studies are listed in the bibliography.

During this time the state of Mississippi experienced an era of rapid growth which had just begun to slacken at the outbreak of the war between the states. The high price of cotton and the fertile new land at a low price drew large numbers of migrants from the older cotton states of the south to the newly organized state. Except for a small area in the southern part of the state most of the land in Mississippi was settled under the provisions of the early land settlement acts of the United States, initiated by the Ordinance of 1785.

Shortly before turning their unoccupied western lands over to the federal government, the state legislature of Georgia passed an enabling act granting large areas of the public domain to a settlement company. The land involved was an ill-defined tract in the present state of Mississippi, which Georgia claimed under the terms of the proprietary charter in 1732. The act was later rescinded when it was publicized that the organizers of the settlement company were also members of the state legislature. Even though the act was rescinded the land claims of the Yazoo Settlement Company were repeatedly brought before the federal courts and Congress until they were finally settled in about 1830.

The first census after the acquisition of the Louisiana Territory from France was in 1810. The territory of Orleans, which had virtually the same boundaries as the present state of Louisiana, had a population of over 76,000. Almost one-fourth of these were living in the city of New Orleans. After some discussion the territory was admitted to the Union as the State of Louisiana. The rate of population growth has been somewhat slower in Louisiana than in Arkansas, Mississippi, or Texas. It differs further from these states in that from 20 to 30 per cent of the population has been enumerated as urban in each census year, except 1820. The population in the early years was concentrated in the southern portion of the state, on the coast and along the Mississippi and Red rivers.

At the time of the first census in 1810 the Territory of Arkansas, which included most of the present state of Oklahoma, had a population of slightly more than a thousand people. By 1820 the population of the same territory had increased more than 14,000. In 1830 the census enumeration showed a population of more than thirty thousand for the present area of the state of Arkansas. The state was admitted to the Union as the twenty-fifth state in 1836. The rate of growth parallels that of Mississippi, but the total population has consistently been slightly under the population for Mississippi. The state differs from Mississippi and Louisiana in that migrants have come to the state from both the North and the South. Cotton farmers and cotton planters settled in the southeastern part of the state, and grain and dairy farmers from the northern states moved into the Ozark-Ouachita Highlands in the northwest section of the state. The people in the southeast were, for the most part, slave owners and pro-slave in sentiment, whereas the settlers in the northwest were primarily anti-slave.

The boundary between the Spanish Southwest and Louisiana Territory had never been clearly defined and it continued to remain indefinite until 1819 when in a treaty between Spain and the United States, the Red River as far west as the 100 meridian was established as the boundary. At the same time the territory was set aside as a reservation for the Five Civilized Tribes. The migration of the Indians from east of the Mississippi into the area did not actually begin for another ten years, but negotiations to effect the movement had been under way for several years before the specific territory to which they were to migrate was designated. The Indian settlements were confined primarily to the eastern half of the present state of Oklahoma but they had been granted treaty rights to the land in all of the present state except the Panhandle, "as long as the grass shall grow and the waters run."

In 1861 the Five Civilized Tribes made alliances with the Confederacy. The federal government considered this a breach of their treaties and contended that they had thereby forfeited their rights to the lands and the guarantees of the early treaties. Though the government threatened to do so, the lands were not opened to white settlement, but the western half of the territory was taken from the Five Civilized Tribes and granted to other Indian tribes. However, the pressure of white settlers both to the north and south of the Indian Territory was making the position of the Indians ever more precarious. Large numbers of white settlers were already infiltrating into the area, thereby complicating the civil affairs of the Indians since these white settlers did not come under the jurisdiction of the tribal government.

The federal government purchased an unsettled tract in North Central Oklahoma from the Creek and Seminole tribes. The territory, known as the Cherokee Strip, was surveyed and opened to white settlement in 1893. Long before this settlers had crossed the south fork of the Red River into the territory known as Greer County, which was claimed by Texas, and lay between the north and south fork of the Red River. In 1895 the United States Supreme Court decided the territory rightfully belonged to Oklahoma. Those who had already settled in the territory were allowed to retain 160 acres as a homestead and to purchase an additional 160 at $1.25 an acre.

Thus, the Indian Territory was being encroached upon from both sides, as well as by infiltration into the territory itself. The clamor for the unsettled lands within the territory became so strong that the federal government through treaties with the several tribal governments purchased the surplus lands. As these lands were opened up for settlement they were sold by lottery rather than by runs as with the Cherokee Strip. The isolation of the Indian was a thing of the past and in 1907 Congress passed the Enabling Act permitting Oklahoma to take the necessary steps to be admitted to the Union as a state.

The first title to land in Texas was issued in 1731, and various grants were made from time to time by the Spanish kings until 1819. By the time of the Mexican revolt Spain was beginning to liberalize her Texas land policy by opening the lands to foreigners. Stephen F. Austin referring to this change says: "This country has lain dormant for ages. It was the policy of the Spanish government to keep it out of reach, and to conceal its natural advantages. The grant to my father, Moses Austin, in January, 1821, by the Spanish Authorities, to settle three hundred families in Texas, was the first deviation from this policy that had ever occurred."[38]

The exact amount of land granted to private owners under the Spanish regime is not known but it is estimated to be at least ten million acres. Large grants of land were held as "mission lands" but an absolute title to them was never granted and the majority of these areas reverted to the government when the financial support of the Royal treasury was withdrawn from them. The net results of more than a hundred years of Spanish attempts at colonization were the settlements at Bexar, present day San Antonio, and LaBahia, now Goliad, with a total white population of 4,000.

The location of Texas and the distribution within it of land suitable for settlement tended to separate it from Mexico and draw it to the United States. Between the most southerly settlements of Texas and the outposts of Mexican settlement was an expanse of semiarid land which served as a more or less natural barrier to the effective extension of Mexican influence and control. Agricultural resources were potent forces in appealing to the Americans. The suitability of the

[38] Quoted in Aldon S. Lang, *Financial History of the Public Lands in Texas*, p. 27.

soil and climate for the production of cotton provided an incentive for migration from the southern slaveholding states.

After the successful revolution against Spain, the Mexican government announced its purpose to colonize the territories of the Republic. It adopted the impresario system of colonization, a method whereby the government enters into contract with the immigration agent. The government agrees to furnish the land for the settlers on easy terms according to law and pay the agent for his services in premium lands, if he will establish a colony of a given number of persons within a definitely described territory and within a given time. The law of 1825 specified that the impresario was to receive five leagues and five labors of land (of which one-half was to be nonirrigable) for each one hundred families that he established within the state. A proportionate amount would be given for any number of families over 100, but no land whatever would be awarded him if he failed to bring that number of families.

The colonization law of 1824 offered free lands to settlers and guaranteed the contracts which impresarios might make with families so far as they were not contrary to law. Furthermore, the imposition of any tax upon the foreigners was prohibited for a period of four years after their entrance. The duty of making such additional laws and regulations as might be necessary to accomplish this purpose was imposed upon the state legislatures. The state of Coahuila and Texas enacted a colonization law which became effective March 24, 1825. According to this act the immigrant should present a certificate of good character, take an oath of allegiance to the Mexican government, promise to observe the Roman Catholic religion, agree to live on the land and cultivate it for a period of six years, and at the end of the six-year period agree to pay a nominal sum, proportional to the class and quality of the land received, as an acknowledgement of the grant.

In 1820 Louisiana and Mississippi to the east of Texas had already accumulated an aggregate population of over 200,000 persons. The land was becoming crowded according to frontier standards. Settlers in Mississippi were still confined to the southern half of the state by treaties with the Indians. There was much dissatisfaction with the federal land policy. Land was too expensive at a dollar an acre and the survey tracts offered for sale by the land office were too large. The country had just experienced a panic. People were restless and looking for a place to begin life anew.

The more liberal colonization policy of Spain and the subsequent

Mexican program opened new frontiers. People by the hundreds found ways to comply with or circumvent the restrictive measures. By 1830 the population of Texas had jumped from 4,000 in 1821 to 20,000, most of the increase coming from the United States. The Mexican government became uneasy over this sudden influx of Anglo-Americans and sought to stem the tide or at least to equalize the population by encouraging Mexican families to settle in the country.

Consequently, in 1830 and the years immediately following, the colonization laws were changed so that only Mexican families could purchase additional land. The law of 1834 abolished the impresario system of land settlement and provided for the survey of the remaining vacant public lands into lots of one labor (177 acres) each. The lots were to be sold at public auction at a minimum price of 10 pesos per lot.

However, it was too late to stop the westward migration into Texas. The restrictive measures merely served to raise the cry of oppression and people came from all over the western frontier to join the fight for "Liberty and Texas." In 1836, Texas became an independent nation and ten years later it was admitted as the twenty-eighth state in the Union. The migration into Texas which had brought the population up to 212,592 by the time of the first census in 1850 continued undiminished for another decade.

On January 9, 1861, Mississippi became the second state to join the Confederacy, thereby seceding from the Union. The other three states which had been admitted to the Union prior to 1860—Arkansas, Louisiana, and Texas—followed shortly thereafter. The Five Civilized Tribes, which held treaty rights to the territory now included in the state of Oklahoma, negotiated a treaty of allegiance with the Confederacy early in the same year. Except for the siege of Vicksburg, none of the major campaigns of the Civil War were fought in the region. However, the war and subsequent reconstruction period seriously disrupted the social and economic life of the states.

The rate of growth for Mississippi was already declining prior to the Civil War but it had been consistently greater than that for the nation. During the decade from 1860 to 1870, however, the population of the state increased by less than 5 per cent. Following 1870, Mississippi again experienced a marked increase in population but the favorable balance of immigration over emigration did not persist and the general trend of a rapidly declining rate of growth became apparent in the following decades. (Figure 5)

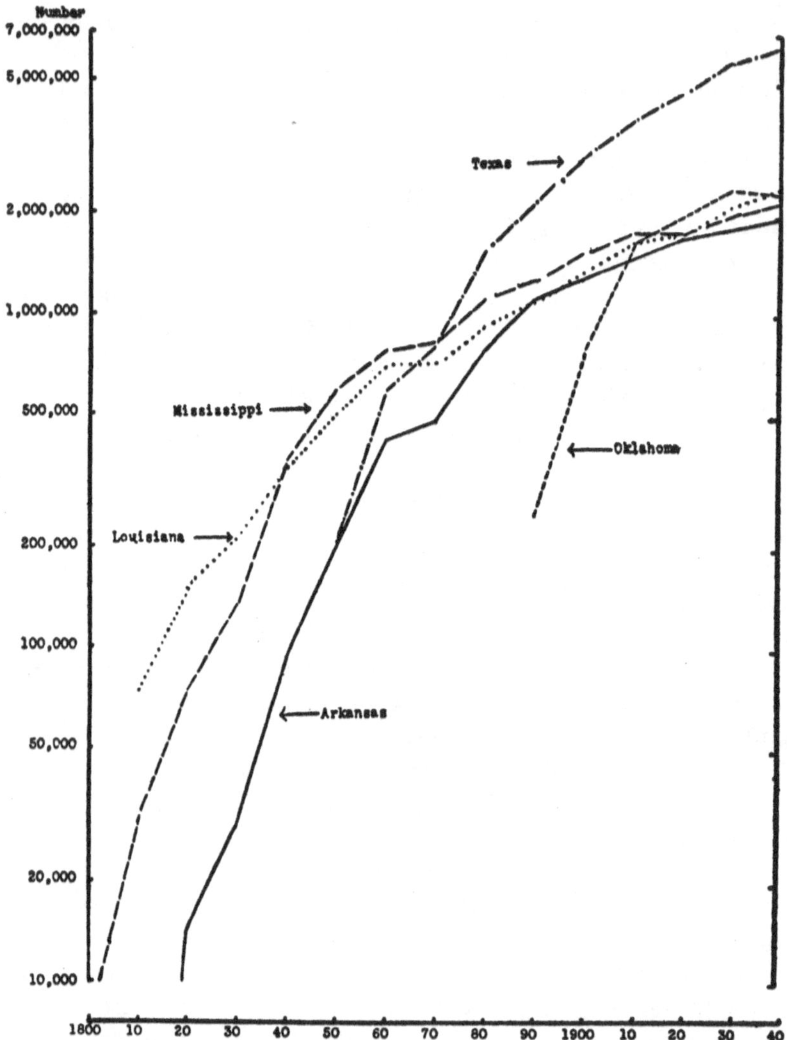

Source: Base figures from the *Sixteenth Census of the United States, Population, 1940.*

FIGURE 5. Rate of population growth from the first census enumeration to 1940 for each of the five states in the Southwestern Region.

Migration was primarily responsible for the rapid growth of Mississippi population prior to 1860. Following the war out-movements exceeded in-movements. Approximately one-fourth of the persons born in Mississippi have been enumerated as living outside the state since 1870. During the same time the proportion of native white persons living in the state but born elsewhere in the United States declined to 13.3 per cent in 1920, increasing slightly in 1930 to 13.9 per cent. During this same period the source of migrants to the state shifted from the South Atlantic states and New England to the neighboring states of Alabama, Arkansas, and Louisiana, migrants also coming to the state in considerable numbers from Texas. In total numbers the native white persons born elsewhere but living in Mississippi increased from nearly 128,000 to approximately 138,000 persons. In contrast, the number of persons born in Mississippi but living elsewhere increased from 81,000 to 321,000 during the same period. Texas is the home of the largest number of Mississippi-born migrants, with Louisiana, since 1900, receiving almost as many. The migration to the northern industrial states of Mississippi-born whites has not increased as rapidly as has the migration of native whites northward in the neighboring states of Louisiana, Alabama, and Tennessee.

Louisiana had accumulated a greater aggregate population at the time of the first census in 1810 than the other states in the region. During the subsequent years the rate of growth was less rapid than in other states and during the decade 1860 to 1870 the population increased by less than 3 per cent. Following the Civil War, Louisiana, like Mississippi, experienced a marked increase in population but the flow of migrants did not persist and the general trend of a declining rate of growth became apparent in the succeeding decades. (Figure 5)

Since 1870 Louisiana has consistently been below the national average, both as a source of migrants to other states, only 14 per cent of the native white persons born in Louisiana lived elsewhere in 1870, and as a place of residence for migrants from other states, since only 21 per cent of Louisiana's native white population were born outside the state. In 1930, 16.6 per cent of the persons born in Louisiana were enumerated as living outside the state and 16 per cent of Louisiana's native white population gave some other state as the state of their birth. Prior to 1890 native white migrants to Louisiana came primarily from the three neighboring states to the east—Mississippi, Alabama, and Georgia. At this time, also, there were in Louisiana 1,000 or more persons who had been born in each of several states to the northeast and east and in Arkansas, Missouri, and Texas, but since 1900 the number who were born in adjacent states has increased more rapidly than those coming from more distant states. New Orleans accounts for a relatively larger proportion of the migrants than all the rest of the state. Louisiana-born migrants have predominantly gone to urban centers and since 1810 there has been a concentration of native whites in the industrial centers of the north and northeast who give Louisiana as the state of birth. Texas and California have also received migrants from Louisiana in considerable numbers.

Arkansas was experiencing a period of rapid growth during the period preceding 1860 and the rate of growth (11.3 per cent) did not drop as low in the next decade as did the rates for Louisiana and Mississippi. Following 1870 the rate increased sharply and remained high until 1900 when it leveled off to a declining rate of growth comparable to that for Mississippi and Louisiana. (Figure 5)

In 1870 more than 52 per cent of the native white population living in the state had been born outside the state. The chief source of immigrants was the neighboring state of Tennessee. Other states which contributed in increasing numbers to the native white population of the state were Texas, Louisiana, Oklahoma, Missouri, Illinois, and Indiana. Since 1900 the number living in Arkansas but born in the South Atlantic states has decreased. The relative importance of the persons born elsewhere but living in Arkansas to the total native white population has decreased in each census year from 1870 to 1930 when only 26 per cent of the native white population had been born outside the state. Since 1900 the number emigrating from Arkansas has exceeded 100,000 in each decade and since 1890 the number born in Arkansas and moving elsewhere has exceeded the number moving into the state from other places so that the state has suffered a net loss from the migratory process. Texas and Missouri were the chief recipients of the outward migration from Arkansas prior to 1900. After 1900 Oklahoma became the primary place of residence for migrants born in Arkansas. Employment opportunities in the industrial states to the north and east caused a change of direction which is particularly noticeable in the migration to Michigan between 1920 and 1930, also there were more persons living in other states, but born in Arkansas, than there were persons from other states living in Arkansas.

Texas had just been admitted to the Union as a state 15 years earlier and was growing phenomenally at the outbreak of the Civil War. Though the stream of migrants to the state slowed somewhat, the population of the state increased by 36 per cent during the decade. In the next decade the rate increased sharply and continued high until 1890 when it dropped off slightly. Since that time Texas has continued to grow at a faster rate than the other three states, Louisiana, Mississippi, or Arkansas.

The favorable balance of immigration over emigration has been the primary factor contributing to the rapid increase of population in Texas. In 1870 one-half of the native white residents gave some other state as the place of their birth. The proportion declined steadily in each succeeding census year and in 1930 the native white residents not born in Texas accounted for less than one-fourth of the native white population. Prior to 1900 the migrants came primarily from the states east of the Mississippi River. Since then, however, the numbers reporting birth places in states west of the Mississippi River have increased at a more rapid rate than the ones coming from the states to the east. In each census year there were many more persons living in Texas and reporting some other state as the place of their birth than there were persons born in Texas and living in other states. However, the persons reporting Texas as the place of their birth and living in other states have been increasing. In 1880 only 5.2 per cent of the persons born in Texas were living elsewhere. The proportion increased to 16.5 per cent in 1930. In 1910 nearly half of the migrants from Texas were living in Oklahoma and in 1930 that state still accounted for almost one-third of the migrants. However, during the latter period there was a considerable increase in the number of persons leaving Texas and migrating westward as well as some migration to the industrial states of the northeast and east.

Oklahoma, which was enumerated by the census for the first time in 1890, experienced an exceedingly rapid growth for the next twenty years. In 1920, however, the rate of increase over the preceding census had dropped to 22.4 per cent. The rate was only slightly smaller in 1930 but the census of 1940 showed that Oklahoma had experienced a decrease of 2.5 per cent during the preceding decade.

Prior to 1890 the number of persons born in the territory that is now Oklahoma, but living elsewhere, was very small since there were few white people residing in the area at that time. The few that were enumerated were living primarily in the neighboring states. In 1890, 15 per cent of the persons born in Oklahoma were living elsewhere, by 1930 the proportion had increased to almost 29 per cent. The direction of migration had also changed sharply during this period. In 1930 the number living in California was four times the number living in that state ten years previously. That the out-migration from the state has continued high since 1930 is indicated by the fact that Oklahoma experienced a net decrease in population during the decade 1930 to 1940.

Nearly 98 per cent of the native white persons living in Oklahoma territory in 1890 were born elsewhere. The proportion decreased to 52 per cent by 1930. The number of native whites living in Oklahoma in 1930 was approximately the same as the number enumerated ten years previously. During the early years of the state's history, homesteading opportunities were the primary incentive for migration into the state. Later migrants came primarily to the towns and cities which were developing to serve the needs of the agricultural areas and to exploit the mineral resources, chiefly oil, of the state.

The establishment of defense industries and later war industries caused a pronounced shift of population in the United States during the period immediately following the 1940 census enumeration. According to estimates by the Census Bureau as of March 1, 1943, the five states in the region all suffered a net loss in civilian population as a result of these shifts. There were numerous large military camps and some defense industries in Texas. The service institutions clustering around these camps and the defense industries attracted workers in sufficient numbers to maintain a stable population despite the transfer of a large number of the young men and women in the state to the armed forces. The state suffered a net loss of 0.6 per cent. Louisiana also was able to almost maintain a stable population due to defense industries, shipping interests, and military posts centered in the state. The net loss in Louisiana was 0.8 per cent.

The population in Arkansas and Mississippi declined about 7 per cent during the three-year period following the 1940 census. The combined out-migration of persons to defense industries in other states and to the armed forces was greater than the rate of natural increase in these states. Both states had been experiencing a net loss due to migration during the preceding decade but the rate of natural increase had been sufficient to effect a net gain. In Oklahoma out-migration had resulted in a net loss in the preceding decade and during the three years following the decennial census the trend continued with the state suffering a net loss of 10 per cent.

Distribution and Composition of the Population

Rural-urban Distribution. The Interior Highlands and the Coastal Plains, with the exception of the Rio Grande Plain in southern Texas, are much more densely populated than the Interior Plains and the Inter-mountain Plateau. The large urban centers, with a population of 250,000 or more, lie within this area. (Figure 6) San Antonio and Dallas in Texas lie on the border between the two major divisions. Aside from these which border the Interior Plains there are only four

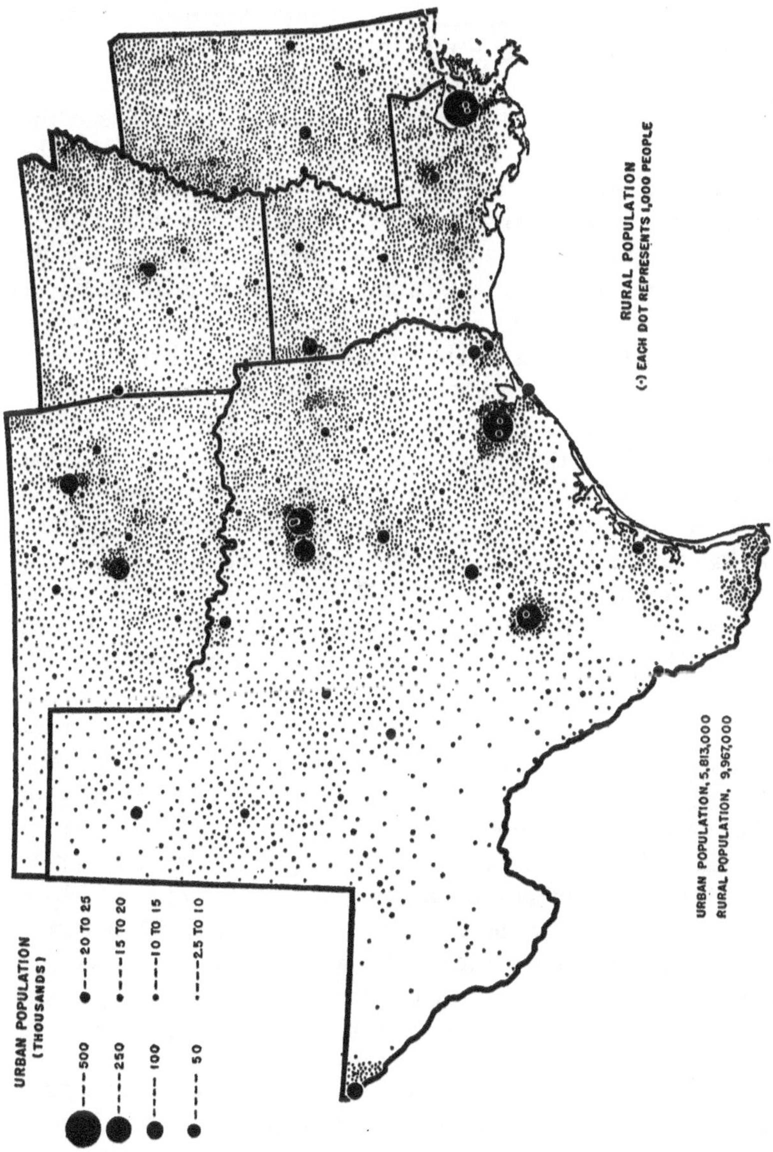

Base figures from the Bureau of Census. U. S. Dept. of Agriculture, Agricultural Post-War Planning Committee.

FIGURE 6. Distribution of urban and rural population in the Southwestern Region, 1940.

centers in the western part of the region with a population of 50,000 or more. Considering the rural population alone, it is definitely more concentrated in the eastern portion of the region than in the west.

Arkansas, with a total population of slightly less than 2 million, was still predominantly rural in 1940. Nearly 78 per cent was classified as rural and 57 per cent of the total were farm people. Since 1860 when the first urban population was enumerated in the state the urban population had been increasing at a more rapid rate than the total population. In 1940 there were only nine urban centers in the state with a population in excess of 10,000 and 33 centers with a population of 2,500. The rural nonfarm population has increased slightly during the 20 years since it was enumerated separately from 18 per cent to approximately 21 per cent. The decrease in farm population has been both relative and absolute with most of the decrease being centered in the upland areas of the Eastern Coastal Plains.

Until 1890 approximately 25 per cent of the population of Louisiana was urban and the greatest proportion of the urban population was concentrated in New Orleans. Since 1890, however, the urban population has increased two and a half times and the number of urban centers has increased from nine to 54. The number over 10,000 was 10 in 1940. Nearly 42 per cent of the 2,364,000 persons in Louisiana were classed as urban residents, and only 36 per cent were classed as farm people. The remaining 22 per cent were rural nonfarm residents composed primarily of villagers, overflow from urban centers, and persons engaged in marsh and swamp and other rural industries.

The number of cities in Oklahoma has increased from two in 1890, at the time of the first census enumeration, to 74 in 1940 with 21 of the cities having a population over 10,000 each. The rural population has decreased during this period from 96.3 per cent of the total to 62.4 per cent. The combined rural, farm, and urban population have comprised an almost constant proportion of the total population from 1900 to 1940 (about 78 per cent). The general trend in the number of farm people in the state has been downward. In 1940, 39.7 per cent of the slightly more than 2 million inhabitants of the state were living on farms and 22.7 per cent were classed as rural nonfarm persons.

There were two cities in Texas in 1850 with a population of 2,500 or more. Their combined population was slightly over 7,000 persons, accounting for less than 4 per cent of the total population of the state. By 1940 the number of cities had increased to 196 with 44 of them over 10,000 and the rural population had decreased from 96.4 per cent

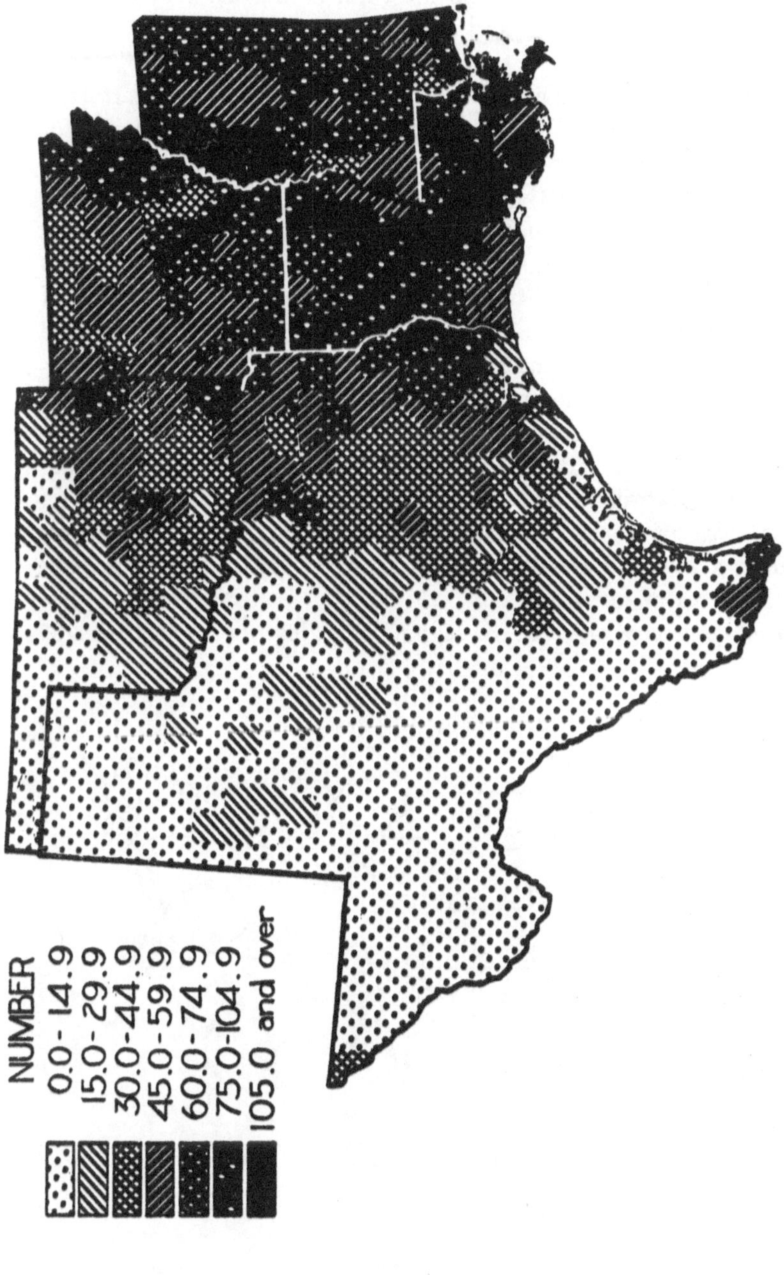

Source: Base figures from the *Sixteenth Census of the United States, 1940.*

FIGURE 7. Number of farm persons per 1,000 acres of farm land for each county in the Southwestern Region, 1940.

to 54.6 per cent of the total population. The farm population accounted for only 33.5 per cent and the rural nonfarm for 21 per cent. The population, both urban and rural, is concentrated in the eastern half of the state.

Population Density. The ratio of farm persons to acres of farmland is a better measure of population pressure on economic resources for the farm population than the above comparisons. It shows an even greater contrast between the Coastal Plains and the Interior Plains. (Figure 7) Nearly all counties in the western two-thirds of Texas fall below 15 farm persons per 1,000 acres of farmland. The concentration in the western half of Oklahoma is slightly greater, but most of the counties fall below 30. The state average for Texas (16) and Oklahoma (27) is below the national average (29). Only a few counties on the eastern border of the states approach the average for the eastern states of the region: Arkansas (62), Louisiana (86), and Mississippi (72). The delta counties have a ratio of over 100 persons per 1,000 acres of farmland and the delta border counties are all over 75 persons. Except for the Ozark-Ouachita Highlands in northwest Arkansas, a few counties in these three states fall below 60 persons per 1,000 acres of farmland.

Racial Characteristics. In the region farm Negroes are concentrated

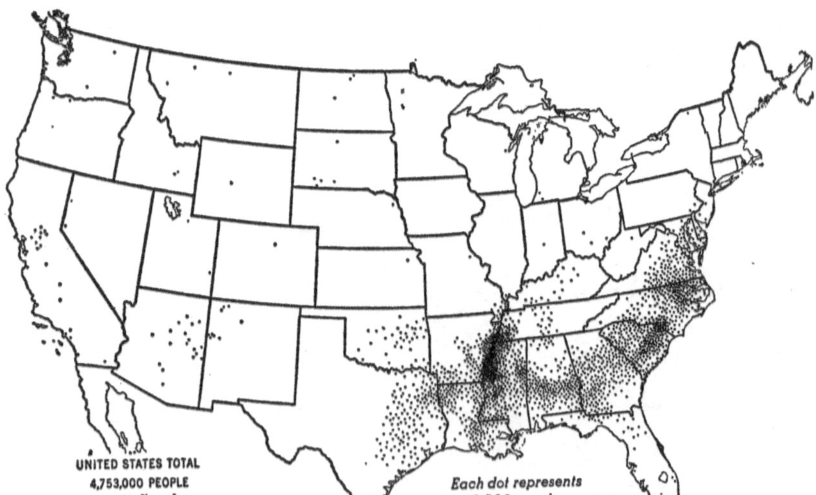

Base figures from the Bureau of the Census. U. S. Dept. of Agriculture, Bureau of Agricultural Economics.

FIGURE 8. Distribution of Negro rural farm population in the United States, 1940.

on the Mississippi Alluvial Plain and on the smaller alluvial plains of the tributary rivers where the plantation system of agricultural organization predominates. (Figure 8) The Negro population reached its highest proportion, in relation to the total population, for any state in the region, in Mississippi in 1900 when 58.5 per cent of the population was Negro. The proportion exceeds 90 per cent in some counties on the Mississippi Alluvial Plain.

For Mississippi the proportion had consistently been over 50 per cent from the first enumeration, but in 1940 it dropped to 49.2 per cent. Negroes are more prevalent in the rural population (55.3 per cent) than in either of the other two population groups—nonfarm, 34.9 and urban 41.1 per cent. The Negro farm population is scattered through the state more so than in any of the other states in the region, but the greatest concentration is in the upper delta.

Prior to 1890 approximately 50 per cent of the population in Louisiana was Negro but since then the proportion of Negroes has declined steadily to 35.9 per cent in 1940. As in Mississippi, Negroes are more prevalent in the farm population (44.7 per cent) than in either the urban (29.0 per cent) or the rural nonfarm populations (32.0 per cent). Negroes are concentrated along the Mississippi and Red rivers and in the sugar parishes of south Louisiana. They become scarcer as subsistence farming becomes more and more prevalent in the economy of the parishes and are present in larger proportions in those areas where the plantation economy is predominant.

Since first enumerated, Negroes have accounted for approximately one-fourth of the population of Arkansas. In the year 1910, which shows the highest proportion, Negroes accounted for more than 28 per cent of the total population. Since that time they have declined in importance until 1940 when 24.8 per cent of the population was returned as Negroes. In 1940 Negroes were more prevalent in the farm population (26.8 per cent) than in either of the other two residence groups—urban 24.3 and rural nonfarm 19.7 per cent. The Negro farm population is concentrated in the delta areas, primarily along the southern and eastern borders.

At the time of the first census in Texas 27.5 per cent of the population were Negroes. The proportion increased to 31 per cent in 1870 after which time the proportion has steadily declined to 14.4 per cent in 1940. The Negroes are more prevalent in the farm population (16.5 per cent) than in either of the other residence groups—urban, 14.4 and nonfarm, 11.1 per cent—and the farm Negroes are further concentrated in the eastern third of the state.

In contrast to the other states hardly 8 per cent of the inhabitants of Oklahoma were Negroes in each census. The highest proportion was 8.4 per cent in 1890 and the lowest 7 per cent in 1900. The proportion in 1940 was 7.2 per cent. The actual number of Negroes increased in each decade from 1890 to 1930 but decreased from 1930 to 1940. Oklahoma also differs from the other states in the region in that the Negroes are more prevalent in the nonfarm population than in the other residence groups. Negroes comprise 9.1 per cent of the rural nonfarm population, 6.4 per cent of the farm population, and 5.7 per cent of the urban population. Because of the mechanization of agriculture, the reduction in the number of farms, the reduction in acreage planted to cotton, and other changes in the agricultural system, the Negro is being displaced on the farms and absorbed by the cities. Also the Negro has advanced culturally at a rapid pace and begun aggressively to seek a higher standard of living. Farm Negroes live primarily in the eastern half of the state.

Another racial group which assumes some prominence in the Oklahoma population is the Indian. However, the census enumeration of Indians varies erratically between census years, presumably because of a lack of consistency in the classification of persons of mixed blood. In 1890, at the time of the first enumeration, there were 64,500 Indians in the territory. The number enumerated in succeeding censuses varies from 57,000 in 1910 to 93,000 in 1930 with 63,125 enumerated in the census for 1940. In 1890 the number constituted one-fourth of the total population whereas in 1940 it was only 2.7 per cent. Even though the classification is not entirely consistent it is apparent that the Indian has steadily declined in importance in the population of the state.

The foreign-born population has not been a very significant element in any state in the region. In Mississippi the proportion has consistently been under 1 per cent and in Arkansas the proportion was 1.1 per cent in 1910 and dropped to less than half of 1 per cent by 1940. In each of these states over half of the foreign-born persons were urban residents. In Oklahoma the foreign-born element dropped from 2.6 per cent in 1900 to less than 1 per cent in 1940. Less than one-third or slightly over 6,000 persons were living on farms in that year.

The foreign-born population in Texas reached its maximum both numerically and as a proportion of the total population in 1920 when there were 360,000 foreign-born persons in the state. The proportion declined from the maximum 7.8 per cent to 3.7 per cent in 1940. Of the 235,500 foreign-born in the state in 1940, 144,000 were enumerated as city residents. Over two-thirds of the foreign-born in the state are Mexican nationals from across the border and are concentrated in the border counties. In addition to the Mexican nationals, born in Mexico, there is a large group of native-born Mexicans who are classed as native white by the census but constitute a distinct culture group, which is distinguishable by the prevalence of the use of the Spanish language and continued observation of Mexican customs. The numerical importance of the group cannot be determined from census data, since they are not enumerated separately.

Nearly 4 per cent of the population in Louisiana were foreign-born in 1900. By 1940 the proportion had dropped to 1.2 per cent of which nearly three-fourths were urban residents. Even in the urban areas the foreign-born population constituted a very minor element, only 2.2 per cent. However, the national or culture characteristics for the state cannot be described entirely on the basis of nativity. Approximately 44 per cent of the native white population of Louisiana in 1930 was estimated to belong to the Louisiana French culture group. The area of French culture lies within a large triangle having its base on the Gulf of Mexico and its apex at the juncture of the Red and Mississippi rivers. The Louisiana French have maintained their language, culture, religion, and mode of living to as great, if not a greater, extent than any other large non-English speaking group in the United States.

Education. The counties showing both the highest and the lowest educational attainment, in terms of the median grade of school completed by persons 25 years old and over, lie within the Southwestern Region. Educational attainments are lowest in the densely settled areas and highest in the sparsely settled areas. The densely settled areas also have the highest proportion of Negroes. In over half the parishes in Louisiana and in the delta counties of Arkansas and Mississippi the median grade attained by the rural farm population, 25 years old or over, was less than 6.0. (Figure 9) There is a marked contrast with the sparsely settled areas of west Texas where there are many counties in which the median grade attained was 10.0 or more.

Within the states there were wide differences in the educational attainments of the various population groups. The highest was among native-white urban Mississippians whose median grade attainment was 11.7, the lowest attainment was 2.8, the median for Louisiana's rural Negroes. Mississippi also ranked highest in educational achievements for native white farm residents. The highest achievement for urban

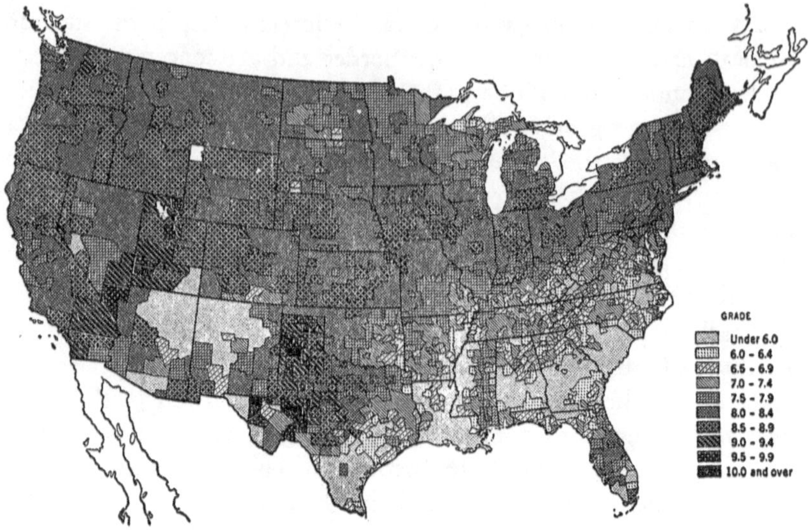

Base figures from the Bureau of Census. U. S. Dept. of Agriculture, Bureau of Agricultural Economics.

FIGURE 9. Median grade of school completed for persons 25 years old and over by counties in the United States, 1940.

and farm Negroes was in Oklahoma. Louisiana ranked lowest for all population groups.

In each of the states at least 50 per cent of the native white urban residents, 25 years old and over, reported that they entered high school; only 30 per cent of those in Mississippi dropping out of school before beginning high school. In the rural farm populations, however, the proportion was smaller, but the range being from 19.4 per cent in Arkansas to 36.9 per cent in Texas. For Negroes the proportions were still lower.

Age and sex. The older age groups are gaining in relative importance in the age composition of the population of the United States. In 1880 persons aged 20 to 64 accounted for approximately 40 per cent of the total population. By 1930 the proportion was 55 per cent. It has been estimated that the relative importance of the people in the older age groups will continue to increase until they comprise 61 to 65 per cent of the total population.

The general trend in the region has been comparable to the trend for the nation. The change in age composition, however, is not progressing to the same degree in all states. The process has progressed most rapidly in Texas, where the proportion of the population aged

20 to 64 increased 26 per cent, in Mississippi 18, in Oklahoma 17, and in Louisiana 16 per cent.

The proportion of the total population in the productive ages varies inversely with the rurality of the state. Mississippi and Arkansas had the highest proportion of rural people and the lowest proportion in the productive ages, 20 to 64, 52 and 53 per cent, respectively. Oklahoma had 54 per cent, Louisiana 55, and Texas, with the lowest proportion of rural people had the highest proportion, 57 per cent, in the productive ages in 1940. The proportions for the rural population of the states are 5 to 7 per cent below the proportions for the total population.

The increase in the proportion of persons in the productive age groups has not been accompanied by a comparable increase in the proportion of the total population in the labor force. In Mississippi the proportion in the labor force decreased by nearly 3 per cent and in Louisiana and Arkansas, though the labor force increased, the increase was less than 3 per cent between 1900 and 1940. Texas, where the increase in the proportion in the labor force was 18.8 per cent, is the only state where the increase even approximates the increase in the proportion in the productive age groups.

The discrepancies between the two may be explained in part by the fact that there is not only a larger proportion in the productive ages, but the proportion in each age group above 50 years has increased and the proportion in the groups under fifty has remained constant or decreased. Assuming the same proportion of the workers over fifty retired, before reaching their 65th birthday, in 1940 as in 1900 the number of workers lost to the labor force would be greater and the proportion which those are of the total population would also be greater. At the other end of the scale persons in the younger age groups, 14 to 25, remained in school for a considerably longer period in 1940 than they did in 1900, thus reducing the proportion in that group who can be considered gainfully employed or in the labor force.

Another factor which has tended to depress the proportion in the labor force in 1940 as compared to 1900 is the sharp reduction in the number of females, and particularly Negro females, in the labor force. In Arkansas and Mississippi the proportion of Negro females in the labor force was reduced by 8 per cent. In Oklahoma and Texas, the two states showing an increase in the proportion in the labor force, the proportion of Negro females in the labor force increased 20 and 7 per cent, respectively.

Farming and Farm Family Living

Occupational Employment. Mississippi had the highest proportion of employed workers engaged in agriculture for any state in the region. The proportion in Mississippi was 57.7 per cent. The other states in order were Arkansas (51.4 per cent), Oklahoma (33.1 per cent), Louisiana (32.2 per cent), and Texas (29.8 per cent). In each state the proportion of the nonwhite persons employed in agriculture was greater than the proportion of white persons, though in Texas there was a difference of only 3 per cent (29.3 for white and 32.3 per cent for nonwhite workers), and in Oklahoma the difference between the two groups was only 2 per cent. The greatest racial difference exists in Louisiana where only 25.1 per cent of the white employed workers but 43.8 per cent of the nonwhite workers are employed in agriculture.

In each state Negroes constitute a greater proportion of the agricultural labor force than they do of the total population. In Louisiana 35.9 per cent of the population is colored and 51.9 per cent of the agricultural labor force are nonwhite, and in Mississippi the difference is almost as great, 15.8 per cent. There is a difference of 7.4 per cent in Arkansas and less than 3 per cent in Texas and Oklahoma. Except for Oklahoma, where the proportion is 3.0 per cent, female workers constitute over 10 per cent of the nonwhite agricultural labor force as compared to around 5 per cent females in the white agricultural labor force of each state.

In each of the states more of the white than of the nonwhite agricultural workers are classed as farmers and farm managers. The proportions range from 61 per cent of the white agricultural labor force in Texas to 76 per cent in Mississippi and for the nonwhite agricultural labor force from 63 per cent in Oklahoma to 47 per cent in Louisiana and Texas. At the other end of the economic scale the proportion of farm laborers and unpaid family workers in the nonwhite agricultural labor force exceeds the proportion in the white agricultural labor force exceeds the proportion in the white agricultural labor force.

In 1940 there were 9.3 million persons gainfully employed in agriculture in the United States. Of these 3.7 million owned all or part of the land they were cultivating and 2.4 million rented all the land operated. The remaining 3.2 million were farm laborers of which one-fifth worked on the home farm and 2.5 million worked for others on larger than family farms. Tenancy increased in the United States from 1880, when the census first reported data on the tenure status of farmers, to 1930 when tenant-operated farms accounted for 42.4 per cent of all farms. By 1940 the proportion of tenancy for the United States had declined slightly to 28.7 per cent.

Farm Tenure. The states in the Southwestern Region have followed the same pattern as the United States, but all states exceed the national average in proportion of tenants. Texas with 48.9 per cent tenancy ranks 39th among the states of the nation, Arkansas, 42nd, Oklahoma, 43rd, Louisiana, 46th, and Mississippi with 66.2 per cent tenancy ranks 48th—the highest in the nation. Eighty-two per cent of the countries in the region are above the national average in the proportion of tenants. LeFlore County in Mississippi has the highest proportion of tenancy for any county in the country with 96.8 per cent of the farms operated by tenants.

In 1880, 7 per cent of the counties in the United States had a tenancy rate of 50 per cent or more. By 1935 this 7 per cent had advanced to a peak of 29 but declined to 24 in 1940. The counties in the region with the highest proportion of tenancy are concentrated on the alluvial plains of the Mississippi and Red rivers with another concentration in the Cross Timbers of Oklahoma and on the Texas Blackland Prairie. (Figure 10)

In general, the best land in the region has the lowest proportion of owner-operated farms and the poorer land shows higher proportions of ownership. Less than 20 per cent of the farms in the delta are owner-operated. (Figure 11) The Coastal Plain is spotted with owner-operated farms constituting over 50 per cent of all farms in southeastern Mississippi and also in southeastern Texas. The Rolling Plains have from 30 to 40 per cent owner-operated farms with isolated counties dropping below 30 and a few others exceeding 40 per cent. The Texas Blackland Prairie ranges from 20 to 30 per cent in the northern part and from 30 to 40 per cent in the southern section with a few counties exceeding 50 per cent ownership.

Part owners constitute less than 10 per cent of the farm operators in the majority of the Coastal Plain counties. (Figure 12) The western part of the region is considerably more spotted with some counties in the wheat and cattle ranch areas exceeding 25 per cent. The southern portion of the Rolling Plains range from 10 to 20 per cent.

In 1935 the value of all farm real estate owned and operated by the farmer constituted 39 per cent of all farm real estate in the United States. In all states in the region the equity was lower than the average for the United States. Oklahoma had the lowest equity with 28 per

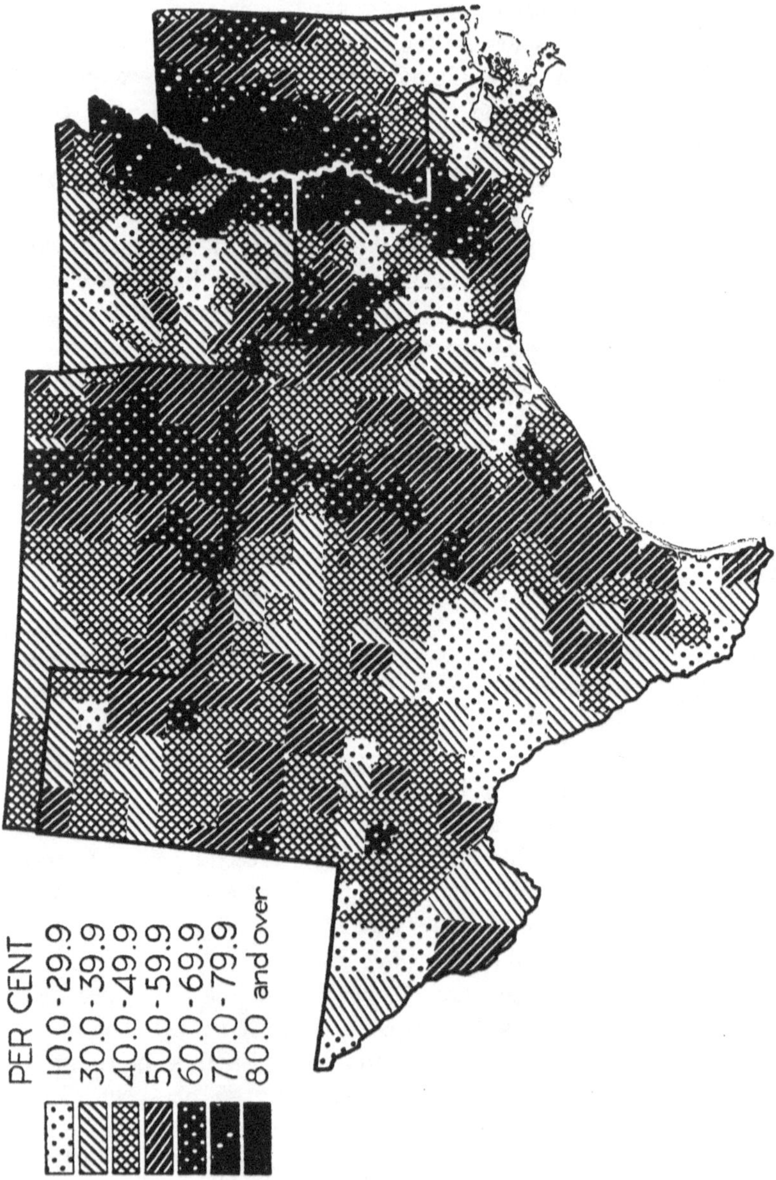

Source: Base figures from the *Sixteenth Census of the United States, Agriculture, 1940.*

FIGURE 10. Percentage of operators who are tenants in each county in the Southwestern Region, 1940.

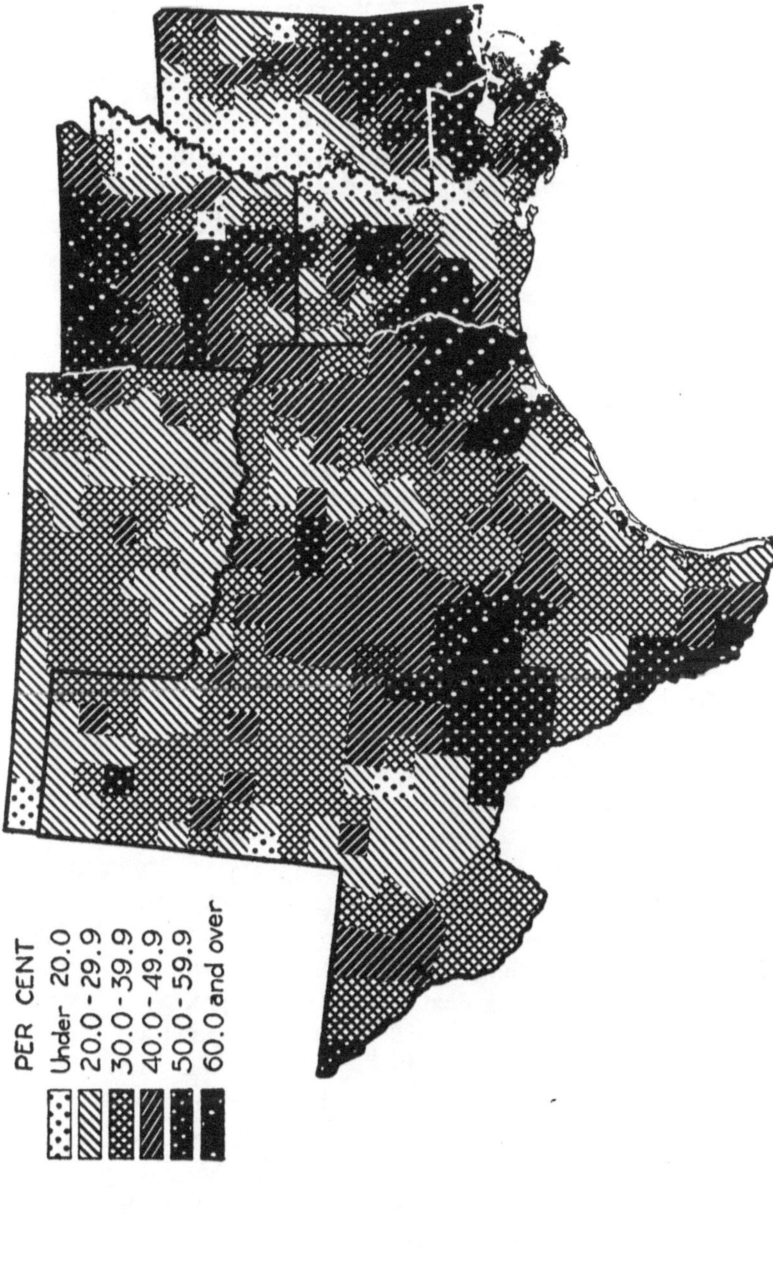

Source: Base figures from the *Sixteenth Census of the United States, Agriculture, 1940.*

FIGURE 11. Percentage of operators who are full owners in each county of the Southwestern Region, 1940.

cent and the other states ranked upward in the order of increasing equity were Texas (32.4), Mississippi (35.0), Arkansas (36.3), and Louisiana (36.6). Only 23.8 per cent of the farm land in the United States was operated by mortgage-free owners in 1940. Counties in the Rolling Plains and the High Plains of the western part of the region and the majority of the counties in the delta have more than 50 per cent of the owner-operated farms mortgaged. (Figure 13) In the Blackland the proportion of owner-operated farms with mortgages drops down to between 30 to 40 per cent. The majority of the counties in the Coastal Plain are under 30 per cent, except in Mississippi where the proportion with mortgages ranges up to 50 per cent with most of the counties clustering in the 40 to 50 per cent groups.

Nearly all forms of tenancy enumerated by the census are found in the areas where tenancy is prevalent. However, two types of tenants account for the major portion of the tenant-operated farms in the region. Croppers are associated with cotton production and are most prevalent in the areas where the average acreage of cotton per farm is less than 15 acres. Over 40 per cent of the farm operators in the alluvial plains of the Mississippi and Red rivers are croppers. (Figure 14) Most of the croppers in this area are colored and in some counties as many as seven-eighths of the tenant-operated farms are handled by colored croppers. The proportion of croppers drops to less than 5 per cent, except in isolated counties, in the western part of the region.

In the Texas Blackland Prairie, the Rolling Plains, and the High Plains where the average cotton acreage per farm is 20 acres or more the share tenant replaces the cropper as the most prevalent type of tenant. Over 35 per cent of the farm operators in these areas are share tenants. (Figure 15) Share tenancy also is prevalent in the rice area of southern Louisiana, the proportion exceeding 35 per cent in these parishes. In the Western Coastal Plain, share tenancy accounts for almost as large a proportion of the farm operators as croppers. In the northern portion of the Rolling Plains and in the Oklahoma Central Prairies the share-renting agreement is frequently supplemented with cash rent for pasture and grazing land. This combination agreement accounts for 5 per cent or more of the farm operators in these areas. (Figure 16) Except for isolated counties elsewhere this is the only section where this form of rental agreement assumes even a minimum significance. The cash tenant is found primarily in the grazing areas of southwest Texas and north central Oklahoma and in the sugar parishes of southern Louisiana. (Figure 17)

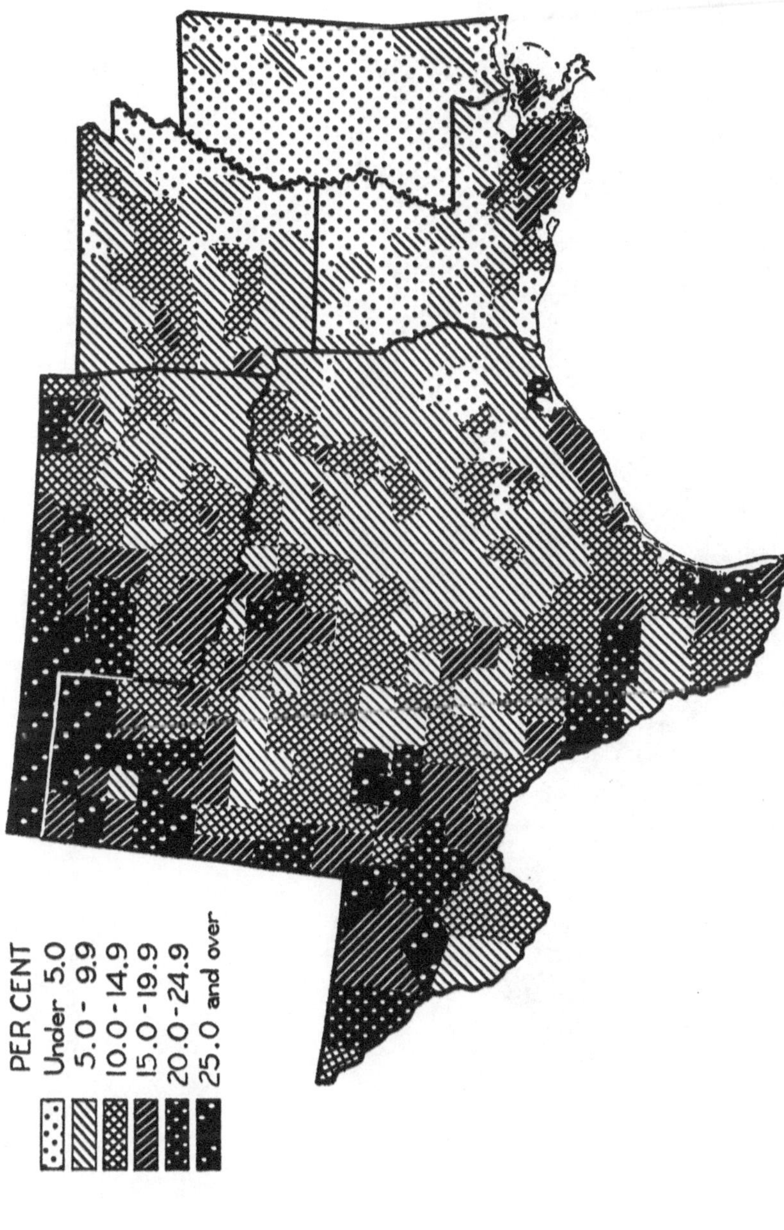

Source: Base figures from the *Sixteenth Census of the United States, Agriculture, 1940.*

FIGURE 12. Percentage of operators who are part owners in each county of the Southwestern Region, 1940.

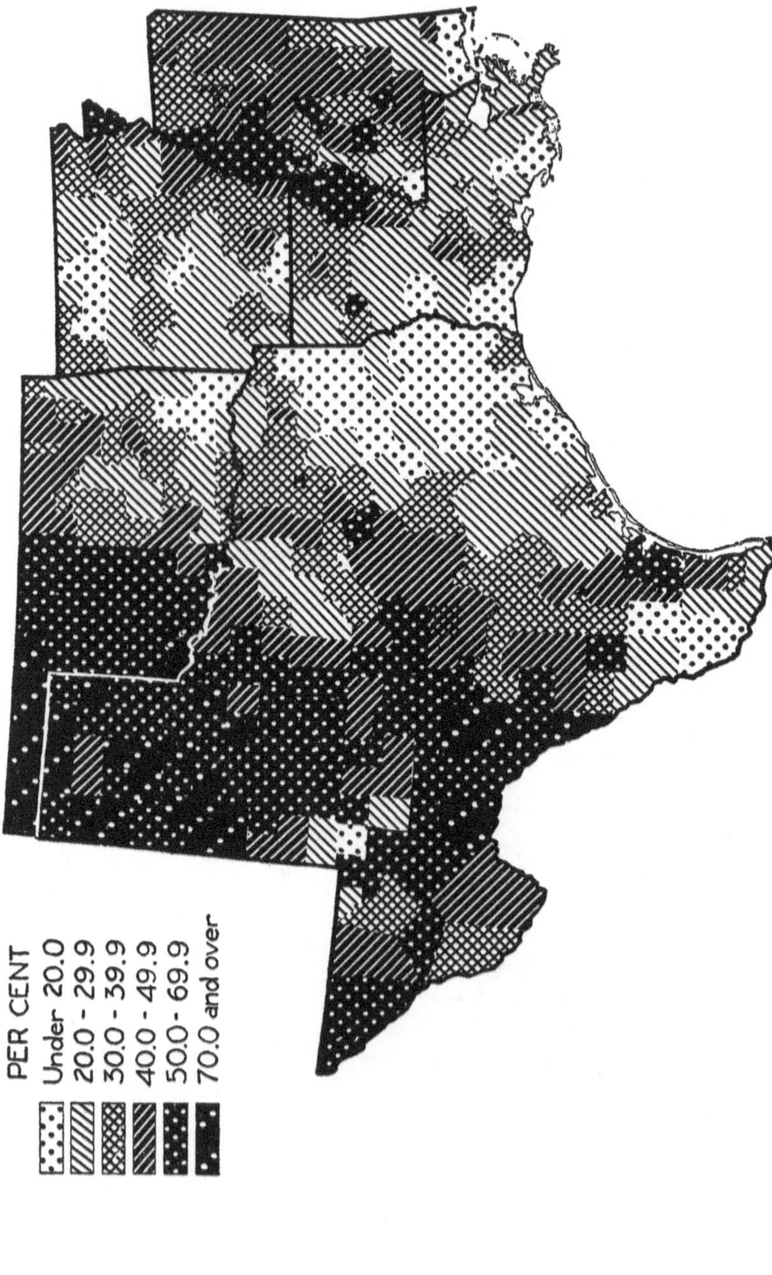

Source: Base figures from the *Sixteenth Census of the United States, Agriculture, 1940.*

FIGURE 13. Percentage of owner operated farms with mortgages in each county of the Southwestern Region, 1940.

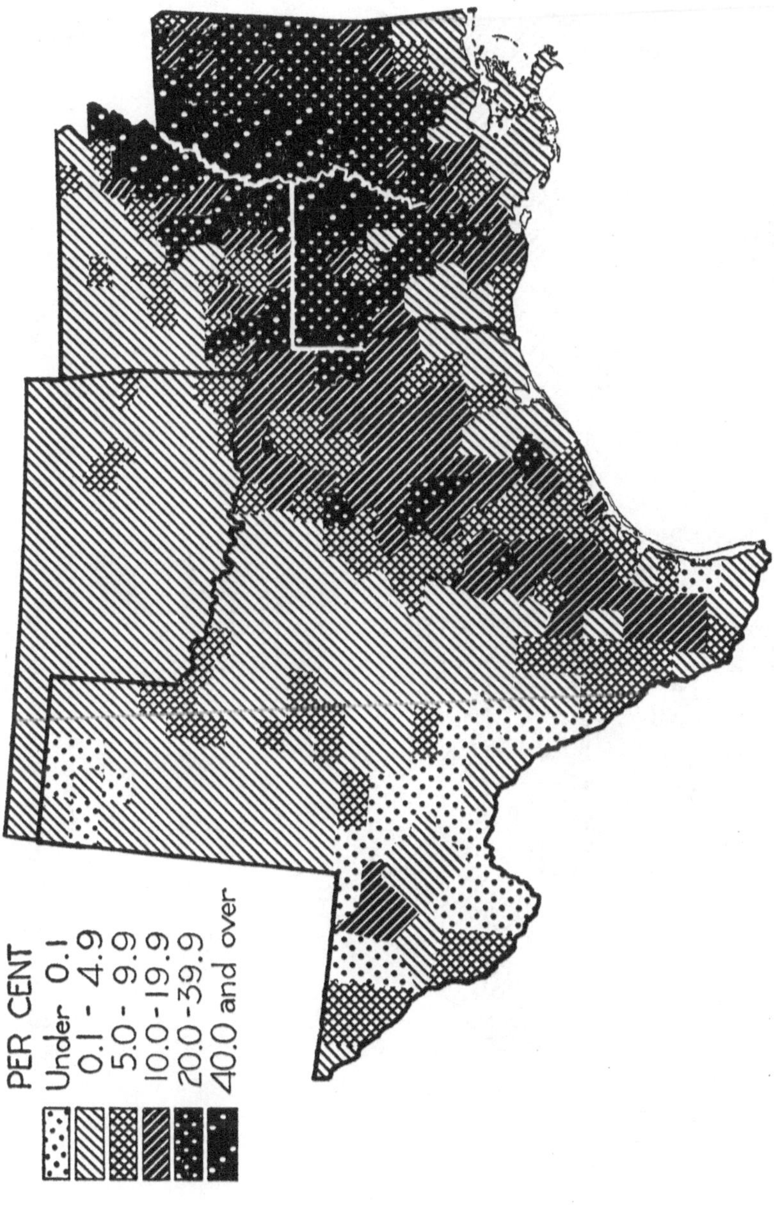

Source: Base figures from the *Sixteenth Census of the United States, Agriculture, 1940.*

FIGURE 14. Percentage of operators who are sharecroppers in each county of the Southwestern Region, 1940.

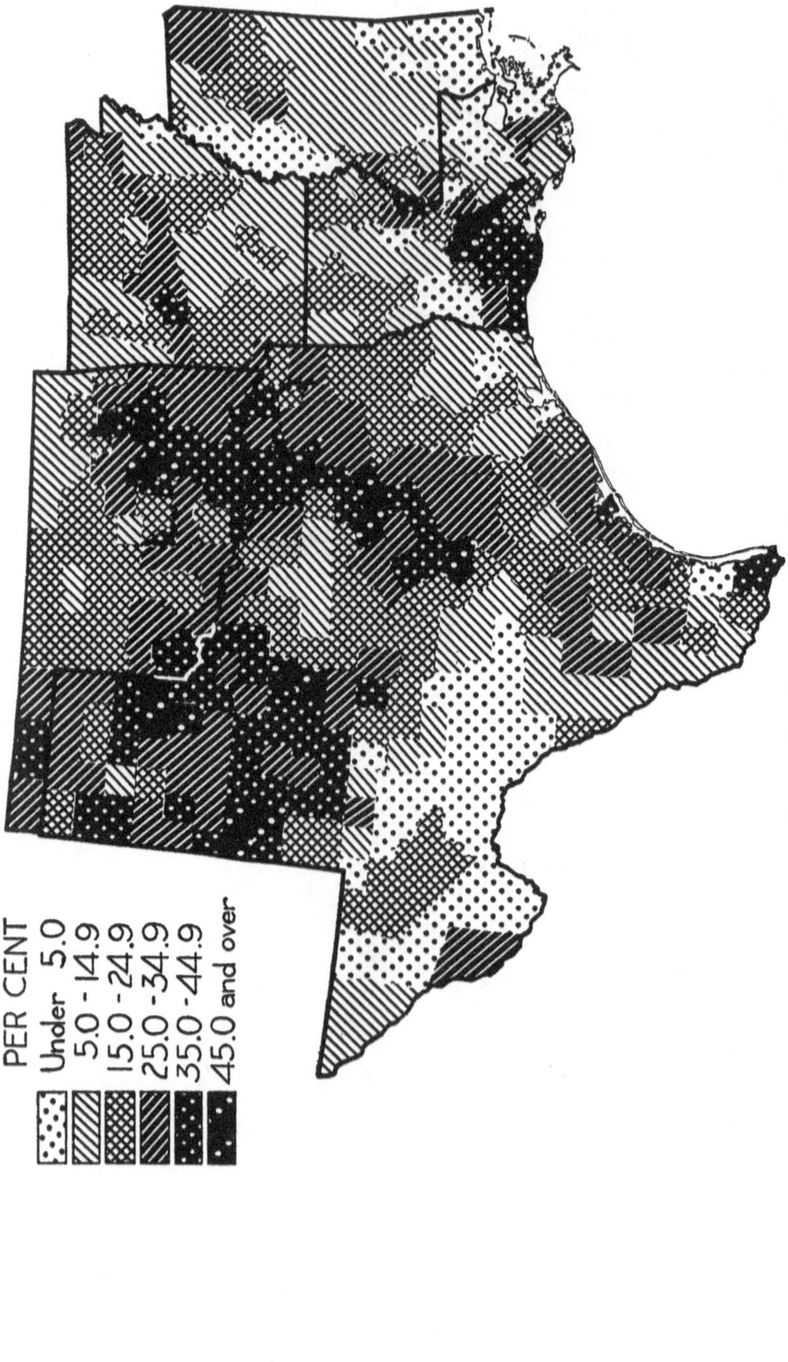

Source: Base figures from the *Sixteenth Census of the United States, Agriculture, 1940.*

FIGURE 15. Percentage of operators who are share tenants in each county of the Southwestern Region, 1940.

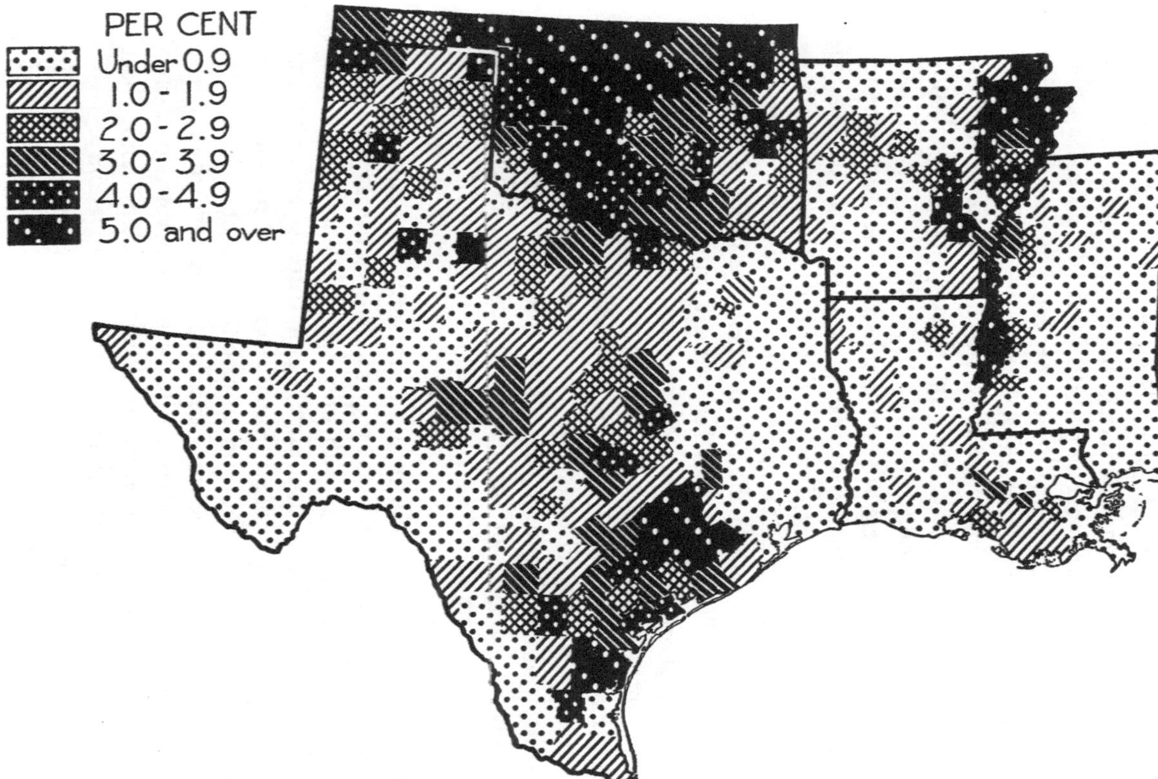

Source: Base figures from the *Sixteenth Census of the United States, Agriculture, 1940.*

FIGURE 16. Percentage of operators who are share-cash tenants in each county of the Southwestern Region, 1940.

The counties which use the most hired labor are in those areas where the chief agricultural enterprise is not adaptable to sharecropping or renting agreements, or in those areas where the average cotton acreage per farm exceeds 15 acres. The grazing area of Texas, the High Plains cotton area, and the Texas Blackland Prairie all have a ratio of 100 or more farm laborers per 100 farms. (Figure 18) Other areas where the ratio exceeds one laborer per farm are the sugar areas in Louisiana and the rice area of Arkansas, south Louisiana, and southeast Texas. In addition there are isolated counties in the delta where the planters have changed from the sharecropping organization to a wage-labor organization.

The proportion of farmers who do not live on the farm operated is not very significant in the region, except in the wheat and grazing areas of west and southwest Texas and western Oklahoma, where over 13 per cent of the farm operators live elsewhere. There are isolated counties elsewhere in the region where the proportion equals this, but the prevailing pattern is for farmers to live on the farm operated. Except for the few isolated counties, less than 5 per cent of the farm operators do not live on the farm operated. (Figure 19)

Size of Farm. The areas of the greatest density of population are also the areas with the smallest farms. The division between large and small farms is almost identical with the division between the dense and sparsely settled areas of the region (Figure 20), except for the border of intermediate-sized farms ranging from 125 to 225 acres that divides the two areas.

The eastern portion of the region is an area of small operating units. Over half of the counties in the eastern area average less than 40 acres of cropland per farm with only isolated counties exceeding 80 acres per farm. (Figure 21) Here again there is a border belt where the cropland acreage ranges from 80 to 120 acres per farm. The spotted character of the western portion results from the type of farming prevalent in the area. The southwestern area is devoted primarily to cattle ranching with only a very small portion devoted to a crop culture. In the northwest the farms are devoted to cotton and wheat so that the greatest portion of the farm is under cultivation.

Types of Cotton Culture. There are four types of cotton culture in the region, as pointed out elsewhere, delta cotton, upland cotton, blackland cotton, and dryland cotton. The extensiveness of cotton is rather sharply delineated by the average acreage of cotton per farm. (Figure 22) In the eastern areas of the region nearly all farmers raise some cotton. The number of acres is largely determined by the supply of labor available for the periods of maximum labor utilization. The Mississippi upland cotton areas, the Eastern Coastal Plain, vary from 5 to 10 acres per farm. The delta areas, the Mississippi Alluvial Plain, and the western upland cotton areas, the Western Coastal Plain, range from 10 to 15 acres per farm. Except for the delta, mechanization had made little headway prior to 1940 in these areas. Chopping and picking, which are the operations of maximum labor demand, were still done by hand labor. In the Texas Blackland Prairie, most of the operations are performed with power equipment and the farmers rely on migratory workers for harvest labor. The acreage of cotton per farm averaged around 20 acres. In the High Plains and the Rolling Plains, scant yields per acre have combined with mechanization to develop a more extensive cotton culture with acreages per farm exceeding 31.6. The average acreage per farm in some of the counties in this area exceeds 70 acres. Since the average is computed on the basis of the total number of farms in the area rather than on the basis of the number of farms reporting cotton, variations downward on the fringes of these several areas are an indication that cotton is a marginal crop and only a fraction of the farmers in the county raise cotton.

Farm Income. The gross income from products sold, used, or traded was under $400 on 34 per cent of the nation's farms in 1939. In each of the states in the Southwestern Region the proportion of farmers in this category was greater than the proportion for the nation. Texas, with only 35.4 per cent, came closest to the national average. Mississippi had 49.2 per cent, and the other states in descending order were Louisiana (42.7), Arkansas (39.9), and Oklahoma (37.0). At the other end of the income scale 8.2 per cent of the Texas farmers and 7.2 per cent of the Oklahoma farmers reported a gross income from all products sold, used, or traded of $2,500 or more. The proportion for Mississippi was only 1.3 per cent with Arkansas and Louisiana slightly higher at 3.1 per cent and 3.7 per cent, respectively.

Louisiana, Arkansas, and Mississippi are over-represented in each of the lower income groups. (Figure 23). The areas of concentration correspond roughly to the areas of population density. (Figure 7) The concentration of farms in the lower income group—$250-$399—is comparable in the three eastern states of the region to the distribution for the South. In the next two income groups—$400-$599 and $600-$999—the concentration is heaviest in the Mississippi Alluvial Plain. Farms in these three groups are sparsely scattered in the United States, except

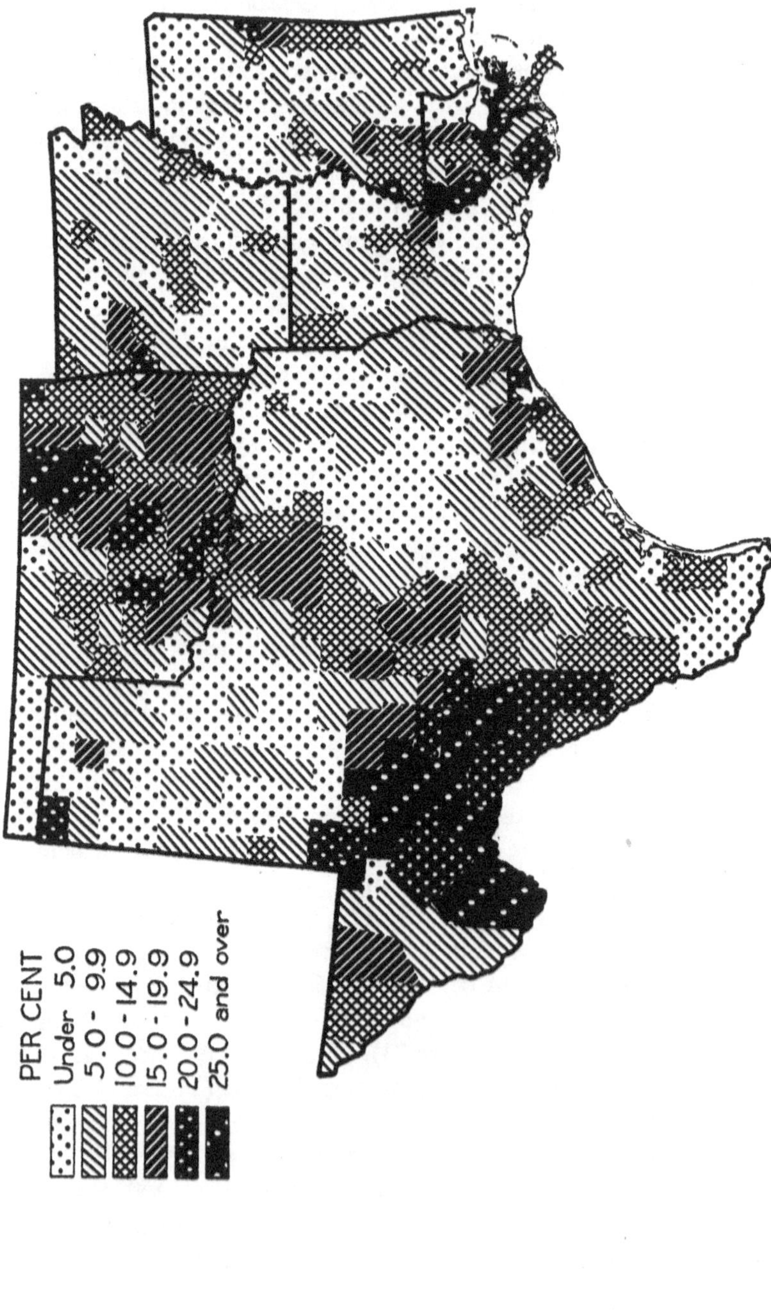

Source: Base figures from the *Sixteenth Census of the United States, Agriculture, 1940.*

FIGURE 17. Percentage of operators who are cash tenants in each county of the Southwestern Region, 1940.

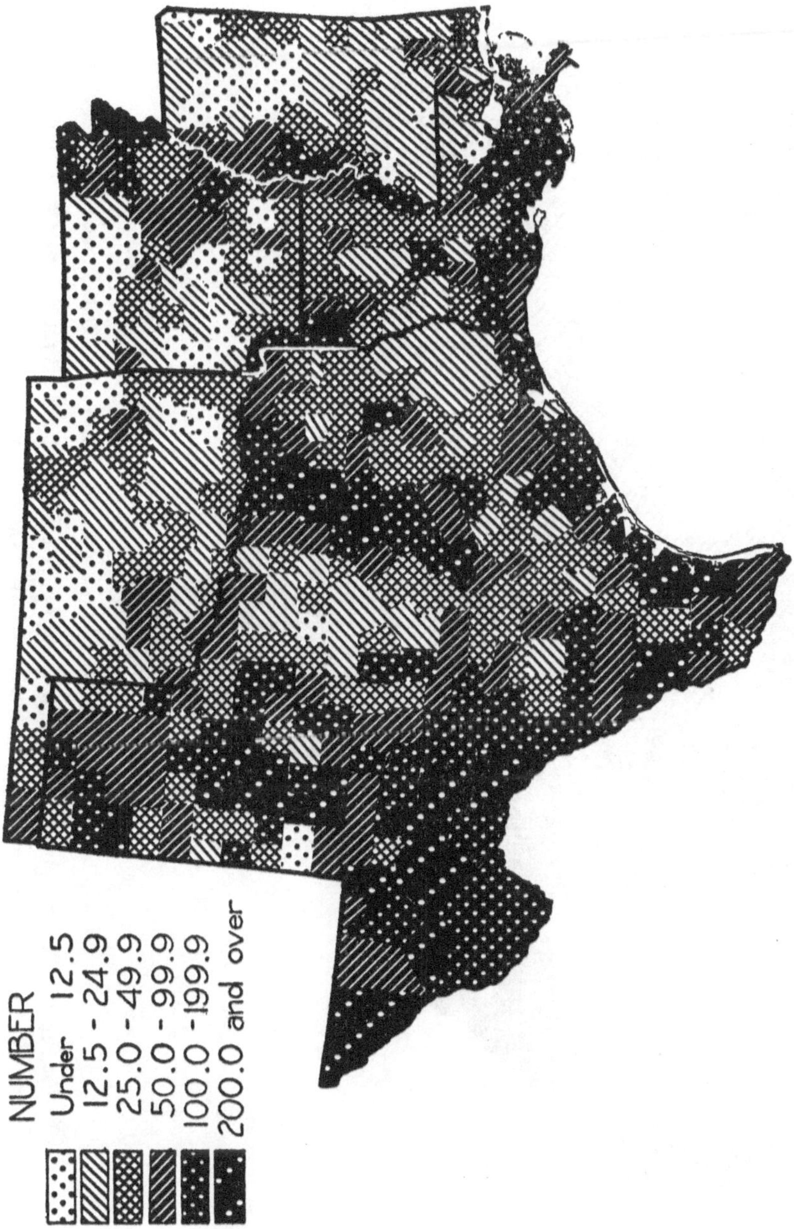

Source: Base figures from the *Sixteenth Census of the United States, Agriculture, 1940.*

FIGURE 18. Number of hired laborers per 100 farms in each county of the Southwestern Region, 1940.

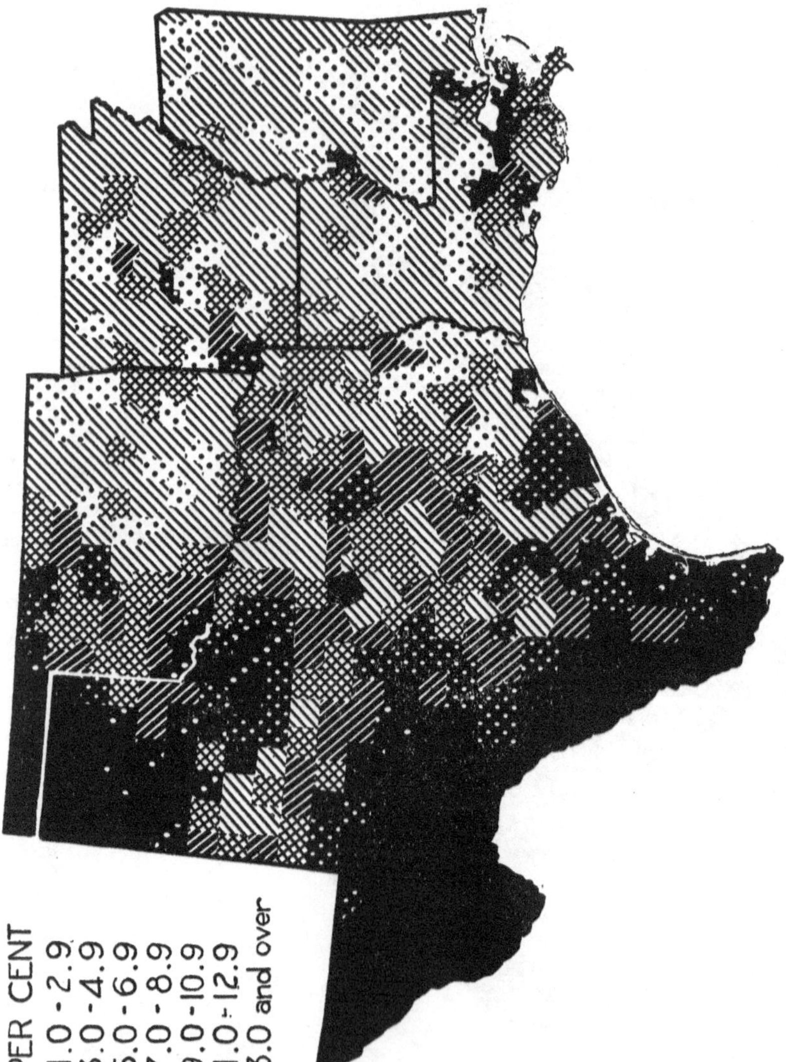

Source: Base figures from the *Sixteenth Census of the United States, Agriculture, 1940.*

FIGURE 19. Percentage of operators who do not live on the farm operated for each county in the Southwestern Region, 1940.

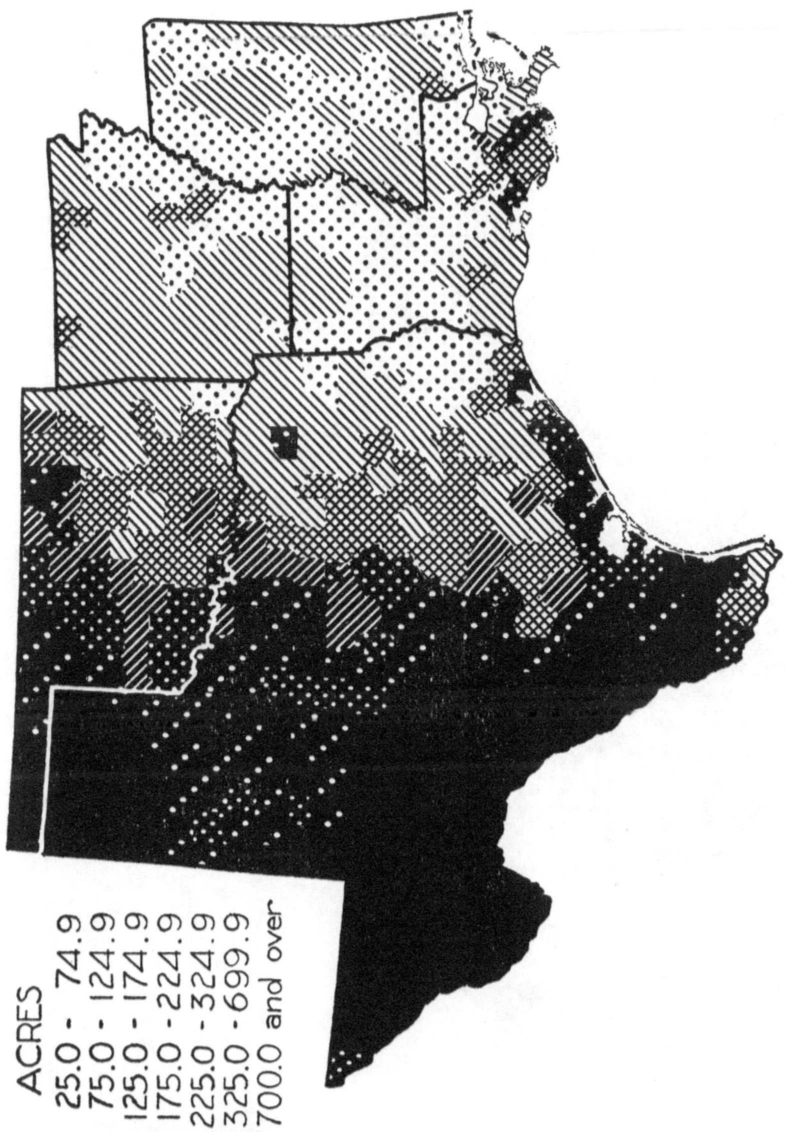

Source: Base figures from the *Sixteenth Census of the United States, 1940.*

FIGURE 20. Average number of acres per farm in each county in the Southwestern Region, 1939.

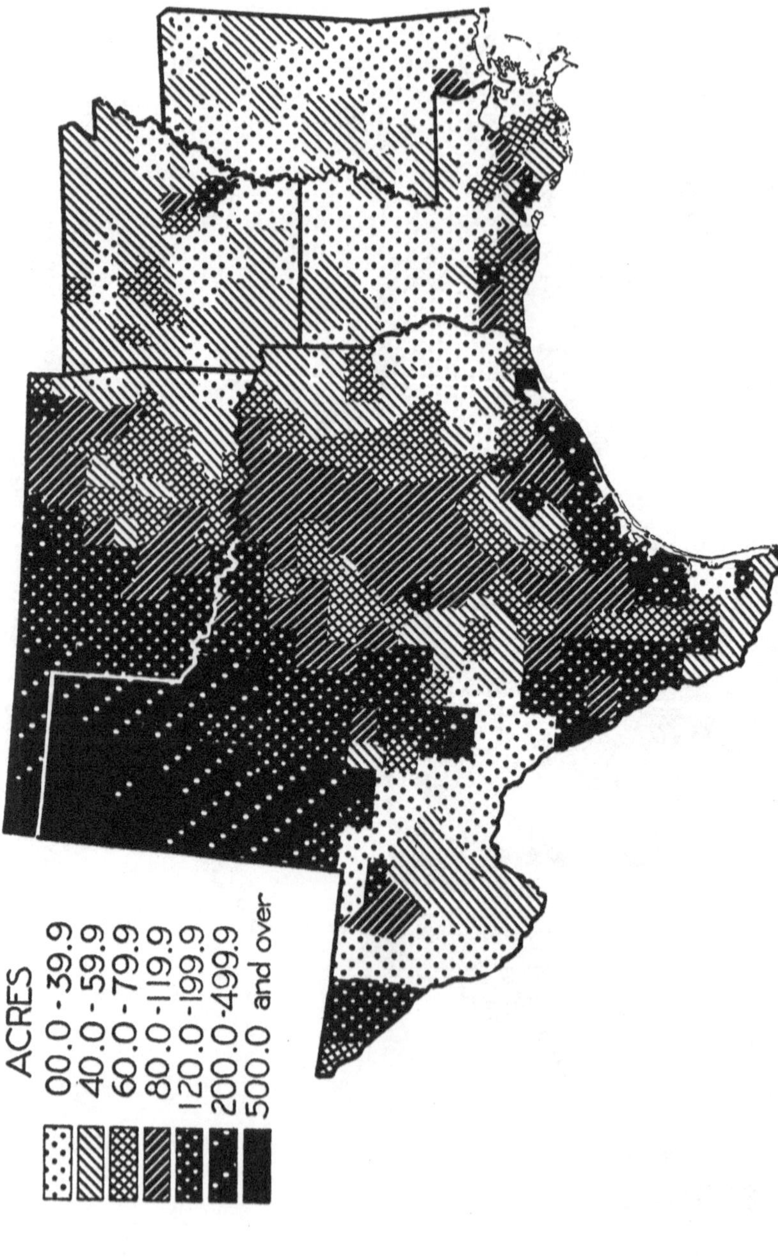

Source: Base figures from the *Sixteenth Census of the United States, Agriculture, 1940.*

FIGURE 21. Average number of acres available for crops per farm in each county in the Southwestern Region, 1939.

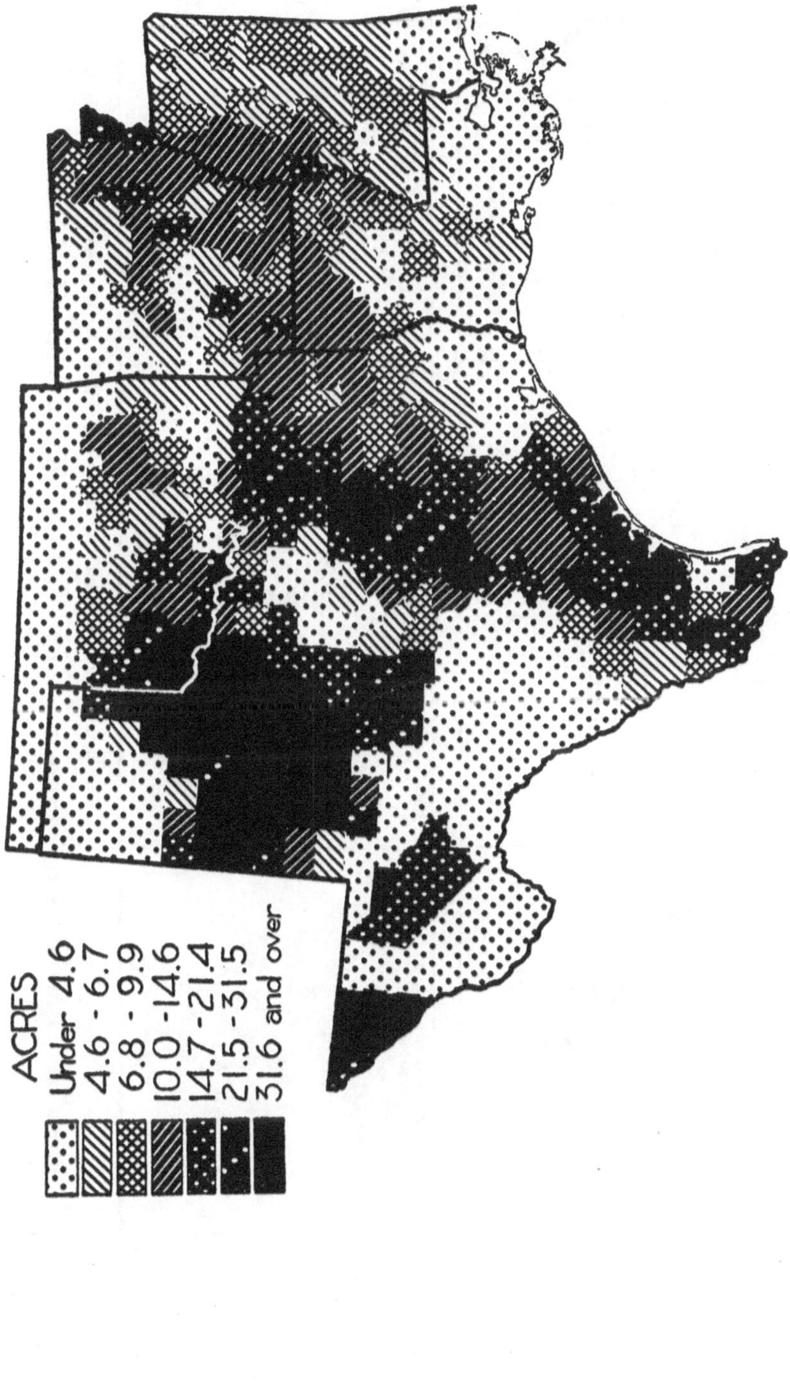

Source: Base figures from the *Sixteenth Census of the United States, Agriculture, 1940.*

FIGURE 22. Average number of acres in cotton per farm in each county in the Southwestern Region, 1939.

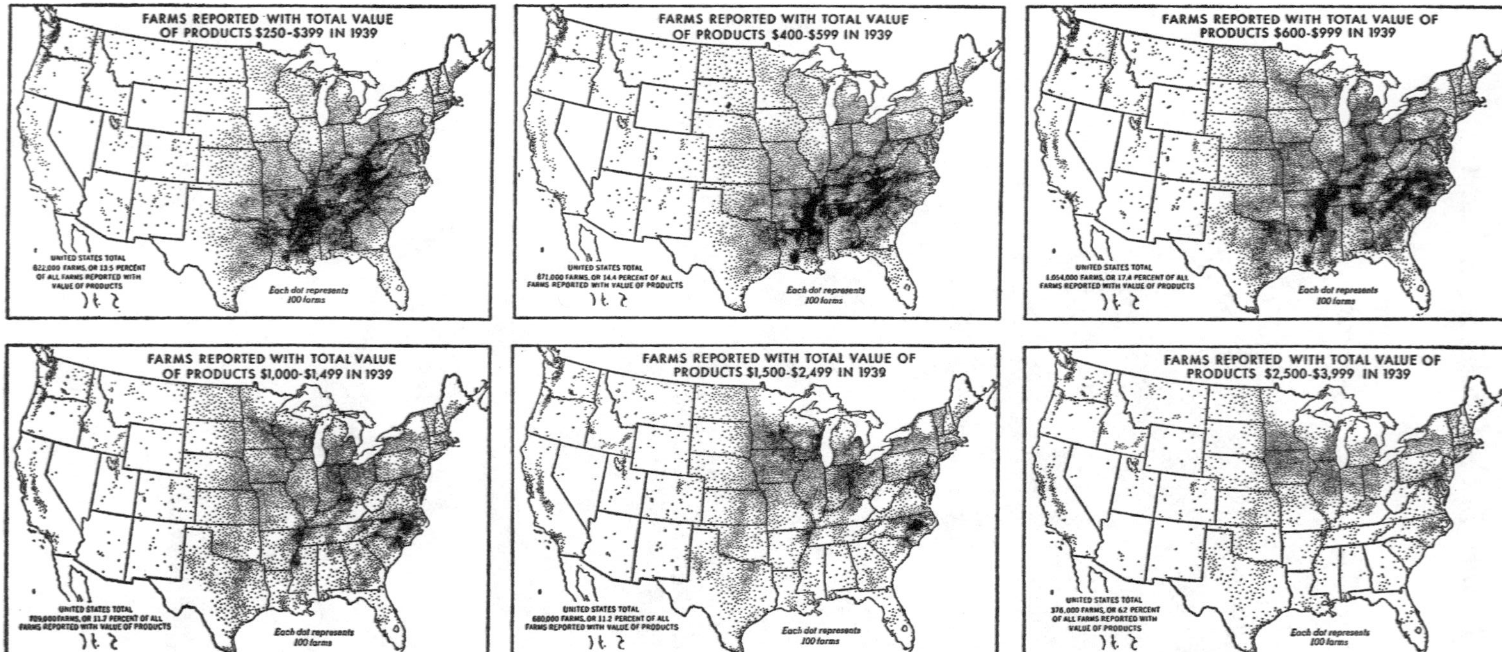

Base figures from the Bureau of the Census. U. S. Dept. of Agriculture, Bureau of Agricultural Economics.

FIGURE 23. Distribution of farms with specified gross income from products sold, traded, or used on the farm in the United States, 1940.

in the Appalachian mountain regions and the South. In each of the income groups above $1,000 the other areas are more heavily represented than the South and the Southwestern Region. In the income group $2,500-$3,999 there are very few farms in the South and a definite concentration in the North Central Region.

The same general relationship exists between the states in the average gross income of farmers. The average gross income for Texas farmers is approximately $1,250 and for Oklahoma farmers $1,000. The average income for Arkansas farmers is slightly under and for Louisiana farmers slightly over $750. Mississippi farmers are at the bottom of the economic scale with an average gross income of $550.

Level of Living. All counties in the Coastal Plain and in the Interior Highlands have a lower level of living for farm people than the average for the United States and all counties in the Interior Plains and in the Inter-Mountain Plateau are equal to or above the level for the nation. (Fgure 24) The presence or absence of an urban population has only a slight effect on the level of living of farm people in the region. The area around New Orleans is in the next to the lowest index group both for the nation and Louisiana. The counties in the Houston-Galveston area and in the Corpus Christi area have a slightly higher index than the surrounding counties but none of

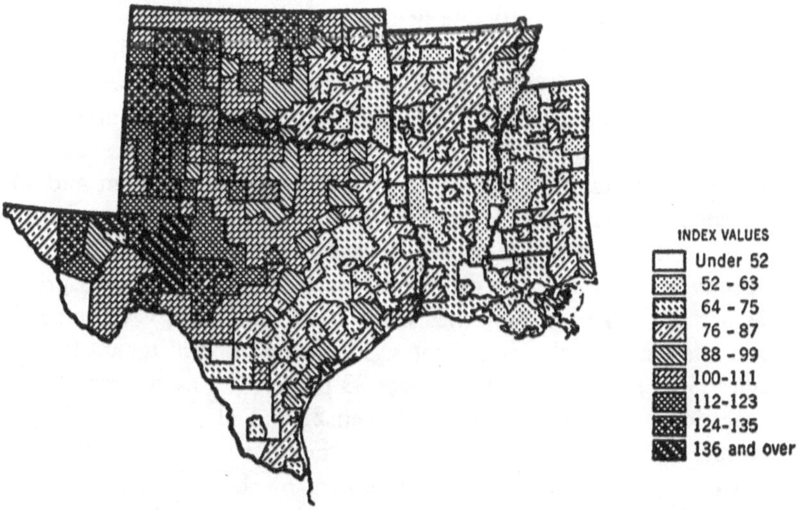

Source: Base figures from the *Sixteenth Census of the United States, Agriculture, 1940.*

FIGURE 24. Rural farm level of living index by counties in the Southwestern Region, 1940.

the other counties with large urban concentrations of population deviate markedly from the general pattern of the surrounding areas.

The indices for the eastern counties are 30 to 40 points below the indices for the western counties. There is an inverse relationship between the ratio of farm persons to farm land and the level of living. With minor deviations, the areas with the largest number of persons per 1,000 acres of farmland are also the areas with lowest index on the level of living scale.

The index of communication (see Appendix A) which is a composite measure of the extent to which people in a given area are being exposed to ideas from other areas, shows a marked difference between the eastern and western divisions of the region. (Figure 25) The Coastal Plains and Interior Plains and the Inter-Mountain Plateau have a high index. Deviations from the general pattern are observed in the New Orleans metropolitan area, in the Houston-Galveston area, and in the Rio Grande Plain, all of which lie in the Coastal Plain but have a high index of communication in sharp contrast to the surrounding areas. The counties in which Dallas, Fort Worth, and other metropolitan areas lie, also have higher indices than the surrounding counties. The counties in the western portion with one exception have indices over 50 and the majority of the counties in the east fall below 50.

Size of Family. Thirty-one per cent of the 1,500,000 farm families in the Southwestern Region have three or more children under 21 years old. Tenant families have more children than owner families. In Oklahoma 23 per cent of the tenant families had no children under 21 years old as compared to 40.9 per cent of the owner families. Among tenant families 37.6 per cent had 3 or more children and 13.4 per cent had 5 or more children under 21 years old. The proportions for owner families in Oklahoma were 24.2 per cent and 7.3 per cent, respectively. Though the difference between the two tenure groups was not as marked in the other states as in Texas and Oklahoma the same relationship exists in all states. The proportion of tenant families having 3 or more children was over 33 per cent in each state and the proportion among owners was between 21 and 31 per cent. The fact that more than 32 per cent of the owner families have no children over 21 years old may in part be accounted for by the fact that the owner families are older and the children may have passed their 21st birthday but it is also due to a lower fertility ratio among owner families.

There are more childless families among Negro than among white

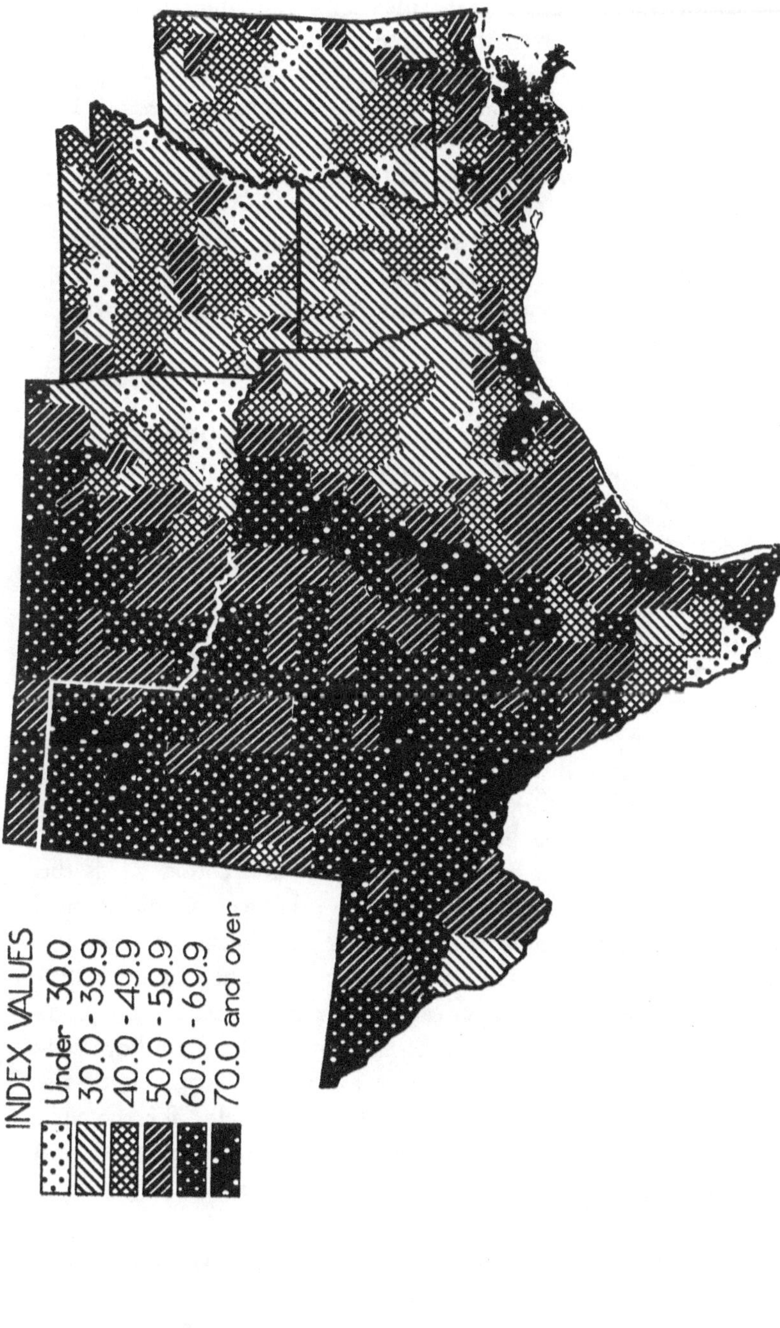

Source: Base figures from the *Sixteenth Census of the United States, Agriculture, 1940.*

FIGURE 25. Communication index for each county in the Southwestern Region, 1940.

families. Forty per cent or more of the nonwhite families in each state in the region do not have any children under 21 years old. Comparable proportions for the total population (including nonwhite) range from 37 to 40.4 per cent. However, the proportions of Negro families with three or more children also exceeds the proportion in the total population in all states except Arkansas where nonwhite families are less than 1 per cent below the proportion for the total. The discrepancy is even greater when the proportion with large families of 5 or more children are considered for the nonwhite and total population. In Oklahoma the proportion of nonwhite families with five or more children is more than 75 per cent larger than the proportion for the total. The smallest difference between the two groups is in Arkansas with a difference of nearly 20 per cent.

The Sample Areas

Now that a broad view of the five-state region has been presented, there remains the need for certain additional details with respect to the local sample areas. The sample areas lie in four natural subregions. The Eastern and Western Coastal Plains and the Texas Blackland Prairie are natural subregions of the Gulf Coastal Plain. The Rolling Plains is a natural subregion of the Interior Plains. Cotton production is a major enterprise in each of these subregions. However, the factors associated with cotton production differ considerably in each. Some of these deviations have been pointed out previously. The differences in yields will serve to establish the relationship between the areas before discussing the characteristics of the individual sample counties. (Figure 26)

The Mississippi sample lies on the western edge of the Eastern Coastal Plain. In terms of both cotton acreage and cotton yields the Eastern Coastal Plain differs from the two other coastal plains subregions. Following the same general trend in acreage to 1936, the acreage increased sharply in 1937, and though it declined again in 1938 it remained at a higher level than the acreage in the other subregions through 1942. Since 1929 yields on the Eastern Coastal Plain have consistently been higher than the five-year average 1928-1932, with the single exception of 1941. However, in 1942 the yields for the area were again up 40 per cent over the average. The higher yields are partly due to the more extensive use of commercial fertilizer by farmers in the Eastern Coastal Plain.

The Arkansas and Louisiana samples lie in the Western Coastal

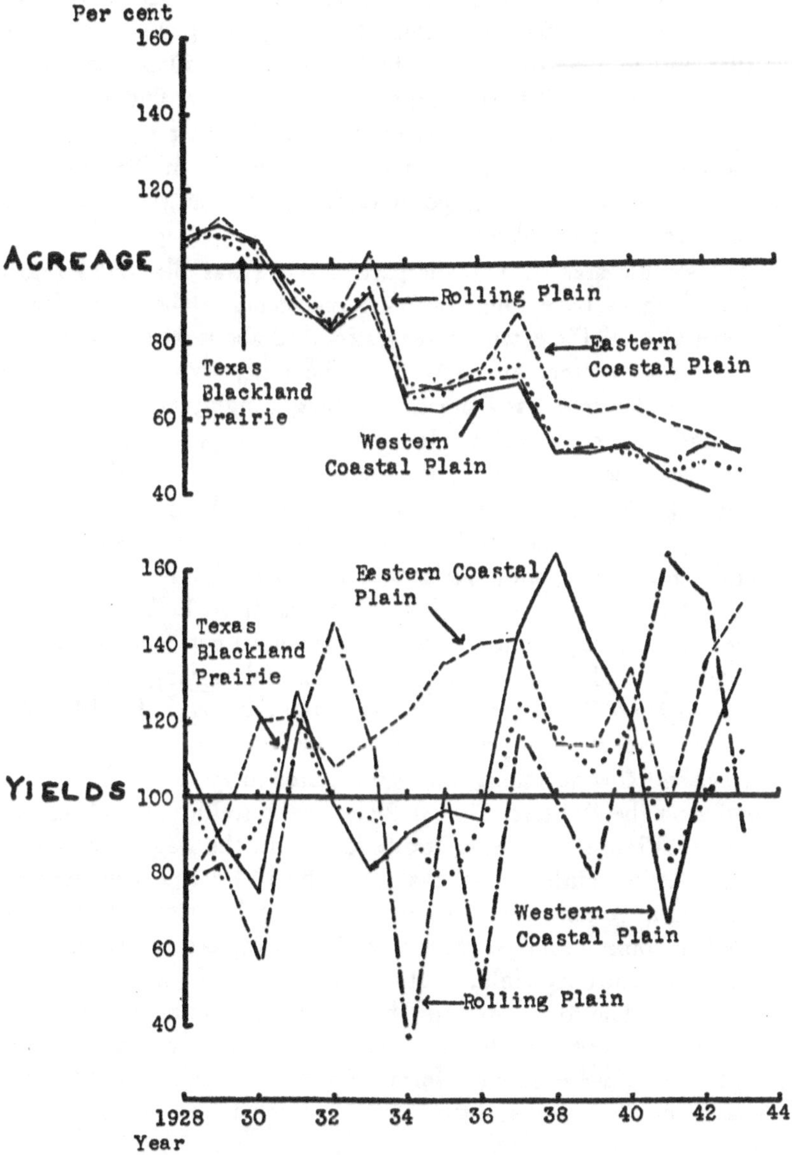

Source: Based on data compiled by the United States Department of Agriculture, Bureau of Agricultural Economics.

FIGURE 26. Trend in cotton acreage and cotton yields in four production areas in the Southwestern Region. (Five-year average 1928-1932 = 100 per cent.)

Plain. In this area cotton acreage has continued to decline with only a slight rise from 1935 to 1937 after which they dropped abruptly again in 1938 and in 1942 the acreage for the area was 50 per cent below the average for 1928-1932. Cotton yields per acre have fluctuated much more in the Western Coastal Plain than in the other two subregions of the Gulf Coastal Plain, ranging from 20 below in 1930 to 60 per cent above the five-year average in 1938. In 1942 the yields were only 10 per cent above the average.

The sample area in Texas is part of the Texas Blackland Prairie. Cotton acreages have followed the same trend as the trend for the Western Coastal Plain with acreages in 1942 about 50 per cent below the five-year average. In contrast to the other two areas, however, yields have deviated less from the average, ranging only 20 per cent above and 20 per cent below. In 1942 the cotton yield per acre in the Texas Blackland Prairie was the same as the average for 1928-1932.

The Oklahoma sample lies in the Rolling Plains. It is in the semiarid climatic zone of the region, which has 24 to 40 inches of rainfall annually. Cotton acreages have followed the same general trend as for other areas except for a slight rise from 1941 to 1942 which brought the acreage in the area up to about 40 per cent of the 1928-1932 average. Yields, however, because of the varying rainfall, have fluctuated from 60 per cent under to 60 per cent over. In 1942 cotton yields per acre were 55 per cent above the five-year average.

Arkansas Coastal Plain. The sample area in Arkansas lies in three counties on the Western Coastal Plain in the south central section of the state. (Figure 1). It is centrally located in the state type of farming area 8, the South Coastal Plain, in which 84 per cent of the farms are classed as cotton farms with a few fruit and vegetable farms interspersed in some localities. (Figure 2) The sample counties lie within the area in which Norfolk, Ruston, and associated soils predominate. (Figure 27) The topography of the area is undulating to gently rolling and was forest covered in its native state. The area in which the sample farms were located forms a crescent beginning in central Nevada moving southeastward into Columbia and western Union County.

Union County which was the only county established in 1830 had 640 inhabitants. By 1850 there were 10,000 inhabitants and, with some fluctuation, the growth continued to 1930 when there were 56,000 inhabitants. The population dropped to 50,000 in 1940. Columbia County was organized prior to 1860 when it had a population of 12,000

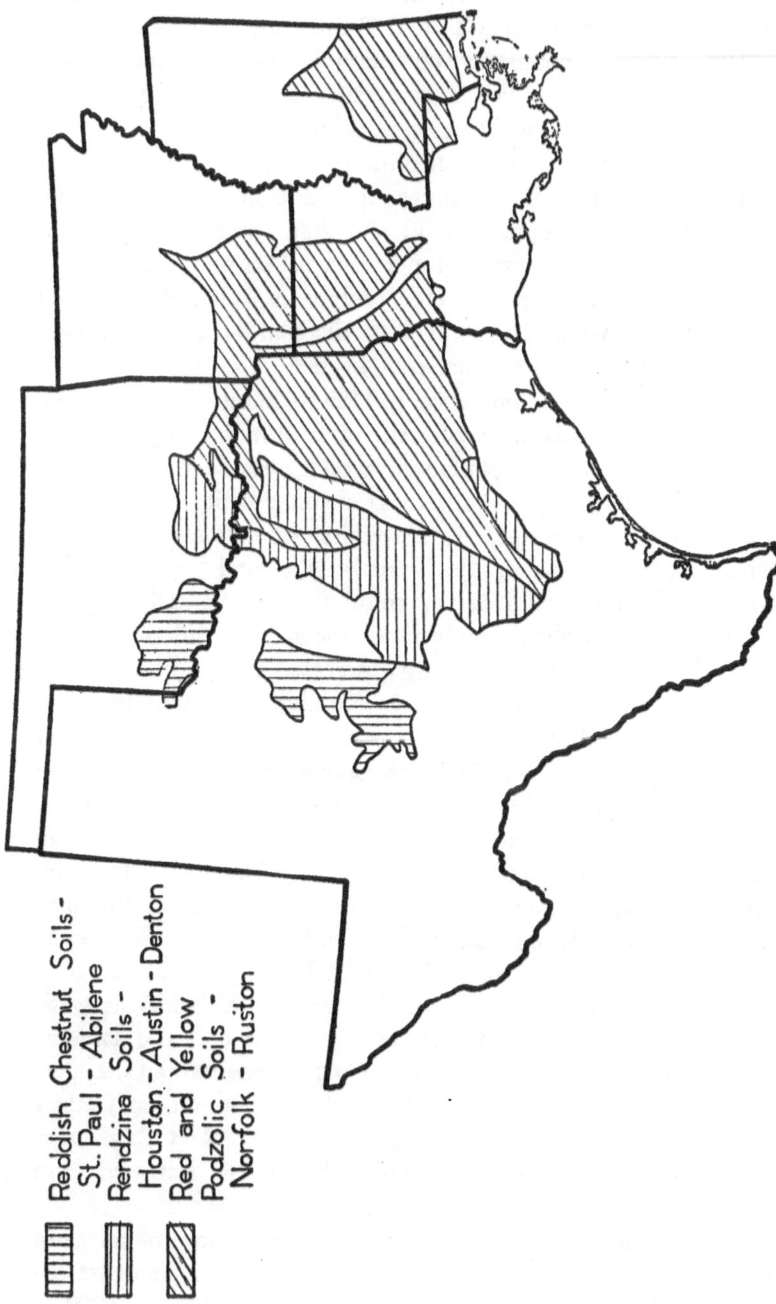

Source: Data on soils adapted from the soils map "Soils of the United States" in the *Yearbook of Agriculture, 1938*, "Soils and Men."

FIGURE 27. Associated soil areas in the Southwestern Region in which the sample counties are located.

which increased to 30,000 by 1940, and Nevada increased from 13,000 in the first census in 1880 to 22,000 in 1920 dropping to 20,000 by 1940. From 1940 to 1943 the population of Union County remained almost stationary decreasing by only 0.8 per cent. Columbia and Nevada counties decreased by 12 and 17 per cent, respectively.

The counties were entirely rural until 1900 when cities were enumerated in Nevada and Union counties. In each county the urban population has increased at a more rapid rate than the rural population and in 1940 Union County was 31 per cent urban and Nevada was 16 per cent urban. None of the trade centers in Columbia exceeded 2,500 prior to 1930 when 11 per cent of the population was urban. The proportion increased to 15 per cent by 1940.

In 1860 over half of the population in Union County were Negroes. The proportion decreased to 31 per cent in 1930 increasing to 35 per cent in 1940. The urban population, which was increasing more rapidly than the rural population, attracted more white persons than Negroes and this increase in the urban white population resulted in a decrease in the importance of the Negro in the total population. In Columbia and Nevada counties the trend is reversed and Negroes, which accounted for only 29 per cent of the total population at the time of the first census in each county, increased in importance to 37 per cent in Nevada and 45 per cent in Columbia County in 1940.

There were over 15,000 persons in the agricultural labor force in the three counties in 1940. In Columbia County over half of the labor force was colored and in the other two counties, Nevada and Union, the proportion of colored was slightly under one-half. In each county the proportion of owners and the proportion of laborers in the total labor force increased. Twenty-four, 23, and 34 per cent of the agricultural labor force in Columbia, Nevada, and Union counties owned the farms they were operating in 1940 and 18, 14, and 20 per cent, respectively, were at the other end of the agricultural ladder as wage laborers. The owners were predominantly white and the laborers were predominantly colored. Columbia County tenants and croppers decreased to 30 and 13 per cent, respectively, and in Union County the comparable decrease was to 24 and 9 per cent. In Nevada County tenants increased from 30 to 32 per cent and croppers decreased from 15 to 12 per cent.

While the population more than doubled, the number of farms in the counties increased by around 80 per cent. Farms increased from 2,000 in Columbia in 1880 to 4,800 in 1930 and dropped to 3,700 in

1940. The same general trend characterized Nevada and Union counties as well. From 1910 to 1940 the most prevalent size of farm in Columbia and Union counties was from 20 to 49 acres per farm. Thirty-six per cent of the farms in each county were in this group in 1940. Ten years earlier the proportion of farms in this group was 46 per cent in Columbia County and 41 per cent in Union County. In these two counties the number of farms with 100 acres or more per farm have increased during the period 1910 to 1940 and the number of farms 100 acres have decreased, with only minor deviations from this general pattern. In Nevada County there has been less stability and a less marked trend. The modal group was 50-99 in 1910, 20-49 acres in 1920 and 1930, and 50-99 in 1940. Farms under 50 acres decreased from 1930 to 1940 and farms over 50 acres increased during this period. Previous to 1930 there was considerable fluctuation in the size of farms in Nevada County.

The trend in acres available for crops is comparable to the trend for the number of farms, except that the maximum acreage in crops was recorded in 1920 for Columbia and Nevada counties and in 1910 for Union County. In Columbia and Nevada counties the acres in crops dropped sharply during the next decade and increased slightly again by 1940 in Columbia County. The increase in Nevada County was more pronounced. In Union County the acres in crops dropped slightly between 1910 and 1920 with an abrupt drop in recorded acreage for 1930. The decline continued to 1940 though not as strong as during the preceding decade.

Cotton acreage in Columbia and Nevada counties increased steadily to 1930 when it reached a maximum acreage of 91,602 acres and 56,418 acres, respectively. In 1940 the acreage was reduced by approximately one-half in these two counties. The number of acres planted to cotton in Union County was much more erratic, fluctuating from 30 to 50 thousand acres and dropping to nearly 22,000 acres in 1940. The trend in acres planted to cotton for the three counties in the Arkansas sample is comparable to the trend for the Western Coastal Plain. (Figure 28) Following the initial loss in acreage in 1934 caused by the cotton control program under the Agricultural Adjustment Administration, the acreage planted to cotton has continued to decline in the area. Production for the area has also declined during the period from 1934 to 1944. Despite a 30 per cent increase in yields for 1942 over the 1928 to 1932 average, production was 40 per cent under the average. Yields per acre in the counties vary considerably from year to year, fluctuat-

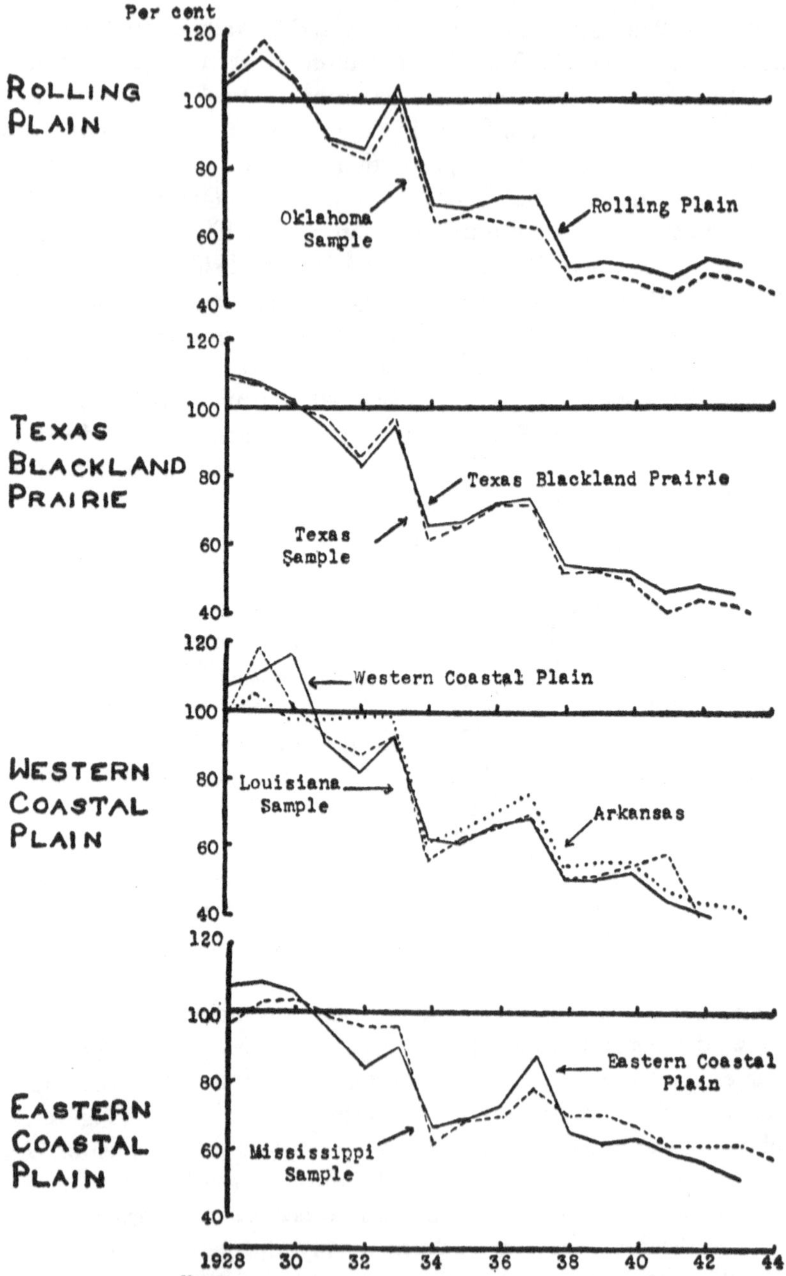

Source: Based on data compiled by the United States Department of Agriculture, Bureau of Agricultural Economics.

FIGURE 28. Comparison of trend in cotton acreage in four production areas in the Southwestern Region with the sample counties studied within each area. (Five-year average 1929-1932 = 100 per cent.)

ing from 40 per cent under the five-year average in 1930 to 50 per cent over the average in 1937.

Louisiana Coastal Plain. The four sample parishes are Bienville, Jackson, and Lincoln in the North Louisiana Upland Cotton type of farming area, and Winn in the Central Louisiana Cutover Pine type of farming area. (Figure 2) Cotton is the predominant crop in both areas with self-sufficing farms more prevalent in the central area. In Louisiana an intensive survey was made of a selected area in each parish.

The four parishes steadily increased in population from the first census to 1910. The increase continued in Jackson Parish to 1920. In Jackson Parish there was a slight decline from 1920 to 1930 followed by a marked increase between 1930 and 1940 bringing the total up to 18,000 persons. In Bienville and Lincoln parishes there was a slight decrease between 1910 and 1920 followed by a marked increase between 1920 and 1930, continuing to 25,000 inhabitants in 1940 in Lincoln Parish. The population in Bienville Parish remained almost stationary at 24,000 persons during the latter decade. In Winn Parish the decline continued from 1910 to 1930 and the increase from 1930 to 1940 was not very marked but brought the population up to 17,000 persons. All parishes in the Louisiana sample decreased in population during the period 1940 to 1943, the rate ranging from 9 per cent in Lincoln Parish to nearly 15 per cent in Bienville Parish. There are no urban centers in Bienville Parish and in Jackson Parish there were none until 1940 when 15 per cent of the population was classed as urban. In Lincoln and Winn parishes over 15 per cent of the population has been enumerated as urban since 1910. The proportion in Winn Parish increased to 27 per cent in 1940. In Lincoln Parish the proportion increased to 43 per cent in 1930 but dropped to 29 per cent again by 1940.

Considerable variation exists in the proportion of colored in the total population since the first enumeration. In Bienville the proportion ranged from 35 per cent in 1850 to 48 per cent in 1880 to 41 in 1920 and back to 48 per cent in 1940. In Lincoln Parish the proportion dropped from 44 per cent in 1880 to 37 per cent in 1920 rising again to 45 per cent in 1940. The proportion in Winn Parish was smaller but the trend was comparable, dropping from 20 per cent in 1860 to 14 per cent in 1890 and rising gradually to 25 per cent in 1940. In Jackson Parish the extremes were more marked, the proportion rising from 39 per cent in 1850 to 45 per cent in 1870 and 1880. In 1890 and

1900 there were 35 per cent colored. The proportion dropped to 28 per cent in 1920 and rose again to 32 per cent in 1940.

The number of persons in the agricultural labor force in the sample parishes in Louisiana decreased from 19,500 to 14,000 between 1930 and 1940. Whereas whites and Negroes left the labor force in about equal numbers for the area as a whole, in Jackson Parish the loss to the white labor force was much greater than the loss in the Negro agricultural labor force. In the other three parishes Negroes left in slightly greater numbers than white workers. The change in the distribution of the agricultural labor force by tenure in Jackson Parish also differs from the change in the other three parishes. Twenty-six per cent of the labor force were owners in 1930 and only 22 per cent in 1940, tenants dropped from 27 to 12 per cent, croppers remained the same at 12 per cent, and wage laborers increased from 7 to 16 per cent with unpaid family workers also showing a marked increase in proportion to the total population, 23 to 32 per cent. In the other three parishes owners and wage laborers increased. Tenants and croppers decreased in Bienville and Winn parishes, and in Lincoln Parish these two groups increased slightly, 3 and 2 per cent, respectively. Winn Parish, with 47 per cent of the agricultural labor force owning their own farms, had the highest proportion of owners for any of the counties sampled.

By 1900 the number of farms in Winn Parish was nearly 1,600 and each census since then had returned between 1,600 and 1,700 farms for the parish. In Lincoln Parish the number of farms reached a peak of 3,400 in 1930 and dropped to 2,800 in 1940. The trend in Bienville was comparable, except the peak was 3,800 and the number dropped to 3,000 in 1940. In Jackson Parish there were 2,000 farms in 1920 and the number dropped to 1,600 in 1940.

From 1900 to 1940 farms with 20 to 49 acres per farm were the most prevalent size of farms in Bienville and Lincoln parishes. Similarly sized farms have predominated in Jackson and Winn parishes since 1920. In 1900 and 1910 there were an equal number of farms in each of the three groups, 20-49, 50-99, and 100-174 acres in these two parishes. The proportion of farms with 20-49 acres was the same in 1940 as in 1930 in these two parishes, 34 and 40 per cent, respectively, but the proportion decreased in Bienville and Lincoln parishes from 52 to 38 per cent and from 43 to 37 per cent, respectively.

The land available for crops increased to 137,500 acres in Bienville Parish and to 140,400 acres in Lincoln Parish. In Jackson Parish the maximum was 74,700 in 1920 after which it dropped to 60,700 in 1930 and continued to decline to 58,500 in 1940. The trend in Winn Parish was comparable to Jackson except the maximum was only 54,300 in 1920 and the acreage dropped to 42,000 in 1940.

In Bienville and Lincoln parishes the acreage planted to cotton increased with slight fluctuation to a maximum acreage in 1929. Jackson and Winn parishes arrived at the maximum acreage in 1929 with much greater fluctuations from decade to decade. In each of the four parishes the 1939 acreage in cotton was approximately half the reported acreage for 1929. The yearly trend in acreage is comparable to the trend for Arkansas and for the Western Coastal Plain. (Figure 28) In 1942 the combined acreage in the Louisiana parishes was 60 per cent below the average for the five-year period 1928 to 1932. With cotton yields only slightly above the five-year average in 1942, production for the year also was down nearly 60 per cent below the average.

Mississippi Coastal Plain. Marion and Jefferson Davis counties in Mississippi lie on the Gulf Coastal Plain east of the Mississippi River in the Eastern Coastal Plain. (Figure 1) They are part of the Mississippi type of farming area 8, the Longleaf Pine Area. (Figure 2) Cotton farms predominate, 77 per cent in 1930, with self-sufficing and general farming interspersed and part-time farming prevalent in some areas. Norfolk, Ruston, and associated soils are the most prevalent soil types in the area. (Figure 27) The topography, as elsewhere on the Gulf Coastal Plain is gently rolling. The area was originally covered with a forest of longleaf yellow pines.

Population increased slowly up until 1880. At this time there was some farming on the bottom lands. Railroads crossed the area between 1880 and 1900 and sawmilling assumed great importance in the economic life. Population increased from 7,000 to 13,500 in Marion County from 1880 to 1900 and continued to increase at a slightly slower rate to 24,000 in 1940. Jefferson Davis County which was established as a separate county in 1910 with 13,000 inhabitants had increased to 16,000 by 1940. Both counties experienced a net loss in population during the period 1940 to 1943, 12 per cent for Marion and 10 per cent for Jefferson Davis County.

There are no urban centers in Jefferson Davis County. Marion County was also entirely rural up to 1920 at which time the census enumerated 16 per cent of the population as urban, which increased to 25 per cent in 1940.

When Jefferson Davis County was organized in 1910, Negroes constituted 38 per cent of the population. The proportion increased to 39 per cent in 1920 and to 55 per cent in 1930, remaining at 55 per cent in 1940. In contrast, the population of Marion County was evenly divided between white and Negro in 1850. The proportion of Negroes decreased to 31 per cent in 1890 and fluctuated to 37 per cent in 1940.

In 1940 there were 10,230 persons in the agricultural labor force which was a net increase of approximately 80 persons over the 1930 figure for the two counties. The increase was the result of a loss of 150 persons in Jefferson Davis and an increase of 230 in Marion County. The increase also was accompanied by a slight change in the relative importance of Negroes in the agricultural labor force from 55 per cent to approximately 50 per cent. In Jefferson Davis County owners increased from 23 to 26 per cent and laborers increased from 6 to 10 per cent. Tenants and croppers decreased from 33 to 30 and from 23 to 20, respectively. Owners increased more sharply in Marion County from 25 to 33 per cent but laborers decreased from 11 to 8 per cent, and tenants and croppers increased by less than 1 per cent with 23 and 16 per cent of the total agricultural labor force in 1940.

The number of farms in Jefferson Davis County increased from nearly 2,000 in 1910 to nearly 3,000 in 1930 and dropped to 2,800 in 1940. The number of farms in Marion County increased in each enumeration to 2,000 in 1910 then dropped slightly in 1920 and increased again to over 2,000 in 1940.

In Jefferson Davis County 43 per cent of the farms in 1930 and 1940 were recorded as having 20 to 49 acres per farm. In 1930, 37 per cent of the farms were 50 acres or larger as compared to 45 per cent with 50 acres or more in 1940. The proportion recorded with 20 to 49 acres in Marion County in 1930 was 46 per cent increasing to over 50 per cent in 1940. The proportion of farms with 50 acres or more also increased between the two enumerations accounting for 37 and 40 per cent in 1930 and 1940, respectively. Farms are increasing in size in both counties but the concentration in the 20 to 49 acre group is more pronunced in Marion County.

In Jefferson Davis there were 74,000 acres available for crops in 1910. The total acreage increased to 109,400 acres by 1940. The acreage available for crops in Marion County was around 20,000 when first enumerated and increased with only minor setbacks in the early years to 93,800 in 1940.

Cotton acreage which was around 26,000 in 1909 increased to 42,400 in 1929 and dropped to 27,000 in 1939 in Jefferson Davis County. In

Marion County the cotton acreage increased from 5,000 when first recorded in 1880 to 35,100 in 1929 and dropped to 23,500 in 1939. Cotton acreage in the area was about 40 per cent under the five-year average for 1928 to 1932 in 1942. (Figure 28) After the initial loss of acreage due to the reduction program under the Agricultural Adjustment Administration, cotton acreage in the two areas has remained 30 to 40 per cent below the five-year average. However, in contrast to Louisi-

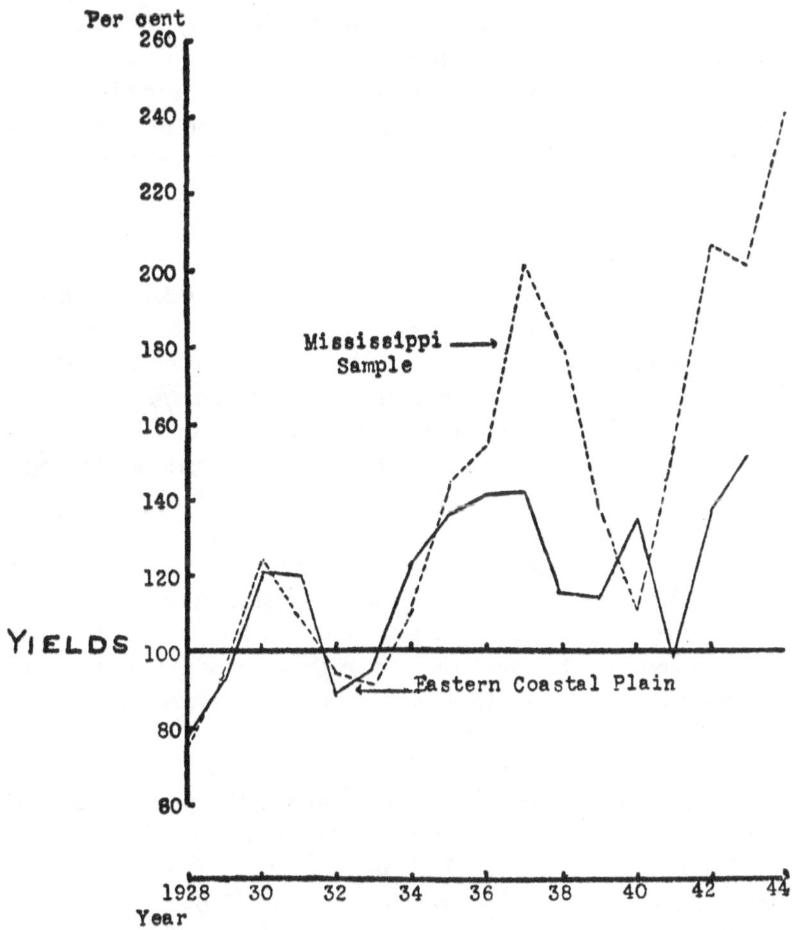

Source: Based on data compiled by the United States Department of Agriculture, Bureau of Agricultural Economics.

FIGURE 29. Comparison of trends in cotton yields in the Mississippi Eastern Coastal Plain sample and the Eastern Coastal Plain as a whole. (Five-year average 1928-1932 = 100 per cent.)

ana and Arkansas the increased yields in Mississippi (Figure 29), over 200 per cent above the 1928-1932 average, was sufficient to raise production for the area in 1942 to more than 20 per cent above the five-year average. The increased yields for the counties result from the introduction of new land to cultivation during the past decade and through extensive use of fertilizer on the land which was already under cultivation. According to 1939 estimates Jefferson Davis and Marion counties have 2.4 per cent of the acreage available for crops in Mississippi and 2.1 per cent of the cotton acreage but they use 4.1 per cent of the commercial fertilizer used in the state.

Oklahoma Rolling Plains. The five sample counties in Oklahoma—Greer, Harmon, Jackson, Kiowa, and Tillman—lie in the western half of the lowland section of the Interior Plains in the subregion of the Rolling Plains. (Figure 1) The area in which the sample farms were selected covers all of Jackson County and adjacent areas in the other four counties. The sample area lies almost wholly in the Oklahoma type of farming area 11. (Figure 2) Cotton is the predominant crop. Small grains and grain sorghums compete for the best land in the counties. Reddish chestnut soils of the St. Paul, Abilene, and associated soil groups predominate in the area. (Figure 27)

Kiowa and Tillman counties were formerly part of the Kiowa, Apache, and Comanche Indian Reservations and were not opened to white settlement until 1901. The other three counties lie between the north and south fork of the Red River in what was formerly claimed by Texas but was declared to be a part of Oklahoma by the Supreme Court of the United States in 1895 and was officially opened to settlement in that year. Originally it was a grazing area but grain farmers moved in between 1880 and 1890 and in 1890, though the territory had not been officially opened to settlement, there were over 5,000 persons in the area.

Population increased rapidly from 1900 to 1930 at which time all the counties had reached their maximum population. In 1930 there were 20,000 people in Greer County, 14,000 in Harmon, 29,000 in Jackson, 30,000 in Kiowa, and 24,000 in Tillman County. By 1940 the population in the counties had dropped to 15, 10, 23, 23, and 21 thousands, respectively. The decline continued from 1940 to 1943 with Jackson County losing 4 per cent and Harmon County losing 18 per cent and the other counties ranging in between with 8, 11, and 12 per cent losses, respectively, for Greer, Kiowa, and Tillman counties.

Cities have developed in all the counties in their brief history and in 1940, 25 per cent of the population lived in urban centers in all counties except Kiowa where the proportion was only 23 per cent. Jackson County with 38 per cent urban dwellers had the highest proportion for the five counties.

Except in Tillman County, where the proportion is 88 per cent, over 90 per cent of the inhabitants are white. In Harmon County the proportion of white persons in the total population is 98 per cent.

In 1930 there were nearly twice as many people in the agricultural labor force as in 1940. Of the 12,300 persons left in 1940, 39 per cent owned all or part of the land they were operating in that year. In contrast to the other areas, where part owners constituted 5 per cent or less of the total agricultural labor force, in the Oklahoma sample counties 10 per cent or more were part owners. Part owners increased from 4 per cent to 12 per cent in Greer County from 1930 to 1940. In Harmon County the comparable increase was from 4 to 11, in Jackson from 6 to 12, in Kiowa from 6 to 14, and in Tillman from 8 to 15 per cent. Farmers who owned all the land they operated also showed a marked increase in each county. Laborers and croppers on the other hand decreased. Tenants increased from 37 to 42 per cent in Greer County and from 36 to 44 per cent in Kiowa County. Tenants showed a gain of 1 per cent over the 1930 proportion to 38 and 34 per cent, respectively, in Jackson and Tillman counties and remained at 38 per cent in Harmon County.

In each county in the Oklahoma sample there were almost as many farms in 1910, the first census subsequent to the time when the present county areas were established, as there were in 1930 and in each county there were fewer farms in 1920 than there were in the other two census years. In 1940 the number of farms had decreased to less than had been reported in the previous census years 1910 to 1930.

In the five counties 35 to 40 per cent of the farms ranged in size from 100 to 174 acres, and 36 to 42 per cent of the farms had 175 acres or more per farm in 1940. In each county the proportion of farms ranging from 100 to 174 acres per farm had decreased from 1930 to 1940 and the proportion of farms with 175 acres or more per farm had increased sharply. In Greer County the proportion with 175 acres or more per farm increased from 22 per cent in 1930 to 36 per cent in 1940. In Harmon County the comparable proportions were 25 to 42 per cent, in Jackson and Kiowa 24 to 39, and in Tillman 30 to 41 per cent.

In Jackson and Tillman counties the maximum acreage available for crops was reported in 1939 when there were 363,200 and 415,600 acres in each of the two counties. In Kiowa County the acreage varied considerably with each enumeration and the 400,500 acres reported in 1939 was about midway between the maximum and minimum acreage recorded in previous census enumerations. The acreage in Greer and Harmon counties increased with each enumeration to 1929 and declined slightly from 1929 to 1939. There were 218,600 acres in Greer County in the latter year and 207,200 in Harmon County.

Cotton acreage in the counties have shown great variations in each enumeration. The maximum acreage was reported for 1929 and was well over twice the acreage reported in any previous census. The acreage for 1929 dropped to approximately one-third the acreage reported for 1929. Cotton acreage in Green County dropped from the maximum of 155,400 acres to 65,700 acres in 1939. In Harmon County comparable acreages were 135,300 to 49,200, in Jackson 244,600 to 92,500, in Kiowa 228,800 to 72,700 and in Tillman 229,900 to 94,700 acres.

The yearly trend in cotton acreage for the five-county area compared to the five-year average, 1928-1932, has continued downward with only minor rises since the initial loss resulting from the initiation of the crop control program. (Figure 28). The acreage in 1942 was approximately 50 per cent below the five-year average. Cotton yields in the area were extremely erratic fluctuating from 80 per cent above to 80 per cent below the five-year average. High yields in 1942 brought production for that year up to within 10 per cent of the five-year average, despite the 50 per cent reduction in acreage.

Texas Blackland Prairie. Bell County, Texas, lies in the border area between the Gulf Coastal Plain and the Interior Plain. The western portion of the county is in the subregion of the Grand Prairie and the eastern portion is in the Texas Blackland Prairie. (Figure 1) The sample farms are located in the eastern portion of the county, the part which is in the Texas Blackland Prairie subregion. The area lies in the Texas type of farming area 14, Blackland Prairie Area. (Figure 2) Cotton and corn are supplemented with small grains on most farms. Heavy black soils of the Houston group are predominant in the area. (Figure 27)

The population of the county rose steadily from 5,000 in 1860 to 49,000 in 1910. During this time the primary emphasis in agriculture shifted from ranching to farming with cotton assuming major importance in the cropping system. The population in the area dropped to 46,000 in 1920 and rose to 50,000 in 1930 after which it dropped again to 45,000. From 1940 to 1943 the population rose to 51,000, an crease of 13.4 per cent. This is in sharp contrast to the sample counties in the other four states where the population decreased in all counties during this period. However, the increase in Bell County was primarily due to the labor demand on army installations in the county, including a large army training center in the western part of the county and a base hospital which was under construction in Temple.

In 1890 there were 4,000 persons in the city of Temple accounting for 21 per cent of the population of Bell County. By 1940 the urban population had increased to 42 per cent of the total population of which 15,000 persons were in Temple and slightly more than 3,000 in Belton, the two urban centers in the county.

In 1860 white persons comprised 79 per cent of the total population in Bell County. The proportion increased to 90 per cent in 1870 and continued around 90 per cent in each census up to 1940.

Beginning with the Nashville or Robertson Colony, which brought settlers from Tennessee to the Mexican state of Texas, the first white settlers who located in what is now Bell County arrived in 1834, on the waters of the Little River.

In 1850, when formed from a part of Milam County, Bell County contained less than 600 people. The population doubled within a year. The drought of 1855 ushered in what was long referred to as the "seven years' drought."

In describing these early years in Bell County, Tyler makes the following comment:[39]

"The great black land prairies of Bell County, where lie the splendidly improved and prosperous farms of today, were then considered as almost worthless except to pasture the growing herds of horses, cattle and sheep. People said that this would never be anything but a stock country. Even so the water supply for the stock, away from the streams, was an uncertain proposition. In selecting his land the colonist, and later the immigrant, looked first for water for his family and stock and for timber for building, fencing and fuel. With these secured he cared not who owned the back lands on the prairie, as the frontage on the stream, with timber and water, was the key to the situation, the vantage ground of supreme control which enabled him

[39] George W. Tyler, *The History of Bell County, Texas*, The Naylor Co., San Antonio, Texas, 1936, pp. 168-69.

to keep out all comers, to throw his stock back on the open prairies and graze them upon the broad acres of the nonresident owners of those unoccupied hills, costing him absolutely nothing but providing him a constant and increasing source of revenue."

The building of the railroads into the cattle country in the eighties was followed by widespread use of barbed wire, windmill wells, and cash crop farming. These ushered in the permanent settlement of the Blackland Prairie in eastern Bell County. Stock raisers converted to the new cash crop farming or they moved west to the pasture areas.

Wheat yielded to cotton in the eighties. The droughts of 1886 and 1887 favored this shift to cotton, which withstood the dry summers better. All of these changes ushered in a new wave of immigration from the lower counties of Texas, along with some from central and eastern Europe. German Lutheran families settled in the Bartlett and Killeen sections of the country. A German Catholic settlement was started at Westphalia in Falls County in 1879 that later grew toward eastern Bell County, where a number of the descendants and newcomers of the German Catholic settlement now live.

During the eighties, when Bell County was changing from cattle range land to intensive farming of cotton a Czech migration from the cotton counties lying within 100 miles southeast of Bell County paralleled the German migration. The present influence of the Czech culture in the Bell County survey area is strong. In 1881 seven Czech families migrated to eastern Bell County from the sandy lands of the counties to the south. The first ones settled at Seaton, another soon developed at Cyclone. In later years the Czechs settled in Ocher, Ratebor, Lost Prairie, Meeks, Oscar, Airville, Red Ranger, and Zabcikville. Some of the Czechs were Catholic, some were Moravian, and some were either members of some other church group or, more rarely, were anti-clerical in their beliefs. They had a common bond in the use of the Czech language, although some had come from Moravia, Bohemia, Slovakia, Austria, Hungary, and other nearby provinces or states of eastern Europe.

Through the language bond they organized the SPJST (Slavonske Podporujici Jednoty Statu Texas) a benevolent lodge of Texas families who identified themselves with the Czech language. The grand lodge headquarters is at Fayetteville, Texas. Organized in 1897, the SPJST is nonsecretarian and nonpolitical. Bell County was reported to have seven lodges in 1936 and to lead in membership. The local lodges have family gatherings that include dances and other social activities.

The state organization is primarily concerned with the operation of a life insurance and a fire insurance mutual company. The capital accumulated therein is loaned on mortgages of farm land. After years of experience with loans to members, the state office has concluded that it is safer to loan to members who live in a lodge community, because group pressure for support of sound farm practices is thereby enhanced, according to the report of lodge officers who live in Bell County.

The present ethnic areas are delineated in Figure 33 (Bell County neighborhoods). The German families have spread over into Bell County from the Falls County communities of Westphalia and Rosebud. A Catholic Parish at Cyclone unites both Czech language and German language families, and even during the conditions of opportunity for resentment over European conflicts, they continued in this by-lingual parish during World War II.

The town of Heidenheimer was laid out by the Atcheson, Topeka, and Santa Fe Railroad shortly after the railroad crossed Bell County in 1882 and the families of German language origin in that community have already become identified with the English language group.

The Czech language groups have spread out in all directions from their original settlements, and in the present decade are moving into an area of expansion that reaches southwest toward Rogers.

Regarding the cultural characteristics of the Czechs in Bell County, the following is quoted.[40]

"Thrift is practiced by the Czechoslovak farmer, for that is about the only way he is able to succeed. Success, in this case, means ownership of a farm with the necessary buildings, farm implements and animals. The farm is not considered to be owned, however, until it is paid for and a little cash money saved for future emergencies. In many cases it is found that the father will attempt to provide a farm for each of his sons by the time the boys are twenty or twenty-two years old. However, it is expected that the whole family, and especially sons, (even those who already have farms of their own) will cooperate to provide the other sons with farms. That is, the family remains not

[40] Sandor Bodousky-Kovacs, *Observations and Impressions of the Czechosolvaks in Eastern Bell County, Texas,* unpublished manuscript, filed with the Department of Agricultural Economics and Rural Sociology, Texas Agricultural Experiment Station. This study was made for the Regional Land Tenure Research Project in the summer of 1944. The author's preparation for this analysis rests partially on his doctoral dissertation, *Czechoslovaks in Virginia,* University of Virginia, 1939.

only a social unit, but also, to some extent, an economic unit as long as the father lives. This is a carry-over from the old world where the so-called *gross familie* is still in existence.

"It should be noted here, however, that the more educated and younger farmers usually are more like 'Americans' in restricting the number of children in their families. Instead of the large family, therefore, it is the family of four or five that predominates among the younger farmers. With the number of children reduced to two or three per family, it is supposed that each child will receive a better education and perhaps a greater share of the family wealth. Yet, there are many women working on the fields with their husbands and children. They plant gardens and keep poultry and make the home as nearly self-sufficient as possible.

"Frequently the mother of a boy will complain because he is going with an American girl. She will admonish him and say, 'What do you want with that good-for-nothing girl? She can't work, can't even cook. Why don't you go with a Czechoslovak girl? She will work with you on the field and raise some good Czechoslovak kids.' Thrift is so much a part of the life of the Czechoslovak farmer that he has no use for a spendthrift, particularly one of his own group. The Czechoslovak farmer does not want relief for he knows other Czechoslovaks will not respect him unless he stands by his own strength.

"The Czechoslovak measures success in somewhat different terms from those used by the average American farmer. The Czechoslovak buys a farm for a home and a living. He is not thinking exclusively of how much money he will make on the transaction. He is interested in seeing a home of his own on a farm that can produce crops to sustain him and his family. Crop rotation, balanced farming, and intensive farming are usually practiced. New methods of agriculture, suitable to special soils and climates, are usually taken up by the Czechoslovaks without much hesitation. The Czechoslovaks in Bell County, Texas, came from the middle-class farming population of Czechoslovakia. They were accustomed to small land holdings. In some parts of the former Austria-Hungary, land was held in the family for generations."

The agricultural labor force in Bell County decreased about one-third between 1930 and 1940. However, in 1940, 23 per cent of the 6,300 persons in the labor force owned their own farms as compared to 14 per cent in 1930. At the other end of the agricultural hierarchy wage laborers increased from 18 to 23 per cent. Croppers and tenants both decreased during the ten-year period, 13 to 4 and 38 to 36 per cent, respectively.

In 1880 there were nearly 3,000 farms in Bell County. The number increased to over 4,000 in 1890 and to over 5,000 in 1900 after which the number declined to 4,500 in 1920 and rose again to 5,400 in 1930. In 1940 the number of farms reported had dropped to 4,004.

The number of farms with 50 to 99 acres per farm declined from 39 per cent in 1910 to 28 per cent in 1940. The number of farms with 100 acres or more per farm increased from 42 to 54 per cent. Whereas prior to 1940 the proportion of farms with 50 to 99 acres per farm had been greater than the proportion of farms with 100 to 174 acres per farm, in 1940 the latter group had 30 per cent as compared to 28 per cent for the smaller farms.

The number of acres available for cropland jumped from 28,000 to 200,000 between 1870 and 1880. In 1890 the acres available as cropland had increased to 378,000 but in the following enumeration only 324,000 acres were reported. From 1910 to 1930 cropland acreage reported increased in each succeeding enumeration to a maximum of 386,000 acres reported for the crop year 1929. By the 1940 census the crop acreage had again dropped to 354,000 acres for the crop year 1939.

The acreage planted to cotton increased from 38,000 to 190,000 acres in 1910. It was 20,000 acres lower in 1920, but rose to 229,000 acres in 1930. The 1939 cotton acreage was less than one-half of the acreage in 1930. The yearly trend of acreage has been consistently downward since 1928. (Figure 28) Acreages in 1942 were approximately 55 percent below the five-year average for the period 1928-1932. Cotton yields for the county have varied 20 per cent above and below the five-year average. The yields in 1942 were nearly 12 per cent above the average. However, the increased yields were not sufficient to maintain production on the reduced acreage in the county and production for 1942 was 50 per cent below the five-year average.

SUMMARY

1. The foregoing introductory statement constitutes an attempt to acquaint the reader with the nature of the study, its focal problems, the social and economic aspects of the region pertinent to an understanding of its tenure conditions, and a description of the sample areas in which the intensive study was carried on.

2. The aim of the project is to relate farm tenure status to farm family performance. On the basis of these findings a separate report

is to be issued with respect to tenure policy. In addition to these specific subject matter objectives the project constitutes an experiment in regional research cooperation which is to be the basis for a second separate report.

3. The approach to this study is more or less unique in that the work was carried on on a regional cooperative basis and fuses the subject matter fields of land economics, rural sociology, and farm management.

4. Realizing the need for a better tenure classification in relating tenure status to performance, the study places especial emphasis on this aspect. The work previously done in the region in this regard is reviewed and a statement made of the plan adopted for this study.

5. The nature of the sampling procedure is stated in some detail.

6. The region shows a wide range in topography, climate, soils, levels of living, type of farming, and farming practices.

7. The Eastern and Western Coastal Plains are areas of relatively great pressure of people on the land. Families are large, farms are small, and tenancy is relatively high. Farm family incomes approach subsistence levels. There are few alternative opportunities for farm people in the area. Out-migration exceeds in-migration resulting in an economic and social loss to the area in expenditures of time and money for education, religion, health, and other group activities.

8. The Texas Blackland Prairie is an area of fertile soils with intermediate-sized farms. Tenancy is high but the proportion of croppers is low. Power driven equipment is prevalent. Cotton yields are high but acreages have been sharply curtailed and total production has been reduced. Farm family incomes are high but operating expenses are also high. Alternative employment opportunities are available in nearby cities.

9. The Rolling Plain is a high risk area. The bulk of the settlement dates back less than 50 years. Farms are large and becoming larger. Farming is highly mechanized. Production is dependent on rainfall. In "wet" years yields are high. "Dry" years mean crop failures. Mobility, both between farms and between tenures, is high. Since 1930 out-migration has caused a net population loss to the area.

CHAPTER II

Tenure and Farm Organization

As pointed out in the introductory chapter, this study represents a synthesis of the three disciples: farm management, land economics, and rural sociology. In this chapter no attempt is made to perform the usual farm management or farm business analysis of the data, but rather to examine what, if any, basic differences in farm organization can be attributed to tenure. The discussion will answer such questions as: Is tenure itself related to differences in the size of operations? Is there a tendency for farmers in different tenure groups to apply the factors of land, capital, and labor in different ways? Do the results of farm operations in the different tenure groups show significant differences?

It should also be noted that, interesting though such a discussion would be, no attempt is made to discuss or evaluate differences in organization as between the several sample areas included in the study except insofar as such discussion would contribute towards an understanding of tenure relationships. The characteristics of these areas have been fully described in the first chapter. It is assumed that the reader realizes the wide differences between farming in the Rolling Plains of Oklahoma, for example, and that in the Eastern Coastal Plain.

In sharecropping areas, the problem of defining a farm operating unit is particularly difficult. While not pretending to distinguish precisely between a farm as an operating unit and as a portion of a farm, the discussion in this chapter proceeds on the assumption that both types exist and that they are not directly comparable. To a considerable degree one type shades into the other so gradually that only by the use of arbitrary criteria can one classify certain tracts of land near the margin. Such shading does not, however, alleviate the necessity for some sort of separation, crude though the method may be.

In the chapter dealing with the classification of tenure types, the complex nature of tenure controls in the operation of farm land was emphasized. It was pointed out that some share renters often do not have full control of the operating unit and that some sharecroppers exercise major control of the unit they operate. Despite this overlapping, the practice followed in this chapter is to treat owners, part owners, share renters, cash renters, and combination share and cash renters as farm operators. Croppers, and the tracts of land with which they are associated, are considered separately.

Analysis of the relation of tenure to the farm business must be predicated upon assumptions relative to the ways in which tenure might exert an influence upon farm operation. In this connection it is well to differentiate between the effects of tenure upon farm performance and upon the distribution of farm income among the several factors of production, that is, the total income of the farm as contrasted with the incomes of those who share it.

Most of the influences of tenure on the farm business are indirect in character. Thus, consideration needs to be given to the criteria appropriate for measuring tenure influences and to the ways and means of isolating tenure from the other factors which have an important bearing on farm performance. Most farm business analyses have shed too little light on tenure relationships. The criterion of farm performance too often has been the operator's net labor income, with differences among tenure groups sometimes adjusted for the influence of other factors. Such results represent a composite for all the influence upon both the total farm performance and the portion of the results of that performance allocated to one individual or family regardless of tenure status.

The results presented in this chapter give an over-all picture of the major characteristics of the farms, classified by race and tenure of the operator, in samples drawn from four areas in the region. Some of the comparisons will suggest tenure implications which only additional research can elucidate.

SIZE OF FARM

The factors used in this study in measuring size of a farm are: labor requirements, total acreage, acres in cropland, acres in a major crop, amount of livestock, and capital invested in the farm business. Brief discussions of these several factors follow. (Table 3)[1]

[1] See statistical tables in Appendix.

1. Labor requirements expressed in productive man-work units.[2] This measure, based on labor input, is the most satisfactory one to be used when there is a wide difference in the spatial size of farms or in types of farm enterprises and helps to put on an equal footing such divergent operations as, for instance, a truck farm and a ranch. A total of at least 240 productive man-work units is generally considered essential for the full-time use of the labor of one man. As the monthly distribution of labor requirements becomes increasingly seasonal, with high labor requirements during certain periods of the year, the total number of productive man-work units required for efficient farm operation increases.

In all areas part owners had the largest farms and the two owner categories had significantly larger units than renters in all areas except the Rolling Plains, where owners operated farms smaller than those of renters. Larger owner farms were particularly significant in the two Negro groups in the Coastal Plains, where more than half of the renters had units requiring less than 200 PMWU, whereas for owners the proportion was less than 40 per cent in each case. Also in all areas a much higher proportion of owners than tenants were on those farms requiring more than 400 PMWU. (Table 4)

2. Total acres in farm. This is the most commonly used measure of size of farm and the measure usually implied when size is referred to and the term not qualified. When significant portions of the farm, however, are not adaptable to agriculture or are usable only in a limited way, the value of this measure as an indicator of the scale of farming operations is greatly reduced. The measure also has limited value when attempting to put on an equal footing such essentially different areas as the Rolling Plains and the Mississippi Coastal Plain.

Using this measure owner-operated farms in most areas averaged larger than rented farms, particularly in the white group in the Mississippi Coastal Plain. In all areas the proportion of farms with less than 50 acres operated by tenants was considerably higher than that owner-operated. (Table 4)

3. Acres in cropland. This measure overcomes some of the handicaps of using total acres in farm as a measure of size. However, with

[2] These units represent the estimated number of days of man labor required under average conditions to produce and care for the crop and livestock enterprises on the farm. They are computd by assigning to each enterprise an estimate, based on labor-use studies, of the number of days normally required by one man to care for that enterprise. Each of the states in this study used a slightly different procedure for computing productive man-work units (PMWU); a full discussion of methods employed is given in Appendix A.

the data used in this study the relationships are much the same as for total acres in farm.

4. Acres in cotton. In cases where one crop or group of crops is dominant in the economy of the area concerned, the number of acres so used has advantages as a measure of size. Since cotton is a major crop common to the farms surveyed in this study, a comparison of size by tenure groups is made on this basis. Average (Table 3) and median figures of acres in cotton for the several tenure and racial groups indicate that there was less close relationship between tenure and this factor than was the case with acres in farm or in cropland, except among farmers in the white group in the Mississippi sample.

5. Animal units of productive livestock.[3] This measure applies only where livestock is the dominant enterprise and it has only limited application in this study. However, there is a significant relationship between number of livestock and tenure of operator in all areas, owners and part owners exceeding renters and part owners exceeding owners. More will be said about this relationship in a later section of this chapter.

6. Value of farm business. This is a measure of the capital invested in a farm and includes the value of real estate (land plus improvements), together with the value of equipment and livestock, regardless of whether these factors are provided by the operator or a landlord. With this measure also, owners are consistently higher than renters in all areas. There were particularly great differences among the Negro farmers in the Mississippi sample, but smaller variation between owners and renters among the white farmers in the Arkansas sample and the Czech group in the Blackland Prairie. (Table 3) There were only a few cases of renters in the higher value groups in the Coastal Plains area and a comparatively large number of owners in the higher value groups in the two western areas.

In summary, then, regardless of the measure of size employed, there is a definite tendency in the areas studied for owner-operated farms to be larger than those operated by renters, but the relationship appears to be more significant in the Coastal Plains area than in the two western regions. This fact is in conformity with the idea of capital rationing, discussed in greater detail in a later chapter. In the western areas, where farm units have to be larger in order to support a family, the amount of capital required to own a farm is so large that operators with limited capital resources who wish to own a farm are forced to

[3] The method of calculation is described in Appendix A.

own either a small unit or else farm on the less expensive land. Added support is given to this theory by the position of part owners in all areas except the Negroes in the Mississippi Coastal Plain, who, as has been explained before, are essentially cropper-owners. In all other areas part owners operated the largest farms, which suggests that some owners, being limited in the amount of capital available to invest in land and yet wishing to operate efficient units, seek the necessary additional land through leasing.

USE OF FARM LAND

Important in any analysis of the relation of tenure to farm organization is the comparative use of resources by those who operate farms under different tenures. One of the major resources used is, of course, land. The use made of it determines, in a large measure, the relative productivity of a farm over a period of years.

The so-called primary uses of the land on farms in the four sample areas of the Southwestern Region differ considerably. (Table 5) In the Coastal Plains the proportion of farm land in woods and available for crops is approximately equal, with a somewhat higher proportion of the woods in the Mississippi sample classified as pastured. Woods represent an insignificant use of land on the sample farms in the western areas, but land which has been termed noncropland open pasture is important, particularly in the Rolling Plains.

Certain tenure differences in the use of land as classified can be noted. In the Arkansas Coastal Plains a larger proportion of the land was available for crops on the farms operated by owners and part owners of both races than on those operated by tenants. The same was true in the Texas Blacklands but to a lesser degree. In the Rolling Plains part owners and share-cash renters had a higher proportion of land in pasture than other groups, which would seem to indicate that part owners to some extent rented pasture in addition to operating their own land and that some renters rented additional land for pasture on a cash basis.

The proportion of land in crops for different sizes of farms as measured by either productive man-work units by acres in cropland does not appear to vary much according to tenure status. Whereas the primary use of farm land generally remains fixed for a number of years, the secondary uses of cropland, for example, may fluctuate widely from year to year. All uses referred to in this report are those applicable to the 1942 calendar year, and hence are comparable between tenure groups insofar as the time factor is concerned.

The intensity of the use of cropland shows significant variations only in the Coastal Plains area. (Table 6) In the Arkansas sample, owners had a higher proportion of land idle than renters and the composite measure of intensity (crop acres in percentage of acres in cropland) is lower for owners than for other groups. In the other areas of the Coastal Plains owners appear to farm more intensively.

Crop organization does not appear to be related directly to tenure. (Table 7) While renters in the Mississippi Coastal Plain have a higher proportion of land in feed grains than do owners, in the Arkansas sample owners have more land in hay and forage crops. Negro renters in the Arkansas sample had more cropland pasture than owners, whereas the reverse is true in the Mississippi section. Obviously factors other than tenure account for these differences. There was, however, a tendency for owner-operated farms to be more diversified than rented farms in all areas. (Table 8)

As the size of farm increases, the proportion of cropland in cotton tends to be greater (Table 8), particularly for owner-operated groups. One factor which accounts, in part, for this tendency is the use of cropper labor. If, as the size of the farm increases, the operators shift more and more to the use of croppers with specific tracts upon which they grow cotton to an above-average extent, which they generally do, the net result is for larger farms to grow a higher proportion of cotton. On the other hand, a farmer with a large farm who decides to grow a large acreage of cotton would probably turn to cropper labor in order to ensure an adequate supply of labor at chopping and picking time. Significant variations in the cotton acreage as between farms of the same size was not to be expected, since the price of cotton was high in 1942 and most farmers planted up to their alloted quota, which was based on acres in cropland, or at least as much as they thought they could handle with available labor and equipment.

COTTON ON FARMS

Because cotton is a major crop enterprise in each of the areas sampled, special consideration is given it in relation to tenure. To a considerable extent, also, the tenure system in each of these areas is an outgrowth of special problems associated with the production of cotton.

Although the number of acres per farm devoted to cotton varied markedly among tenure groups and among the races represented (Table 10), these differences disappeared when cotton acreage was expressed as a percentage of the total number of acres in the farm. A partial explanation constitutes the effect of the cotton quota on acreage, as explained above. On the farms studied, acreage in cotton ranged typically from 25 to 35 per cent of total cropland, which was approximately the quota set by the Agricultural Adjustment Administration for most counties in the area.

Cotton yields seem to be related more to race than to tenure. The Negro operators in both areas of the Coastal Plains had significantly lower yields than white operators. While in many cases owners had higher yields than renters in the same area, the relationship is not consistent. However, no adequate appraisal of the relationship of yields to other factors can be made except by comparing farms with identical soils and other productivity factors, which was not done in this study.

Cotton sales, expressed as percentages of total crop sales, and total gross income, serve as summary indicators of the relative importance of cotton. The results emphasize the dominating position of cotton as the leading cash crop in all areas. It is also of major importance as a contribution to total gross income. Tenure differences indicate a generally higher proportion of crop sales represented by cotton for renters than for owners.

The relationships between cotton acres and yields on farms standardized by size (Table 11) reflect the complex nature of the influences which were brought to bear on the situation. Among the factors which account for these results was the tendency under some circumstances for the operators of large farms to produce cotton on a less intensive basis than was generally the case on smaller farms, with a lower yield resulting. In other instances, the larger farms were operated to a greater extent with croppers who, with their small tracts, tended to produce cotton on an intensive basis, securing higher-than-average yields. Thus, two important counteracting forces were at work with the net results dependent, to a considerable extent, on their relative importance in a given situation.

USE OF CAPITAL IN RELATION TO TENURE

The total capital investment in the farm business, together with its allocation in real estate, equipment, and livestock for the farms in the sample areas, by race and tenure, shows great diversity for the various groups. (Table 12) For example, the average white part owner in the Oklahoma sample had at his disposal over seventeen times as much in the way of capital investment as the Negro share renter in the Mississippi Coastal Plain. In both the Arkansas and Mississippi Coastal Plains white part owners operated with over three times as large a business, on the average, as Negro share-cash renters and with considerably larger farms, when measured in terms of capital invested, than white renters.

Since the discussion in Chapter VIII is focused on the details of the capital aspects of the tenure problem in its broader sense, the intention here is merely to present an over-all picture of the use of capital as a factor in farm operation. Such matters as the extent to which differences among tenure groups may be due to the relative availability of capital to operators of different tenure or to the sources of credit at their command are not considered.

In general, as might be expected, owners and part owners operated with a larger capital investment than renters. (Table 12) The relative proportions of investments which are represented in real estate, equipment, and livestock are not, however, significantly different among the tenure groups. It is of interest that although part owners had the largest total investments and also the largest farms by other measures, the proportion which real estate is of the total is not the highest in all cases. The figures also illustrate the very small amount of equipment found on rented farms in the Coastal Plains, about which more will be said below.

The real estate values were broken down into those for land, improvements other than dwelling, and dwelling. (Table 13) The separation of the dwelling from other improvements was made for the purpose of giving special consideration to those improvements on the farm which relate most directly to farm operation. The dwelling, although a necessary and important part of the farm is not a productive resource in the same sense as are land, equipment, and livestock.

In the Arkansas and Oklahoma samples the proportion of the real estate values represented by land is higher for renters than for part owners and higher for part owners than for owners. The data for Texas largely substantiates this, whereas in Mississippi on the sample farms the reverse situation existed. The varying influence of the value of the dwelling among tenure groups showed the relative importance for improvements other than dwelling. In Arkansas and Oklahoma, part owners had a larger proportion of the farm investment in improvements other than dwelling than did owners, and renters had the smallest proportion so invested.

The results indicate that dwellings on farms operated by owners have a higher value than those of farms operated by part owners, but it is not known from the data to what extent part owners lived in their own or in rented homes. Likewise, the value of the dwelling on the farms operated by part owners exceeded the corresponding figure for renter-operated farms in all areas. The value of improvements other than dwelling was greatest for part owners, except for the Negro operators in Mississippi, with the owners in all cases having the next to highest valuation.

One difficulty with the valuation figures is that they are estimates which contain certain biases possessed by the persons making them. Owners, for example, frequently have a tendency to place a higher value on a piece of property they own than a renter would, unless, of course, they are providing, or think they are providing, information for the tax assessor.

To further compare the total value of the farm business among tenure groups the farms have been classified according to size based on PMWU. (Table 14) The total value of the farm business is expressed both as the actual amount and as a ratio to acres in cropland. The latter figures are intended to reflect relative changes in two measures of size which are highly correlated—total value of farm business and acres in cropland.

Although the results do not permit very definite conclusions, there appears to be some tendency for tenure differences to decrease as other factors are taken into account. For example, on medium-sized farms alone, where the situation is more comparable than for all farms, the total investment for operators with different tenure is not generally very significant. This particularly is true when the investment is expressed as a ratio to acres in cropland.

LIVESTOCK ON FARMS

Livestock is a major enterprise only in the Rolling Plains and Blackland Prairie areas of the study. However, the fact that tenure is so often considered an important factor in livestock production justifies some discussion of these relationships. For the purpose of analysis livestock are divided into two groups, workstock and productive livestock. Generally the latter group is referred to in this study when the term livestock is used without qualification. Numbers are expressed in animal units.

In all areas owners had more livestock than renters, and in most cases part owners had more than owners and share-cash tenants more than share tenants. This was true both for all livestock and productive livestock. (Table 15) Furthermore, in none of the areas studied were there any owners with no livestock and few cases with less than one animal unit, whereas the number of renters in these categories was much higher. (Table 16) Likewise in the Coastal Plains there were only very few renters with more than 7 animal units of livestock, whereas many owners and part owners had that many. In the Rolling Plains and Blacklands samples the number of owners, especially part owners, with above average livestock numbers was significant. Similar results are obtained from an analysis of the investment in livestock on different groups of farms. (Table 12)

As might be expected there are differences among tenure groups with respect to the maintenance of breeding stock. (Table 17) Owners more frequently than renters possessed a bull, and white groups more often than Negroes. The difference is not so pronounced with respect to sows and boars; this can probably be explained in that breeding stock are not differentiated from other stock to as great an extent in the case of hogs and in the enumeration it is likely that male and female hogs were entered as breeding stock even though they were not especially set aside for that purpose.

Even when farms are grouped according to size, owners generally had more livestock than renters. On small farms part owners in the Rolling Plains and Blacklands samples had more livestock than owners, but on median farms share-cash tenants in both the Arkansas and Oklahoma samples had the largest number of livestock. On large farms part owners had more than owners and share-cash renters more than share renters. Much the same trend is observed when farms are grouped according to PMWU but less marked. On large farms share-cash tenants had the largest number of livestock per 100 acres of cropland in most areas.

TYPE OF POWER EQUIPMENT ON FARMS

Total investment in equipment (Table 12) is higher for owners than for renters, but there is little difference in the percentage of total farm investment which is in the form of equipment. The larger investment on the part of owners is to be explained largely in terms of the larger size of farms operated by them. It is probable, however, that tenants who move frequently do not acquire much in the way of machinery that would be difficult to move. It should be noted that in the Mississippi sample none of the renter groups averaged as much as $100 investment in equipment.

The extent of mechanization would seem to be more closely related to size of farm than tenure. In the Coastal Plains those few operators who farmed with tractors were mostly owners. (Table 18) In the

Rolling Plains and Blackland Prairie samples, part owners had the highest use of tractors, but otherwise there were no differences between tenure groups. In the Coastal Plains there were very few cases of Negroes with more than horse equipment and there was a tendency for more owners to have more-than-one-horse equipment than renters.

There are certain racial and tenure differences with respect to the ownership of special equipment. (Table 19) Although most groups had similar proprietorship of a car there were more whites than Negroes with cars in the Coastal Plains area samples, which was also true of trucks, of which owners also had more than renters. However, Negroes had more cane mills than whites, reflecting Negro partiality for syrup and its manufacture. In the two western areas where combines are frequently used, part owners had the most, reflecting their larger operating units. However, the matter of owning a combine is associated with whether or not the operator plans to do custom work with it, since only the very largest farmers generally have a combine only for their own farms. Presumably the choice of doing or not doing customs work would be little influenced by tenure. Part owners had also the most grain binders, and in Oklahoma more share tenants than owners owned their own binders. With haying equipment there was a definite tendency in all areas for owners to own such items more than renters, and whites more than Negroes. This is partly a reflection of the larger acreage in hay and meadow mentioned earlier.

USE OF LABOR ON FARMS

An important factor in farm operation is the efficient use of labor. Unfortunately not as much emphasis has been placed on this aspect as the subject deserves. One major reason for such neglect is the complexity introduced by cropper arrangements. On account of the peculiar semi-independent status of croppers on farms, the labor-use information for farms with croppers is not complete. It does not include the use of labor on the cropper tracts which are considered a part of the farm operating unit for most types of information.

An analysis of farms operated without croppers in the Coastal Plains area shows that for farms with between 20 and 40 acres in cropland, the average number of days of labor used varied from 245 for Negro renters in Mississippi to 364 for Negro renters in Arkansas. (Table 20) In the Arkansas sample, Negro operators, both owners and renters, used more labor than the white operators. Also, renters of both races used more labor than the corresponding owner groups. In Mississippi, on the other hand, the two white operator groups were in between the two Negro groups in the number of days of labor used, with owners of both races using more labor than corresponding renters.

The source of labor used varied more between areas and between races within an area than between tenure groups of the same race in the same area. For the groups of farms with between 20 and 40 acres in cropland, the white operators provided approximately 70 per cent of the labor in Arkansas and 60 per cent in Mississippi. The corresponding figures for Negro operators were 60 and 50 to 55 per cent. In both areas a relatively larger proportion of the labor used on the farms operated by Negroes consisted of family labor (other than the operator) than was the case on the farms operated by whites. Tenure differences were generally insignificant.

As the size of farm increased, the total number of days of labor used increased and the proportion of labor provided by the operator generally decreased. Most of the labor not provided by the operator represented the labor of other members of the family, particularly on the farms operated by Negroes, although hired labor became important on some of the largest farms. In the Arkansas sample hired labor accounted for a significant proportion of the total labor used on the larger farms with white operators. The Negro operators, as a rule, used relatively little hired labor.

A comparison of the number of days of labor used with the number of days of labor normally required to perform the amount of productive work indicated for a farm provides a rough measure of the efficiency of the labor used. Since the number of productive man-work units is designed as an indicator of labor requirements, a ratio of its value to the number of days of labor used gives what might be called an index of labor efficiency. The higher this index, the higher the labor efficiency, for the fewer the number of days of labor used in relation to the number of days normally required. Unfortunately, comparisons of the index of labor efficiency cannot be made satisfactorily between areas because each area used a different basis for computing PMWU. Within areas the data are presumably comparable.

In the Arkansas sample white operators of farms with between 20 and 40 acres of cropland had labor efficiency indices of 66 and 68 for owners and renters, respectively. The corresponding figures for Negro operators were 50 and 49. White operators appeared to be somewhat more efficient on the average than Negro operators. There was a pronounced tendency for labor efficiency to increase with the size of farm for both white and Negro operators and for both owners and renters.

In the Mississippi sample differences in labor efficiency between tenure groups appear to be about as great as between races. Moreover, whereas the white owners are shown to be more efficient than the white renters, the reverse situation held for Negro operators, with the renters shown to be the more efficient. Labor efficiency of white owners increased with size of farm much as in the Arkansas section. For the other tenure groups, however, the relation is quite different. In the case of Negro owners, no relation at all is indicated while for white renters and Negro renters, the larger the farm the lower was the index of labor efficiency.

GROSS INCOME

Although the usual detailed net farm income analysis is beyond the scope of this study, a background picture of gross income and the sources thereof seems highly desirable.

Total gross income varied significantly with tenure of operator in all sample areas (Table 21), owners and part owners having consistently higher incomes than renters. However, it is obvious that the most important factor here is not tenure but size. When incomes on farms are grouped according to size of farm (Table 22) the relationship between gross income and tenure is not so consistent. Nevertheless there is a tendency for owners to have higher incomes than renters, particularly in the two western area samples. A significant feature of these tables is the higher incomes earned by whites than Negroes of equal tenure status in the Coastal Plains.

The major sources of the operators' gross income are from the farm, work off the farm, and other nonfarm sources such as royalties from oil. (Table 21) Naturally, the most important source is from the farm, but many farmers derive considerable income from work off their farms, such work being either on other farms or in some nonfarm occupation. In the two western sections farm operators were largely full-time farmers, receiving a relatively small proportion of their total gross income from other work off their farms or from other nonfarm sources. In the Mississippi Coastal Plain sample, on the other hand, off-farm work was very important, providing, on the average, close to one-fourth the gross income of farm operators. The situation in the Arkansas sample was intermediate, with off-farm work less important than in Mississippi but more so than in either of the western sample areas. Nonfarm sources, other than work off the farm, assumed major proportions only in the Arkansas sample where white owners and white part owners received significant percentages of their income from oil royalties or leases.

Although only that portion of gross income which comes from the farm is the direct result of farming operations, the income which a family derives from nonfarm sources may be an important factor in farming operations and, hence, have an indirect effect upon the gross income from the farm. A sizable nonfarm income might, under some circumstances, lead to increased efficiency in farming, by providing additional working capital and more profitable use of labor. On the other hand, it could lead to neglect of the farm and inefficient production because of the decreased dependence on the farm for a livelihood and the interference of nonfarm interests with farming operations.

The major sources of gross income by tenure groups are rather significant. While no consistent differences in the relative importance of the farm income are apparent, off-farm income sources for different tenure groups show a marked contrast. In most cases, renters received a larger proportion of their incomes from work off the farm than did owners and part owners. Similarly, the owners and part owners averaged the larger incomes from nonfarm sources other than work off the farm. The proportion of income derived from the farm did not vary much with the size of farm. (Table 22)

Gross farm income is a rough measure of the results achieved by farm operators with the resources at their command, regardless of who provides them, and if there are significant differences in farm organization among tenure groups, such differences should be reflected in gross income figures. Both median and average (Table 23) figures show that owners earned considerably higher farm incomes than renters in all areas, but when farms are first grouped according to size the differences are less significant. Among small farms (less than 200 PMWU) owners had higher incomes than renters in groups except Negroes in the Mississippi Coastal Plains sample. In the medium size group incomes in the Coastal Plains were much more uniform and no tenure relationships were evident, and in the largest size groups only the Mississippi sample showed significant tenure relationships, although the sample for renters is too small to warrant definite conclusions.

Approximately one-half of the gross income from the farm in all four sample areas resulted from the sale of crops. (Table 24) The major crop sold was cotton which accounted for around 90 per cent of the total crop sales value. (Table 10) Tenure differences in the relative importance of the various sources of the gross income from the farm are not very great. Moreover, such differences as do appear are primarily the result of factors other than tenure. For example, the proportion of the total gross income from the farm which is represented by the value placed on products used in the home tends to be somewhat greater for renters than for owners. To a considerable extent, this is the result of differences in the average size of farms and families for the two groups and to the tendency for the estimates of the dollar value of products produced on the farm and used in the home to approximate a uniform figure for all farm operators. Since renters generally operate somewhat smaller farms than owners, the proportion of the income of the farmer represented by the value of products used in the home is usually larger. The proportion of total income coming from livestock sales tended to be highest for part owners and share-cash renters, which groups, as has been pointed out before, had more livestock than other groups.

FARMS WITH AND WITHOUT CROPPERS

For some purposes, separate consideration of farms operated with and without croppers seems desirable. Then, too, some types of data have meaning only for farms operated without croppers. For example, due to the semi-independent status of croppers, many operators are unable to furnish satisfactory information concerning certain characteristics, such as labor used, which relate to the cropper tracts as well as to the remainder of the farm. Also, the use of cropper labor has a direct influence on farm organization. Differences among tenure groups might well be due to the use of a cropper organization and the tendency of some tenure groups to use croppers more than others.

A comparison of selected characteristics for farms of white owners with and without croppers in the samples for the Arkansas Coastal Plain and Mississippi Coastal Plain shows that the white owners with croppers operated approximately 50 per cent larger farms than those without croppers. In Mississippi they were over twice as large. Whether size of farm is measured in terms of productive man-work units, acres in farm, acres in cropland, or value of farm business, the relationship is much the same.

Differences in factors other than size are also present. In the Arkansas sample, 20 per cent of the cropland on the farms operated by white owners without croppers was in cotton. On the farms operated by white owners with croppers, the percentage rose to 28. In Mississippi, on the other hand, the proportion of cropland in cotton was the same for the two groups, and the average acreage change was directly proportional to the size of farms.

The average number of animal units of productive livestock on farms operated by white owners with croppers and without croppers was approximately the same in Arkansas, despite the 50 per cent difference in the average size of the farms operated by the two groups. In Mississippi, however, differences in the amounts of productive livestock for the corresponding groups were in about the same ratio as the size of the farms included in those groups. In other words, the white owners in the Mississippi sample who operated with croppers had twice as large farms as the white owners without croppers but maintained much the same internal balance among enterprises.

In the Arkansas sample, in addition to differences in average size of farms, the white owners with croppers had relatively more cotton and relatively less livestock than white owners without them. Differences in cotton yields are also to be noted. Whereas in Arkansas white owners with croppers and white owners without croppers averaged similar yields of cotton per acre, the average yields in Mississippi for the former group were nearly 10 per cent larger than for the latter.

In the case of the Negro owners with and without croppers, the contrasts between the two sample areas were generally less than have been indicated for whites. (Table 25) However, the differences between the situation on the farms operated by Negro owners with croppers and on those operated by Negro owners without croppers in each area were about as great. In Arkansas, the Negro owners with croppers operated farms approximately 45 per cent larger than the Negro owners without croppers. For the Mississippi sample area, the corresponding percentage is about 75, the exact figure dependent upon the particular measure of size used. Incidentally, in neither of the two sample areas do the various measures of size check as closely for Negro owners as for white owners. Consideration of the major characteristics of the tracts and of the croppers' incomes from them seems desirable.

In the sample from the Arkansas Coastal Plain, 20 white croppers had tracts averaging 69 acres in size. (Table 26) On an average, 42 of these acres were in cropland, with 16 in cotton. The tracts of the

Negro croppers in the same sample area consisted of 40 acres in total, with 31 in cropland, and 14 of them in cotton. The cropper tracts in the Mississippi sample area were generally smaller, for the corresponding racial group, than those in Arkansas. Both the whites and the Negroes average 9 acres in cotton and approximately 25 in cropland, but the total acreage for the former was 44 as compared with 31 for the latter. Since, in both sample areas, relatively little cropland was left idle and much was double-cropped, the number of crop acres exceeded the acreage in cropland by approximately 10 per cent in Arkansas and 15 per cent in Mississippi.

The smaller cotton acreage per cropper tract in the Mississippi sample area as contrasted with Arkansas was more than compensated for by a much larger cotton yield per acre in the former area. More favorable weather conditions and heavier applications of fertilizer were the major factors accounting for this greater yield. Considering both acreages and yields, the production of cotton per cropper tract was about 20 per cent greater for the Mississippi sample than for Arkansas. In the Arkansas sample, the tracts of white croppers produced 40 per cent more cotton than the tracts of Negro croppers. In Mississippi, on the other hand, 10 per cent more cotton was produced on the tracts of Negro croppers than on those of whites.

CROPPER TRACTS

As already indicated, many farms, particularly in the Arkansas and Mississippi sample areas, were operated with tracts of land which they "crop," contributing their labor in return for a share of the crop produced.

Although the average size of the white cropper tracts in Arkansas was 69 acres (Table 26), over half consisted of less than 50 acres (Table 27). Likewise, over half of these tracts had between 20 and 40 acres in cropland and between 7 and 15 acres in cotton. In contrast, 91 per cent of the Negro-cropper tracts in Mississippi were under 50 acres in size, with 74 per cent having between 10 and 30 acres in cropland. On 77 per cent of these tracts the acreage in cotton ranged from 3 to 11 acres.

In terms of productive man-work units, the white croppers had larger tracts than the Negroes, particularly in the Arkansas sample. They also used more days of labor but that percentage of labor which was hired was about equal in Mississippi and all but 6 per cent of total days of labor were provided by the cropper and his family.

The amount of productive work on most cropper tracts required between 100 and 300 days of labor. (Table 28) Few required less than 100 or more than 400 days. Variations in the number of days required to do the productive work on cropper tracts (productive man-work units) were similar for the Negro croppers in the Arkansas sample and for the croppers of both races in Mississippi. White croppers in Arkansas, with larger average-sized tracts than the other groups, had none with less than 100 productive man-work units and but one with over 600.

The average gross income of 18 white croppers in the Arkansas Coastal Plain sample area was $1,028. (Table 29) Eighty-two per cent of this amount represented income from the cropper's tract, most of the remainder coming from work off the tract but not necessarily off the farm of which the tract was a part. Of the gross income from the tract, 59 per cent represented the sale of crops, cotton accounting for 92 per cent of total crop sales, 54 per cent of gross income from the tract, and 45 per cent of total gross income.

Differences in income between white and Negro croppers in the same area and between corresponding racial groups in the two areas were due mainly to differences in the size of the tracts from which the income was derived. However, in both areas Negroes received much smaller income from work off the tract than whites, despite their having smaller tracts as a source of income. In relation to the gross income from the tracts, Negro croppers depended relatively more on cotton sales, less on sales of other crops, and less on sales of livestock products than whites. The major differences between the corresponding racial groups in the two areas were the smaller tracts and the greater importance of work off the tract in Mississippi.

In contrast to the gross income of the croppers is the gross income of the cropper tracts. This represents the gross value of the total production of the tracts, including both the portion which went to the croppers for their labor and to the farm operators for their contribution of land, capital, and supervision or management. In the Arkansas sample, the average gross income of the tracts of white croppers amounted to $1,302. Negro-cropper tracts in the same area had an average of $896 gross income. In Mississippi, the gross income averaged $1,107 for the tracts of white croppers and $1,063 for those of Negroes.

Comparisons made among the gross incomes of the cropper tracts, classified by size, indicate no significant differences, with the possible exception of the Negro-cropper tracts in Arkansas. The gross incomes for these were consistently lower than those for the corresponding sized tracts of the other groups. In Mississippi, there was some tendency for Negroes to produce more on a given sized tract than the whites, with the opposite the case in Arkansas.

SUMMARY

Below is a list of the most important points brought out in the preceding discussion, following which is an attempt to assess the significance of these results in a brief general statement.

1. Regardless of the measure of size used there was a tendency on the farms studied in the four sample areas for farms operated by owners and part owners to be larger than those operated by renters. The trend was more consistent in the Coastal Plains than in the two western areas. For all groups, except the Negroes in the Mississippi Coastal Plain, part owners operated the largest farms.

2. Land use and crop organization on the farms studied showed little variation as between operators of different tenure.

3. In all areas owners and part owners operated with a larger capital investment than renters. The relative proportions of this investment which were in real estate, equipment, and livestock, were not, however, significantly different among the tenure groups.

4. Owners and part owners had more livestock than renters. Although much of the difference disappeared when farms were grouped according to size, the trend remained the same in many cases. However, share-cash tenants emerged as the biggest livestock groups on large farms in the same areas.

5. Investment in equipment and the extent of mechanization is related primarily to size of farm, tenure of operator having little influence. However, there appeared to be certain differences among races with respect to the ownership of cars and trucks, white operators having more than the Negroes of similar tenure status.

6. Use of labor and labor efficiency on the farms studied indicated considerable variation, but no tenure relationships were clearly established.

7. Owner and part owner operators showed higher total gross incomes than renters even when size of operation was held constant. This was particularly marked in the two western areas. In the Coastal Plains areas white operators received higher incomes than Negroes of similar tenure status. Renters in the region in general received a higher proportion of total income from farm work off the farm than

did owners. However, owners averaged more from nonfarm sources than renters. Gross farm income was highest for owners and part owners but elimination of the size factor reduced the difference. Part owners and share-cash renters received the highest proportion of farm income from livestock sales.

8. Although croppers throughout most of this report are analyzed along with the other tenure groups, from the standpoint of the farm business, cropper units in many respects are only partially comparable to complete farm units. From this standpoint, a cropper tract is designed to meet a special purpose within the framework of the larger farm and as such possesses certain characteristics not common to the entire unit. As a rule, cropper tracts contained a larger percentage of cropland than the entire farm and a larger proportion of this cropland was devoted to cotton. Also more intensive methods of cotton cultivation tended to be used, resulting in larger yields. In addition, little cropland was left idle and much of it was double cropped.

Although most of the cropper's income comes from his share of the crop on a specific tract, he also received in most cases a significant amount in the form of wages for work off his tract but on other parts of the farm. Most of the income from the home tract represented sales from cotton plus the value of products used in the home. For the crop year 1942 the gross income of cropper tracts compared very favorably with complete farm units of corresponding size. One major factor in this situation was the unusually favorable position of the cotton enterprise that year. Good yields, particularly in the Mississippi sample area, coupled with high prices, resulted in better than average incomes for those who grew cotton. Since cropper tracts tend to be devoted to cotton more exclusively than the farm as a whole, they generally benefited from this situation.

Croppers in the Coastal Plains areas tended to be full-time croppers to a greater extent than in the other areas. The majority of those in the Texas area worked for wages, whereas those in Oklahoma were about equally divided between operating croppers and wage laborers, the latter receiving a share of the production of cotton, poultry, eggs, or milk as a bonus payment. In the Coastal Plains the cropper arrangements were closely associated with the white, male, resident landlord.

It has been shown in the preceding pages that the only significant farm organization factor which appears to be related to tenure of operator at all closely is that of size. Other items such as total investment, gross farm income, amount of equipment and workstock, which are apparently tenure-related, are in reality related primarily to size of farm, and when size of farm is held constant, tenure differences disappear or become much less significant, and even size of farm does not bear as consistent a relationship to tenure in the western areas as it does in the Coastal Plains. The question naturally arises as to whether it is mere chance that owner-operated farms in the Coastal Plains are larger than rented farms, or is there a further explanation? It is possible that in an area of heavy population pressure on the land, such as this area, land in owner-operated farms tends to remain intact and in owner-operatorship; pressure on it is reflected only in higher land prices. Heavy pressure on farms usually rented, however, might result in a certain amount of subdivision or chopping off of fields, with the end result that rented tracts become smaller. On the other hand, perhaps it is that those renters with less than average managerial ability who consequently have to operate smaller tracts bring down the average size of rented farms. In the two western areas, where there is a tendency for some renters to own larger farms than owners, it has already been suggested that the explanation might be found in the theory of capital rationing. Since operating an economically sized unit in these areas requires such a large amount of capital, many owners, because of limited capital resources, are forced to be content with small units; some of them rent additional land to increase the size of their units, as seen in the large size of part-owner-operated farms.

It was expected that some differences would be found between different tenure groups in land use and crop organization. The fact that there were no major differences might be due to several factors. It might point to the tendency for all farmers in a given type of farming area to be almost identical in their organization. Indeed this is frequently; significant differences appear most usually in minor enterprises only.

However, a factor which should not be overlooked is the tremendous influence on the Agricultural Adjustment Administration in determining crop organization. Once the acreage in conserving and nonconserving crops has been established for the farm, the choice is limited. Few operators, in fact only those with above-average managerial skill, risk experimenting with new crops. Usually, with the acreage of the major crop established, other crops are arranged in accordance with the need for feed for the workstock and other livestock, including temporary pasture, and finally, the farmer plants whatever conserving crops he is acquainted with and which yield him an economic return. The choice of crops adaptable to the particular soil and climatic conditions of a given area is not a wide one.

There is nothing in the Agricultural Adjustment program which limits or standardizes livestock enterprises, and in the farms studied there was a considerable amount of variation in this respect. The tendency for owners to have more livestock than renters in general is fairly easy to explain. Livestock enterprises require some length of time before returns on investment are realized and also require certain improvements which a landlord may be unwilling to furnish, such as larger barns, fences, ponds, etc., and which a tenant hesitates to put up himself in case he should move. The landlord sees no point in putting money into items from which his return will be small and which might be wasted should there be a change of tenant. Of course, on rented farms where such improvements are already in existence, such impediments do not arise, nor do they in cases where the landlord is willing to become a partner in a livestock enterprise and a livestock lease is drawn up. It is not meant to be implied that there is something inherent in ownership which means more livestock, but rather that ownership generally makes livestock enterprises easier to introduce. There is a definite implication in the data in this study to the effect that those who want to maintain large livestock enterprises need larger units and therefore rent additional land for pastures, owners thus becoming part owners and share tenants becoming share-cash tenants. This is not true of all part owners or share-cash renters, however.

CHAPTER III

Tenure and Family Status

The rungs in the land tenure ladder are frequently regarded as synonomous with those of the social status ladder. In general, this statement of relationship has considerable foundation in fact, but unless qualified it is likely to be misleading. It has been shown that owners average higher on the socio-economic status scale than renters, and that renters in turn average higher than croppers. (Table 30)[1] But it is also true that this can be attributed more to earning capacity over a period of years than to the present tenure of the operator.

SOCIO-ECONOMIC STATUS AND TENURE

A group of 36 items describing the family in measurable terms was constructed into a scale to measure the socio-economic status of the family, in relation to that of all the other farm families of the county, state, or region. This socio-economic status scale had been devised for use in Oklahoma and was tested in other culture areas of the region to verify its accuracy and its validity for measuring the family well-being.

Originally this scale was standardized for use as a combined measure.[2]

---

[1] See statistical tables in Appendix.

[2] For a discussion of its standardization for Kansas farm families and for white and Negro families in Lincoln Parish, Louisiana, see William H. Sewell, "The Restandardization of a Sociometric Scale," *Social Forces, XXI,* (March 1943), pp. 302-11. Sewell compares the Lincoln Parish scores for white and Negro families thus: "The main difference is probably in the extent to which the Negroes participate in the material culture of the white group. The item analysis reveals that many of the best material culture items in the scale are possessed by so few of the Negroes that they have very little value, so far as the Negro group is concerned, in a scale which attempts to differentiate between successive as well as extreme status groups. This does not mean that interracial comparisons cannot be made. Actually, the socio-economic status of Negroes can be evaluated in terms of the standards of the whites by using a scale designed for whites, but it must be remembered that the measurement will be in these terms."

In this study it was considered desirable to also separate the scale into three parts. One of these is called the housing index. Twelve items that are concerned with the comforts, the livability, and the farm standards of good house construction were grouped into this measure of family socio-economic status as indicated by the construction and maintenance of the house, including primarily the items that are furnished by the owner.

The second part of the total scale is called the movable possessions index. The 16 items in this group measure the family goods and equipment that contribute to comfortable living and that are readily moved from house to house when the family seeks a new domicile. These are the responsibility of the occupant, whether owner or nonowner.

A third part of the total scale includes eight items that measure the social participation of the farm family insofar as this reflects the socio-economic status of the family. This index does not measure how much the family attends meetings or how many offices the husband and wife fill. Rather it measures the extent to which these participations indicate the total well-being of the farm family. It is, therefore, an indirect measure of the position of the family in the total number of families rather than how busy it is in community affairs or how much office holding it does. These eight items of participation, in other words, were selected because they were indicators of the well-being of the family.[8]

Index of Socio-economic Status

Comparing the 1,580 farm families of the five sample areas as a whole, the part owners rank first in socio-economic status (with a regional index of 110) and croppers are at the other end of the scale, with a regional index of 87. (Table 30) Full owners rank next below part owners, followed by renters. The share renters and the share-cash renters have essentially the same index level.

Comparisons of separate areas and races show certain differences in socio-economic status. In the Mississippi Coastal Plain, the white full owners have a slightly higher index than the white part owners, and in the German ethnic group of the Texas Blackland Prairie, the full owners very significantly exceed the part owners in socio-economic status. Is this exception an indication that these full owners have re-

[8] For a list of the items in each component part of the scale see the Appendix, "The Farm Family Socio-economic Status Scale," p. 484.

versed the usual pattern by exceeding the part owners in size of business and earning power?

Arrayed into five groups, based on socio-economic status scores, it is observed that no croppers are in the highest status group and that all tenures are represented in the lowest status in at least some of the sample areas. (Table 31) The wide spread in each of the tenures demonstrates that tenure alone does not determine the status of a farm family and that it rarely sets the limits for such status.

Index of Housing

The housing index is one of the three components of the index of socio-economic status and would be expected to reveal similar tenure contrasts. Certain reversals, however, are noted. For the Negro farmers, full owners exceed part owners in the combined sample from the five areas. This is true in Arkansas and Louisiana but not in the Mississippi Coastal Plain. (Table 32)

Although there is considerable flucation in the region, the housing index among white farmers is in general higher for part owners than for full owners.

Considering only the three broad tenure groups, owners exceed renters and renters as a whole exceed croppers in the housing level as measured by this index. The comparisons between the two owner subgroups and also the comparisons between the two renter subgroups are not consistent in direction and not sufficiently large to indicate significant differences.

Index of Movable Possessions

This is a measure of the part of the family possessions for which the operator is himself primarily responsible, in contrast with the index of housing, for which the landowner is largely in a position to determine the level of use. The broad tenure comparisons show that the combined renter group has an index considerably above that of the cropper, and the combined owner group has an index slightly above that of renters. (Table 33)

For the index of movable possessions renters as a whole are farther along the scale from croppers to owners: 83, 101, 106, than for the index of housing: 83, 98, 108. (Table 32) This indicates that the tenants have used their consumer purchasing ability to improve their socio-economic status, even though they could not do so for housing facilities.

Index of Social Participation

Although the combined owner group has a higher index than the renter group and renters in turn are followed by the croppers, the entire spread among these averages is much less than for the housing or the movable possessions. (Table 34) Moreover, the difference is reversed as among owner and renter groups for the Negro sample in all areas. This is particularly marked in the Arkansas and Mississippi Coastal Plains. It is concluded that for social participation the differences between the owner and renter groups are not particularly significant. The renter and owner groups have a higher social participation than croppers for all areas except in the Oklahoma Rolling Plains.

The Negro croppers consistently have a higher index of social participation than white croppers. At the same time they have a lower housing index and a lower index of movable possessions. These reversals are likewise true for both renter groups. The single variant in this pattern is in the housing index of Mississippi share renters where whites have a lower housing index than Negroes.

Can these differences in social participation be explained in terms that are associated with, rather than causally identified with, race? It may be pointed out that present tenure has already been removed as a factor, since race differences are noted within the specific tenures of cropper, share renter, and share-cash renter.[4]

SCALE OF FARM OPERATION AND QUALITY OF BUSINESS

Gross farm income is a measure of the size of the farm business, but among other factors it is influenced by the two quality factors, yield and the price received per unit of production.[5] Therefore, for the purposes at hand a measure of the size of operation was developed which depends only on the three input factors: value of the farm business, productive man-work units of labor required, and acres

[4] While it is believed that the explanation of these differences lies either in race or closely associated factors, it is possible that the instrument of measurement used is not adequate for the purpose at hand. The status scale was originally constructed to measure differences among white farm families and was not successfully standardized for Negro families. It is in the social participation part of the index that the scale is least adapted for use in measuring socio-economic status of Negro farm families. Church membership and attendance are so nearly universal among Negro farm family adults that these six out of the eight items do not reliably measure socio-economic status differences. See William H. Sewell, "The Restandardization of a Sociometric Scale," *Social Forces*, 21 (March 1943), p. 308 for Table 5, "Church Attendance Percentages for Husbands and Wives in Negro Farm Families of Lincoln Parish, Louisiana."

[5] For further discussion of measures of size, see Chapter II, "Tenure and Farm Organization."

in cropland. Using these three, the gross farm income for this combination of production factors is computed for each farm. This computed gross farm income, based on average conditions of management, is called the scale of operation.[6] The attained gross farm income, expressed as a percentage of the predicted or expected gross farm income, becomes a measure of the quality of the farm business for each race and tenure group.

Within each race group, in each area, the cropper group of tracts shows a higher gross quality of business than does any other tenure when holding size constant by using the scale of operation. On the whole, the full owners make the poorest record, although the Mississippi Negro full owners rank second among their race groups, exceeded only by croppers. Share renters are below other tenures in the Arkansas white and the Mississippi Negro groups. They fare better in the other areas.

Another measure of quality of business is the operator's earnings, expressed as a percentage of the predicted or expected gross farm income. This ratio of net returns to the operator per hundred dollars of scale of operation is a measure of the net efficiency of production after due allowance is made for expenses of operation. On this measure, the croppers rank first among all the selected tenure groups for Arkansas Negroes, and among Mississippi whites and Negroes. They are decidedly surpassed by share-cash renters in the Arkansas white sample. In the Oklahoma sample the croppers drop to the bottom of the list on this measure of performance. Evidently their expenses were high for operating equipment, picking, or other labor costs. However, the variation in actual percentage was very narrow among all tenures in Oklahoma.

The full and part owners rank fourth or fifth in the Arkansas Coastal Plain white or Negro sample, and in the Mississippi white sample. For the Mississippi Negro sample, full owners rank second, followed by share renters, part owners and share-cash renters, respectively. The 26 Arkansas white share-cash renters stand exceedingly high (75 per cent) and the five Mississippi Negro share-cash renters stand exceedingly low (11 per cent) on this measure of net performance in earning capacity for the given size or scale of operation.

The scale of operation and the gross quality of business together account for the variation in gross farm income among farms and among tenure groups. The scale of operation and the net quality of

[6] See Appendix B, p. 501 for further explanation of this scale.

business by definition account for the variation in operator's earnings among farms and among tenure groups. There is quite general agreement between gross quality and net quality of business. This agreement would lend support to the opinion that farm profits first of all depend upon large production per unit of input. In this analysis the input is measured by the scale of operation. It is when the expenses of production mount at a faster rate than the gross production that net quality will fail to keep pace with gross quality of production.

The five cropper groups have the highest gross quality of business, each exceeding 115 on this index. They are proportionally low on net quality of business, although they average as high on this measure as does any other tenure group. The share-cash renter groups have the greatest amount of deviation from the line of average relation for gross and net quality of business.

Implications for Tenure

The scale of operation measures the size of the farm business by combining the three input factors in proportion to their respective effects upon the gross farm income and expresses this size as dollars of expected gross farm income. The attained gross farm income expressed as a percentage of the scale of operation is the gross quality of the farm business and is, therefore, independent of the size factor. The operator's earnings total, expressed as a percentage of the scale of operation, is the net quality of the farm business and is likewise independent of the size factor.

The cropper groups already have such high gross quality that they can only achieve higher net returns by getting more returns through increasing the size of their operation or through more favorable leases. They run the risk of obtaining less productive land and hence less gross quality of production if they seek more favorable leasing arrangements through change to share-renter leases. For both races in Arkansas and Mississippi, the croppers exceed share renters in operator's earnings. Among Oklahoma native white families, croppers have less operator's earnings than share renters, but most of them operate considerably smaller units with highly efficient gross quality and low efficiency in net quality of business.

If they have these opportunities, the real problem facing the cropper families is one of going from intensive farming on high quality land, under conditions of supervision that result in high gross quality of business and average net quality of business, to a more extensive type of farming that requires a significant amount of capital, managerial ability, and risk taking. The transfer to share renting does not bring advantages, either in increased operator's earnings or in socio-economic status. Moreover, their experience as supervised croppers does not necessarily or even probably equip them for managerial responsibilities that go with farming as an operating tenant who has care of livestock added to that of cash-crop production. It is no small achievement for a son of a cropper to acquire the managerial experience of an operating tenant, if he must do so without the benefit of parental tutelage and in competition with the landlords' sons. Neither does it help nor is the problem solved by acquiring a small unproductive farm at even mortgage-free ownership.

The problem faced by the families who are operating tenants on farms of average or larger size is somewhat more simple than the above. The only additional step they face is one of landownership, and this can be one of part owner, preferably the purchase of the house and barns on land that can become part of the operating unit. They already have the experience of management that can be readily tested for gross quality and net quality, in relation to the stage of the business cycle and its influence on the desirability of making a purchase of land.

When these two steps on the agricultural tenure ladder are contrasted, it is apparent that the risks and the problems associated with going from supervised cropper to the status of managing or operating tenant are quite different in kind from those faced by an operating tenant who faces the choice of becoming a landowner. The comparison of croppers' achievements with those of other croppers in any one of the three sample areas, when measured by the gross and the net quality of their farm business, enables one who counsels with them, whether he be county agent, vocational agriculture teacher, or farmer friend, to advise whether or not they are ready for the next step up the agricultural ladder. This includes the steps toward increased scale of operation in addition to or in place of increased equity in the farm business.

SCALE OF FARM OPERATION AND FAMILY STATUS

In all tenure groups the larger the scale of operation, the higher the average socio-economic status score. (Table 35) This continuous positive relation of scale of operation and socio-economic status holds for each race and for the four areas under consideration. (Table 36 and Figure 30)[7]

[7] The graphic presentation of these data (Figure 30) reveals a consistently higher

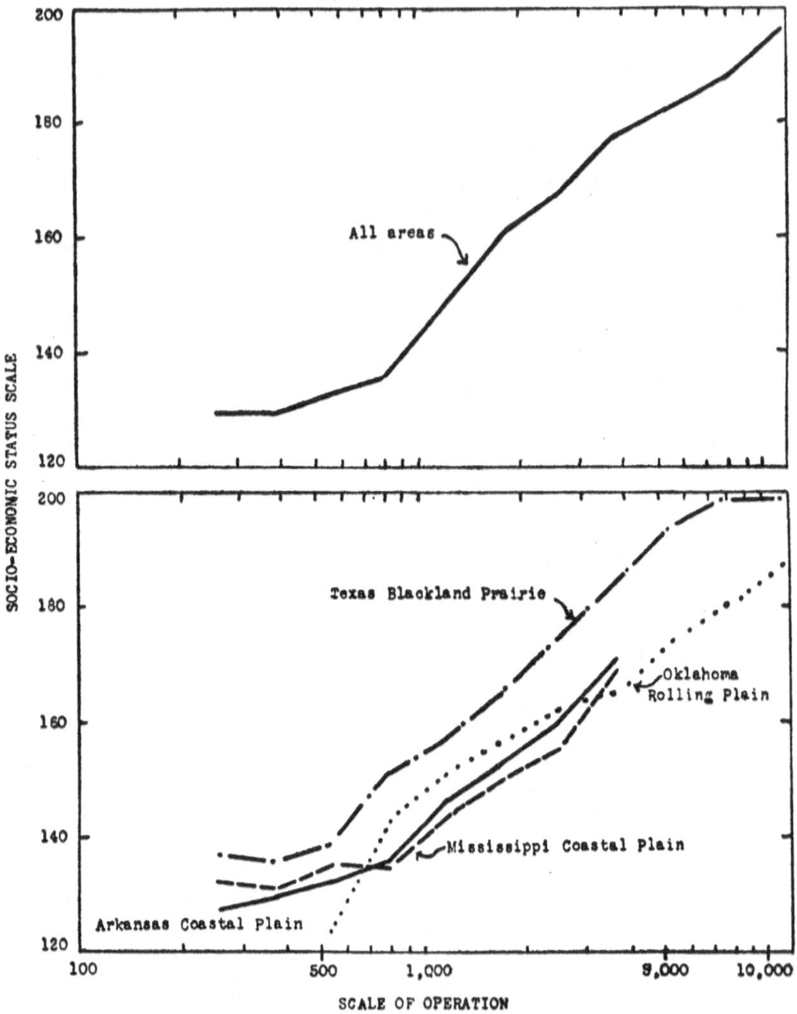

FIGURE 30. Socio-economic status related to scale of operations of the farm in four sample areas in the Southwestern Region.

socio-economic status score for each given scale of operation in the Texas Blackland Prairie than in the other three areas. This is primarily a result of the relation of 1942 gross farm income to the 1930-1944 average in each sample area. Data for these adjustments are taken from Wylie D. Goodsell, Ronald W. Jones, and Russell W. Bierman, *Typical Family-Operated Farms, 1930-45, Adjustments, Costs, and Returns*, F.M. 55, Processed, April 1946, 91 pp. See especially pp. 74-77 and 78-81. On the basis of these computations the Texas Blackland area had an index of 143 in 1942. The 1942 gross farm income of $1,987 adjusted to the 1930-1944 base period is $1,390 which is to be compared with a socio-economic status score of 169, the average for the 1942 Texas Blackland sample. The Oklahoma Rolling Plains area had an index of 193 in 1942. The 1942 gross farm income of $3,682 adjusted to the 1930-1944

Net Family Income and Socio-economic Status

In addition to the influence of size of operation on socio-economic status, what other factors are known to affect it? Holding scale of operation constant, the data show that full owners rank higher on the socio-economic status scale than the renters and that the renters in turn rank higher than the croppers. (Table 35) Analysis of the part owners for the Oklahoma and Texas area samples shows a socio-economic status not consistently lower than that of full owners, but consistently higher than that of renters.

It is known that the socio-economic status of a family is dependent upon the earnings of the family, but just how direct is this dependence? In the three area samples for which net family income was determined, the Oklahoma Rolling Plains families show the nearest to a direct linear relation, closely paralleled by the Arkansas Coastal Plain families. (Figure 31) The Mississippi Coastal Plain sample reveals a decidedly curvilinear relation between net family income and socio-economic status, with a tendency of all families below $800 in net family income to level off at a socio-economic status scale of 130 to 135.

The Arkansas and Mississippi Coastal Plain samples show a very similar socio-economic status at the lower range of net family income, below $1,800, but a divergence occurs at the income range above $2,000. A possible explanation lies in the fact that a large number of white families, formerly in the Arkansas Coastal Plain sample area, inherited a comfortable standard of living and are now transferred from farming to the oil industry in nearby counties. This has drained off from the sample of families who would be expected to have a higher socio-economic status in relation to their present net family income. The highest Mississippi sample income group is too small to give a reliable average. (Table 37)

Measures of Family Status

A number of measures of farm family status are presented for the selected tenure groups of each area. (Table 38) First of all, it is neces-

---

base period is $1,908 which is to be compared with a socio-economic status score of 172, the average for the 1942 Oklahoma Rolling Plain sample. These adjustments of the expected gross farm income to the base period of 1930-1944 result in moving both the Texas and the Oklahoma lines of relationship to the left in Figure 30. The new positions are much closer to each other, although the line of relationship for the Texas area sample is still at a slightly higher level on the socio-economic status scale for any given point on the scale of operation. Similar adjustments should be made to the 1942 gross farm incomes of the Mississippi and Arkansas Coastal Plain samples. However, much less satisfactory yearly trend data are available for this type of farming area.

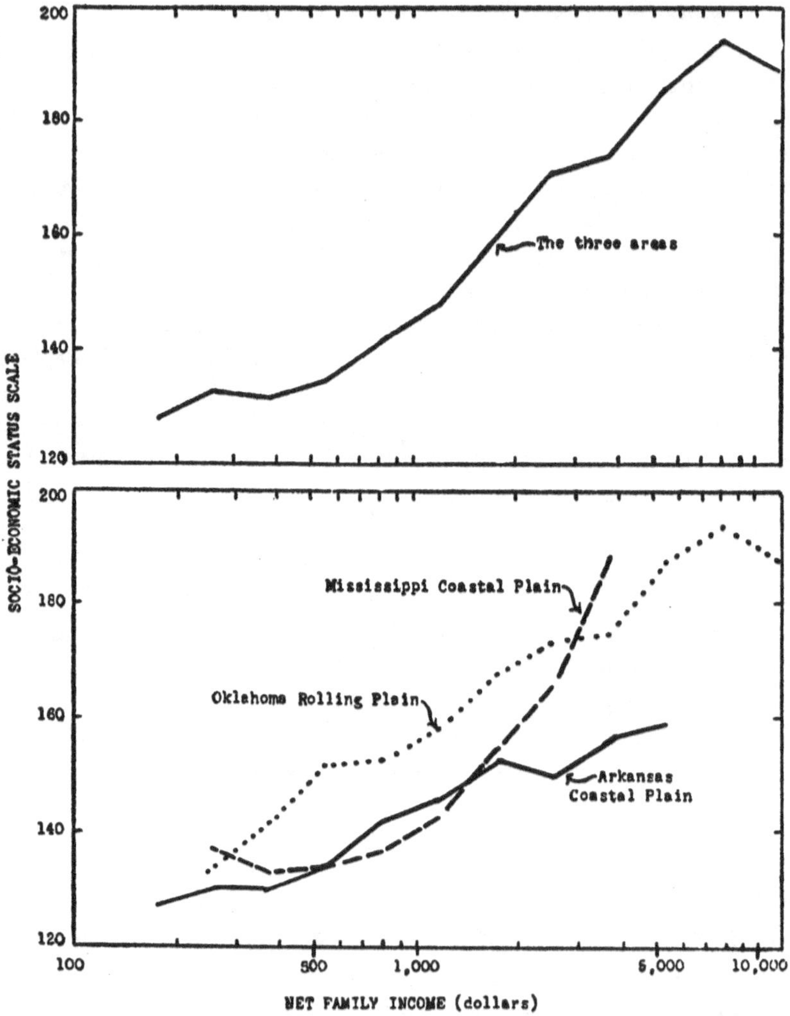

FIGURE 31. Socio-economic status related to net family income in three sample areas in the Southwestern Region.

sary to emphasize that scale of operation ignores quality of the farm business. This latter factor is included in the operator's earnings (column 3 of Table 38). Also many families have sources other than the farm business to enlarge their net family income. Hence, the farm is not their only source of funds to purchase their consumption goods and items of family and household equipment. Moreover, the present annual income may not be representative of the income which has been received over a period of years. This long-time earning record of the family is reflected in the present net worth. In this analysis only the farm net worth was ascertained. It reflects the influence of previous accretions of capital, either by inheritance or savings, as these are now used in the farm business. Other forms of net worth, including household goods and nonfarm investments such as life insurance and stocks or bonds, would be significant in their combination with farm assets to affect jointly the socio-economic status score of the farm family. It is well-known from previous studies that the accumulation of net worth is a function of years of earning life, hence this latter is expected to influence socio-economic status.

The highest grade completed by the husband or wife is averaged for each tenure group. This is termed the average education (of higher spouse). The tenure groups rank somewhat differently on this measure of status than on the others. The education of the husband and of the wife are separate items in the socio-economic status scale.[8]

Data are not lacking to support the claim that the higher education of either spouse is a more discriminating measure than either one taken separately.[9] The assumptions underlying the discovery of this joint relationship of education of the spouses can be inferred from the commonplace observation that when two people of widely different formal schooling are mated, they usually have closer pairing of native ability than of schooling. Therefore, although the education of husband and of wife are two separate items in the socio-economic status scale, the item as here used is a joint relationship that is expressed as the higher education of either spouse.

Implications for Tenure Programs

It is necessary to know the values held by any occupational and tenure group if the programs designed to serve their needs are to have predictable results or even reasonably high usefulness to them. Often these values are understood and implied without formal recognition. It is first of all necessary to know to what extent each tenure group is striving to achieve the next rung on the ladder and what amounts

[8] Sewell found that the two separate items were highly discriminating graduated response items in the scale. See William H. Sewell, *The Construction and Standardization of a Scale for the Measurement of the Socio-Economic Status of Oklahoma Farm Families*, Oklahoma Agricultural Experiment Station Technical Bull. 9, April 1940, pp. 78, 81.

[9] See for example, Merton D. Oyler, *Neighborhood Standing and Population Changes in Johnson and Robertson Counties, Kentucky*, Kentucky Agricultural Experiment Station, Typewritten manuscript, 1946. See pp. 9-11 for the relation of neighborhood standing to level of living.

of sacrifice they are making in their present levels of living in order to take the next step on the ladder. The socio-economic status, as measured by possession of material items, has been ascertained for each tenure group and for each size of farm business.

From the data in the areas sampled for this tenure analysis, it is concluded that the Oklahoma renters are prepared to and are maintaining a high level of movable possessions and a high investment in farm operating equipment, both of which are more directly associated with the scale of operation than with tenure status. It appears that the renters in the Rolling Plains are more concerned with maintaining these two groups of possessions than with land purchases as a life goal.

Because the housing index is low in relation to the movable possessions index, it is probably to be expected that any farm housing program in the Rolling Plains would necessarily need to be geared to improvement of rented houses rather than based on improvement of owner-occupied houses. These are already higher in relation to income earning capacity than are renter homes.

A similar approach is suggested for a soil conservation program. It is only when the soil conservation is geared to maintenance of the operating unit, whether owned or leased, that the large-scale operating tenant can be expected to find his personal or family goals in harmony with the goals for the general welfare.

Because the scale of operation for all farms, owned and leased, tends to be larger in the Rolling Plains than in the Coastal Plains and the Blackland Prairie sample areas, it is in the Rolling Plains area that the permanent goals of socio-economic status might be more completely expected to replace the goals of land ownership. The extreme swings in the income cycle in this area that result from adding weather cycle to business cycle make this emphasis on separation of land ownership and socio-economic status all the more pronounced.

SIZE OF FARM AS A FAMILY AND A NATIONAL GOAL

What principle can be used in harmonizing the maximum returns to the individual farm family and the returns to the general welfare? These two objectives in agricultural production are fundamental and must be brought into agreement if an agricultural policy is to be sound and workable.

The data presented in this chapter show that the most effective method of increasing the socio-economic status of the farm family is through the increased size of business as measured by the scale of operation. As the scale of operation increases, the socio-economic status increases. This relation is semi-logarithmic; for each increase of 18 per cent in the scale of operation there is an addition of 10 points on the socio-economic status scale within the range from $1,000 to $10,000 in expected gross income from farming. (Figure 30) Although this is a comparison among 1,200 farm families in one year rather than a history of changes made by families who have increased their size of farm business, it is however, a very good indication of what would result if farmers who have the capacity to operate larger businesses were to do so.

Increasing the size of business results in higher socio-economic status only when the operator has sufficient managerial ability to maintain a quality of business that would lead to an increase in his net earnings as a farm operator. The operation of the economic principle of diminishing returns suggests that many of those farmers who already have above average gross quality and net quality of business can probably increase their operator's earnings by applying their managerial ability to farm businesses of larger size. An increase in the size of business operated by those whose present quality of business is below average will probably result in no increase in operator's earnings and might even lead to a reduction in earnings.

How large can the farm business become when viewed from the general welfare? Assuming that the attained gross income for farms of all tenure groups is the expected gross income for that type of farming area and accepting average gross quality and net quality of farm business in the given type of farming area as the yardstick, the following principle is here proposed for application to this problem.

If the operator of a given farm, regardless of tenure, continuously obtains average or above average gross and net quality of business, he contributes, other things being equal, to the general welfare in such use of the resources of production. It is presumed that he continues to allot to the labor so used on the farm a wage or family level of living that is average or above for that type of farming area. This yardstick of the general welfare presupposes that maximum total production is an essential factor in maximum total consumption.

This yardstick for reconciling the maximum net operator's earnings of the individual operator and the maximum total production for the given type of farming area first looks toward the optimum scale of operation as a result of managerial performance independent of tenure arrangements. The tenure aspects can then be considered for the various resulting sizes of business in the same manner that tenure policy has always reckoned with a wide variation in size of farm.

This principle, when applied to farm operations as going concerns, calls for many related decisions. Is the local community concerned with the ever widening opportunity of farm youth to become efficient operators? It is well recognized that the farm boy is first of all trained as a family member. The socio-economic status of his parental family in large part determines the type of social and pre-occupational training he will receive during his formative years. It still is a vital factor in the opportunities that become available to him through the high school program in vocational agriculture.

The application of a principle of equilibrium that is based on managerial results rather than on an absolute upper limit in the use of the factors of production is not new in our economy. It has been widely used in the income tax structure, the corporation tax structure, and during wartime in British agriculture it has been used as a basis for classification of farms to determine who shall have the right to remain in operation of the farms.[10]

But before this principle can be applied, it must be related in some effective way to the aims and aspirations of the individual farm families in each type of farming area. Access to the means of production is now regulated through the cash transaction of purchase and the private rental contracts of leasing. This principle of optimum managerial efficiency can be gradually substituted for maximum returns to the individual in a manner similar to the steps by which public welfare aims in health are added to private incentives for medical care. If the principle is acceptable in American democratic ideals, then effort can be directed toward implementing it.

FERTILITY OF THE FARM FAMILY

Because fertility of the various tenure groups would in large part influence the replacement rates of each tenure, this subject becomes a major factor in population pressure on land resources. If the birth rate of the farm families of low socio-economic status and low-capital assets is quite high in comparison with the birth rate of families having a high socio-economic status and a high amount of owned capital, then this would have certain important implications for the man-land ratio and for the ratio of farm wage rates in comparison with farm land rentals. It would add importance to a rural school program that keeps open the road to urban industrial employment, in order to help

[10] The basis for classification of farms in the British wartime agriculture into types A, B, and C, based on tests of performance, was described to Agricultural College faculties in the United States in a series of addresses by Leonard K. Elmhirst.

restore the balance between farm labor supply and availability of agricultural land.

The fertility ratio as used in this analysis is based on the number of children ever born to the male head in the family. Two considerations led to this decision. First, the economic and social characteristics that are presumed to influence the fertility ratio can be more directly stated in relation to the male head. Second, where the present marriage was not the first one, the history of the male head's offspring was more completely obtained in the farm and family interview than that of the female head.

The fertility index is based on the children ever born to the male head divided by the number expected for his given age, using the entire farm population of the United States as the yardstick. This standardizes age for male heads. In the plan of tabulation it was necessary to create an index for each family head, in order to facilitate sorting by ten or more factors related to land tenure. This was accomplished by using the geometric mean of these family fertility ratios when comparing groups of families with various combinations of tenure factors. While these geometric means of the fertility for each group of families are always somewhat lower than comparable ratios of children under 5 years per 1,000 females of child-bearing age (or per thousand males of comparable age), the ranking of the groups as a series of high to low population fertility remains the same. This type of analysis measures relative fertility. The absolute fertility of the farm families in each county is presented elsewhere.

Using the ratio of observed children to expected children as the measure of fertility, the relative differences of these ratios for the race and tenure groups of each sample area are expressed as index numbers. (Table 45) In fertility rates, the white part owners exceed the white full owners in the Arkansas and Texas samples, they are equal in the Louisiana sample, and are considerably lower in fertility than the part owners in the Mississippi area sample. In the Texas sample, the native white families are the reverse of the Czech and German families. The 17 part owners in the latter groups have farms that average larger in scale of operation than the farms operated by the 42 full owners that are of Czech and German origin. When the farms are sorted into the same sizes as measured by the scale of operation, the part owner farm families have lower socio-economic status than the full owner families, in all three ethnic groups, with the single exception of the native white owners and part owners having farms expecting a gross income (scale of operation) of from $1,000 to $2,153. (Table 35)

In all three ethnic groups of the Texas Blackland sample full owners are older than part owners, nine years older in the native white group, seven years in the Czech, and only one year on the average in the German group. (Table 39) The age differences do not affect the fertility comparisons because the data have already been adjusted to remove any fertility differences due to age of the operator. The age diffrences do indicate that the German, and to some extent the Czech, part owner families are larger operators on the average when compared at the same age levels.

In summary, the Czech and German part owners are probably having somewhat larger families than the full owners in the Texas Blackland sample, because they are families of inherited frugality and ambition with a greater tendency toward retention of the large family patterns of their ancestors. The full owner families are about a generation earlier than the part owners in the transfer from large to moderate-size family patterns.

A similar explanation holds for the 15 white part owners in comparison with the 116 white full owners in the Mississippi Coastal Plains sample. The part owners average three years younger than the full owners, but at comparable ages they have somewhat higher socioeconomic status scores than the full owners. (Table 40) They are operating farms that compare equally in size with the full owners as measured by the scale of operation. They are, therefore, presumed to be a generation later than the full owners (on the average) in going from the large family patterns of their ancestors to the moderate family patterns of the selected full owners who operate farms of equal scale of operation. The 15 white full owners have farms with expected gross incomes ranging from $464 up to $6,800, with only one below $680 and only one above $3,160. With this range in scale of operation, it is evident that income can be more important than tenure in relation to patterns of family size.

In the Arkansas and Mississippi sample areas renters of both races have significantly higher fertility rates than croppers of the respective races. In the other three areas croppers have the higher fertility rates. This reversal demonstrates that income factors and other factors associated with tenure (or method of wage payment) can be more important than tenure itself.

In every area sample and for each ethnic group or race, the renters average higher scores on the socio-economic status scale than the croppers. Why then do the croppers have lower fertility rates? Why this departure from the general inverse relation of income and the birth rate? Or is socio-economic status an incorrect indicator of cropper versus renter income?

The index of communication is higher for Negro croppers than for Negro renters in each of the three Coastal Plain samples. For the white families in only the Mississippi Coastal Plain sample is the index for croppers higher than for renters. A high communication index is associated with a lower birth rate when income is held constant.[11] The white croppers have a higher migration index than white renters in all sampled areas except the Mississippi Coastal Plain. For Negroes, croppers exceed renters in only the Mississippi sample.

A slightly larger percentage of the white croppers than of white renters are single in the Mississippi Coastal Plain sample (6.9 versus 4.2 per cent and in the Oklahoma sample 6.2 versus 3.7 per cent). These differences do not explain differences in the standardized birth rate because the marriage rates may be similar when standardized for age.

An array of the families in intervals of progressively higher fertility ratios shows that the distributions for owners, renters, and croppers have parallel midpoints. The length of the range in fertility, however, is influenced by the size of the respective tenure sample. This is another way of saying that unusually small and unusually large families are found in each tenure class in approximately direct proportion to the number of families in each tenure sample.

SUMMARY

The larger the scale of operation, the higher the average socio-economic status score of the farm family. For any given scale of farm operation, full owners rank higher in socio-economic status than renters, and renters rank higher than croppers. The socio-economic status of part owners is not uniformly lower than that of full owners but is uniformly higher than that of renters.

In general, the socio-economic status of farm families increases in linear relation to the percentage increase of the net family income,

[11] This was demonstrated for the farm population of Kentucky counties. See Merton D. Oyler, *Fertility Rates and Migration of Kentucky Population, 1920 to 1940, as Related to Communication, Income, and Education.* Kentucky Agricultural Experiment Station Bull. 469, November 1944, p. 33.

but there is a lower minimum of approximately $300 of net family income below which the socio-economic status remains constant at approximately 130. Net family income is not as reliable an indicator of the family's socio-economic status as is the scale of operation of the farm business. Annual fluctuations due to weather and prices affect the income but not the scale of operation.

Using six measures of farm family well-being, the scale of operation agrees more closely with the socio-economic status of each tenure classification than do any of the other four measures.

An array of the families into five groups, based on their socio-economic status score, shows that no croppers are in the highest status and that all tenures are represented in the lowest status in at least part of the sample areas. The wide spread in each of the tenures demonstrates that tenure alone neither determines nor limits the status of a farm family.

Because the scale of operation for all farms, owned and leased, tends to be larger in the Rolling Plains, it is in this area that the permanent goals of socio-economic status might be expected more completely to replace the goals of landownership.

As a yardstick of how large a single farm operation can become and still contribute to the maximum good of the nation, it is proposed as a result of this analysis that so long as the operator, regardless of his tenure, continuously obtains average or above average gross and net quality of business, he continues to have a suitable size of farm, provided he continues to allot to the labor so used a wage or family level of living that is average or above for that type of farming area.

CHAPTER IV

Factors Related to Changes in Tenure Status

The factors underlying change in individual tenure status may be understood by analyzing the tenure life cycle as it applies to different types of individuals. The tenure status of an individual in any one year is regarded as one stage in a series rather than as a static position. While it is true that for many the present tenure is likely to be permanent, the problem is to predict for each type of individual the amount of change or stability that may be expected within a given institutional setting.

The measurement of tenure change necessitates the acceptance, or at least the use, of specific tenure categories. In secondary source materials, such as census and Agricultural Adjustment Administration data, the classification used by the agency in question must largely be followed. The project data allow more freedom of classification excepting that much of the detail apply only to the single year of 1942. The necessary common ground for the use of the various types of data is found in the categories of owner, renter, cropper, wage laborer, and family worker — the terms usually used by the farmers themselves. These categories, however, might more properly be regarded as status positions in the occupation of agriculture rather than tenures since tenure is customarily defined in terms of rights and it is doubtful if laborers, or croppers as defined in some states, have property rights.[1]

Theoretically, those with no rights in property would be assigned a value of zero in a continuum of tenure rights. On the other hand, the owner has all the rights which society allows individuals to possess. Those rights may be alienated through mortgaging or leasing

[1] The word "right" as herein used refers mainly to authority as prescribed by law and not to a functional "right" of doing what is permitted even though contrary to law nor does it refer to a moral "right."

to others, but basically they reside with the owner of the land. The renter has the right to use land within certain limits of time and use dependent upon the agreement. The cropper has little control over the farming operation yet is dependent upon the value of the production for his income and well being and has rights to a share of the physical production of the land.[2] The wage laborer has the right of occupancy through sufferance and has contracted to work for a definite wage which is independent of the value of production. He has no right to any part of the land or production thereof except through sufferance. The family laborer, usually mislabeled as "unpaid family laborer," does not have any right to a specific wage although he may receive even more returns than the wage laborer.

The tenure situation of an individual in any particular year and the changes that can be predicted are influenced by a large number of factors, many of which are beyond his control. The entire complex of factors may be classified into three groups: (1) The environmental setting in which the individual applies his resources. (2) The type of individual considered, determined largely by his experience, training, and parental background. (3) The use made of the alternatives available to each type of individual within a given environmental setting. The items in the first two categories are for the most part beyond the direct control of the individual. Environments, however, can be changed by moving. For example, a net worth of $5,000 for farm operations in a given locality may be quite inadequate to achieve ownership or to obtain the tenure necessary to assure a satisfactory income. In another locality, however, the same net worth offers different limits to the possibilities of tenure and income performance and a different set of chances for achieving the desired goals.

ENVIRONMENTAL SETTING

Land Settlement

One of the first subjects of inquiry about an area is that of settlement. How long has the area been settled? By whom? By what method? Answers to these questions are related to the tenure pattern directly. They also aid in predicting the type of farming, the credit structure, the labor organization, and the stage in technological development. These latter factors in turn are related to the

[2] A comparison of the legal rights of croppers and tenants is summarized by states in Chapter VII, Legal Aspects of Land Tenure and Farm Credit. Also see *Crop-Sharing Contracts (Appendix Section of Special Study-Plantations)*, Agriculture Census of the United States, 1940, Washngton, 1943.

tenure composition of the farmers and limit the choice of possibilities of an individual in achieving various levels of tenure.

On the frontier new land is free, or nearly so, for the labor cost of clearing land or breaking sod. Little capital is needed to become a land owner. However, an individual is required to move from his former location, to wait a few years for returns from his labor, and to secure capital for seed, equipment, and family living. The expense of moving and the capital required to meet the immediate expenses are usually secured through the use of credit at a high rate of interest. The risk is extremely high. It has been said that three bankruptcies are needed to settle a new area. The length of time since settlement is associated with the stability of the type of farming, the tenure pattern, the credit organization, and the income.

The Coastal Plain is an area of long settlement, stable types of farming, and little risk of income although the amount of the income is fairly low in comparison with that received by farmers in 1942 in the Rolling Plains and the Blacklands. While most of the better lands were settled by native whites from the Carolinas, Negro ownership neighborhoods and isolated Negro ownership in other areas are today quite common. Negro ownership neighborhoods are on poorer land and in more isolated sections. The productivity of the soil in a few of these neighborhoods has been improved so that it is only slightly less desirable than the average for the whole sample area.

Jefferson Davis County, Mississippi, is an old agricultural county. Settlement began shortly after 1811 by people from the states to the east and northeast.[3] Descendants of these pioneers make up the present population. (Table 41)[4] Cotton was the staple money crop before the Civil War and continues to be of primary importance. Truck crops are second in importance and although the particular crop has varied somewhat, the importance of trucking has remained about the the same. Farm land has been cheap and to a large extent is owned by resident operators. Some land either in woods or in stump is owned by lumber companies. Some of this land reverted to the state for nonpayment of taxes and some has been opened for settlement since 1930. Greenscreek neighborhood is an example of "new land" settlement in the county.

Marion County, Mississippi, is a much younger agricultural county than Jefferson Davis although the first permanent settlement was

[3] T. M. Bushnell and L. Vincent Davis, *Soil Survey of Jefferson Davis County, Mississippi*, Washington, 1916, p. 6.

[4] See statistical tables in Appendix.

made as early as 1809. Growth was very slow before 1870.[5] Early settlers came largely from the Carolinas with smaller numbers from Virginia and Tennessee. The agricultural history of Marion County is interwoven with that of the lumber industry. As timber was removed from the land during the period from 1910 to 1930, the cutover land was being utilized for farming. What with high taxes and low income from the cutover lands in the early thirties, large tracts of nonfarm lands reverted to the state and new settlement was quite common.

Much of the land in Marion County is rolling to steep and is in a mature stage of erosion. Soils in some of the neighborhoods in Marion County are equal to the better lands of Jefferson Davis County but on the whole there is less of the good soil. At the time of the soil survey (1935) about 20 per cent of the total land area was owned by four or five large landowners. These were probably lumber companies. Slightly over half of the total land area is in farms. In several stranded sawmill neighborhoods farming on a part-time basis is being carried on with work at Columbia in one of the numerous plants there or in sawmill work.

The history of the sample counties in the Arkansas Coastal Plain closely follows that of Jefferson Davis County, Mississippi. (Table 41) Income from oil leases during the past ten years has caused a tendency for owner-operators to move into the villages and to leave the farming to the renters and croppers. This lessening of interest in the farm as a source of income is reflected in the higher percentage of the family income from sources other than farm or off-farm work for owners (Table 21) and the fact that more freedom of management is allowed both renters and croppers in Arkansas than in Mississippi. (Table 42) The residence of the landlords for Arkansas was a bimodal distribution with one-fourth of them located less than one-half mile from the tract and the remainder falling in a fairly normal distribution with about ten miles being the mode. (Table 43) Over one-half of the Mississippi landlords were less than one-half mile from the rent tract and only about 12 per cent were over five miles.

Oklahoma was one of the last states settled, yet it has one of the highest rates of tenancy, excluding croppers, of any state in the United States. Land was homesteaded with little cash cost to the settler.

[5] J. W. Moon, *et al*, *Soil Survey of Marion County, Mississippi*, Washington, 1938, p. 4.

However, only about one-half of those filing for homesteads completed the requirements and actually operated the farms as owners. Two-thirds of the farmers sampled were native of either Oklahoma or Texas. (Table 41) One of the first things a homesteader did was to get a mortgage on the farm. Most of these mortgages are still active. This fact indicates that over a period of 40 years, it has generally not been possible for the land to pay the costs of improvements, finance the operating capital requirements needed to operate the farms, and maintain suitable levels of living. The farms were settled by native white homesteaders or purchased from them in family-sized farm units. Change of title due to mortgage foreclosure and tax adjudication in the early 1930's may have added to the tenancy rate. Nominal ownership with high mortgage rates, high risk of income, and title to land tends to prevail in 1942.

The homestead tract in southwestern Oklahoma was the quarter section of land (160 acres). While it was possible to purchase additional quarter sections, and the Texas law allowed larger tracts in Old Greer County, such cases were the exception. In some neighborhoods such as Martha, the quarter section has been subdivided into 80's and even 40's. These latter neighborhoods have high priced land, relatively low risk on yields, and less than a quarter section will support a family. There has been practically no tax foreclosures in such areas and very few foreclosures of mortgages. With the large tractor units, some consolidation of the smaller parcels has taken place. On the poorer soils and on the lands more suitable for small grain farming, the shift has been toward concentration of holdings so that farms of two quarters or larger in size predominate. The unit of measure for ownership tracts is still the quarter section. The size of farm, measured in terms of labor requirements, is the family farm. The change in total acres has been toward, rather than away from, the "ideal" of the operator and his family doing all of the work. Nearly all farmers sampled hired their cotton harvested but very little other labor was hired. Wheat was harvested with combines and was also sowed at a fixed rate per acre. Only one farmer in seven owned a combine and one in twelve owned a grain drill. (Table 19)

The Blackland of Texas has been cultivated about 60 years and was settled first by native whites from areas to the east and north. The livestock ranches of the first settlers were replaced with crop-growing farms and cotton became the chief source of income in the latter part of the nineteenth century. A later settlement of Germans and Czechs on the heavier bottom soils occurred between 1880 and 1910. The heaviest immigration of Germans to Bell County occurred between 1880 and 1890 while the Czechs came between 1900 and 1910. (Table 44) Bell County has a higher proportion of the Czech and German groups than other Blackland counties, but these culture groups are quite common throughout the Blackland area. More recently the type of farming has been shifting from cotton to general farming with livestock and feed crops. Farms have increased in size as measured by total acres, but with the increase in the use of tractors, the labor requirements have actually decreased. These changes are associated with less need for croppers, resident wage laborers, and seasonal laborers. The farmers who survive these changes will likely be owners rather than renters. Absentee owners will rent land to owner-operators who will thereby become part owners. Acreage operated by renters decreased between 1930 and 1940 while the acreage rented by part owners increased. Blackland counties with the greatest increases reported for part owners by the census are Collin, Falls, Ellis, Kaufman, Rockwall, McLennan and Travis; all of these practically doubled the acreage between 1935 and 1940.

Stage in Technological Development

Plantations, depending upon croppers or other hired labor, are associated with southern agriculture. It should be pointed out, however, that interspersed with their large holdings are many family-sized units. With the introduction of large power machinery, either horse or tractor, the need for a large number of agricultural workers has been reduced. Along with this trend has been the introduction of livestock on a commercial basis so that those remaining in agriculture have become more skilled and receive larger incomes. Thus, some of the interspersed family farms have increased in size as measured by labor requirements and by acres. Since land is physical in nature and has inflexible size in a given area, it is only reasonable to assume that as some farms increase in size, others must decrease or disappear entirely. The Oklahoma sample area is representative of the highest degree of mechanization, Texas is next, Louisiana third, Mississippi fourth, and Arkansas last. (Table 12) Large power units are more efficient on large farms and are more likely to be found there. Large farms also mean large net worth which provide the ability to purchase tractors as well as to operate them.

Some of the practical applications of these generalizations are illustrated in the fact that Farm Security Administration borrowers in

Oklahoma were purchasing tractors with their credit while those in Mississippi and Arkansas purchased one row or even half-row equipment. The technological development of the area established limits for farm management behavior and for tenure behavior. Both skilled labor for operation and agencies for giving adequate servicing for tractor operation are lacking in the Coastal Plains. Likewise, credit agencies in 1942 were not yet willing to advance $1,000 for a set of tractor equipment. These factors limit the activities of any one individual but as more and more individuals demand them, such services will become available. A tenant must accumulate capital according to the established practices of the community in which he is farming.

The cotton picker and the flame cultivator will further revise the tenure composition of each area of the South. This equipment will be readily used in areas of large operating units. It can be adopted in other areas as custom work or through the aid of cooperative ownership. A large investment in machinery tends to force farmers to larger farms in order to realize the maximum efficiency from the equipment. This process entails the bidding for land and forces the less efficient renters out of the area or out of agriculture. Some of these displaced renters will doubtless remain in the area seeking employment from the agencies servicing the equipment and as wage laborers on farms. If the pressure for land becomes too great or takes place too quickly, it may be possible to secure land only through ownership. Western Oklahoma is approaching this stage at the present time. As ownership becomes more desirable, the selling price of land increases to meet the demand.

In general, mechanization has increased the size of farms and the incomes of those remaining in agriculture as operators and has tended to lessen the differential between tenure groups. The livestock enterprise on the other hand is still limited on many farms to a cow, a couple of hogs, and a few chickens. In a livestock area such as the Corn Belt, there is no limitation to the size of the livestock business for a non-landowner. Other factors operate to determine a limit but the Corn Belt area has accepted livestock as a cash enterprise and arrangements have been worked out by which the farmer and the owner of the land can cooperate in a partnership arrangement.

Population Pressure

Fertility. Within each area the relationship between size of family and tenure status shows little significance. For the five samples taken in the current study renter families had a significantly higher fertility index than owners for Arkansas and Mississippi, while the difference was only slight for Oklahoma. (Table 45) For Texas and Louisiana the owner families were slightly higher. Croppers exceeded renter families only in the Louisiana sample. Traditionally farm children have been regarded as economic assets in that they augment the labor force. On the other hand there is a tendency for larger families to be poor economically. Duncan and Sanders concluded that large families neither aid nor hinder a family in climbing the tenure ladder.[6] In a more recent study by McMillan and Duncan, utilizing data from the current study and others, a more refined conclusion is offered; "Families with one to five children tend to exceed the average of all farmers in the proportions of farm owners. Apparently children do not handicap families in the achievement of farm ownership until their number reaches at least six or seven. . . . The absolute number of children per family is not the all-important factor in the matter."[7] They pointed out that their observations were taken during a period of rising prices and that the degree of mechanization also influenced their generalizations. To summarize, those families that achieve ownership have about as many children as those who do not when standardized for age of parents. In some cases the children are economic assets utilized in the labor force possibly at the sacrifice of their educational opportunities and in other cases they are economic liabilities. An examination of fertility of the families sampled showed no significant differences by tenure of parents.

Out-Migration. From two-thirds to three-fourths of the children of the sampled farm families have gone into or married into families of nonfarm occupations. (Tables 46 and 47). Other studies have shown the same general trend of heavy out-migration of farm young people to urban areas and to nonfarm occupation. Dicken's study of Mississippi cotton farmers children indicated a considerably lower percentage (25 per cent) in non farm occupation.[8] Mississippi as a whole offers little opportunity for nonfarm employment within its boundaries and the percentage retained in agriculture is greater in the more rural areas.

---

[6] O. D. Duncan and J. T. Sanders, *A Study of Certain Economic Factors in Relation to Social Life Among Oklahoma Cotton Farmers*, Oklahoma Agricultural Experiment Station Bull. 211, April 1933, p. 15.

[7] R. T. McMillan and O. D. Duncan, *Social Factors of Farm Ownership in Oklahoma*, Oklahoma Agricultural Experiment Station Bull. B-289, November 1945, pp. 20-21.

[8] Dorothy Dickins, *Occupation of Sons and Daughters of Mississippi Cotton Farmers*, Mississippi Agricultural Experiment Station Bull. 318, May 1937, p. 16.

A high tenure status of the parental family is associated with higher educational attainment by the children and also with a higher income level and socio-economic status of the parental family. Tenure, education, income, and socio-economic status are interrelated and increases in each tend to increase the percentage of the children who migrate to urban centers and to nonfarm occupations. This relationship was generally true for the cases sampled in 1942 although for the white families in Mississippi, children of renters had gone to nonfarm occupation to the greatest extent and children of owners to the least extent. There was little difference by tenure for the Texas sample. Negro children remained in the occupation of agriculture to a greater extent than white children and in general children of all nonowners to a greater extent than children of owners.

A number of theories have been developed on the subject of selective migration of children from the farm. Most of them agree on selection by age, sex, and educational attainment but differ as to physical, moral, intellectual, economic, and social qualities.[9] The data obtained in the current study emphasizes the effect of education as a factor in selective migration. For the racial groups in the areas in which children of the higher tenure groups also received the higher educational advantages, the children of the higher tenure group left agriculture for nonfarm occupations to a greater extent than children of the lower tenure groups. In those groups which had little or no difference in the education of the children (Mississippi whites and Texas Czechs and Germans) the difference in transfers to other occupations followed the difference in education rather than the difference in tenure status. (Tables 46 and 48)

A recent statistical study in Kentucky showed low income and education to be of greatest influence in determining the incidence of out-migration.[10] Fertility was of little importance and communication was related to fertility and income in such a way that the net result was not highly related to migration. The evidence of the current study is in partial agreement with conclusions drawn from the Ken-

---

[9] For a summary of the more recent studies see T. Lynn Smith, *The Sociology of Rural Life*, Harpers, New York, 1947, pp. 185-91. Also see P. A. Sorokin, C. C. Zimmerman, and C. J. Galpin, *Systematic Source Book in Rural Sociology*, III, 479-534, University of Minnesota Press, Minneapolis, Minn., and Dorothy Swain Thomas, *Research Memorandum on Migration Differentials*, Social Science Research Council Bulletin 43, New York, 1938, pp. 70-167.

[10] Merton D. Oyler, *Fertility Rates and Migration of Kentucky Population, 1920-1940, as Related to Communication, Income and Education*, Kentucky Agricultural Experiment Station Bull. 469, November 1944.

tucky study and is quite different from the results McMillan obtained in his study of Oklahoma migrants. For Oklahoma, McMillan found that during the drouth and depression years with the government crop control program and increases in mechanization, nonowners in a five-county sample moved to a much greater degree than owner.[11] The current study is also more optimistic than the statement of the National Resources Planning Board which stated: "Young people now provided with the most meager educational advantages are the ones who, in largest numbers, will find it necessary to seek occupational opportunity outside the communities in which they were born."[12]

Whatever the cause of selective migration, when it occurs, it has its effect on the tenure opportunities of those remaining. As children of owners, or nonowners, leave an area in disproportionately large numbers, the pressure is eased for those remaining. And further, the establishing of channels of migrations for children of one tenure group to leave an area makes it easier for those of the same tenure group to follow and thereby establish a pattern of differential migration. If children of owners leave an area to the extent that they are not replacing themselves, children of nonowners have greater opportunities of becoming owners either through marriage or by farm purchases. If children of nonowners are leaving in excessively large numbers (as McMillan observed in Oklahoma), nonowners may be completely eliminated as they are not replacing themselves. The nonmigrant owners add the "rent land" of the area to their owned farms. Either differential migration or competitive bidding for "rent land" by owners may be the casual factor and the other the resulting situation, but the two processes take place at the same time.

VARIATIONS AMONG INDIVIDUALS

Cultural Origin

The matter of cultural origin is of interest in tenure analysis as a relatively simple way of labeling peoples with different attitudes, techniques, ideas, habits in regard to educational standards, practices with regard to borrowing money, soil conservation, levels of subsistence farming, governmental programs, out-migration of children, etc. For the samples studied the groups are: native white in the

[11] Robert T. McMillan, *Migration of Population in Five Oklahoma Townships*, Oklahoma Agricultural Experiment Station Bull. B-271, October 1943, p. 31.

[12] National Resources Committee, *The Problem of a Changing Population*, Washington, 1938, p. 211.

Arkansas, Mississippi, Oklahoma, and Texas samples; the whites originating from Germany and Czechoslovakia in the Texas sample; Negroes in all samples; and a few Mexicans in Oklahoma and Texas. The Negro and the Mexican can be separated fairly easily from the white on the basis of race. The separation of the whites into their significant subdivisions is a more difficult matter. The difficulty lies in a satisfactory label rather than the actual classification. Native white is used for those families originating from the British Isles and actually includes one case in the Arkansas sample of a family head born in England. (Table 41) This isolated case as well as the three cases of foreign born (Swedish, Russian, and German) in Oklahoma has been so well assimilated that little difference was noted between them and the other people in the area sampled. The Czechs and Germans of the Texas sample, although the majority were born in Texas, represented a difference from the people living in other neighborhoods because they retained their language to some extent and maintained their own institutions. It might have been significant to have separated the Oklahoma sample into those born in southern states and those born in midwestern states but the small number of cases born outside the South rendered this plan impractical.[13]

While the preponderance of the white people in the South are "Old Americans" there are a number of well defined "cultural islands" within the five states. Some of these are the Italian settlements of northwestern Arkansas; the French area of southern Louisiana; Hungarian settlements in Tangipahoa, Livingston, and Ascension parishes; Hungarian, Czech, Belgian, and German settlements in Rapides Parish; and Italian settlements in areas near New Orleans. Practically no "cultural islands" are to be found in Mississippi. Oklahoma has important Indian concentrations (2.7 per cent of the total population) and Negroes (7.2 per cent of the total population). In Texas, the Mexican is the most important minority group and is located mainly in the southwestern part of the state. Czechs are located in both Texas and Oklahoma and a large concentration of Germans is located in Llano, Gillespie, and Mason counties, Texas.

Sufficient evidence has been presented from other studies to warrant a separate treatment of the Czech and German culture groups.[14]

---

[13] McMillan and Duncan found that fewer Oklahoma farmers born in the South achieve farm ownership than those born in other regions. R. T. McMillan and O. D. Duncan, *Social Factors of Farm Ownership in Oklahoma*, Oklahoma Agricultural Experiment Station Bull. B-289, November 1945.

[14] R. W. Lynch, *Czech Farmers in Oklahoma*, Oklahoma A. and M. College Bulletin Vol. 39, No. 13, 1942; Joe R. Motheral, *Type of Farm Tenancy Areas in Texas*,

In each of these other studies, the Old World culture group exhibited a much higher degree of stability, percentage of ownership, soil conservation practices, diversification of agriculture, and self-sufficiency. Shryock stated that the English settled on "loose dirt," which meant bottom land and sandy uplands while the Germans tended to settle on the "more permanently fertile, heavy-textured wooded lands among which the clay loams of limestone origin are conspicuous."[15] He went on to say that these were the lands that they knew to be good for farming. He further stated that the Scotch-Irish also settled on lands with which they were familiar but that, unfortunately for them, these lands were inferior in quality and often found on hilly terrain. Length of settlement was a common factor in the studies made and in most cases the land had been cultivated for 50 years or longer. Whether from better husbandry, location on more productive soils, harder work by the entire family while sacrificing educational opportunities for the children and sacrificing farm-family living, those retaining the Old World cultural ideas in general conserve the soil, diversify the farming operations, and achieve ownership to a greater extent than the "Old American" group. Security is attained more by belonging to the culture group than through the use of governmental programs of relief, Agricultural Adjustment Administration benefits, etc. Whether this emphasis on farming as a way of life is a more important criterion of success than the profit motive of the "Old Americans" is for the group itself to say. There are two distinctly different goals.

The Negro is more important numerically than the Old World culture groups. Beginning in 1865 with practically no ownership of land, he has increased his holdings considerably although the ownership of land by Negroes is still disproportionately low. Standardizing for tenure of parents the difference between present tenure status for the two races largely disappears. Sample Negro families within the same tenure of parent groups began their occupational life at about the same station with somewhat less ownership and considerable

U. S. Department of Agriculture, Bureau of Agricultural Economics, Washington, 1941, Mimeo., p. 13; Walter M. Kollmorgen, *The German Settlement in Cullman County, Alabama,* U. S. Department of Agriculture, Bureau of Agricultural Economics, Washington, Mimeo., 1941; Walter M. Kollmorgen, *The German-Swiss in Franklin County, Tennessee,* U. S. Department of Agriculture, Bureau of Agricultural Economics, Washington, Mimeo., 1941; R. H. Shyrock, "Cultural Factors in the History of the U. S.," *The Journal of Southern History,* V (August 1939).

[15] R. H. Shryock, "British Vs. Germans in Colonia Agriculture," *Mississippi Valley Historical Review,* XXVI (June 1939), 46-48.

more of the farm laborer status. (Table 49) The percentage who were owners was two to three times as great for the whites with less than 20 years of earning life, but after 40 years the difference in favor of whites is somewhat less. (Table 50) The low tenure status of Negroes is due mainly to the fact that Negroes as a group are nonowners and have very little land to pass down from generation to generation. Negroes with owner parents achieve ownership to only a slightly less extent than whites with comparable tenure of parents. Children of the family heads sampled show the same tendency. Children of Negro families with comparable tenure status are staying in agriculture to a greater extent than those of white families. (Tables 46 and 47) A higher percentage of Negro children are at present working as laborers and croppers and a lower percentage are in the owner status than those children of white families. Within tenure of parent groups, Negroes enter the higher status nonfarm occupations to a slightly less degree than whites.

Education is another factor in which culture groups differ. Since the Negroes have separate schools from the whites, the two systems can be evaluated in themselves. Negro schools in general are for shorter terms, are held in more crowded conditions (number of pupils per teacher), have teachers with less academic training, and have less equipment with which to teach. Considering both cultural background and educational attainments, Negroes in the regional sample rate below whites. (Tables 48 and 51) When evaluated according to standards for the total population, Negroes are not achieving higher tenure or occupational status than whites. However, within their own racial group the same set of factors (tenure status of parents and education) are operative to about the same extent as for native white. Those whites with the Old World cultural set of attitudes have a high percentage of farm owners but use formal education to a much lesser extent than the "Old Americans." The combined effect is that their children leave school at a somewhat earlier age than the children of "Old Americans" but are retained on the farm and in the community to a greater extent.

Age

Fundamental to the term "agricultural leader," so popular in the 1920's, is the matter of age. Logically, a young man begins his earning life with little or no capital accumulation or managerial experience. With this lack of resources his only choice in agriculture is either wage laborer or cropper, and as he accumulates capital it is possible for him to buy equipment and power and to finance his crop production and living expenses through the use of his own capital or by using credit. He also gains in experience and supposedly in managerial ability in the process of aging. The successful renter accumulates still more capital or credit standing so that he can purchase land. If he is successful as a renter, he has also increased his managerial ability. The owner who inherits land or is aided by his parents in a financial way is seldom given a deed to land the first year he farms. Therefore, he too must go through approximately the same steps.

Age is a most important factor affecting tenure status. For a detailed consideration of the relationship between age and tenure status, questions as to definitions and gaps of information necessarily arise. Farming is only one of several occupations and nonfarm employment is an important rung in the agricultural ladder in some areas. Then too, should age be measured in terms of years since birth or in years of occupational age? If occupational age is used, further choices are possible such as "years since beginning on own," "years since completing education" and "years since marriage." If years since birth are used, an arbitrary age of 18 (or 21) is usually set as the lower limit for considering occupational characteristics. Each of these measures has been used at various times in other studies, and each has its merits.

The farming activity of children in school is not a major field in the present study, but the years spent in the schoolroom are by no means sterile ones in the process of producing farmers. In most cases, however, any farm work is incidental to the use of the boy's time in the schoolroom and "in school" is his chief occupation. This statement in no way depreciates the amount or quality of the farm work done by children in school.

Children are recognized to be a part of the labor force in the experiment station studies in all of the five states. While each state varied slightly as to age intervals and the exact unit assigned for each interval, in general, boys of from 8 to 16 were regarded as equal to a grown man. Females were assigned slightly less equivalents. These assumptions appear to be justified in that the family (spouse and children) performed nearly as much of the total labor as did the operator. (Table 52) Since the family labor was concentrated during periods of peak labor needs, its importance is greater than is indicated by a comparison of the percentage distribution of the total labor used.

Schools are in session for five days of the week and for a term of from six to nine months in southern states. Many children are kept out of school during the planting and harvesting season and at other times when the farmer is "in a tight place." In some areas, the schools are closed during periods of peak labor requirements, so that both pupil and teacher may work on farms. This practice is followed in the Eldorado area of Jackson County, Oklahoma, during the cotton harvest season and it is also followed in the strawberry area of Ascension Parish, Louisiana. Children living on farms gain considerable experience at farming while in school. In addition to their experience, it is possible in an increasing number of schools for children to learn the theory of farming and farm life in courses in vocational agriculture, home economics, and in 4-H Club work. These activities include work at home in developing skills and managerial ability. During a four-year course in vocational agriculture a boy should accumulate considerable livestock and possibly a little equipment in his own name. Many of the children in families sampled had bank accounts in their own names. In addition, over twenty owners are shown to have accumulated cash for the initial down payment from "farming" even though their previous occupational experience had been that of unpaid family laborer. Work for neighboring farmers or in nonfarm occupations are other possible sources of income. Some farmers give their children livestock or the crop productions from designated acres in order to stimulate their interest in farming or in lieu of an allowance. However, it has been said that too often "the boy's calf becomes the father's cow; the boy's pig the fathers sow." This illustrates possible ways in which some farm children gain in farm net worth, in acquiring skills and managerial experience in farming during their school years.

No attempt was made in this study to secure data on the subject so the extent of the activity by racial or tenure groups was not determined. Those farmers with large units and especially those with considerable amounts of livestock are in a better position to give their children such opportunities. One case was sampled in Greer County, Oklahoma, in which the son's purebred cattle acquired in 4-H Club and Vo-Ag work was gradually replacing the father's grade cattle and the father was being forced out of the livestock business.

Children of owner families remain in school about one year longer than children of renters for each racial group in the four sample areas. (Table 53) The Czech and German families sampled in

Texas were an exception. The children of Czech and German owner families left school about one year earlier than children of native white owners. No consistent difference was noted between children of croppers and those of renters. Little difference was noted in the average age left school between whites and Negroes. In general the differences in "age left school" are repeated in the grade attainment of children 20-29 years of age. (Table 48) The notable exception occurs in the comparison of whites and Negroes in the Coastal Plains samples. With approximately the same age at time of leaving school, the white children were from one to four grades more advanced. The difference was greater for children of older ages. The grade retardation for all children who completed schooling shows the same relationships more directly. (Table 54) Negroes were about three grades more retarded than whites for each tenure group in the Coastal Plains samples. Children of Czech and German families in the Texas sample were slightly more retarded than those of native white families. Children of owners were less retarded for each racial group in each sample area than children of nonowners.

Following the completion of formal schooling at an average age of from 16 to 18 years, sons in each tenure group averaged a period of about three years before marriage and the beginning of an occupational career. Daughters averaged about two years between time of leaving school and marriage. Little difference was noted between tenure groups for "age at marriage" for children of whites in Arkansas and Mississippi and the native whites sampled in Texas. Among children of native whites in Oklahoma, Czechs and Germans in Texas, and the Negroes in the Coastal Plains, sons of owners married about one year later than children of renters.

With the earlier age at leaving school for children of the Czech and German families, a total period of over five years was given the sons to work full time with their fathers at home before marriage and beginning an occupation of their own. For other racial groups in other sample areas the period was three or four years. Although there were slight differences in the length of the period between completion of schooling and marriage or going into an occupation on their own, when a comparison of tenure groups of races in made, an apprentice period of from three to five years on the average is available to each son and from one to three years for each daughter in which the young person is at home full time under the influence of the teaching of the parents regardless of tenure status. Children of farmers owning livestock have an opportunity to begin in a modest way the management of livestock enterprises as owners themselves. Skills can be perfected. It is quite evident that the father can pass on to the son only those skills, decisions, and managerial functions that he is making himself. This means that sons of owners and operating tenants have much more opportunity to learn from their fathers than those of supervised tenants (croppers) or laborers.

The first business decision that a son must make during the period between leaving school and marriage is the choice of an occupation. Of the family heads sampled, over one-half began their occupational life and got married within the same year. This situation held for all areas and racial groups. Marriage brings the question to a head if it has been delayed. A study in Livingston County, New York, in 1919 showed that for sons at home between the ages of 18 and 24 the usual arrangement with their fathers was that no definite wages were paid the son.[16] Above the age of 25, however, arrangements were made whereby either: (1) the son purchased the farm, (2) a definite plan was agreed upon for inheritance (3) a tenancy was established, (4) a partnership was arranged, or (5) the boy worked for wages. Over three-fourths (77 per cent) of the sons over 35 years old at home had worked out plans to own the home farm. The father-son arrangement allows the son to benefit from the experience of the father and to utilize the capital and operating equipment that the father has accumulated during his lifetime. If the son is not allowed to "grow" under such an arrangement, it works a hardship on both father and son. Sons of croppers and laborers do not have the advantage of the experience and capital accumulation of their fathers since the father himself has little capital and has had little experience in making decisions. The importance of father and son getting along well together as a factor in the success of such arrangements has been emphasized by a number of writers in recent publications on this subject.[17] In the regional study, two or three times as many of the

---

[16] E. C. Young, *The Movement of Farm Population,* New York Agricultural Experiment Station Bull. 426, March 1924.

[17] Elton B. Hill, *Father and Son Farm Partnerships,* Michigan Agricultural Experiment Station Spec. Bull. 330, April 1944; H. C. M. Case and J. B. Cunningham, "The Illinois Father-Son Business Agreement," *Illinois Farm Economics* (January 1943), pp. 419-23; H. C. M. Case and Joseph Ackerman, *Farm Leases for Illinois,* Illinois Agricultural Experiment Station Cir. 503, May 1940; North Central Regional Land Tenure Committee, *Capital Needed to Farm in the Midwest,* Minnesota Agricultural Experiment Station Bull. 389, January 1946; Kenneth H. Parsons and Eliot O. Waples, *Keeping the Farm in the Family,* Wisconsin Agricultural Experiment Station Res. Bull. 157, September 1945.

children of owners are in the owner category as for children of renters in each racial group for each area. (Table 46) The farm operators sampled who were sons of owners also showed the same high proportion of owners for their first farm tenure status. (Table 49)

Numerous other studies have presented data showing that as age increases there is an increase in the percentage of farmers who are owners.[18]

This increase in ownership is the more striking when tenure of parents is considered. Negroes are about on a par with whites when only those with owner parents are considered. (Table 50) Negro sons of owners with less than 20 years of earning life are much lower in percentage ownership than whites. In the Arkansas sample there were about one-third as many owners proportionally among Negroes as there was among whites and less than half for the Mississippi sample. At 20 to 39 years of earning life, Negroes were approaching whites, and for those with 40 and over years of earning life, 75 per cent of the Negroes in the Arkansas sample were owners as compared to 82 per cent of the whites. For the Mississippi sample in the older age grouping, Negroes exceed whites in achieving ownership—93 per cent as contrasted with 87 per cent. In the Coastal Plains there were few cases of white farmers whose parents were other than owners so the comparison between races for that group is not conclusive. However, those with nonowner parents had lesser percentages in the owner group in each age group and as age increased the percentage of owners increased. The generalization applies equally well to the samples taken in Oklahoma and Texas.

Increases in the percentage of farmers who are owners occur with increases in years of earning life and are parallel for both whites and Negroes in the Coastal Plains and for the whites in the Bell County, Texas, areas. The difference between the groups at the first year of earning life remained approximately the same throughout the life span. The whites in the Coastal Plains leveled off at about 85 per cent and the other groups at about 65 per cent owners at 35 years of earning life. For single individuals the process of climbing the tenure ladder is not so direct nor is the direction always upward. Over 20 per cent of the renters in the Coastal Plains areas had been owners sometime during their occupational career. (Table 55) The same proportion of white croppers in Mississippi had been owners but only

[18] See H. A. Turner, *A Graphic Summary of Farm Tenure*, U. S. Department of Agriculture, Misc. Pub. 261, Washington, 1936; and L. C. Gray *et al*, "Farm Ownership and Tenancy," *Agriculture Yearbook*, 1923, Washington, 1924, pp. 507-600.

10 per cent of the croppers in the Arkansas area. Negroes in the Coastal Plains and the whites in the Oklahoma and Texas samples had experienced about half the loss of ownership as the Coastal Plain whites as measured by the percentage of nonowners who had been owners.

The cases reporting loss of ownership had experienced an average of about 10 years as owner. From a third to a half of the owners in the Coastal Plains had passed through a renter experience while three-fourths of the owners in Oklahoma and Texas had at one time been renters. The Coastal Plains owners passing through the renter stage had spent about three years less time as renters than similar cases in Texas and Oklahoma. Ten years represented the average for all areas. These owners reporting a cropper status had spent an average of about five years in that status. A cropper arrangement was reported by about one-half of the Negro owners and one-fourth of the white owners in the Coastal Plains areas, while less than one-fifth of the owners in the Oklahoma and Texas areas reported such a status. Part of the difference in cropper status as a step to ownership between areas was compensated by work as farm laborers. If cropper and laborer were combined, the differences between areas would be only slight.

Tenure of Parents

The influence of the tenure, education, economic and social status, attitudes, and ideals of parents on the life of the offspring is many sided and often difficult to measure. Numerous other studies have shown that the occupation and the status of the father is transmitted to the son to a high degree.[19] The status of the father must be taken at a particular time as must the status of the son. Either may have fluctuated considerably so that the influence the father actually effected on the son may be different from that assumed from the reported status of the father. The status reported for the son may not have fully reflected the total effect of the influence of the father as the influence may have been dissipated at the time of measurement. Standardizing for age of children would help to minimize these differences.

The influence of parents is cumulative in that children tend to marry within their own occupational grouping and within their own

[19] P. A. Sorokin, *Social Mobility*, Harpers, New York, 1923, pp. 414-62. After examining a number of studies, the author reached the conclusion that: "Its maximum (transmission of occupational status) seems to be at about 70 percent; its minimum at about 3 to 10 percent."

tenure grouping.[20] The family heads sampled showed over 80 per cent of the male heads who were sons of owners to have married daughters of owners for the whites in Mississippi and the Czechs and Germans in Texas. (Table 56) The percentage was over 60 for all racial groups in all sample areas. Similarly the children of each tenure group tended to marry within their own tenure except that children of renters married children of owners about as frequently as they did children of renters. This might be partially explained by the fact that there was a higher proportion of children of owners in the areas sampled than of children of renters. Characteristics transmitted from father to son were also transmitted from father to daughter.

No data were gathered on the parents of the heads of families sampled other than their tenure or occupation at the time the male and female heads were married. For each racial group in each of the Coastal Plains samples the marriage of son of owner with daughter of owner resulted in about twice as high a proportion of owners for first tenure reported as other combinations. The lower the tenure of parents the lower the beginning tenure status. (Table 49) The difference is first tenure by tenure of parents was only slight for the samples taken in Oklahoma and Texas.

Children of the family heads sampled exhibit similar characteristics. There is a slight bias favoring children of owners in that they average about four years older than children of renters, who in turn are about four years older than children of croppers. The children of the higher tenure status families had gone into nonfarm occupations to a greater extent and were farming with a higher tenure status than the children of families with lower status. (Table 46) Of the children who had nonfarm occupation, those from owner families were consistently more concentrated in the higher status nonfarm occupations. (Table 47)

The difference in average age of children of different tenure groups suggests that the difference in tenure of families sampled by tenure of parents may be due to age difference more than to differences in the characteristics of the parents. The data show this hypothesis to be correct in part. Changes in the tenure composition of the family heads varies more by years of earning life than by tenure of parents. As occupational age increases the percentage of owners

[20] This characteristic is even more pronounced if the data are corrected for the excess farm population which is forced to migrate to urban centers with the marriage following migration.

increases consistently for each tenure of parent group with about the same difference between the tenure-of-parent group in each age group. (Table 50) Sampled families in the owner-owner category with 40 years or more of earning life had three-fourths or more classified as owners in each of the racial groups for the four areas studied.

The Oklahoma sample showed differences in percentage owners by tenure-of-parents groupings in the younger age groups but practically no difference for the older farmers. The older farmers in the Oklahoma area are affected more by the settlement of the area through homesteading than by age or tenure of parents. None of the lesser tenure-of-parent groups (combinations other than owner-owner) in the Arkansas and Mississippi sample reached as high as 50 per cent ownership at the older ages for those groups which had numbers sufficient to be considered reliable. In the Texas sample, the difference was less than in the Coastal Plain sample but in the same direction.

Farm net worth showed the same results by years of earning life and tenure of parents for the racial groups in the areas sampled as did percentage owner.

McMillan's study of 618 farm families in Oklahoma showed that 65 per cent of the husbands and wives married within their own tenure group with approximately the same differences by specific tenure and by sex as found in the current study.[21] Specific items that McMillan found to have the greatest significant difference by tenure of parents were: family income, net worth, educational attainment, rate of farm-to-farm migration, housing index, socio-economic status score, use of tractors, and the growing of wheat as a principal crop. In all of the items families of owner-owner parents were higher than families of nonowner parents for both husband and wife. Of lesser significance were the differences by which those of owner-owner parents excelled in total number of acres, location on best grade of soil, cotton as a principal crop, membership in church by the husband, and number of persons in the family. Those with nonowner parents received public assistance twice as frequently as those in the other group.

Education

Differences in retardation of children who had completed their education were slight between tenure groups but white children were rather consistently about three grades ahead of the Negroes. (Table

[21] Robert T. McMillan, "Farm Ownership Status of Parents as a Determinant of the Socio-economic Status of Farmers," *Rural Sociology*, 9, (June 1944) 151-160.

54) The low rate of retardation for Texas is due in part to the 11-grade-school system which existed until 1941. Children of the higher tenure families completed more grades than the nonowner families. (Table 48) Schuler found white children to have completed about three more grades than Negro children, and that children of families in the higher tenure status in the South had about one grade advantage per step in the tenure status hierarchy.[22] Children of renters, croppers, and laborers who were related to their landlords/employers were higher than those cases in which they were not related. An Oklahoma study published in 1933 indicated that realtively higher educational attainment of children was related to high tenure status of the parents, net wealth of the parents, educational attainment of the parents, and the percentage of children who entered nonfarm occupation (particularly the professions.)[23] The advantage of educational attainment to farmers was summarized as follows: "Parents are generally desirous to have their children better prepared for the problems of life when they start for themselves than they (the parents) were at the same age. The more advanced the parents are, educationally and culturally, the greater this desire (or the ability of both parents and child to satisfy it) is as a general rule."[24]

In general the school is the most important urban factor in a rural community and as such a positive relationship exists between schooling and out-migration of children. The introduction of vocational agriculture into the curriculum has been a step in adapting education to rural needs but business courses were introduced at about the same time in order that the children would be better prepared for urban life. It is common knowledge that larger proportions of all children are now entering high school. For the children sampled, the Negroes have made greater progress than the whites. (Table 48) The high school has become a reality to a majority of the rural children, and at the same time its primary function has ceased to be that of a preparatory school for college but it has become a preparatory school for life.[25]

---

[22] E. A. Schuler, *Social Status and Farm Tenure—Attitudes and Social Conditions of Corn Belt and Cotton Belt Farmers*, Social Research Report No. IV, U. S. Department of Agriculture, Farm Security Administration and Bureau of Agricultural Economics, Washington, April 1938, p. 147.

[23] O. D. Duncan and J. T. Sanders, *A Study of Certain Economic Factors in Relation to Social Life Among Oklahoma Cotton Farmers*, Oklahoma Agricultural Experiment Station Bull. 211, April 1933.

[24] *Ibid.* p. 28.

[25] The problems and objectives of general education, and of the secondary educational system in particular, have been subject to reorganization in recent years. One

The studies of Oklahoma families have indicated that "schooling and tenure status are related but the degree of association is not large."[26] It was pointed out that while the amount of schooling has had little influence on tenure status, the relationship will likely become more important as the effect of the free land by homesteading becomes less.[27]

Education is a process which is not confined to the school. The parents may do the educating as illustrated by the Czechs and Germans sampled in Texas and the Amish of Lancaster County, Pennsylvania.[28] The vocational agriculture teacher and the agricultural extension service workers are emphasizing the theoretical and practical aspects of farming in work with rural youth and adult farmers. The importance of the extension service is brought out by the fact that over one-third of all owner and renter families of each racial group in the Arkansas, Mississippi, and Oklahoma samples reported some contact with either the farm or the home agent. (Table 57) The percentage with contacts in Texas was somewhat lower.

In general owner families had the greatest number of contacts, renters were second, and croppers lowest. This might be interpreted to mean that the tenure factor in and of itself was largely responsible. On the other hand, it is possible that those who used these services were those who achieved operatorship. More than 10 per cent of all families in each area and for each important racial group participated in 4-H Club work. This measure, however, was not corrected for the variation in percentage of families with children of eligible ages so that the comparisons are not entirely valid.

LIMITATIONS IMPOSED BY INDIVIDUAL FACTORS

The previous discussion has shown what the average person is doing or has done within a given environment considering his age, tenure of parents, education, and general background. Variations

---

of the more recent compilations dealing with education of all the people in a democratic society is the Report of the Harvard Committee, *General Education in a Free Society*, Cambridge, 1945. The U. S. Chamber of Commerce has also emphasized the value of education in relation to purchasing power and living standards in two publications: *Education Steps Up Living Standards*, and *Education, an Investment in People*, Washington, 1945.

[26] Robert T. McMillan and O. D. Duncan, *Social Factors of Farm Ownership in Oklahoma*, Oklahoma Agricultural Experiment Station Bull. B-289, November 1945, p. 15.

[27] Robert T. McMillan and Marylee Mason, "Social Background and Farm Ownership," *Rural Sociology*, 10, (December 1945), 414-16.

[28] Walter M. Kollmorgan, *The Old Order Amish of Lancaster County, Pennsylvania*, Rural Life Studies: 4, Culture of a Contemporary Rural Community, U. S. Department of Agriculture, Bureau of Agriculture Economics, Washington, 1942.

from the average have been described. However, for any individual a number of choices are available within limits. Farming is only one of a number of occupations. It has been suggested by some writers that the easiest road to ownership is for a young man to work at a nonfarm occupation until his ownership tract is free from mortgage. This means that he purchases a farm on credit, rents it out until the mortgage is completely paid, and then becomes a farmer. To clarify the discussion, let us make certain assumptions. First, that a boy is to become a bona fide farmer. Second, that he falls in either one of two categories in regard to parents—his parents can offer him financial assistance or they are unable to do so. Since practically all farmers are married (Table 58), the financial status of the wife's parents is given equal consideration with that of the husband.

For Farmers With Owner Parents

The term "owner parents" is used primarily as an indicator of parents with considerable net worth although the effect of attitudes instilled by parents is also of considerable importance. Sons of owner parents begin their earning life with very little more capital than those of nonowning parents. (Table 59) However, they are in better position to secure credit either directly from their parents or through the sponsorship of the parents. At any rate the son has an heir interest in the home farm upon which he can count sometime in the future. The limits placed upon tenure status by the amount of available capital are clearly brought out by the data in the current study. Those sons who begin farming as renters, croppers, or laborers do not stay in such categories very long, but because of financial assistance and the drive to equal the parents they soon rise to a higher status. (Table 50) Many sons of owners begin their occupational life as owners. The sample of whites in Mississippi represents the greatest percentage in this category with 42 per cent reporting owner as the first tenure. (Table 49) The whites in Mississippi reporting inheritance and gift as methods of ownership acquisition were quite young at the time of such acquisiton being under 30 years of age on the average. (Table 60) Over half of the white owners sampled in Arkansas and Mississippi achieved that status before the age of 25. (Table 61)

With such large proportions of sons of owners beginning their occupational life as owners and a large proportion of the remainder becoming owners in a relatively short time, it appears that sons of owners have few problems in regard to ownership acquisition or in becoming farm operators. It has been pointed out earlier that the son taking over the home farm is usually only one of several heirs. This means that although his title is assured, the other heir interests must be purchased. If the father has a mortgage on the farm, the demands of the mortgage holder must likewise be met. The equity inherited is often quite small. Until a definite arrangement is worked out with the other heirs, there is a strong inclination to mine the soil as any improvement made to the value of the farm must be shared with the other heirs. The inheritance represents an opportunity to get an early start but is no assurance of success in and of itself. A study of human factors in agricultural efficiency in 1932 in Minnesota indicated that "those not inheriting any property were making the higher current earnings and showed superior ability on the agricultural test."[29] The conclusion reached in the Minnesota study of the operator's economic status or earning being the result of his own ability is in agreement with the conclusion of L. C. Gray, in 1923, "efficiency is less a matter of the class of tenure than it is of the personal qualities of the farmer, the character of the land, and the adequacy of farm equipment and operating capital."[30] It is important to note that sons of owners have an initial advantage in all of these factors with the possible exception of the quality of the land.

For Farmers with Nonowner Parents

There is little choice within agriculture for the son of parents with little net worth to be other than a farm laborer or a cropper at the beginning of his earning life. Begining with little or no capital or credit, he is forced to accumulate enough capital as a cropper or as a laborer to buy equipment, power, and livestock in order to become a farm operator. At the same time he must meet his expenses of family living. Since croppers and laborers are in demand on the more productive soils and by the operators with the most managerial ability, a fairly high cash income is to be expected in good years. Croppers in the Arkansas and Mississippi samples equaled or exceeded renters in net farm income for 1942. (Table 62) As these farmers accumulate capital in one year or over a period of years, the real test of the man occurs. Where the son of an owner is assisted in securing a productive tract of land by relatives, the son of a nonowner has dif-

[29] W. W. Wilcox, Andrew Boss, and George A. Pond, *Relation of Variations in the Human Factor in Financial Returns in Farming*, Minnesota Agricultural Experiment Station Bull. 288, June 1932, p. 42.

[30] L. C. Gray, *et al*, "Farm Ownership and Tenancy," *Agricultural Yearbook, 1923*, Washington, 1924.

ficulty in securing land as a renter which will give him opportunity to increase his capital. On the other hand he has little opportunity to invest capital as a cropper. He has limits as to size of farm as a cropper which are more restrictive than those imposed upon renters. The son of a nonowner can achieve the status of son-in-law of an owner family and thereby get at least some of the advantages of the children of owner parents through marriage.

Capital Limitation

With a given amount of capital and available credit, a farmer has the choice of: (1) accepting a lower tenure status, less proportion of income for family living, but with limited opportunity to invest capital in his own business, or (2) a higher tenure status on a smaller farm, on less productive soil, a higher proportion of total farm income from the value of home-used products and possibly more from the capital invested. The lower the tenure status the higher the productivity of the land available as a general rule. With the higher tenure, more acres are under control of the operator, but the productivity of the soil tends to be lower. Likewise the equipment and supervision which contribute to higher yields and higher income tend to be lacking. To offset these factors, a larger quantity of food is raised for family living and a greater sense of security is felt in stability of location which encourages an accumulation of capital goods. In too many cases the income producing capacity of these owner tracts is too small to meet more than the minimum requirements of family living.

The hypothesis stated above applies between cropper and renter and between renter and owner. A comparison of white owners on poor soils with white croppers on good soils of Mississippi indicated that for the years studied the owners realized a somewhat higher income but the greatest difference was by source of income rather than the amount.[31]

The total amount of the income was not strictly comparable since the data were secured for different years but the observation in regard to source of income appears valid for all years. Croppers received income mainly from the sale of crops but owners had a more diversified program. A few cases in the current study represent an ideal utilization of capital. These operators owned a farmstead which gave them stability of location of residence and a site for the construction

[31] Dorothy Dickins, *Owner Farm Families in Poor Agricultural Areas and Cropper Farm Families in Rich Agricultural Areas,* Minnesota Agricultural Experiment Station Bull. 359, June 1941.

of barns and other structures needed for livestock enterprises. For all except control over the acres in the farm and the investment of capital in such acreages, such farmers were owners. The difficulties which might be encountered are that not enough reasonably productive land would be available in a given year to provide the most efficient use of labor, equipment, and operating capital. This procedure separates the farmstead from the cropland and pasture. It separates the farm as a place to live from the farm as a place to grow crops. Many farmers in the Oklahoma sample were operating several tracts of land which were not contiguous. Distances of as great as 20 miles between tracts offered few complications when trucks and tractors were used. The system combines the best features of ownership and tenancy.

Nonfarm Work

On the surface, income from off-farm work appears to be equal to farm income dollar for dollar. The additional income to the family can be invested in land, operating capital, savings, or family expenditures. And about one of every ten farmers sampled had experienced some full-time nonfarm employment during his occupational lifetime. (Table 55) The Czechs and Germans in the Texas sample had less experience at nonfarm work while other groups appeared to vary according to the opportunity for such work. The majority of those sampled who had experienced full-time nonfarm work returned to the farm because of adverse employment opportunities. A few had managed to accumulate enough capital at the nonfarm work to get started in farming. In general, however, the average man going from a nonfarm occupation to farming brings little capital to the farm. Off-farm work represents an opportunity to accumulate capital for the purchase of a farm but it is an opportunity which is not easy to utilize. An examination of individual cases shows that those who achieved ownership through other occupational routes took from five to ten years longer than those who achieved it through farming alone.

A second possibility is that of off-farm work in addition to the farming operations. While those with the smaller farms and with the lower tenures worked more days off-farm, the total value of such labor was lower than for those with the larger farms and the higher tenures. (Tables 63 and 64) Those farmers with small units and those in a cropper status in general were those doing unskilled labor, while the better farmers (size of farm and tenure) were those tending to do skilled labor and to get the higher wage rates. Further examination showed that those giving the highest proportion of their time to their farms were those doing the best job. The cash received from the off-farm work is a gross figure and certain additional costs must be met such as the expense of transportation, board, tools, and equipment. In addition, as off-farm work increases there is a tendency to increase the expenditures for commercialized recreation and store purchases of food and clothing. These expenditures add little to the comforts of farm family living as measured by the socio-economic status scale and contribute nothing to the value of farm production goods.

While nonfarm work or off-farm occupation may add very little to the farm status of most individuals, it does represent an opportunity by which any individual may acquire ownership or operatorship of a farm adequate to meet his needs.

Farm-to-Farm Migration

Every change in farm is made for what seems to be a "good" reason. From a tenure viewpoint, however, approximately two-thirds of all changes in farm were made with no tenure change in the Mississippi and Texas areas. (Table 65) It may be that within the same general tenure status some progress is made by obtaining a higher proportion of the management function, by getting a more advantageous leasing arrangement or a larger and more productive farm. On the positive side of the ledger, about three-fourths of all tenure changes are accompanied by changes in farms. Those improving their tenure without moving were mainly tenants renting from relatives. This conclusion is in agreement with those reached in the consideration of leasing arrangements—that the landlord largely determines the tenure under which a tract of land is operated and that the lessee must fit into the pattern as established by the landlord.

A second aspect of changes in farm is the change in type of soil. Capital accumulated by nonowners on productive land is most frequently invested in the ownership of poorer land. This is a choice made by the man. Much less capital is required to become an owner of a family-type farm on poor land than on good land. The general migration picture is that a man accumulates capital in a lower tenure status on good land, but as he progresses up the tenure ladder, he tends to move to land of lesser productivity. This tendency is particularly true in areas where the cropper system is followed. Of course, the phenomena of those with the higher tenure using the poorer soil does not apply to those inheriting as they inherit land of all varieties and qualities.

Tenure Goals

The particular alternative which the individual will choose is largely determined by his goals, his abilities, resources, and his opportunities. If ownership is the goal, farmers achieving the goal with limited capital too often are forced to accept small farms and low income. If income and level of living is the primary goal and tenure is merely a means to that end, a lower tenure status on productive land (with adequate equipment and livestock for efficient use of labor, with sufficient assurance of stability of location to secure the maximum benefits from the better practices, and with as large a farm as possible) is the alternative to be chosen. Most people in all occupations do more efficient work and thereby receive more income under supervision. Supervision or control over operations may be done by a landlord, an agency supplying credit, or a governmental agency such as the Agricultural Adjustment Administration. If the farmer can have a partnership arrangement with the supervisory agency on a basis of equality, it is possible to retain the dignity that is commonly associated with the ownership of land and at the same time enjoy a level of living above the minimum standards. If the residence is separated from the farm business financially, any farmer can own his dwelling and secure his income in a tenure status suited to his abilities, ambition, and capital accumulation. Mechanization and rapid transportation facilities make such a plan possible as demonstrated by individual cases in the Oklahoma area. By such an arrangement it is possible to combine the best features of ownership and tenancy.

SUMMARY

1. The tenure arrangements of an individual at any given time are meaningful chiefly in relation to the environmental setting in which the arrangements occur. Capital and land requirements, use of equipment, and income distribution were quite different in the Coastal Plain from those in the other two areas sampled. In order to state the minimum requirements of land, operating capital, managerial ability, and skills needed to become a farmer with specified tenure arrangements, it therefore becomes necessary to examine the pattern of such items in the area for which the recommendations are to apply.

2. Individuals climb the tenure ladder or achieve success in a given tenure status within the institutional framework of the environment in which they live, utilizing the farming practices and the managerial opportunities available in that area. Action programs are necessarily conditioned by these limitations.

3. Within each area studied, ownership increased with age. The percentages appeared to reach a maximum of 60 per cent for Negroes and 80 per cent for whites in the Coastal Plain at around 35 years of earning life. Each of the white groups in the Texas sample were slightly higher than the Negroes in the Coastal Plain in the older age groups. The settlement of the Oklahoma area was not old enough to warrant a conclusion in this regard. All racial and ethnic groups increased in ownership at about the same rate, the difference being accounted for by the percentage who were owners at the beginning of earning life.

4. The tenure and economic status of the parents had an important bearing upon the tenure at which the children began their earning life but was not related to the age at which earning life began. Parents of husband and wife appeared to have equal influence upon the tenure status of the family. Higher tenure status of the parents was positively associated with a higher educational attainment for the children, a relatively heavier out-migration of the children to nonfarm occupations, and a higher beginning farm tenure status. The difference in the rate of out-migration was probably more closely related to the educational attainment than to the tenure status of the parents.

5. Young people tend to marry within their tenure groups and thereby concentrate the farm wealth within a relatively few families. However, many of those inheriting land receive only a share of the total inheritance and must purchase the balance from those brothers and sisters who have migrated to nonfarm occupations. On the whole those owners who purchased their farms farmed more efficiently than those who inherited them.

6. Three-fourths of the farm-to-farm changes involved no change in tenure status. On the other hand, four-fifths of all tenure changes were accompanied by changes in farm. A majority of all farmers had never moved over 10 miles. Consequently major community ties were unbroken by such moves. Full owners and share-cash renters in the Oklahoma sample had moved the greatest distances—a situation probably linked with the relative newness of the area.

7. Within any of the areas studied little difference was noted in the birth rates between tenure groups. A significant difference was observed between areas and between ethnic groups. In general the high birth rates occur on low priced and low productive land. This land is found in areas of high percentage ownership.

CHAPTER V

Leasing Arrangements and Landlord-Tenant Relationships

The tenure and leasing arrangements in a given area are largely conditioned by the ownership pattern. If the farm land area is owned mainly by resident operators, the leasing arrangements and other landlord-tenant relationships are likely to partake of the character of the cropper system. In the case of absentee owners a large variety of types exist, including those based on method of acquisition, reasons for retaining ownership, policy toward conservation, form and length of lease, extension of credit, and amount of control exercised over farming operations.

TYPE OF LANDLORD AS A FACTOR IN THE LEASE

The owners of land offer as wide a variety of situations as its occupiers. In general, land in the United States is held in fee simple by the owners. However, the regulations involved in taxation, police powers, and eminent domain establish conditions which must be met annually to satisfy the state. Then too, many so-called owners are in effect holders of purchase contracts, others are restricted by law to ownership for a limited number of years, and still others have titles which are not clear so that custom rather than law allows them to continue as owners.

The owners of rural[1] lands are divided into four principal groups: (1) public agencies (2) institutions (3) estate and joint ownerships, and (4) individuals. Public agencies include all branches of government; federal, state, county, and incorporated cities and towns. Each of these governmental branches has its own department for handling the land under its jurisdiction in its own particular way. For example, lands administered by the Forest Service and the Biological Survey are usually leased to private users for grazing only, while Indian

[1] The term, *rural* lands is employed rather than *land* in farms since practically all rural lands have some agricultural use.

lands may be of any character and require consideration accordingly. School lands owned by the state or county are administered quite differently than lands acquired through tax adjudication. Institutions are divided into those extending real estate credit and others. This classification is based on the assumption that credit agencies are unwilling owners who acquired their holdings through foreclosure while other institutions own land as an investment or for use. In the eastern part of the United States, lumber companies own large tracts of land which are being held for future use. Railroads are important owners in the mountain states of the West. Corporations own and operate cattle ranches, fruit farms, and sugar cane farms to some extent. Estate and joint ownership of land represents privately owned land held in severalty or, in some cases, communal ownership. In order to relate ownership to operatorships, individual owners of land are classified by color, sex, kinship to the lessee and the distance from the rental tract.

Public Agencies

The first great division in type of owner is between private and public ownership. The latter is more extensive than is frequently appreciated. In many of the mountain states more than one-third of the total land area is owned by the public[2] which is rented to farmers for grazing.

In the Southwestern Region, Indian land is of considerable importance, particularly in Oklahoma. Although most of the Indian lands are privately owned it is under the administration of the Department of Interior so that Indian land as a whole might well be said to be in quasi-public ownership. The General Allotment Act of 1887 permitted land in Indian Reservations to be divided among the Indians of the Reservation giving each Indian an allotted acreage in fee simple after a period of 25 years, during which time the United States acted as guardian. Over 19 million acres of land in Oklahoma were allotted under this system. By 1934 over 16 million acres of this allotment were alienated to either white or Indian ownership. Since the Indians lacked both capital and agricultural education to farm this land, and with the partitioning of land caused by inheritance,

[2] See R. R. Renne, *Who Owns Montana's Land,* Montana Agricultural Experiment Station Mimeo. Cir. 15, April 1939; National Resources Planning Board, *Land Classification in the United States,* Washington, p. 98, 1941; L. C. Gray *et al.* Farm Ownership and Tenancy, *Agriculture Yearbook,* Washington, pp. 522-525; and Philip Greisinger, *Land Ownership in the Eleven Western States,* U. S. Department of Agriculture, Bureau of Agricultural Economics, Berkeley, California, March 1943.

most of the lands during the interim period were leased to white tenant operators.[3] With the exception of reservation lands, all Indian holdings in the Southwestern Region have been allotted to individuals and generally are subject to alienation. The location of the type of ownership (privately owned, tax free, corporately owned, and unclassified lands) for Oklahoma has been presented in map form as it existed in 1938.[4] Tax free lands are concentrated in the Old Indian Territory and the Oklahoma School Land Commission has concentrations in the north central part of the State and in Cimarron County. Corporation ownership is heaviest in the eastern and southeastern parts of the state. The Commissioners of the Land Office of the State of Oklahoma use a preference lease with cash method of rental payment for a five-year period.[5] The lessee is entitled to purchase the land at the highest bid in the event of sale. He is also granted the preference right to release. Rental is due annually and is covered by promissory notes signed by the lessee and one qualified person, a resident of the state. If the lessee's improvements are three times the value of the rental, no surety on the notes is required. First lien on all crops and improvements are given as security. Subleasing and transfer of the lease is possible with the written permission of the lessor. The amount of the cash rent is 2 per cent of the appraised value of the land without improvements. This applies to both the preference and the nonpreference types of leases. The nonpreference lease of the Oklahoma Land Office requires a cash payment in advance and is for a period of from one to five years. The land can be subleased with written permission of the Land Office. There is no preference given to the lessee in case of sale or to release. Because of low crop yields, a few tenants have been permitted to pay a share of the crop as rent on nonpreference leasing arrangements. Leasing of Indian lands owned by adults may not exceed five years for farming purposes or three years for grazing purposes. Rental varies in that cash, share of crop, or improvements may be accepted.

[3] A comprehensive treatment of the problems of Indian land tenure is given in *Indian Land Tenure, Economic Status, and Population Trends*, Part X, of the Supplementary Report of the Land Planning Committee of the National Resources Planning Board, Washington, 1935. Also see *Indians and Their Land*, Contributions by the Delegation of the United States, Washington, First Inter-American Conference on Indian Life, Patzcuaro, Mexico, April, 1940.

[4] Randall T. Klemme, *Oklahoma Land Ownership Study:* Preliminary Report (Land Ownership Pattern Map), Oklahoma Agricultural Experiment Station Mimeo Cir. No. 50, October, 1939.

[5] W. J. Coleman and H. Alfred Hockley, *Legal Aspects of Landlord-tenant Relationships in Oklahoma*, Oklahoma Agricultural Experiment Station Bull. 241, August 1940, pp. 36-38.

Before 1938, when the State began selling some of its lands, the School Land Commission owned about 1,300,000 acres. Considerable land has been sold since that time. The Commission also makes loans to farmers at 3 per cent interest on real estate mortgages and amortized over a period of 25 years.

Each state holds title to some land through the process of tax adjudication and the ownership of school lands. In Oklahoma and Texas, school land is held by the state but in the other three states of the region it is held by the county. Land reversion occurs mainly during periods of low income. For Mississippi the seriousness of the problem is indicated by the fact that 1,700,000 acres of tax reverted land was on the state land rolls as of January 1, 1936.[6] This represents 5.8 per cent of the total land area of the state. The larger part of this acreage consisted of unimproved lands.

While it has been commonly accepted that the penalty for nonpayment of taxes is loss of title, in many cases the land is not reverted and there is no actual penalty of any kind. Mississippi has the right to remove occupants of land owned by the state through tax reversion, but it has not always followed the practice.[7] When general property taxes in Mississippi are delinquent the law provides for sale of such lands to the highest bidder on February 1 of the year following. The owner is allowed two years in which to redeem the land. If not paid within the designated time, title passes to the state or to the tax purchaser. Any person may secure a patent to such land by paying to the State Land Commissioner an amount at least equal to the back taxes plus costs and damages. By an Act of 1936, tax reverted lands may be sold on a contract to purchase with no down payment. The Land Commissioner, with the approval of the Governor may lease such lands for a period not exceeding one year.

Tax reverted lands in 1936 were concentrated in four areas of the State: (1) The Delta overflow area located in Tunica, Quitman, and Panola counties in the northwestern part of the state—an area subject to periodic overflow. Drainage taxes were high and cutover timber lands had little annual income to meet tax payments. (2) The Delta Backwater Area located in Issaquenna, Humphreys, and Sharkey counties. (3) Submarginal farm land in Clay, Webster, Choctaw, and Chicasaw counties. (4) Cutover lands owned by lumber companies

[6] C. O. Henderson and John T. Caldwell, *Lands Owned by the State of Mississippi through Tax Reversion*, U. S. Department of Agriculture, Farm Security Administration and Bureau of Agricultural Economics, Mimeo. No. 4, November, 1937.

[7] *Ibid.*, p. 7.

in Stone, Perry, George, Harrison, and Greene counties. In all of these counties the amount of land reverted in 1936 exceeded 10 per cent of the land area of the county. Tax delinquency reached its maximum around 1930 at which time state-owned land became a factor of considerable importance. In 1937 state lands were re-sold at $1 per acre without classification of any kind by the state. The ninety-nine year leases on school lands are recorded in the county clerks offices and taxes are paid on the land by the lessee. Beginning about 1936, fifteen-year leases on rural lands and twenty-five year leases on urban lands were instituted to take the place of the ninety-nine year leases as they terminated.

In Arkansas, before the Land Policy Act of 1939, state lands were sold for $1 per acre, were donated in tracts not exceeding 160 acres upon payment of a $10 donation fee, or were redeemed by the former owner upon payment of back taxes, costs, and penalties.[8] The Land Policy Act provided for the classification of land into (1) land to be retained in public ownership (2) land to be sold at an assessed valuation, and (3) land to be opened for settlement.[9] Formerly, mineral rights were retained by the state on all land sold or donated but the law has been repealed. The fee for donation is $10 but the qualifications of both man and land are considered and the donee is limited to what is considered to be a family-sized ownership unit. Between November 1939 and September 1942, a total of over 43,000 acres were involved in donation certificates on tax reverted lands. These lands were located in the Mississippi Delta counties to a very large extent, Cross County alone having over 11,000 acres of donated land. During the period from September 1939 to October 1942, over 323,000 acres were sold under the Land Policy Act regulations. Between March 1939 and September 1942, a total of 202,000 acres were redeemed by the original owners. The extent of delinquency in Arkansas is indicated in a study made in 1934.[10] Each year between 1928 and 1933 showed an increase with total sales, in 1933 mounting to more than ten million acres of rural land, sold because of delinquent taxes. While the Mississippi Delta area was the most important contributor to this situation, northwest Arkansas and the Arkansas River Delta areas were also important. All of these are areas of high producing

[8] *Arkansas Tax-Forfeited Land, Manual of Policies and Procedures*, Land Use Committee of the State Planning Board, August, 1941.

[9] Erling D. Solberg, *The Arkansas Land Act Policy in Operation*, Department of Agriculture, Bureau of Agricultural Economics, Little Rock, Arkansas, December, 1942.

[10] C. O. Brannen, *Tax Delinquent Rural Lands in Arkansas*, Arkansas Agricultural Experiment Station Bull. 311, November 1934.

soils but all except the Benton County area have drainage district taxes in addition to the customary taxes.

Institutions

Most land owned by institutions is operated by tenants rather than directly by the institutions as such. A survey made by the Bureau of Agricultural Economics based on income taxes paid for the year 1921 by corporations showed that only 7,428 corporations in the entire United States were operating farms.[11]

An analysis of questionnaires returned by 1689 of these corporations showed 42 per cent were operating farms classified as cattle farming and 56 per cent as fruit farming. Cotton farming made up less than 1 per cent of the sample farms. A number of the states have passed laws restricting the operation, and to some extent the ownership, of farm land by corporations. Cattle ranches, fruit farms, and sugar cane farms therefore represent most of the cases of corporations operating farms on the land they own.

The State of Oklahoma passed a Corporate Land Holding Act in the 1937 Session of the legislature which limited the time of holdings to seven years for real estate located outside of incorporated cities or towns and for lands not necessary and proper for the transaction of the business for which the corporation was licensed or chartered.[12] The Attorney General in his opinion of March 16, 1938, stated that because schools were exempt from taxation, they were also exempt from the provisions of the Corporate Land Holding Act. However, taxes had been collected from Baker University, domiciled in the State of Kansas, by reasoning that it was a "foreign corporation" and was not chartered under the laws of Oklahoma.[13] Corporations in Kansas are restricted by a law passed in 1931 from engaging in the business of operating farms.[14] A later law restricted the time during which corporations can hold title to real estate after such property has been conveyed to them in satisfaction of debts. Howe points out that the landlords affected by such legislation do not wish to make commitments in the form of leases for any longer time than necessary.[15]

---

[11] L. C. Gray, *et al.*, "Farm Ownership and Tenancy," *Agriculture Yearbook 1923*, Washington, 1924, p. 537.

[12] See Session Laws of 1937, Ch. 46, for details of the Act and for a statement of the penalties.

[13] See Chapter VII on "Legal Aspects of Land Tenure and Farm Credit" for further discussion of legal items.

[14] Harold Howe, *Facts on Farm Tenancy in Kansas*, Kansas Agricultural Experiment Station, Mimeo. No. 20, December 1943, pp. 17-18.

[15] *Ibid.*, p. 18.

California has had legislation restricting insurance companies from owning land longer than five years, and Nebraska prohibits charitable and fraternal organizations from holding real estate other than that necessary for a hospital, asylum, or the transaction of its business for more than a period of 25 years.[16]

Institutions have a higher percentage of written leases than other types of landlords. A study by Howe of 256 corporate landlords owning 7,937 farms in Kansas for the year 1941 showed a strong concentration in regard to a number of characteristics.[17] For all corporations studied, 94 per cent acquired their tracts either through foreclosure or by deeds to avoid foreclosure. One-fourth employed a fieldman and an additional fourth employed a local agent. Seventy-three per cent had writen leases and 87 per cent reported one-year leases. Eighty-six per cent used crop-share leases but a great many received a cash payment in addition for the use of buildings, equipment, or pasture. Thirty-eight per cent extended credit to their tenants for the operation of the farm. Ninety-six per cent of all farms were for sale which made all leasing arrangements subordinate to the desire on the part of the corporate owner to dispose of the land. Insurance companies were the most important corporations having written leases while local commercial banks extended credit to a larger extent than other corporations.

Included in the institutional landlord category for the survey farms in the Southwestern Region are state and county School lands in Mississippi and Oklahoma. These account for nearly all of the long-term leases observed in those states. Insurance companies and other "foreign" corporations accounted for the high percentage (over 90 per cent) of written leases in the Oklahoma Rolling Plains and the Texas Blackland Prairie. (Table 66)[18] Local banks were important in the Arkansas sample. While the percentage of written leases by banks exceed those of other types of landlords, when the influence of the Farm Security Administration is considered, the percentage is only slightly over 30. Institutional landlords were twice as frequent in Oklahoma and Texas as in the Mississippi and Arkansas samples. (Table 67) Institutional landlords rented on a cash or share-cash basis to a greater extent than any other type of landlord. The share-

[16] Arthur B. Jebens and Ernest Engelbert, *1941 Summary of Outstanding Federal and State Legislation Affecting Rural Land Use,* U. S. Department of Agriculture, Bureau of Agricultural Economics, June, 1942, p. 35.

[17] Harold Howe, *Corporations as Landlords of Kansas Farms,* Agricultural Economics Report No. 17, Kansas Agricultural Experiment Station, Mimeo., January, 1943.

[18] For tables mentioned in this chapter refer to statistical tables in Appendix.

cash lease was relatively frequent for the Texas and Oklahoma samples.

Since the ownership of land by corporations partakes of some of the character of tax adjudicated land in that it is acquired by the foreclosure of mortgages, it is to be expected that the tracts would be larger and have less agricultural value than those owned by individuals. Data by ownership tracts in seven selected parishes of Louisiana for 1939 show that corporations have much larger tracts than individuals. In some parishes they are over ten times as large. (Table 68) Farm credit agency holdings have about the same percentage of land classified as farm land as do individuals.

Estates

Estate ownership as herein used refers to the ownership situation which exists after the death of an individual owner of real estate until such time as the title is passed to another individual. There is great legal variation among states in this regard. As of 1942 seven states, including Louisiana and Texas, had community property laws which permitted varying degrees of separate and community property ownership by husband and wife.[19]

In general an undivided estate is created upon the death of an individual owner or the death of the husband in case of married couples. For an estate to operate a farm, it would mean that all interested parties would operate the farm as "tenants in common."[20] In most cases, the entire farm is rented to one person. In this study the category of "indeterminate" was used for those farmers operating farms in which they had an heir interest but no title.

Estates occupy a fairly important position in the consideration of types of landlord and landowners. The legal status of estate ownership is common to a large proportion of all land passing from generation to generation. While the title to land is in the status of estate, some form of renting is the usual method of farm operation. The percentage of landlords falling in this category in the Oklahoma and Texas samples was around 8 per cent, in Arkansas 11 per cent, and in Mississippi 3 per cent. The difference in the Arkansas and the

[19] Harriet Spiller Daggett, "The Modern Problem of the Nature of the Wife's Interest in Community Property — A Comparative Study," *Legal Essays on Family Law*, Louisiana State University Press, Baton Rouge, 1935.

[20] Kenneth H. Parsons and Clara J. Legrid, *Planning for the Descent of Property in the Family*, Wisconsin Agricultural Extension Service Circ. 364, October 1945, outlines the different legally possible ways by which real and personal property may be handed down to heirs according to Wisconsin law.

Mississippi data is due to some extent to differences in the tenure of the lessees sampled. The Arkansas sample is composed of 233 renters and 98 croppers while the Mississippi sample includes 39 renters and 87 croppers. The estates rent out land on a cash, share, or no rent basis while the cropper usually secures his land from male landlords. (Table 69) The ownership of land by estates and joint ownership by individuals in Louisiana showed a range of from 8 per cent to over 28 per cent for seven selected parishes. (Table 70)

Lands in estate ownership are in larger tracts than those owned by individuals but have a smaller proportion in farm land and therefore tend to have less value per acre. (Tables 68 and 71) Estate lands are often rented to one of the interested parties for paying the taxes, keeping the place in repair, and possibly taking care of the aged mother or father. Two-thirds of all estate landlords in the Mississippi sample had such arrangements, slightly over one-third in Arkansas and lesser proportions for the other samples. Apart from the FSA borrowers living on estates, all of whom have written leases, the tenants living on estates have relatively fewer written leases than any other type of tenant save those related to their landlords. The FSA was responsible for all written leases on estates in the Arkansas sample. (Tables 66 and 67)

Individuals

The great bulk of farm landlords are individuals. Of the total sample of landlords, individuals comprised 86 per cent in Arkansas, 93 per cent in Mississippi, 84 per cent in Oklahoma, and 81 per cent in Texas. (Table 67) Individuals made up over 90 per cent of the owners of rural lands in each of seven selected parishes in Louisiana in 1939. (Table 70) In view of this the characteristics of leases in general are those associated with the individual landlord.

Male landlords have over 90 per cent of the cropper leases sampled. Individual landlords in general and males in particular are associated with the straight crop share lease. Institutions have more cash and share-cash leases while estates more frequently use taxes, upkeep of farm, and "care of landlord" as a method of rental payment. (Table 69) Fewer individuals than other types of landlords use written leases. The high degree of association of the individual landlord with the cropper lease, which is almost always oral, is one important factor. Then too, individuals may be related to the lessees and individuals live nearer the farms than other types of landlords. All of these factors contribute to the high percentage of oral leases.

Individuals rent out their land because of retirement from active life, other occupations, concentration of holdings, and other miscellaneous reasons. The study of L. C. Gray, *et al*[21] based on 1920 data showed that concentration of holdings occurred mainly in the South. This tendency still exists but care should be exercised in this area in measuring the size of a concentration simply by the number of farms under the operatorship of a given owner. Many of these so-called farms are nothing more than small cropper tracts. Concentration of holdings appears to be higher in the Corn Belt than in the South when measured in terms of value of land. While the use of croppers increases in the Southwestern Region as acres of cropland in the farm increases, larger equipment is being used as an alternative to croppers. There are however a number of difficulties which arise from the use of tractors in replacing the more intensive farming as practiced with croppers. The comparison of the degree of mechanization and the labor organization for the sample farms in Texas and Oklahoma with those in Mississippi and Arkansas offers interesting speculation. Judging from the smallness of some of the farms with croppers in the Arkansas and Mississippi samples it would almost appear that no farm is so small but that a cropper may not be used on it. Two stituations were sampled of croppers using other croppers. For these cases the cropper and the subcropper each received one-fourth of the production while the owner of the land and equipment received his customary one-half share.

Separation of individual landlords into resident and "absentee" indicates that the latter give a relatively smaller amount of supervision. The cropper method of rental payment usually indicates a considerable amount of supervision. Only a few cash, share, or share-cash renters in the sample are closely supervised. An approximately equal number of croppers have relatively complete freedom of management. The middle group of divided management includes some of both groups and is characterized by a complicated set of offsetting and contradictory factors. Examination of Agricultural Adjustment Administration data for two parishes of Louisiana shows that six times as many landlords are landlords of croppers than are landlords of operating tenants for the Upland Cotton Parish.

Race. While Negroes owned as many as 15 per cent of the ownership tracts in one of the parishes studied in Louisiana, many of these

[21] L. C. Gray, *et al.*, "Farm Ownership and Tennancy," *Agriculture Yearbook*, 1923, Washington, 1924, pp. 529-33.

tracts were only farmsteads of less than five acres in size and had little or no cropland. (Tables 68, 70, 71) White male resident owners in the seven parishes of Louisiana on their ownership tracts ranged from 32 per cent of all owners in Calcasieu Parish to 67 per cent in Concordia Parish. Parcellation resulting from inheritance in cutover grazing land in the northern part of Calcasieu and the high percentage of non-cropland in West Feliciana and St. Mary are responsible for the low percentage of resident ownership in those parishes. The presence of a relatively large number of small, self-sufficient owner-operated farms in the Black River portion of Concordia Parish is responsible for the high percentage of resident owners in that parish so that the data for Concordia Parish are not representative of a Delta situation. Negro owners had a higher percentage of residence on their tracts than did white owners. Female owners of both races were lower in terms of residence on ownership tracts than were male owners.

Around 20 per cent of the landlords of Negroes in the Arkansas sample, renting cropland by methods other than the one-half share, were Negro landlords. Over 50 per cent of the Negroes in the Mississippi sample with similar methods of renting leased land from Negro landlords. In general there is a strong tendency for farmers to lease land from those of their own ethnic group regardless of the concentration of ownership in other ethnic groups. In the Texas sample over 75 per cent of those with renter leases leased from landlords within their own ethnic group. On the other hand, the cropper lease is primarily an arrangement between white, male owner-operators and either white or Negro landlords. In most cases this may more properly be regarded as a type of labor organization rather than as a leasing arrangement. (Table 72)

Sex. While male landlords far outnumber females, the female landlord constitutes a definite type which is numerically important in local areas. The study of landlords in 1920 by the United States Department of Agriculture showed 15 per cent of the owners of rented farms were women, 58 per cent of whom acquired their holdings through inheritance or marriage.[22] By eliminating the landlords of croppers in the samples taken in 1942 the percentage of individual landlords who were women is about 30 per cent. Female ownership of land was the highest in West Feliciana Parish, Louisiana, of any

[22] H. A. Turner, *The Ownership of Tenant Farms in the United States*, U. S. Department of Agriculture Bull. 1432, Washington, September 1926, p. 38.

of the parishes surveyed. (Table 70) A study of leasing arrangements in East Feliciana Parish, Louisiana, in 1940 showed that 28 out of 58 individual landlords (including landlords of croppers) were women.[23]

Female landlords use a written lease and tend more toward cash rent than male landlords. (Tables 66 and 69)

Residence. Increase in the distance from farm to residence of the landlord shows a consistent increase in the percentage of written leases. (Table 73) However, many landlords living close to their farms have cropper leases, of which none of those sampled were written. The distribution of cases by residence was bimodal for the Arkansas and Mississippi samples. (Table 43) In Mississippi 55 per cent of the landlords lived less than one-half mile from the tract leased out as compared with only 23 per cent for Arkansas. This is essentially a measure of the cropper lease. Ignoring those with distances under one-half mile, the sample of Arkansas, Texas, and Oklahoma landlords showed somewhat the same distribution except that Texas was higher for those living over 100 miles from the farm, and Oklahoma was extremely high for that class interval—28 per cent of all landlords. A high inverse relationship exists between distance and the amount of supervision given to the lessee by the landlord but as indicated below this tendency is less marked where landlord and tenant are kin to each other.

Kinship to Lessee. Landlords related to the lessee and living near the farm supervise the farming operations only to a slightly less extent than those living at some distance. It is difficult, however, to weight these factors and it is possible in this instance that the supervision administered through correspondence has been overweighted in comparison with that given through direct contact by the landlord who is close at hand. Quite a little variation exists in the details of the leasing arrangements between lessor and lessee when the two are related. In general related landlords use the oral lease and use the "no rent," "upkeep of place," "payment of taxes," and "care of landlord" methods of rental payment to a greater extent than other individual owners. Related lessees on the average are more independent of the landlord in making farming decisions. On the other hand, sons renting from their fathers are often supervised more closely than the average cropper regardless of the method of rental payment. In such cases the son is usually quite young.

---

[23] Unpublished data of Bureau of Agricultural Economics and Louisiana Agricultural Experiment Station.

THE LEASE

Property Covered by Lease

The most prevalent type of farm lease covers an entire farm unit. This most commonly consists of a farmstead with cropland and some pasture or non-cropland. (Table 74) Such farm units constituted 45 per cent of the properties rented by part owners in Texas and 47 per cent in the Oklahoma samples. The farm units in the Texas and Oklahoma areas were usually 160 acres in size. Many of these quarter sections had no buildings but otherwise conformed to the definition of farm units. Quite a few of the part owners lived in the dwelling on the rent tract rather than the dwelling on the owned tract. Multiple dwellings raised a problem if both dwellings were insured and thereby required occupancy. One part owner in Oklahoma allowed a family to live in the rent tract dwelling rent free and did the machine work on the garden without charge in order to assure occupancy of the dwelling. This case illustrates the pressure for land and the excess of farmsteads in the area.

The cropper arrangement which provided cropland, a farmstead, power, and equipment with an occasional undesignated acreage of pasture land for a cow was restricted nearly altogether to lessees of cropper tenure. A majority of those classified as croppers in Oklahoma had no cropland, other than possibly a garden, but received a share of livestock and/or livestock products as a bonus to insure the stability of the labor force on the farm. Such cases were essentially wage laborers.

The practice of renting single fields was more common in the Coastal Plains of Mississippi and Arkansas than in the Oklahoma and Texas areas. The high percentage of part owners renting farm units in the Oklahoma and Texas samples tends to support this conclusion. Field renting was more important in Mississippi than in Oklahoma, one factor being the renting of small separate tracts for the growing of cane where the soil on the main tract was not suitable for that purpose.

The renting of additional cropland involved a relatively high rental since such land was usually put in a cash crop and subject to a high labor input. (Table 75) In addition, these field and cropland tracts included no farm buildings. Cropland rental rates were over twice the rental rates for farm units for the Arkansas and Mississippi samples but only slightly higher in the other two areas.

Leasing of pasture land was a minor item in the sample studied, there being a total of only 17 such leases, most of which were on a cash basis. Another type of pasture rental constitutes a necessary part of the family "milch cow lease." Under this arrangement a nonowner "leases" or "borrows" a milk cow and pays the owner for her use by caring for the calf. The owner of the cow (usually the landlord or employer of the nonowner) furnishes pasture which both parties use in common. The nonowning user of the pasture helps the owner at such jobs as repairing fence or may assume all of the labor obligation of repairing the pasture fence. Both the milch cow arrangement and the pasture arrangement are accepted as customary and may exist between any two parties regardless of any other relationship which they may have.

Ratio of Rent to Value

Farmers renting farm units paid relatively lower rental rates than those renting pasture land, cropland, or single fields. This is due in part to the fact that the value of the farm unit includes some land and improvements on which no share rent is paid. With a single field or all cropland, rent is paid directly on all property rented and a minimum of nonproductive property is involved. For years when yields and prices are high, such as 1942, the difference between rentals for the two kinds of property would be greater than for years with poor returns.

Cash rent had the lowest rental rate of any method of rental payment for 1942 in the areas studied. (Table 76) Share rent (one-third and one-fourth) was slightly higher than cash and the half share was from three to four times as high as the ratio to share for rent. Rental rates were computed on a gross basis and the net rates would lessen the difference to some extent between the three methods of payment. The landlord usually pays the same share of the fertilizer and ginning expense as he shares in the crop. (Table 77).

The relationship between cash rentals, land values, and related factors was studied in 1924 using 1920 census data by counties.[24] Using averages for groups of counties, southern areas showed coefficients of correlation of .87 between value per acre and the productivity factors of yield and percentage that improved land was of the total; .70 between average cash rents and the same two productivity factors; and .85 between adjusted rent and value per acre. The survey data for the four sample areas of Southwestern States in 1942 showed

[24] Clyde R. Chambers, *Relation of Land Income to Land Value*, United States Department of Agriculture Bull. 1224, June 1924.

that the related tenants who paid cash or share rent paid a higher rental rate than nonrelated and that Negro tenants paid higher rentals than white tenants for cash, one-third and one-fourth share and one-half share rent. This agrees with the results of the study made in 1924. About two-thirds of the southern counties in the 1924 study showed lessees related to their landlords had higher ratios of rent to value than those not related. It also showed that Negroes paid higher ratios in three-fourths of the counties studied. Census data of 1940 revealed similar relationships.

High rental rates are explained in a publication of the agricultural census as being related to the use of intensive crops requiring large amounts of hand labor and to farms with relatively large gross farm incomes per acre.[25] The value of management contributed by the landlord was discussed in the same publication, but it is more likely that management increases the gross farm income and would have an effect upon the rental rates in that way rather than there being an additional rental for management *per se*. An areal analysis of the relationship between value of rental per acre and value of land per acre on crop rent farms showed a definite positive relationship.[26]

The extreme differences in the ratios of crop rental payment are due in large part to the yields, use, and the productivity of the land. Croppers are located on the more productive soils and for their units the percentage of the total acreage planted in cotton is very high. (Tables 5 and 10) They also had the highest yields as expressed in terms of cotton or the crop yield index. The one-fourth rental payment involves a lesser share of high yields and income and a lesser ratio is to be expected. In a year of crop failure one-fourth and one-half of no income is identical but as incomes increase the difference in the ratios increases likewise. It is quite obvious that the additional one-fourth share of cotton is paid for equipment, power, and seed for planting and a larger share of expenses for fertilizer and ginning. Not so obvious is the management of the landlord which is associated with the cropper arrangement, and the higher natural productivity of the land farmed by croppers. Whether it is soil as such or management, croppers get much higher yields than renters.

While yields measure the effect of management on the soils variable, management can be measured to some extent as a pure factor. Croppers have a higher percentage of property in income-producing

---

[25] *Cash Rent*, Agriculture Census, 1940, Washington, 1944.
[26] *Ibid*, p. 5.

crops. They have the advantage of the use of more equipment. It is probable that improved seed, more effective fertilizer application, and disease and insect control are practised to a greater extent on the larger units which include croppers. Certainly the larger units with croppers have an easier access to production capital or credit. While croppers in Arkansas and Mississippi paid a very high rental rate yet they had net incomes equal to or greater than share renters. Also, share-cash renters in Texas paid cash in addition to the usual share and thereby paid a higher rental than the straight share renters but received a higher gross income.

Share-cash renters in Oklahoma represent a different kind of rental arrangement. Although the gross farm income of straight share renters in Oklahoma was higher than that of share-cash renters, the share-cash renters had a slightly higher operator's earnings or net income. It is evident that in years of high yields and prices, a farmer can well afford to pay a larger share or more cash rent for better land or more services. A budgetary analysis of rentals of cash and share renters from 1909 to 1920 for Brazos, Dallas, and Williamson counties in Texas showed only slight variations for cash rents but variations from 4.2 to 7.3 for Dallas County, from 3.9 to 11.0 for Williamson County, and from 4.8 to 15.1 for Brazos County for share rent expressed in terms of net rental per $100 sales price on total land in farms.[27] The variations were even greater when computed on the basis of price of land less improvements.

Form and Length of Lease

The form of the leasing agreement places definite limits on the time period to which it applies. Under the laws of most states an oral contract is valid for a period of time not to exceed one year. If the agreement is to be for a longer period of time, usually it must be written to be legally valid. The details of the agreement may or may not be adequately covered or may be discriminatory to either party. In its more complicated forms the lease clearly states the rights, duties, privileges, and responsibilities of each party together with a complete description of the property covered in the contract.

A long-term lease with an automatic renewal clause may continue for many years provided the stated obligations are met. Easements allowing the use of land for some special purpose may be either writ-

[27] F. A. Buechel, *The Relation Between Rents and Agricultural Land Values in Theory and in Practice*, Texas Agricultural Experiment Station Bull. 318, February 1924, pp. 59-61.

ten or oral in character. Water rights for irrigation or other purposes comprise another set of legal rights. It is interesting to note that rice farmers in Louisiana customarily "lease" irrigation water for one-fifth or one-fourth of the rice crop.

Since nearly all corporations require written leases, it is to be expected that corporate (institutional) landlords exceed all other types in this respect. (Table 66) The usual lease form used by institutions is for one year with no renewal clause. Since most corporations such as banks and insurance companies are unwilling owners, they are usually looking for a buyer. Renting a farm under such circumstances tends to render the position of the renter insecure.

Not all institutions, however, fit into this pattern. School lands in Mississippi are in the hands of the county school authorities so that a personal relationship between the agent and the renter is possible. In Oklahoma school lands are administrated by the Oklahoma School Land Commission on a statewide basis. Two types of leases are offered, the usual one-year written lease without automatic renewal and a preference lease of five years duration. The preference lease gives preference to the lessee for renewal and for purchasing in case the farm is sold. In both Mississippi and Oklahoma the renters on school lands usually own all of the improvements on the land. Preference leases in Oklahoma are sold, handed down to sons, or otherwise transferred in the same manner as deeds to land. The commission must give its approval but if the new lessee meets the qualifications stated in the lease, little difficulty is encountered in securing approval.

In general female landlords, landlords renting to lessees not related to them, and landlords living at a distance from the rent tract are the individual landlords using the written lease to the greatest extent. (Tables 61 and 73) The activity of the FSA program has tended to increase the number of written leases, particularly with individual landlords.

In order to evaluate the effects of the written lease, consideration of the types of landlords and the effect of the FSA participation must be taken into account. Renters using written leases are slightly older than those with oral leases. On the other hand, when it is considered that no cropper in the sample reported written leases and that the difference in the ages of croppers and renters is greater than that between lessees with written leases and those with oral leases, a relationship between written leases and tenure is suggested rather than a relationship between written leases and age per se. Although renters with written leases exercise a higher proportion of the management and have more diversified farms than those with oral leases, the factors of type of landlord and effect of participation in the FSA program may be the real causal factors rather than the form of the lease. In regard to method of rental payment the same set of complications arise. Those lessees paying cash and share-cash rent have the highest percentage of written leases; straight share rental are next followed by the miscellaneous methods and the one-half crop-share group is lowest with no written lease in the samples taken.

While the written lease allows a long-term agreement which outlines the obligation of both parties and gives assurance of a relatively permanent contractual arrangement, the written lease is more a measure and indication of the degree of the formal, contractual, legal relationship between the two parties than it is of the number of rights which may be granted to either party. Those lessees with an oral, indefinite lease have been most stable on the present rent tract. (Table 78) Those with long-term written leases followed next. Those with one-year written leases show the least stability. These data do not, however, present a complete picture of the situation. Many renters and croppers who had been on the present tract over ten years have farmed each year with the expectation of moving. In other words, the *sense of stability* may have been lacking although the operator may have experienced a relatively long period of residence.

Method of Rental Payment

The nomenclature used for the classification of tenants according to method of rental payment has become so attached to the characteristics of the tenants that it is sometimes more confusing than definitive. Fundamentally there are two methods of paying rent on productive capital goods: (1) sharing the production and (2) paying rent independent of the volume of production or earned income. These two methods are combined in a "cash plus a share of production" arrangement as they also are and also in the case where the renter pays a stated quantity of production as rent. Other less frequent methods of rental payment are the payment of taxes, upkeep of the property, labor for the landlord, care of the landlord, and recently the Agricultural Adjustment Administration check has been sometimes paid as rent. All of the last named methods could be classified as either sharing of production or as rent whose value is independent of production. Any and all of the methods named may apply to the rental of land or livestock or both.

The method of rental payment is quite commonly used as a label for a type of tenancy or a system of renting. Although such labeling is justified it must be realized that it is meaningful only in limited geographic areas. In fact, from the local viewpoint, practically every tenant rents land "in the customary manner." Actually this means that considering the resources and characteristics of the lessee, the lessor, the productivity of the land, the stage in the business cycle, the relative pressure of population (labor supply and demand for land), availability of credit, and free land, there is no other method of renting expected than the one the farmer in question is using. Variations from the share or cash rent methods represent adjustments that lessee and lessor have made to fit their own situations. Leasing land "rent free" for a definite number of years for clearing the land or breaking the sod was formerly considered customary but certainly was no bargain for the renter. For a tenant to pay the real estate taxes in lieu of rent or in addition to other rents was more common in the frontier days than at present. Efforts on the part of large landowners to reduce taxes and to offset the threat of discriminatory rates contributed to the birth of tenancy in the New World even though "free land" was available further to the West. The payment of taxes by the renter relieved the landlord of that obligation and caused local civil officials to be more careful in their tax program since the payments were made by friends and neighbors rather than by absentee owners.[28]

Crop-share Rental. The usual crop-share rental consists of one-fourth of the cotton and other cash crops and one-third of the feed grain and hay crops. In the sample studied more than 97 per cent of the share rentals in Texas and Oklahoma and 92 per cent in Arkansas followed this pattern. (Table 77) For the Mississippi sample cotton was shared in the same proportions as in the other states but for feed crops more than 70 per cent of the renters sampled paid one-fourth rather than one-third of the feed crops. For most of the other crops the one-third rental share prevailed. The straight one-fourth rental was more commonly found in Marion than in Jefferson Davis county.[29] Peanuts were a relatively new cash crop for the Mississippi

[28] The custom of the tenant paying taxes on real estate rented persist to the present day in some areas of New York State according to findings of Neil Adams McNall, *The First Half-Century of Wadsworth Tenancy*, Cornell University Press, Ithaca, New York, 1945.

[29] *Report on Land Use*, Marion County, Mississippi, Agricultural Policy and Planning Committee, 1939-1940, p. 5.

area and a definite share had not been determined. The crop was planted for the government and in many cases no division of the crop was agreed upon by either party. Since on most of the farms the crop was not harvested, the question of actual division did not come up. Alfalfa seed and hay production was divided half and half in the Oklahoma area although only a few cases were sampled. Landlords of rice farms in Louisiana usually received one-fifth share of the crop as land rent. For expenses in cotton production the landlord shares in the costs of fertilizer and ginning to the same extent that he shares in the cotton crop. The tenant furnishes the seed, equipment, labor, and his share of the fertilizer and ginning expense.

In the matter of spray materials considerable variation occurs. In the areas of the region where it is practised most—Arkansas and Texas—the expense is usually divided in the same manner as the crop and other cash expenses. Few of those cases studied, however, included the expense of spray materials in the formal rental arrangements. Usually it was assumed that the tenant would bear all of the expense. The tenant is expected to do small jobs of repairing the dwelling and other improvements but variation exists as to who pays for "major" repairs and cash costs on any repairing. Since repairs are not annual costs, they are not usually a part of the lease itself, but are commonly arranged for as the need arises.

Cash Rental. Rentals in the form of cash follow a much closer pattern of uniformity with respect to what is furnished by each party, division of production and expenses, and other details than any other type of rental payment. In nearly 100 per cent of the cases the tenant furnished everything except the land, paid in cash rental, and received all of the production. Cash rentals in the southeastern states and in the Florida parishes of Louisiana show a variation from the typical arrangement described here in that the renter either rents the mule and equipment from his landlord or is buying them on credit and is closely supervised. Many of those paying standing rent in those areas follow the same procedure. Cash rentals in the areas sampled are more similar to the cash rental of the Corn Belt than to those of the Black Belt and the Southeast in general.

Sharecropper Rental. The designation of cropper is not mutually exclusive of the crop-share rental and the cash rental methods of payment. Croppers are defined by the census as, "share tenants to whom their landlords furnish all of the work animals, or tractor power in lieu of work animals." Analysis of 846 mailed questionnaires in 1940 in Louisiana showed that 90 per cent of those tenants owning no workstock paid one-half share rent and that 94 per cent of those paying one-half share rent did not own workstock.[30]

For over 90 per cent of the cases in the Arkansas and Mississippi samples the croppers and those paying one-half share rental were synonomous. (Table 74) Usually the landlord furnishes everything to "make the crop" except the labor, the cropper is charged one-half of the costs of fertilizer and ginning, and the cotton and feed crops are divided equally.

Share-cash Rental. Share-cash rental represents a crop-share rental with additional cash payment. This combination is an important method of rental payment in Texas and Oklahoma but was of much less importance in the Arkansas and Mississippi areas. In Oklahoma the additional cash payment was considered as payment for the use of a house, or pasture, or it was unassigned to any particular piece of property. The extent to which it was considered a bonus payment was justified on the basis that under the Agricultural Adjustment Administration less acreage was planted to cash crops and more to crops from which the landlord received no share of the production. Meanwhile the tenant realized a pasture usage. In Texas the cash rent consisted of rent per acre on part of the feed grain acreage while share rent was being paid on the balance of the acreage in the same crop. On acreages in crops which might or might not be harvested, such as Sudan, cash rent was paid only if such crops were actually harvested. If the crop were left, no cash rent was charged. In both areas, the share-cash rental appeared to be an adjustment to the changes made in land use and crop organization brought on by the Agricultural Adjustment Administration program.

Miscellaneous Methods of Rental. Standing rent was rather rare in the areas sampled, there being only seven such cases in all. Five of the seven rentals were in Arkansas; also five of the seven cases were Negro. (Table 79) The single, unique case in Oklahoma represented a dairy farmer who paid all of the cotton as rent in exchange for which he operated the farm as he pleased. Cotton was planted according to Agricultural Adjustment Administration regulations and was turned over to the landlord after the last cultivation. A total of 36 tracts—most of them in the Arkansas and Mississippi samples—were rented at "no rent." Payment of taxes, upkeep of farm in the form

[30] Ralph J. Ramsey, *Criteria for Classifying Louisiana Tenants*, Louisiana State University, Unpublished Master's Thesis, 1940.

of labor and/or cash expense, and providing food and shelter for the landlord accounted for 28 leases in all areas. An additional 53 rentals did not fall in any of the designated classes chiefly because of combinations of methods of payment.

Livestock Leases. While numerically unimportant in the survey sample, livestock leases are of considerable potential importance in the region. A total of 12 rentals of livestock on a share basis was included in the sample studied and only two of these were the crop and livestock-share rental so typical of the Corn Belt.[31] In addition to the arrangements made for sharing livestock and livestock products, in the sample taken there were five joint family arrangements for livestock production, three arrangements for sharing the poultry enterprise receipts, 54 arrangements for using a cow and giving the calf as rent, and 16 other miscellaneous arrangements.

Except for the few cases noted above, livestock leasing in the Southwestern Region appears in the main to be that of a cropper getting a cow for an indefinite time, feeding and caring for her to get the milk, and giving the owner the calf at a specified time. Poultry in small numbers is handled in a somewhat similar manner. Egg production and friers are divided equally between landlord and tenant, the landlord owning all of the mature birds and contributing a share of the grain fed. The Oklahoma sample included some cases of larger herds of milk cows and flocks of chickens handled on this basis. This general type of arrangement resulted largely from a shortage of help and was utilized as a bonus to labor in the attempt to maintain a stable labor supply. The laborer, or cropper, was given a share in the production of milk, cream, eggs, or young chickens for performing the labor required incident to the cows or chickens from which he shared production. In some instances additional livestock was cared for in which he did not share in the production.

Geographic Distribution. The crop sharing arrangements in the

---

[31] The crop and livestock-share rental of the Corn Belt is a sharing of the cash crops and joint ownership of livestock and feed crops. Livestock productions, inventories, and expenses are likewise shared between landlord and tenant. Some areas in the Corn Belt have as high as 70 per cent of the rental arrangements made in this manner, see John F. Timmons, *Landlord-Tenant Relationships in Renting Missouri Farms*, Missouri Agricultural Experiment Station Bull. 409, August 1939; John H. McCoy and W. E. Grimes, *The Stock-Share Lease*, Kansas Agricultural Experiment Station Cir. 213, 1942; W. H. Scofield and H. C. M. Case, *Farm Leasing Practices in Illinois*, Cooperative study of Illinois Agricultural Experiment Station and U. S. Department of Agriculture, Bureau of Agricultural Economics, October 1942; and I. W. Moomaw, *Farm Tenancy Areas in Ohio*, Ohio Agricultural Experiment Station Department of Rural Economics Mimeo. Bull. 144, August, 1941.

southern states are not as varied as those in the Corn Belt or the dairy and hay type of farming areas. The third and fourth system and the half and half system of the cotton South are by far the most important methods of rental payment. Within the five states included in the regional survey, the half share rental payment predominates in Mississippi (except for the extreme northeastern corner and the extreme southern part), the northern half of Louisiana, and the Deltá counties and the southermost tier of counties of Arkansas.[32] Share rental (third and fourth) was the most frequent method of rental payment in the five states with the exception of Trans-Pecos and Edwards Plateau, Texas, and Osage and Comanche counties, Oklahoma, which have a large number of tracts owned by Indians and a few other isolated counties in which the cash or share-cash method is most frequent. In 1920 share rental predominated, with the half share crop arrangement the second most frequent type. In those counties in which the half share crop arrangement predominated, other types of share rental were the second most frequent.[33]

Within the cotton South the cash renters are mainly Negroes and are located in southern Alabama, central Georgia, and in South Carolina. According to the 1920 census these are the same areas in which standing renters were most concentrated.

Relation of Rental Payment to Other Factors

The value of using method of rental payment as a basis of classification for tenancy systems is contingent upon an understanding of the relationship of the classes thus established to other tenure factors. Cash rentals and share-cash rentals are associated with institutional landlords and such landlords in turn with the written lease. The cropper system of rental is associated with the resident individual male white landlord who closely supervises the cropper, rarely has a written lease, and furnishes credit both for production and for farm family living. Share rental arrangements fall between the cash rental and the cropper arrangements but are more like the cash rent system in regard to tenure factors.

Although the cropper system is sometimes thought to apply only to Negroes, there are more white than Negro croppers in the South. For the sample taken in Mississippi 53 per cent of the white croppers were related to their landlords. Those using various degrees of "no

[32] *Cash Rent,* Agriculture Census, 1940, Washington, 1944, p. 9.

[33] L. C. Gray, *et al.,* "Farm Ownership and Tenancy," *Agriculture Yearbook, 1923,* Washington, 1924, pp. 584.

rent" (no rent, taxes, upkeep of place, etc.) had a consistently high percentage related to their landlord for both white and Negro. Those using the cash and share-cash rental payments had more freedom of management (measured by the division of management score), those with third and fourth method of payment had a lesser share in management, and those with cropper arrangements had the least share in the function of management. Since at least some of the Negroes rent from white landlords and practically none of the whites rent from Negroes, the division of management score for Negroes was lower (lesser share in the management function) than for whites for each method of rental payment.

Likewise the results of operating under different methods of rental payment are related not so much to the method of payment itself but to other associated factors. In the Mississippi area, low efficiency of Negro renters of all types is probably associated with the fact that over half of them rent from Negro landlords. Although an accurate measure of natural soil productivity is difficult to determine, it appears that land owned by Negroes is less productive than that owned by whites. Croppers farm portions of relatively large operating units which have the equipment, power, and flexibility that allow for efficient management. In addition, cropper tracts are small in size and have the advantage of the intensive application of human labor by the cropper and his family. The results are not due simply to the utilization of the share or cash methods of rental payment but to the quality of soil, the size of the over-all operating unit, and the influence on the farming operations of the person responsible for management.

The relationship between method of rental payment and the ratio of value of rental payment to market value of property rented is rather definite and is the theoretical basis for the categories used for method of rental payment. Chambers has advanced the theory that income is the prime causal factor of both rent and land value.[34]

It follows that income must also be the chief determinant of the relationship between rent and value.[35]

Cash rents fluctuate with income and land prices but somewhat behind both. The value of rent for crop-share rental varies with shifts in income year by year with no time lag. The landlord does not share in the risk of production or of price with the cash rental, so he is satis-

[34] Clyde R. Chambers, *Relation of Land Income to Land Value*, U. S. Department of Agriculture Bull. 1224, Washington, June 1924.

[35] It is quite probable that prevailing interest rates are an additional factor or that interest rates are in part determined by the ratio of rent to value.

fied to accept a cash rent that is equivalent to interest rates from alternative investments. The cash rental for a supervised tenant is somewhat higher than this theoretical figure in that the renter is paying for management, assurance of production, farm family living, credit, and the other items which are common to the cropper arrangement.

In these situations the landlord is assuming part of the risk of price and production. In years of low farm income, adjustments are made in the cash rent; in years of high farm income, the cash rent is collected in full. It follows that the greater the share interest of the landlord in the production, the more he tends to protect his risk by contributing his ability to manage the farming operations.

The above is not intended as a complete discussion of the cropper system but is merely a brief résumé of the motivating economic forces which tend to make the system possible and workable.

KINSHIP TO LANDLORD

The significance of kinship is largely contingent upon the characteristics of the landlord and the family to which he belongs. The fundamental consideration therefore is the type of landlord to which the tenant is related. If he has little to offer by way of supervision or credit standing, and particularly if the land is of low productivity, the fact of kinship may have little influence on the performance of the tenant. On the other hand a related tenant is from a landowning family so that "related tenant" becomes a partial substitute for a tenure of parent criterion. Tenants related to their landlords are involved with the economic affairs of the parental family. Under such circumstances there is a tendency for family money to be "loaned" back and forth according to relative need and supply rather than according to strict economic practices. Since distribution of wealth within the kinship group is likely to be dependent on need as well as upon input factors, a greater range of rental arrangements is to be expected for related than for nonrelated tenants.

The incidence of related tenants is associated with types of owners. In the South with 90 per cent or more of the farm land held by white owners and with one-third of all tenants Negro (including croppers), the percentage of tenants related to their landlords is relatively low. In the consideration of related tenants, the question arises as to what comparisons should be made. In other studies, comparison of related and nonrelated tenants has been essentially a comparison of tenants from landowning families with those from nonowning families. As such they are owners-in-prospect and have the characteristics as herein ascribed to tenants with owner parents. Such comparison is treated in this study under the subject *Tenure of Parents.* Therefore the comparison made here is between tenants related to their landlord and tenants with the same type of landlord but not related.

Some of the characteristics of related tenants are: (1) they are younger than other tenants (2) they are of landowning families (3) they have been aided financially by their own relatives (4) their net worth and socio-economic status are higher (5) they participate in the community activities more like owners than other tenants (6) they have had schooling more comparable to owners than to other tenants. These characteristics apply to renters, croppers, and laborers related to their landlords or employers.

In addition, related tenants: (1) vary more from the traditional third and fourth or half share lease arrangements than the unrelated (2) more frequently have oral leasing arrangements (3) more often have leases of indefinite length (4) show a low ratio of rent to value and sometimes pay no rent (5) with landlords living near the farm received less supervision than similar non-kinship tenants but those with landlords living more than 25 miles away received more supervision.

DIVISION OF MANAGEMENT

The division of management between landlord and tenant is an old subject in American agriculture. The Bureau of the Census has been under attack since 1910 for enumerating croppers as farm operators. The basis for saying that the cropper unit is not a farm is one of control over the operations of the unit or division of management between landlord and tenant. In an area containing sharecroppers, such measures as type of farming, crop organization, land use, land values, amount of livestock, value of equipment, farm incomes, age of operator, kinship to landlord, and many others become relatively meaningless when croppers are included with real operators. It is readily apparent that the use of county averages in these areas is misleading and relatively meaningless. In a comparison of tenure groups, as in the present study, additional complications arise. Factors such as crop yields, soil conservation practices and efficiency of farming in general are related to "the personal qualities of the farmer, the character of the land and the adequacy of farm equipment and operating capital."[36] In the case of supervised tenants and croppers the human factors involved in the success of a farming operation are those of the landlord and not those of the cropper. Without sorting the cases by some measure of "who is responsible for the failure or success of the farming operations," the personal characteristics of the wrong man would be related to the efficiency measures in the case of all cropper tracts.

Schuler, in his comparison of Corn Belt and Cotton Belt farmers, devoted one section of his report to a discussion of the amount of control the landlord exercises over the farming operations.[37] Data were presented as to frequency of supervision and four degrees of control: (1) leave decisions entirely up to tenants/employees (2) simply discuss problems with them (3) usually suggest what to do but do not command (4) give strict orders. He found that for the southern states, a few renters, croppers, and laborers were to be found in all categories. This suggests a continuum of control, or supervision, or division of management. A later study in Louisiana set up an index of division of management combining the following factors: (1) frequency of supervision by the landlord (2) landlord's part in marketing the tenant's crop (3) presence of a commissary on the farm (4) landlord's part in supplying credit for tenant's living expenses (5) proportion of production credit supplied by landlord and tenant and (6) nearness of landlord's residence to tenant's farm.[38] The index resulting from the weighting of these items was handled as a continuum and a number of other characteristics of both landlord and tenant were related to the index.[39]

---

[36] L. C. Gray, *et al.*, "Farm Ownership and Tenancy," *Agriculture Yearbook, 1923*, Washington, 1924, p. 576. Also see W. W. Wilcox and O. G. Lloyd, *The Human Factor in the Management of Indiana Farms*, Indiana Agricultural Experiment Station Bull. 369, August 1932; and W. W. Wilcox, A. Boss and G. A. Pond, *Relation of Variations in the Human Factor to Financial Returns in Farming*, Minnesota Agricultural Experiment Station Bull. 288, June 1932.

[37] E. A. Schuler, *Social Status and Farm Tenure—Attitudes and Social Conditions of Corn Belt and Cotton Belt Farmers*, Social Research Report No. 1, V., U. S. Department of Agriculture, Bureau of Agricultural Economics, Washington, April 1938, pp. 153-61.

[38] Ralph J. Ramsey and Harold Hoffsommer, *Procedure in Delineating Types of Tenancy Areas in Louisiana*, U. S. Department of Agriculture, Bureau of Agricultural Economics, Washington, Mimeo., 1941, p. 5.

[39] Analysis of the Louisiana mailed questionnaire data showed that independence of management by the tenant increases as the percentage of tenants owning workstock, and the percentage who were white, increased. At the same time the size of the landlord's farm (measured by average number of families per farm) and the percentage of tenants reporting work for their landlord for wages decreased. Cash renters and standing renters were independent, share renters (share other than one-half) were next, and the one-half share tenants were supervised to a greater extent than those

A statistical index of the division of management was developed from data secured in the present study. Scores were computed for each leasing arrangement and a composite score was computed for those lessees with more than one landlord. Scores were computed based upon the distribution of answers for each sample and for the total of the Arkansas, Mississippi, Oklahoma, and Texas samples.[40]

Due to the method by which it was computed, the division of management score is closely related to the division of the individual items of management. (Table 80) These items are as follows: the selection of the kinds of crops, acres in each crop, kinds of livestock grown, amount of such livestock, when and how planting is done, when and how cultivating is done, when and how crops are harvested, selection and purchase of fertilizer, securing of production credit, securing of credit for family living, establishing a crop rotation system, marketing the cash crops, keeping records, and signing the Agricultural Adjustment Administration forms as operator of the farm. In addition two other items of a somewhat different nature were also included in the score: frequency of supervision by the landlord and distance from the tenant tract to the residence of the landlord. The relationship of the two latter items to the total score was also high. (Table 81)

Landlords exercised less control over the operations of planting, cultivating, and harvesting than any of the other management items. These operations are fairly well fixed by local custom and are limited to a large extent by the nature of the type of equipment available. The "business operations" were supervised by the landlords to the greatest extent. These were signing the Agricultural Adjustment Administration forms, record keeping, deciding upon a long-time crop rotation program, selection of individual crops and acreages in each for each year, marketing the cash crop, and securing production credit.

Division of management is associated closely with the method of rental payment. Those paying cash or standing rent had the most independence of management and those paying one-half share rent had the least in all areas sampled. (Table 82) Negroes in the Coastal Plains were consistently more supervised than whites for each method of rental payment, but as between methods of rental payment they

---

with other methods of rental payment. The age of both tenant and landlord increased with increases in independence of management by the tenant. Colored landlords and related landlords for both white and Negro were concentrated in the middle group of divided responsibility of management. The written lease and stability on the same farm showed some association with independence but was not so pronounced as the items mentioned above.

[40] See Appendix for complete statement of method.

followed the same pattern. Differences within method of rental groups between native whites and the Czechs and Germans in the Texas sample were not conclusive. Part owners exercised more freedom of managment than renters regardless of method of rental payment in all areas except Mississippi. (Table 42) Croppers were the most supervised although some overlapping occurred in all areas. In the Mississippi sample a few white and Negro part owners were essentially croppers on their rent tracts even though they farmed some land which they owned.

No conclusive relationship was noted between size of farm (productive man-work units) and division of management within tenure groups. (Table 83) Apparently, independence of management is associated both with large units and with units too small to be worth the cost of supervision. Within each racial and tenure grouping the value of livestock and equipment owned increased as the proportion of management increased for the tenant. (Table 84) Several inconsistencies were noted but the generalization appears to hold. Part owners had more livestock and equipment than renters, who in turn exceeded croppers with the same management score. In the Coastal Plain samples, whites owned more than Negroes when division of management was held constant. Since the ownership of workstock automatically raises the cropper to the renter status, differences in those two tenures were to be expected.

In general, the more the supervision, the higher the crop yield index within each race and tenure grouping. (Table 85) White renters and croppers in both Coastal Plain samples had the highest crop yield index when the management was divided more or less equally between landlord and tenant. Supervision, therefore, appears to increase yields, or it may be stated that it pays to add supervision to land which will respond to management. The result is increased yields. The effects of freedom of choice on the part of the tenant is reflected in increased diversification with increases in the proportion of management allotted the tenant. (Table 86) A part of the increased diversification is accounted for by increases in the value of products used in the home. (Table 87) While a number of inconsistencies occur in this relationship, the direction is quite definite and consistent within tenure groups for the Texas and Oklahoma samples.

The division of management is influenced in about the same way as tenure status with regard to length of time on a given tract of land. A farmer gets a higher proportion of management or a higher tenure status by moving to another farm. Practically no difference was noted in the distribution by division of management between groups with varying number of years on rent tract for the Coastal Plains samples either for renters or croppers. (Table 101) In Oklahoma and Texas, however, the proportion in the independent management group increased with the number of years on the rent tract. This fact is probably more a matter of age of tenant and type of arrangement than of a changing division of management with increased stability. Very few cases were noted in which an increased share in management had been achieved without moving to another farm.

Once a set of relationships is established between landlord and tenant at the beginning of their contractual period, it is likely to persist. It appears to be much easier for each of the two contracting parties to work out different arrangements with other individuals than it is to change the arrangements in the current relationship. For those to whom the latter applies, this is one of the more serious defects in the functioning of the tenure ladder. For a young farmer to become more of a managing tenant, or to climb the ladder from laborer to cropper or from renter to owner, it becomes almost necessary for him to change farms. In addition to the economic and social costs of moving, it becomes necessary to learn the peculiarities of the new farm.

Participation of the tenant in the Farm Security Administration program transfers part of the management from the landlord to the Farm Security Administration supervisors or it is turned over to the tenant. (Table 88) Part of this transfer is inherent in the Farm Security Administration program itself which provides credit to the tenant, aids in securing fertilizer, encourages a diversification program, encourages cooperative marketing through Farm Security Administration sponsored channels, and gives on-the-job instruction in both farm management operations and farm skills. Since some of the cooperators have recently been croppers with little managerial experience and others are related to their nearby landlords, the transfer of managerial functions is not so complete as might be inferred from the foregoing statement of Farm Security Administration policy. Part owners in the Coastal Plains samples with the most freedom of management have a lesser percentage in the Farm Security Administration program than those with more supervision.

Supervision by the landlord varies directly with the extension of production credit to the tenant in each racial and tenure group in each area sampled. Croppers in general get credit from their landlords to a greater extent than renters or part owners. Within the same division of management grouping, Negro renters in the Coastal Plains samples obtained credit from their landlords to a greater extent than did Negro croppers. This suggests that credit operates independently of the other aspects of management associated with rent and care of workstock and equipment. Kinship to landlord as related to division of management is a complex phenomenon both as to amount and as to direction. It has been pointed out elsewhere that landlords who live at a distance from the farm exercise more control over the operation if related to the tenant than do those with tenants who are not related. However, if the distance is short, the control is less than with those who are not related. Those croppers who exercise most management functions are more frequently related to their landlords than those with less management responsibilities. (Table 89) On the other hand, part owners and renters who are most independent in their operation are less frequently related to their landlords than those with more supervision. The number of cases in each group is not sufficiently large however to warrant a valid conclusion except for the cropper group. Both races in the Coastal Plains sample followed this pattern.

Both age and education of tenants increased with a greater degree of management. Although this held for all race and tenure groups the nature of the data are such that the evidence is not regarded as conclusive. (Table 90) The two factors have somewhat opposite effects in that each separately is positively associated with a higher proportion of management, yet the older farmers are the ones with the least formal education. This is especially noticeable in the Oklahoma and Texas samples.

SUMMARY

1. The pattern of the leasing arrangement is largely conditioned by the type of landlord who owns the land. Institutional, nonresident, nonrelated, and female landlords use the cash method of rental payment and the written lease more often than do other types of landlords. Other types of landlords tend to use an oral, informal arrangement which is typical of folk practices.

2. Those renting land tend to select farms owned by landlords of the same ethnic or racial group regardless of the quality or size of the farm or the proportion of the total land area owned by that partic-

ular ethnic group. In leasing a farm, the renter gives important consideration to both land and the landlord.

3. The great bulk of farm land in the areas surveyed was owned by individual males. Females constituted around 15 per cent of the individual landlords although in some areas as high as 40 per cent were females. Estates accounted for less than 10 per cent of all landlords sampled. While this percentage is not high in a given year, essentially all farm land goes through this stage sooner or later in the transfer of ownership from one generation to another. The amount of land owned by governmental agencies and by agencies extending credit on real estate varies from year to year depending upon farm incomes. Because of the high rate of foreclosures in the thirties, the amount was high, but during the ensuing war years much of the land was sold to individual buyers.

4. Most leases in the sample areas covered an entire farm unit. Renting of single fields was more common in the Coastal Plains than in the other areas. Renting milch cows was fairly common for croppers.

5. In 1942 the value of rental per $100 valuation was highest for those paying one-half share rent. This was followed by the third and fourth rentals. Cash rentals were lowest, being near the usual interest rate. Differences in the ratios vary according to yields and prices so that conclusions based upon 1942 data should be carefully weighed.

6. The written lease showed little or no relationship to the number of years on the rent tract or to measures of soil conservation practices. It was associated with the types of landlords who had formal, contractual relationships with the lessees and with those lessees who were participating in the Farm Security Administration program. Aside from the school land leases sampled in Oklahoma and Mississippi, the written lease apparently contributed little to the stability of the renter on a given tract of land. None of the croppers sampled had written leases.

7. The third and fourth system of renting, with its variations, was the most prevalent method of rental payment in each area sampled. The cash-share variation in the Oklahoma areas represented additional cash payments for pasture or dwelling while in the Texas area it represented cash on a specified acreage of feed crop and share on the balance. In general those paying cash-share rent were making the most money.

8. Croppers in the Coastal Plains tended to be full-time croppers

to a greater extent than in other areas. The majority of those in the Texas area worked for wages, whereas those in Oklahoma were about equally divided between operating croppers and wage laborers, the latter receiving a share of the production of cotton, poultry, eggs, or milk as a bonus payment. In the Coastal Plains the cropper arrangements were closely associated with the white male resident landlord.

9. Renters related to their landlords were younger than other renters and a considerable number of them did not pay conventional rent. Since they were of landowning families, their education was relatively high as was also their socio-economic status.

10. The measure of the division of management between landlord and tenant is, among other things, a means of determining to which party the success of the farm operation should be attributed. Some overlapping occurred among the traditional tenure classes in regard to the division of management as measured by the scale. Several part owners were essentially croppers. In general, the more the landlord furnished and the nearer he was to the farm, the more he supervised the operations. The management index was closely related to the method of rental payment and to the extension of credit by the landlord to the lessee. Net worth, livestock, education, and age appeared to have some relationship to the division. As in the case of tenure change, renters usually acquired a larger share in management by moving. The Farm Security Administration transferred supervision for its borrowers from the landlord to the credit agency.

CHAPTER VI

Land Tenure and Soil Conservation

The problems of land tenure and soil erosion have long been interrelated in the study of agricultural problems of the South. It is well recognized that certain relationships exists between the manner in which a farmer holds his land (his tenure status) and how he uses that land. If ownership is in fee simple the owner has to recognize only the public's right to tax, the police power, and the right of eminent domain. Such an owner may do as he pleases with the land. On the other hand, if the occupant of the farm is a tenant, his rights are more restricted and a different pattern of relationship to the land ensues. The purpose of this chapter is to re-examine some of the basic tenure qualities in their relation to conservation.[1]

In using the term conservation, broad as well as more limited applications of the term have been used. An all inclusive definition is "the wise use of land resources for the greatest good of the greatest number—and that for the longest time."[2] Limited definitions usually refer only to the physical performance of soil saving without regard for economic costs or benefits. Unfortunately, some of the ardent advocates of soil saving have created the impression that this is what is implied by conservation. All too often a picture of rolling farmland, terraced and farmed on the contour, is the only image which the term conservation stimulates. For discussion here neither of these concepts of conservation will suffice. While one permits too much latitude and is vague, the other is too limiting since it treats only of the physical act of soil saving without consideration of economic implications. Conservation should denote more of the maintenance

[1] The term *conservation* as herein used is generalized to include the commonly accepted broad meaning of the term. Since the field survey of the Regional Project only partially covered the subject at hand, data in this chapter are drawn from a variety of sources.

[2] C. R. Van Hise, *Conservation of Our Natural Resources*, The Macmillan Company, New York, 1930, republication, p. 527.

of the exhaustible resource (farmland) and the present level of productivity of the soil.[3] Concomitantly with certain practices and techniques used in conservation methods, the level of productivity actually may be increased. This definition does not preclude this latter concept of increasing productivity. Also, conservation might suggest or include a "reduction in the rate of consumption"[4] of farmland or a "redistribution of rates of use over time in the direction of the future."[5]

This latter concept becomes very important in considering the problems involved in land tenure-conservation relationships, particularly under tenant operations. Furthermore, conservation as used here must always be considered as having socio-economic implications or involving costs and benefits. Under normal socio-economic processes the term must have more implication than the aesthetic reaction aroused by the beauty of a green and well-farmed countryside. It is a term used to denote more than soil saving and erosion control or only "plugging of gullies on eroded hillsides."

THE PROBLEM

Fundamental to the problem of conservation in the region is the nature of the land tenure process as it has developed historically. The first aspect of this lies in the fact that ownership of farmland has not been stable. That is, title to land has not rested in the same individual for a long period or within the same family for more than a generation. In all states of the region, with the exception of a limited number of small areas inhabited by groups from European cultures, there has been no general permanent attachment to land as a basic pattern of rural life. Primarily, the motive for landowning has been economic returns in terms of income from crops and livestock. However, all too often for the sake of those who occupy and till the land, the motive for owning apparently has been for resale at higher prices. Recent as well as long-time trends in land transfers are indicative of the more or less transitory interest of the landowner in the soil. It may be said that conservation is influenced by ownership stability for the reason that some degree of permanence of ownership is required in order to carry out any land improvement measure. Most owner-

[3] A. C. Bunce, *The Economics of Soil Conservation*, The Iowa State College Press, Ames, Iowa, 1942, p. 7.

[4] *Ibid.*, p. 3.

[5] S. V. Ciriacy-Wantrup, "Private Enterprise and Conservation," *Journal of Farm Economics*, XXIV (February 1942), 76.

ship tenures of short duration discourage establishment of conservation programs.

In Jackson County, Oklahoma, during the period of 1941 to 1945, almost one-third of the total acreage in farm land changed hands. During this same period, one-fifth of the land in Nevada County, Arkansas, and one-fourth of the land in Covington County, Mississippi, changed hands. Rapid and widespread turnover of land titles in these sample areas is indicative of the region-wide nature of this characteristic of tenure. From these sample studies it is reasonable to assume that about one-fifth of all farm land in the states included in this study changed hands in the five-year period, 1941-1945. During the last decade when conservation was receiving its greatest impetus it is estimated that from one-third to one-half of all farm land in the region changed hands.

It is, of course, recognized that many land transfers are necessary to enlarge and otherwise adjust operating farm units to a more profitable basis. And many tracts are bought by farmers who desire to become owner-operators. This type of transfer may favor conservation. On the other hand, the volume of change in title indicates that these may not be the primary motives for buying and selling land tracts. Tenure policies, designed to allow free access and easy transfer of land, probably encouraged "cashing in" on rising land prices.

Coupled with this desire of "cashing in" has been the impact of actual and speculative mineral development on nearly all agricultural localities of the region. Many owners have been and are interested in the land primarily as a source of mineral wealth. About one-fifth of nonoperating owners in Jackson County, Oklahoma, fell in this class, indicating that title to farm land was being held in anticipation of oil development.[6] Almost one-third of absentee out-of-state owners intended to hold title to land to await mineral development. In a Texas area "the owner frequently obtains a greater return from mineral leases than from crop and grazing rentals. The possibility of mineral development tends to keep the price of land above its value for agricultural production."[7] And some significance to conservation lies in the fact that much of the land affected by mineral development is also the land most nearly ruined by erosion and exploitation.[8]

---

[6] Reports from absentee owners.

[7] A. C. Magee and C. A. Bonnen, *Information Basic to Adjustments in Rice Production in Texas*, Texas Agricultural Experiment Station, Bull. 676, November 1945, p. 41.

[8] P. Nelson, "Land Tenure and Agricultural Conservation," *Current Farm Economics*, Oklahoma Agricultural Experiment Station, Stillwater, Vol. 11, No. 2, April 1938, p. 27.

However, regardless of the motives of the owners, land parcels have changed hands quite freely. Rather than being an object of permanent investment for an individual or a family, land perhaps has been just another commodity only slightly different from crops in that the period of maturation is longer. And for programs requiring years for installation and realization of benefits this maturing period has been altogether too short. The allocation of costs and benefits involved has not been feasible for many landowners. This unstable tenure base has been one of the difficult problems recognized by the United States Department of Agriculture in its attempts to further conservation through the Soil Conservation Service.

Each time a parcel of land under conservation agreement changes hands this agreement to carry out certain practices and reorganization for conservation is automatically cancelled.[9] Of course, in some instances the new owner elects to continue the conservation program. But in any case the program is retarded to the degree that effort and time is required to obtain a new agreement. The extent of this difficulty is indicated by the fact that in one conservation district where 692 farms were under agreement at the end of 1945, 113 agreements had been cancelled due to changes in ownership.[10] Another district had 251 farm plan agreements with 26 cancelled because of change in ownership.[11] To be sure some new conservation agreements are made possible by changes in ownership.

The second basic aspect of tenure-conservation history in the region is the fact that settlers brought with them little or no heritage of a conserving, or a nonexploitive, agriculture. Again an exception should be made of some of the groups settling in the region directly from continental Europe. Fostered by free lands and a rapid westward expansion, until recent years the attitude of the landowner and farm operator, as well as the general public, was that soils are an inexhaustible resource.

These two aspects of tenure-conservation relationships—(1) the ease and rapidity of change in landownership resulting in the ultimate treatment of land as a negotiable commodity, and (2) the lack of a conservation heritage and knowledge due partially to the fact that exploitation had paid—have resulted in rather widespread land misuse and rapid soil erosion in portions of the region.

---

[9] *Farm Plan Agreement,* a document used to facilitate cooperation between landowners and conservation districts.

[10] Summary of Soil Conservation District activities published in *Northwest Arkansas Times*, Fayetteville, Arkansas, May 21, 1946.

[11] From records of Dal-Worth Soil Conservation District, Ft. Worth, Texas, April 1946.

An example of what can happen physically to soil resources in a short period of time under the influence of these basic factors is shown in the following table regarding erosion conditions of Oklahoma farm land in 1944:

Erosion class*	Acres (Add 000)	Per cent of total land in farms
Little or no erosion	4,900	14.1
Moderate erosion	6,222	17.9
Severe erosion	13,460	38.6
Other	10,221	29.4
Total farm land	34,803	100.0

* Adapted from 1944 records of Soil Conservation Service, United States Department of Agriculture, Region 4, Ft. Worth, Texas. "Other" in the table includes shallow and stony soils, wasteland, and all other land in farms.

An area with little erosion only 50 years ago now has more than one-third of the total farm land in a "severely eroded condition" as defined by soil technicians. Not all of this should be charged to land tenure but it is held to have a significant relationship. More than one-half of all Oklahoma farms lie in such areas.

TENURE AND LAND UTILIZATION

After discussing the above basic characteristics of tenure and conservation the following more immediate items and their relation to conservation are analyzed: size of farm, land use and practices, land ownership, and methods of leasing.

Size of Farm

Although tenure denotes the legal and socio-economic implication of rights in land, the spatial extent or areal size of a land tract is a tenure characteristic. This is significant to the degree that land settlement policies and other institutional influences have molded the spatial pattern of farm units.[12]

[12] To a relative degree the acreage sizes of farms within the region are related to the original settlement pattern utilized by the federal and the various state authorities involved. In other words present farm units sometimes are tied closely to the original title of land insofar as size is concerned. The institution of land ownership has not been flexible enough to throw off entirely the size limitation implanted by early settlements. In a large area of western Oklahoma the quarter section was the homestead unit. At the present time, nearly one-half century later, the usual size of ownership tract is still the quarter section although the farm operating unit is much larger. Other areas of the state are represented by various sizes of tracts as allotted originally to the Indians of the various tribes. In Hemphill County, Texas, conterminous to Roger Mills County, Oklahoma, the development of ranching was probably partially the result of early allotment of large land tracts. Across the 100th meridian in Roger Mills County, land was allotted in quarter sections and crop farm units developed.

Otherwise, size may be a reflection of a more profitable farm business, or it might reflect the managerial ability of an individual operator. Areal character determines the space or size of the parcel in which rights are granted, and this size or acreage extent of a unit in many instances determines the ensuing prosperity or poverty for an occupant.

The significance of farm unit size lies in the fact that application of conservation measures and soil-saving practices depend in a large measure upon the size of the operating farm. Size-conservation relationships have been recognized and studied in various areas of the region, and invariably the findings have shown that conservation as now constituted is more compatible with large farms. A small unit in a given type of farming area must depend upon the largest amount of land cultivated in the cash crops of that area. And the unfortunate situation existing is that cash crops and soil-depleting crops are too frequently synonymous. Thus, the small operator may not be able to adopt a comprehensive conservation plan without too greatly reducing his cash income.

The following comparison of "conserving" with "eroding" farms, from a study in Payne County, Oklahoma, shows that in each year the farms were studied the average size of unit practicing conservation was significantly larger than the one not following conservation.[13]

	Year			
Conservation practices	1933	1937	1938	1939
Conserving farm (acres)	169	238	226	223
Eroding farm (acres)	152	166	185	178

In Okfuskee County, Oklahoma, small farms did not earn as large a proportion of allowed conservation payments as did large farms. "There was a definite tendency for small farms to fall in the no-payment group," while large farms tended toward earning the entire conservation allowance.[14]

This same study indicates that individual practices vary by size of farm with the small farms tending toward contour cultivation of intertilled crops. The larger units did more terracing. In the southwestern part of the state small farms have the greatest proportion of land in

[13] Adapted from E. A. Tucker and P. Nelson, "Does a Program of Conservation Interfere with Farm Operations? *Current Farm Economics*, Oklahoma Agricultural Experiment Station, Stillwater, Vol. 13, No. 5, October 1940, p. 131.

[14] D. L. W. Anker, "Agricultural Conservation in Okfuskee County," *Current Farm Economics*, Oklahoma Agricultural Experiment Station, Stillwater, Vol. 13, No. 6, December 1940, pp. 156-61.

crops and the greater part of these are row crops tending to promote rapid run-off and consequent erosion.[15] In regard to application of a program it was concluded that on the "basis of the distribution of farms and the land use of the several sites it may logically be assumed that water-flow retardation (resulting from a conservation program) probably can be best accomplished on the larger size units." An examination of available information indicates that the experience of conservation agencies in the area has been in accord with the above assumption.

In the work programs of several soil conservation districts actual farm units planned for conservation invariably have been larger than the average farm of the district. For all districts the planned farm was nearly one-third larger than the average farm. In areas with large numbers of small farms the evidence of size as related to conservation application becomes more striking. The situation for southwestern Oklahoma is indicated in the following table:[16]

District	*Average size of farms*		Per cent planned farm is of average size
	In district	Planned	
Garvin-Murray	165	214	130
Stephens County	187	212	113
Canadian-Walnut	125	170	136
Arbuckle	196	213	109
Grady County	144	169	117
Upper Washita	257	315	122
N. Fork of Red River	166	232	140
Total	180	233	129

In the Trinity River Watershed of Texas a study of farms shows that "many are too small to support their operators without exploiting the land."[17] In one locality of this watershed a committee of farm operators in a conservation district found that "on farms of less than 50 acres there is seldom sufficient equipment or income to execute a conservation program."[18] Nearly one-half of all farms in this district

[15] *Flood Control Survey, Washita River Watershed, Oklahoma* (unpublished), United States Department of Agriculture, 1942, Appendix G, p. 58.

[16] Adapted from unpublished data collected in Flood Control Survey, *Washita Watershed, Oklahoma,* United States Department of Agriculture. Includes farms planned to December 31, 1940.

[17] *Survey Report on the Trinity River Watershed, Texas,* United States Department of Agriculture, House Document No. 708, p. 8.

[18] *District Work Program and Plan,* Ellis-Prairie Soil Conservation District, No. 504, Texas, 1941.

were less than 100 acres, or within the range size where dependable participation in a conservation program was questionable.

The Soil Conservation Service reports that, "in parts of Oklahoma, Louisiana, Arkansas, and Texas . . . the problem consists of the fact that these small farms in many cases contain a comparatively large percentage of land which must be retired from cultivation in order to halt erosion."[19]

Another report states: "Planning for conservation farming on these farms (where not enough land is available) is difficult. On many such farms no solution can be found unless additional land can be leased or purchased or a supplementary source of income for the farmer can be established."[20]

In the early years demonstration projects in conservation, where the interest was primarily in displaying soil saving and soil-saving methods, were highly subsidized and costs to the individual farmer were held to a minimum. Size of an operator's resources meant little. However, in recent years conservation has grown up, so to speak, and the economic implications of conservation to all operators must be considered. Plans are made on an individual unit basis, and, generally speaking, an operator or owner must see some benefits accruing to himself before participating.

Land Use and Practices

It is often stated that the tenure status of a farmer does not imply either conservation or exploitation of the land. "The complexity of the whole problem and the indicated influences of various factors included show definitely that ownership does not necessarily mean conservation, that tenancy does not necessarily mean soil erosion and depletion, and that differences in farming practices on owner and tenant farms may be a reflection of many causes other than differences in tenure."[21] There are examples in the region of comprehensive practices applied to land by operators in each of the various tenure status groups, owner-operators and tenants alike. Even though some operators of all tenure groups are practicing conservation, there is an apparent tendency for certain types of conservation performance to

---

[19] *Conservation Planning for Small Farms,* Soil Conservation Service, Region IV, Ft. Worth, Texas, mimeo.

[20] R. D. Hockensmith and J. G. Steele, *Classifying Land for Conservation Farming,* United States Department of Agriculture Farmers' Bull. 1853, February 1943, p. 45.

[21] Otis T. Osgood, "Some Observations on the Relation of Farm Land Tenure to Soil Erosion and Depletion," *Journal of Land and Public Utility Economics,* XVII (November 1941), 422.

be associated with tenure. This relationship has been observed and studied in various other sections of the nation.[22]

To evaluate conservation performance differences between owner-operators and tenants it has been necessary in this study to examine the problem indirectly through land use, land use practices, and farm organization. It is felt that a close relationship exists between these factors and the actual carrying out of conservation practices. And, of course, the actual participation experience of farm operators in a conservation program is a final measure of performance.

From the standpoint of major land use and type of farming there is almost always some degree of difference between owners and tenants in a given area. In the regional study the index of diversification shows greater diversification for full-owner farms than for tenant farms. The difference is not great but the trend is consistent. Also, tenants who are related to their landlords show a greater degree of diversification. Sons had greater diversification than other related tenants, indicating that those operators who expect to become owners through family kinship farm more like owner-operators. In so far as diversification reflects a less exploitive or a less wasteful land use then it may be said that owner-operators belong to a more conserving group.

Another evidence of tendency toward conserving operations on the part of the owners exists in the amount of productive livestock kept. The usual livestock enterprises found in this region are less exploitive of land than the common crop enterprises. In most areas owner-operators exceed tenants in productive livestock units kept by a considerable margin. (Table 15)[23] The tendency for more livestock on owner farms still is true when size of units is held constant. (Table 91) It follows since livestock is a medium of marketing conserving crops that owner-operators tend more to grow such crops in connection with livestock enterprises. And the stability and long-time characteristics of livestock growing definitely facilitates more conservation on the part of owner-operators. Generally speaking, tenants operate the cash crop farms and owners, while operating cash crop

[22] For example see: R. Schickele, J. P. Himmel and, R. M. Hurd, *Economic Phases of Erosion Control in Southern Iowa and Northern Missouri*, Iowa Agricultural Experiment Station Bull. 333, June 1935. P. L. Slagsvold, *Land Ownership and Tenure*, Huntley Irrigation Project. Montana Agricultural Experiment Station Bull. 385, January 1941. M. R. Cooper, W. J. Roth, J. G. Maddox, R. Schickele, and H. A. Turner, "The Causes: Defects in Farming Systems and Farm Tenancy," *Soils and Men, Yearbook of Agriculture 1938*.

[23] For tables mentioned in this chapter refer to statistical tables in Appendix.

farms, also operate the general, self-sufficing, livestock, and dairy farms[24] or those which tend to be more conserving of resources.

A recent study of farm types and tenure status of operators in Oklahoma states that "farms which include combinations of cotton, small grain (usually wheat) and some livestock, are more frequently owner-operated than those farms which depend chiefly upon cotton and some livestock."[25]

In the southwestern portion of the state 88 per cent of all livestock farms were owner-operated. In southeastern Oklahoma this proportion was 81 per cent. These are much greater proportions than owner-operators were of all farmers. In the Tallahatchie Watershed Area of Mississippi, tenants "cash cropped" a higher proportion of the farm and had less pasture of all types.[26] In the sample of farms in the regional study there is a noticeable trend for owners to have a smaller proportion of cropland in intertilled crops when size is held constant. (Table 92) This trend is quite marked in the Arkansas area. Also the proportionate amount of income from cotton (a depleting crop) tends to be less on owner farms. (Table 10)

A more direct measure of active conservation performance is that of conservation participation as related to tenure status. In the regional study some information was obtained with reference to conservation performance of the various tenure types. Of 48 operators actively participating in a district conservation program, 36 or three-fourths of the total were owner-operators. Owner-operators make up one-half or less of the total operators in the region. Total participation, including contacts with the conservation district office for information, was much higher among owner-operators. (Table 93) Payments for conservation practices were invariably higher for owner-operators. (Table 94) In some instances this may be explained by larger-sized owner farms, but this is true only to a limited degree.

In an Oklahoma area, including seven soil conservation districts, during the period studied less than one-fourth of all cooperators were tenants.[27] This is in an area where more than one-half of all farmers were tenants. In some districts where tenancy was proportionately

[24] J. H. Southern, *Farm Tenancy in Oklahoma,* Oklahoma Agricultural Experiment Station Bull. 239, December 1939, p. 29.

[25] R. T. McMillan and O. D. Duncan, *Social Factors of Farm Ownership in Oklahoma,* Oklahoma Agricultural Experiment Station Bull. 289, November 1945, p. 31.

[26] *Survey of the Little Tallahatchie Watershed in Mississippi,* United States Department of Agriculture, House Document No. 892, 1942.

[27] *Flood Control Survey, Washita Watershed, Oklahoma,* United States Department of Agriculture, unpublished data, 1941.

higher the actual participation of tenants in the program was less. Another investigation in the conservational aspects of the Agricultural Adjustment Administration program in this state concluded that "tenants have generally entered into the conservation program as a result of landlord insistence or in order to earn Government payments" for conservation practices.[28] Tenants worked out only three-fourths as much of "soil building" payments as owner-operators did in the Little Tallahatchie River Watershed Area.[29] It was found also that tenant conservation practices vary somewhat from those of owner-operators. They perform certain practices primarily concerned with year to year operations. For example, contour cultivation is practiced, but terraces or other permanent types of water holding and soil-saving structures are not built.

In a former demonstration project area near Lindale, Texas, practically all those indicating a desire for continuation of conservation under the districts program were owner-operators.[30] Most of the reasons given for not continuing conservation were of a tenure nature. Six units had absentee landlords who were not interested. Four had been sold or were for sale. Others were in estates or had tenants who were not interested in conservation practices.

Thus, variations in land use and practices are due partially to the tenure arrangements under which a farmer operates. After size of unit and other factors are considered there is still an apparent trend toward a more conserving use on the part of owner-operators. And the performance in conservation of owner-operators is much greater than that of tenants as measured by participation in public programs for conservation.

Land Ownership

Type of farm ownership is of primary importance in the initiative of any program for the land. This character becomes especially important in the consideration of a long time program of conservation. It is obvious that some types of owners have interests that are outside conservation investment while others are enthusiastic about its potentialities. In the former category fall those whose intent is to sell

[28] E. A. Tucker, "Conservation on Small Cotton-Corn Farms," *Current Farm Economics*, Oklahoma Agricultural Experiment Station, Stillwater, Vol. 14. No. 6, December 1941, p. 192.

[29] *Survey of the Little Tallahatchie Watershed in Mississippi*, United States Department of Agriculture, House Document No. 892, 1942.

[30] *Lindale Project Records*, 1946, Soil Conservation Service, Region IV, Ft. Worth. Texas.

at an early date. A clue to this intent is indicated by the previous information given on land transfers. The latter category includes some landowners of all the various types.

From the standpoint of tenure the unencumbered owner-operator perhaps is in the most favorable position for conservation. There are no specific tenure relationships standing in the way of his participation. He holds all the rights in his land tract and is in a position to achieve maximum conservation if other factors are favorable. Information in the previous section of this chapter demonstrated that owner-operators actually tend to farm in a more conserving manner than other operators. It is within this group that public agency efforts in conservation finds greatest cooperation and the most sustained interest.

Another group of owner-operators include those of encumbered status. That is, the owner's rights to the land in fee simple have been modified to the extent that a second party now holds a mortgage right in the land. If conservation requires cash outlay or a temporary reduction in income the operator must choose between these costs and paying off the mortgage. If the burden of payments becomes proportionately large in relation to his income, this type of owner may find it necessary to further exploit land for present returns rather than conserve for future benefits. The numbers of owner-operators found in this group decreased during the war years of agricultural prosperity. However, there are yet relatively large numbers of mortgaged owner-operators. Also, wartime trends in land sales indicate that about two-fifths of the farm buyers are financing a portion of their purchase prices through mortgaging.[31] There is always a potential if not an actual threat to conservation performance in a large proportion of these mortgages. If farm commodity prices sag the mortgage operator may find himself in an untenable position in so far as the early years of a program is concerned. Conservation planning on mortgaged farms must consider the fact that a certain minimum income is necessary to meet fixed payments during the period of installation. In many instances this may preclude the initiation of conservation practices by these owners.

In general, the remaining owners of farm lands in the region fall in the landlord category. That is, they hold ultimate control of the rights in land but have contracted use and occupancy rights to others

[31] E. C. Ford, *Wartime Land Market Activity, The South Central Region, 1941-44*, U. S. Department of Agriculture, Bureau of Agricultural Economics, Little Rock, Arkansas, 1945.

for a period of time. For purposes of analysis in relation to conservation these landlords may be grouped in the following classes:[32] (1) Individuals: resident, male and female; (2) Estates; and (3) Corporations. The "individual" type landlord is by far the most prevalent in the region. (Table 67)

In so far as residence of landlord is concerned the available evidence indicates that landlords at great distances from their farms show a minimum of interest in conservation. Many of these landlords hold land for speculative mineral development. About 40 per cent of nonresident landlords in Jackson County, Oklahoma, indicated this intent. A Chicago, Illinois, landlord expresses the following typical attitude, "My father previously owned this farm. He purchased it with the possibility that it had oil. I personally feel there are good chances."[33] Another characteristic feature of absentee owned land is that over it hangs a potential threat of sale. About one-third of the landlords indicated that their land was for sale. Tenants of these landlords know that occupancy is highly insecure and that long-time conservation programs hold little for them. One landowner reports he is "too far away to go and see how it (his farm) is tended." Another reports, "I have been too far away to really know what was going on." Nearly all indicated that no conservation measures had been instituted on their farms other than through "government regulations"—which in most cases refers to the Agricultural Adjustment Administration program. A practical problem of administration in public conservation efforts caused by absentee ownership is pointed out by a soil conservation district committee in Texas which reports, "It is hard to get in touch with these absentee owners and complete the necessary arrangements for a conservation program for their farms. And it is especially hard to arrange any cooperative action on a community or watershed basis."[34] In the Oklahoma and Texas areas, about one-fifth to one-fourth of all landlords live over 100 miles from their farms. (Table 43)

The evidence from the Jackson County, Oklahoma, survey indicates that female landowners, both resident and nonresident, show relatively little interest in conservation practices. A common response

[32] Public landlords are not included. The two chief types in the region are school lands and lands supervised, but not owned, by the Indian Service of the Department of the Interior. A brief discussion bearing on these types is included in the chapter, Leasing Arrangements and Landlord Tenant Relationships.

[33] Reports from Jackson County landlords.

[34] *District Work Program and Plan,* Ellis Prairie Soil Conservation District No. 504, Texas.

was, "I let the tenant take care of that." Reasons for this attitude among female landlords are readily apparent. In many cases they live at great distances from the farm, and the above discussion on non-resident landlords is applicable in their case. In most other instances the woman has been left a "life estate" interest in the farm, and upon her death the land goes to the children. Actually, this leaves the land suspended somewhere between individual ownership and an estate. Therefore, no one of the interested members feels free to go ahead with conservation. And the woman landowner, because of advanced age or other reasons, sees no advantage in changing a system of farming.

A further type of ownership which complicates the execution of conservation is the estate mentioned above. Here the whole web of rights in land becomes involved among several parties and the uncertainty surrounding decisions of the court. In the main no one member of an estate has the authority or the incentive to proceed with farm reorganization and improvement. And the power of the administrator of an estate in many instances does not include questions connected with land except in the case of minors. The matter of clearing title to estate-held lands usually involves a period of time that frequently runs into a number of years. The difficulty of making settlements grows as the distance of residence of estate members becomes greater and as the number involved becomes greater. Conservation agencies have had little success in cooperation with members of estates, the usual procedure being to wait for settlement before a practical approach is made.

By 1942 corporate owned lands in the region had reached an all time low, and their significance to conservation has decreased accordingly. This significance lies in the fact that in almost all instances corporate ownership is only a temporary phenomenon due to mortgage foreclosure, and the land is always for sale. Generally, corporations, in view of their nonagricultural structure, have not seen fit to participate in detailed programs for soil improvement. Land is held for sale rather than for further investment. The influence of this factor, though not important at present, can become great if any considerable proportion of present mortgaged lands should be foreclosed for indebtedness.

A new type of owner, apparently holding some promise for conservation, has come into prominence during the war period. This is the urban business and professional individual who buys land, generally in the vicinity of his residence. The proximity of this type of owner to the farm allows him to participate in its management. A localized study[35] indicates that many of these owners actually manage the farm and operate with hired labor or with a hired manager. No definite information is available to measure the extent of this urban landownership. However, at the time of the regional survey 90 such owners were counted in the county seat town of Altus, Oklahoma. Their occupations included mainly banking, real estate, medicine, and law. Their specific relation to conservation appears to lie in the fact that they believe in it and are financially able to carry through. Income is chiefly from nonagricultural sources and land has become a depository for investment. "In some cases, nonfarmers may be buying farm land as a means of lowering their income taxes. The expense of improvements, deductions for depreciation, and the cost of conservation measures may decrease income taxes at present, while the rate of tax is high."[36]

Leasing Arrangements

Primarily, there are three characteristics of lease provisions that are related to conservation. These include (1) length of occupancy and renewal (2) type of lease or method of rental payment, and (3) provisions regarding conservation or related items.

While there are notable exceptions to short-term tenure in the region, the typical farm lease situation provides for only one year occupancy with no provision for renewal.[37] More than one-half of the tenants studied had been on their present unit less than five years. The usual oral lease agreement is prohibited by law from extending more than one year. Occupancy may be longer, but there is the ever present knowledge on the part of the tenant that each year may terminate it. Every aspect of insecurity of tenure not only discourages conservation but it further encourages a continuation of malpractices. The change to a system of conservation may require increases in pasture lands and in productive livestock which need a production period of several years. Uncertainty of occupation creates a risk in connection with such enterprises that the typical tenant cannot afford to bear. In regard to this aspect, it perhaps is significant to conservation that the

[35] Area included in the Dal-Worth Soil Conservation District, Ft. Worth, Texas.

[36] E. C. Ford, *Wartime Land Market Activity, The South Central Region, 1941-44*, U. S. Department of Agriculture, Bureau of Agricultural Economics, Little Rock, Arkansas, November 1945, pp. 11-12.

[37] See Chapter V for a detailed discussion.

tenants with longer term agreements also show greater diversification. (Table 95)

That the land tenure system has more or less withheld the right of long-term occupancy from the tenant is evidenced in law and in the customary contracts. A typical provision regarding length of occupancy states, "This contract terminates on the 31st day of December, 1942, without further notice and can only be renewed by written agreement, and no holding over on the part of said tenant shall be construed as a renewal, and said tenant agrees to surrender peaceful possession of said premises upon expiration of this contract."[38] Further insecurity of occupancy is embodied in most written leases in the "sale clause." Here the tenant usually agrees that upon sale of the farm and upon payment of a certain stipulated amount for his work in cultivation up to time of sale, he will vacate and give possession to the new owner if so required.

The type of lease or method of rental payment in vogue in any area may influence conservation. The most commonly used rental payment is the crop share, or one-third and one-fourth system. (Table 96) In adhering to this form of lease payment both owner and tenant tend to restrict farm organization to the usual and customary crops. The cash crops of the region on which shares are paid are usually the depleting crops. Landlords and tenants alike tend to avoid new crops and enterprises which, though soil conserving, call for new arrangements and relationships. The course of least resistance tends to be followed. The net result to land resources and the prospects for future conservation has been stated succinctly as follows: "It (crop-share renting) is predominantly a system of single-cash-soil-depleting-crop farming offering no security of tenure, and promoting exploitative management practices."[39]

A third feature of leasing which is related to conservation of soils arises from the amount and kinds of improvements provided for on tenant-operated farms. It will suffice to point out briefly that certain farmstead and other improvements are required if comprehensive measures for conservation are to be instituted. Barns, sheds, fences, permanent pastures, and watering facilities are necessary if the tenant is to grow certain crops and livestock which appear to be a part of

[38] From lease forms obtained in this study.

[39] S. B. Schneider and H. A. Graham, "Improving Rental Agreements as a Means of Encouraging Development of a Permanent Agriculture," *Current Farm Economics*, Oklahoma Agricultural Experiment Station Stillwater, Vol. 11, No. 4, August 1938, p. 90.

conservation practices in most localities of the region. There are other improvements usually in the form of soil-and-water-saving structures that also are included in farm plans for conservation. The relationship between these improvements and present conservation is obvious. The amount, kind, and quality of improvements on tenant farms, and some owner farms as well, are usually inadequate. The value of these structures are only about one-half the value of those on owner-operated farms in the survey sample. (Table 13)

The ultimate feature regarding improvements is the fact that lessees are not encouraged by the statutes of the states to make improvements for themselves. Statutory enactments and court decisions in all states of the region hold that improvements of a permanent character made by the tenant on leased premises must remain, provided there is no contractual understanding to the contrary. No state in the region has a legal provision granting the tenant compensatory rights for the unused portion of improvements he may construct. The practical result of such leasing arrangements amounts to a retardation of conservation practices.

Soil Erosion and Tenure Impacts

What has been the result of these tenant impacts on soil resources? Is there greater erosion on tenant than on owner farms? This problem is complex and difficult of measurement though it is reasonable to expect certain physical differences between land regularly farmed by tenants and land with a history of owner operation. Available data, though limited, do indicate some differences.

In Oklahoma studies, a relationship between the type of operators and erosion was found. The evidence indicated that "the tenants occupy the less sloping land but show an equally higher degree of erosion."[40] Data with wider application perhaps are available from the watershed conservation surveys mentioned earlier. Here an "erosion index" was prepared based on soil type, slope, erosion, and cover qualities. This index was then related to the tenure history of sample farms. The evidence, while not conclusive, indicates that soils with a 20-year history of tenant operation are more eroded than similar soils with a 20-year history of owner-operation. In a Texas watershed, covering several major physiographic areas, erosion on

[40] Peter Nelson, "Land Tenure and Agricultural Conservation," *Current Farm Economics*, Oklahoma Agricultural Experiment Station, Stillwater, Vol. 11, No. 2, April 1938, p. 29.

tenant farms was slightly though invariably greater as indicated in the following table:

Area*	Full owner	Mortgage owner	Tenant
West Cross Timbers	100	102	113
Grand Prairie	100	105	101
East Cross Timbers	100	102	105
Blackland Prairie	100	108	115
Gulf Coastal Plain	100	104	139
Total	100	105	108

* *Watershed Flood Control Survey, Trinity River, Texas,* United States Department of Agriculture, unpublished data based on 424 farms. Erosion index equals 100 on full owner farms.

And on the mortgaged owner-operated farms there was some indication of greater relative erosion. In southwest Oklahoma,[41] in an area including parts of the regional sample area, similar measurements on farms with 20-year histories of various types of operators shows an erosion index of 126 for the mortgaged owner farm and 144 for the tenant-operated farm as compared to the full owner index of 100. Thus, erosion apparently varies between farms depending to some extent on the tenure history of those farms.

The preceding discussion has shown that there are some features of the land tenure pattern and conservation practices that are not in harmony. It is necessary to study these features and to the extent possible determine why these relationships exist between tenure and conservation. In the face of a nationally recognized need for conservation why is the actual application making such little headway on many farms? And what is the effect of the tenure system in this regard?[42]

Despite the broad appeal for stewardship of the land as an investment for posterity, a basic question of the owner-operator, or even the tenant, rests on the answer to the question "Does it pay me?" An examination into this question and the additional question "When does it pay me?" is revealing.

Costs and Benefits of Conservation

Each individual in the tenure system, lacking other incentives, builds his plans for a conservation program around the economic concepts of costs and benefits. It serves the individual operator no

[41] *Watershed Flood Control Survey, Washita River, Oklahoma,* United States Department of Agriculture, unpublished data.

[42] Some of the difficulties presumably lie within the conservation programs. However, an examination of these programs, as such, is not an objective of this discussion.

apparent gain if he performs something only for posterity or for those operators who follow him on a particular farm. He must ask, "What is the likely return to me for the period of time that I may remain on this unit?" He begins to think in terms of farm reorganization, new crops, new enterprises, and actual physical costs of conservation installation. These costs include (1) temporary reduction in crop production during the first few years of the program (2) maintenance costs which are relatively high during the first two to five years (3) recommended shifts from cash to noncash crops (4) increased investment in livestock (5) temporary reduction in livestock where overgrazing is marked and (6) annual recurring costs in connection with new enterprises and maintenance. Any one or several of these costs may result on any one unit during the installation period.

Let it be assumed that the economic benefits to the individuals involved will exceed costs after a certain period of time. The time period necessary to realize net benefits may be two, five, or fifteen years. The length of time matters little. All parties sharing rights in land have to *wait.* This wait occurs regardless of the fact that title to land has changed at rather rapid rates throughout the region. Tenant operators change even more rapidly.

In the sample of farmers included in this study more than one-half of all tenant operators had resided on their present farm less than five years. (Table 97) In Oklahoma almost one-third of the owner-operators had lived on their units less than this period. Occupancy for a five-year period is significant since the usual comprehensive conservation program requires at least this length of time for installation and some realization of benefits. This is true particularly of additional livestock enterprises where the usual operator must "grow" into the business with both livestock and pastures.

Thus, the period of waiting for benefits to exceed costs becomes paramount in the conservation performance of an individual. An excellent example of the time involved in realization of economic benefits from conservation is available from recent conservation surveys.[48] In the installation of a program in a range area the rate of grazing had to be reduced about 35 per cent. The total period involved in this reduction amounted to nine years. After about ten years the benefits are great enough to increase the stocking rate to slightly above that previous to installation of a program. Thereafter, economic

[48] *Survey Report on the Trinity River Watershed,* United States Department of Agriculture, House Document No. 708, 1942.

benefits increase proportionately with a grazing capacity of about 150 per cent of that at the beginning of the program.

Another example of delayed benefits and the subsequent loss in income to the farm and to a tenant operator is illustrated in the following table showing the cumulative farm income due to conservation for the first 15 years of a program on a normal-crop farm, West Cross Timbers Area, Texas:

Year of Program*	Farm	Landlord	Tenant
	Dollars	*Dollars*	*Dollars*
1st	-121	- 66	- 35
2nd	-247	-175	- 72
3rd	-380	-269	-111
4th	-520	-368	-152
5th	-667	-472	-195
6th	-518	-136	-382
7th	-361	- 94	-267
8th	-197	- 52	-145
9th	- 24	- 6	- 18
10th	157	41	116
11th	348	91	257
12th	547	143	404
13th	757	198	559
14th	977	255	722
15th	1,209	317	892

* Unpublished data from *Trinity River Watershed Flood Control Survey, Texas.* United States Department of Agriculture.

An increasing loss is shown each year up through the first five years for the farm and through six years for the tenant. This total loss for the tenant amounts to $382 before gains begin to cancel cumulative losses. In the tenth year all cumulative losses have been regained and a net income over-all losses results.

These examples illustrate that over a long period this farm operator would have economic benefits from range and farmland conservation practices. But what about the period of years when the number of grazing animals are reduced to restore favorable pasture conditions and when crop income was reduced due to reorganization? This is the critical point of conservation and constitutes the period that determines performance of the individual operator. The tenant with only short-term occupancy hardly can afford to participate in a practice that requires nine years for economic realization. Also, many owner-operators will hesitate to expend funds on such a venture.

To indicate the magnitude of the problem of costs, the above study reports, "At the beginning of the program about one-half the farms will experience some decrease in income." More than 10 per cent of all the farms would require four years or more for increases in income to amortize costs of the program. Some farms were found to be so badly eroded and depleted in fertility that benefits would never exceed the costs to the individual. On such farms there is little likelihood that the operators would cooperate in a program unless it is heavily subsidized. A recent report on conservation in the West Cross Timbers Area of Texas says, "The cost of applying the land treatment is far more than present owners of the poor farms can afford to pay. It has been calculated that the cost of erosion and run-off control on a typical farm would be as much as the net income that could be expected from the land in 13 years."[44] In a north central area of Mississippi "it will take approximately three years for his (the farmer's) annual cash income to equal or exceed the annual costs" on a typical farm of 135 acres.[45]

In view of these costs the individual tenant operator, and too often the short-term owner, has little prospect of capitalizing expected future benefits into present value. Direct installation costs of a comprehensive conservation program may not, and perhaps does not, cost the tenant directly in terms of cash expense. This is usually the case in light of the generally used leasing arrangements that permit little or no improving on the part of the tenant. His costs are due to temporary reductions in income, a cost which, though indirect, is none the less real, and sometimes sizable in amount.

It is not difficult to see why many tenants cannot participate in active conservation programs. Moreover, under certain conditions there may be realistic objection to renting farms with a recently installed program. A tenant moving to a new farm must keep in mind certain factors in regard to his status and its relationship to conservation. If his tenure promises to be of short or uncertain duration (the usual situation existing), it will be to his economic interest to inquire relative to any temporary reductions in livestock numbers or acres in

---

[44] Soil Conservation Service, United States Department of Agriculture, statement as reported in *Ft. Worth Star Telegram*, Ft. Worth, Texas, April 21, 1946.

[45] *Survey of the Little Tallahatchie Watershed in Mississippi*, United States Department of Agriculture, House Document No. 892, p. 70.

cash crops due to the installation of conservation practices. It is under such influences that the tenant might refuse a farm unit with a newly executed program. On the other hand, if the program has become an established part of a farm's practices and has had sufficient time to obtain benefits, then tenants may find that farm more desirable and bid for it. Landowners should be benefited in the long run by the quality of tenant obtained if they can afford the costs involved during the early years of a program, and if they can keep progressive installation going with frequent changes of operators.

Exploitation vs. Conservation

In addition to the direct and indirect costs and the delayed benefits involved in a conservation program other factors tend to operate to discourage conservation on the part of the individual operator. Among these factors the most important one appears to be that exploitation, on a short-time basis at least, apparently has paid the individual operator. An example of how exploitation pays under certain conditions is shown by a study of pasture management practices in Oklahoma.[46] An owner-operator, by overgrazing or exploiting his rangeland in 1945, could increase his income from $2,402 to $3,337 on 640 acres of pasture. A renter, leasing 640 acres of pasture on a per acre basis, gained $794 net by overgrazing. "The owner-operator received not only the highest total net return for the overgrazed unit, but also a higher rate of return on the larger total investment in steers and land."

And for a renter the conclusion reached was that under a situation where grazing land was rented out at so much per acre, "it was clearly to the cattle owner's (a tenant in this case) immediate interest to overgraze."

In so far as the individual renter is concerned, loss of capital assets through his misuse has to be borne by the landlord. As one writer states, ". . . the gain from exploitation is shared between the tenant and the landlord, but the total capital loss will generally be borne by the landlord. When this is true, it is to the tenant's advantage to exploit the soil as long as the exploitive system gives a higher annual return than conservation, regardless of the permanent damage done to the land."[47] To carry this a bit further, what has been the position of

---

[46] Peter Nelson, "Land Tenure and Pasture Conservation," *Current Farm Economics*, Oklahoma Agricultural Experiment Station, Stillwater, Vol. 18, No. 6, December 1945, pp. 142-43.

[47] A. C. Bunce, *The Economics of Soil Conservation*, The Iowa State College Press, Ames, Iowa, 1942, p. 95.

the landowner in regard to exploitation? In the instance where an owner-operator exploits the land where does the capital loss fall? Perhaps on the owner himself if the period of ownership is long enough. However, in the long run the capital loss falls on society as is evidenced by the great public effort in conserving and restoring the capital plant.

Conservation Programs and Tenure

Probably the greatest effort in conservation is being carried on by the United States Department of Agriculture through the Soil Conservation Service. Cooperation of this public agency is obtained by individual farmers through state-organized soil conservation districts. What are some of the actual experiences in tenure performance of this public conservation agency?

Certain trends have been noted in the previous information given in this chapter. Large farms participate in an action program for conservation to a greater extent than small ones. Owner-operators performance in conservation is at a greater rate than that of tenants. The administrative problem of obtaining cooperation of absentee and certain other types of landowners is difficult. There are other tenure factors which have been recognized by the Department of Agriculture in its program.

One of the most important of these is the necessity of planning for conservation on the basis of ownership tracts. In other words, the operating unit has to be ignored unless it happens to be synonomous with the ownership tract. This results in conservation planning for a particular tract of land rather than a unit of land as a "going concerns" or for an operating unit of land as the base of a farm family's welfare. Thus, the necessary integrated reorganization of the unit for conservation becomes highly improbable on many farms. The basis on which such conservation rests may be too tenuous to be of a permanent nature. The practice of planning for ownership tracts was a practical recognition by the Soil Conservation Service that the landowner is responsible for conservation under present leasing arrangements. The tenure system has given the owner the larger share of the rights associated with use and possession, thereby leaving with him the decision and responsibility for conservation.

A recent development in public policy re-emphasizes the differences in rights in land and conservation performances between tenure groups. A Federal Reserve Bank has announced a credit plan to finance a program of land improvements and conservation.[48] The practical application of this credit plan extends only to landowners. The final result of this type of credit may mean an enhanced rate of conservation. It may serve also to bring out greater tenure differences in conservation performance in favor of the landowners.

SUMMARY AND CONCLUSIONS

The chief objective of this chapter was to show the relationship, if any, between tenure and conservation performance. Conservation performances differ between tenure groups in relationship to land use, farm practices, and the actual participation in conservation programs.

1. Land parcels in the region are subject to frequent transfer thus retarding and discouraging long-time conservation programs. Related to this is a lack of conservation philosophy, resulting from an attitude born in the past when judicious use of soil resources appeared unnecessary.

2. Spatial size of a farm unit is related to conservation. Settlement policies have anchored the farm production pattern to what is now an outmoded ownership pattern. Large numbers of farms are now too small to adjust their enterprise organization to requirements of conservation. Therefore, performance of the smaller tracts in conservation practices is relatively low.

3. Certain land uses and land-use practices are characteristic of conservation or nonexploitive farming. The performance of tenant-operators in these conservation uses and practices is at a lower rate than owner-operators. Renters tend more toward cash crops which for the region are also soil depleting. Smaller numbers of livestock are kept and therefore fewer acres of hay and pasture are necessary.

4. Participation in conservation programs is relatively greater among owner-operators. The experience of active public agencies in field operations has been that the task of executing conservation plans on tenant farms depends largely on the efforts of the landowner.

5. The type of landowner influences the progress of conservation programs. Female landholders, estates, and those who own land primarily for anticipated mineral values show a relative lack of interest in conservation. In certain areas of the region these types of owners are of considerable significance.

6. Leasing arrangements, frequently oral and depending primarily

[48] For a discussion of this plan see J. D. Black, "Tailored Credit for Land Improvements," *Journal of Farm Economics*, XXVIII (May 1946), pp. 596-604.

on custom, are usually for only one year at a time. The tenant feels that he does not have enough rights in the land to justify the initiation of conservation practices. Terms of most written leases as well as the law discourage better farming improvements on the part of the tenant. Incentives are lacking for both the tenant and the owner, the former because he cannot expect to reap future benefits of conservation, the latter because he feels any investment he makes for conservation may be jeopardized by a rapid turnover in operators.

7. Installation of a comprehensive program for conservation is generally accompanied by costs, either directly in cash outlay or indirectly through temporary losses of income. Because of short-time leasing arrangements the tenant usually foregoes practices that promise to pay off at a distant future date. Similarly, in any given year, exploitive practices apparently pay the individual renter-operator. These factors create widespread passiveness toward, and nonparticipation in, public programs of conservation.

8. Leasing arrangements and statutory enactments have established and maintained the owner's position with respect to possession and use. Consequently, the set-up of active conservation programs assumes that conservation is primarily the responsibility of the landowner.

9. The greatest tenure obstacles to conservation at the present time constitute high tenure mobility, few leases that include conservation practices, legal obstacles, and frequent land transfers.

10. A class of new landlords, of the urban occupation and residence groups, are participating to a marked degree in conservation programs. This is due partly to the fact that land has become a place of investment for their surplus nonfarm income.

11. It is recognized that factors other than land tenure concern the application of conservation programs. Education in the matter of soil-saving techniques, costs, and benefits are urgently needed.

12. Of great importance to conservation are the general price relationships existent at a given time. For example, high prices for beef and dairy products tend to promote conservation while the same situation for hogs, cotton, and cash grain tend to promote more exploitation.

13. Those tenure practices which are impediments to conservation are difficult to change since many of them are based on traditional procedures and attitudes.

CHAPTER VII

Legal Aspects of Land Tenure and Farm Credit

HISTORICAL BASIS OF TENURE LAW IN REGION

All states in the Southwestern Region except Louisiana, where the civil law[1] prevails in civil matters,[2] have adopted the common law as the basis of their jurisprudence.[3] The English-speaking colonists brought the common law of England[4] with them when they settled the Eastern Seaboard. As settlement moved westward, the settlers established their system of law in the new states, and the common law became established in so far as such principles were applicable to the new conditions. However, where new states were formed from territory in which other systems had originally prevailed, as was true particularly in Louisiana and Texas, it became necessary to choose between the common law and other legal systems.[5]

The common law was adopted by statutory enactment in Arkansas, Oklahoma, and Texas and by court decision in Mississippi.[6] Under the acts of the three former states, the common law is declared in force only to the extent that it is not inconsistent with the Constitution and laws of the state; and, as is added in the Arkansas act, "so far as the same is applicable and of a general nature."[7] An Oklahoma enact-

[1] Civil law is that "system of jurisprudence held and administered in the Roman Empire, particularly as set forth in the compilations of Justinian and his successors . . . as distinguished from the common law of England and the canon law." Black, *Law Dictionary*, 3rd Ed. p. 332.

[2] Civil matters include all matters other than criminal.

[3] Jurisprudence is "the philosophy of law, or the science which treats of the principles of positive law and legal relations." Black, *Law Dictionary*, 3rd Ed., p. 1039.

[4] "The common law is that body of law and juristic theory, which was originated, developed, and formulated and is administered in England . . ." as distinguished from the Roman law, the modern civil law, the canon law, and other systems. Black *Law Dictionary*, 3rd Ed. p. 368.

[5] 11 *Am. Jur.*, pp. 156-157.

[6] Pope, *Dig. Stat. Ark.*, 1937, sec. 1679; *Okla. Stat. Ann.*, 1937, Tit. 12, sec. 2; Vernon, *Tex. Civ. Stat.*, 1947, Art. 1; *Hemingway* v. *Scales* (1868), 42 Miss. 1, 16.

[7] Pope, *Dig. Stat. of Ark.*, 1937, sec. 1679.

ment declares, "The common law, as modified by constitutional and statutory law, judicial decisions, and the conditions and wants of the people, shall remain in force in aid of the general Statutes of Oklahoma . . . ."[8]

The courts in Arkansas, Mississippi, Oklahoma, and Texas have leaned heavily on the common law in decisions involving tenure questions. For example, in these four states only a small part of the tenancy law is statutory, and the remainder is an adaptation of the common law to local conditions. The common law, however, is always in the background and fills in the many gaps not covered by statute. In contrast, Louisiana has a very detailed tenancy code.

The legal system of Louisiana, and to a lesser extent of Texas, reflects the early influence of two civil law nations, Spain and France. For many years preceding formation of the Republic in 1836, Texas was under Spanish law and, later, Mexican, a product of the former. Only a few years after establishment of the Republic, however, by act of the Fourth Congress, the common law of England was made the rule of decisions in the Republic. Since the fathers of the Republic of Texas were mostly Anglo-Saxons, emigrants from the United States, such action was to be expected. Having adopted the common law, the Texas Congress enacted various important modifications. Among others, "the Spanish community system of marital property rights was retained . . ."; and, "the laws exempting property, including the homestead, from forced sale were taken from Spanish prototypes . . ."[9] Both are a part of present Texas law.

French law had a marked influence on the legal system of Louisiana. Before 1700, law in Louisiana was imperfectly administered by military commanders. In 1712 an early French code, the Custom of Paris, became the law of Louisiana. The territory known as Louisiana then included that part of the Southwestern Region west of the Mississippi except Texas and remained under French sovereignty until 1763 when it was ceded to Spain. In 1769 all French law, excepting the "Black Code" or slave code, was abrogated by proclamation, and Spanish law took its place. Not until 1801 was Louisiana territory ceded back to France; and in 1803 France delivered possession to the United States.[10]

[8] *Okla. Stat. Ann.*, 1937, Tit. 12, sec. 2.

[9] George C. Butte, "Early Development of Law and Equity in Texas," 26, *Y. L. J.*, 1917, p. 699.

[10] John H. Wigmore, "Louisiana: The Story of Its Legal System," *So. L. Quar.*, 1916, Vol. I, p. 2.

During this latter short period of French ownership, France did not promulgate a system of laws, and Spanish law remained in force. Even after purchase by the United States, the territory continued under Spanish law, except that the Federal Constitution became supreme. The Act of Congress authorizing the President to take possession of the province (Oct. 31, 1803) vested in new officers the power to administer them. Subsequent acts passed in 1804 and 1805 expressly declared "that all laws in force in the territory at the passage of the act and not inconsistent with it, should continue in force until altered by legislation."[11]

In 1804 a territorial government was established for the new region, and in 1805 "the district of Orleans, substantially corresponding to the present state of Louisiana, was set apart and a separate government given." The ensuing 20 years saw Spanish, French, and common law all cited as authorities by lawyers.[12] During the next quarter century the foundations of the present laws of Louisiana took form. In this period a series of codes on various legal subjects was compiled and enacted. Louisiana codifiers took as their model the French code, "and in their discretion pruned from it unsuitable clauses, or added to it desirable provisions taken from other systems or suggested by their own experience. All helpful sources were freely sought, and there is no servile adherence to any model." It was not until March 28, 1928, that the last Spanish laws were repealed.[13]

On the following pages, the contrast between legal systems evolving from the civil law, particularly in Louisiana, and the laws of states following common law principles is sometimes very marked. Only a few of the many legal aspects of tenure which impinge on the problems statistically studied are examined here.

LEGAL RIGHTS IN LAND OF OWNERS, TENANTS, AND CROPPERS

The legal rights of farm people in the land they farm are important factors influencing how it is used. A fee simple owner has the maximum legal control over his land, subject of course to the rights of society to tax, to condemn and purchase for public purposes, and in various ways to regulate its use. However, the nature and scope of an owner's rights in land will depend on the estate or interest conferred by his particular title, which, as is revealed in the discussion below, frequently is less than a fee simple estate. Moreover, control

[11] *Ibid.*, p. 6.
[12] *Ibid.*, pp. 5, 9.
[13] *Ibid.*, pp. 13-14.

over use of an owner's land may be further restricted by covenants or conditions in deeds, purchase contracts, and mortgages.

Somewhat lower in the tenure hierarchy in terms of control over land farmed is the tenant and below him the sharecropper. The rights of a tenant or cropper are conferred by contract, written or oral, expressed or implied. The landlord or employer can confer upon his tenants or croppers no greater rights in the land than he himself possesses, but, within the limitations of legality, he is free to restrict them as he desires. Cognizance should also be taken of various social and economic factors influencing use of farm land, including local customs, adequacy of earnings of the farm family, credit arrangements, and types and availability of markets.

Types of tenure in the Southwestern Region, as has been indicated, fall into 3 broad classes: owners, tenants, and croppers. These broad groups have been further segregated into subclasses. Owners may be either public or private, and private owners have been subdivided into the institutional, individual, and estate groups. Under another classification, owners are listed as full and part owners. Tenants have been subclassified, based on types of rental payments, as cash, share-cash, and share tenants.[14] The legal arrangements under which these various categories of owners (including public), tenants, and croppers hold their land have a material bearing on how it is farmed.

Geographical Distribution of Tenure

The greater proportion of the land area of the 5 states in the Southwestern Region is in private ownership. A relatively small percentage of the total was held by the federal government and by the states. Federal agencies owned 2.8 per cent in 1940 and 3.8 per cent in 1945. Another 2 per cent was owned by the states. (Table 98)[15] A summation of acreage owned by counties, municipalities, and various other local units of government was not available. In Oklahoma tax-delinquent lands forfeit to the counties. Other local governmental units in all 5 states often acquire farm lands on foreclosure of assessment liens.

The proportion of the total land area in 1940 in farms ranged from 34.6 in Louisiana to 81.6 in Texas.

The percentage of tenancy in the 5 states of the Southwestern Region in 1940 was as follows: Mississippi, 66.2; Louisiana, 59.4; Okla-

[14] For discussions and definitions of various classes of owners, tenants, and croppers, see succeeding sections in this chapter.

[15] For tables mentioned in this chapter refer to statistical tables in Appendix.

homa, 54.4; Arkansas, 53.3; and Texas, 48.9.[16] All states in the region exceed the national average in the proportion of farmers who are tenants or croppers. In general, the counties with the poorer land show the highest proportion of owner-operators (Figures 11, 12, and 13), and the better lands the higher proportion of tenancy (Figures 14, 15, 16, and 10).

The greatest concentration of part owners is found in counties in the western half of Oklahoma and Texas. (Figure 12) Major concentrations of full owners are found in central and eastern Texas; northern, western, and central Arkansas; western, central, and southeastern Louisiana; and in southeastern Mississippi. (Figure 11)

The counties with the highest proportion of tenancy are concentrated on the alluvial plain of the Mississippi River in Arkansas, Mississippi, and Louisiana, along the Red River in Arkansas and Louisiana, with another concentration in the Cross Timbers of Oklahoma and on the Texas Black Prairie. (Figure 10) The largest concentrations of cash tenants are found in Oklahoma and Texas (Figure 17); of share-cash tenants in Oklahoma (Figure 16); of share tenants in Oklahoma and Texas (Figure 15); and of croppers in Arkansas, Mississippi, and Louisiana (Figure 14).

Use of farm wage laborers was most prevalent in Texas and southern Louisiana, with minor concentrations in the 3 other states. (Figure 18)

Rights in Land of Owners

Rights in land of the various categories of owners are far from uniform. Equally dissimilar are purposes or reasons for holding title to rural land. Necessarily, the deviations in these reasons, purposes, and rights influence the way farm land is used.

Public Lands. Public agencies owning land in the region include the federal government and its instrumentalities, and state and local units of government.

The principal federal agencies holding rural land in the region in 1941 were the Indian Service, the Forest Service, the Fish and Wildlife Service, the General Land Office, the Grazing Service, and the Military services. Title to some farm land obtained by mortgage foreclosure was also held by federal lending agencies in all 5 states. Except for temporary ownership by its lending agencies, no rural land was reported held by the federal government in the sample areas.

Acreage of state-owned lands in the Southwestern Region in 1940

[16] U. S. Census, 1940.

varied from 141,466 acres in Mississippi to 3,660,418 acres in Texas. (Table 98) Some additional land was held by counties and local governmental units. Nonfederal, publicly-owned farm lands may be divided into two types: school and other grant and trust lands, and tax-forfeited lands. Ownership of both types, with some important exceptions, is temporary pending sale. Rural trust and school lands occurred in the samples, particularly in Mississippi and Oklahoma. Some tax-forfeited lands were found in each of the 5 areas.

Procedures for management of state trust and school lands and of tax-forfeited rural lands vary considerably from state to state. When land is offered at tax sale in Arkansas, Mississippi, Louisiana, and Texas and no person offers the amount of the taxes plus other sums due, the land is bid in for the state.[17] In Oklahoma, on the other hand, tax-sale land is bid off in the name of the county in which the sale takes place.[18] While state land officers in the former 4 states are generally responsible for the management and leasing, pending resale, of tax-forfeited land,[19] in Oklahoma these functions are performed by the boards of county commissioners.[20]

State school lands, swamp lands, and various grant and trust lands in Arkansas, Texas, and Oklahoma are also under the jurisdiction of the state land offices.[21] The same is true in Mississippi, except for sixteenth section school lands.[22]

Although rural lands owned by states or local governments in the region, particularly tax-forfeited lands, usually are for sale, there are some interesting exceptions. One such exception in Arkansas is state-owned land which is not suitable for private ownership. Under provisions of a 1939 act all state lands must be classified, based on their suitability for retention as public lands, or return to private ownership by sale or donation. The land commissioner selects the lands to be retained and administered by appropriate state or local agencies.[23]

[17] Pope, *Dig. Stat. Ark.*, 1937, sec. 13849; *Miss. Code Ann.*, 1942, sec. 9923; Dart, *La. Gen. Stat.*, 1939, sec. 8441; Vernon, *Tex. Civ. Stat.*, 1939, Art. 7288; see Vernon, *Tex. Civ. Stat.*, 1939, Art. 7345b secs. 2 and 9, authorizing a taxing unit to foreclose on tax-delinquent real estate and take title thereto for other inpleaded units. Also, in all states in the region improvement districts, necessarily, may foreclose to collect delinquent assessments.

[18] *Okla. Stat. Ann.*, 1942, Tit. 68, sec. 391.

[19] Pope, *Dig. Stat. Ark.*, 1937, sec. 8610; *Miss. Code Ann.*, 1942, sec. 4070; Dart, *La. Gen. Stat.*, 1939, secs. 8464 and 8470; Vernon, *Tex. Civ. Stat.*, 1947, Art 5251.

[20] *Okla. Stat. Ann.*, 1942 Tit. 68, sec. 432i.

[21] Pope, *Dig. Stat. of Ark.*, 1937, secs. 8621 and 8626; Vernon, *Tex. Civ. Stat.*, 1947, Arts. 5251, 5306, and 5307; *Okla. Stat. Ann.*, 1937, Tit. 64, secs. 1 and 241.

[22] *Miss. Code Ann.*, 1942, sec. 4070.

[23] *Acts of Ark.*, Act 331, p. 863, 1939.

Provision also is made for appraisal of all land before sale or donation.[24] Only unimproved land may be donated,[25] and then only in tracts no larger than can be worked by a farm family and no smaller than will produce for them an adequate living, considering location, fertility, and type of farming.[26]

Another exception of interest is sixteenth section school lands, and lands held in lieu thereof, in Mississippi. These lands may never be sold but, if rural, may be leased by public or private contract for terms not exceeding 15 years.[27] In contrast, other state lands in Mississippi may be leased for periods of only a year or less.[28] The county board of supervisors, under the general supervision of the state land commissioner, has general jurisdiction over sixteenth section school and lieu lands. However, the superintendent of education of each county, with the approval of the supervisors, is charged with leasing these rural lands.[29] In Louisiana, if voters in a township reject sale, sixteenth section school lands are leased by the parish board of school directors.[30]

The land office in Louisiana has jurisdiction over only a part of the state's public rural lands. A general law permits public landowning agencies, including the land office, penal, charitable and educational institutions, other state agencies, school, levee and drainage districts, and municipal or parochial subdivisions to lease their rural lands for terms not exceeding 5 years.[31] Leasing may be for trapping, grazing, hunting, agricultural, or any other legitimate purposes, except for oil, gas, or mineral development.[32] The maximum area which may be leased to any one person or corporation is 640 acres. Tracts to be leased must be advertised. Applicants are required to submit sealed bids. Annual rentals may not be less than 25 cents per acre. The lessor is empowered to include in each lease proper stipulations for the development of the land. All leases are heritable but are not subject to mortgage, pledge, hypothecation, or seizure and sale.[33]

Unsold state lands in Texas, also, may be leased for terms not exceeding 5 years, but all leases are subject to termination on sale of

[24] *Acts of Ark.*, Act 286, p. 626, 1943.

[25] Pope, *Dig. Stat. of Ark.*, 1937, sec. 8665.

[26] *Acts of Ark.*, Act 331, p. 863, 1939.

[27] *Miss. Code Ann.*, 1942, secs. 6597 and 6609.

[28] *Ibid.*, sec. 4095.

[29] *Ibid.*, secs. 6598 and 6609.

[30] Dart, *La. Gen. Stat.*, 1939, Supp. secs. 7245 and 7249.

[31] *Ibid.*, secs. 7317-7117.10.

[32] Another act, *ibid.*, secs. 7118-7318.7, permits some of the same public landowning agencies to lease land for mineral, oil, and gas purposes and developments.

[33] *Ibid.*, Supp. 1947, secs. 7317-7317.10.

the land.[34] Improvements made by lessees on state-owned land in Texas are declared to be personal property and may be removed by the lessees at expiration of the lease or within 60 days thereafter.[35]

The Oklahoma Land Office uses two types of lease contracts in renting rural state-owned lands, the preference and the nonpreference right lease. Under the preference right lease, which is authorized for renting only some classes of state lands, the tenant is granted an initial 5-year term, with a preference right to renew.[36] He also is entitled to a preference right to purchase the land leased at the highest bid at time of sale, or, in case of no bid, at an appraised value.[37] If preference right lands are sold to persons other than the lessee, the buyer must reimburse the lessee for the value of all agricultural and grazing improvements and structures erected on the premises.[38] Rental rates of preference right lands are 3 per cent of the fair market value thereof, exclusive of improvements. However, if the market value of the land is greater than its value for the purpose for which it is being leased, a rental of not less than 3 per cent of that latter value may be charged.[39]

Where state-owned lands in Oklahoma are leased under a nonpreference right lease, the maximum lease term is also 5 years. In the event existing improvements thereon need repair or new improvements are needed to attract more desirable tenants, the commissioners of the land office may, in their discretion, grant a preference right lease in favor of a tenant who will make the repairs or improvements. However, before a preference right lease is issued, the tenant must pay the state for existing improvements on the lease tract.[40]

Institutional Lands. Included in the institutional landowner category are insurance companies, banks, and corporations. Insurance companies and banks are usually unwilling owners temporarily holding title acquired in collecting debts. This, also, is frequently true of leases in the Arkansas area, 4.0 per cent in Mississippi, 8.4 per cent in Oklahoma,[41] and 10.2 per cent in the Texas sample area. (Table 67) Institutions, including minor holdings by government in 7 selected

[34] Vernon, *Tex. Civ. Stat.*, 1947, Art. 5331.

[35] *Ibid.*. Art. 5337.

[36] See *Noel* v. *Barrett* (1907), 18 Okla. 304, 90 Pac. 12; *Okla. Stat. Ann.*, 1937, Tit. 64, sec. 89.

[37] *Okla. Stat. Ann.*, 1937, Tit. 64, sec. 184.

[38] *Ibid.*, sec. 188, See *Okla. Stat. Ann.*, 1937, Supp. 1947, Tit. 64, sec. 86.1.

[39] *Ibid.*, Tit. 64, sec. 86.1

[40] *Okla. Stat. Ann.*, 1937, Tit. 64, sec. 86.

[41] State and county school lands were included in the institutional landlord category in Mississippi and Oklahoma.

parishes in Louisiana, own 4.8 to 17.8 per cent of the ownership tracts. (Table 70)

Laws in all 5 states in the region regulate and limit ownership of rural land by institutional owners. For example, insurance companies in Arkansas within 5 years must sell real property acquired as a result of default in payment of loans. Five years are also allowed in Mississippi and Louisiana and 10 years in Texas, unless the time for disposition is extended by state insurance officials.[42] In Oklahoma a general law, discussed below, limits rural land ownership by all types of corporations.[43]

Comparable laws require banks to dispose of real estate acquired in liquidation of debts. National banks may not hold such realty for a longer period than 5 years. The same is true of banks operating under state laws in Louisiana and Oklahoma, but in the latter state the time of sale may be extended an additional 2 years. If state banks in Arkansas or Mississippi hold real estate acquired through collection of debt longer than the initial 5-year period, plus any extension granted by state banking officials which in Mississippi may not exceed an additional 5 years, such real estate cannot be carried as book assets of the bank. Although an old Texas act, now repealed, required banks to dispose of real estate acquired in settlement of debts within 5 years, no such provision was found in the Texas Banking Code of 1943.[44]

Corporations are artificial beings created by statute and have authority to perform only such acts as are granted by law and are expressed or implied from their charters. In Arkansas, Mississippi, and Louisiana private corporations may be formed for any lawful business purposes,[45] including owning and leasing land.[46] A Mississippi act specifically provides that no restrictions shall obtain against a corporation holding land for farming uses, "except that no one corporation shall hold and cultivate for agricultural purposes more than ten thousand acres of land in any one year."[47] The constitution

---

[42] Pope. *Dig. Stat. Ark.*, 1937, sec. 7683; *Miss. Code Ann.*, 1942, sec. 5653; Dart, *La. Gen. Stat.*, 1939, Supp. 1947, sec. 4006; Veron, *Tex. Civ. Stat.*, 1940, Art. 5008.

[43] *Okla. Stat. Ann.*, 1937, Supp. 1947, Tit. 18, sec. 86, 86a-1.

[44] *U. S. C. A.*, Tit. 12 sec. 29; Dart, *La. Gen. Stat.*, 1939, sec. 543; *Okla. Stat. Ann.*, 1936, Supp. 1947, Tit. 6, sec. 108 f; Pope, *Dig. Stat. Ark.*, 1937, sec. 777; *Miss. Code Ann.*, 1942, sec. 5216; see Vernon, *Tex. Civ. Stat.*, 1925, Art. 514; and Texas Banking Code of 1943 in Vernon, *Tex. Civ. Stat.*, 1947, Arts. 342-101, *et seq.*

[45] Certain exceptions irrelevant here are listed. See Pope, *Dig. Stat. Ark.*, 1937, sec. 2129; *Miss. Code Ann.*, 1942, sec. 5309; Dart, *La. Gen. Stat.*, 1939, sec. 1081.

[46] Pope, *Dig. Stat. Ark.*, 1937, sec. 2134; *Miss. Code Ann.*, 1942, sec. 5329; Dart, *La. Gen. Stat.*, 1939, sec. 1092.

[47] *Miss. Code Ann.*, 1942, sec. 5329, Miss. Laws 1926, Ch. 253.

in Louisiana forbids corporations possessing land, "except for legitimate corporate purposes for a longer period than ten years."[48]

Statutes in Texas and Oklahoma list specific purposes for which private corporations may be formed. Inferentially, purposes not enumerated are forbidden. Corporations in Texas, excluding all nonagricultural activities, may be formed to grow nursery seeds and plants, fruit, vegetables, tobacco, sugar cane, and rice; to raise livestock; and to carry on an apiary business.[49] A statute enacted before the turn of the century forbids private corporations whose main purpose is the acquisition of land to acquire thereafter any land within the state by purchase, lease, or otherwise. All other private corporations doing business in the state may acquire only such real estate as is necessary to enable them to carry on their business, and all other, including that acquired for debt, must be sold in fee simple within 15 years after acquisition.[50]

Farming or ranching is not included in the enumeration of purposes for which private corporations may be formed in Oklahoma. Moreover, a Corporate Land Holding Act passed in 1937, later embodied in the Business Corporation Act of 1947, forbids corporations from holding or owning any real estate located outside of incorporated cities or towns, except real estate acquired in the collection of debt, which is not necessary or proper for the transaction of the business for which the corporation was chartered. Real estate acquired for debt must be disposed of within 7 years after acquisition.[51]

Individually Owned Land. Fifty-four to 77 per cent of the owners of land in seven selected parishes in Louisiana in 1939 were individuals. (Table 70) Although data by type of owners are not available for the other 4 states, the great bulk of the landlords sampled were individuals. Individuals, both male and female, comprised 86 per cent of the sample landlords holding leases in Arkansas and 93, 84, and 81 per cent, respectively, in Mississippi, Oklahoma, and Texas. (Table 67)

Title to land in the individual ownership category may be held by unmarried individuals, by husband or wife as his or her separate property, by the spouses, or by other persons in one of several forms of common ownership. Laws of the 5 states relating to individual ownership of property vary greatly.

[48] *La. Const.*, Art. XIII, sec. 1.
[49] Vernon, *Tex. Civ. Stat.*, 1945, Art. 1302, sub-sec. 8, 20, 22, 25, 26, and 28.
[50] *Ibid.*, Arts. 1359-1362; Texas Acts 1893, p. 36; 1897, p. 48.
[51] *Okla. Stat. Ann.*, 1937, Supp. 1947, Tit. 18, sec. 1.20; Okla. Laws 1937, pp, 314-17; 1947, p. 92, Sec. 20.

Two schemes of marital property rights are found in the region. One, developed from the common law, is found in Arkansas, Mississippi, and Oklahoma. The other, the community property system, an institution of the civil law, is established in Louisiana and Texas, and is optional in Oklahoma.

—Under the common law. At common law, the husband during marriage is entitled to possession and control of real estate owned by his wife, whether owned by her at wedlock or acquired during coverture. The husband is absolute owner of the rents and profits from his wife's real estate, and this right he can alienate to another.[52] If a child capable of inheriting is born of the marriage, the husband becomes entitled to enjoy the land during his lifetime. This right, known as curtesy initiate, becomes consummate or vested if the wife predeceases him.[53] During the marriage, the wife has no power to alienate her land without her husband's consent.[54] Similarly, under the common law a widow is entitled for her life to one-third of the realty of which her husband was seised[55] of an estate of inheritance at any time during the marriage.[56] The right of dower is a contingent interest during coverture and becomes consummate upon the husband's death.[57] Even before his death she cannot be deprived of dower by any voluntary act of the husband.[58]

—Under adaptations of the common law. The common law system of marital property rights has been revolutionized in Mississippi and Oklahoma and partially in Arkansas, the three states in the region which in 1942 followed its general scheme. Common law disabilities of married women have been abrogated. In all three states, under present laws, the real and personal property acquired by a woman before or after marriage remains her separate property which, except in Oklahoma, she may dispose of without consent of her husband.[59]

When land is conveyed or devised to both husband and wife a

---

[52] See Thompson, *Real Property*, Perm. Ed., 1939, Vol. 2, sec. 835; and Pollock & Maitland, *History of English Law*, 2nd Ed., 1923, Vol. 2, pp. 403, 407.

[53] Thompson, *Real Property*, Perm. Ed., 1939, Vol. 2, sec. 842.

[54] Pollock & Maitland, *History of English Law*, 2nd Ed., 1923, Vol. 2, p. 404.

[55] "The word 'seised' is used to express the 'seisin' or owner's possession of a freehold property . . ." "Seisen" applies exclusively to the possession of land of a freehold tenure, and not to possession of leaseholds. At common law " 'Seisen' imported a feudal investiture of title by actual possession. With us it has the force of possession under some legal title or right to hold." Black, *Law Dictionary*, 3rd Ed., p. 1597.

[56] Tiffany, *Real Property*, 3rd Ed., 1939, Vol. 2, secs. 487 and 489.

[57] Thompson, *Real Property*, Perm. Ed., 1939, Vol. 2, sec. 869.

[58] Tiffany, *Real Property*, 3rd Ed., 1939, Vol. 2, sec. 487.

[59] *Ark. Const.*, Art. 9, sec. 7; *Miss. Const.*, Art. 4, Sec. 94; *Miss. Code Ann.*, 1942, sec. 451; *Okla. Stat. Ann.*, 1937, Supp. 1947, Perm. Ed. Tit. 32, secs. 4 and 8.

tenancy in common, unless provided otherwise, is created in Mississippi[60] and each owns an undivided one-half interest therein.[61] The same rule applies in Oklahoma,[62] but in Arkansas a deed to a husband and wife jointly creates an estate by the entirety,[63] and the survivor takes the whole fee.[64] Neither owner by the entirety can impair the rights of the other by his or her sole act;[65] nor can acts respecting the title by one tenant in common bind the other.[66]

A widow's dower in Arkansas entitles her to a life interest in one-third of all the lands of which her husband was seised of an estate of inheritance at any time during marriage, and to one-third absolutely of the personal estate which he possessed at death.[67] If the husband dies leaving no children, the widow's dower is one-half of his personalty absolutely and one-half of the real estate in fee simple of which he died seised, except ancestral realty[68] of which she is endowed one-half for life. Against creditors her dower portion is one-third of the real estate in fee simple, if a new acquisition; one-third for life, if ancestral realty; and one-third of the personalty absolutely.[69] A married woman of course may release her dower.[70]

The surviving husband under Arkansas law has a right of curtesy only in the estate not disposed of during his wife's life or by her will. If she leaves descendants, he is entitled to one-third of her realty for life and one-third of her personalty absolute. If she leaves no descendants, his portion is one-half of her personalty absolute and one-half of her realty in fee, except for ancestral real estate of which he is entitled to a life estate in one-third. His portion is further reduced if there are creditors.[71]

---

[60] *Miss. Code Ann.*, 1942, sec. 834.

[61] *Conn* v. *Boutwell* (1912), 101 Miss. 353; 58 So. 105, 106.

[62] *Haugh* v. *Continental Oil Co.* (1943), 192 Okla. 345; 136 P. (2d) 691, 692; *Hamra* v. *Fitzpatrick* (1916), 55 Okla. 780; 154 p. 665, 667.

[63] "A 'tenancy in common' is where two or more hold the same land, with interests accruing under different titles, or accruing under the same title, but at different periods, or conferred by words of limitation importing that the grantees are to take in distinct shares. . . . A 'tenancy by the entirety' is created by a conveyance to uhsband and wife, whereupon each becomes seized and possessed of the entire estate and after the death of one the survivor takes the whole." Black, *Law Dictionary*, 3rd Ed., pp. 711, 713.

[64] *Naler* v. *Ballew* (1907), 81 Ark. 328; 99 S. W. 72, 73.

[65] *Pope* v. *McBride* (1945), 207 Ark. 940; 184 S. W. (2d) 259, 262.

[66] Tiffany, *Real Property*, Vol. 2, 1939, sec. 426.

[67] Pope, *Dig. Stat. Ark.*, 1937, secs. 4396 and 4420.

[68] "Ancestral realty" has been defined as that "which comes to one by descent or devise from a now dead ancestor, or by a deed or actual gift from a living one; there being no other consideration than that of blood . . . ." Black, *Law Dictionary*, 3rd Ed., p. 108.

[69] Pope, *Dig. Stat. Ark.*, 1937, sec. 4421.

[70] *Ibid.*, sec. 1815.

[71] *Ark Acts*, 1939, No. 313, sec. 1, p. 767, amending Pope, *Dig. Stat. Ark.*, 1937, sec. 4422.

Dower and curtesy have been expressly abolished in Mississippi and Oklahoma.[72]

—Under the community property system. The community property system of marital rights has been incorporated into the statutes of 3 states in the region: Louisiana, Texas, and Oklahoma. In the latter state the husband and wife may elect to come under the provisions of the statute. This system of marital property rights was established by the Spaniards in their possessions in America and later was incorporated into the Code Napoleon. The first community property system in Louisiana combined French and Spanish elements. Traces of Louisiana origin also are found in the early Texas Code.[73] Present community property systems in the 3 states however indicate much statutory and court decision development.

Under the community property laws of Louisiana, Texas, and Oklahoma, all property, both real and personal, owned by either spouse before marriage and that acquired by each individually during coverture by gift, devise, or descent remains his or her separate property.[74] Also separate property in Louisiana is that which either party "acquires during marriage by separate funds";[75] the "increase" in Texas of all separately owned lands;[76] sums received as "compensation for personal injuries" by the husband or wife in Oklahoma;[77] and by the wife in Louisiana and Texas.[78]

Under the community property system in the 3 states all property acquired by either husband or wife during marriage, except that heretofore defined as separate, belongs in common to the community, one-half to each spouse.[79] Acquests or gains in Louisiana are presumed to be community property, unless there is an agreement to the contrary;[80] and in Texas, unless it is proved otherwise.[81] In Oklahoma,

[72] *Miss. Code Ann.*, 1942, sec. 453; *Okla. Stat. Ann.*, 1937, Tit. 32, sec. 9, and Tit. 84, sec. 214.

[73] Chester G. Vernier, *American Family Law*, Stanford Univ. Press, 1935, Vol. 3, sec. 178, p. 208, citing George McKay, *The Law of Community Property*, sec. 6, p. 4.

[74] Dart, *La. Civ. Code*, 1945, Art. 2334; Vernon, *Tex. Civ. Stat.*, 1940, Arts. 4613 and 4614; *Okla. Stat. Ann.*, 1939, Supp. 1947, Tit. 32, secs. 66 and 67; *Okla. Laws*, 1945, p. 118.

[75] Dart, *La. Civ. Code*, 1945, Art. 2334.

[76] Vernon, *Tex. Civ. Stat.*, 1940, Arts. 4613, 4614.

[77] *Okla. Stat. Ann.*, 1937, Supp. 1947, Perm. Ed. Tit. 32, sec. 66, 67.

[78] Dart, *La. Civ. Code*, 1945, Art. 2402; Vernon, *Tex. Civ. Stat.*, 1940, Art. 4615.

[79] *Ibid.*, Arts. 2334, 2386, 2402, 2406; *Phillips* v. *Phillips* (1926), 160 La. 813, 825; Vernon, *Tex. Civ. Stat.*, 1940, Art. 4619; *Okla. Stat. Ann.*, 1937, Supp. 1947, Tit. 32, sec. 68.

[80] Dart, *La. Civ. Code*, 1945, secs. 2399, 2400.

[81] Vernon, *Tex. Civ. Stat.*, 1940, Art. 4619; but see Art. 4622 providing that bank deposits in the name of either husband or wife are presumed separate property.

of course, the husband and wife may elect to hold real and personal property as joint tenants, tenants in common, or as community property.[82]

Under the law in all 3 states, each spouse has management and control of his or her separate property, but the husband as head of the household administers the community estate.[83] The husband generally may alienate community effects without consent of the wife;[84] but in Louisiana he may not mortgage or sell community property without his wife's consent, where title is in her name;[85] and in neither Texas nor Oklahoma may he sell the family homestead, whether separately or community owned, without her consent.[86]

The two schemes of marital property rights found in the region may be briefly summarized and differentiated as follows: In the so-called common-law states, Arkansas, Mississippi, and Oklahoma, "all of the property of the spouses is owned separately by either the husband or the wife, or perhaps by both as tenants in common, joint tenants, or tenants by the entirety." In the community property states, Louisiana, Texas, and optional in Oklahoma, " . . . the property of the spouses is either the separate property of the husband, the separate property of the wife, or a part of 'the common fund of matrimonial gains' called the community property."[87] It is this fund of marital gains, owned by the community of husband and wife, which formally differentiates the community property system from the marital property system found in Arkansas, Mississippi, and, unless the spouses elect otherwise, in Oklahoma.

Estate Lands. As the term is here used, lands are deemed estate lands from the time of death of an individual owner until both title and right to immediate possession is passed to another owner. This period of time may be relatively short, pending administration of the estate by the courts; or it may be prolonged during the minority of children, and during the life of a surviving spouse who holds dower, curtesy, or homestead rights in the premises. The period may be

[82] *Okla. Stat. Ann.*, 1937, Supp. 1947, Tit. 32, sec. 8.

[83] Dart, *La. Civ. Code*, 1945, Art. 2404; Vernon, *Tex. Civ. Stat.*, 1940, Art. 4613; see Art. 4614; *Okla. Stat. Ann.*, 1937, Supp. 1947, Tit. 32, sec. 69.

[84] Dart, *La. Civ. Code*, 1945, Art. 2404; Vernon, *Tex. Civ. Stat.*, 1940, Art. 4619; *Okla. Stat. Ann.*, 1937, Supp. 1947, Tit. 32, sec. 69.

[85] Dart, *La. Civ. Code*, 1945, Art. 2334.

[86] Vernon, *Tex. Civ. Stat.*, 1940, Art. 4618; *Okla. Stat. Ann.*, 1937, Supp. 1947, Tit. 32. sec. 70.

[87] Chester G. Vernier, *American Family Law*, Stanford Univ. Press, 1935, Vol. 3, sec. 178, p. 208, citing George McKay, *The Law of Community Property*, sec. 178, p. 208.

further prolonged pending sale of the property jointly owned by several heirs or devisees.

Since estate lands usually are operated under some form of rental agreement, the proportion of all landlords falling into this category also quite accurately measures the percentage of all farms that are estate controlled. Estate landlords held 11.6 per cent of the sample leases in Arkansas, 3 per cent in Mississippi, 7.5 per cent in Oklahoma, and 8.4 per cent in Texas. (Table 67)[88] In 7 selected parishes in Louisiana, the percentage of all ownership tracts controlled by estates ranges from 2 to almost 30 per cent. (Table 70)

Title to land may be passed to others upon the death of the owner by will or, in the absence of a will, by state laws of descent. A "will" is a testamentary instrument, executed by any person who is competent, whereby he makes a disposition of his property to take effect after his death.[89] "Descent," or hereditary succession, is the title whereby a person on the death of his ancestor acquires his estate as his heir at law.[90]

—*Types of wills.* Real and personal property may be devised by every soundminded person aged 21 years and upwards in Arkansas and Mississippi, 18 years in Oklahoma, 16 years in Louisiana, and, in Texas, 21 years, or "who may be or may have been lawfully married or may be a member of the armed forces or maritime service."[91]

Three general types of wills are recognized: the formal written will, the holographic will (entire will intestator's handwriting), and the nuncupative (oral) will.

The formal written will is authorized for the disposition of both real and personal property in Arkansas, Mississippi, Oklahoma, and Texas. A will of this type must be subscribed by the testator the testatrix, or by some other person at his or her request, and attested by two or more creditable witnesses in the presence of the maker.[92]

---

[88] The difference in the percentage of estate landlords in Arkansas and Mississippi is due in part to differences in tenure of the lessees sampled. The Arkansas sample is composed of 233 tenants and 98 croppers, while the Mississippi sample is composed of 39 tenants and 87 croppers. Estates usually rent on a cash, share, or no-rent basis; croppers most frequently obtain land from male landlords. (Table 69.)

[89] *Harris* v. *Harris Estate* (Tex. C. A. 1925), 276 S. W. 964, 966.

[90] *Barclay* v. *Cameron* (1860), 25 Tex. 232, 241; *Parrish* v. *Mills*, (1908), 101 Tex. 276; 106 S. W. 882, 886.

[91] Pope, *Dig. Stat. Ark.*, 1937, sec. 14510; *Miss. Code Ann.*, 1942, sec. 657; Dart, *La. Civ. Code*, 1945, Arts. 1470, 1479; *Okla. Stat. Ann.*, 1938, Tit. 84, sec. 41; Vernon, *Tex. Civ. Stat.*, 1941, Supp. 1947, Art. 8281.

[92] Pope, *Dig. Stat. Ark.*, 1937, secs. 14512, 14513; *Miss. Code Ann.*, 1942, sec. 657; *Okla. Stat. Ann.*, 1938, Tit. 84, secs. 55, 56; Vernon, *Tex. Civ. Stat.*, 1941, Supp. 1947, Art. 8283.

A somewhat comparable type, called the mystic or sealed testament, is allowed in Louisiana. The testament or will must be drawn in writing by the testator, or under his direction, and signed by him. After it has been enclosed in an envelope and sealed, the testator, in the presence of a notary and witnesses, must declare that it contains his signed will. The notary then writes his superscription upon the envelope and it is signed by the testator, notary, and witnesses.[93]

A second general type of will, the holographic, may be used in all 5 states for devising realty or personalty. Holographic wills must be entirely written, dated, and signed by the hand of the testator and is established from the handwriting.[94] The third type, the nuncupative or oral will, is allowed in all states in the region except Louisiana where it has been expressly abolished.[95] A usual requirement for validity is that the will be made during the last illness or after injury and in expectation of immediate death. Also, the will must be proved by two or more witnesses who were present during the pronouncement and heard the decedent call upon someone to bear witness. Amounts that may be bequeathed by oral will may not exceed $500 in Arkansas or $1,000 in Oklahoma. In Texas and Mississippi the maximums are $30 and $100 respectively, unless the will is proved by two or more witnesses as above indicated.[96] Land, according to a Mississippi holding, cannot pass by nuncupative will.[97]

Although oral wills as such are not recognized in Louisiana, two variations thereof are allowed. Both real and personal property may be devised by either. When executing the first type, called nuncupative testament by public act, the testator dictates his will, in the presence of 3 to 5 witnesses, to a notary public who writes it down as it is dictated. The will is then read to the testator in the presence of the witnesses and signed by him and by the witnesses, or at least by one of them for all, if the others cannot write.[98] The second variation is called nuncupative testament under private signature. To effect this type, the testator may write the will himself or dictate it, in the presence of 3 to 7 witnesses, to some person who writes it

---

[93] Dart, *La. Civ. Code*, 1945, secs. 1574, 1575, 1584-1587.

[94] Pope, *Dig. Stat. Ark.*, 1937, sec. 14512; Dart, *La. Civ. Code*, 1945, Art. 1588; *Miss. Code Ann.*, 1942, sec. 637; *Okla. Stat. Ann.*, 1937, Tit. 84, sec. 54; Tit. 58, sec. 31; Vernon, *Tex. Civ. Stat.*, 1941, Supp. 1947, Arts. 8284, 3344.

[95] Dart, *La. Civ. Code*, 1945, sec. 1576.

[96] Pope, *Dig. Stat. Ark.*, 1937, secs. 14515-14518; *Miss. Code, Ann.*, 1942, secs. 663-665; *Okla. Stat. Ann.*, 1938, Tit. 84, secs. 46, 51; Vernon, *Tex. Civ. Stat.*, 1941, Arts. 8286-8289.

[97] *Sadler* v. *Sadler* (1882), 60 Miss. 251, 253.

[98] Dart, *La. Civ. Code*, 1945, Arts. 1577-1580.

down. The will is then read in the presence of all and signed by the testator and by at least 2 witnesses, the unlettered affixing their mark.[99]

—*Limitations on disposition by will—laws of descent.* The right to make a will is not a natural right but is a creature of statute. The legislature may subject the right to such regulations and restrictions as it sees fit.[100] The laws of the 5 states controlling the disposition of property by will vary greatly. Much variation is also found in laws transmitting property by descent, in the absence of a will.

Using broad language, an Arkansas statute empowers every sound-minded person over 21 years old to devise all his real and personal estate.[101] Restrictions on such sweeping powers, however, are soon apparent, when consideration is given to dower, homestead, and other rights of the surviving spouse and minor children. For example, if the husband devises land to his wife, or makes other provisions by will in lieu of dower, the widow may elect between taking under the will or claiming her dower in the lands and personal property of which he died seised.[102] Moreover, if the owner of a homestead[103] dies, leaving a widow without a separate homestead of her own, the rents and profits of his homestead vest in her during her life; if he also leaves minor children, she must share the income, giving one-half to any children who are under 21 years, and then all goes to the widow. She may reside on the homestead or not, as she desires.[104] The homestead insures to the benefit of the minor children after the decease of the parents.[105] An executor or administrator who undertakes to disturb the widow or minor children in the enjoyment of the homestead is both civilly and criminally liable.[106]

Under present Arkansas laws a married woman has greater leeway than her husband in devising her estate. She is free to dispose of or will her separate real and personal property, acquired either before or after marriage, to whomever she may choose.[107] The surviv-

[99] *Ibid.*, Arts. 1581-1583.

[100] Thompson, *Real Property*, Perm. Ed., 1940, Vol. 5, sec. 2681.

[101] Pope, *Dig. Stat. Ark.*, 1937, sec. 14510.

[102] *Ibid.*, sec. 4410, and sec. 4425 as amended by Ark. Acts, No. 66.

[103] A rural homestead in Arkansas consists of not exceeding 160 acres, with improvements, of a value not over $2,500, and in no event shall it be reduced to less than 80 acres, without regard to value. *Ark. Const.*, Art. 9, sec. 4; Pope, *Dig. Stat. Ark.*, 1937, sec. 7179.

[104] *Ark. Const.*, Art. 9, sec. 6; Pope, *Dig. Stat. Ark.*, 1937, sec. 7162.

[105] *Ibid.*, sec. 10; Pope, *Dig. Stat. Ark.*, 1937, sec. 7163.

[106] Pope, *Dig. Stat. Ark.*, 1937. sec. 7177

[107] *Ark. Const.*, Art. 9, sec. 7.

ing husband's right of curtesy attaches only to property not disposed of by her prior to death or given by will. [108] Neither husband or wife can devise an estate held by the entireties, since upon the death of one, the estate is the property of the survivor.[109] Except for the homestead rights of minors, a person may disinherit any or all his children, provided he names them in his will.[110]

When property is not disposed of by will, its transmission to the heirs is governed by laws of succession. In Arkansas real and personal property of an intestate descends, subject to dower, curtesy, and homestead rights, to the following classes of heirs, each class of which a member is living inheriting to the exclusion of the following classes: (1) to children, or their descendants, in equal parts; (2) to parents; (3) to brothers and sisters; (4) to grandparents; (5) to uncles and aunts, and so on without end, passing to the nearest lineal ancestor.[111] If the intestate dies without descendants, leaving an ancestral estate, it ascends to the parent through which it came, to the exclusion of the other parent.[112] If the deceased leaves no descendants nor kindred, the whole estate goes to the surviving spouse.[113]

Under Mississippi laws a parent may disinherit any or all children.[114] Neither spouse, however, may disinherit the other. If the will of either fails to make provision for the other, or makes an unsatisfactory provision, the survivor may elect to take the legal share of the estate, real and personal, he or she would be entitled to by descent, which may not exceed one-half of the estate.[115] There is one exception, however. If the surviving spouse has separate property equal in value to his or her lawful share of the decedent's estate, the survivor cannot defeat the will; but to the extent that such separate property is less than the lawful portion, the deficiency must be made up from the estate.[116] A co-tenant, or tenant in common, can devise his undivided interest in the property and no more.[117]

Under Mississippi succession, if either spouse dies intestate leaving no descendants, the surviving spouse inherits all the estate; but if the

---

[108] Pope, *Dig. Stat. Ark.*, Cum. Ann. Supp. 1944, 1939, sec. 4422a.
[109] Tiffany, *Real Property*, 3rd Ed., 1939, Vol. 2, sec. 435, p. 235.
[110] Pope, *Dig. Stat. Ark.*, 1937. sec. 14525; *Yeates* v. *Yeates* (1929), 179 Ark. 543 16 S. W. (2d) 996, 999.
[111] *Ibid.*, sec. 4338.
[112] *Ibid.*, sec. 4347.
[113] *Ibid.*, sec. 4344.
[114] *Miss. Code Ann.*, 1942, secs. 658 and 659.
[115] *Ibid.*, secs. 668, 669.
[116] *Ibid.*, sec. 670.
[117] Page, *Wills* (Lifetime Ed. 1941), Vol. 1, sec. 197, p. 399.

decedent left children, or descendants of children, he or she gets only a child's share.[118] Otherwise, the estate descends as follows, each class in which a member is living taking to the exclusion of the following classes: (1) children and their descendants, in equal parts; (2) brothers and sisters, father and mother; (3) next of kin in equal degree, computed by the rules of civil law.[119]

When the husband in Mississippi disposes of the family homestead[120] by will, the widow, even though she renounces the will as inadequate, cannot claim that specific property but only her share of the estate generally.[121] If, on the other hand, the husband or wife dies intestate, the homestead descends to the survivor, unless there are living children or grandchildren of the marriage. In the latter case the descendants and the surviving spouse inherit as tenants in common. However, if the surviving spouse owns a residence of equal value to the homestead and the deceased has descendants of a former marriage, the homestead descends to the latter.[122] The homestead, in cases of intestate succession to the widow and others, is not subject to partition without her consent during widowhood.[123] She may occupy the homestead free of rent,[124] or she may use the income from the property and reside elsewhere.[125]

Either spouse in Oklahoma may devise separate property[126] and also his or her share of the community estate.[127] Although children may be disinherited,[128] neither spouse may will the other less in value than would be obtained by succession at law, which, if the devise or bequest is of separate property, need not exceed one-half.[129] Except that either spouse may devise the homestead[130] to the other, neither may by will dispose of property which could not be alienated while

[118] *Miss. Code Ann.*, 1942, sec. 470.

[119] *Ibid.*, sec. 468.

[120] A rural homestead in Mississippi must not exceed 160 acres in area, nor $3,000 in value. *Miss. Code Ann.*, 1942, secs. 320, 322.

[121] *Nash* v. *Young*, 1856 (156), 31 Miss., 134, 135.

[122] *Miss. Code Ann.*, 1942, sec. 476; this section is operative only in case of intestacy. *Norris* v. *Callahan* (1881), 59 Miss. 140, 143.

[123] *Miss. Code Ann.*, 1942, sec. 478.

[124] *Martin* v. *Martin* (1904), 84 Miss. 553, 559.

[125] *Tiser* v. *McCain* (1917), 113 Miss. 776, 785.

[126] *Okla. Stat. Ann.*, 1938, Tit. 84, sec. 41, 42.

[127] *Ibid.*, 1937, Supp. 1947 Tit. 32, sec. 80.

[128] *Ibid.*, 1938, Tit. 84, sec. 132.

[129] *Ibid.*, 1938, Supp. 1947 Tit. 84, sec. 44.

[130] A rural homestead in Oklahoma shall consist of not to exceed 160 acres of land. *Okla. Const.*, Art. 12, sec. 1. *Okla. Stat. Ann.*, 1937, Tit 31, secs. 1, 2. It may consist of separate property of either spouse or of community or common property of both. *Okla. Stat. Ann.*, 1937, Supp. 1947, Tit. 32, sec. 70.

living, without consent of the other.[131] Upon the death of the husband or wife, the survivor may continue to occupy the whole homestead, and upon his or her death it may be occupied by the children until the youngest becomes of age. During this period the homestead is not subject to administration proceedings.[132] In addition to the homestead, there shall be set aside to the survivor, or minor children, all money and personal property used with the homestead as is exempt by law from levy and sale on execution.[133]

The estate, real and personal, of an intestate in Oklahoma descends one-half to the surviving spouse and one-half to children, if only one child or lawful issue of one child survive; one-third to the surviving spouse and two-thirds to the children, if two or more; one-half to surviving spouse and one-half to the parents, if there be no issue; one-half to surviving spouse and one-half to brothers and sisters, if there be no issue or parents; or all to the surviving spouse, if there be no issue, parents, brothers or sisters. If there be no surviving spouse, the estate descends as follows, each class in which a member is living inheriting to the exclusion of the subsequent classes: (1) children, or their issue; (2) parents; (3) brothers and sisters, or their descendants; (4) to next of kin; (5) escheats to the state.[134]

Either husband or wife in Texas may dispose of by will, as prescribed by law, all their separate property and their share of the community estate.[135] Neither spouse, however, may devise the community property of the other, and when this is attempted the survivor may elect between taking under the terms of the will or claiming the community interest to which he or she is entitled.[136] A parent may by will empower the surviving spouse to keep the decedent's separate estate together and manage it as if it were community property, until minor heirs, children of the deceased, become of age.[137]

Although children may be disinherited, a parent may not by will so dispose of his homestead[138] as to prevent its occupation and use by minor children,[139] or by the surviving spouse.[140] The homestead,

[131] *Okla. Stat. Ann.*, 1938, Supp. 1947 Tit. 84, sec. 44.

[132] *Ibid.*, 1937, Supp. 1947 Tit. 58, sec. 311 and Tit. 32, sec. 81.

[133] *Ibid.*, Tit. 58, sec. 312.

[134] *Ibid.*, 1938, Tit. 84, sec. 213.

[135] Vernon, *Tex. Civ. Stat.*, 1941, Supp. 1948, Arts. 8281, 8282.

[136] *Dunn* v. *Vinyard* (Tex. Com. App. A, 1923), 234 S. W. 99; 251 S. W. 1043, 1046.

[137] Vernon, *Tex. Civ. Stat.*, 1941, Art. 8298.

[138] A rural homestead in Texas consists of not more than 200 acres, with improvements thereon. *Tex. Const.* Art. 16, secs. 50, 51.

[139] *Hall* v. *Fields* (1891), 81 Tex. 553; 17 S. W. 82, 86.

[140] *Lindsley* v. *Lindsley* (1942), 139 Tex. 512; 163 S. W. (2d) 633, 636.

whether separate or community property, may not be partitioned among the heirs so long as the surviving husband or wife or guardian of minor children elect to use or occupy it.[141]

In Texas, with the community estate, upon the death of the husband or wife leaving no will, all descends to the surviving spouse, if there be no children or their issue; or, one-half to the surviving spouse and one-half to children, if one or more or their issue survive.[142] Other intestate property is transmitted as follows: If the decedent leaves a surviving spouse, one-third of the realty for life and one-third of the personalty absolute descends to the survivor, and the balance to the children, or their issue; or, if there be no children or their issue, then all the personalty and one-half of the realty in fee goes to the surviving spouse, and the balance to other heirs; or, if there be no surviving parents or brothers or sisters, or their issue, then all the estate goes to the surviving spouse.[143] If a person dies intestate leaving no surviving spouse, his property, real and personal, descends as follows, each class in which there is a living member taking to the exclusion of all succeeding classes: (1) children and their descendants; (2) parents equally, or all to the survivor unless the intestate's brothers or sisters, or their issue, are living, who then inherit the deceased parent's share; (3) brothers and sisters and their descendants; (4) grandparents and their descendants.[144]

All persons in Louisiana having testamentary capacity may by will dispose of their property,[145] subject, of course, to restrictions imposed by law. A married woman may devise her property without consent of her husband.[146] Community gains at dissolution of the marriage are to be divided equally between husband and wife or their heirs.[147] A spouse can devise only his or her share thereof.[148]

Legitimate children and their descendants and the decedent's parents are called "forced heirs." They cannot be disinherited except for just cause.[149] Ten grounds are recognized for disinheritance of children, and seven for parents.[150] A child may be deprived of his legal portion of the estate if he has struck the parent; been guilty of

[141] Vernon, *Tex. Civ. Stat.*, 1925, Arts. 3496, 3498, 3501.
[142] *Ibid.*, 1942, Art. 2578.
[143] *Ibid.*, Art. 2571.
[144] *Ibid.*, Art. 2570.
[145] Dart, *La. Civ. Code*, 1945, 2nd Ed., Art 1470.
[146] *Ibid.*, Art. 1480.
[147] *Ibid.*, Art. 2406.
[148] *Succession of John Geddes* (La. S. C. 1884), 36 La. An. Rep. 53, 54, 56.
[149] Dart, *La. Civ. Code*, 1945, Arts. 1493-1495.
[150] *Ibid.*, Arts. 1621, 1623.

cruelty, a crime, or grievous injury toward the parent; attempted to take either parent's life; accused a parent of a capital crime; refused sustenance, or when parent was insane, failed to take care of him; refused to ransom or provide bail; hindered by force making of the will; and, when a minor, married without the parents' consent.[151] A child may disinherit his parent if the parent has accused the child of a capital crime, attempted to take the life of the child or of the other parent, hindered by force making of the will, refused sustenance, neglected the child when insane, or failed to provide ransom.[152]

A parent can by will or gift dispose of only two-thirds of his property, if he leaves at his decease a legitimate child or his descendants; one-half if he leaves 2 children; and only one-third if he leaves 2 or more.[153] If he has no children but leaves one or both parents surviving, he may dispose of two-thirds of his estate.[154] If neither legitimate descendants nor parents survive, the entire estate may be donated or devised.[155] The disposable portion of an estate may be given in whole or in part to one or more of the disposer's descendants to the prejudice of the others[156] or to the surviving spouse.[157]

Acknowledged illegitimate children may be disinherited and adulterous children must be, except for sustenance.[158] When there are no legitimate descendants, the illegitimate may receive the whole amount of the mother's succession[159] and one-fourth of the father's if he leaves legitimate ascendants or legitimate brothers or sisters or their descendants; and one-third if he leaves only more remote relatives.[160] The balance of the father's estate must go either to his legitimate relatives or to some public institution.[161]

In Louisiana, if a person dies intestate leaving community property, the intestate's share of the community all goes to the descendants; if there be no descendants, one-half goes to the surviving spouse and one-half to the parents; and if there be no descendants or parents, all shall be inherited by the surviving spouse in full ownership.[162] The surviving spouse, where there is left issue of the marriage, has the right to use for life, or until remarriage, so much of the community property as may be inherited by the issue.[163]

---

[151] *Ibid.*, Art. 1621.
[152] *Ibid.*, Art. 1623.
[153] *Ibid.*, Art. 1493.
[154] *Ibid.*, Art. 1494.
[155] *Ibid.*, Art. 1496.
[156] *Ibid.*, Art. 1501.
[157] See *Succession of Eastman* (La. Ct. App. 1942), 6 So. (2d) 788.
[158] Dart, *La. Civ. Code*, 1945, Arts. 1483, 1488.
[159] *Ibid.*, Art. 1484.
[160] *Ibid.*, Art. 1486.
[161] *Ibid.*, Art. 1487.
[162] *Ibid.*, Art. 915.
[163] *Ibid.*, Art. 916.

Other property of an intestate in Louisiana descends in the following manner, each class in which there is a member taking to the exclusion of subsequent classes: (1) legitimate children or their descendants, or acknowledged illegitimate children of mother, there being no legitimate descendants;[164] (2) parents and brothers and sisters, or descendants of these last;[165] (3) lawful ascendants;[166] (4) lawful collateral relatives;[167] (5) surviving wife and surviving husband, unless the wife has acknowledged an illegitimate child;[168] (6) husband's illegitimate descendants;[169] (7) the state.[170]

The benefit of homestead exemption in Louisiana[171] may be claimed by a surviving spouse who has some person dependent upon him or her for support.[172] A widow holding property in indivision, one-half her share of the community in fee and use of the other half belonging to her minor children, is entitled to homestead exemption against creditors on the whole property.[173]

Mention should also be made of a Louisiana act authorizing the creation of private trusts which may be either *inter vivos*[174] or testamentary. The trust must terminate 10 years from the settler's death as to a beneficiary who is of full age at that time and as to a beneficiary who is a minor, 10 years from his majority. The act does not affect the law of forced heirship, save that a trust may be created upon the heritage of the forced heir, who must be paid the income therefrom at least once a year.[175] There may be one or more beneficiaries.[176]

Any type of property, including land, may be held in trust. The trustee may be a bank or trust company, or one or more individuals. A trust may be created for any legal purpose.[177]

One likely explanation of the high proportion of ownership tracts controlled by estates in selected parishes in Louisiana (the percentage ranging from 8 to nearly 30—Table 70) may be Louisiana's restrictive laws of forced heirship. The owner, unable to freely dispose of his

164 *Ibid.*, Arts. 902, 918.
165 *Ibid.*, Arts. 903, 904, 911-913.
166 *Ibid.*, Arts. 905-910.
167 *Ibid.*, Art. 914.
168 *Ibid.*, Art. 924.
169 *Ibid.*, Art. 919.
170 *Ibid.*, Art. 929.
171 A rural homestead in Louisiana exempt from forced sale may not exceed 160 acres, with improvements, livestock, farm equipment, etc., to a total value of $4,000. *La. Const.* Art. 11, sec. 1. In case the husband fails to file a homestead declaration, the wife may file one but not to exceed 20 acres. Dart, *La. Gen. Stat.*, 1939, sec. 3807.
172 *Baker & Co.* v. *Davis* (1918), 143 La. 215; 78 So. 473.
173 *Tinney* v. *Vittur* (1914), 134 La. 549; 64 So. 407, 408.
174 "Between the living; from one living person to another." Black, *Law Dictionary*, 3rd Ed., p. 994.
175 Dart, *La. Gen. Stat.*, 1939, secs. 9850: 1-8.
176 *Ibid.*, secs. 9850: 23-25.
177 *Ibid.*, secs. 9850: 11-22.

property to whomever he deems most deserving, can, by creating a trust, delay division of the estate and in that manner protect the surviving spouse and minor heirs.

Legal Rights of Tenants and Croppers

The rights of tenants and croppers in the land they farm are conferred by contract, written or oral, or implied by law from the conduct of the parties. One of the inherent rights incident to ownership of property is that of controlling its use. The landlord may restrict the extent of a tenant's (or cropper's) rights by any lawful agreement.[178]

Tenants, as previously stated, have been subdivided, based on type of rental payments, into 3 classes: cash, share-cash, and share in harmony with United States Census classifications.[179] Although project and census classifications of tenants and croppers generally conform to the legal classification, this is not necessarily so. In legal theory, a tenant is one who pays the landlord cash or a share of the crop, or both, for the use of the land, whereas a cropper is one who receives a share of the crop from his employer as payment for his labor and is merely an employee.[180]

The division of the crop, the nature of the rental or wage payment, and the provision of power and equipment by either party is not conclusive of the legal relationship between a landowner and his tenants or croppers. Either rent or wages may be paid in cash, in a share of the crop, or both, as well as by other arrangements. Moreover, it is as possible for a landowner to hire a man and a team as it is for him to hire the man alone and to pay a share of the crop rather than a cash wage. Or, it is possible for a tenant to rent teams and farming equipment along with the land and to pay a share of the crop as rent for team, equipment, and land. In short, the landlord may make any arrangement he chooses for supplying his tenant with farming equipment without altering the fact that he has made a lease.

The criterion for ascertaining whether the legal relationship be-

[178] *Celli and Del Papa* v. *Galveston Brewing Co.* (Tex. C. A. 1916), 186 S. W. 278, 280.

[179] The Agricultural Census definition of tenants and croppers is as follows: "Tenants operate hired or rented land only. *Cash* tenants pay a cash rental, such as $4.50 per acre for the cropland or $500 for the use of the whole farm. *Share-cash* tenants pay a part of their rental in cash and part as a share of crops or livestock production. *Share* tenants pay a share only of either the crops or livestock production or both. *Croppers* have been defined as share tenants to whom their landlords furnish all of the work animals or tractor power in lieu of work animals. *Other* tenants include those whose rental agreement was unspecified and those who did not fall definitely into one of the other sub-classes."

[180] *Barnhardt* v. *State.* (1925), 169 Ark. 567, 570; 275 S. W. 909.

tween the contracting parties is landlord-tenant or employer-cropper is their intent as evidences by their agreement or contract.[181] A most important determinant of this intent is the owner's disposition of his legal possession or "dominion" over the land to the other party. Expressions of this basic distinction are found in court decisions in each of the 5 states.

In a 1902 decision the Arkansas court held that ". . . a contract for the cultivation of land on shares, where the occupier was to have the exclusive possession of the land . . . created the relation of landlord and tenant."[182] In a later decision, a similar conclusion was reached in construing a share agreement under which the operator ". . . had dominion over the lands and controlled the processes of agriculture unhampered by interference on the part of the landlord . . . ."[183] However, when the possession of the land is not surrendered[184] and the contract does not vest "any interest in the freehold" in the operator, he is a sharecropper, an employee hired to make the crop.[185] In describing a particular contract held to create the relation of employer-employee, the court said, "There is no language in the contract indicating . . . possession of the land was surrendered . . ." nor that the operators ". . . had either exclusive dominion of the land . . . or of the crops to be planted thereon, giving them the right to pursue their own methods in the cultivation thereof . . ." On the contrary, the landowner had the right to direct the operators "as to how they should perform the labor necessary for the cultivation and harvesting of the crop."[186]

Similarly, in Louisiana a contract to cultivate land for a share of the crop was held a contract of lease, where there was no showing that the landowner ". . . reserved the right to direct, supervise, or control . . . planting, cultivating, or harvesting the crop. . . ."[187] On the other hand, a cropper is defined as ". . . one who agrees to work the land of another for a share of the crop, without obtaining any interest in the land. . . ." The cropper has ". . . no legal possession of the premises further than as an employee; the legal possession is in the employer."[188]

---

[181] *Tinsley* v. *Craige* (1891), 54 Ark, 346; 15 S. W. 897, 898; *Jones* v. *Dowling* (La. Ct. App. 1929), 12 La. App. 362; 125 So. 478, 479; *Betts* v. *Ratliff* (1874, 50 Miss. 561, 569; *Cry* v. *Bass Hardware* (Tex. C. A. 1925), 273 S. W. 347, 350.

[182] *Neal* v. *Brandon* (1902), 70 Ark. 79; 66 S. W. 200, 202.

[183] *Campbell* v. *Anderson* (1934), 189 Ark. 671; 74 S. W. (2d) 782, 783.

[184] *Tinsley* v. *Craige* (1891), 54 Ark. 346; 15 S. W. 897, 898.

[185] *Hammock* v. *Creekmore* (1886), 48 Ark. 264. 266; 3 S. W. 180.

[186] *Hardeman* v. *Arthurs* (1920), 144 Ark. 289; 222 S. W. 20, 21.

[187] *Jones* v. *Dowling* (La. Ct. App. 1929), 12 La. App. 362; 125 So. 478, 480.

[188] *Holmes* v. *Payne* (1926), 4 La. App. 345, 348.

An early decision in Mississippi held that "a tenant or lessee has an interest in the soil";[189] but it is equally well settled that one party may cultivate the land of another for a part of the crop, where the parties are tenants in common of the crop and do not sustain the relation of landlord and tenant.[190]

According to the Oklahoma court, a "tenant has exclusive right to possession of the lands he cultivates and an estate in the same for the term of his contract. . . ."[191] A cropper, however, ". . . is a hired hand paid for his labor with a share of the crop he works to make and harvest. He has no exclusive right to possession and no estate in the land. . . ."[192] If ". . . the landowner is to have supervisory possession of the land to be cultivated, and the party working the land is to be a wage-earner, whether in terms of money or part of the crop, the relation is that of landowner and sharecropper."[193]

The same rules apply in Texas. As stated by the court: "One of the essentials of a valid leasing of premises, whereby the relation of landlord and tenant is established, is that exclusive possession of the premises rightfully belonging to one party is transferred to another . . . ."[194] The distinction between a cropper and a tenant is that the latter has possession of the premises for a fixed time exclusive of the landlord. On the other hand, possession of the land is with the owner as against the cropper, who "is in the status of an employee, one hired to work the land and to be compensated by a share of the crop raised with the right only to ingress and egress on the property."[195]

Rights Under Various Types of Leases. For purposes of statistical analysis, contracts between owners and tenants or croppers have been grouped into 4 types of agreements referred to as "leases": oral indefinite, oral 1-year, written 1-year, and written 2-years or over. In legal theory, as has been pointed out, a cropping contract is not a lease. Under the common law a lease, besides being a contract between

---

[189] *Betts* v. *Ratliff* (1847), 50 Miss. 561, 568.

[190] *Betts* v. *Ratliff* (1874), 50 Miss. 561, 569. Also see a recent decision *Jackson* v. *Jefferson* (1935), 171 Miss. 774; 158 So. 486, where the court recognizes but does not define the relationship conferred by the "usual sharecrop contract." But see *Williams* v. *Sykes* (1934), 170 Miss. 88; 154 So. 267, 727, and cases there cited, regarding tenure relationship created by a sharecropping contract; also see *Miss. Code Ann.*, 1942, sec. 336.

[191] *Elder* v. *Sturges* (1935), 173 Okla. 620, 49 P. (2d) 221, 222.

[192] *Elder* v. *Sturges* (1935), 173 Okla. 620, 49 P. (2d) 221, 222.

[193] *Halsell* v. *First Nat. Bank of Coweta* (1925), 109 Okla. 220, 235 P. 532, 533.

[194] *Brown* v. *Johnson* (1929), 118 Tex. 143; 12 S. W. (2d) 543, 545.

[195] *Brown* v. *Johnson* (1929), 118 Tex. 143; 12 S. W. (2d) 543, 545, quoting *Cry* v. *Bass Hardware* (Tex. C. A. 1925), 273 S. W. 347, 350.

the parties, is also regarded as a conveyance.[196] It involves an interest in the land passed to the tenant[197] and a possession exclusive even of the landlord, except as the lease permits his entry.[198] In contrast, a cropper has no possessory interest in the premises he occupies;[199] he has no estate in the land but has merely a right to possession incident to and dependent upon the performance of his personal engagement.[200]

—*Written leases.* About 10 per cent of the individual landlords[201] sampled in Mississippi and Texas used written leases compared with approximately 25 per cent in Oklahoma and Arkansas. Written leases were in somewhat greater favor with female than with male landlords. Types of leases used by estate landlords closely parallel types used by individual landlords. Use of written leases was far more prevalent with Farm Security Administration then with other landlords in all 4 states, the proportion ranging from 57 to 70 per cent. Institutional landlords in the sample areas in Oklahoma and Texas used written leases almost exclusively. Generally, the written 1-year lease was in greater favor than those for 2 years or longer, the notable exceptions being Farm Security Administration clients in Mississippi and Oklahoma. (Table 66)

The written memorandum of lease or cropping contract may be a formal document or it may be only an informal written statement. A single letter setting forth the essentials of the agreement has been said to be a sufficient memorandum of the lease, when it names the parties, identifies the property leased, the length of time the lease is to run, the rental to be paid, and it is plainly inferable from the letter that an agreement to lease has been made.[202] The same rules of law generally apply to the written lease, whether for 1 year or for 2 years or over. A caution is in order, however, since requirements of signa-

---

[196] Under the civil law a lease is regarded as a "wholly bilateral agreement by which the lessor instead of making a conveyance, promises a continuing permission to occupy the premises," and the tenant "covenants to pay rent and render such other performance as the lease requires of him." Williston, *Contracts.* Vol. 3 sec. 890, p. 2520 (Rev. Ed. 1936).

[197] *Betts* v. *Ratliff* (1874), 50 Miss. 561, 568.

[198] *Tips* v. *United States* (Cir. Ct. App. 1934), 70 F. (2d) 525, 526.

[199] *Webb* v. *Garrett* (Tex. C. A. 1902), 30 T. C. A. 240, 70 S. W. 992; *Woodson* v. *McLaughlin* (1921), 150 Ark. 340; 234 S. W. 185, 186.

[200] *Ellis* v. *Bingham* (Tex. C. A. 1912), 150 S. W. 602, 603.

[201] Over 80 per cent of the landlords in the Arkansas, Mississippi, Oklahoma, and Texas samples were individual landlords, male and female; and of this total, 13 to 28 per cent were female, the percentage varying by states. The remainder were estate and institutional landlords. (Table 67)

[202] *Halsell* v. *Scurr* (Tex. C. A. 1927), 297 S. W. 524, 527.

ture, acknowledgment, and recording vary from state to state, depending on a number of factors.

In all 5 states of the Southwestern Region tenancies for a definite term, whether oral or written, terminate at the time agreed without further notice. Statutes in Louisiana, Mississippi, and Oklahoma expressly so provide.[203] In Arkansas and Texas the rule has been adopted by court decision.[204]

—*Oral leases.* Oral or verbal leases, sometimes referred to as parol leases, were the most prevalent type of rental agreement used by individual landlords in the sample areas in Arkansas, Mississippi, Oklahoma, and Texas. The proportion of individual landlords, male and female, using oral leases varied by states from about two-thirds to nine-tenths. Related landlords used verbal leases a little more frequently than did unrelated landlords. (Table 66) About the same proportion of estate landlords as individual landlords used oral leases and, in the Arkansas sample area, 69 per cent of the institutional leases were oral. Of interest is the fact that in the Oklahoma and Texas sample areas very few institutional landlords used oral leases. Nor were verbal leases in as great favor with Farm Security Administration landlords as written contracts, and, when used, the oral 1-year contract was most popular.

Frequently, in negotiating an oral lease or cropping contract only a few words are said as to time, rental payment—whether cash, third and fourth, or half-and-half—and sometimes "furnish." The other terms of the leases are those customary to the community and, unless varied in the oral agreement, become an implied part of the contract.

For purposes of analysis of project data, oral leases have been classified into two main groups: the oral 1-year lease, and the oral lease for an indefinite term. Rules of law governing each type differ widely.

—*Oral 1-year leases.* Oral leases or cropping agreements are binding in all 5 states for any length of term not exceeding 1 year. If a lease is oral and for a longer term than 1 year, it is unenforceable in Arkansas, Mississippi, Oklahoma, and Texas. Sharecropping agreements for similar terms are voidable under the same acts.[205] In Louisi-

---

[203] Dart, *La. Civ. Code*, 1945, Art. 2727; *Okla. Stat. Ann.*, 1937, Tit. 41, sec. 8; *Miss. Code Ann.*, 1942, sec. 946.

[204] See *Henry* v. *Gulf Refining Co.* (1929), 179 Ark. 138; 15 S. W. (2d) 979, 982; *Shipman* v. *Mitchell* (1886), 64 Tex. 174, 176; and see *Hendrick* v. *Cannon* (1849), 5 Tex. 248, 250.

[205] Pope, *Dig. Stat. Ark.*, 1937, sec. 6059; *Miss. Code Ann.*, 1942, sec. 264; *Okla. Stat. Ann.*, 1937, Tit. 15, sec. 136; Vernon, *Tex. Civ. Stat.* 1945, Art. 3995.

ana, "leases may be made either by written or verbal contracts";[206] but a farm lease, when the length of the term has not been agreed upon, is presumed to be for 1 year.[207]

Although oral leases for terms longer than 1 year are voidable, such leases are sometimes enforced by the courts, under an exception to the above general rule. For example, where either party in reliance upon a verbal lease has so changed his position by acts or forbearance that he will be defrauded by failure to carry out the oral agreement, the courts will enforce it under the equitable doctrine of part performance.[208] Just what facts are sufficient to make the oral lease enforceable for the full term agreed upon must be determined from the particular circumstances of each case and the laws of the state having jurisdiction.

Possession of the premises, plus the making of valuable improvements with the consent of the landlord, has been held such part performance of an oral lease, invalid as to its duration, as to render it enforceable.[209] Slight repairs to fences were held insufficient to extend to an oral tenancy beyond a year,[210] and so was payment of rent for the time the farm was actually occupied, plus work usually done in cleaning up and preparing land for cultivation.[211] However, the combination of entering on the land, fencing and cultivating it, paying taxes, and putting up 4 tenant houses was sufficient to warrant specific performance of an oral lease beyond 1 year.[212] Sufficient also was possession by the tenant, clearing 10 acres of a 20 acre leasehold, plus erecting a fence.[213] "Improvements, to constitute part performance . . . need not necessarily consist of erections on the land but may arise from skill and labor bestowed in cultivation, which, however, must enhance the land in value."[204]

A verbal or oral lease of land extending beyond a year when regarded retrospectively is valid, since the Statute of Frauds applied to such leases only for years to come.[215]

—*Oral, indefinite-term leases.* Oral tenancies of indefinite duration may be created either expressly, by a lease for an indefinite term, or impliedly, from an occupation of premises under an unenforceable oral

[206] Dart, *La. Civ. Code,* 1932, Art. 2683. [207] *Ibid.,* Art. 2687.

[208] *Halsell* v. *Scurr* (Tex. C. A. 1927), 297 S. W. 524, 528.

[209] *Wanscaffe* v. *Pantoga* (Tex. C. A. 1901), 63 S. W. 663, 664; also see *Anderson* v. *Anderson* (Tex. C. A. 1896), 13 T. C. A. 527; 36 S. W. 816, 817.

[210] *Storthz* v. *Watts* (1915) 117 Ark. 500, 175 S. W. 406.

[211] *Garner* v. *Starling* (1919) 137 Ark. 464; 208 S. W. 593, 594.

[212] *Morrison* v. *Peay* (1860), 21 Ark. 110, 115.

[213] *Wanscaffe* v. *Pantoga* (Tex. C. A. 1901), 63 S. W. 663, 664.

[214] *Anderson* v. *Anderson* (Tex. C. A. 1896), 13 T. C. A. 527; 36 S. W. 816, 817.

[215] See *Robb* v. *San Antonio St. Ry.* (1891), 82 Tex. 392; 18 S. W. 707, 709.

or written lease, or from a holding over after expiration of a definite term without a new agreement.

The first type, the express oral lease of indefinite duration, which may or may not end within a year, depending upon the occurrence of some contingency, is enforceable.[216] Among leases of this type which have been upheld in Texas even though oral, to mention only a few, are a lease of a farm for the duration of the landlord's life,[217] an agreement for possession pending sale of the farm,[218] and a lease which was to continue until a controversy over another farm was settled.[219] Similarly, a lease under which the landlord let the tenant occupy and cultivate a farm for taking care of it and paying the taxes until such time as the owner demanded possession could have been fully executed within a year and, therefore, was enforceable though not in writing.[220]

A second type of oral lease of indefinite duration results from a tenant holding under a voidable oral or written lease. For example, in Mississippi an oral lease for a term of years, voidable under the Statute of Frauds may be "changed into a tenancy from year to year, by payment and acceptance of rent annually, and by other circumstances indicating that to be the intention of the parties."[221] An invalid 5-year oral farm lease under which the tenant took possession of the premises, made contracts with hands for the farming year, and was improving the property for the purpose of making a crop was held to create a periodic tenancy good from year to year. Under this latter oral lease, no rent had been paid but the agreement provided for settlements at the end of each year.[222]

The same conclusions were reached in Oklahoma regarding the rights of tenants in possession under void written leases. In 1913 a controversy arose over land held by a tenant under a 5-year written lease negotiated with an Indian allottee. The lease was void. It was held, however, that entry under a void or defective lease for a term of years creates a tenancy at will, and if periodical rent be paid the tenancy becomes one from year to year, which continues until termi-

---

[216] *Betts* v. *Betts* (Tex. C. A. 1920), 220 S. W. 575, 576; see *Dallas Joint-Stock Land Bank of Dallas* v. *Wise*, (Tex. C. A. 1931), 40 S. W. (2d) 931, 933.

[217] *Betts* v. *Betts* (Tex. C. A. 1920), 220 S. W. 575, 576.

[218] *Dallas Joint-Stock Land Bank of Dallas* v. *Wise* (Tex. C. A. 1931), 40 S. W. (2d) 931, 933.

[219] *Bostick* v. *Haney* (Tex. C. A. 1919), 209 S. W. 477. 479.

[220] *New York & Texas Land Co.* v. *Dooley* (Tex. C. A. 1903), 33 T. C. A. 336; 77 S. W. 1030, 1031; *Hintze* v. *Krabbenschmidt* (Tex. C. A. 1897), 44 S. W. 38, 40.

[221] *Scruggs* v. *McGehee* (1915), 110 Miss. 10; 69 So. 1003, 1005.

[222] *Montgomery* v. *Hollingsworth* (1921) 127 Miss. 346, 90 So. 79, 80.

nated by 3 months' notice in writing.[223] The rule of this case was followed in a later decision resolving the rights of a tenant in possession of a farm for a term of years under another void and defective lease.[224]

—*Leases created by holding over.* A third type of lease of indefinite duration is created in some states when a tenant holds over after expiration of a definite term without a new agreement. This type of lease of indefinite term is probably most prevalent. Requirements for creation of, and rights conferred by, a holdover lease vary by states.

Under the common law, holding over by consent, expressed or implied, and payment of rent after termination of a previous lease for years creates a tenancy from year to year.[225] Such lease can be terminated by either party by giving notice ". . . at least a half-year before the expiration of the current year of the tenancy."[226]

The common law tenancy from year to year is recognized in Arkansas. Such a tenancy ". . . may be created either by an express agreement or by a lease for 1 or more years and the holding over by the tenant and payment of an annual rental after the first year without a new contract."[227] A 6-months' notice is necessary in Arkansas to terminate a common law tenancy from year to year.[228]

Under the same rule, however, the rural tenant is at a disadvantage, for in the usual agricultural tenancy the rent is not due until the end of the year or at the time the crop is harvested. A concurring opinion in one Arkansas decision observes that holding over of the farm and the landlord's acquiescence in the planting of the crop doubtless would be sufficient without the offer and acceptance of rent to justify any court in holding that a tenancy from year to year has been created. Moreover, according to dictum in the same decision, "when a tenant after the expiration of the term fixed by the lease at one year or less, continues to occupy the premises without any new contract, this may, at the election of the landlord, be considered a renewal of the prior lease for a like period and upon like terms."[229]

Mississippi courts recognize 2 types of tenancies which may be created by holding over: a tenancy for another year and a tenancy from year to year.

---

[223] *Peters* v. *Holder* (1913), 40 Okla. 93; 136 P. 400, 401.

[224] *Guffey* v. *Pollan* (1918), 73 Okla. 219; 175 P. 817, 818.

[225] W. Blake Odgers, K. C., and Walter Blake Odgers, *The Common Law of England*, 2nd Ed., II, p. 872.

[226] *Ibid.*, p. 877.

[227] *Lamew* v. *Townsend* (1921), 147 Ark. 282; 227 S. W. 593, 594.

[228] *Peel* v. *Lane* (1921), 148 Ark. 79; 229 S. W. 20, 22.

[229] See *Lamew* v. *Townsend* (1921), 147 Ark. 282, 227 S. W. 593, 594, 595.

The first type, the tenancy for another year, is created whenever a tenant, without a new contract, continues to occupy the property which he has held under an annual lease. Such a holdover tenant becomes liable as tenant for another year at the same rate and under the same terms.[230] When the lease term has expired it is the duty of the tenant to either surrender the premises or procure a new contract. If he fails to do either, the landlord at his option may treat him as a trespasser or as a tenant under the previous terms.[231] The same rule applies where a tenant at the expiration of the first 1-year term enters into a definite, different contract for the coming year. The tenant is not entitled to 2 months' notice to vacate at the end of the second year. The lease, being for a definite 1-year period, terminates without notice.[232] In other words, where a series of annual leases begin and end on specified dates, no notice to quit or vacate is necessary, and the landlord has the option to treat the tenant as a trespasser after each termination date.[233]

Under different circumstances the second type of tenancy, tenancy from year to year, may be created by holding over. This latter type also may be created by express agreement. Mississippi statutes require 2 months' notice in writing to terminate a tenancy from year to year.[234]

Just what is required in Mississippi to create a tenancy from year to year is not too clear. In a recent decision, where a tenant had occupied a farm without any express agreement for termination and continued in possession for 4 years, paying annual rent, the court held a tenancy from year to year was created. "After the year (first year) 1930, a tenancy by the year was created by implication. The occupancy alone . . . did not create the year to year tenancy, nor did the payment alone of money, but the course of dealing here by the parties, undenied, did so create a holding from year to year. The tenant, without the statutory notice to the contrary, held over . . . plowed the land, planted his oats, and had a right to presume that the relation would be continued for that year." In the same opinion the court, citing previous decisions, said, "Where the relation of landlord and tenant exists, and there is a holding from year to year, with no definite period

[230] *Tonkel* v. *Riteman* (1932), 163 Miss. 216, 141 So. 344, citing *Usher* v. *Moss* (1874), 50 Miss. 208, 211, and *Love* v. *Law* (1880), 57 Miss. 596, 598.

[231] *Tonkel* v. *Riteman* (1932), 163 Miss. 216; 141 So. 344.

[232] *Graham* v. *Cauthen* (1936), 169 So. 58, 59.

[233] *Copiah Hardware Co.* v. *Johnson* (1924), 123 Miss. 624, 100 So. 31, 33.

[234] Miss. *Code Ann.*, 1942, sec. 946; *Scruggs* v. *McGehee* (1915), 110 Miss. 10, 69, So. 1003, 1005; see *Hamilton* v. *Federal Land Bank* (1936), 175 Miss. 462, 167, So. 642, 644.

for the termination of the lease, notice to terminate the tenancy is essential . . ."[235]

A 1918 decision involving a business lease was in the same vein. It was there held that a letting of real property to continue indefinitely according to the wishes of the contracting parties terminated at the end of the term then pending by giving the statutory notice.[236] The rule of this decision applied to a month-to-month tenancy requiring 1 week's notice to terminate also would apply to a year-to-year tenancy, where the requisite notice is 2 months.[237]

In Louisiana, if after a lease term has expired the farmer continues in undisturbed possession for 1 month, the former lease continues on the same terms and conditions for the next year.[238] Moreover, if the tenant holds over for the required period, the lease may be continued, 1 year at a time, from year to year.[239] To effectuate a lease for the next year an "indispensable prerequisite is that the lessee must remain in undisturbed possession of the premises, for thirty days immediately following the expiration of the terms of the lease."[240] The act has no application" . . . when either party has clearly announced his intention not to renew the lease on the same terms or for a full year. . . ."[241]

[235] *Hamilton* v. *Federal Land Bank* (1936), 175 Miss. 462, 167 So. 642, 644, citing *Scruggs v. McGehee* (1915), 110 Miss. 10, 69 So. 1003, and *Wilson v. Wood* (1904) [84 Miss. 728], 36 So. 609.

[236] *Lay* v. *Great Southern Lumber Co.* (1918), 118 Miss. 636, 79 So. 822, 824.

[237] *Miss. Code Ann.*, 1942, sec. 946. A number of Mississippi opinions, in which the question of the notice required to terminate leasing was an issue, recognize the year-to-year tenancy. These decisions throw some light on the legal requirements for creating a year-to-year tenancy. An 1874 decision held that a tenancy from year to year ". . . could be terminated only at the end of the year, unless stipulated otherwise in the contract." Continuing, the court said, "Where a tenant continues to occupy and enters upon another year without objection from the landlord, and with his silence or tacit consent and approval, a tenancy for another year is thus created and cannot be terminated in the middle of the term, and in the midst of the crop, but only at the end of the year."—*Usher* v. *Moss* (1874), 50 Miss. 208, 211. Similarly, in another early holding it was said to be ". . . firmly established that where a tenant continues to occupy land which he has held upon a contract of leasing, without a new contract, he is liable as a tenant from year to year, at the same rate that he paid before . . . ."—*Love* v. *Law* (1880), 57 Miss. 596, 598. More recently, the court held that a tenant who held over and paid rent after the expiration of an annual lease, with the consent and acquiescence of the landlord but without any new agreement therefor, became a tenant from year to year.—*Viator* v. *Moses* (1939), 186 Miss. 419, 191 So. 412. In another opinion it was said that a tenant who leased the land for one year, held over and paid rent, thereby acquired the right of becoming a tenant thereof from year to year by remaining in possession after the expiration of his lease without objection from his landlord.—*Richardson* v. *Neblett* (1920), 122 Miss. 723, 84 So. 695, 697.

[238] Dart, *La. Civ. Code*, 1945, Art. 2688.

[239] *Dyer* v. *Wilson* (La. Ct. App. 1939), 190 So. 851, 853.

[240] *Dyer* v. *Wilson* (La. Ct. App. 1941), 1 So. (2d) 126, 128.

[241] *Ashton Realty Co.* v. *Prowell* (1928), 165 La. 328, 115 So. 579, 581.

In Texas, when a tenant holds over after expiration of a definite term for a year or for a term of years, without a new agreement, a tenancy for "another year" is created;[242] and this is true whether the holding over follows a 1-year oral lease[243] or a written lease.[244] Similarly, where the tenant holds over for a full year and continues in possession, a lease for a second holdover year is created.[245] The creation of a lease for a holdover year is not affected by the length of time a tenant holds over after the one or more years expiring term but will arise if the tenant holds over a few days or a single day, unless the circumstances are such as to excuse the holding over.[246]

"The essential difference between the general doctrine of a tenancy from year to year and the Texas doctrine of a tenancy for another year is that the former tenancy continues indefinitely unless the required notice before the end of the rent year is given, while in Texas each year constitutes a separate distinct tenancy. . . ."[247]

Texas law is uncertain as to the exact length of time required to terminate a tenancy for another year. However, in the absence of an agreement to the contrary, it is terminable only at the end of the lease year and not at any intervening date.[248] One court indicated that such holdover tenancy is terminable at the pleasure of either party at the end of any year "upon giving requisite notice." In its decision involving a farm lease, without discussing whether "requisite" notice had been given, the court granted possession to the landlord on the first of January, as requested, following notice to vacate given by the landlord to the tenant on the preceding 17th of October.[249]

An Oklahoma statute, enacted during the 1910-11 legislative session, provides, "When premises are let for one or more years, and the tenant, with the assent of the landlord, continues to occupy the premises after expiration of the term, such tenant shall be deemed to be a tenant at will." Further, it is "provided that no lease or rental contract of premises shall be continued, unless the original contract

[242] *Shipman* v. *Mitchell* (1885), 64 Tex. 174, 176; *Bateman* v. *Maddox* (1894), 86 Tex. 546; 26 S. W. 51, 53.

[243] *Bateman* v. *Maddox* (1894), 86 Tex. 546, 26 S. W. 51, 53; also see *Dallas Joint-Stock Land Bank* v. *Rutherford* (Tex. C. A. 1938), 115 S. W. (2d) 1160, 1163.

[244] See *Shipman* v. *Mitchell* (1885), 64 Tex. 174, 175; *Abeel* v. *McDonnell* (Tex. C. A. 1905), 87 S. W. 1066, 1067.

[245] *Bateman* v. *Maddox* (1894), 86 Tex. 546, 26 S. W. 51, 54; *Hunger* v. *Toubin Bros.* (Tex. C. A. 1942), 164 S. W. (2d) 765, 766.

[246] *Hunger* v. *Toubin Bros.* (Tex. C. A. 1942), 164 S. W. (2d) 765, 767.

[247] Frank Bobbitt, "Tenancies from Year to Year and Related Estates," 8 *Tex. Law Review,* (1930), p. 331.

[248] See *Bateman* v. *Maddox* (1894), 86 Tex. 546, 26 S. W. 51, 54.

[249] *Hill* v. *Hunter* (Tex. C. A. 1913), 157 S. W. 247, 253.

was in writing, and all other leases or contracts shall expire by limitation with the calendar year, without notice."[250]

This act, as construed by the Oklahoma courts, is clear as to the rights of the parties when a rural tenant holds over beyond the end of an annual oral lease. What the rights are when a rural tenant holds over after expiration of a written lease of 1 or more year's duration is confusing.

In two decisions settling controversies over the rights of rural tenants who continued in possession after the end of 1-year oral lease terms, the Oklahoma court held that oral 1-year leases, where there was no agreement for extension, terminated at the end of the calendar year without notice. Under this rule a tenant will acquire no right to another lease year by holding over without consent of the landlord.[251] The same conclusion was reached in resolving another dispute over possession of a farm leased under an oral lease for the year 1924. Here the tenant held over and was given 3 days' notice to move, which notice was served about 8 days after expiration of his term. The court, citing the 1910-11 statute, said the tenant who held over without consent of the landlord was a tenant at sufferance and might be treated as a trespasser. Furthermore, notice was not required to terminate the tenancy at sufferance.[252] The same rule has been applied where urban tenants have held over after annual oral leases.[253]

A number of opinions construing the 1910-11 act[254] in controversies

---

[250] *Okla. Stat. Ann.*, 1937, Tit. 41, sec. 2; Okla. Laws 1910-11, Ch. 64, p. 146, sec. 1. The same enactment amended a previous 1901 law which read as follows: "When premises are let for one or more years, and the tenant, with the assent of the landlord, continues to occupy the premises after expiration of the term such tenant shall be deemed to be a tenant from year to year."

[251] *Parsons* v. *Root* (1926), 122 Okla. 25, 250 P. 503 (rural), citing Comp. St. 1921, sec. 7342, now *Okla. Code Ann.*, 1937, Tit. 41, sec. 2; *Westheimer* v. *Sterling* (1926), 123 Okla. 7, 251 P. 738, 739 (rural), citing Comp. St. 1921, sec. 7342, now *Okla. Code Ann.*, 1937, Tit. 41, sec. 2.

[252] *Bardwell* v. *Riverside Oil & Refining Co.* (1929), 139 Okla. 26, 280 P. 1083, 1087, citing sec. 7341, C. O. S. 1921, now *Okla. Stat. Ann.*, 1937, Tit. 41, sec. 2.

[253] *Berry* v. *Opel* (1944), 194 Okla. 670, 154 P. (2d) 575, 576 (urban), citing *Hancock* v. *Maurer* (1924), 103 Okla. 196, 229 P. 611 (rural residence); in this dispute an urban tenant entered under an oral agreement for a term of 1 year and thereafter continued in possession for a number of years, with express or implied consent. The court held a tenancy at will was created. "It is settled law that where a tenant goes into possession of real estate for a definite term under contract and continues to hold possession of the property after expiration of the fixed tenancy, with the consent, express or implied, of the landlord that the possession is thereafter a tenancy at will and requires no notice from either of the parties to terminate the relation. It is also settled law that where a tenant for a term holds over after the expiration of the term without consent, either express or implied, of the landlord that the tenancy becomes one of sufferance," and the tenant is not entitled to notice to terminate the tenancy. Also see *Hickey* v. *Whitfield* (1931), 153 Okla. 1, 4 P. (2d) 761, 762 (urban).

[254] *Okla. Stat. Ann.*, 1937, Tit. 41, sec. 2.

involving holding over after expiration of written lease terms of 1 or more year's duration have been written. These opinions leave little doubt as to the meaning of the act when applied to disputes with tenants over the right to continue in possession of urban or business premises. Such holdover tenants are tenants at will, and the lease is terminable by a 30-day or shorter notice.[255] It is not clear whether the court would apply the same rule in settling a similar rural dispute, particularly if an attempt was made to terminate the tenancy during the crop year.

A number of opinions in which the issues were the rights acquired by rural tenants holding over after the end of written lease terms have been written since the law was amended. Some of these decisions, though of interest, do little to clarify the meaning of the act as it relates to such farm holdover disputes because the court applied the law as it appeared before amendment in 1910-11.[256] In 1936, however,

[255] An urban tenant who, after expiration of a written 2-year lease of business premises, held over for several months with the landlord's consent and paid rent monthly, was held a tenant at will and not liable for another year's rent.—*Jacobson* v. *Knee* (1924), 103 Okla. 253, 229 P. 814, 816, (urban), citing sec. 7342, C. S. 1921. now *Okla. Stat. Ann.*, 1937, Tit. 41, sec. 2, In an opinion resolving another urban dispute, it was said that when "a tenancy terminates and the tenant holds over, the landlord may elect to create a tenancy at will by merely giving assent."—*Rourke* v. *Houghes-Bozarth-Anderson Co.* (1929), 141 Okla. 22, 283 P. 561, 562 (urban), citing sec. 7342 C. S. 1921, now *Okla. Stat. Ann.*, 1937, Tit. 41, sec. 2. The same conclusions were reached in settling a controversy involving a holding over and payment of monthly rent following expiration of the second of two annual written leases on a sales barn. The tenant, citing an 1890 act (now *Okla. Stat. Ann.* 1937, Tit. 41, sec. 35), claimed a tenancy for another year was implied from holding over an acceptance of rent. The court held that the last legislative expression enacted in 1910 and 1911 governed (*Okla. Stat. Ann.*, 1937, Tit. 41, sec 2); and under this latter act "a tenant holding over is a tenant at will. The tenancy was held terminable by a thirty day or shorter notice."—*Stephenson* v. *O'Keefe* (1945), 195 Okla. 28, 154 P. (2d) 757, 758, 759 (urban). See *Anthony Co., Inc.* v. *Stroud* (1941), 189 Okla. 104, 114 P. (2d) 177, 178 (urban), where the court found it unnecessary to reconcile *Okla. Stat. Ann.*, 1937, Tit. 41, sec. 35 and Tit. 41, sec. 2, since the decision was based on an "acceptance" of an offer to renew for another year.

[256] In the first, a 1912 decision, a tenant who had leased a farm under written contract during 1907, and held over pending negotiation of a new lease for 1908, was held to be a tenant from year to year, but, since a new lease was under negotiation, not under the terms of the 1907 lease. This controversy arose before enactment of the new act, which therefore would not apply.—*Turner* v. *Wilcox* (1912), 32 Okla. 56, 121 P. 658, 660 (rural). Another of the series of decisions was made in 1918. In this case, the tenant had leased a farm for the year 1913, and again leased the property by written lease for 1914, under a contract which did not fix the expiration date of the tenancy. The tenant continued in possession into 1915 and cultivated a crop. In October, he was ordered to vacate. The court cited sec. 3784, R. L. O. 1910, as it appeared before amendment and held that the tenant "was entitled to occupy these premises until the expiration of the year 1915."—*Wolverton* v. *Ward* (1918), 74 Okla. 40, 176 P. 924 (rural). Again in 1926, the court, relying on section 3784 as it appeared before amendment, construed a farm lease to be a tenancy from year to year. This controversy was between two tenants, one of whom during the crop year attempted to gain possession under an overlapping

the court in settling a rural dispute relied on the 1910-11 act, but the right to the farm premises during the crop year was not an issue. The question was whether a tenant had the right to sell water; and in deciding that question, the legal effect of a farm tenant holding over was pertinent. In this decision the court said that if the tenant held over he would be a tenant at will.[257]

A year later a dispute between a landlord and a farm tenant reached the Supreme Court, and again the 1910-11 act was cited. The tenant had leased the premises in 1923 and remained in possession continuously until March 18, 1935, when he was ousted by threats of the landlord. The tenant claimed an oral lease for 1935 and brought legal action for repossession. The landlord alleged the lease expired at the end of 1934, and, therefore, under Title 41, section 2,[258] the tenancy was at will. The court held that Title 41, section 2, *supra* did not repeal Title 41, section 1,[259] which provides that "any person in possession of real property is presumed to be a tenant at will unless the contrary is shown. . . ." Also that Title 41, section 2, *supra* "has no application to a case where the person in possession of real estate continues over with the assent of the owner. It merely provides that no lease . . . shall be continued unless the original contract was in writing, and further provides that . . . oral contracts shall expire by limitation with the calendar year without notice." The question of whether the person in possession remains on the land with the assent of the owner, and thus becomes a tenant at will under the provision of the preceding act, Title 41, section 1, was a fact to be determined from all of the evidence. In affirming judgment for the tenant the court said there was evidence warranting a finding of either a new

---

lease. The record discloses that the tenancy construed began as a 5-year written lease in 1912 or 1913. This 5-year lease contract was purchased in 1914 by the tenant who was in possession at the beginning of the controversy. He remained in possession after expiration of the original 5-year lease, paying annual rent until 1921, when the controversy arose. The equities in the case were in favor of the tenant in possession, since the owner of the overlapping lease was being financed by a third party, whom the court said was obviously "buying a lawsuit." The court in its opinion relied on three acts, two of which had been amended or repealed during the 1910-11 session but made no mention of the new act enacted at that time. The tenancy was held not terminated without legal notice.—*Harley* v. *Paschall* (1926), 115 Okla. 294, 243 P. 167, 168 (rural), citing R. L. O. 1910, sec. 3784, was amended by Ch. 64, sec. 1, Laws of 1910-11, now as amended the act appears as *Okla. Stat. Ann.*, 1937, Tit. 41, sec. 2; R. L. O. 1910, sec. 3787, now *Okla. Stat. Ann.*, 1937, Tit. 41, sec. 5; R. L. O. 1910, sec. 3788, repealed by Ch. 64, sec. 2, Laws 1910-11.

[257] *Continental Oil Co.* v. *Logan* (1936), 177 Okla. 273, 58 P. (2d) 554, 559 (rural), citing *Okla. Stat.*, 1931, sec. 10898, now *Okla. Stat. Ann.* 1937, Tit. 41, sec. 2.

[258] *Okla. Stat. Ann.*, 1937, Tit. 41, sec. 2.

[259] *Ibid.*, Tit. 41, sec. 1.

contract for 1935 or that the tenant was in possession with assent of the landlord.[260]

—*Types of oral leases favored.* With the individual landlord using oral leases, the oral 1-year lease was in predominant favor in all 4 state sample areas for which data are available, and this is particularly true in Mississippi and Texas. Oral indefinite leases found considerable favor with individual landlords reported in the Texas and Oklahoma samples. Related landlords used oral indefinite leases two to five times as frequently as nonrelated landlords. No discernible preference for oral indefinite leases by male compared with female landlords was indicated. (Table 66)

Institutional landlords in the Arkansas sample area made some use of oral indefinite leases, but it is of interest that no leases of this type were reported used by institutional landlords in Oklahoma and Texas. Oral indefinite leases were quite extensively used by individual and estate landlords.[261] Where oral indefinite leases were used by estate landlords, a larger proportion of such leases no doubt were the type of oral lease for an indefinite term, which may or may not end within a year, depending on the occurrence of some contingency, which type of lease is enforceable.

Oral leases were favored over written leases by landlords charging cash or standing, third and fourth, and half-share rent. In fact, all farmers on the "halves" had oral contracts, the oral 1-year contract being most preferred. When share-cash rent was charged, the oral 1-year lease was favored in Mississippi and Texas and the written 1-year lease in Arkansas and Oklahoma. The preference for written 1-year leases in Oklahoma, when share-cash rent was charged, has been ascribed to a choice of this type of lease by institutional landlords. Landlords charging "other types of rent," who most frequently were related landlords or estates, favored oral leases. (Table 96) Also of some interest is the fact that half-share contracts were more favored by male than by female, estate, or institutional landlords. (Table 69) In fact, such contracts were seldom used by female landlords. (Table 99) Moreover, landlords using half-share agreements on the average were a few years younger than other landlords. (Table 100)

Generally, as the distance from the landlord's residence to the

[260] *Turner* v. *Bishop* (1937), 181 Okla. 61, 71 P. (2d) 1088, 1089.

[261] In view of the Texas legal doctrine that a tenancy for "another year" is created by holding over, most of the oral indefinite leases reportedly used by individual landlords in Texas most likely were oral 1-year leases. In Oklahoma, hold-over tenants probably were only tenants at will. See *supra* "Leases created by holding over," p. 255.

leasehold increased, landlords tended to use fewer oral and more written leases. (Table 73)

Remedies for Breach of Tenancy Agreements. Remedies available to an aggrieved landlord, tenant, or cropper to redress violation by the other contracting party of a lease or cropping agreement vary, depending on the nature of the transgression and the state of jurisdiction. Generally, the remedy is in the civil courts and, depending on the facts of each case, may consist of an action for money damages, for possession of specific chattels or crops, for repossession of the premises, or, sometimes, for specific performance of the agreement. Relief is permissible in the criminal courts where the transgressor breaks a criminal law, as, for example, if lien-crops are wrongfully removed or sold, if the Federal Peonage Act is violated, or, in some states, if there is an unlawful holding over after the end of the lease term.

Another type of statute designed to discourage abandonment of tenancy contracts is found in 3 states in the region. These acts impose both civil and criminal liability on anyone who entices a tenant, cropper, or laborer away from his contract. Under the Arkansas act, one who induces a laborer or renter under present contract to leave his employer or leased premises without consent, before expiration of the contract, upon conviction may be fined not less than $25 nor more than $500, and such person is also civilly liable for all advances made under the contract and for any other damages sustained by the breach.[262] A similar act in Mississippi imposes fines of $25 to $100.[263] In Louisiana, the statute authorizes fines of from $10 to $200 on conviction for each offense and, in addition, civil liability equal to twice the amount of the debt due for advances.[264] However, the Louisiana act does not apply to any farming contract made for a period longer than 1 year.[265] The new landlord or employer is not liable under these acts if, before entering into the agreement, he acted in good faith in believing that the tenant or employee had already made up his mind to quit the prior contract.[266]

Louisiana, in addition to imposing criminal and civil liability on the enticer, also imposes civil liabilty for all damages resulting from violation of the lease on any third person who assists, aids and abets,

[262] Pope, *Dig. Stat. Ark.*, 1937, secs. 8600 and 3493.
[263] *Miss. Code Ann.*, 1944, sec 2129.
[264] Dart, *La. Gen. Stat.*, 1939, sec. 4384.
[265] *Ibid.*, sec. 4386.
[266] *Coolidge* v. *Howe* (1930), 180 Ark. 952, 23 S. W. (2d) 609; *Thompson* v. *Box* (1927), 147 Miss. 1, 112 So. 597, 600.

and entices a tenant to violate his contract.[267] Further, it is unlawful in Louisiana for any person to go upon premises or a plantation between sunset and sunrise to move or assist in moving any laborer or tenant or his property without consent of the landowner or proprietor.[268] Any person found guilty of violating this act may be fined $50 to $1,000 or imprisoned from 10 days to 6 months.[269]

No comparable statutes relating to the enticement of tenants, sharecroppers, or laborers from their contracts were found in Oklahoma or Texas.

Variation of Tenure Factors by Lease Types. Tenure stability, division of management scores, and other tenure factors varied with lease types. Whether types of leases used were casual or merely an adjustment to other forces, historical, social, and economic, is not decided. Probably all had an influence.

—*Tenure stability.* In the terms of actual years spent on the rent tract by the lessee, the oral, indefinite lease resulted in the most stable tenure. Twenty to 50 per cent of the tenants farming under oral, indefinite leases reported having resided on the present rent tract for 10 years or over. In contrast, tenure under both oral or written 1-year leases, when regarded retrospectively, was far less stable, and the record under written leases of 2 years' duration and over was not much better. The highest percentage of tenants in each of these latter 3 lease categories were found to have been farming the present tract for only 1 to 2 years.

Tenure under half-share, oral 1-year cropping contracts appears less stable than under oral or written 1-year leases. Also, although the sample was small, tenure under oral indefinite cropping contracts is less stable than under oral indefinite leases. (Table 78)

When looking toward the future, one reasonably would expect the greatest tenure security from written leases of 2 years' duration or over. However, a written lease for a term of several years, which may be terminated sooner on the happening of some event, is not conducive to security of tenure. Similarly, when looking forward toward years to come, an oral indefinite lease offers little assurance of tenure security. In Arkansas, Mississippi, and Oklahoma, where a year-to-year tenancy is implied under certain circumstances when a tenant holds over, the new lease term may be terminated at the end of each year by either party giving the requisite notice. Moreover, in Texas

[267] Dart, *La. Gen. Stat.*, 1939, sec. 6606.
[268] Dart, *La. Code Crim. Law and Pro.*, 1943, sec. 1291.
[269] *Ibid.*, sec. 1293.

and Louisiana a tenant holding over obtains only a lease for another year, which terminates at the end of the year with little or no notice.[270]

Security of tenure, when looking ahead, also appears illusory under another type of oral indefinite lease sometimes used, the oral lease of indefinite duration, which may or may not end within a year depending on the occurrence of some contingency.[271] Although occupancy under this type of lease may continue for years, the contingency ending the lease term may occur at any moment.

—Division of management. Division of management scores are indicative of the proportion of the details of farm management exercised by various categories of tenants or croppers. In a measure, these managment scores describe in statistical terms the number and types of rights in the land farmed actually exercised by tenants and croppers under prevailing leasing and cropping agreements, and the quantity and kinds of rights reserved by the landlords and landowner-employers. A high score indicates that a high proportion of the management was done by the farmers in that tenancy class, and a low score, that the reverse was true. (Table 82)

In the sample areas of Arkansas, Mississippi, Oklahoma, and Texas management scores of farmers paying cash or standing rent were highest. Such scores in the order named progressively decreased for farmers paying share-cash rent, having other rental arrangements, or paying "third and fourth" rent. Management scores of farmers on the "halves" were perceptibly lower, ranging from 23 to 51, compared with scores of 61 to 91 for the other tenancy classes. Scores of Negro farmers in all tenancy groups were lower than scores of comparable white classes and considerably less for Negro half-share farmers. Scores of farmers on the halves on the Coastal Plain in Arkansas were 51 for whites and 28 for Negroes. Comparable scores in Mississippi were 38 and 23, respectively.

As the distance from the residence of the tenant or cropper to the rent tract increased, the frequency of supervision decreased and the management score increased. (Table 81) There is no definite relation between management scores and years on rent tracts. (Table 101)

One no doubt can validly conclude from the distribution of management scores that farmers on the half-shares most frequently were legally croppers, or employees, with little control over the details of farm operations and that farmers in all other tenancy categories most often were legally tenants. However, it is highly probable that some

[270] See *supra,* "Leases created by holding over," p. 255.

[271] See *supra,* "Oral, indefinite-term leases," p. 253.

farmers on the halves were not croppers but were legally tenants and that some farmers in the other tenure classes legally should be classed as croppers. This latter supposition is confirmed where a number of renters are found in the two low-score class intervals and a number of croppers in the two high-score class intervals. (Table 42) It is well to bear in mind that the highest average management score of a half-share farmer was 51 and the lowest average management score of tenants paying rent in other ways was 61. (Table 82)

—*Miscellaneous factors.* Migration indexes in all sample areas of tenants operating under oral indefinite leases were lower, indicating a more stable tenure than similar indexes of tenants with other types of leases. Indexes of tenants in all lease classes in Texas were considerably lower than in other sample areas. (Table 95)

The average tenant's years of earning life since beginning of independant earning, except in the Arkansas sample area, was lowest for tenants farming under oral indefinite leases. The average years of earning life for tenants in the oral 1-year, written 1-year, and written 2-year and-over types of lease classes, in the order named, generally tended to increase slowly but progressively. Management scores of tenants in the various type of lease classes showed the same general trend of increase by class, except for tenants operating under oral indefinite leases, who, in the Oklahoma and Texas sample areas, had the highest scores for those areas.

Diversification indexes of tenants operating under written leases of 2 years' term or over, in all 4 sample areas, were higher, an indication of more diversification, than similar indexes of tenants in the other type of lease classes. Of interest is the finding that diversification indexes of tenants farming under oral indefinite leases in Mississippi, Oklahoma, and Texas areas had higher scores than tenants with oral or written 1-year leases.

Improvements and Repairs

One measure of improvements on farms in the Southwestern Region is the value placed upon such improvements by the farmers. Estimated value of dwellings of owners, except for the Texas and Oklahoma sample areas, averaged less than $825. Comparable values placed on homes of tenants and croppers in all areas ranged from slightly over $700 to less than $200 per unit. The dwelling usually represented a little over half of the value of all improvements on the farm. (Table 13)

An indicator of interest in the condition of improvements on farms is the annual cash repair costs. Expenditures for repairs in 1942, not including labor contributed by the farm operator, on dwellings and other improvements, were highest for owners and part owners in Oklahoma, averaging $112 and $135 respectively. Such average expenditures in Arkansas and Texas by white farmers in the same two tenure groups ranged from a high of $72 to a low of $34. No data were available for Mississippi and Louisiana. Cash expenditures for repairs on cropper farming units in the 3 states reporting all averaged under $12. Renters fared considerably better, except for Negro renters in Arkansas.

Repair costs when compared with value of improvements are perhaps more revealing of the relative attention given to repairing farm improvements in the various tenure groups than is a mere listing of the amounts expended for repairs for each group. Ratios of cash repair costs of value of all improvements indicate that relatively equal attention was given to repairs on owner, part owner, and renter operated farms. Ratios in the Oklahoma sample area were 4.4 for owners, 5.1 for part owners, and 5.1 for renters; and in the Arkansas area, 2.3, 2.7, and 2.9, respectively, for white farmers in the same tenure groups. Generally, the same relationship between the ratios was maintained in the Texas area.

All measures of improvements on farms, that is, value of dwellings, value of all improvements, average cash repair costs, and the ratios between the latter two, usually were lowest for the cropper tenure group. (Table 102)

Condition of Leased Premises at Time of Entry. Laws of the several states in the Southwestern Region relating to the duty of the landlord to provide a habitable dwelling for his tenants vary. Three states deny the existence of such a duty and two states impose the duty, with reservations.

Unless otherwise agreed, the tenant in Arkansas takes the premises as he finds them. There is no implied covenant that the leased premises are tenantable or suitable for the uses for which they are leased, or even suitable for occupation, or that they will continue suitable for the tenant's purposes. In the absence of fraud or concealment by the landlord, the rule of *caveat emptor* applies and the tenant leases at his peril.[272]

The same rule applies in Mississippi. As stated in an early decision,

[272] *Little Rock Ice Co.* v. *Consumers Ice Co.* (1914), 114 Ark. 532, 170 S. W. 241, 243; *Oliver* v. *Hartzell* (1926). 170 Ark. 512, 280 S. W. 979, 980.

"The intended tenant must use his own facilities, and judge for himself if the premises he desires to lease are in repair, and are suitable for his use. . . . He takes the premises for better or for worse . . . as he finds them."[273] This decision is still being followed.[274]

The law is similar in Texas. "In the absence of a covenant on the part of a landlord to repair, there is no implied warranty that the leased premises are in a tenantable condition . . ." or that the leased structure is fit for occupancy.[275] "The tenant, in the absence of an agreement to the contrary, takes the rented premises as he finds them, under the doctrine of *caveat emptor,*"[276] unless, of course, there is fraud or concealment by the landlord as to their condition.[277] In the words of another court, "There is no implied covenant . . . that the premises are tenantable, or reasonably suitable for occupation."[278]

The rule that the landlord, in the absence of agreement in the lease, is not bound to put the premises in a condition fit for occupancy, also applies in Oklahoma when premises are leased for business and trade.[279] The rule has been applied to a grazing lease under which the tenants refused to pay rent because the premises were unfenced. The court held, "In the absence of warranty, deceit, or fraud, the rule of *caveat emptor* applies . . . and it is the duty of the tenant to make examination of the demised premises to determine their safety and adaptability to the purposes for which they are hired."[280] A different rule in Oklahoma pertains to premises leased for "occupation of human beings." The landlord of such a building, in the absence of an agreement to the contrary, must put it in a condition fit for occupation, and thereafter keep it in repair, except that the tenant must repair all injuries due to his ordinary negligence.[281]

In contrast, Louisiana landlords are bound to deliver the leased premises to the tenant in good condition.[282] In fact, the landlord guarantees the tenant against all the vices and defects of the thing

---

[273] *Jones* v. *Millsaps* (1893), 71 Miss. 10, 14 So. 440, 441.

[274] *Green* v. *Long* (1928), 152 Miss. 117, 118 So. 705, 706; *Causey* v. *Norwood,* (1934), 171 Miss. 874, 156 So. 592, 593.

[275] *American Exchange Nat. Bank of Dallas* v. *Swope & Mangold,* Tex. C. A. (1907), 46 T. C. A. 64, 101 S. W. 872, 873.

[276] *Walling* v. *Houston & T. C. R. Co.* (Tex. C. A. 1917), 195 S. W. 232, 237.

[277] *Archibald* v. *Fidelity Title & Trust Co.* (Tex. C. A. 1927), 296 S. W. 680, 682.

[278] *Jackson* v. *Amador* (Tex. C. A. 1934), 75 S. W. (2d) 892, 893.

[279] *Tucker* v. *Bennett* (1905), 15 Okla. 187, 81 P. 423, 425; *Horton* v. *Early* (1913), 39 Okla. 99, 134 P. 436, 437; *Enterprise Seed Co.* v. *Moore* (1915), 51 Okla. 477. 151 P. 867, 868.

[280] *Arbuckle Realty Trust* v. *Rosson* (1937), 180 Okla. 20, 67 P. (2d) 444, 445.

[281] *Okla. Stats. Ann.,* 1937, Tit. 41, sec. 31.

[282] Dart, *La. Civ. Code,* 1945, Art. 2693.

leased, which may prevent its being used, even if he knows nothing of such defects at the time of making the lease or if they arise later without fault of the tenant.[283]

Obligation to Repair During Lease Term. State laws placing responsibility, in the absence of contract, for maintaining repair in dwellings and other improvements on leased premises also vary, the variation parralleling closely by states the law relative to the duty to provide tenants a habitable dwelling. Under Arkansas law there is no implied obligation upon landlords to keep leased premises in repair. Unless the landlord agrees to repair he cannot be compelled to do so.[284] Similarly, in Mississippi the landlord is not under a duty to make repairs to leased premises so as to keep them in suitable condition for the tenant, unless such obligation is specifically undertaken by contract.[285] The same rule is followed in Texas, and "a landlord is not bound to repair leased premises unless there is a covenant or agreement on his part to do so."[286] Moreover, "the mere relation of landlord and tenant creates no obligation on the landlord's part to repair or keep in repairs the leased premises."[287] Nor will the prevalence of a general custom among landlords in the community to repair impose such obligation.[288] In fact, unless the landlord agrees to repair or premises are let with a nuisance upon them, the tenant, and not the landlord, is obligated to repair the premises leased to him and is responsible for damages resulting from want of repair.[289]

In Oklahoma, in the absence of an agreement to the contrary, the landlord must put premises leased for "occupation of human beings" in a condition fit for occupation and thereafter keep them in repair, except that the tenant must repair all injuries due to his ordinary negligence.[290] If the landlord after reasonable notice fails to repair, the tenant may repair and deduct the cost thereof from the rent.[291] On the other hand, in Oklahoma there is no implied duty on the owner of premises leased for business purposes to keep them in re-

---

[283] *Ibid.*, Art. 2695.

[284] *Rundell* v. *Rogers* (1920), 144 Ark. 293, 222 S. W. 19, 20; *Delaney* v. *Johnson* (1910), 95 Ark. 131, 128 S. W. 859, 860; *Jones* v. *Felker* (1904), Ark. 404, 80 S. W. 1088.

[285] *Causey* v. *Norwood* (1934), 171 Miss. 874, 156 So. 592, 593; *Jones* v. *Millsaps* (1893), 71 Miss. 10, 14 So. 440, 441; *Rich* v. *Swalm* (1931), 161 Miss. 505, 137 So. 325, 326.

[286] *Weinstein* v. *Harrison* (1886), 66 Tex. 546, 1 S. W. 626, 627.

[287] *Ross* v. *Haner* (Tex. Com. App. A, 1924), 258 S. W. 1036, 1037; 244 S. W. 231.

[288] *Weinstein* v. *Harrison* (1886), 66 Tex. 546, 1 S. W. 626, 627.

[289] *O'Connor* v. *Andrew* (1891), 81 Tex. 28, 16 S. W. 628, 629.

[290] *Okla. Stats. Ann.*, 1937, Tit. 41, sec. 31.

[291] *Ibid.*, Tit. 41, sec. 32.

pair. Such duty can arise from contract only.[292] The statute imposing a duty on landlords to repair a building intended for occupation by human beings[293] has no application to business buildings.[294]

The landlord in Louisiana is under an implied obligation to maintain the thing leased in a condition to serve the use for which it is hired[295] and to make all repairs which may accidentally become necessary.[296] Excepted are repairs to the hearth, chimney, plastering of lower part of interior walls, floors, except when decayed, accidentally broken window panes, windows, partitions, locks and hinges, and everything of that kind which, according to the custom of the place, the tenant is bound to make,[297] unless otherwise agreed.[298] The expense of repairs of a nature usually done by the tenant, when caused by unforeseen events or decay, must be borne by the landlord.[299] If the landlords fails to deliver the leased thing in good condition, or fails to repair when necessary during the lease term, the tenant, after request and on refusal or neglect by the landlord, may make such repairs as are indispensable and deduct the price thereof, when just and reasonable, from the rent due.[300]

Area Practices Regarding Repairs. Although under the laws of Arkansas, Mississippi, and Texas the tenant, unless otherwise agreed, takes the premises as he finds them under the rules of *caveat emptor,*[301] and repairs, if desired, at his own expense,[302] the most frequent practice in the Arkansas and Texas sample areas was for the landlord to provide all cash outlays used to make repairs to dwellings used by both tenants and croppers. In the Mississippi sample area the usual practice, except for cash renters, was for the landowner and his tenants or croppers to contribute equally towards the cash expense required for repairing tenant and cropper dwellings. Labor for repairing dwellings in all sample areas was usually furnished by the tenant or cropper, except where a cash outlay for hire of labor was involved. (Table 77)

[292] *Enterprise Seed Co.* v. *Moore* (1915), 51 Okla. 477, 151 P. 867, 868; *Wick* v. *Wasson* (1943), 193 Okla. 209, 142 P. (2d) 124, 125; *Gordon* v. *Reinheimer* (1934), 167 Okla. 343, 29 P. (2d) 596, 598.

[293] *Okla. Stats. Ann.*, 1937, Tit. 41, secs. 31, 32.

[294] *Barker* v. *Findley* (1929), 136 Okla. 55, 275 P. 1054, 1055; *Gordon* v. *Reinheimer* (1934), 167 Okla. 343, 29 P. (2d), 596, 598.

[295] Dart, *La. Civ. Code*, 1945, Art. 2692.

[296] *Ibid.*, Art. 2693.

[297] *Ibid.*, Art. 2716.

[298] *Ibid.*, Art. 2715.

[299] *Ibid.*, Art. 2717.

[300] *Ibid.*, Art. 2694.

[301] See *supra*, "Condition of Leased Premises at Time of Entry," p. 267.

[302] See *supra*, "Obligation to Repair During Lease Term," p. 269.

Modal arrangements, that is the arrangements between landowners and tenants or croppers that occur most frequently, regarding repair of leased dwellings in Arkansas and Texas sample areas indicate that in 74 to 100 per cent of the cases the landlord contributed all cash expenses of repairs on dwellings. In the Mississippi area similar modal arrangements reveal that the landlord contributed half the cash cost of repairs to dwellings of share-renters and croppers in 90 to 99 per cent, respectively, of the samples. No modal arrangement in Mississippi for sharing cash cost of repairs to dwellings of share-renters was found. Modal arrangements also show that all labor requirements, not involving cash outlays, for repairing dwellings in all 3 sample areas usually were provided by the occupant, except for croppers in Mississippi and Texas.

In contrast, in Oklahoma, where under the law the landlord, in the absence of an agreement to the contrary, must put premises leased for "occupation of human beings" in a condition fit for occupancy and, thereafter, keep them in repair,[303] the most frequent practice in the sample area was for the tenant to assume responsibility for all repair costs, both cash outlays and labor requirements, on his residence. Modal arrangements also disclose that all labor costs were paid by cash and share-renters 100 per cent of the time, and by share-cash renters 67 per cent of the time. No comparable data were available for Louisiana.

Modal arrangements regarding repairs to improvements on leased premises in Oklahoma no doubt were influenced by the fact that a greater proportion of the tenants in Oklahoma than in the other states owned some or all of the improvements on leased premises.

Of considerable interest is a comparison of the incidence of the obligation to repair leased farm dwellings under prevailing practices in the sample areas and the legally implied incidence of that obligation when unchanged by contractual arrangements. The relationship, except for labor costs, appears generally inverse. In view of the laws in each state,[304] one would reasonably have expected prevailing practice to place all costs of repairing dwellings in the Arkansas, Mississippi, and Texas areas on the tenants, and in Oklahoma on the landlord, but the reverse, except for labor costs in Arkansas, Mississippi, and Texas, appears most frequently true. (Table 77)

Responsibility for repairing improvements other than dwellings

[303] See *supra*, "Obligation to Repair During Lease Term," p. 269.

[304] See *supra*, "Condition of Leased Premises at Time of Entry," p. 267; and "Obligation to Repair During Lease Term," p. 269.

parallels closely by states the practices regarding repairs to dwellings. In the Arkansas and Texas areas in 60 to 94 per cent of the samples, varying with the type of rental payment, the landlord bore all cash costs of such repairs; and in the Oklahoma area, in 72 to 100 per cent of the cases, all such cash costs of repairs were borne by the tenant. In the Mississippi area, the landlord usually paid all cash costs when share-renters or croppers were involved, but in 56 per cent of the cases cash renters were responsible for the cash repair costs of improvements other than dwellings. On farms employing sharecroppers 42 per cent of the landlords in the Mississippi area provided all the labor on improvements. In the Texas area no modal arrangement for provision of labor for improvements on farms using croppers was found.

Again, the incidence of the obligation of repair under prevailing practices, compared with its incidence as implied when unmodified by contract, under the laws of each state is of interest. Under the laws of Arkansas, Mississippi, and Texas the tenant must keep improvements on leased premises in repair, unless otherwise agreed. The same rule applies in Oklahoma to all improvements on leased premises, excepting those leased for "occupation by human beings."[305] However, in the sample areas in Arkansas, Texas, and in Mississippi, except for cash renters, the prevailing practice was for the landlord to bear all costs of repair. In the Oklahoma area, the usual practice was for the tenant to assume both cash and labor costs of "other improvements," which is where Oklahoma law places that obligation unless shifted by agreement of the parties.

Compensation for Improvements. State laws in the Southwestern Region, except for Louisiana under some circumstances, uniformly do not impose a duty on the landlord to pay for improvements erected by tenants or croppers on leased premises, unless the landlord has expressly or impliedly agreed to pay for them. However, in all 5 states the parties by contract may bind the landlord to pay his tenants or croppers for their equity in improvements left on the premises at the end of the lease or contract term.

As stated by the Arkansas court, "The law imposes no obligation upon a landlord to pay his tenant for improvements made by him upon the demised premises. The tenant is presumed to repair and improve for his own benefit; and his right to the result of his labor expended for that purpose is to reap the enhanced benefit during the term. . . . It is only by virtue of an express agreement by the

[305] See *supra*, "Obligation to Repair During Lease Term," p. 269.

landlord to pay for improvements that the tenant can recover their value of him. . . . The mere fact that the landlord permits the tenant to make permanent improvements, without protest or warning that he will not pay, raises no presumption that he intends to do so."[306] The same general rule applies in Oklahoma, Texas, and apparently in Mississippi, where it was applied in a decision concerning repairs only.[307] Similarly, in Louisiana, a tenant cannot recover from the landlord the value of improvements made without consent of the landlord;[308] but if the improvements were made with lime and cement, the landlord may retain them on paying a fair price.[309] Another act permits a landlord, on payment of material and labor costs, to keep plantings, construction and works made by third persons on his premises.[310]

Removal of Agricultural Improvements and Fixtures. Under the common law rule whatever is annexed by a tenant to the land becomes a part of it and cannot afterward be removed by him without consent of the landlord. An exception, however, exists favoring removal of fixtures erected by tenants for purposes of trade and manufacture. This exception does not include erections "solely for agricultural purposes."[311] This common law rule, of course, applies only where the landlord and tenant have made no agreement regarding removal of improvements or fixtures. Under the laws of all 5 states, the contracting parties are free to agree to disposition of agricultural fixtures and improvements made on leased premises by a tenant or cropper in any manner they see fit.

Oklahoma by statute has re-enacted the common law rule on this subject.[312] Under one Oklahoma act, fixtures are defined as things affixed to land "by roots, as in the case of trees, vines, or shrubs, or imbedded in it, as in the case of walls, or permanently resting upon it, as in the case of buildings, or permanently attached to what is thus permanent, as by means of cement, plaster, nails, bolts, or screws."[313] Another act provides that a fixture thus attached belongs

[306] *Gocio* v. *Day* (1888), 51 Ark. 46, 9 S. W. 433.

[307] *Hull* v. *Semple* (1924), 103 Okla. 112, 229 P. 1042, 1044; *Randolph* v. *Mitchell* (Tex. C. A. 1899), 51 S. W. 297, 298; *Thomas Hinds Lodge No. 58, F. & A. M.* v. *Presbyterian Church of Fayette* (1912), 103 Miss. 130, 60 So. 66, 71, 72.

[308] *Benton* v. *Jacobs* (1926), 3 La. App. 274, 278; *Dreyfuss* v. *Process Oil & Fuel Co.* (1918), 140 La. 50, 77 So. 283, 285.

[309] *Elrod* v. *Hart* (La. C. A. 1933), 146 So. 797, 798, citing *Civ. Code*, Art. 2726; *Dreyfuss* v. *Process Oil & Fuel Co.* (1918), 140 La. 50, 77 So. 283.

[310] Dart, *La. Civ. Code*, 1945, Art. 508.

[311] *Van Ness* v. *Pacard* (U. S. S. Ct. 1829), 2 Pet. 137, 143, 27 U. S. Rep. 137.

[312] *Winans* v. *Beidler* (1898), 6 Okla. 603, 52 P. 405.

[313] *Okla. Stat. Ann.*, 1937, Tit. 60, sec. 7.

to the owner of the land and may not be removed, unless he chooses to require or permit its removal. An exception to this general rule permits tenants, during the lease term, to remove "any thing affixed thereto for purpose of trade, manufacture, ornament, or domestic use, if the removal can be effected without injury to the premises, unless the thing has, by the manner in which it is affixed, become an integral part of the premises." The parties, of course, may by agreement permit removal of improvements.[314] This latter act does not authorize the removal by the tenant of agricultural fixtures placed by him on leased premises, except by agreement.

Apparently in Texas there is no discrimination against rural tenants removing their agricultural fixtures. According to dictum in one Texas decision, "trade fixtures, agricultural fixtures, and fixtures established for ornament, convenience, or domestic use . . . are removable on termination of the lease, if that can be effected without substantial injury to the freehold."[315] Similar dictum is used by another Texas court: "As between landlord and tenant, there may be many fixtures attached by the latter which he may remove during or at the termination of his lease without the consent of the landlord. These are classed as trade fixtures . . . agricultural fixtures; and fixtures set up for the purpose of ornament or convenience, or for domestic use."[316] However, improvements of a permanent character made by the tenant on leased premises without the consent of the landlord and without an understanding that they might be removed from the premises at the expiration of the tenancy may not be removed by the tenant.[317]

Neither Arkansas nor Mississippi have statutes dealing with removal by tenants of their agricultural improvements or fixtures from leased premises. Further, in both states there is a paucity of court decisions on the subject in which some agreement regarding removal was not involved. Court decisions in Arkansas, however, follow the modern trend in favor of removal of articles affixed to the freehold by the tenant for purposes of trade or manufacture, unless it appears that the fixtures were intended to be permanently attached.[318] In deciding whether an improvement should remain or be removed, the Arkansas court looks to the intent of the tenant as determined from

[314] *Ibid.*, Tit. 60, sec. 334.

[315] See *Nine Hundred Main* v. *City of Houston*, (Tex. C. A. 1941), 150 S. W. (2d) 468, 471.

[316] See *Bovet* v. *Holzgraft* (1893), 5 T. C. A. 141, 23 S. W. 1014, 1015.

[317] *Williams* v. *Gardner* (Tex. C. A. 1919), 215 S. W. 981, 984.

[318] *Bennett* v. *Taylor* (1932), 185 Ark. 794, 49 S. W. (2d) 608, 610.

expressed intent, from manner of annexation to the premises, and from suitability of the chattel to the tenant's purposes.[319] Arkansas decisions have permitted the removal of a cotton gin as a trade fixture. The gin was not intended to be permanently attached to the realty and was constructed so that it could be put on rollers and taken away.[320] Similarly, temporary employees' houses erected by tenants to house sawmill employees have been held to be removable trade fixtures.[321]

Also in Mississippi, a cotton gin, placed on a plantation by a tenant with intention of removing it, has been held removable. In this decision the court, in discussing the removal of fixtures, said " . . . there have always been generous exceptions in favor of trade, manufactures, and, as in the case before us, tenants. The placing of gins, condensers, etc. on plantations cultivated largely in our staple product, cotton, is essential to the preparation and manufacture of the article for market; and the rights of tenants, as against their landlords, are not to be doubted."[322] In an earlier Mississippi decision, the court said it would have no difficulty in holding that a tenant has the right, at the termination of his tenancy, to remove a sawmill, engine, and appurtenances.[323] The court in referring to an early United States Supreme Court decision, said that although "the English courts seem to have made no relaxation in favor of erections for agricultural uses . . . it is otherwise in the United States." Further, "there has been considerable modification of the old rule, that the erection must not be attached to the freehold, so as to be incapable of removal without some disturbance of the soil."[324]

In Louisiana, "the lessee has a right to remove the improvements and additions which he has made to the thing let, provided he leaves it in the state in which he received it. But if these additions be made with lime and cement, the lessor may retain them, on paying a fair price."[325] The tenant, under this article, cannot claim compensation for the improvements, but may remove them, in case the removal can be effected and the premises left in the condition in which they were

[319] *Arkansas Cold Storage and Ice Co.* v. *Fulbright* (1926), 171 Ark. 552, 285 S. W. 12, 13.

[320] *Field* v. *Morris* (1910), 95 Ark. 268, 129 S. W. 543, 545.

[321] *Rogers* v. *Vanderbilt* (1928), 175 Ark. 977, 1 S. W. (2d) 71; *Barnes* v. *Jeffus* (1927), 173 Ark. 100, 291 S. W. 990.

[322] *McMath* v. *Levy* (1896), 74 Miss. 450, 21, So. 9, on error, 74 Miss. 450, 21 So. 523.

[323] *Perkins* v. *Swank* (1870), 43 Miss. 349, 362, citing *Van Ness* v. *Pacard* (U. S. Sup. Ct. 1830), 2 Pet. 137. 144.

[324] *Ibid.*

[325] Dart, *La. Civ. Code*, 1945, Art. 2726.

leased, except where the improvements were made with lime and cement and the landlord elects to retain them.[326] Another Louisiana act permits the owner of the soil either to keep or to compel removal or demolition of plantings, construction, and works made by third persons on his premises. If the owner elects to keep the works, he must reimburse the material and labor costs of construction; but, if he requires their demolition, the cost thereof must be borne by the person who erected them.[327] Under this act, a tenant has been held entitled to retain possession of the property, without being chargeable with rent, until the landowner makes his election, and if the election is to keep the improvements, until he is reimbursed. The tenant, however, cannot compel the landowner to elect to keep and reimburse him for the value of improvements placed upon the land.[328]

LEGAL ASPECTS OF FARM CREDIT

The availability of adequate farm credit, both long-term and seasonal, is a prerequisite to a healthy rural economy. Credit needs of landlords, tenants, and croppers are often dissimilar and so also is the security offered. The terms of a loan to finance purchase of, or improvements on, a farm necessarily are different from the terms of a production loan. The former generally and properly is a long-term loan, with a mortgage on land and improvements as security; the latter often is a short-term loan made on personal security or secured by a chattel mortgage on farm machinery, equipment and crops, or secured by a contract or statutory lien on the current crop only.

Many factors conditioned the extent to which credit was used by farmers in the various sample areas and the type and sources of credit used. Important was the tenure of the borrower, his net worth and annual income, the purposes of the loan, the type of crops raised and the power used, and, most significant, the security available to assure repayment of the loan.

Credit was extensively used by sample farmers in the Southwestern Region for buying farms, for making farm improvements, for buying livestock and equipment, for paying production and family expenses, and for other purposes. (Tables 113 and 106) The proportion of farm owners having mortgages on their real estate varied by race and state from slightly under 15 to over 70 per cent. Other-than-

[326] *Dreyfus* v. *Process Oil & Fuel Co.* (1918), 140 La. 50; 77 So. 283, 285.
[327] Dart, *La. Civ. Code*, 1945, Art. 508.
[328] *Hammonds* v. *Busbee* (1930), 170 La. 573, 128 So. 520, 521.

real-estate credit was extensively used by farmers in all the principal tenure groups. (Table 103) A considerable proportion of farmers in all tenure groups, particularly renters and croppers, used credit to finance farm production and farm family living. Credit for such purposes was extensively used by Negro farmers. (Table 104)

Although credit is sometimes extended as a personal favor, creditors in the long run usually look to a debtor's net worth or anticipated earning for assurances of repayment. Farmers in all tenure groups in the 2 western states had both a higher net worth and a higher annual income than in the eastern sample areas. (Tables 62 and 105)

Real Estate or Long-Term Credit

The main purpose as reported by sample farmers for using real estate credit in the Southwestern Region was to buy the present farm. Of the 282 owners reporting purposes in all sample areas, 213 used it for farm purchase. Twenty-one used real estate credit to refinance old mortgages or other debts and 13 to finance improvements. Real estate credit was infrequently used for financing purchase of livestock and equipment or for paying production and family expenses, only 12 cases being reported. (Table 106)

Credit alone, or together with some cash, was used by farmers in 60 per cent of the cases for acquiring the first tract of their present farms. By comparison, acquisition of such first tracts was by cash purchase in only 15 per cent of the cases, with a similar proportion acquired by inheritance. (Tables 107 and 108)

The average real estate loan outstanding per farmer in the sample areas was about $800 in Mississippi, around $1,100 in Arkansas, $3,950 in Oklahoma, and from $3,500 to $6,500 in Texas. (Table 109)

Of the 829 farm owners sampled in the 5 areas, 363 used real estate credit. Sources of such loans, ranked by numbers of loans, were as follows: Federal Land Bank, 195; insurance companies or societies, 37; individuals, 35; local banks, 27; mortgage companies, 15; Farm Security Administration, 15; local merchants, 14; Oklahoma School Land Commission, 11; lumber companies, 6; and others, 8. (Table 110)

Rights Under Real Estate Mortgages. Several theories of real estate mortgages prevail in the states in the region. In Louisiana, Oklahoma, and Texas "a mortgage is regarded as merely a lien upon the property both before and after breach of conditions. It passes no title or estate in the property to the mortgagee and gives him no right to possession before foreclosure." Under the Mississippi doctrine, "the mortgagee has, before default, merely a lien, but after default and entry by the mortgagee, the latter has the legal title, and, as owner, may take possession, or may adopt any legal remedies to obtain possession." Arkansas retains the common law doctrine and regards the mortgage deed as passing at once the legal title to the mortgagee, subject to defeasance on performance by the mortgager of the conditions of the mortgage. "The right of possession follows the title so that the mortgagee may enter into possession of the mortgaged property immediately unless restrained by express provisions, or necessary implications, of the mortgage; and in any case upon breach of the condition he becomes entitled to the possession and may recover it by action." As between the mortgagee and mortgagor in Arkansas, the legal title is in the mortgagee only for the protection of his interests; as to all others, legal title is in the mortgagor, and the property may be conveyed by him subject to the mortgage.[329]

In all 5 states, if mortgaged property at foreclosure sales does not sell for a sum sufficient to satisfy the amount due, a judgment for the deficiency may be had.[330] However, if a mortgagee in Louisiana elects to foreclose without first having the mortgaged property appraised, he loses his right to a deficiency judgment.[331] Moreover, in Arkansas mortgaged real property may not be sold at first offering at foreclosure sale for less than two-thirds of the appraised value. Twelve months later at a second offering it may be sold to the highest bidder without reference to appraisement.[332]

There is no statutory right of redemption after foreclosure sale in Louisiana, Mississippi, Oklahoma, or Texas.[333] In Arkansas, on the other hand, a period of 1 year is allowed after sale for redemption of the property by the mortgagor, his heirs, or legal representatives.[334] All 5 states in the region during the 1930 depression years enacted

[329] Thompson, *Real Property*, Perm. Ed., Vol. 9, sec. 4657; see also Jones, *Mortgages*, 8th Ed., 1928, Vol. 1, secs. 21, 34, 40, 52, and 59.

[330] Pope, *Dig. Stat. Ark.*, 1937, sec. 9478; *Salzman* v. *His Creditors* (La. S. C. 1842), 2 Robinson, *Reports* 241, 242; *Miss. Code Ann.*, 1944, sec. 1386; *Okla. Stat. Ann.*, 1937, Tit. 12, sec. 903; John F. Franki, *Vernon's Tex. Rules of Civ. Pro.*, Rule 309 (1942).

[331] Dart, *La. Gen. Stat.*, 1939, sec. 5021.6; *Home Finance Service* v. *Walmsley* (La. Ct. App. 1937), 176 So. 415, 417.

[332] Pope, *Dig. Stat. Ark.*, 1937, secs. 9460-9464.

[333] *Suthon* v. *Cambon Bros.* (1924), 159 La. 134, 105 So. 252, 253; *Payne* v. *Long-Bell Lumber Co.* (1900), 9. Okla. 683, 60 P. 235, 238; *Maulding* v. *Coffin* (1894), 6 Tex. C. A., 416, 25 S. W. 480, 482; regarding redemption in Mississippi, see Martindale-Hubbell, *Law Dictionary*, 1946, Vol. 2, Title "Mississippi," subtitle "Mortgages," and Jones, *Mortgages*, 8th Ed. 1928, Vol. 3, sec. 1720.

[334] Pope, *Dig. Stat. Ark.*, 1937, sec. 9473.

temporary moratorium legislation authorizing delay in sale or in other steps in foreclosing real estate mortgages.[335]

Federal Long-Term Loans. The Federal Land Bank made over 50 per cent of the real estate loans on farms in sample areas of 4 states in the region. In Texas the percentage was 25.

Federal Land Bank loans, secured by first mortgages on farm land, may be made to finance purchase of land, equipment, fertilizer, or livestock; for making improvements; to liquidate indebtedness; or to obtain funds for general agricultural uses. No loan shall exceed 65 per cent of the normal value of the mortgaged farm. Provision must be made for amortization within a period of from 5 to not more than 40 years.[336]

In addition to Federal Land Bank credit, it is possible for a farmer also to obtain a Land Bank Commissioner loan. Such loans may be made on the security of a first or second mortgage on the farm property, real or personal, including crops. Commissioner loans are made for the same purposes as Land Bank loans and, in addition, for refinancing purposes. Amounts loaned ordinarily may not exceed 75 per cent of the normal value of the property. The debt is repayable over similar periods as Land Bank loans. Commissioner loans under present acts may be made until July 1, 1947.[337]

Federal Land Bank real estate loans in the Arkansas and Mississippi sample areas averaged near $600 per loan and around $3,000 in Oklahoma and Texas. (Table 123) These averages by states are considerably lower than averages of all realty loans from all sources. (Table 109)

Another Federal agency, the Farm Security Administration, is also authorized to make loans secured by real estate mortgages. Under the provisions of the Bankhead-Jones Farm Tenancy Act,[338] the Secretary of Agriculture is empowered to extend credit to qualified farm tenants, farm laborers, sharecroppers, veterans, and certain other individuals to enable such persons to acquire farms.[339] Loans must be secured by first mortgages and may be in such amounts, not in excess of the farm's value, as may be necessary to enable the borrower to acquire

[335] Wiltsie, *Mortgage Foreclosure*, 5th Ed., 1938, Vol. 3, secs. 1297, 1306, 1310, 1322, and 1327.

[336] 12 *U. S. C. A.*, sec. 771, 1945, Supp. 1947. As amended June 30, 1945, Ch. 204, sec. 4, 59 Stat. 267. Under previous acts loan maximums were lower.

[337] *Ibid.*, sec. 1016, 1945, Supp. 1946. As amended June 30, 1945, Ch. 204, secs. 11-13, 59 Stat. 269; July 12, 1946, Ch. 570, sec. 1, 60 Stat. 532.

[338] 7 *U. S. C. A.*, sec. 1000 *et seq.*, 1939, Supp. 1947.

[339] *Ibid.*, sec. 1001.

the farm and make necessary repairs and improvements thereon. The contract shall provide for amortization in not more than 40 years.[340] Numbers of loans that can be made annually are limited by the funds available, which are distributed among the states on the basis of farm population and the prevalence of tenancy.[341] An administrative ruling limits the maximum loan to $12,000.

Only 15 of 363, the total number of real estate loans from all sources, were Farm Security Administration loans. (Table 110) A few occurred in the samples from each state, except Mississippi. Farm ownership loans outstanding with the Farm Security Administration averaged over $3,100 per loan in Arkansas and nearly $8,000 in Oklahoma and Texas. (Table 111)

Oklahoma Land Office Loans. Loans on the security of first mortgages on improved farm lands also may be made by the Commissioners of the Land Office in Oklahoma. No loan may be made for an amount greater than 50 per cent of the cash value of the land, disregarding improvement, nor for more than $50 per acre, regardless of value. Loans may not be made on tracts smaller than 20 acres, nor may a loan exceed $10,000. Provisions must be made for amortizing the debt in 25 years. Moreover, the fair rental value of the premises must be equal to the annual payments which are to be made by the borrower. Payment of a part or all of the principal may be made on any interest paying date.[342]

Eleven of the 107 real estate loans in the Oklahoma sample were made by the Oklahoma Land Office. (Table 110)

Real Estate Loans by Local Banks. Local banks operating under either national or state banking laws are authorized to extend farm real estate credit. Loans can be made for only a limited number of years but may be renewed.

Any national bank may make real estate loans secured by first liens upon improved real estate, including improved farm land. The amount loaned must not exceed 50 per cent of appraised value nor run for a longer term than 5 years. However, a 10-year loan in an amount not to exceed 60 per cent may be made if secured by an amortized mortgage providing for retirement of 40 per cent of the principal in installments within a period of not more than 10 years. The above limitation does not prevent the renewal or extension of the loan. Loans to mature in less than 6 months may be made by national

[340] *Ibid.*, sec. 1003.
[341] *Ibid.*, sec. 1004.
[342] *Okla. Stat. Ann.*, 1937, Supp. 1947, Tit. 64, sec. 52.

banks, with or without real estate mortgage security, to finance the construction of residential or farm buildings.[343]

The power of banks operating under state laws to lend money on real estate is subject to state statutes and regulations. Statutes of Oklahoma and Texas are quite similar to the Federal Act. For example, the Oklahoma act permits state banking associations to make real estate loans secured by first mortgages on improved or productive farm land. Loans not exceeding 50 per cent of the appraised value of the real estate offered as security may be made for a term not over 3 years; but loans up to 70 per cent of such values may be made under amortized mortgage providing for retirement of 40 per cent or more of the principal within a period of not more than 10 years. Both types may be renewed or extended. Loans, whether or not secured by real estate mortgages with maturities of less than 6 months, may be made to finance construction of residential or farm buildings.[344]

A similar Texas statute authorizes loans on real estate not to exceed 50 per cent of appraised value, secured by first liens; or not to exceed 60 per cent of such values, when 40 per cent of the loan is to be amortized in 5 years; or 66 2/3 per cent of appraised value of "residential real estate" when the loan is to be completely retired by equal monthly installments over a period of 20 years.[345]

No detailed statutory regulation of loans made on the security of farm real estate by state supervised banks was found in the other 3 states in the region. Language in a Louisiana act merely empowers banks to lend money on real estate security.[346] Similar authority is granted Arkansas banks when loans are "secured by deeds of trust."[347] No acts restricting this type of credit were found in the Mississippi code.[348]

Twenty-seven real estate loans were made by local banks. All state sample areas were represented, but 16 of the total were in Louisiana. (Table 110) Since real estate credit in 213 out of 283 cases reported was used to buy the present farm which requires a long-term loan, local banks, because of the legal limitation on the length of the loan period, cannot as effectively meet the needs of the typical borrower as can federal loan agencies.

---

[343] 12 *U. S. C. A.*, sec. 371, 1945, Supp. 1947.

[344] *Okla. Stat. Ann.*, 1936, Supp. 1947, Tit. 6, sec. 108b.

[345] Vernon, *Tex. Civ. Stat.*, 1947, Art. 342-504.

[346] Dart, *La. Gen. Stat.*, 1939, Vol. 1, sec. 543.

[347] Pope, *Dig. Stat. Ark.*, 1937, sec. 715.

[348] See *Miss. Code Ann.*, 1942, secs. 5153-5287.

Other sources of real estate mortgage credit that should be mentioned are insurance companies and insurance societies, commercial loan companies, and local merchants. Loans by individuals were reported in all sample areas.

Short-Term Farm Credit

Sixty-five per cent, of the 1463 families sampled in Arkansas, Mississippi, Oklahoma, and Texas used other-than-real-estate credit. (Table 112) The principal purposes of this type of credit were to finance current crop production, to buy livestock and farm equipment, and to finance family living. (Table 113) The average amount of non-real estate credit used per family was $221 in Mississippi, $259 in Arkansas, $499 in Texas, and $905 in Oklahoma. (Table 109)

Security offered for other-than-real-estate loans by 945 families in the Arkansas, Mississippi, Oklahoma, and Texas sample areas, as reported by the borrowers was: crop liens, 279; chattel mortgages, 240; chattel mortgages and crop liens, 198; personal note, 38; and other security, 6. No security was offered for 77 loans, and the type of security was not reported for 114. (Table 114)

These types of security fall into 3 major classes: (1) personal security, embracing the no security and personal note classifications; (2) crop liens, both contractual and statutory; and (3) chattel mortgages, either on animals or equipment, or on animals, equipment, and crop.

Only 115, or 14 per cent of all the loans for which the type of security is known, were made on the personal security of the borrowers. In contrast, 85 per cent, or 717 farmers, reported their other-than-real-estate credit secured by either a crop lien, chattel mortgage, or by a combination of the two. In other words, the predominant credit base for short-term loans in the 4 sample areas was the debtor's crops and chattels.

Effect of Assets and Income on Loan Needs and Credit Risks. Important factors influencing the type of security used for other-than-real-estate credit are the farmer's net worth and expected income and the ratio of the loan used to his net worth and income. By way of background, a brief discussion of all 3 factors is desirable.

Net worth of owners and part owners was materially higher than the net worth of farmers in the other tenure groups in all 5 state sample areas. Net worth of all tenure groups, except croppers, was considerably higher in the 2 western states. (Table 115) A comparison of the relative assets, expressed in percentage of operator's equities in the farm business, of the various tenure groups is revealing. While median percentage equities in the farm business of owners range by states from 76 to over 90 per cent and of part owners, excluding Negroes in Louisiana, range from 50 to 78 per cent, median equities in the farm business of most renter groups are under 20 per cent and of cropper groups under 10 per cent. (Table 116)

Differences in gross income of farm operators in the various tenure groups, however, are not as impressive. Nevertheless, average gross incomes of owners and part owners were higher than for other tenure groups, and this holds true both as to gross farm income (Table 24) and gross income from all sources. (Table 21) The greater proportion of the farmers in all tenure groups in the Arkansas and Mississippi samples reported net family incomes falling in income classes under $1,000. In Oklahoma, on the other hand, most incomes of farmers were over $1,000. (Table 117)

A comparison of value of operators' earnings in the 3 states shows the same general distribution. The greatest proportion of such earnings of all tenure groups in Arkansas and Mississippi fell in the 4 income classes under $568. In contrast, in Oklahoma most earnings exceeded $927. (Table 105) The highest median operator's earnings in the 2 eastern states was $492 in Arkansas and $441 in Mississippi. Median operator's earnings of all tenure groups in Oklahoma were appreciably higher. (Table 62)

Differences in size of loans used were not as great as differences in net worth or of income. The average amount of non-real-estate credit used by reporting farm families of all tenure groups was $221 in Mississippi, $259 in Arkansas, $499 in Texas, and $905 in Oklahoma. (Table 109)

Crops as a Pledge for Loans. Thirty-three per cent, or 279, of the farmers reporting types of security for short-term loans obtained their credit with a crop lien as security and another 198, or 24 per cent, of the loans were secured by chattel mortgages and crop liens. (Table 114) Since crop liens alone or with chattel mortgages on crops and other chattels were the declared security for 57 per cent of such loans, the variations in legal rights of the several tenure groups in the crop are of great importance to a creditor.

Crop liens may be either statutory or contractual. Statutory liens are conferred by statute on landowners and landlords only for rent owing or for advances of cash or supplies to their tenants and croppers for purposes of making, harvesting, and marketing the crop. A contractual lien, on the other hand, may be conferred, usually by mortgage, on anyone supplying credit. Landowners, landlords, tenants, and croppers can pledge as security for a loan only their particular interest in a crop. Further, a chattel mortgage on the crop of a tenant or cropper is generally junior, unless latter liens are waived, to the landowner's or landlord's liens for rent and advances. Title to crops prior to division and the priority of statutory liens thereon are basic factors determining the crop's availability as security for loans.

—*Under a tenancy.* Under laws of Arkansas, Mississippi, and Texas, where a tenancy exists, whether under a cash or share lease, title and possession of the crop prior to division generally is in the tenant, subject to prior statutory liens for rents and advances.[349] In Louisiana and Oklahoma, when land is leased on the share "the crop produced belongs to the lessor and lessee, respectively, in the proportions fixed by the contract between them."[350] Under a cash lease, the rule existent in the other 3 states applies, and the landlord in both Louisiana and Oklahoma would have a lien for rent,[351] and in Louisiana also for advances.[352]

Although in Louisiana a landlord is entitled to a privilege on the tenant's share of the crop for advances, the landlord's claim has been held inferior in rank to that of another creditor to whom the tenant had pledged his crop to secure advances.[353] One statute specifically provides that the privilege of a laborer on the crop for wages and of the landlord for rent, but not for furnish, shall be superior to a pledge of a tenant to a third party for furnish.[354] Priority of pledges for advances in Louisiana, including the landlord's, depends on order of recordation. All privileges and pledges on crops are ranked in the following order of preference: first, privilege of the laborer; second, privilege of the lessor; third, privilege of the overseer; fourth, pledges

---

[349] *Hammock* v. *Creekmore* (1887), 48 Ark. 264, 3 S. W. 180; *Tinsley* v. *Craig* (1891), 54 Ark. 346, 15 S. W. 897; *Barnhardt* v. *State* (1925), 169 Ark. 567, 275 S. W. 909, 911; Pope, *Dig. Stat. Ark.*, 1937, sec. 8845; *Mississippi Cooperative Cotton Assn.* v. *Walker* (1939), 186 Miss. 870, 192 So. 303, 305; *Williams* v. *Sykes* (1934), 170 Miss. 88, 154 So. 267; 154 So. 727, 728; *Tignor* v. *Toney* (13 Tex. C. A. 1896), 518, 35 S. W. 881, 882; *Curlee* v. *Rogan* (Tex. C. A. 1911), 136 S. W. 1126, 1127; Vernon, *Tex. Civ. Stat.*, 1947, Art. 5222.

[350] Dart, *La. Gen Stat.*, 1939, sec. 5065; *La. Farm. Bur. Cotton Growers Co-op Assn.* v. *Bannister* (1926), 161 La. 957, 109 So. 776, 777. *Okla. Stat. Ann.*, 1937, Tit. 41, sec. 24; see *Elder* v. *Sturges* (1935), 173 Okla. 620; 49 P. (2d) 221, 222.

[351] Dart. *La. Civ. Code*, 1945, Arts. 2705, 3218; *Okla. Stat. Ann.*, 1937, Tit. 41, sec. 23.

[352] See *Ibid.*, Arts. 3217, 2705.

[353] *Landreneaux* v. *Dergin* (La. Ct. App. 1932), 19 La. App. 542, 134 So. 283, 286; 139 So. 505, citing Dart, *La. Civ. Code*, Art 3217.

[354] Dart, *La. Gen. Stat.*, 1939, sec. 5058.

in order of recordation; and fifth, privileges of furnishers of supplies and of money, and of physicians.[355]

In Oklahoma a landlord does not have a statutory lien on the tenant's part of the crop for supplies furnished to make the crop.[356]

—Under a "tenancy in common" in the crop. In Arkansas, Mississippi, and Texas, when the relationship between the parties is that of "tenants in common" in the crop, each has title to his share prior to division,[357] and in the first two states the landlord or landowner has a lien on the cropper's share for advances.[358] In Louisiana and Oklahoma, under a share-lease or cropping contract, the statute definitely fixes each party's ownership in the crop to be the proportion stipulated by his agreement.[359] However, the landlord in Louisiana has a statutory lien or privilege on the tenant's share for advances.[360] Oklahoma laws do not confer a statutory lien for advances, but a contractual lien is recognized.[361]

—Under a "cropper" relationship. In all 5 states when the relationship between the parties is that of employer and cropper or laborer, title and possession of the crop is in the employer prior to settlement and division,[362] but the sharecropper has a lien thereon[363] or interest therein for his labor.[364]

---

[355] *Ibid.*, sec. 5064.

[356] *Hallsell* v. *First Natl. Bank of Coweta* (1925), 109 Okla. 220, 222, 235 P. 532.

[357] *Hammock* v. *Creekmore* (1887), 48 Ark. 264, 3 S. W. 180; *Tinsley* v. *Craig* (1891), 54 Ark. 346, 15 S. W. 897, 898; *Barnhardt* v. *State* (1925), 169 Ark. 567; 275 S. W. 909, 911; *Williams* v. *Sykes* (1934), 170 Miss. 88, 154 So. 728; *Tignor* v. *Toney* (13 Tex. C. A. 1896), 518; 35 S. W. 881, 882; *Williams* v. *King* (Tex. C. A. 1918), 206 S. W. 106, 107.

[358] *Tinsley* v. *Craige* (1891), 54 Ark. 346; 15 S. W. 897, 898; Pope, *Dig. Stat. Ark.*, 1937, secs. 8844, 8846; *Miss. Code Ann.*, 1942, sec. 908.

[359] Dart, *La. Gen. Stat.*, 1939, Art. 5065; also see Art. 6602. *Okla. Stat. Ann.*, 1941, Tit. 41, sec. 24.

[360] *Dixon* v. *Alford* (La. Ct. App. 1932), 143 So. 679, 682, citing Dart, *La. Civ. Code*, 1932, Art. 3217.

[361] See *Hallsell* v. *First Natl. Bank of Coweta* (1925), 109 Okla. 220, 222; 235 P. 532.

[362] *Hammock* v. *Creekmore* (1887), 48 Ark. 264. 3 S. W. 180; *Tinsley* v. *Craig* (1891), 54 Ark. 346, 15 S. W. 897, 898; *Barnhardt* v. *State* (1925), 169 Ark. 567; 275 S. W. 909, 911; *Holmes* v. *Payne* (1926). 4 La. App. 345, 347; see *Jackson* v. *Jefferson* (1935), 171, Miss. 774; 158 So. 486, 487; *Elder* v. *Sturges* (1935), 173 Okla. 620 49 P. (2d) 221, 222; *Tignor* v. *Toney* (13 Tex. C. A. 1896), 13 518, 35 S. W. 881, 882; *Rentfrow* v. *Lancaster* (321 Tex. C. A. 1895) 10, 31 S. W. 229, 231.

[363] *Barnhardt* v. *State* (1925), 169 Ark. 567, 275 S. W. 909, 911; *Miss. Code Ann.*, 1942, sec. 336; *Stalling* v. *Key* (1937), 180 Okla. 238, 68 P. (2d) 842, 843, citing *Okla. Stat. Ann.*, 1937. Tit. 42, secs. 92, 96; see also *First Natl. Bank* v. *Roger* (1909), 24 Okla. 357, 103 P. 582, 583; Vernon, *Tex. Civ. Stat.*, 1941, Art 5483.

[364] *Holmes* v. *Payne* (1926), 4 La. App. 345, 349; see Dart, *La. Civ. Code*, 1945, Art. 3217.

Rights Under a Chattel Mortgage. Fifty-two per cent, or 438 of the 838 families in the Arkansas, Mississippi, Oklahoma, and Texas sample areas, reporting types of security used to obtain other-than-real-estate credit gave a chattel mortgage on their livestock and farm equipment (240) or on both chattels and crops (198) as security for their loans.

There are two distinct theories of chattel mortgages recognized in the region. The first, called the legal title or common law theory, is followed in Arkansas. Under the common law rule, "a chattel mortgage operates as a sale vesting legal title in the mortgagee subject to defeasance by performance of the conditions of the mortgage."[365] Similarly in Mississippi, deeds of trust commonly used to secure loans on chattels have been held to confer title to the property embraced instead of merely a lien.[366] Under the lien theory, followed in Louisiana, Oklahoma, and Texas, a chattel mortgage is regarded as creating a lien only in favor of the mortgagee as security for the debt.[367]

At common law an oral chattel mortgage is valid.[368] However, under the statutes of all 5 states, if a chattel mortgage is to be effective against creditors or subsequent purchasers, it must be in writing, signed (in some states also acknowledged), and recorded with the proper official in the county where the mortgagor resides or, under certain circumstances, where the property is located.[369]

Personal chattels, including livestock, farm machinery, equipment, and crops may be mortgaged. So also may crops not yet planted but which are to be planted on land in which the mortgagor has a present interest. However, if the mortgage is to be valid, in Arkansas such crops must be planted within a 12-month period.[370] In Mississippi it "is good at law if given at any time during the year or when . . .

[365] Leonard A. Jones, *Chattel Mortgages and Conditional Sales*, 6th Ed., 1933, Vol. 1, sec. 1; *Perry County Bank* v. *Rankin* (1905), 73 Ark. 589, 84 S. W. 725, 86 S. W. 279; *Monongahela Ins. Co.* v. *Batson* (1914), 111 Ark. 167, 163 S. W. 510, 512; but see *Fincher* v. *Bennett* (1910), 94 Ark. 165, 126 S. W. 392, 393.

[366] *Elson* v. *Barrier* (1879), 56 Miss. 394, 396; see *Miss. Code Anno.*, 1942, secs. 851-853.

[367] Jones, *Chattel Mortgages and Conditional Sales*, 6th Ed. 1933, Vol. 1 sec 1; *Baton Rouge Rice Mill* v. *Fairbanks, Morse & Co.* (1927), 164 La. 729, 114 So. 633, 634; *Edmisson* v. *Drum-Flato Commission Co.* (1903), 13 Okla. 440, 73 P. 958, 960; *First Nat. Bank of Commerce* v. *Young* (1932), 155 Okla. 282, 8 P. (2d) 1108, 1109; *Preston* v. *Carter* (1891), 80 Tex. 388, 16 S. W. 17, 18; *Barr* v. *White* (Tex. C. A. 1932), 47 S. W. (2d) 910, 915.

[368] Jones, *Chattel Mortgages and Conditional Sales*, 6th Ed. 1933, Vol 1, sec. 2.

[369] Pope, *Dig. Stat. Ark.*, 1937, secs. 9434, *et seq.*; *Miss. Code Ann.*, 1942, Arts. 851-853, 858-861, 863, 868-871; Dart, *La. Gen. Stat.*, 1939, Supp. 1947, secs. 5022.1 *et seq.*; *Okla. Stat. Ann.*, 1937, Tit. 46, secs. 51, *et seq.*; Vernon, *Tex. Civ. Stat.*, 1941, Supp. 1948, Arts. 5489, *et seq.*

[370] Pope, *Dig. Stat. Ark.*, 1937, secs. 9445, 9446.

executed within a time so close to the beginning of the year that it could be reasonably held that preparations were being made for the planting and production of the particular crop."[371] A mortgage on unplanted crops in Louisiana is good only to secure advances for the production of the current crop.[372] By way of contrast, in Texas "one may execute a valid chattel mortgage not only upon his crops about to be planted for the current year . . ." but the instrument may "extend to any number of succeeding years."[373] The latter rule also apparently is followed in Oklahoma.[374]

Personal property which is exempt to every family from forced sale[375] for payment of debt may be validly mortgaged in Texas, Louisiana, Oklahoma, and Mississippi. The exemption is personal and may be waived by the debtor.[376] In Arkansas, on the other hand, such personal property reserved to every family is "exempt from seizure or

---

[371] *Coffey* v. *Land* (1936), 176 Miss. 114, 167 So. 49, 50.

[372] Dart, *La. Gen. Stat.*, 1939, sec. 5058.

[373] *South Texas Implement & Machine Co.* v. *Anahanc Canal Co.* (1926), 280 S. W. 521, 522; 269 S. W. 1097.

[374] *Okla. Stat. Ann.*, 1937, Tit. 42, sec. 8. See dictum in *Payne* v. *McCormick Harvesting Mach. Co.* (1901), 11 Okla. 318, 66 P. 287, 288.

[375] State laws exempting personal property from forced sale by unsecured creditors vary considerably. Wearing apparel, plus personal property valued at $200 to a single person and $500 to the head of a family is exempt from forced sale in Arkansas.—Pope, *Dig. Stat. Ark.*, 1937, secs. 7183, 7184. In Louisiana every family may claim exempt from seizure and sale for debt all wearing apparel, bedding and household furniture, and, in addition, agricultural implements, workstock, fodder and seed necessary for carrying on the plantation for the current year, plus 1 work horse and wagon, 1 yoke oxen, 2 cows, 25 hogs and the necessary fodder.—Dart, *La. Code Prac.*, 1942, Supp. 1947, 2nd Ed. 1942, secs. 644, 645. Mississippi statutes exempt to every family from forced sale for payment of debt certain personal property including wearing apparel, agricultural implements for two laborers, 2 work horses, mules or oxen, 2 cows and calves, 10 hogs, 20 sheep and 20 goats, all poultry, all colts under 3 years old, certain seed, fodder, and meat, 1 wagon, 1 cart, harness and saddle, household furniture ($200), and 1 mower and rake, or, in lieu of these articles, personal property not to exceed $250 in value. — *Miss. Code Ann.*, 1942, secs. 307, 318, Oklahoma statutes exempt from forced sale to every family personal property, including all wearing apparel and household furniture,. all implements of husbandry, tools of a trade or profession, 5 milch cows and their calves, 1 yoke oxen, 2 horses, 2 mules, harness, saddles, wagon and cart, 10 hogs, 20 sheep, and provisions and forage for 1 year. Single persons have reserved wearing apparel, tools of a trade or profession, 1 horse and saddle or a yoke of oxen, and a certain percentage of earnings. — *Okla. Stat. Ann.*, 1937, Tit. 31, secs. 1, 4. In Texas, personal property exempt to every family from forced sale for debt includes all household furniture and wearing apparel, all implements of husbandry, tools of a trade or profession, 5 milch cows and their calves, 2 mules, 2 horses and 1 wagon, saddles and harness, 20 hogs, 20 sheep, 20 goats, 50 chickens, 30 turkeys, 30 ducks, 30 geese, and 30 guineas. To a single person is exempt all wearing apparel tools of his trade or profession, 1 horse with saddle and bridle, and a percentage of wages.—Vernon, *Tex. Civ. Stat.*, 1945, Art. 3832, 3835.

[376] Vernon, 1945, *Tex. Civ. Stat.*, Art. 3840; *Kay* v. *Furlow* (1933), 178, La. 637, 152 So. 315, 316; *McComb* v. *Watt* (1913), 39 Okla. 412, 135 P. 361, 362; see dictum in *Adkinson & Bacot Co.* v. *Varnado* (1908), 91 Miss. 825, 47 So. 113, 117.

attachment, or sale on execution, or other process from any court, issued for the collection of any debt by contract," except for debts contracted for the purchase money thereof.[377] It is unlawful in all 5 states for the mortgagor to sell or remove from the county any mortgaged property with intent to defraud the creditor.[378]

The legal rate of interest, in the absence of an agreement as to the rate, in Arkansas, Mississippi, Oklahoma, and Texas is 6 per cent,[379] and in Louisiana, 5 per cent per annum.[380] The maximum rate of interest that may be legally charged under any contract, either directly or indirectly, in Arkansas, Oklahoma, and Texas is 10 per cent per annum, [381] and in Louisiana and Mississippi 8 per cent per annum.[382]

Procedures in the 5 states for foreclosing a chattel mortgage vary greatly. In no state is there a right of redemption after the foreclosure sale.[383] Arkansas foreclosure law is unique in that it prohibits per-

---

[377] Pope, *Dig. Stat. Ark.*, 1937, sec. 7183, 7184.

[378] *Ibid.*, secs. 3212, 3215; Dart, *La. Gen. Stat.*, 1939, Supp. 1947, sec. 5022.8; *Miss. Code Ann.*, 1944, secs. 2250. 2252; *Okla. Stat. Ann.*, 1937, Tit. 21, sec. 1834; Vernon, *Tex. Pen. Code*, Supp. 1947, Art. 1558.

[379] Pope, *Dig. Stat. Ark.*, 1937, sec. 9391; *Miss. Code Ann.*, 1942, sec. 36; *Okla. Stat. Ann.*, 1937, Tit. 15, sec. 266; Vernon, *Tex. Civ. Stat.* 1947, Art. 5070.

[380] Dart, *La. Civ. Code*, 1945, Art. 2924.

[381] Pope, *Dig. Stat. Ark.*, 1937, sec. 9392; *Okla. Stat. Ann.*, 1937, Tit. 15, sec. 266; Vernon; *Tex. Civ. Stat.*, 1947, Art. 5071.

[382] Dart, *La. Civ. Code*, 1947, Art. 2924; *Miss. Code Ann.*, 1942, sec. 36. In Arkansas, all contracts that provide for a greater interest rate than 10 per cent per annum are usurious and void as to principal and interest.—Pope, *Dig. Stat. Ark.*, 1937, secs. 9401-9405. Where interest is charged for advances at a higher rate than 10 per cent per annum, the transaction is void and neither principal advanced nor interest can be recovered in a court action by the lender.—*Hall Bros.* v. *Johnson* (1914), 111 Ark. 593, 164 S. W. 278, 280. If usurious interest is paid in Louisiana, the whole amount paid as interest may be recovered within 2 years from the time of payment. —Dart, *La. Civ. Code*, 1947, Art. 2924. Similarly, in Mississippi, if a greater rate of interest than 8 per cent shall be stipulated for or received, all interest shall be forfeited and may be recovered. Moreover, if a rate in excess of 20 per cent per annum is contracted for or received, directly or indirectly, the principal and interest shall be forfeited and any amount paid, both principal and interest may be recovered by the borrower.—*Miss. Code Ann.*, 1942, sec. 36; *Taylor* v. *Copeland* (1938), 183 Miss. 85, 181 So. 742; 183 So. 519. In Oklahoma, if usurious interest is reserved or charged, twice the amount of interest which the debt carries shall be forfeited, and if paid, twice the amount paid may be recovered.—*Okla. Stat. Ann.*, 1937, Tit. 15, sec. 267. Further, a suit foreclosing a mortgage or lien involving $300 or less must be accompanied by an affidavit setting forth that the debt sued on is not usurious. Upon trial, if found usurious, the action shall be dismissed. — *Okla. Stat. Ann.*, 1937, Tit. 15, sec. 271. Persons paying usurious interest in Texas may recover double the whole amount of interest paid. — Vernon, *Tex. Civ. Stat.*, 1947, Art. 5073. Further, a Texas statute authorizes the Attorney General or any district or county, attorney to bring suit to enjoin anyone "habitually" charging usurious interest.—Vernon, *Tex. Civ. Stat.*, Supp. 1948, Art. 4646b.

[383] Pope, *Dig. Stat. Ark.*, 1937, secs. 9460-9465; see Dart, *La. Gen Stat.*, 1939, Supp. 1947, sec. 5022.9. In Mississippi, foreclosure is under the general jurisdiction of courts of equity. See Jones, *Chattel Mortgages and Conditional Sales*, 6th ed., 1938, Vol. 2, sec. 735, and Jones, *Mortgages*, 8th ed., 1928, Vol. 3, sec. 1720. See

sonal property from being sold at first offering for less than two-thirds of appraised value; 60 days later, at a second offering, it may be sold to the highest bidder.[384] Unless an appraisal is made before foreclosure sale in Louisiana, a deficiency judgment is denied.[385]

Annual Conservation Assistance Payment as Security. Another potential asset of landowners, tenants, and croppers available as a basis for obtaining annual credit is the conservation assistance payments earned under the agricultural conservation program. Payments earned in carrying out soil building practices in 1941 in all 5 states were payable to the landowner, tenant, or cropper in proportion to the value of labor, equipment, or material, not including land, contributed by each in carrying out the conservation practices.[386] Regulations provide that payments "shall be computed and made without regard to questions of title under state law; without deduction of claims for advances . . ." except indebtedness to the United States; "and without regard to any claim or lien against any crop, or proceeds thereof, in favor of the owner or any other creditor."[387] However, any person entitled to any conservation payment "may assign his interest in such payment as security for cash loaned or advances made for the purpose of financing the making of a crop." No assignment will be recognized unless made in writing in accordance with Agricultural Adjustment Administration regulations.[388]

Laws Protecting Liens. All 5 states have laws protecting statutory or contractual liens on crops or chattels against certain actions of debtors.

Under Arkansas law it is unlawful "to sell, barter, exchange, or otherwise dispose of" or remove from the county or state any property upon which there exists a landlord's, laborer's, mortgagee's, or other

---

Okla. Stat. Ann., 1937, Tit. 46, secs. 52-56. See Franki, *Vernon's Tex. Rules of Civ. Pro.*, Rules 621, 656 (1942); and Jones, *Chattel Mortgages and Conditional Sales*, 6th ed., 1938, Vol. 2, sec. 751.

[384] Pope, *Dig. Stat. Ark.*, 1937, secs. 9460-9464.

[385] Dart, *La. Gen. Stat.*, 1939, sec. 5021.6.

[386] *Arkansas Handbook* (B Area) 1941, Agricultural Conservation Program, p. 22. *Louisiana Handbook* 1941, Agricultural Conservation Program, p. 17. *Mississippi Handbook* 1941, Agricultural Conservation Program, p. 14. *Oklahoma Handbook* 1941, Agricultural Conservation Program, p. 22. *Texas Handbook* 1941, Agricultural Conservation Program, p. 20.

[387] *Arkansas Handbook,* supra., p. 27; *Louisiana Handbook,* supra., p. 23; *Mississippi Handbook,* supra., p. 20; *Oklahoma Handbook,* supra., p. 27; *Texas Handbook,* supra., p. 25.

[388] *Arkansas Handbook,* supra., p. 28; *Louisiana Handbook,* supra., p. 24; *Mississippi Handbook,* supra., p. 20; *Oklahoma Handbook,* supra., p. 28; *Texas Handbook,* supra. p. 26.

lien, with intent to defraud the owners of such lien.[389] Such act is a felony if the value of the debt secured exceeds $10 and a misdemeanor if worth a lesser sum.[390] It is also a criminal offense knowingly to aid or assist any person in the disposal of property subject to an unpaid lien.[391] In order to convict under section 3212, criminal intent to defraud the lienholder must be shown; therefore a mortgagee's consent to the sale is a good defense,[392] even though the mortgagor failed to turn over the proceeds as agreed.[393] Later ratification of the sale by the landlord is also a good defense.[394] A conviction of a cash tenant who failed to pay the landlord in full was obtained in a case in which, because of bad weather, according to the defendant, the entire crop would not pay the $1,000 cash rent agreed and the cash tenant, without consent of the landlord, sold some cotton turned over to him by his subtenants.[395]

A Louisiana law declares it a misdemeanor punishable by fine and imprisonment ($1,000 and 1 year) for a tenant to sell or dispose of the part of the crop belonging to the landlord.[396] Another act authorizes the tenant to pledge his share of the crop for supplies to make and harvest the crop. This pledge is subordinate to the claim of laborers for wages and of the landlord for rent[397] but not for furnish.[398] It is a misdemeanor for any pledgor to sell or otherwise dispose of any crops, or part thereof, with intention to deprive the pledgee of his pledge thereon, unless consent is given in writing.[399]

Under a Mississippi act, any person who with notice of a landlord's lien on agricultural products shall conceal or remove the crop from the premises where produced, without consent of the landlord, with intent to defeat the lien, may be punished by fine or imprisonment.[400] Another statute declares it a crime to remove from the county, conceal, sell, or dispose of all or any part of lien-property, without consent of the lienor, unless immediately thereafter such lien is discharged. The act applies whether the sale takes place before or after maturity of the debt.[401] Sale of cotton in the county, without more, under this

---

[389] Pope, *Dig.. Stat. Ark.*, 1937, sec. 3212.
[390] *Ibid.*, secs. 3214, 3215.
[391] *Ibid.*, sec. 3213.
[392] See *Osborne* v. *State* (1913), 109 Ark. 440, 160 S. W. 215, 217.
[393] *Lawborne* v. *State* (1913), 108 Ark. 474, 158 S. W. 113, 114.
[394] See *Murray* v. *State* (1921), 150 Ark. 461, 234 S. W. 485, 487.
[395] *Royal* v. *State* (1933), 159 Ark. 601, 252 S. W. 601.
[396] Dart, *La. Gen. Stat.*, 1939, sec. 5066.
[397] *Ibid.*, sec. 5058.
[398] *Ibid.*, sec. 5064.
[399] *Ibid.*, secs. 5061, 5062.
[400] *Miss. Code Ann.*, 1944, sec. 2251.
[401] *Ibid.*, sec. 2252.

latter act, has been held not to constitute an offense.[402] Similarly, merely selling mortgaged property before the debt is due, without consent and without immediately discharging the debt, is not an offense.[403] Other Mississippi acts authorize the landlord to attach the tenant's goods and chattels if the tenant removes from the leased premises, or the landlord has just cause to suspect and believe that the tenant will remove, agricultural products or any part thereof on which the landlord has a lien.[404]

Any person in Oklahoma who shall remove any crop from leased premises with intent to deprive the owner or landlord of the rent due shall be deemed guilty of embezzlement.[405] Under this act removal of the crop with intent to deprive the landlord of rent due is a material ingredient of the offense and must be proved. Removal and sale of cotton, proceeds being applied on the rent, does not show intent to deprive the landlord thereof.[406] Moreover, the person entitled to rent may recover from the purchaser of the crop, with notice of the lien, the value of the crop purchased, to the extent of the rent due plus damages.[407] When any person liable for rent, whether due or not, if due within 1 year thereafter, intends to remove, is removing, or has within 30 days removed his property or crops or any part thereof from the leased premises, the person to whom rent is owing may bring an action of attachment and seize the crop, or so much thereof as may be necessary.[408] Since Oklahoma does not confer a statutory lien on landlords for advances on tenants or croppers, a law in aid of such liens would be superfluous.

Mortgaged property in Texas may not be sold or removed from the county without consent of the mortgagee, and if so sold or removed, the mortgagee is entitled to its possession and he may sell it for payment of the debt whether due or not.[409] Further, sale or removal out of the county or State with intent to defraud of any "personal or movable property or growing crop of farm produce" on which a written mortgage or other lien has been given is a crime punishable by imprisonment for a term of 2 to 5 years.[410]

---

[402] *Polk* v. *State* (1888), 65 Miss. 433, 4 So. 540 citing sec. 2909, *Code of 1880*, now *Miss. Code Ann.*, 1944, sec. 2252.

[403] *State* v. *Sullivan* (1902), 80 Miss. 596, 32 So. 55, citing *Ann. Code* 1892, sec. 1184, now *Miss. Code Ann.*, 1944, sec. 2252.

[404] *Miss. Code Ann.*, 1942, secs. 920, 921.

[405] *Okla. Stat. Ann.*, 1937, Tit. 41, sec. 25.

[406] *Crittenden* v. *State* (1922), 21 Okla. Cr. 347, 207 P. 747, 748.

[407] *Okla. Stat. Ann.*, 1937, Tit. 41, sec. 26.

[408] *Ibid.*, Tit. 41, secs. 27, 28.

[409] Vernon, *Tex. Civ. Stat.*, 1941, Art. 5496.

[410] Vernon, *Tex. Pen. Code*, 1925, Cum. Supp. 1947, Art. 1558.

Moreover, in Texas, while rents and advances remain unpaid, a tenant may not remove from leased premises, without consent of the landlord, agricultural products produced thereon or animals, tools, or property furnished.[411] Further, while any part of the rent remains unpaid it is not lawful for the tenant to remove or permit to be removed from the rented premises any portion of such crops, without consent of the landlord;[412] and an unauthorized removal of a portion, leaving enough upon the premises to pay the rent, will not defeat the landlord's lien on the portion removed, since the lien extends to all of the crop, regardless of the amount due the landlord or the value of the crop remaining.[413] However, "the law imposes no restraint whatever upon the right of the tenant to sell or otherwise dispose of the crop upon which the landlord may have a lien. It is the removal of those crops from the rented premises without the landlord's consent which the statute forbids."[414] A tenant has the right to sell a crop (cotton) matured in the field, and the purchaser has the right to ingress and egress to gather it, and to sell it, subject to the landlord's lien for rent and advances.[415]

Under another Texas act, a landlord may consent to the removal of agricultural products raised on leased premises for preparation for market without losing his lien.[416] The landlord's lien continues so long as lien-crops are stored in public or bonded warehouses, provided negotiable receipts have not been issued therefor.[417]

Security Offered for Loans Used. Other-than-real-estate credit was used by 952 of the 1,463 families of all tenures and races interviewed in the sample areas of Arkansas, Mississippi, Oklahoma, and Texas. This type of credit was not used by 511 families. (Table 118) Full owners far more frequently (48 per cent) failed to use such credit than did other tenure groups. (Table 103) Moreover, in the two western areas, both the numbers and proportion of full and part owners not using other-than-real-estate credit were greater than in the two eastern areas. (Tables 131 and 132) It is of interest that 47 out of 62 laborers did not use credit, compared with only 29 of 215 croppers. (Table 103)

[411] Vernon, *Tex. Civ. Stat.*, 1947, Art. 5225.

[412] *Watson* v. *Cox*, 1884, 2 *Willson Civ. Cas. Ct. App.* sec. 277, citing *R. S.* Art. 3108, now shown in Vernon, *Tex. Civ. Stat.*, 1947, as Art. 5225.

[413] *Wilkes* v. *Adler* (1887), 68 Tex. 689, 5 S. W. 497, 499.

[414] *Adams* v. *A. A. Paton & Co.* (Tex. C. A. 1915), 173 S. W. 546, 548.

[415] *Elliott* v. *Dodson (Tex. C. A. 1927)*, 297 S. W. 520, 523; see *Dodson* v. *Moore* 272 S. W. 263.

[416] Vernon, *Tex. Civ. Stat.*, 1947, Art. 5226.

[417] *Ibid.*, Arts. 5223, 5606.

The most common use of other-than-real-estate credit was to finance farm production and family living and, secondly, to buy livestock and farm equipment. (Table 113) The percentage of farmers in the various tenure groups using credit for farm production and for farm family living tends to increase with decline in tenure status. Some exceptions are noted, however, particularly Negroes in all tenure groups. Twelve farm owners in 4 states sample areas supply their needs for short-term credit to purchase livestock and equipment and to finance production and family expenses with loans secured by real estate mortgages. (Table 106)

All the three principal types of security for short-term loans, that is, personal, crop liens, and chattel mortgages, were reported used to obtain credit by some farmers in each of the major tenure classes. (Table 119)

—*Personal credit loans.* Personal credit as here defined embraces the "no security" and "personal note" classifications. Owners and part owners relied on their personal credit more consistently than renters and croppers. In the Oklahoma and Texas samples, 33 out of 112, or 30 per cent, of other-than-real-estate loans to owners and part owners were made on personal security. In contrast, only 16 of the 227 other-than-real-estate loans reported by owners and part owners of both races in Arkansas and Mississippi were obtained on personal credit. The balance of such loans of which the nature of the pledges is known, in these latter states, except for two, were made on the security of liens, either statutory or contractual, on crops or other chattels.

Some tenants and croppers in all 4 state sample areas reported short-term loans made on personal credit. Where it was obtained by tenants or croppers from sources other than the landlord, no statutory lien on either crops or chattels exists in favor of the creditors in any of the states. However, if the landlord provided so-called personal credit to his tenants or croppers, as was reported in some cases in 4 state areas (Table 120), and the advances were used for financing crop production on the leased premises or for family living, the landlord, under the laws of Arkansas, Mississippi, and Texas, had a statutory lien for such credit, unless waived (which is improbable) on the tenant's or cropper's share of the current crop and, except in Arkansas, on the chattels furnished to make the crop. In Oklahoma, only contractual liens for advances are recognized.[418]

---

[418] See *supra,* "Crops as a Pledge for Loans," and subtitles thereunder, pp. 283 ff.

If credit or supplies are furnished a tenant or cropper from other credit sources, but the landlord is primarily liable for the obligation incurred by the advancement, and not merely secondarily as a surety, the landlord has a statutory lien on the tenant's or cropper's share of the crop for such advances though furnished indirectly.[419] Generally, the taking of a tenant's note as additional security for rent or advances does not amount to a waiver by the landlord of his statutory liens.[420]

—*Loans secured by crop liens.* Liens on crops may be either statutory, that is, conferred by law without act of the parties, or contractual, usually as a result of a chattel mortgage. The crop lien was the type of security for short-term credit most frequently reported. Of all farmers reporting loan security, 279, or 33 per cent, used crop liens and another 198, or 24 per cent, pledged chattels and crops. (Table 114) Liens on the crop alone were popular with all tenure groups in the Arkansas, Mississippi, and Texas sample areas as a basis for credit. In Oklahoma, only 1 loan was reported secured by a lien on the crop alone, and this loan was made to an owner.

—*Crop loans to owners.* A lien on the crop of an owner can only result from a contract pledge. The same applies to a crop raised by a part owner on the land he owns. Moreover, if the owner conducts his farming operation with the use of tenants or croppers, he can pledge only his interest in the crop, which will vary depending on the particular legal relationship between the owner and his tenants or croppers.

Under a cash tenancy in all 5 states title and possession of the crop is in the tenant, but the landlord has a statutory lien for his rent. The same applies under a share lease in Arkansas, Mississippi, and Texas. In Louisiana and Oklahoma, the crop under a share lease or cropping agreement belongs to the contracting parties in the proportion fixed by the contract. Dividend ownership of a crop may also result in Arkansas, Mississippi, and Texas, where the agreement between the landowner and his tenants or croppers creates the relationship of a "tenancy in common" in the crop, with each party having title to his share prior to division. Finally, when the relationship between the parties is that of landowner and cropper or employee, title

---

[419] *Morrilton Cotton Oil Co.* v. *Frauenthal and Schwartz* (1924), 162 Ark. 597, 258 S. W. 628, 629; *Monroe* v. *Gaylor* (Tex. C. A. A., 1925), 268 S. W. 724, 725; 260 S. W. 929; 221 S. W. 330, 332.

[420] *Franklin* v. *Meyer* (1880). 36 Ark. 96, 112; *Merchants and Planters Bank* v. *Meyer* (1892), 56 Ark. 499, 20 S. W. 406, 407; *First Nat'l. Bank of Quitaque* v. *Pointer* (Tex. C. A. 1932), 51 S. W. (2d) 781, 783; see *Henneman Grain and Seed Co.* v. *Hill* (Tex. C. A. 1934), 68 S. W. (2d) 525, 526.

and possession of the crop is in the employer, and the cropper has a lien or interest therein for his labor.[421] Multiplicity of legal interests in a crop is further increased where a head tenant is also involved. In any event, a landowner can pledge for a loan only his particular interest in the crop.

—*Crop loans to tenants and croppers.* Liens on tenants' and croppers' share of the crop for loans or advances may be either statutory or contractual. If the advancement is made by the landlord and is used for making, harvesting, and marketing the crop, the law in Arkansas, Mississippi, and Texas confers on the landlord a prior statutory lien on his tenant's or cropper's share of the crop for such advances. The law in Mississippi and Texas also confers on the landlord a prior statutory lien on animals and equipment furnished on credit to make a crop. In Louisiana, too, a landlord has a statutory lien for furnish, but its priority depends on the order of recordation. A landlord in Oklahoma has no statutory lien on his tenant's or cropper's part of the crop for advances. However, a contractual lien may be created.

A landlord instead of relying solely on his statutory lien may insure repayment of his loans or advances to his tenants or croppers by taking a chattel mortgage on their share of the crop. However, the taking of a chattel mortgage on the crop as additional security for advances does not operate as a waiver of the landlord's statutory lien on the crop in the absence of an intent to do so.[422]

When credit on the security of crops is obtained by tenants and croppers from other sources than their landlords, the lien on the crop can only be conferred by contract or chattel mortgage. Of course, the interest in the crop of such borrowers which they can pledge will vary with the nature of the lease or cropping agreement.[423]

Although a tenant or cropper may pledge his interest in the crop as security for a loan to be obtained from sources other than the landlord, such pledge or chattel mortgage will be junior in Arkansas, Mississippi, and Texas to the landlord's statutory lien for advances unless the latter lien is waived or surrendered.[424] In these 3 states, the landlord's statutory lien for advances has preference, unless waived, over

[421] See *supra,* "Crops as a Pledge for Loans," and subtitles thereunder, pp. 283 ff.

[422] *Franklin* v. *Meyer* (1880), 36 Ark. 96, 112; *Merchants and Planters Bank* v. *Meyer* (1892), 56 Ark. 499, 20 S. W. 406, 407; *Smith* v. *Miller* (Tex. C. A. 1927), 300 S. W. 953, 954; citing *Daugherty* v. *White* (Tex. C. A. 1924), 257 S. W. 976, 979; and *Griffin* v. *Mangrum* (Tex. C. A. 1924), 267 S. W. 279, 280.

[423] See *supra,* "Crops as a Pledge for Loans," and subtitles thereunder, p. 283 et seq.

[424] Pope, *Dig. Stat. Ark.,* 1937, secs. 8838, 8844, and 8846; Vernon, *Tex. Civ. Stat.,* 1947, Art. 5222; see *Orange County Irri. Co.* v. *Orange National Bank* (Tex. C. A. 1910). 130 S. W. 869, 870.

a chattel mortgage whether the rental agreement is a cash lease, a share lease, a cropping contract or, except in Texas, provides for a "tenancy in common" in the crop. In Arkansas, a landlord may orally waive his lien for advances on crops grown by his tenants,[425] such waiver to be valid where croppers under oral contracts are concerned must be in writing, endorsed upon such mortgage.[426] In contrast, in Louisiana, liens on the crop for advances, irrespective of source of the credit, are given priority in order of recordation; and in Oklahoma, where landlords' statutory liens on the crop for advances are not recognized, a waiver is redundant.

It is also observed that landlords, in addition to their prior statutory liens for advances discussed above, also in all 5 states have prior statutory liens for rent if, under the lease contract, title to the entire crop is in the tenant.[427] Creditors sometimes require waiver of both the landlord's statutory furnish and rent liens before extending credit. This is particularly propitious where the lease provides for cash or cash-share rental and there is danger of crop failure. Since a landlord's lien for rent is good against all crops for any rent due under the contract, the landlord may attach all the crop if the crop produced on acreage rented for cash does not yield enough to pay the cash rent.[428]

—*Loans on chattels.* A chattel mortgage on livestock and equipment may be required by anyone supplying the loan, including the landlord.[429] In fact, in Oklahoma, where a statutory lien for advances is not conferred by law, and also in Arkansas, it is necessary for the landlord to take a chattel mortgage on livestock and equipment furnished his tenants and croppers in order to obtain a lien prior to general creditors. In Louisiana, liens for advances take priority according to order of recordation. Under laws of Mississippi and Texas, landlords have a prior statutory lien on chattel furnished tenants and croppers to make a crop.[430] Even in states where a landlord has a statutory lien on chattels furnished his tenants or croppers to make, harvest, and market the crop, he may sometimes find it advisable to

[425] *Wilson* v. *Citizens Bank* (1926), 170 Ark. 1194, 282 S. W. 689, 692; *Griggs* v. *Horton* (1907), 84 Ark. 623, 104 S. W. 930; *Meyer* v. *McKenzie* (1934), 189 Ark. 76, 70 S. W. (2d) 505, 506.

[426] Pope, *Dig. Stat. Ark.*, 1937, sec. 8844; *Tinsley* v. *Craige* (1891), 54 Ark. 346, 15 S. W. 897, 16 S. W. 570.

[427] See *supra*, "Crops as a Pledge for Loans," and subtitles thereunder, pp. 283 ff.

[428] *Stephenson* v. *Lewis* (1922), 152 Ark. 361, 238 S. W. 61, 63.

[429] See *supra*, "Rights Under a Chattel Mortgage," p. 00, for a discussion of mortgages on personalty exempt to every family from forced sale.

[430] See *supra*, "Crops as a Pledge for Loans," p. 283.

take a mortgage on such chattels because a mortgage can have greater flexibility and scope. For example, a chattel mortgage may be given on farm machinery, horses, and crops to secure "indebtedness now due and owing" as well as for indebtedness to become due.[431] In fact, a landlord's mortgage lien upon "all goods, chattels and property of every kind belonging to his tenant, given to secure payment of all indebtedness now owing . . . or which may hereafter be owing, including rentals, during the existence of the lease" has been upheld.[432] Moreover, the taking of a chattel mortgage as additional security does not, as a matter of law, operate as a waiver of the landlord's lien conferred by statute.[433]

Tenants or croppers are free to mortgage their chattels in all states without consulting their landlords, unless the chattels have been furnished by the landlord to make the current crop and have not been fully paid for, in which case, in Mississippi and Texas, the landlord has a prior statutory lien thereon.

Value of chattels owned or in process of purchase is the basis for extension of chattel mortgage credit. The part-owner tenure group reported the highest average value of livestock and equipment owned and, in descending order, full owners, share-cash renters, share renters, and croppers reported progressively lower values. Reported values in the 2 western states for all tenure groups, except croppers, were 3 or more times as high as values of equipment and livestock of comparable tenure groups in the 2 eastern states. Excluding croppers, average values of such chattels owned by tenure groups of both races ranged from around $200 to over $1,000 in Arkansas and Mississippi and from slightly under $1,200 to over $4,000 in Texas and Oklahoma. By comparison, average amounts of non-real-estate credit used were $221 in Mississippi, $259 in Arkansas, $499 in Texas, and $905 in Oklahoma. (Table 109)

Twenty-eight per cent, or 240 of the families in the Arkansas, Mississippi, Oklahoma, and Texas sample areas reporting the types of security used to obtain other-than-real-estate credit gave a chattel mortgage on livestock and farm equipment as a pledge for their loans. (Table 114) Renters and croppers pledged their livestock and equipment as security for loans far more frequently than owners. (Table 119) Parenthetically, purchase of livestock and equipment was the

[431] See *Askey* v. *Stroud* (Tex. C. A. 1922), 240 S. W. 339.
[432] *Pair* v. *Scoggins* (Tex. C. A. 1932), 54 S. W. (2d) 841, 842.
[433] *Gulf C. and S. Ry. Co.* v. *Enloe* (Tex. C. A. 1928), 5 S. W. (2d) 545.

sole purpose for which short-term credit was used by 78 families, of which 64 were in Oklahoma and Texas. Another 317 families reported such purchases in combination with other uses as the reason for their loans. (Table 113)

Local banks and federal agencies were the principal sources of short-term funds loaned on the security of chattels in all 4 states. (Table 120)

—*Loans on pledge of crops and chattels.* A pledge of chattels and crops as security for loans may be either statutory or contractual, depending on the tenure of the borrower and on the source of the loan. Where the lender is someone other than the landlord, the pledge must be contractual. The same is true where the borrower is an owner, and, if a part owner, it is true of crops raised on land he owns. Of course, if the owner or part owner obtains his labor supply by use of tenants and croppers, such owner can pledge for a loan only his particular interest in the crop, which will vary depending on the legal relationship between him and his tenants and croppers.[434]

Where credit on the security of chattels and crops is obtained by tenants and croppers from other sources than the landlord, a contractual lien, as was noted above, is required. Like the landlord, tenants or croppers can pledge only their interest in the crop, which will vary with the type of rental agreement, and in Arkansas, Mississippi, and Texas, obtaining a waiver of the landlord's prior statutory lien on the crops for advances may be expedient. No such waiver is needed in Louisiana and Oklahoma.[435]

Although landlord creditors in Arkansas, Mississippi, and Texas have prior statutory liens on their tenants' or croppers' share of the crop for advances to make, harvest, and market the crop, and in the latter 2 states on chattels furnished for the same purposes, landlords in all 3 states may take a chattel mortgage on such crops and chattels as additional security for the advances. In Louisiana and Oklahoma a chattel mortgage is essential to give the landlord's loan priority over other creditors.[436]

Twenty-four per cent, or 198 of the families in the Arkansas, Mississippi, Oklahoma, and Texas sample areas reporting types of security used to obtain other-than-real-estate credit pledged both chattels and crops as security for their loans. Owners, renters, and croppers alike in all states offered this type of security for short-term

[434] See *supra*, "Crops as a Pledge for Loans," p. 283.
[435] *Ibid.*, and "Loans secured by crop liens," p. 294.
[436] See *supra*, "Crops as a Pledge for Loans," p. 283.

loans. Funds obtained on the security of this type of pledge in the greater proportion of cases were provided by local banks and federal agencies except in Mississippi where they were provided by merchants.

Sources of Short-Term Credit. The principal sources of non-real estate credit of sample families in 4 state areas ranked by numbers of loans made were federal agencies, 300; local banks, 263; landlords and landlord-merchants, 166; merchants, 142; and individuals, 49. Banks and federal agencies made the greater proportion of the loans of $500 and over. (Table 121)

—Landlord credit. The landlord in addition to providing tenants and croppers with land, and often with mules and equipment, sometimes also provides them throughout the growing season with credit. "Furnish," or advances, as this form of credit is often called may be in the form of a cash loan, or it may consist of provision of food and other necessities, and supplies needed to grow the crop. It may be extended by periodic rations from the plantation commissary, by periodic distribution of cash, or by guaranteed credit at a local store.

Landlords in 1942 extended credit to 152 sample families in 4 sample areas in the Southwestern Region. Credit for another 14 families was supplied by merchant-landlords. All but 10 of the families using landlord credit lived in Arkansas or Mississippi. (Table 112) Croppers, especially Negroes in the 2 eastern sample areas, were the chief recipients. Eighty-four per cent of the Negro croppers in the Arkansas sample and 72 per cent in Mississippi obtained all their short-term credit from landlords. Comparable percentages for white croppers in these 2 states were 59 and 27. Some part owners and renters, most frequently Negroes, also obtained such credit. (Table 122) Eighty of the loans made by landlords were for less than $100 and 65 were from $100 to $499. Only 6 loans exceeded $500. Loans by merchant-landlords were all less than this latter sum. (Table 121)

Landlords, particularly in Arkansas, Mississippi, and Texas, can influence sources of credit available to tenants and croppers by refusing to waive their statutory liens on the crop for rents and advances, the inclusiveness of which varies from state to state, depending on the nature of the leasing agreements.[437]

The landlords and not the tenants made the decisions as to the securing of production credit in 93 per cent of the cases where tenants had management scores under 20, and in 73 per cent of the cases

[437] See *supra,* "Crops as a Pledge for Loans," p. 283, and "Loans secured by crop liens," p. 294.

where the scores ranged from 20 to 39. The same was true regarding furnish credit in 82 and 53 per cent of the cases, respectively, for these 2 score classes. (Table 80) The greater proportion of the farmers in the 2 lower management score groupings were Negro croppers. (Table 42) As the management scores of tenants increased, however, the landlords less frequently made credit decisions. Tenants with scores of 60 or over in 97 and 99 per cent of the cases did the deciding. (Table 80)

Ninety-five to 100 per cent of the production credit used by croppers of both races, with management scores of from 10 to 19, in the Arkansas area was obtained from landlords. Comparable percentages in Mississippi were 63 and 43. The percentage of credit supplied by landlords varied inversely with the management scores. Only an insignificant proportion of the production credit used by part owners, renters, or croppers was supplied by landlords in the Oklahoma and Texas areas.

—Local bank, merchant, and individual credit. Banks in all 5 states may grant short-term loans on the personal credit of the borrower, or on the pledge of land, farm machinery, livestock, or crops as security. The same applies to credit from merchants and individuals.

Local banks in the 4 state areas made 263 loans to sample farmers, of which 72 were for sums of $500 or over. (Table 121) Farmers in the 2 western areas, particularly in Texas, relied heavily on local banks for short-term credit. In the latter state, 120 of the 193 short-term loans used by sample families were obtained from local banks. (Table 112) In these 2 western states local banks were the favored source of production and family living credit for sample farmers in all tenure groups, except share-cash renters in Oklahoma and Czech and German croppers in Texas. Owners and white part owners in the Arkansas sample also favored local banks as a source of short-term credit. (Table 122) Banks depended primarily on pledges of crops and chattels as security for their short-term loans. (Table 120) It is of interest that in the Oklahoma area, where the law does not confer a statutory lien for advances on the tenant's or cropper's share of the crop and they are free to pledge their crops, giving chattel-mortgage-creditors a first lien without obtaining a waiver from the landlord, the crop was seldom pledged. Instead, short-term loans in Oklahoma were usually secured by chattel mortgages on livestock and equipment.

Although merchants supplied some non-real-estate credit to sample farmers in all 4 state areas, 93 of the 142 families using merchant credit were in Mississippi. (Table 112) Merchants in that state supplied a greater proportion of production and family living credit used by most tenure groups than was obtained from any other single source. Loans by merchants were usually under $500, only 14 being in excess of that sum. (Table 121) Crops, or crops and chattels, were the primary security for merchant credit in the Mississippi sample area. In that state, unless the landlord waives his prior statutory liens, only a junior lien on the crop will be obtained by a chattel mortgage.

Related individuals supplied 27 and unrelated individuals 22 non-real-estate loans to sample farmers. Ten of the kinship loans were in Texas, and 16 of the unrelated loans were in Arkansas. This geographic distribution partly explains the more frequent occurrence of larger loans between relatives. In Texas, most of the individual short-term credit was made on the personal security of the borrowers. This was also true to a slightly lesser extent in Oklahoma. On the other hand, in Arkansas chattel mortgages on crops and/or livestock and equipment were more often required. (Table 120)

—*Federal short-term loans.* Short-term loans for farm purposes are available through several federal agencies. So-called production credit for general agricultural purposes, or for home alteration, repair, and improvement is authorized on such terms, conditions, rates of interest, and security as may be prescribed by the Production Credit Corporation. Loans may be made in amounts from $50 up[438] and are usually secured by first mortgages on crops and livestock, and sometimes they are on other personal property of the borrower. Repayment is planned to fit the individual's farming operations. Loans generally are repaid when the farm products financed are sold, but 12-month loans can be renewed if satisfactory progress has been made.

Seventy-one production credit loans were made to sample farmers in 4 sample areas. Owners and part owners used credit from this source to a greater extent than other tenure groups. Moreover, loans to owners, except in Oklahoma, were larger than loans to renters or croppers. (Table 123)

The Secretary of Agriculture also is empowered to make rehabilitation loans through the Farm Security Administration to eligible farm owners, tenants, farm laborers, sharecroppers, and certain other individuals, "for the purchase of livestock, farm equipment, supplies,

[438] 12 *U. S. C. A.*, secs. 1131-g, 1131-g-1 (1945).

and for other farm needs (including minor improvements and minor repairs to real property), for the refinancing of indebtedness, and for family subsistence." Such credit must be secured by a chattel mortgage, a lien on crops, or by an assignment of the proceeds from the sale of agricultural products, or by one or more of the foregoing.[439] Loans for as much as $2,500 can be made.

Rural rehabilitation loans were made to 162 sample farmers in 4 states. Such credit was used by all tenure groups and was especially favored by share renters. Loans by tenure groups averaged from $250 to over $700. (Table 111)

Federal agencies usually made loans on the security of crops and other chattels. (Table 120) Of course, before tenants or croppers can pledge their crops and confer a first lien, it is necessary, except in Oklahoma, to obtain a waiver of the landlord's prior statutory liens. In Louisiana, pledges take priority in order of recordation.

SUMMARY

Two legal systems have influenced the development of tenure law in the Southwestern Region. The Common Law of England was adopted as the basis of jurisprudence in Arkansas, Mississippi, Oklahoma, and Texas. French and Spanish civil law had a marked effect on the legal system in Louisiana and to a lesser extent on the law of the other states. The community property system and homestead exemption laws are both of Spanish origin.

The legal rights of farm people in the land they farm are important factors influencing how it will be used. The full owner has the maximum control over his land, subject of course to certain prior rights of society, and limited by the nature and scope of his title and by miscellaneous contractual restrictions in deeds, mortgages, or purchase contracts. Somewhat lower in the tenure hierarchy in terms of control over lands farmed is the tenant and below him the cropper. Their rights in the land are conferred by contract with the landlord, either written, oral, or implied. Obviously the landlord or employer can confer upon his tenants or croppers no greater rights in the land than he himself possesses, but, within the limitations of legality, he is free to restrict them as he desires.

Rights in farm lands held by various categories of owners in the region are far from uniform, and so also are the reasons for holding title. Variations in these rights and in the reasons for having title

[439] 7 *U. S. C. A.*, sec. 1007 (1939).

influence the way farm land is used, and this is true whether actual operation is by the owners or by tenants or croppers.

Landowners have been classified as public, institutional, individual, and estate. Ownership of farm land by agencies of the state usually is intended to be temporary, pending sale. This is equally true of tax-forfeited lands, school and other trust lands. An important exception is 16th section school land in Mississippi, which may never be sold but may be leased. Leases of publicly-owned land, reflecting the purposes of the holding, are drawn to facilitate sale. Lease terms are short, ranging from 1 to 6 years, the exception being 16th section school lands in Mississippi, where the term is 15 years.

Institutional land, like much public land, frequently is held by unwilling owners temporarily holding title acquired in collecting debts. Laws in all 5 states limit the maximum period of ownership. Leases, necessarily, must be for relatively brief periods or may be subject to termination on sale.

Title to land in the individual ownership category may be held by unmarried individuals, by the husband or wife as separate property, by the spouses or others in one of several forms of joint ownership. Two schemes of marital property rights are found in the region.[440] One, developed from the common law, is found in Arkansas, Mississippi, and Oklahoma. The other, the community property system, an institution of the civil law, is established in Louisiana and Texas, and is optional in Oklahoma. In the so-called common-law states "all the property of the spouses is owned separately by either the husband or the wife, or perhaps by both as tenants in common, joint tenants, or tenants by the entirety." In the community property states the property of the spouses is either the separate property of the husband, the separate property of the wife, or a part of the "common fund of matrimonial gains called the community property."

Title to land is passed to others upon death of the owner by will or, in the absence of a will, by descent. The right to dispose of property by will is not a natural right but is a creature of statute, and therefore subject to regulation and restriction by the state. Laws of the 5 states transmitting property by will and descent vary greatly.

[440] The probable extent to which differences in the nature of the titles under which spouses hold farm land may influence the way it is used poses an interesting question. More specifically, is the community property system of farm land ownership preferable, from the point of view of land use, to other systems evolved from the common law? Secondly, would a marital system of property rights under which all property of the spouses (individual and common) was merged in a common fund result in better use of farm land?

A testator's right to freely devise his separate property, and his interest in common property, is limited by the nature and scope of the title under which he holds it, by dower or curtesy rights, by homestead rights of the surviving spouse and minor children, and by other miscellaneous rights of the survivors. Title to land descends to the heirs subject to many of these same limitations. In Louisiana, children and their descendants and the decendent's parents, known as "forced heirs," cannot be disinherited, except for certain statutory reasons. Only a portion of the estate can be willed to whomsoever is deemed most deserving, and that person must be a legal heir.

The period of time land is under estate control may be relatively short, pending administration of the estate by the courts, or it may be prolonged during the minority of children and during the life of the surviving spouse holding dower, curtesy, or homestead rights.[441]

In legal theory, a tenant is one who pays the landlord cash or a share of the crop, or both, for the use of land, whereas a cropper is one who receives a share of the crop from his employer as payment for his labor and is merely an employee. The criterion for ascertaining whether the legal relationship between the contracting parties is landlord-tenant or employer-cropper is their intent as evidenced by the contractual agreement. A most important determinant of intent is the owner's disposition of his legal possession or "dominion" over the land to the other party.

Where, by the terms of the contract, the landlord surrenders dominion over the land to the other party, the relationship of landlord-tenant is created. On the other hand, where, under the agreement, the landowner does not surrender the land but agrees to pay the occupant a share of the crop for cultivating and gathering, the cultivator is a cropper, not a lessee, and the relationship is that of employer-employee. The cropper has no estate in the land but merely a right to possession incident and dependent upon the performance of his personal engagement.

[441] It is common knowledge that farm "estates" are frequently mishandled. The degree of misuse is often related to the duration of the estate, sex of the surviving spouse, and age of heirs. Of interest in this connection is whether the Louisiana heritage system of devolution to "forced heirs" or the systems prevailing in the other 4 states, which allow greater freedom to the testator, results in better operated farms, both before the parent's decease and afterwards, during the existence of the "estate"? Also, whether the granting to the surviving spouse and minor heirs of rights to the rents and profits of the family homestead, particularly under Oklahoma and Texas laws, is more conducive to properly operated farms as going concerns, than are arrangements possible under the laws of the other states, including the creation of trust estates under Louisiana law.

Distribution of management scores of sample farmers indicates that croppers have little control over details of management.

Farm leases prevalent in the region have been grouped into 4 main types: written 1-year, written 2-years and over, oral 1-year, and oral indefinite. Rights under each type are limited by the terms of the agreement as interpreted by state laws, which vary considerably. Oral leases were favored, the oral 1-year lease being most frequently used.

Under the laws of Arkansas, Mississippi, and Texas, a tenant, unless it is otherwise agreed, takes leased premises as he finds them and repairs, if he desires, at his own expense. The same rule applies in Oklahoma to improvements other than dwellings. In that state, in the absence of an agreement to the contrary, the landlord must put premises leased "for occupation of human beings" in a condition fit for occupancy and thereafter keep them in repair. In Louisiana, the landlord, unless otherwise agreed, is bound to deliver premises to the tenant in good condition and also maintain them, except for certain minor repairs which the tenant must make.

A comparison of the obligation to repair leased farm dwellings under prevailing practices in the sample areas, and the legally implied incidence of that obligation when unchanged by contractual arrangements, is of considerable interest. The relationship, except for labor costs, appears generally inverse. In view of the laws in each state, one would reasonably have expected prevailing practice to place all costs of repairing dwellings in the Arkansas, Mississippi, and Texas areas on the tenants and in Oklahoma on the landlords; but the reverse, except for labor costs in Arkansas, Mississippi, and Texas, appears most frequently true.

Laws relating to removal by tenants or croppers, in the absence of agreement, of their agricultural fixtures or improvements placed on leased premises are restrictive in Oklahoma and most liberal in Louisiana, with the other 3 states somewhere in between. In Louisiana, the landlord may compel removal or he may elect to keep the improvements, paying therefore a fair value. In the absence of an election by the landlord to retain the improvements, the tenant may remove them, provided he leaves the premises in the condition he received them. No state, except as noted in Louisiana, imposes any legal duty on a landlord to pay his tenants or croppers for the unexhausted value of improvements left on leased premises, unless he has expressly or impliedly so agreed.

Two principal types of credit, long-term secured by real estate mortgages and short-term obtained without security or secured by pledge of crops or chattels, were used by farmers in the region. The main reason for using real estate credit was to buy the present farm. The principal purposes of short-term credit were to finance current crop production, to buy livestock and farm equipment, and to finance family living.

Both the lien and title theories of real estate mortgages prevail in the region. Deficiency judgments may be had in all states. Only in Arkansas is a period for redemption allowed after foreclosure sale.

The predominant credit base for short-term loans in the region is the debtor's crops and chattels. Liens on crops or chattels to secure a loan may be either statutory or contractual. Statutory liens are conferred on landlords only for rent owing or for advances of cash or supplies made to tenants and croppers by the landlord for purposes of making, harvesting, and marketing the crop. A contractual lien may be conferred on anyone supplying credit, but it is junior to the statutory liens, unless these latter have been waived. A statutory lien for advances is not conferred on landlords in Oklahoma.

A landowner, landlord, tenant, or cropper can pledge, as security for a loan, only his particular interest in a crop. This interest varies by states, and also varies depending on whether the rental agreement creates a tenancy, a "tenancy in common" in the crop, or a cropper relationship.

Not only crops already planted but crops which are to be planted within the current year may be mortgaged. In Texas a mortgage on unplanted crops may extend to any number of succeeding years. Obviously, chattel mortgages on livestock, farm machinery, and equipment also may be made and, except in Arkansas, the pledge may include personalty exempt to every family from forced sale.

Landlords generally made the decisions relating to obtaining production and family living credit for croppers and tenants in the lower management score brackets. As management scores increased, these decisions with increasing frequency were made by the tenants.

CHAPTER VIII

Use and Sources of Capital

Whether or not a man succeeds at the business of farming depends to a large measure upon the use that he makes of the land, labor, capital, and management factors of production over which he has control.[1]

All of these factors are important in their time and place. In many farming areas and particularly in the South, however, capital has often seemed to be the one really scarce factor of production. Because of this fact, the ability of the farmer to accumulate or acquire access to capital and to use and manage the capital at his disposal has more often than not exerted a strategic influence upon his tenure performance.

The interrelationship between the tenure performance of the farmer and his use of capital involves a number of problems. How much investment capital does the farmer need to start as a cropper, a renter, or as an owner? How much money must he have for his current production and consumption needs? How and from what sources can he get the money? Beyond these immediate questions are those of its relation to the other factors of production and the importance of the various sources of capital and their general relationship to the tenure behavior of individual farm operators.

USE OF CAPITAL AND TENURE PROGRESS

All business activity, and particularly farming, involves some use of each of the four chief factors of production—land, labor, capital, and management. Before a man can farm he must own, lease or otherwise have access to a tract of land. To make this land productive

[1] As used here the term *capital* deals primarily with money and with those worldly goods that are bought and sold in the market place. In so far as farm land costs money, it is treated as farming capital and as part of the capital investment that one must control if he is going to farm.

he must apply his own labor or that of his family or hire the labor of others. Since his farming activities involve the use of land, buildings, livestock, equipment, feed, seed, fertilizer, and supplies, and perhaps hired labor, he must have access to the use of capital. In securing this capital he might draw upon his own capital savings and accumulations, borrow from credit agencies or others who have money to lend, or lease the capital investment of other people. Whether or not he finds farming profitable will also depend upon his ability as a manager. In addition to the operation of the productive factors, the farmer's prospects for success are also conditioned by such other factors as weather conditions, market prices, institutional and community settings, health, family, his ambition to get ahead, his drive and capacity for farming, and a certain element of luck.

All of these factors operate in influencing the workings of the tenure process. On any given day or during any given crop season a single factor such as a short supply of labor, the receipt of an inheritance, or adverse weather conditions might have a decisive impact. Yet on most other occasions this factor might operate in a routine fashion and seem comparatively unimportant. This condition of fluctuating relationships and the fact that any factor, even those ordinarily taken for granted such as good health or family happiness, can suddenly loom up as the strategic or limiting factor, makes it difficult to label any one factor as most important.

Importance of Capital

The importance of capital as a factor of production is borne out in many ways by the regional data. In general this importance is measured by two different standards, operator's net worth and value of farm business used. Neither of these standards provides an exact measure of the amount of the farmer's capital input. But the net worth data reflect the operator's status so far as past acquisitions of real estate and accumulations of capital goods are concerned while the value of the farm business data are generally indicative of the capital investment value of the land, buildings, improvements, livestock, and equipment.

Comparisons based upon the use of these two measures show wide differences between the sample areas. But within each sample area farm owners almost invariably have the highest average net worth followed very closely by part owners. For the four areas the average net worth of the renters runs between 10 and 25 per cent of that of the owners while the croppers are worth between one-fourth and one-half as much as the renters.[2] Comparisons based on the value of farm business used show that the part owners usually operate the largest investments followed by the owners, renters, and croppers. On the average, the farm businesses operated by owners are worth between 70 and 90 per cent as much as those of part owners, while the renters have farms worth between 50 and 70 per cent of those operated by owners, and the croppers use farm investments worth between 25 and 80 per cent of those operated by renters. (Tables 124, 115 and 125)[3]

Within the area samples the net worth of the different farmers varies considerably. On the one extreme some of the croppers and renters and even a few owners have a negative net worth while on the other extreme a few owners have clear ownership to more than $50,000 worth of farm real estate, livestock, and equipment. In general the owners cluster into the higher net worth classes but there is considerable overlapping between the renters and croppers and between the low owners and the high renters. In the Arkansas and Mississippi areas many of the owners have extremely low net worth while in the Oklahoma and Texas areas several of the renters have relatively high net worth. (Table 126)

Wide ranges also exist between the values of the farm businesses used in the four sample areas. By areas these values range from $400 to $19,100 in Arkansas, from $100 to $16,400 in Mississippi, from $1,300 to $90,200 in Oklahoma, and from $300 to $56,600 in Texas. Since these farm business values are a measure of capital investment used rather than owned, there is a general overlapping between tenure groups with the owners, particularly in the Arkansas and Mississippi areas. In the Oklahoma and Texas samples the renters tend to operate the larger farm businesses about as often as the owners. In the Arkansas and Mississippi areas, however, the larger invest-

[2] The entire problem of analyzing the effect that various factors such as capital, land use, etc., have upon tenure performance is complicated by the land tenure classifications now in use. Throughout this report the conventional classification of owners, part owners, renters, and croppers is used even though it is recognized that this breakdown is at times unsatisfactory. While this classification reflects the division of the rights in property, it permits considerable overlapping between tenure groups when such other measures of performance as size and stability of operations, income, quantity and quality of management, and relative security are considered. For the sake of convenience and comparison those farmers classified as croppers will be treated as operators throughout the remainder of this chapter even though it is recognized that they very often are actually laborers rather than operators.

[3] For tables mentioned in this chapter refer to statistical tables in Appendix.

ments are usually owner operated with the renters and croppers handling the lower valued farms. (Table 127) The farm business, farm real estate and farm livestock and equipment values, reported in the Arkansas and Mississippi areas tend to be lower than those of the Oklahoma and Texas samples. Generally speaking, land (exclusive of dwellings and improvements) accounted for between one-half and two-thirds of the farm real estate values in the Arkansas and Mississippi samples and for between three-fourths and seven-eighths of the real estate values reported for the Oklahoma and Texas areas. (Tables 12 and 13)

Comparison of these two measures of farm capital with the average income data for the various tenure groups shows that the value of the farm business used, and to a lesser extent net worth, bear a positive relationship to the average gross farm incomes, gross incomes, and family net incomes received by the various tenure groups. (Table 124) A positive relationship also exists between the value of the farm business used and operator's earnings and family earnings in the Oklahoma area. The fact that the white and Negro croppers in the Arkansas area and the Negro croppers in the Mississippi area had higher operator and family earnings than the owners in 1942 makes this relationship seem less clear in these two states. But when the data are organized to show the effect of the use of varying amounts of capital upon gross farm incomes and operator's earnings, it becomes apparent that the higher farm incomes are usually realized by those operators who work with the larger farm business investments.[4] (Table 128)

The importance of capital (as measured by value of farm business) also is indicated by its high positive correlation with production man-work units and with acres in crop land, the measures used in describing farm labor requirements and land use. (Tables 129 and 114) Its importance as a measure of size of business and as a factor affecting

[4] The fact that the operator and family earnings data for the Arkansas and Mississippi samples do not show the owners earning more than the croppers can be explained in terms of: (1) the large number of small and poorly managed owner tracts in these two sample areas (2) the higher than usual yields and receipts from cotton enjoyed by the renters and croppers of these states in 1942 (cf. discussion in Chapter IV and (3) the high operating costs (hired labor, supplies, etc.) borne by some owners in 1942. Coupled with this is the fact that a considerable number of operators, about half of whom were owners, were either so interested in off-farm work or were such poor managers that they had negative earnings for their labor and services as farm operators. Included in this group are two part owners in the Arkansas area, one white and one Negro, who operated businesses valued at over $11,500 but who realized operator earnings of -$830 and -$1104 respectively. Both of these operators, however, had substantial incomes from miscellaneous and non-farm sources.

gross farm income is also demonstrated by its high correlation with gross farm income. For the sample as a whole the size of business measure representing capital contributes more to the multiple determination of gross farm income than do the size of business measures representing the labor and land inputs of production. (Table 130)[5]

Capital Requirements for Farming

The average farmer has few delusions about the importance of investment and operating capital. Before World War II it was not uncommon for men in good health, with agricultural backgrounds, reasonable managerial ability, and ambition to get ahead to ask: "How can I buy a farm? How much will I be safe in paying?" and "How much credit can I safely use and still hope to pay off my mortgage?" The problems presented by these questions are real even in areas of low land values. The war years with their tremendous inflationary effect upon farm prices, profits, and land values have disrupted the average farmer's perspective on these issues. But the problem of high capital requirements must still be dealt with by the farm operator who would climb the agricultural ladder.

To how much capital must a man have access if he is to farm on a profitable basis? For the five states covered by the sample the 1940 census reports an average value of land and buildings per farm of $1,632 in Mississippi, $2,108 in Arkansas, $2,359 in Louisiana, $4,625 in Oklahoma, and $6,196 in Texas. These average farm values are for the states as a whole and reflect differences in farm sizes. The average acreage values of the farms in these states in 1940 ranged as follows: Texas, $18.81; Oklahoma, $23.88; Mississippi, $24.80; Arkansas, $25.32; and Louisiana, $35.40. The average value of the implements and machinery used per farm ranged as follows: Mississippi, $215; Arkansas, $223; Louisiana, $292; Texas, $510; and Oklahoma, $514.

[5] Table 130 indicates that capital (value of farm business) has greater relative importance in the Oklahoma and Texas areas than in the two eastern states. This difference can be explained partly in terms of the higher land values in the two western states and the greater reliance upon the use of tractors and mechanized equipment. Inter-area differences and differences in the methods used in computing the size of business measures used for the four state areas make comparisons based upon these multiple correlations unsound. For example, it is generally recognized that the use of commercial fertilizer is one of the most important factors affecting crop yields and farm incomes in the Arkansas and Mississippi areas while it has no importance in the Oklahoma and Texas areas. Yet the measure of capital used in this multiple correlation does not include the cost of fertilizer or other operating expenses. Similarly, the measure of productive man-work units was computed on a different basis for each of the state areas.

By sample areas the Farm and Family Survey data show median farm business values ranging from $924 for colored croppers to $3,375 for white full owners in Arkansas, from $750 for colored share-cash tenants to $2,667 for colored owners in Louisiana, from $778 for colored croppers to $2,828 for white owners in Mississippi, from $6,500 for croppers to $16,543 for part owners in Oklahoma, and from $2,250 for native white croppers to $17,682 for native white part owners in Texas. (Table 125) Stated in terms of arithmetic averages these values usually run somewhat higher, the range by areas being from $1,209 to $4,376 in Arkansas, from $819 to $3,467 in Mississippi, from $6,725 to $18,887 in Oklahoma, and from $2,244 to $15,937 in Texas. (Tables 12 and 124)

These average values give some indication of the minimum capital requirements that the farm operator should figure on although in many cases these average values are too low for profitable farming. This is equally true of owners, part owners, renters, share tenants, and croppers. The distribution of cases for the Arkansas, Louisiana, and Mississippi areas by value of farm business clearly shows that a considerable proportion of the owners, tenants, and croppers in these states operate farm business of extremely low values. In the Mississippi area, for example, 38 per cent of the owners operated businesses valued at under $2,000 while 72 per cent operated businesses valued at less than $3,500. With the other tenure groups 80 per cent of the renters and 97 per cent of the croppers operated farm businesses valued at less than $2,000 in 1942.

In the Mississippi sample area 5 full owners, 4 part owners, 5 renters, and 22 croppers reported farm business values of less than $500.[6]

These small investments can be explained largely in terms of small acreages, low land values, marginal improvements, and poor farming equipment. Needless to say the owners and renters of these low value farms are frequently worse off financially than are the croppers and wage hands on other farms. Ownership or tenancy under such conditions, particularly where the operator fails to supplement his income with off-farm earnings or by renting in additional land, can operate as a definite handicap in preventing him from achieving economic success. Such low capital value farms usually provide an unsatisfactory medium for the efficient employment of the operator's

[6] Most of these operators are colored and several of them should properly be considered as part-time operators.

labor and management, which in turn results in low returns for labor and management, lack of real profits, and usually low levels of living for the operator and his family.

USE OF CREDIT AND TENURE PROGRESS

Although the data show a high correlation between gross farm income and value of farm business, the important thing so far as the use of capital is concerned is not so much the amount but the efficiency with which it is used.

To achieve the maximum return from his supply of capital the operator must be mindful of the operation of the economic law of diminishing returns. He must proportion and balance his inputs of capital, land, and labor in such a manner that he will secure the most profitable combination of these factors. If his supply of these three factors of production is limited he should, of course, attempt to put them all to their most remunerative use, thus utilizing each factor to the point of equi-marginal return. If, however, his problem is one of dealing with a short supply of capital and with extensive and relatively inexpensive supplies of land and labor, he can and probably should operate on a broader scale even to the point of making rather wasteful and less efficient use of his land or labor. The fact that many of the operators in the three eastern states use their capital to buy fertilizer, supplies, land, and the minimum essentials in farm equipment shows that these operators want to make the maximum use of their capital even though this often involves the lavish and inefficient use of labor.

Farm operators have three major sources for investment and operating capital: (1) savings and capital accumulations; (2) borrowing from credit agencies and others by putting up suitable security; and (3) agreeing to pay cash or share rent for leasing farm capital investments owned by others.

In the discussion that follows, primary consideration will be given to the significance and importance of the roles played by the first two of these sources of farming capital.

The use of borrowed money has provided a major source for the investment capital used by many farmers in the past. This has given rise to the development of an active farm credit market, and the availability and use made of the facilities and credit provided by this market have exerted an important influence upon the tenure performance of most farm operators. The effect that the credit market has upon his field of choice and his opportunities for action is certain to have a significant impact upon his tenure behavior. This is particularly true in the Southwestern Region where distinctions in tenure status are frequently tied up with the operation of the credit system.[7]

Use of Farm Credit in 1942

Much of the credit advanced to croppers, renters, and owners in the South goes for consumption rather than for production purposes. The operators who find it necessary to use this type of credit usually anticipate a profit that will permit them to accumulate savings and perhaps to advance their tenure status and with it their earning capacities. Very often, however, the use of high cost consumption credit has a negative rather than a positive effect upon the farmer's ability to advance his economic and tenure status. But even if the borrower has little hope of profit, his credit arrangements give him an opportunity to continue in farming. Thus the use of furnish credit helps to guarantee him a job, a living, and a home. If the farmer who needs consumption or production credit is unable to secure credit he may be forced to sell part of his property or in some other way slip down the agricultural ladder. In this way, the lack of adequate farm credit can and has at various times forced renters and croppers to offer themselves as farm wage hands or to seek employment in other fields.

As has been suggested, the South has long suffered from what many people consider a deficient supply of farm capital. This has forced the various credit agencies to ration the limited supply of real estate, production, and consumption credit that has been available at times during years past. In 1931 and 1932, for example, the available supply of credit was far too short to meet the need that practically every farmer had for borrowed capital. The credit picture in those years was further complicated by low farm prices, poor prospects for debt repayment, and an unusually large number of mortgage foreclosures. By 1942 the farm credit picture had changed considerably. Good harvests and rising farm prices in 1940 and 1941 brought an

[7] Credit needs and the problems of rationing an inadequate supply of capital are not new to the South. Historians have stressed the relationship between the use of credit in the plantation economy even in early colonial times and the decisions of the planters to rely upon a one commercial crop type of farming. The need for farm capital and credit also provided the basis for the development of the sharecropper and furnish systems after the War Between the States. A deficient supply of investment capital and constant reliance upon imported capital are also partially responsible for the lack of industrialization and the lack of agricultural progress found in many parts of the South.

increase in farm earnings and profits. This made it possible for many farm operators to pay off their back debts, to add to their savings at the local banks, to buy war bonds, and in some cases to switch to farming on a cash rather than a credit basis.

All of this reduced the demand for farm credit and served to make 1942 an "easy" credit year—a year during which practically every cropper, tenant, or owner whose personal record or production plans made him at all acceptable as a credit risk was able to get all the production or real estate credit he really needed.

The regional survey indicates that 75 per cent of the farmers interviewed in Arkansas, 76 per cent of those in Mississippi, 48 per cent of those in Oklahoma, and 60 per cent of those in Texas reported the use of non-real-estate (production or consumption credit in 1942.[8] Table 112) By tenure groups the number of farm operators using non-real-estate credit varied from 34 per cent for the white owners to 93 per cent for the colored share renters in the Arkansas area, from 53 per cent for the white part owners to 100 per cent for the colored croppers in the Mississippi area, from 34 per cent for the owners to 72 per cent for the share-cash renters in the Oklahoma area, and from 10 per cent for the Czech part owners to 81 per cent for the native white share renters in the Texas area. (Table 104) So far as the use of real estate credit in 1942 is concerned, the proportion of the full and part owners using real estate credit by sample areas was 19 per cent in Arkansas, 44 per cent in Louisiana, 46 per cent in Mississippi, 72 per cent in Oklahoma, and 42 per cent in Texas. (Table 110) The average amount of real estate credit used in these state areas in 1942 was $1,130 for Arkansas, $792 for Mississippi, $3,950 for Oklahoma, and $5,084 for Texas. (Table 109) Almost 88 per cent of these loans involved the purchase of farm real estate, the financing of farm improvements or the refinancing of old mortgages. A smaller number involved in the financing of current crop production and family living costs, the refinancing of old furnish debts, and the purchase of livestock and equipment. (Table 106)

Sources of Credit. Sources for both real estate and non-real-estate credit were provided by the various government sponsored agencies,

[8] Lack of uniformity and lack of detail in the schedule data makes it difficult if not impossible for one to make an exact division between real estate, production, and consumption or furnish credit. Throughout this discussion two classifications are used: real-estate credit and non-real-estate credit (also variously referred to as other-than-real-estate credit, and as production and consumption or furnish credit). This classification is based upon whether or not the operator gave a real estate mortgage as security.

by the local banks and merchants, and by some private investors and sellers of land. Real estate loans were also made by commercial mortgage and insurance companies, by lumber companies, landlords, and in Oklahoma by the Oklahoma School Land Commission. (Tables 112 and 110) While there are similarities, there are also some rather significant differences between the credit facilities of the five sample areas. The most used single source of non-real-estate credit is provided by the landlords in Arkansas and Louisiana, by the merchants in Mississippi, and by the local banks in Oklahoma and Texas. In the real estate credit field differences also exist with the insurance and mortgage investment companies operating extensively in Texas and Oklahoma but not in the other sample areas.

The principal differences between the credit facilities provided in the sample areas can be secured through a brief description of the facilities that served the needs of the Mississippi and Texas farmers in 1942. These two states have been selected as examples because the facilities provided in Mississippi roughly parallel those found in Arkansas and Louisiana and those found in Texas approximate the facilities available in Oklahoma.

The principal sources of short term production and furnish credit in these two states are provided by the three government sponsored agencies, the Farm Security Administration, the Production Credit Administration, the Feed and Seed Loan Section of the Farm Credit Administration, and by the landlords, merchants, local banks, and private investors. The credit services provided by the government sponsored agencies are essentially alike in all of the states.

The Production Credit Associations are set up on a county or local area basis to supply production credit for farm operators. Their loans are made for periods of one year or less and carry an interest charge of 4.5 per cent (5 per cent up until July 1, 1942). In addition to this interest charge the borrower must pay a loan service fee equal to about 1 per cent of his loan, pay for the filing of his crop lien or chattel mortgage, and own or buy stock in the local Production Credit Association up to 5 per cent of the amount of his loan. The average Production Credit Association loan made in Mississippi in 1942 ran between $300 and $400 while the Texas average was $750 with an average of around $1,200 for livestock loans.

The Feed and Seed loans affect approximately the same group of operators as the Production Credit Association but these loans are usually smaller and more risky. Although loans can be made for as much as $400, all loan requests for over $100 in Mississippi and over $200 in Texas must be passed on by the local Production Credit Association officials before Feed and Seed loans can be granted. These loans call for 4 per cent interest and a crop lien as security. The loans made in 1942 averaged around $100 each in both states.

A third type of government sponsored short term credit is provided through the Rural Rehabilitation Loan Service of the Farm Security Administration. This agency aims specifically at the rehabilitation of underprivileged farm people and at giving them an opportunity to establish themselves in farming on a sound basis. Two general types of credit are granted: the Rural Rehabilitation loans and the farm ownership loans. The farm ownership loans are of a long-term nature while the Rural Rehabilitation loans are granted for periods varying from one crop season, if the loan is made for subsistence or for production or consumption purposes, up to five years if a capital loan is made for the purchase of equipment or livestock or for building repairs or improvements. All of the Rural Rehabilitation loans, regardless of whether they are short term or intermediate term in nature, pay an annual interest rate of 5 per cent. Except for the filing fee on the chattel mortgage taken as security for the loan no other costs are associated with the use of this type of credit. The Farm Security Administration, however, provides varying amounts of farm and home management supervision to all the farms included under its program and all farmers securing Farm Security Administration credit receive this supervision as a condition of their loans. The average Rural Rehabilitation loan made in Texas in 1942 amounted to around $545. The average Mississippi loan was somewhat smaller.

As has been pointed out, the most important single source of production and furnish credit in Mississippi is provided by the local merchants. In this respect the credit facilities provided in Mississippi are not exactly typical of those in the other two eastern states and are quite unlike those provided in Oklahoma and Texas in 1942. In all of these states, Mississippi included, the merchant furnish business has lost considerable ground during the last 25 years. It has declined in relative importance, partly because of the competition provided by government sponsored credit agencies and partly because of the effect that the depressions of the 1920's and the early 1930's had in forcing many furnish merchants out of the credit business, if not out of business entirely.

Most of the furnish credit available in the Mississippi area in 1942 was provided by a few large and comparatively well-managed mercantile establishments. Some of the more successful of these merchants take considerable interest in the lives and affairs of their furnish clients and broadly interpret the word "furnish" to include a vast array of goods and services. They not only provide the farmer with a place where he can buy food, clothing, implements, fertilizer, furniture, feed, seed, and even livestock, but they also supply him with the credit for buying his goods, with markets for much of the produce he raises, and in some cases with guidance in his financial affairs and with advice on how he can best operate and manage his farm.

The details of the merchant credit system are by no means standardized. The farmer who wants credit for the purchase of production and consumption goods during the cropping season, however, usually makes his furnish arrangements with his merchant rather early in the year. As security for his loan, the furnish client is asked to give a deed of trust on his crops and chattels and in some cases on his real estate. These mortgages are given at the beginning of the crop season and the merchant releases them at harvest time if the farmer pays up his account. If he has a poor crop and is unable to pay his debts, supplementary arrangements are made to carry him over until the next spring when he will again arrange for furnish credit. At that time he is asked to sign a personal note for the amount of debt still due and the merchant's books are wiped clean. Then a new deed of trust is made out for the new loan to help secure the farmer's note.

Most of the furnish merchants in Mississippi use a double price system (cash and time prices) rather than carrying charges on their credit accounts. A few merchants use a 10 per cent carrying charge on furnish accounts but this practice runs counter to the usury laws of the state and thus jeopardizes the merchant's prospects for collection. At the larger stores the time or credit price is usually posted along with the cash prices. In many instances this represents a 10 to 20 per cent interest charge.

In the Texas sample area the importance of the furnish merchant has declined much more than in Mississippi. Only a few furnish merchants were still to be found in 1942, and those that once did 75 to 80 per cent of their business on a credit basis have now reduced it to 20 to 25 per cent.

Another type of merchant credit is provided by the farm equipment companies. This is particularly important in Texas and Oklahoma. Practically all of the large tractor and equipment companies have developed special credit terms to encourage sales. As a general rule they require a 30 to 40 per cent down payment and charge 6, 7, or 8 per cent interest on the balance. If this balance is not paid off in the first year an additional 5 or 6 per cent carrying charge (not charged in Mississippi) is applied to the credit carried into the second year. The dealer, of course, takes a chattel mortgage on the equipment sold. In the past many of the dealers have financed these loans out of their own capital. If they are unable to handle them they can always find a ready market for their tractor mortgage paper at the local banks and with the equipment producer companies.

With respect to local bank credit, the Mississippi sample area is served by four local banks. Three of these banks are closely associated with large mercantile stores and tend to supply the credit needs of the better fixed farmers who do not care to use furnish credit. In this respect the facilities provided by these banks complement those provided by the merchants in much the same way that the Production Credit Associations supply the needs of those farmers who are not eligible for or who have graduated from the use of Farm Security Administration credit. These local banks usually write their loans at the full 8 per cent interest rate permitted by law, but in actual practice usually collect only 5 or 6 per cent interest. Most of their farm loans in 1942 were for between $200 and $300 and they usually required a chattel or real estate mortgage as security.

The local bank credit provided in the Texas area in 1942 was supplied by two types of banks: the rural banks that did 90 to 100 per cent of their business with farmers and the larger city banks that made about a fourth of their loans to farmers. These banks made a flat 10 per cent interest charge on most of their farm loans, and some of them made a practice of discounting this interest charge in advance. A few of the larger banks made their interest charges on an annual basis and reduced their rates to 7 or 8 per cent on the larger loans. Bank credit was provided on a very similar basis in the Oklahoma area with the interest rates varying from 4 to 10 per cent according to the farm operator's bargaining power, the security he was able to offer, and his credit standing.

Landlord credit was particularly important in the Arkansas, Louisiana, and Mississippi areas. It was used most generally by the croppers who were in a poor position to put up the necessary security for bank or merchant credit. In some cases the landlords took their croppers to the merchants and helped them make their credit arrangements. In other cases, particularly in Louisiana, many of the landlords operated their own furnish stores or commissaries. Generally, however, the landlords arranged to furnish their croppers a set sum, say $15 to $18 a month, during the crop season. The interest or carrying charges applied in these cases of landlord furnish are often far from definite. This informality and lack of definiteness has frequently given rise to serious differences of opinion between landlords and their tenants.

With respect to the long-term credit facilities in the two state areas, it is noted that the government-sponsored agencies are again very important. The Federal Land Bank loans made through the local National Farm Loan Associations provide the most used single source of real estate credit in each of the five states. The terms of this National Farm Loan Association credit are essentially the same in all the states. To supplement these loans Land Bank Commissions loans at 5 per cent interest can be made on up to 75 per cent of the appraisal value of the farm land and buildings. Due to congressional action the actual interest payment rate on both of these types of loans has been temporarily reduced to 3.5 per cent interest. The interest rate, however, is not the only charge made for this type of credit. The borrower must pay a land appraisal fee, an application and loan service fee equal to about 1 per cent of the loan and the filing fee on his real estate mortgage. He must also join the local National Farm Loan Association and subscribe stock equal to 5 per cent of the amount of his loan. The Federal Land Bank can make real estate loans of between $100 and $50,000. These loans can be written for from 5 to 40 years but most of the loans in the survey areas are amortized over a 20 year period.

The Farm Security Administration also makes farm ownership loans. These loans usually go to a limited number of selected tenants who want to become owners. They are written for 40 years at 3 per cent interest with the provision that the amount of the annual payments is to be adjusted to the operator's income, that the loans can be paid off in as little as five years, and that the new owners will accept a certain amount of Farm Security Administration supervision. These loans are usually 100 per cent loans and the number made has been limited by the size of the federal appropriations for this purpose and by the provisions made in these appropriations concerning the selection and maximum value of the farms to be purchased.

In Mississippi, and more particularly in Louisiana, the local banks sometimes make real estate purchase loans. Ordinarily these loans are of a short or intermediate term nature, and they usually must be paid off within one or two years. The lumber companies have provided another important source of farm purchase capital in the Mississippi area. As these companies have cut the lumber off of their holdings they have attempted to sell these for farming purposes. The usual arrangement has involved the use of purchase contracts. The lumber companies have often accepted small down payments and given the buyers five or more years to pay the balance at 6 per cent interest.

A considerable number of real estate loans in the Texas area have been made by the large insurance companies. These companies are for the most part interested only in the larger loans where the average per dollar cost of placement and administration is reasonably low. Many of the insurance companies will make loans of over $3,000 at 5 per cent interest on up to 50 per cent of a farm's appraisal value. A large number of loans in the Texas survey area have also been made by the SPJST, a Czechoslovak lodge and benevolent society. This society makes real estate loans on up to 50 per cent of the value of the farm to its members and to farmers residing in communities where it has local lodges. These loans are written for from 10 to 20 years and call for 5 per cent interest (4.5 per cent interest in cases of prompt payment).

The credit facilities described above for the Mississippi and Texas areas are fairly typical of those available in 1942 in the Southwestern Region. An additional statement might be made, however, concerning the long-term facilities available in the Oklahoma area. In addition to the real estate credit provided by insurance companies and local banks, a considerable number of long-term real estate loans have been made in that state by commercial mortgage companies and by the State School Land Commission.

Use Made of Credit Facilities. The distribution of cases by race and by volume of non-real-estate credit used in 1942 shows that a larger percentage of Negro operators than whites used credit in the Arkansas and Mississippi samples but that of those using credit a larger proportion of the Negroes than of the whites used small amounts of credit. The data also show that a smaller proportion of the Oklahoma and Texas operators used credit than in the other two state areas but that those who used credit tended to use more of it than was the case with the Arkansas and Mississippi operators.

(Tables 118 and 109) For all state areas and for all color and national origin groups the largest group of loans falls in the $100 and $499 class. Broken down by $100 intervals, the largest number of cases falls in the $100-$199 group for the Arkansas, Oklahoma, and Texas areas and in the less-than-$100 group for the Mississippi area. The largest percentage of those reporting no use of non-real-estate credit in 1942 comes from four tenure groups: owners, part owners, laborers, and others (non-operators). (Table 103) While very few of the croppers used more than $500 in production and consumption credit, some of the renters in the Oklahoma and Texas areas used considerable amounts of non-real-estate credit, sometimes even more than the owners.[9] (Tables 131 and 132)

Consideration of the relationship between volume of non-real-estate credit used and its source shows that landlords usually granted less than $100 in credit, that most of the merchant loans were for around $100 (usually between $100 and $200), and that the bulk of the bank, Feed and Seed, Production Credit Association, and individual loans involved between $100 and $499. Most of the Farm Security Administration loans involved credit for more than $500. The great majority of the larger loans were granted by three agencies: the Farm Security Administration, the Production Credit Association, and the local banks. (Table 121)

Approximately 97 per cent of the non-real-estate credit used in 1942 went for three general purposes: to buy livestock and farm equipment (78 cases), to finance current crop production (306 cases), for family living (59 cases), or for various combinations of these purposes (418 cases). The use of crop production credit was important in all four of the sample areas studied. The greatest use of family living credit was made in the Arkansas and Mississippi areas, while the Oklahoma and Texas farmers made the greatest use of credit for the purchase of livestock and farm equipment. (Table 113) The data on the security offered for this non-real-estate credit shows that a few operators, mostly owners, received credit on their personal note or without putting up security, but that most of the operators gave crop liens, chattel mortgages, or both. (Tables 114 and 119)

Not all the non-real-estate credit used during 1942 was repaid during the year. Actually the average amount of this credit outstanding

[9] The field interviews indicate that very few lenders discriminated against tenants simply because they were tenants. Most lenders were quite willing to lend to anyone who seemed to be a good credit risk and who could put up the required security.

at the end of the year was roughly proportionate to the average amount of non-real-estate credit used in each of the sample areas. The average amount of this credit outstanding at the end of 1942 by areas was $92 out of the average of $259 used in Arkansas, $44 out of the average of $221 used in Mississippi, $345 out of the average of $905 used in Oklahoma, and $185 out of the average of $499 used in Texas. (Table 109)

Effect of Use of Credit Upon Tenure Performance

The data indicate that the availability and use of farm credit does and has played a significant role in influencing the tenure progress made by farm operators. For instance, in 78 out of the 890 cases, in which the purpose for which the non-real-estate credit was used is given, the credit was used to finance the purchase of livestock and equipment. In an additional 36 per cent of the cases the credit was used for this in connection with other purposes. (Table 113) Similarly, practically all of the real estate credit used in 1942 involved the purchase of farm real estate, improvements, livestock, or equipment. (Table 106)

Further evidence pointing to the significance of the relationship between the use of credit and tenure progress is found in the data reported by farm owners concerning the methods used in acquiring ownership to the first tract of their present farms. These data show that in all areas and with all color and national origin groups that more farms were acquired through the use of a cash down payment plus the use of some credit than by any other single method of acquisition. At least some credit was used in the acquisition of 61 per cent of these first tracts. By state areas the percentage of these farm tracts acquired through the use of credit was 54 per cent in Arkansas, 57 per cent in Mississippi, 70 per cent in Oklahoma, and 67 per cent in Texas. (Tables 108 and 107) Higher land values and a consequent lower percentage of straight cash purchases account for the greater reliance placed upon the use of credit in the acquisition of farms in the Oklahoma and Texas areas than in the other two states.[10]

It should not be forgotten, however, that it takes more than just

[10] The fact that these farm acquisition data refer in some cases to farms that were acquired as long as 50 years ago suggests that this sample might be unrepresentative of recent trends. Examination of the case histories of the 144 Mississippi owners who reported the acquisition of 195 tracts of farm land in the 15 years between 1927 and 1942, however, lends support to these findings. Of these more recent farm acquisition cases, 61 per cent involved the use of credit, 24 per cent were paid for in cash, and 15 per cent were acquired through inheritance.

the use of credit to insure tenure progress. Examination of the 327 Mississippi case histories, for instance, shows that at least 25 operators have slipped down the ladder from the status of owner to a lower status. Of the 20 cases in which the details are available, the operators in 19 cases lost their farms through foreclosure or voluntarily sacrificed the titles to their farms to meet the demands of their creditors.

Does the tenure performance of farm operators reflect their use of credit? So far as the use of non-real-estate credit is concerned, comparison of those who did and who did not use credit in 1942 shows but few significant differences. As has been pointed out, a larger percentage of owners than renters or croppers were able to conduct their farming operations in 1942 without the use of credit. This fact tends to give the non-user group a slightly higher average net worth than the credit using group. But aside from this and associated differences the farmers who used credit and those who did not behaved very much alike in 1942.

Much the same conclusion holds when the cases of the owners having real estate mortgages are compared with the cases of debt-free ownership. On the whole, those owners who have 100 per cent equity in their farm real estate tend to be slightly older and have somewhat greater net worth than the owners who have real estate mortgages. So far as gross income, socio-economic status, and crop yield and crop diversification indices are concerned, however, there seem to be few if any significant differences between the performance of the debt-free and mortgaged owners. (Table 133) Those owners who operate with small real estate mortgages often operate larger units, have greater net worth, and receive larger gross incomes than the debt-free owners.

SOURCES OF OWNED CAPITAL

As has been pointed out, the farmer's supply of investment and operating capital is usually drawn from one of three sources: (1) credit; (2) savings and capital accumulations; and (3) from the leasing or use of farm business investments owned by others. The following discussion is concerned with savings and capital accumulations. The more important of these are: (1) farm earnings; (2) gifts, inheritances, and family help; (3) off-farm work receipts; and (4) oil lease funds and royalties.

Farm Earnings as a Source of Farming Capital

Farm earnings are basic to the operation of the agricultural ladder and tenure progress concept. Farm earnings and the use of credit provide the chief sources of his capital, and it is the saved earnings that permit the prospective farm owner to pay for his use of credit and to get ahead. Moreover, it is the earnings and profits from farming that provide the incentive that keeps him in the farming business.

The regional data suggest that the agricultural ladder concept has worked out to some extent in the Oklahoma and Texas areas but not so well in the Arkansas, Louisiana, and Mississippi areas. In these areas the ladder concept of tenure progress has broken down in two important respects: (1) a large proportion of those who have started out to climb the ladder to ownership have never succeeded in arriving at the top rung, and (2) a large proportion of those operators who have succeeded in becoming owners started far up the ladder. The first of these limitations grows out of small farm earnings, lack of opportunities, and limited abilities, while the second reflects the use of other sources of capital than farm earnings and credit.

Some indication of the importance of savings as a source of capital is provided by the regional data on operator's earnings in 1942. The distribution of the cases by value of earnings shows a wide range in earnings for the various tenure groups in each of the state areas. The distribution also shows that even though 1942 is usually considered a "good" farm income year, the majority of the farm operators in Arkansas, Mississippi, and a large portion of those in Oklahoma had rather small (if not negative) incomes for their labor and management. (Table 105) By areas these average operator's earnings varied from $201 for colored owners to $693 for white share-cash renters in Arkansas, from $79 for colored share-cash renters to $423 for white part owners in Mississippi, and from $866 for croppers to $2,091 for part owners in Oklahoma. (Table 124) The exact amount that they can save, however, for their farming investments and operations depends upon living costs and buying.

The net family income data for 1942 provides a more complete picture of the resources that the various farm operators and laborers in the three state areas were able to draw on in financing their current living costs and their future farming operations. By areas these net family incomes varied from an average of $804 for white croppers to $1,351 for white part owners, from $539 for colored croppers to $931 for colored part owners in Arkansas, from an average of $747 for white share-cash renters to $1,304 for white part owners, from $540 for colored share-cash renters to $824 for colored owners in Mississippi, and from an average of $1,345 for croppers to $3,483 for part owners in Oklahoma. (Tables 124 and 117)

Even though these net family income data include the value of unpaid family labor, the farmer's return on the value of his capital investment, the Agricultural Adjustment Administration's farm practices payments, off-farm work receipts, oil royalties and lease funds, and other miscellaneous nonfarm income, a large proportion of the operators, particularly in Arkansas and Mississippi, had net family incomes of less than $1,000 in 1942. To be exact, 59 per cent of the white and 84 per cent of the colored owners, renters, and croppers in the Arkansas area, 51 per cent of the white and 81 per cent of the colored owners, renters, croppers, and laborers in the Mississippi area, and 16 per cent of those in the Oklahoma area had net family incomes of less than $1,000 in 1942. For all cases, these percentages by sample areas are 72 per cent for the Arkansas farm families, 64 per cent for the Mississippi families, and 17 per cent for the Oklahoma families.

Inheritance and Family Help as a Source of Capital

Approximately a fifth of all the transfers of real property that are made from year to year in the United States takes place in whole or in part through gift, will, or the laws of descent. This suggests that family help and the inheritance of family wealth provides one of the more important sources for the capital used by farmers in improving their economic and tenure status.

Effect Upon Tenure Progress. Those operators who through inheritance or gift acquire substantial equities in farm real estate or funds that they can use as farm capital have a particular advantage over those who must start on the bottom rung when they climb the ladder to ownership. However, the receipt of capital from this source does not always have a beneficial effect upon tenure performance. For an operator to make the most effective use of capital during his lifetime it is important that he start making constructive use of it rather early in his earning life. When the inheritance comes late in life, however, the heir's opportunities for advancement are often definitely limited. Similarly, the fact that gifts and inheritances usually provide an easy source of capital that one can use in his farming operations does not mean that these gratuities are always received by persons who have either the ability or the inclinations to put them to their most productive use.

Despite these possible negative aspects, however, family help, inheritances, and arrangements to encourage family succession on farms are usually considered as desirable. They are desirable because they usually have a favorable effect upon economic, social, and tenure behavior of the recipients, because they help to raise farm living standards, and because they permit the younger generation to profit from the use of the capital accumulations of the retiring generation.

Use Made of Inheritances and Family Help. The regional data indicate rather clearly that family help, gifts, and inheritances have played significant roles in influencing tenure progress.

Of the 664 cases in which method of acquisition of first tract of present farm is reported, 102 farms were acquired through inheritance, 17 through inheritance plus a cash payment or a mortgage arrangement, and 16 through gift. (Tables 108 and 107) This means that 20 per cent of these farm tracts were acquired in whole or in part through inheritance or gift. For the individual state areas these percentages are 22 per cent in Arkansas, 24 per cent in Mississippi, 11 per cent in Oklahoma, and 24 per cent in Texas. The comparatively low percentage of transfers growing out of inheritance in the Oklahoma area can be explained by the recent settlement of the area.

A breakdown of these farm acquisition data on the basis of race and national origin shows that 21 per cent of the white owners in the Arkansas and Mississippi areas and 24 per cent of the colored owners received their farms through inheritance or gift while 20 per cent of the native whites, 29 per cent of the Czechs, and 28 per cent of the Germans in the Texas area received their farms from this source.

These data indicate that inheritances and gifts have provided an important source of farm investment capital. The data reported, however, fail to present the complete picture. They deal only with land and real estate that has come to the present owners directly as a result of inheritance or gift. They do not report the extent to which the non owners have benefited from family help or inheritances, and they do not deal with those instances where owners or other operators have received livestock, equipment, cash, or other property through inheritances or gift.

Other data reported by the survey strongly imply that many operators have benefited to a considerable extent from various types of family help. The answers reported by the 603 full owners and 255 croppers whose first occupation was farming concerning their beginning farm tenure status, for example, show that 34 per cent of the present owners (45 per cent in Arkansas, 38 per cent in Louisiana, 49 per cent in Mississippi, 12 per cent in Oklahoma, and 9 per cent in Texas) and 4 per cent of the present croppers began their farming careers as owners. These data strongly suggest that many of the operators, particularly in Arkansas, Louisiana, and Mississippi areas, had some help from their families before or at the time they started out as owners.

In the Arkansas sample 50 per cent of the white owners and 8 per cent of the white croppers, as compared with 36 per cent of the colored owners and 1 per cent of the colored croppers, began farming as owners. In the Louisiana sample 39 per cent of the white owners and 30 per cent of the colored owners began as owners. In the Mississippi sample 57 per cent of the white owners, 16 per cent of the white croppers, 21 per cent of the colored owners, 2 per cent of the colored croppers started as owners. (Table 107) Since it usually takes some family help to enable a farm operator who has no record of nonfarm work to start out as an owner, these data would seem to indicate that the white operators in these states have received considerably more help from their families than have the Negro operators.

Further evidence of the fact that a considerable percentage of the present owners received at least some family help is suggested by the findings relative to their ages at the time they acquired ownership. Of the 771 owners in the four sample areas, 26 per cent acquired farm ownership before they were 25 years of age (39 per cent of the white owners in Arkansas and Mississippi), while another 23 per cent achieved ownership before they had reached the age of 30. (Table 61)

The data also show that between 80 and 100 per cent of those operators in each of the survey areas who acquired ownership at an early age were sons or sons-in-law of owners. (Table 134) These data together with the fact that only 26 per cent of those who became owners before they were 25 and only 16 per cent of those who became owners between the ages of 25 and 29 reported receiving their farms through inheritance or gift (Table 135) provide evidence pointing to the extensive use of family help.

Off-farm Earnings as a Source of Capital

Effect upon Farm Tenure. Briefly stated nonfarm employment opportunities have four general effects upon the land tenure pattern. (1) Some farm people accept alternative job opportunities as a way of leaving agriculture entirely. (2) Many persons who desire to farm accept full-time employment in nonagricultural occupations as a means to gaining sufficient capital to purchase a farm or to get a start in farming. (3) Others get a small start in farming but attempt to supplement their farm incomes by looking for off-farm work during the months of the year when they have little or no farm work to do. (4) Still another group of farmers—usually the laborers and sharecroppers—alternate farming with nonfarm work as circumstances dictate.

Off-farm Earnings. For the average farmer 1942 was an unusual year so far as off-farm work and off-farm work opportunities were concerned. During most years many of the farm operators of the South have had opportunities to work on other farms, to work part-time at various skilled and unskilled trades, to hold public office, and in some areas to work at lumbering or in local industries. During the depression years many farmers also supplemented their incomes by earnings from participation in the various state and federal public work relief programs. The war years, however, with the large number of army camps and war production programs that centered in the South brought a considerable increase in the off-farm employment opportunities that were available to the southern farmer. These new opportunities, of course, had a definite effect upon the amount of off-farm work reported in 1942. Most of the operators indicated that they both worked more and made more from their off-farm work in 1942 than they did during the "usual" year.

Seventy per cent of the Arkansas operators, 82 per cent of those in Mississippi, 53 per cent in Oklahoma, and 36 per cent in Texas reported off-farm work and earnings. Further examination of the data shows that 44 per cent of the Arkansas operators, 60 per cent of those in Mississippi, 43 per cent in Oklahoma, and 29 per cent in Texas reported off-farm earnings of $50 or more. A few of the operators profited to a considerable extent from their reliance upon off-farm employment. This was particularly true in Mississippi where 11 per cent of the white operators and in Oklahoma where 7 per cent of the native white operators reported off-farm earnings of between $950 and $3,000.

Broken down on the basis of race these data show that a larger percentage of Negroes than whites worked off their farms in Arkansas and Mississippi but that a smaller percentage of the Negroes than whites reported off-farm earnings of over $50. In the Arkansas area 61 per cent of the whites and 78 of the Negroes reported some off-farm work. Yet of those doing off-farm work, 74 per cent of the whites and 55 per cent of the Negroes reported earnings of over $50, while 43 per cent of the whites and 23 per cent of the Negroes reported earnings of over $150. In the Mississippi area 79 per cent of the whites and 87 per cent of the Negroes reported some off-farm work, while of those who worked off their farms 82 per cent of the whites and 62 per cent of the Negroes earned over $50 off-farm earnings, and 57 per cent of the whites and 37 per cent of the Negroes earned $150 or more. In the Texas area all of the Mexicans and Negroes, all of whom were classified as sharecroppers or laborers, reported extensive off-farm work. The other national origin groups, however, reported much less off-farm work with only 36 per cent of the native whites, 30 per cent of the Czechs, and 12 per cent of the Germans reporting work off their home farms.

From the standpoint of tenure status the data indicate that for practically all the sample areas fewer owners than renters worked off their farms and fewer renters than croppers reported off-farm work. (Table 136) For the four samples as a whole, 53 per cent of the owners, 58 per cent of the renters, and 89 per cent of the croppers reported off-farm work. As a general rule most of the higher incomes from this source were reported by owners and renters but off-farm earnings of over $1,000 were reported by four croppers. Examination of the data also shows that those who worked off their farms tended to be younger than those who reported no off-farm work. There were, however, no significant age differences between those who reported large amounts and those who reported limited off-farm work. The full-time farmers had larger farms as measured by value of farm business, net worth, and labor requirements than the part-time operators, and their farms were slightly more diversified than those of the part-time operators.

Special tabulations of the Mississippi data indicate that the off-farm work reported for that sample area can be classified as work: (1) on the landlord's farm; (2) for other farmers; (3) trucking operations; (4) timber industries; (5) army camps; (6) war industries; (7) local processing industries; (8) skilled or semi-skilled trades; (9) other work. (Table 29)

Thirty-three croppers and laborers reported working for their landlords.[11] The rate paid was usually $1.00 or $1.25 per day. The total volume of earnings was accordingly not considerable. One wage hand and one cropper-laborer, however, reported earnings of $150 and $160 respectively from this type of work. A larger number of operators reported cash receipts from work for other farmers. Of the

[11] This tabulation includes only those cases where the worker received cash.

87 farmers who reported this type of work 44 made less than $25 and 69 made less than $50. Most of those who reported earnings of more than $50 from this type of work were either colored owners of small farms who depended on off-farm work for much of their regular year-to-year income or white operators who received payment for operating tractors or hay mowing equipment. Forty-four of these 87 farmers were owners, 11 were renters, and 32 were croppers. Of these 44 owners, at least four did work of a skilled or semi-skilled nature and of the remaining 40 owners, 24 had a net worth of less than $1,500 while an additional 13 had a net worth of less than $3,000.

Another type of off-farm work closely associated with agriculture is performed by some of the local farmers who do custom hauling of farm produce, fertilizer, feed, and other supplies. Twenty-five Mississippi operators reported receipts from farm trucking operations in 1942. All but two of these operators were owners, and these two were owners-in-prospect, using their fathers' trucks. Ten of these operators reported earnings of less than $100 while the other 15 indicated that they had earned up to $750 from trucking work.

Work in the various timber industries provided off-farm work receipts for 56 of the operators covered by the Mississippi sample in 1942 and provided the major source of off-farm earnings for 45 of these men. The types of work done varied from logging and timber peeling to work in sawmills, veneer mills, paper mills, and on stump clearing crews. Altogether 25 owners, 10 renters, and 21 croppers reported this type of work. Most of these operators reported earnings of less than $100. Even though many owners reported small earnings it is interesting to note that the nine cases of earnings of more than $500 involved six owners, two renters, and one sawmill owner who operated as a cropper during his spare time. In some cases these larger incomes resulted from longer periods of employment while in other cases they resulted from higher rates of pay. Information relative to the daily wage or income rate is available for 50 of these cases. An array of these data shows that the wages received varied from the $.75 a day received by a colored renter to the $6.50 a day received by a white owner who worked part time in a paper mill. The largest group of these part-time timber workers received a wage of $2.00 a day while a smaller number received $3.00. No colored operators, no croppers, and only five owners and one renter received more than $3.50 a day.

In 1942, 57 of the Mississippi operators had off-farm earnings from work around the army camps and in the "defense" industries.[12] Much of this work was done by men who had made a general practice of doing carpentering and other construction work in addition to their farming activities. Altogether 31 owners, eight renters, and 18 croppers reported earnings from this type of work. Of these 57 operators, 21 owners, four renters, and three croppers earned over $250, while 16 owners, 1 renter, and two croppers earned over $500 each.

Here again the highest earnings were reported by the owners. The volume of these earnings, of course, reflects both the number of days spent in off-farm work and the size of the daily wage received. In this last respect the data show that while some of the owners worked for the same unskilled labor wages earned by most of the croppers, still practically all the workers receiving the higher wages were owners. For example, of those receiving $9.75 per day and over, all were owners—eight whites and one Negro. Of the 11 receiving from $2.75 to $3.75 per day, eight were renters and croppers and only three were owners.

Since some of these operators spent the major portion of their time in off-farm work, farming operations for the most part were left to their families, hired hands, or tenants. A detailed analysis of the nine operators who worked 150 days or more in war industries shows that while all nine of these operators relied upon their families, tenants, or hired labor to do most of their farm work, none of them really profited to any great extent from their farming operations and a few of them actually lost money.

In the Mississippi sample, 30 operators (22 owners, 3 renters, and 5 croppers) reported earnings from processing work in 1942. Because of the short periods of employment most of the earnings reported from this work was small. Of the 11 men who reported earnings of over $100, 7 worked in cotton gins, and 1 each at a cotton compress, a canning plant, an ice cream plant, and as a cucumber grader.

In addition to the work reported by the men five white women reported work at the canning plant and two of them earned $400 and $450 respectively as contributions to their family incomes. Even larger contributions to these family incomes were made by the 13 white farm women—11 of them wives or daughters of owners—who live on farms and commute to Columbia, Mississippi, where they work in the garment plant. Only two of these women reported working at this

[12] For 47 of these men, work in the various war industries accounted for the major portion of their off-farm earnings.

plant for a full 12 months. Yet 10 had earnings of over $150, 7 earnings of over $450, and 3 earnings of over $700.

The Mississippi sample also included 22 cases of operators who worked part time in skilled and semiskilled trades. An enumeration of these trades shows that the sample included eight storekeepers and clerks, three railroad men, three well-boring technicians, two bakers, a blacksmith, a laundry worker, a service station employee, a taxi driver, an undertaker, and a veterinarian. Fifteen of these workers were owners, five were renters, and two were croppers. Of those reporting earnings of over $150 five were owners and two were renters. To this list might be added the cases of the farm woman who worked full time as a saleslady in a Columbia store, and the 10 Negro women who reported earnings of up to $130 from taking in washing.

As is true in many rural areas, some of the farm operators in Marion and Jefferson Davis counties in Mississippi also rely upon part-time public employment for part of their annual income. Altogether 35 operators (26 owners, four renters, and five croppers) reported earnings from this type of work.[13] Most of the operators reported earnings of between $100 and $750. The three mail carriers, however, all had off-farm earnings in excess of $1,500.

In addition to the above types of employment a few operators also reported earnings from miscellaneous part-time activities such as preaching, Works Progress Administration work, fishing, trapping, cleaning yards, and boarding teachers. A few of the farm women also reported incomes from cooking and housecleaning for others, and a few families reported dependency allowances from the government for sons or husbands in the armed services.

This brief analysis of the various types of off-farm work reported by the Mississippi operators for 1942 indicates the importance of the several types of work done and the general extent to which the owner, renter, and cropper groups profited from their off-farm work.[14]

[13] Enumeration of the types of work done shows that 16 worked on the county roads, eight drove school buses, three (including a woman) taught school, three were mail carriers, one was a road patrolman, one a constable, one a janitor, one a sanitation project worker, one a Farm Security Administration committee member, one measured Agricultural Adjustment Administration crop land, and one, a woman, was secretary of the draft board.

[14] Further analysis of these Mississippi data shows that of the 321 farm operators 224 were men under 55, 83 were men over 55, and 13 were women. All but 33 of the men under 55, 36 of those over 55, and 4 of the women operators reported off-farm earnings. The importance of this reliance upon supplementary employment opportunities is further indicated by the fact that 44 per cent of the Marion County and 28 per cent of the Jefferson Davis County farmers in the Mississippi sample depended upon off-farm earnings for at least 40 per cent of their net incomes in 1942.

Although the Mississippi sample cannot be regarded as entirely typical of the off-farm work picture in the other state areas, it shows that while the war had an indirect effect upon wages and employment opportunities in general, direct employment in war industries accounted for only a fifth of the off-farm work cases reported in 1942. Actually, the receipts from war work account for a larger percentage of the total earnings than the number employed would suggest. (Table 29) But the fact that a large percentage of the off-farm work opportunities are more or less permanent indicates the extent to which farm people rely upon their use.

Impact upon Tenure Performance. The above discussion indicates that the highest off-farm incomes often accrue to the owners rather than to the renters or croppers and that the owners frequently receive the highest daily wages from their off-farm work. In a few cases where class prestige is involved, it is possible that owners have received the higher paying jobs because they were owners. In the vast majority of the cases, however, the relationship appears to be the reverse. They are owners because they have the ability, the skill, and the earning power that makes it possible for them to hold the high wage jobs.

While it seems natural to presume that the receipt of off-farm earnings should have some effect upon tenure performance, and while the field enumerators in Arkansas, Louisiana, and Mississippi observed that the owners with the greatest net worth were often men who had a reliable and steady source of off-farm income, it is not clear that off-farm earnings always have a positive effect upon tenure performance. If an operator treats his off-farm earnings as investment or production capital he has the same chance to advance his tenure status as if he were using capital acquired from a different source. If, however, his earnings go for consumption purposes, for feeding and clothing the family, for raising family living standards, or for luxury products, the expenditure at best is likely to have no more than an indirect effect upon tenure performance.

The regional farm income data indicate that many of the farmers with low operator's earnings in 1942 depended rather heavily upon off-farm work and other nonfarm sources of income. Of the 60 cases (24 owners, 27 renters, four croppers, and five others) of negative operator earnings in Arkansas, four owners, a renter, and a cropper reported incomes from outside sources over $1,000; eight owners, three renters, and a cropper reported outside incomes of over $500; and ten owners, seven renters, and a cropper reported outside incomes of over

$300. Of the 37 cases (28 owners, five renters, and four croppers) of negative operator earnings in Mississippi, five owners reported outside incomes of over $1,000; 12 owners and one renter reported outside incomes of over $500; and 15 owners and three renters reported outside incomes of over $300. Of the 126 Arkansas farmers with operators incomes of less than $100, nine had outside incomes of over $1,000, 29 over $500, and 47 over $300. Of the 58 Mississippi farmers with operators incomes of less than $100, eight had outside incomes of over $100, 20 over $500, and 24 over $300. Of the 47 Oklahoma farmers with operator incomes of less than $100, 16 had outside incomes of over $1,000, 33 over $500, and 40 over $300.

The farmers with low operator earnings were not the only ones, however, who benefited from other sources of income. Of the 68 Arkansas farmers with operator incomes over $600, nine had outside incomes of over $1,000, 29 over $500, and 47 over $300. Of the 55 cases of Mississippi farmers with operator incomes over $600, eight had outside incomes over $1,000, 14 over $500, and 23 over $300. Of the 88 Oklahoma farmers with operator earnings over $2,000, nine had outside incomes over $1,000, 33 over $500, and 59 of over $300.

What has been said here of the effect of off-farm earnings upon tenure performance applies equally well to the cases of those who work full time in nonfarm occupations for periods involving a crop season or more. If the farm operator who has worked at a nonfarm occupation has been able to save part of his earnings and if he uses his saved capital for farm purposes, he should find it easier to gain control over a going farm.

The effect that these extended experiences with nonfarm occupations can have upon tenure performance is brought out by a detailed analysis of those cases in the Mississippi and Oklahoma sample areas who report from one to 10 or more years of nonfarm employment. Approximately a third of the operators in both areas have worked in nonfarm occupations for at least a year. Many of these people have spent a considerable portion of their earning lives in nonfarm work. On this basis it might be assumed that many of the large number of owners who worked in nonfarm employment probably used capital saved from nonfarm work in becoming owners. This assumption is supported by the fact that the individual tenure histories show that 19 of the Mississippi owners stepped directly from off-farm employment to farm ownership while another three operators followed the same course but have since lost or sold their farms. So far as the croppers, laborers, and Mississippi renters are concerned, however, the data suggest that nonfarm employment experiences had no particularly beneficial effect upon their tenure progress.

The assumption that experience in nonfarm occupations has stimulated the tenure progress of owners is substantiated to some extent by the data on methods of ownership acquisition. Twenty-six per cent of the owners for whom method of ownership is reported have had nonfarm work experience. (Table 137) The findings, though not uniform for all the sample areas, do suggest that many of these owners and particularly those who made cash purchases drew upon their nonfarm earnings and savings for farm investment capital while the other operators had to draw their supplies of farming capital from other sources.

Oil Leases, Royalties, and Other Income

Brief attention needs be given to the importance of such other nonfarm sources of income and capital as receipts from oil leases, oil royalties, pensions, bonuses, and rents from other properties. As one might expect, the data indicate that no one of these sources has provided farm operators with a great deal of farm investment or operating capital. Yet in isolated cases, the receipt of oil royalties, of soldier's bonuses or pensions, or of retirement pensions have provided some farmers with the capital that they have needed in their farming operations.

Of these miscellaneous sources of capital, the funds derived from oil leases and royalties have been most important. Of the 1,463 sample farm families in the region for which these data were available, 107 operators received some income from oil rights or leases. Nine operators in Arkansas and a similar number in Oklahoma profited to the extent of $750 or more each from their oil leases or royalties during 1942. A third of the total number receiving such incomes received from $50 to $150. Oil royalty and lease funds practically always go to the owners, not to the renters or croppers. The continued receipt of these payments usually results in their capitalization into higher land values.[15] This, of course improves the lot of the present owner

[15] General observation seems to indicate that the discovery and production of oil in the Arkansas sample area (the areas of most concentrated oil development were not included in the sample) has brought higher farm land values. While some of the farmers have tended to capitalize their oil lease payments into higher land values, others still differentiate between the value of their farms for farming and the value of the sub-surface oil and mineral rights. Examples are seen in the cases of the owners who split their real estate values "$25 an acre for the land and $30 an acre

as against that of the prospective buyer, and by increasing the capital requirements for buying a farm it tends to widen the breach between ownership and tenancy.

Oil is found and produced in all five states of the region and as a result farm land in many areas has become valuable for its subsurface oil and mineral rights. This fact, of course, has several important implications so far as land tenure conditions are concerned.[16] It has brought higher land values and this has made it harder for farmers to buy and pay for their land. It has encouraged some owners to hold on to their land or at least to the mineral and oil rights when they might otherwise have been willing to sell. It has forced bona fide farmers to speculate on the value of oil rights at times when they might have been interested only in acquiring ownership to the earth's surface. Also, in oil production areas it has at times seriously affected the agricultural use made of land.

SUMMARY

1. Of the factors of production in the Southwestern Region, capital has frequently been the limiting factor. Therefore, much of the success of operators in advancing their economic and tenure status has been contingent upon the skill they have shown or the fortune they have had in acquiring the use of farm capital.

2. Farmers draw their supplies of capital from three general sources: (a) their own savings and capital accumulations; (b) the use of credit; (c) leasing or using the farm businesses belonging to others.

3. The bulk of the owned capital used by the farmers in the five sample areas comes from farm earnings, inheritances, gifts, off-farm earnings, and miscellaneous sources such as oil royalties and pensions.

4. Approximately two-thirds of the farmers included within the sample used production or furnish credit in 1942, the distribution by

---

for oil value" and "$9 an acre for the land and $100 an acre for the oil and mineral rights." Several owners had oil leases paying from $.50 to $3 an acre a year and still reported land values of less than $10 an acre. One operator who reported receiving $10,000 in oil royalties and lease funds in the preceding five years placed a value of $1,265 on his 40 acre farm.

[16] Cf. James Salisbury, Jr. and Loris A. Parcher, "Agriculture and Other Surface Land Uses as Influenced by Mineral Developments," *Current Farm Economics*, Vol 14, No. 1, Oklahoma Agricultural Experiment Station, February 1941, pp. 18-24; James Salisbury, Jr. and Leonard A. Salter, Jr., "Sub-surface Resources and Surface Land Economics," *Journal of Land and Public Utility Economics*, XVII (August and November 1941), 270-79 and 385-93; and R. D. Davidson and Kenneth Wernimont, "Tenure Arrangements in Oklahoma Oil Fields," *Journal of Land and Public Utility Economics*, XIX (February 1943), 40-58.

survey areas being 75 per cent in the Arkansas Coastal Plain, 77 per cent in the Mississippi Coastal Plain, 48 per cent in the Oklahoma Rolling Plains, and 60 per cent in the Texas Blackland Prairie.

5. Production Credit Associations and local banks provided the most important sources of short term credit for the farmers in the Oklahoma and Texas areas, landlords the most important source in Arkansas, and merchants the most important source in Mississippi. Other credit sources were provided by the Farm Security Administration, Feed and Seed loans, equipment dealers, and private investors.

6. In general, a greater proportion of croppers and renters than owners used non-real-estate credit in each of the areas.

7. Although a large proportion of the owners reported no use of non-real-estate credit in 1942, those owners who did use production or furnish credit often used larger amounts than were used by the renter and cropper groups.

8. The following percentages of owners and part owners used real estate credit in 1942: Arkansas Coastal Plain, 19; Louisiana Coastal Plain, 44; Mississippi Coastal Plain, 46; Oklahoma Rolling Plain, 72; Texas Blackland Prairie, 42. Most of this real estate credit was provided by the Federal Land Bank.

9. The average amount per sample farm of real estate credit outstanding for each of the areas in 1942 was $1,130 for the Arkansas Coastal Plain, $792 for the Mississippi Coastal Plain, $3,950 for the Oklahoma Rolling Plains, and $5,084 for the Texas Blackland Prairie.

10. Those owners who had full equity in their farm real estate tended to be older than those who had real estate mortgages, but aside from this and related factors there is little evidence to show that the mortgaged owners behaved differently as farmers than the debt free owners.

11. Much of the accumulated capital utilized by the farmers in the region in financing farming operations as owners or as tenants has come from farm earnings. These earnings have frequently been small. Even with the "good" farm income conditions prevalent in 1942, 82 per cent of the owners, renters, and croppers in the Arkansas area, 81 per cent of those in the Mississippi area, and 25 per cent of those in the Oklahoma area had operator's earnings of less than $568. The net family incomes were considerably higher but still 72 per cent of the farm operators in the Arkansas area, 63 per cent of those in the Mississippi area, and 10 per cent of those in the Oklahoma area had net family incomes of less than $1,000 in 1942.

12. The survey data do not indicate the full extent to which the various operators have benefited through the receipt and use of inheritances, gifts, and family help. Data on farm ownership acquisitions, however, show that 22 per cent of the farm owners in the Arkansas area, 24 per cent of those in the Mississippi area, 11 per cent in the Oklahoma area, and 24 per cent of those in the Texas area acquired the first tract of their present farms in whole or in part through inheritance or through gifts. Further evidence of the importance of inheritances, gifts, and family help as a source of farming capital is suggested by the fact that a large proportion of owners, particularly in the Arkansas, Louisiana, and Mississippi areas, started as owners or acquired ownership status at a relatively early age.

13. Off-farm earnings have provided an important source for the capital used by the owners and tenants in their farming operations. In 1942, 70 per cent of the farmers covered in the Arkansas sample, 82 per cent of those in the Mississippi area, 53 per cent of those in the Oklahoma area, and 36 per cent of those in the Texas area reported receipts from work off their farms. Almost three-fourths of these farmers had off-farm earnings of over $50 and a fair number of operators, particularly in the Mississippi and Oklahoma areas, reported off-farm earnings of over $1,000 for 1942. For the four sample areas, 53 per cent of the owners, 58 per cent of the renters, and 89 per cent of the croppers reported off-farm work. In general, most of the higher incomes from off-farm work were received by the owners and renters.

14. In the Arkansas and the Oklahoma Rolling Plains oil royalties and lease funds provided an important source of farming capital. Other miscellaneous sources of capital and income of importance in scattered individual cases were supplied by pensions, soldier's bonuses, and rental payments on other property.

15. The various sources of capital are not uniformly important in all cases. Some farmers look to one source for farming capital, some to another. Taken altogether, however, the various sources control the use that the individual operators can make of capital as a factor of production.

16. Important as it is, the availability and use of capital is not always the bottleneck or determining factor affecting tenure status. Very often the availability and use of capital has only a routine influence on tenure behavior while other factors such as weather conditions, market prices, farm labor, or the operator's managerial ability frequently become the strategic and limiting factors.

CHAPTER IX

Impacts of Federal Programs on Tenure

The evolution of American agriculture extends from the pioneer problem of securing settlers for unused land to the present day problem of limited land available to landless people. The federal policy toward agriculture and toward that segment of the total population engaged in or desiring to engage in farming follows a pattern which reflects the change from one extreme to the other. Throughout most of this period, the federal land program has been primarily directed to encouraging ownership and owner operation. Illustrative of this attitude is the homestead program and the early lending activities of the Farm Credit Administration.

Most of the federal programs for agriculture have been set up with little regard to differences in the socio-economic status of subgroups. In recent years there has been more concern with the relative situation of the economically less favored groups. Approximately one-fourth of the agricultural producers are hired laborers and approximately one-half of the productive farm land is cultivated by persons who are nonowners. Typically, these nonowners have a lower economic status than owner-operators. Greater effort, therefore, might be directed effectively to the specific subgroups whose relative status is to be affected.

A review of the development of federal programs and their objectives as stated in the statutory provisions for such programs is herein presented. Further, the data accumulated in this project affords an opportunity to observe the extent of participation of the several tenure groups in the different federal programs. The following observations are intended to orient more adequately the thinking with respect to the impact of such programs on tenure. Since the Farm Security Administration is the only program concerned primarily with minimum standards and with the greater relative improvement in the status of substandard groups, a more intensive study, therefore, has been undertaken with respect to its impacts.

OBJECTIVES OF SPECIFIED FEDERAL FARM PROGRAMS

Before undertaking to examine the impact of certain of the federal farm programs on the various tenure groups, it seems appropriate to consider the purposes for which these programs were established. It is recognized that the legislative history of an act, as well as its text, may influence the interpretation placed upon it. After an act is passed, any amendments, and often the language of applicable appropriation measures, may further affect the accepted interpretation of the objectives of the original act. If the purposes for which farm programs were established do not adequately comprehend differences in tenure status, and as a result some tenure groups are adversely affected, the legislative background should be recast.

Administrative attitudes and actions further modify program objectives. If the purposes for which the agencies were established adequately comprehend tenure differences, but the tenure status of some groups is adversely affected by their operation, the administrative operation of the programs needs examination together with the techniques by which the objectives are sought.

This brief statement reviewing the more significant and currently applicable legislation pertaining to the specified programs is presented in the chronological order of the initial legislative actions relating to the present functions of the agencies. These programs did not evolve as integral parts of a composite whole. We are, nevertheless, justified in examining them as a composite. The challenge to research and planning is so to visualize them for purposes of developing the basis for future legislation.

Agricultural Extension Service

On May 8, 1914, the Smith-Lever Act (7 U.S.C. 341)[1] was approved, providing for cooperative agricultural extension work between the agriculture colleges and the United States Department of Agriculture. Its purposes were:

To aid in diffusing among the people of the United States useful and practical information on subjects relating to agriculture and home economics and to encourage the application of the same. . . . Cooperative agricultural extension work shall consist of the giving of instruc-

[1] U. S. Code citations are to the 1940 Edition. In the absence of code references in the following citations, the references are to the U. S. Statutes at Large.

tion and practical demonstrations in agriculture and home economics to persons not attending or resident in said colleges in the several communities, and imparting to such persons information on said subjects through field demonstrations, publications, and otherwise.

The purpose of the agricultural extension service is reasonably capable of distinction from the purposes of the other agencies under study. In so far as the value of knowledge, skills, and techniques accrue to the individual, it appears that the affected individual gains the full benefit of his educational progress and that such benefits cannot be capitalized into the price of other factors of agricultural production. Of course, more efficient production ultimately will result in lower production costs and lower per unit prices, but not necessarily lower net income.

Farm Credit Administration

On June 17, 1916, the Federal Farm Loan Act (12 U.S.C. 641) became law. It established the Federal Farm Loan Board. Its purposes were:

To provide capital for agricultural development, to create standard forms of investment based upon farm mortgage, to equalize rates of interest of farm loans, to furnish a market for United States bonds, to create government depositories and financial agencies for the United States, and for other purposes.

On March 4, 1923, the Agriculture Credit Act (12 U.S.C. 1151-1322) was passed, authorizing the chartering of twelve federal intermediate credit banks which make loans to and discounts for production credit associations, banks for production credit associations, banks for cooperatives, state and national banks, agricultural credit corporations, livestock loan companies, and similar financing institutions. Its purposes were: "To provide adequate credit facilities for the agriculture and livestock industries in the United States; to amend the Federal Farm Loan Act; and for other purposes."

On June 15, 1929, the Agricultural Marketing Act (12 U.S.C. 1141) was approved. This act established the Federal Farm Board. Its purposes were: "To promote the effective merchandising of agricultural commodities in interstate and foreign commerce and to place agriculture on the basis of economic equality with other industries."

On May 27, 1933, by Executive Order No. 6084, dated March 27, 1933, all federal agencies and activities providing or supervising farm credit in the United States were consolidated into the Farm Credit Administration, an independent office.

On June 16, 1933, the Federal Credit Act (12 U.S.C. 1131-48) authorized creation of twelve production credit corporations and the establishment of production credit associations and thirteen banks for cooperatives. On January 31, 1934, an act (12 U.S.C. 1020) created the Federal Farm Mortgage Corporation to supply funds for land bank commercial loans and to make loans to and buy bonds from the twelve Federal Land Banks.

Emergency federal feed and seed loans have been available to farmers under special circumstances in five years prior to 1929 and each year since. The first such loan was made available to drought stricken southwestern wheat growers in 1918. The nature and purpose of this type of loan is set forth in the language of an act (7 U.S.C. 1007) passed June 29, 1937, which authorized the governor of the Farm Credit Administration to make emergency crop and feed loans. Its purposes were:

> To make loans to farmers in the United States . . . for production of crops . . . and for feed for livestock. . . . No loan shall be made under this Act to any applicant who shall not have first established to the satisfaction of the proper officer or employer of the Farm Credit Administration . . . that such applicant is unable to procure a loan in an amount reasonably adequate to meet his needs for the purposes for which loans may be made under this Act. . . . However . . . no loans made under the provision of this Act to any borrower shall exceed $400. . . . Each loan shall bear interest at the rate of 4 per cent per annum.

By order of the President under Reorganization Order No. 1, the Farm Credit Administration became a part of the United States Department of Agriculture on July 1, 1939. The institution and administration of the federal farm credit program no doubt has contributed to the stabilization of agricultural credit, and probably to the establishment of interest rates at levels lower than otherwise would have been the case. Interest rates under federal agricultural lending policies are uniform and are not made to vary with risk, by geographic areas, or by type of enterprise.

To the extent that favorable interest rates are available to landowners generally, such rates may readily be capitalized into the price of land. Higher land prices tend to enhance the bargaining position of land and, thus, may operate against the interests of tenure groups other than owners. On the other hand, the type of loan typified by the emergency feed and seed loan, the use of which is restricted to certain described groups, would tend to improve the bargaining positions of those groups. Thus, the restricted type of loan may be relatively more favorable to tenure groups with limited capital.

Soil Conservation Service[2]

On March 25, 1935, the Soil Erosion Service of the Department of the Interior was transferred to the Department of Agriculture under authority of Executive Orders No. 6252 and No. 6929. On April 27, 1935, the Soil Erosion Act (49 Stat. 163) established the Soil Conservation Service. Its purposes were: "To provide for the protection of land resources against soil erosion and for other purposes."

By this simple statement of the purpose of this act, it would seem that the accent is on land and the concern with man is only in his relation to land. No obligation to the preservation of equitable income relationships between tenure groups is implied. In so far as tenure is involved, the achievement of this objective is concerned, therefore, primarily with impact of tenure on soil erosion than the impact of erosion control on tenure.

Agricultural Adjustment Administration

The original Agricultural Adjustment Administration Act which became effective in 1933 was invalidated by Supreme Court decision on January 6, 1936. Since its provisions are no longer applicable and since subsequent legislation describes adequately the objectives of the present program, no discussion of the original act seems to be required here.

The Soil Conservation and Domestic Allotment Act was amended March 29, 1936 (49 Stat. 1148). This amendment reads in part:

> It is hereby declared to be the policy of this Act to secure, and the purpose of this Act shall also include:
>
> (1) Preservation and improvement of soil fertility.
>
> (2) Promotion of economic use and conservation of land.
>
> (3) Diminution of exploitation and wasteful and unscientific use of national soil resources.
>
> (4) The protection of rivers and harbors against the results of soil erosion in aid of maintaining the navigability of waters and water courses and aid of flood control.
>
> (5) Establishment, at as rapid a rate as the secretary determines to be practical and in the public interest, of the ratio between the purchasing power of the net income per person on farms

[2] See Chapter VI, "Land Tenure and Soil Conservation."

and that of the income per person not on farms that prevailed during the 5-year period, August, 1909-July, 1914 . . . .

The above purposes are altogether desirable. On the other hand, certain of the objectives as stated may be achieved and at the same time admit of increased inequities in the distribution of agricultural income among tenure groups.

The Agricultural Adjustment Act of 1938 (7 U.S.C. 1281-1407) further provides that:

Payments made by the secretary to farmers under subsection (b) shall be divided among the landlords, tenants, and croppers of any farm with respect to which such payments are made in the same proportion that such landlords, tenants, and sharecroppers are entitled to share in the proceeds of the agricultural commodity with respect to which such payments are made . . . .

Thus, a basis was established for the distribution of benefit payments among tenure groups. The long-range benefits of higher price level of agricultural commodities and the increased efficiency of production resulting from the achievement of specific program objectives likewise would be shared by all tenure groups except as the bargaining position of the man (labor and management) versus the land varies with economic change. It does not appear that the Agricultural Adjustment Administration's objectives as stated contemplate the improvement of the economic status of one tenure group over another.

Farm Security Administration[3]

On June 16, 1933, the National Industrial Recovery Act (48 Stat. 201) was passed. Section 203 of this Act read in part: "To provide for aiding the redistribution of the over balance of population in industrial centers . . . to be used . . . for making loans for and otherwise aiding in the purchase of subsistence homesteads . . ."

On April 30, 1935, the Resettlement Administration was established by Executive Order No. 7027, pursuant to the Act of April 8, 1935, Emergency Relief Appropriation (49 Stat. 115). The Resettlement Administration was established:

(a) To administer projects involving resettlement of destitute or low-income families from rural and urban areas, including the establishment, maintenance, and operation, in such connection, of communities in rural and suburban areas.

(b) To initiate and administer a program of approved projects with respect to soil erosion, stream pollution, seacoast erosion, reforestation, forestation, and flood control.

[3] Changed to the Farmers Home Administration in 1946.

(c) To make loans, as authorized under the Emergency Relief Appropriation Act of 1934, to finance, in whole or in part, the purchase of farm lands and necessary equipment by farmers, farm tenants, croppers, or farm laborers.

On December 31, 1936, by Executive Order No. 7530, the Resettlement Administration was transferred to the Department of Agriculture.

On July 22, 1937, the Bankhead-Jones Farm Tenant Act was approved (7 U.S.C. 1000-29) creating the Farmer's Home Corporation. Its purposes were: "To promote more secure occupancy of farms and farm homes; to correct the economic instability resulting from some present forms of farm tenancy and for other purposes . . ."

By a memorandum of the Secretary of Agriculture, the Farm Security Administration was created September 1, 1937, as successor to the Resettlement Administration.

The Emergency Relief Appropriation Act of 1938 (32 Stat. 809) provided that funds appropriated to the Secretary of Agriculture "shall be available for administration, loans, relief, and rural rehabilitation for needy persons."

On August 11, 1939, the so-called Wheeler-Case Act (16 U.S. Code 590y) was approved. The responsibilities of the Department of Agriculture under the act were assigned to the Farm Security Administration. This act was for the purpose of:

Stabilizing water supply and thereby rehabilitating farmers on the land and providing opportunities for permanent settlement of farm families. . . . To construct water conservation and utilization projects in the Great Plains and arid and semi-arid areas of the United States, and to operate and maintain each such project . . . .

In the series of legislative acts and orders relating to the functions of the Farm Security Administration may be observed the development of a federal program specifically directed to benefit less favored tenure groups, to develop improved standards of living for farm people, and to promote more stable conditions of tenure. In consideration, therefore, of the several legislative acts noted above, it would appear that federal responsibility for special attention toward improved tenure status of less favored tenure groups rests largely with the Farm Security Administration.

Farm Labor

Apart from placement services, there has been no well-defined federal policy concerning agricultural labor. Aside from the provisions of the Sugar Act of 1937, the farm laborer receives no direct benefits from any of the federal farm programs, excepting as he may change to a different tenure status. If those who till the soil for hire and those who cultivate it as tenants or owners are alike a part of the human problem of agricultural production, there is no less obligation to provide for the maintenance of minimum standards for those who remain as laborers than for those who seek to become tenants or owner-operators. Farm laborers obviously are an integral part of the farm tenure picture.

Approximately four million hired workers are employed annually in agricultural production, which constitutes upwards of 25 per cent of all agricultural workers. The wage level of agricultural laborers is closely related to the general economic situation. Numerous studies disclose that in times of industrial unemployment real farm wage rates are low. In such times the hired laborer is in a poor bargaining position because of the relative abundant labor supply.

Generally speaking, the farm wage hand has fared less well relatively in the last 30 years than have other workers. The level of living capable of being maintained on prevailing farm wages has been a matter of concern over a long period of time.

PARTICIPATION IN FEDERAL PROGRAMS

A review of literature on tenure leads to the conclusion that an effective study of the relative impacts of federal programs on tenure groups must be confined either to case studies or to clearly described areas of research. Even so the results can be reported only in broad generalizations.

The following observations on participation in government programs are intended to be factual and descriptive and do not of themselves measure the effectiveness of the respective programs. They indicate, however, the relative extent to which the major tenure groups participate. For this purpose the following three tenure combination groupings are used: (1) owners, including part owners; (2) renters, including cash, standing, share, and share-cash; (3) croppers. These groups are further separated by color. It should be noted that the Oklahoma and Texas croppers operate on a substantially larger scale than those in Mississippi and Arkansas.

Not all of the benefits of agricultural programs are fully realized by the individual or by tenure groups. As noted elsewhere, apparent benefits tend to be capitalized into the price of land. In such cases a relatively earlier attainment of ownership based on more extended credit might be more appropriate than a longer term of tenant or laborer status. At any rate, to make sure that a program will aid the farmer in his ascent of the tenure ladder it is necessary that emphasis be placed on programs especially designed for those in the economically less favored groups.

Agricultural Adjustment Administration

Participation in the Agricultural Adjustment Administration program is the most nearly universal of the several government programs. Participation by colored and white farmers is closely comparable in Arkansas and Mississippi. However, the cropper in Oklahoma was the only tenure group which did not have practically 100 per cent participation. (Table 94)[4]

According to regulations, the division of A.A.A. payments between participating landlord, tenant, and cropper has been made in recent years upon the basis of equity in crops produced. The program benefits represented by cash payments were distributed essentially as other farm income; hence, owners received somewhat higher average A.A.A. payments than renters and substantially more than croppers under the provision of the program. The improved productivity of land resulting from conservation practices and balanced production accrue primarily to the owner of the land.

It is noted that not all croppers and tenants on participating farms reported having received A.A.A. payments. The complaint has been made from time to time that many croppers and some tenants were deprived of payments due them in accordance with A.A.A. regulations. The findings of this study support this assumption to a limited extent but no data are available for comparison as to whether or not such practices may have been more prevalent prior to 1942.

It should be borne in mind that diversion of payments which were in the nature of farm income, resulted from the relative bargaining position of the landlord and tenant or cropper and is not inherent in the program itself. Such diversion would tend to take place in the same way as the diversion of other returns. There is considerable evidence that the relative bargaining position of the tenant and cropper changes with changing economic conditions and in 1942 was much improved over that in the middle and late thirties.

[4] For tables mentioned in this chapter refer to statistical tables in Appendix.

Agricultural Extension Service

The extension program depends upon many different types of contacts. Observations in this study were made only with respect to county farm and home demonstration agents. (Table 138) A substantial proportion of all farmers were in contact with county agents running as high as 45 to 50 per cent among colored farmers in Arkansas and Mississippi. In general, the higher the tenure status the greater the number of contacts. The study also discloses substantial participation in 4H Club activities by members of farm families in the area.

Farm Security Administration

The Farm Security Administration undertakes to provide credit to farmers who are unable to get credit from other sources and to provide limited supervision. While the program is available to, and participated in by, a significant number of owners whose net worth is low, it is especially attractive to renters and to croppers who are to become renters. (Table 111) Approximately 35 per cent of the white renters and 20 per cent of the colored renters participated in the F.S.A. program in the Mississippi and Arkansas samples. The participation in Oklahoma and Texas is notably less for both classes.

Croppers generally do not participate in the F.S.A. program for two reasons: One is that croppers who are eligible are likely to become renters as a direct result of such participation. The other is that the nature of the cropper arrangement is such that the landlord usually provides the necessary credit for the cropper to operate.

The extent to which the F.S.A. program may have influenced the relative tenure position of borrowers is reported elsewhere in this study.

Farm Credit Administration

The farm credit program has provided sufficient opportunity and incentive to induce up to 43 per cent of farm owners from whom schedules were obtained to participate in this program. A substantially smaller proportion of tenants than owners and still fewer croppers participated. (Table 123) Of course, that phase of the program which has to do with real estate credit is available only to owners.

The average amount loaned for production credit is larger for owners than for tenants or croppers. No partiality, however, seems to be shown to the various tenure groups in advancing feed and seed credit. Under this program the basis for making such loans is essentially different than those for real estate or production credit.

Borrowers under the Farm Credit Administration secure loans at a universally low rate of interest. The study discloses that the costs of various other types of advances, while not always charged as interest in the conventional manner, frequently run as high as 20 to 30 per cent of the amounts advanced. This fact makes it evident that, while the impact of the Farm Credit Administration program has been substantial from the point of view of participants, much improvement in the credit situation in the sampled area remains to be made.

Soil Conservation Service

The participation in the Soil Conservation Service program is confined almost entirely to owners. (Table 93) Approximately 10 per cent of the white owners and 6 per cent of the colored owners participated in the sample taken (excluding Mississippi) as compared with less than 4 per cent of the renters. The immediate benefits of the Soil Conservation Service program accrue primarily to landowners; hence, the incentive to participate by croppers and other than the more permanently situated tenants is largely lacking.

All Government Programs

A composite measure of participation in the several programs studied discloses that with the exception of the few white croppers in Oklahoma and Texas, practically all farmers in each of the several tenure groups participated in 1942 in one or more of these programs. (Table 139) Measured in this way, it appears that either government programs provide a relatively greater attraction to farm owners or that a higher proportion of owners are able to qualify for participation. Renters come second and croppers third.

Any one farmer may be interested in more than one of the programs offered. On the other hand, these programs are of such nature that they are not likely to afford an inducement for the individual farmer to participate simultaneously in all of them. The programs of the Agricultural Adjustment Administration and the Agricultural Extension Service are essentially universal in their appeal; the program of the Soil Conservation Service appeals more especially to landowners and participation is limited by the scope of activities of the service itself. The credit facilities of the Farm Credit Administration and the Farm Security Administration are arranged to meet the needs of different types of borrowers; hence, there is little duplication of participation in these two programs.

In general, the data indicate the need for serious consideration of the more adequate adaptation of the federal programs to the needs of tenure groups which are less favored by the existing economic institutions and changing economic circumstances.

IMPACTS OF FARM SECURITY ADMINISTRATION ON TENURE

Under the conditions existing between World Wars I and II a significant portion of the farm population was unsuccessful in maintaining an acceptable level of living as independent farm operators, not to mention the possibility of ascending the tenure ladder. Many farmers operated as croppers under managerial supervision provided by private enterprises.

These people fell below an acceptable minimum standard of living during the early 1930's. The nature of their circumstances tended to inhibit the improvement of their bargaining position through organizations corresponding to labor unions. However, the government has assumed increasing major responsibilities which it had no occasion to assume in earlier days.

The National Industrial Recovery Act passed in June 1933 made provision for the extension of certain types of relief to rural and urban people. This relief program was further extended by the Emergency Relief Appropriation in 1935. During the initial period, a considerable number of relief grants were made to clients without regard to the feasibility of their rehabilitation as farmers.

In 1937, with the creation of the Farm Security Administration within the Department of Agriculture, fortified by the Bankhead-Jones Farm Tenant Act, a program of rehabilitation was added to the relief activities previously undertaken. The activity of the Farm Security Administration materially differed from any program in which the Department of Agriculture had previously engaged. By reason of the administrative structure of the organization, significant local variations in administration have existed. Therefore, it should be observed that any study of the impacts of the F.S.A. is primarily applicable to the local setting in which the study is made.

A number of studies have been made of the progress of farm security borrowers toward the attainment of the objectives of that program. Because of the procedure used in making such studies, the reports are largely descriptive and none of them so far as can be ascertained have undertaken to measure the progress of borrowers in contrast to progress which might reasonably have been expected without the direct aid of the F.S.A. program. This seems to be a serious deficiency inasmuch as the measure of current progress of any group is materially affected by the industrial situation and economic trends during the period studied.

Measuring Impacts by the Matching Method

The present study undertakes to measure the impact of the Farm Security Administration by observing the status of its borrowers as contrasted with comparable nonborrowers. To do this, control groups were established by matching the schedules of clients with those of comparable nonclients. In this comparison 1942 is the last year for which data are available. The observations made are believed to be valid for the area from which the sample is drawn and are such as to warrant the application of the technique used to other data on a much wider scale. In observing the impacts of the F.S.A. program, the chief interest is to determine to what extent the program is successful in accomplishing the rehabilitation of people engaged in agricultural production in order that they may continue to operate on a stable and secure basis and improve their tenure status.[5]

The Matching Procedure

Although the following discussion is not intended as an exhaustive statement of method, it is included partly as an aid to the reader in evaluating the conclusions which follow and partly as an indication of the extreme caution necessary in studying a problem of this kind.[6]

The characteristics deemed important for the individual matching of cases and for which information was available are as follows: (1) tenure of parents (2) stage in family cycle (3) age of head (4) education (5) number in family at home (6) kinship to landlord (7) tenure status, and (8) migration ratio. Prior to matching on the above points the cases were separated by race and sex. The above characteristics used in the matching are believed to be such as to warrant the assumption of comparability between the resulting groups for the purpose of observing contrasts in certain characteristics of their 1942 status. The descriptive items thus observed for purposes of further comparison by group averages are as follows: (1) net worth (2) value of business (3) acres in farm (4) crop acres (5) yield index (6) productive man-work units, and (7) credit used.

---

[5] See Donald C. Blaisdell, *Government and Agriculture*, New York: Farrar and Rinehart, 1940, for an objective treatment of the functions and activities of the Farm Security Administration.

[6] See C. C. Peters and W. R. Voorhees, *Statistical Procedures and Their Mathematical Bases* for a general statement of the techniques employed.

After having been matched on the basis of the above points the F.S.A. and non-F.S.A. groups were then compared on the following items relating to rehabilitation and tenure progress: (1) degree of management index (2) index of diversification (3) labor efficiency rating (4) net income per farm (5) net income per man equivalent unit, and (6) socio-economic status. An additional process is an accurate evaluation of net worth of the client and the nonclient prior to the time when the client entered upon the F.S.A. program. The absence of initial net worth, however, need not be of great concern. Observations are made in other studies bearing upon change in net worth of clients,[7] and net worth in 1942 is only one of the characteristics being observed.

In carrying forward the work of matching, two major considerations were involved for each criterion used: (1) Is the criterion of crucial importance? (2) What amount of variation between two cases may be allowed in setting up pairs of matched cases? Obviously no two cases were identical and certain rules of tolerance had to be established. Comments on these two points follow under the headings of the several matching criteria used. It is impossible within the scope of this presentation to set down in detail all of the considerations involved in proceeding with the matching process. A very wide variety of items from the schedules was used in screening for those which were eligible for matching. This involved a careful study and scrutiny of each schedule. The procedure usually involved arranging several sets of matched pairs, in some of which the matching was more rigorous than in the others. The less rigorous sets were then put through a testing and refining process, pairs being discarded until all that remained were sufficiently matched to meet the requirements.

In the Arkansas Coastal Plain sample, for example, 89 pairs were originally set up but 30 of these were later discarded as not sufficiently rigorously matched. The Arkansas sample consisted of 155 F.S.A. borrowers and 407 nonborrowers. It was hoped that a match could be found for each one of the 155 F.S.A. cases among the nonborrowers. The final matched sets, however, consisted of only 59 pairs, it being impossible to pair properly the other 96 cases.

Schedules were first arranged with respect to type of F.S.A. borrower, race, tenure of parents, and stage in family cycle, after which simultaneous consideration was given to the various other characteris-

[7] While no specific reports have been made on average change in net worth, studies by the Bureau of Agricultural Economics and others do not encourage the assumption that any substantial increase in net worth of clients took place prior to the end of 1942.

tics. Schedules that failed of pairing within the permissible degree of tolerance were then rearranged by age groups for a further attempt at pairing. Only schedules in agreement with respect to race and sex of head were paired, and married couples were paired only with married couples.

After trial pairs had been matched, a rigorously matched group was selected within which there was a tolerance of not more than two degrees, as described below in respect to any one characteristic, and not more than a total of five degrees with respect to the seven characteristics tabulated. On this basis it was found that 46 of the 155 F.S.A. cases, although possible of pairing, could not be matched within the permissible range of the tolerance. An additional 20 cases were screened out at the beginning of the process as ineligible because of single person families, broken families, borrowers for less than a year, families for whom the migration ratio could not be computed, and families with unusual incomes or losses.

Tenure of Parents. The tenure of parents is looked upon as a significant characteristic influencing performance. The social and psychological factors were considered no less significant than the economic factors. All characteristics that have an influence may be negative or positive but cooperators paired with respect to these and other characteristics may be expected to result in groups most nearly comparable in the performance later to be observed.

The following table shows the values assigned to tenure of parents and the tolerance in comparison of matched pairs.

		6	5	5	4	3	3	2	2	1
	XX	O-O	O-R	O-NF	O-C	R-R	R-NF	R-C	C-NF	C-C
6	O-O	. .								
5	O-R	1	. .							
5	O-NF	1	. .	. .						
4	O-C	2	1	1	. .					
3	R-R	3	2	2	1	. .				
3	R-NF	3	2	2	1	. .	. .			
2	R-C	4	3	3	2	1	1	. .		
2	C-NF	4	3	3	2	1	1	. .	. .	
1	C-C	5	4	4	3	2	2	1	1	. .

The numbers at the extreme left of the chart indicate the values assigned to the tenure combinations of the parents of the family under consideration. The first letter refers to the tenure status of the husband's parents, the second to the wife's parents. For example, 0-0 indicates that both husband's and wife's parents were owners; 0-R, husband's parents owner, wife's parents renter; O-NF, husband's parents owner, wife's parents nonfarm; O-C, husband's parents owner, wife's parents cropper. The higher the figures in the center of the chart the less close the matching. In general, combinations with scores above 2 were regarded as not sufficiently matched for the purposes of the study.

Stage in Family Cycle. The method of determining this factor is treated elsewhere in this report. In general, families are divided into ten types, five for married families with both husband and wife living and five for broken families. The types are based upon number of children and age. The stage in the family cycle is believed to be significant as a matching factor. Degrees of tolerance were utilized in matching on this factor by a method similar to that indicated above for tenure of parents.

Age of Head. This characteristic is considered of major importance and lends itself to relatively easy manipulation as a matching factor.

Grade Attainment. The matching in this instance was done on the basis of the highest grade attained by either spouse. This item is believed to reflect family and experience background and capabilities. It is not assumed, however, that the differential in subject matter obtained by grade attainment has a significant bearing on the performance of the individual in his specific farming practices.

Number at Home. This item is recognized as giving some indication of the earning capacity and labor supply of the family unit. It is recognized, however, that children of certain ages are an economic liability rather than an asset. Children may contribute more or less to the labor supply, depending upon the time spent in school, the time parents required them to work, and other factors. It is believed, however, that group comparison of these characteristics will tend to result in balancing of these factors for the matched groups.

Kinship to Landlord. It is recognized also that a business-like leasing arrangement which would be appropriate in all instances would tend to minimize the difference that results from kinship to landlord. However, it is believed that consideration of this characteristic in pairing will improve the comparability of the matched groups.

Tenure Status. Comparison on the basis of tenure status although fundamental affords certain difficulties. It is believed that scope of operation and experience as indicated by farm and crop acres and other factors should be given careful consideration. The simplest and possibly the most satisfactory pairing is as of the last year prior to the year when the F.S.A. borrower became a client. A consideration of tenure status in subsequent years may depend upon the influence of the program whereas status in preceding years may not recognize the relative position of the families compared before program influence was brought to bear.

The following table summarizes the general method of computing tolerance between the matched pairs and the relative emphasis of each characteristic:

Characteristic	Range in Intervals		Degree of Tolerance (Cumulative fraction of range)				Approximate order of emphasis
	Actual	Net	0°	1°	2°	3°	
Age of head	20-80	60	1/10	1/7	1/5	1/4	More
Education of husband/wife	0-16	16	1/16	2/8	3/4	1/4	More
Number at home	1-13	12	0	1/12	1/6	3/6	More
Tenure of parent	1-16	5	0	1/5	2/5	3/5	Less
Tenure status	1-4	4	0	2/4	2/4	3/4	Less
Kinship to landlord	0-3	3	0	1/3	2/3	All	Least
State in family cycle	1-5	4	0	1/4	All	...	Least

Before undertaking to describe the matched groups, it is important to note that neither the farm security clients nor the nonclients are necessarily typical of all clients of the samples (or the universe) from which they are taken. Only such schedules are included in either group as are found to compare, within the described limits, with a schedule selected from the other group. Thus, the group description of clients satisfactorily matched would tend in the direction of the nonclient group and vice versa. If clients as a whole have less net worth than nonclients, then the matched nonclients are likely to average lower in net worth than the nonclient group as a whole.

Borrowers and Nonborrowers in the Arkansas Coastal Plain

Credit. A comparison of F.S.A. rural rehabilitation borrowers with nonborrowers, both white and colored, shows that the ratio of production credit used is about four dollars for the former and one dollar for the latter.

In the comparison of real estate credit for farm owner borrowers and nonborrowers, the ratio is much higher than this, due partly to the fact that many nonborrowers who are matched with farm owner borrowers continue as tenants and the real estate credit used by them is negligible as compared with that of the borrowers. These differences are to be expected since the principal function of the F.S.A. is to give liberal extension of credit, especially to those whose economic status is such that it is difficult to get credit elsewhere.

It is possible that the indebtedness of farm security clients might have been more adequately reported in the survey than that of nonclients. If this is true, the difference between the matched groups is less than is indicated. It is believed, however, that any disparity in these data is not sufficient to affect the validity of the general observations made. The effectiveness with which this greater amount of credit is used, together with the benefits of supplemental activities of the F.S.A., may be evaluated in part by observations concerning the performance of these borrowers. (Table 140) In this connection, it is important to bear in mind that the liberal use of credit has a greater advantage during an up-trend period of the economic cycle than in the down-trend.

Degree of Management. It will be seen that a higher degree of management is exercised by colored clients than by the comparable non-clients. This may be achieved in part through better leasing arrangements and in part by the change in tenure status from croppers to renters and renters to owners. A comparison of the degree of management is not made for the farm owner group, since the essential change is that of tenant to owner, with a substantial difference in the degree of management obtained by the client. This increase in responsibility marks progress up the tenure ladder, provided clients are capable of exercising a higher degree of management advantageously when the supervision of the F.S.A. is no longer available to them.

Diversification. F.S.A. clients diversify to a greater extent than comparable nonclients. This diversification involved a shift to a somewhat less acreage of cotton and to more livestock. There is evidence that clients under F.S.A. supervision have been somewhat more successful in their management of the livestock than nonclients. Farm owner clients produced more cattle but fewer hogs and less poultry than comparable nonclients and also place somewhat more emphasis on minor cash crops. The effects of a diversified program of farming in stabilizing year-to-year income is not necessarily apparent in any single year and, therefore, may not be fully reflected in the report for 1942. Such effects could be better observed over a period of years.

It is obvious that the productive man-work days per man equivalent year[8] is higher for nonborrowers than for borrowers except in the farm owner loan groups. White rural rehabilitation borrowers have approximately the same number of crop acres as nonborrowers and have a slightly higher yield index. In the case of colored borrowers, there is a larger average number of crop acres per farm but with a substantially lower yield index. The larger acreages of farm owner borrowers and the substantially higher yield index explain why the PMWU/MEW ratios are so much higher than that of the comparable nonborrowers group.

Net Income. The average net income per farm for both white and colored rural rehabilitation borrowers is less than that for comparable nonborrowers. The net income per man equivalent unit is also less for rural rehabilitation borrowers than for comparable nonborrowers. This situation is again reversed when farm owner borrowers are compared with their respective matched group.

With the exception of the farm owner group, the comparison of production man-work days per man equivalent year and/or net income is decidedly disappointing from the point of view of the F.S.A. The data indicate a need for more detailed planning of farm operations with a view to a fuller utilization of available labor. It is obvious that the farm owner group is more rigorously selected than the rural rehabilitation group; also that the farm owner operates substantially larger units.

Socio-economic Status. The socio-economic status scale averages slightly higher for all groups of F.S.A. borrowers than for the respec-

[8] The formula for arriving at this efficiency factor is as follows:

PMWU — Man Days Hired Labor = Factor
Man Equivalent — Off-farm Work
Units Family Labor (Days/300)

Certain indeterminate situations involved in deriving the components of this formula might influence the validity of the results: These are: (1) the evaluation of the man equivalent of woman labor (2) the amount of hired labor utilized, and (3) inaccuracies arising out of fractional years of family labor not precisely accounted for although in a large sample it is assumed that these would compensate. It is not contemplated, however, that the proposed formula would be applicable without further modification to farms utilizing sharecroppers. It is to be hoped that the present study will stimulate further work along these lines.

tive non-F.S.A. groups. This may be taken as partially indicative of the relative level of living of the groups compared. However, no attempt is made to evaluate the benefits F.S.A. clients derive through membership in cooperative health groups and similar related activities.

Borrowers and Nonborrowers in the Mississippi Coastal Plain and The Oklahoma Rolling Plains

The study of matched groups in Mississippi and Oklahoma in general bear out the observations made above with respect to the Arkansas groups. (Tables 141 and 142) However, it should be borne in mind that the data presented are considered applicable only to the areas from which they were collected.

In Mississippi the F.S.A. borrowers in the matched groups were largely owners. While the borrowers in the white groups were somewhat lower in average net worth than the average of the entire sample, the colored borrowers and matched nonborrowers average substantially above the average of the standard sample.

With respect to income, both the Mississippi and Oklahoma samples show higher net income per man equivalent unit for nonborrowers than for comparable borrowers. In making comparisons between states, however, it should be pointed out that the method of computing the PMWU differed slightly in each state. Hence there is less stability in the comparison of this item across state lines than in the other items.

SUMMARY AND CONCLUSIONS

1. Each of the several government programs now operated for the benefit of agriculture has evolved as a separate provision to meet some new and current problem. Taken as a whole, they bear a rational and appropriate relationship to the conditions which gave rise to their development. However, the composite of programs does not clearly visualize a complete and adequate set of ends or objectives.

2. The lack of a completely comprehensive and integrated governmental program is due in part to the fact that it has not been possible to determine a complete set of long-run ends with which the majority of the people would be in substantial agreement.

3. The prosperity of those engaged in farming depends: (a) on a high level of general employment, and (b) on an active demand for the available supply of agricultural products. Hence, any program for the benefit of agriculture should be undertaken as a segment of a

comprehensive plan for the improvement of the living standards of all people.

4. The productive power of man-hour labor spent in "on farm" work has increased markedly during the past few years. With a fixed amount of available agricultural labor this tends further to weaken its bargaining position in relation to landownership. Industry must be the active or potential employer of the residual labor resulting from improved farm technology if a reasonably satisfactory bargaining position for the tenant and laborer is to be maintained.

5. A recurrence of the situation of the early 1930's seems likely if business cycles continue as in the past. However, there is a serious question as to whether the present system under private enterprise may be improved upon. The burden of proof of any alternative intended to establish a more efficient and acceptable type of operation for this submarginal income group in agriculture must rest with the proponents of such alternatives. The ability of the government to provide such an alternative has not yet been established.

6. Little progress has been made in rehabilitating those who have reached the least acceptable status. It should be observed that those most in need of assistance are generally least capable of rehabilitation.

7. It may be necessary to distinguish more sharply between programs intended to improve the economic level of the farming group as a whole and programs intended to improve the status of certain disadvantaged subgroups if the latter programs are to be effective.

8. As an alternative to the present pattern of agricultural programs it is conceivable that a general program might be devised which would provide for a level of minimum conditions for those engaged in farming without undertaking specifically to influence the tenure status by which the individual operates. Such an approach is in keeping with the concept of job insurance and the social security program in general.

CHAPTER X

Community and Institutional Factors in Tenure

The system of institutions in a local area results from the interaction of many factors, including the source of the settlers, physical environment, stage of technological development, and length of time which the institutions have had to approach a stable equilibrium.

Because land tenure is a fundamental aspect of the institution called private property, it is here viewed in relation to community institutions. The description of the pattern begins with the history of the local settlement and is carried through into the present era of increased communication, mechanization, and the urban centered supplementary farm occupations. The objective is to point out the relations of land tenure to community and neighborhood functions, particularly as they concern the organizations and attitudes in the present day setting.

The study of these factors was not carried on in a uniform manner throughout the region. This was partly because of the physical limitations of the study, which necessitated less intensive work in some areas than others, but also because of the vastly differing community and institutional arrangements in the eastern as compared with the western sections of the region. The work done in the Coastal Plain area of Mississippi was the most intensive. Here a series of neighborhoods are described and classed as to type. In more or less contrast with these types, two community areas representative of the Rolling Plains areas are described in some detail. Throughout these analyses, it should be born in mind that complete coverage of the region is not assumed. The materials presented are to be regarded as suggestive rather than inclusive.

COASTAL PLAIN AREA IN SOUTH CENTRAL MISSISSIPPI

This area has all the contrasts in community and neighborhood patterns of tenure and socio-economic status that would be expected to accompany the development of recent cutover timber operations amidst scattered communities of old plantations. The ante bellum estates were located along the water course of the Pearl River. As clearings expanded on the upper reaches of the watershed, the silting of the river channel eventually led to their abandonment. In addition, the highway system favored plantation areas more removed from the river valley.

The logging era was ushered in with the coming of the railroads. The development of cutover lands into farms can be traced by degrees as a sequel to timber operations.[1] This sequence from timber to crops is paralleled in the sequences of tenure patterns and institutional services.

The analysis of these neighborhoods was carried forward in terms of the sample households and additional materials obtained by special observations in the area. (Figure 32)

Neighborhood Differences

Neighborhoods Classified by Tenure and Race. For the purposes at hand the 20 sample neighborhoods were classified (Table 143)[2] into the following types:

—*Mixed type.* The most numerous type in the area. It consists of a combination of both races and all types of tenures.

—*Single racial type.* Either (1) all white or (2) all colored. Both subtypes include a variety of tenure types.

—*Owner type.* Either (1) all white owners or (2) owner families of both races.

—*Plantation type.* White owners with either white or Negro croppers or laborers.

—*Plantation transition type.* Transition type that is changing from the plantation economy to a new emphasis on livestock, truck, or general farming. It is approaching the *Mixed type.*

The Mixed type neighborhoods are heterogeneous in several ways. Pinebur, for example, is the recently abandoned site of a sawmill. The farms of the central valley are surrounded by new ones developed in the cut-over area. Both races and all tenures are found in this as in the other neighborhoods of this type. The other six neighborhoods in this group have had a long history of farming, with evidences of

[1] For a description of this sequence in a county adjoining the sample area, see Harold Hoffsommer and Herbert Pryor, *Neighborhoods and Communities in Covington County, Mississippi,* Washington, D. C., U. S. Department of Agriculture, Bureau of Agricultural Economics, July, 1941, processed, 31 pp.

[2] For tables mentioned in this chapter refer to statistical tables in Appendix.

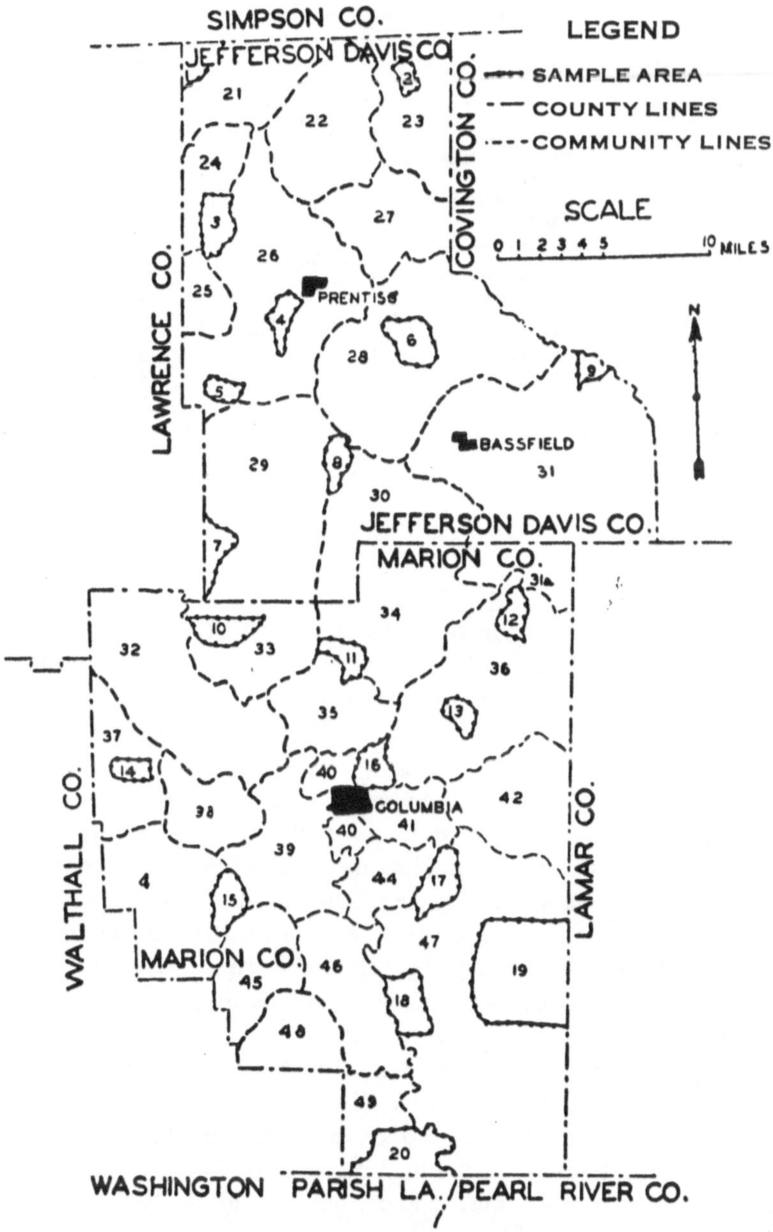

FIGURE 32. Community areas and sample neighborhoods in the Eastern Coastal Plain Sample area, Marion and Jefferson Davis Counties, Mississippi.

Figure 32—Continued

JEFFERSON DAVIS COUNTY

Sample Neighborhoods	*Communities*
1. New Hebron	21. Hebron
	22. Red House
2. Clem	23. Clem
3. Spring Hill	24. Spring Hill
	25. Lucas
4. Prentiss, 5. Progress	26. Prentiss
	27. Mt. Carmel
6. Carson	28. Carson
7. Oakvale	29. Son's
8. Greenscreek	30. Greenscreek
9. Good Hope	31. Bassfield

MARION COUNTY

Sample Neighborhoods	*Communities*
	31a Broom
	32. Morgantown
10. Hathorn	33. Goss
11. Conerly	34. Bunker Hill
	35. Cedar Grove
12. Crawley, 13. Stringer	36. Improve
14. Darbun	37. Darbun
	38. Buford
15. Bedwell	39. Foxworth
16. Ras Pitman	40. Columbia
	41. East Columbia
	42. Baylis Chapel
	43. Kokomo
	44. Lampton
	45. New Hope
	46. Hopewell
17. Edna, 18. Spring Cottage, 19. Pinebur	47. Hub
20. Sandy Hook	48. Hurricane Creek
	49. Sandy Hook

plantation development in their earlier history. Two of the neighborhoods (Prentiss in Jeff Davis County and Ras Pitman in Marion County) are adjacent to the county seat.

Essentially all of the families in the Owner type neighborhoods are owners. In one neighborhood (Greenscreek) all are of one race. The fact that this neighborhood recently developed following cutover timber operations and that it was settled largely by related families makes it probable that it may become a Single Racial type neighborhood as it matures in farming development and becomes more homogeneous in socio-economic status. The other Owner type neighborhood (Sandy Hook) more nearly resembles the Mixed type. This neighborhood had an early history of plantation organization but now tends more toward general farming.

Neighborhood Differences in Type of Farming. Of the farms surveyed in the Mississippi Coastal Plain 72 per cent are cotton type farming, 12 per cent cotton-livestock, 5 per cent truck, 6 per cent general, 3 per cent subsistence, and 2 per cent unclassified. All but 5 of the 58 Negro cropper units, and all but one of the 28 white cropper units are cotton type farms.

Among the Single Racial type neighborhoods cotton type farms predominated but were least common in the Owner neighborhoods. Plantation type neighborhoods show a much higher percentage of cotton type farms than the Plantation Transition type. The latter approaches the Mixed type, which tends more to livestock and mixed farming.

Neighborhood Differences in Socio-economic Status. The sharpest contrast exists between the Single Racial and the Plantation Transition type neighborhoods. The Single Racial type, either all white or all Negro, is homogeneous in the socio-economic status of its families. It shows a strong modal group and a tendency for a normal distribution to extend above and below this mode.

In the Plantation type neighborhoods the croppers cluster in the three lower intervals of the socio-economic status scale. Owners are in much higher intervals, with broad gaps separating them from the cropper families. It is this discontinuous nature of the distribution that characterizes the Plantation type neighborhoods. The Plantation Transition type neighborhoods retain a remnant of this same characteristic, depending on the degree to which they retain the earlier plantation organization of farming in contrast to the transition to cotton-livestock, cotton-truck, or general farming.

Neighborhood Differences in Scale of Farm Operation. Only three of the twenty sample neighborhoods in the Mississippi Coastal Plain included farms in the largest size scale of operation group. (Table 144) All of these were Plantation type neighborhoods. The Owner neighborhoods have the narrowest range among farms in scale of operation. Of these, the Greenscreek neighborhood, a new farming area converted from cutover land of the first World War period, has an extreme sameness in the scale of operation. All of the neighborhood types, except the Plantation Transition type, have one or more neighborhoods with farms falling into the smaller scale of operation groups.

Neighborhood Differences in Quality of Farm Business. The neighborhoods in the sample have a wide diversity in average quality of the business of their farms. (Table 145) The Plantation type neighborhood is consistently high in this regard, and is followed, less consistently, by the Plantation Transition type. Wide contrasts among neighborhoods occur within the other tenure types of neighborhoods. Especially is this true of the Mixed type neighborhoods which range from an average index of 79 for Carson to 122 for Prentiss.

Neighborhood Differences in Operator's Earnings. This measures the extent to which the farms of the neighborhoods support the family from the operator's labor. This computation reveals that some of these neighborhoods do not maintain themselves on the basis of the farm operator's earnings. For example, the farms of the Pinebur neighborhood were operated at a net loss in 1942. This is primarily a result of absentee operation by able-bodied husbands who worked elsewhere at other jobs while family members looked after the crops. In the Ras Pittman, Sandy Hook, and Spring Cottage neighborhoods, operator's earnings averaged less than $60 per farm, all three neighborhoods relying on off-farm work to support their families. In Sandy Hook, timber work was most important. Work in urban industrial plants was most important in the other two neighborhoods.

A different situation is presented by the Good Hope and Greenscreek neighborhoods, each of which has an average operator's earnings per farm of above $500. These are full-time farmers. Good Hope has four croppers and Greenscreek none. Greenscreek is a recent settlement of newground cotton, cotton-truck, and general farms, with nine out of ten farmers landowners.

Averaged for each neighborhood, there is general agreement in rank order between the gross quality of the farm business and operator's earnings. (Table 145)

Neighborhood Differences in Value of Farm Business. The two neighborhoods having the lowest average for value of farm business are also lowest for the average of operator's earning (Pinebur and Sandy Hook). Value of farm business is influenced by the value of the house, hence nearness to the city and other factors of site value, such as location on a trunk highway, increase the value of the farm business out of proportion to the earning capacity of the farm. For example, the farms in Ras Pitman neighborhood, suburban to the county seat, average 14 in neighborhood rank for value of farm business, but their neighborhood rank is 19th for operator's earnings.

Greenscreek, Stringer, and Good Hope are high ranking neighborhoods on all three measures of size of business, that is operator's earnings, net family income, and value of farm business. However, Progress, a Negro neighborhood, ranks high only in value of farm business. This sustains the opinion of field enumerators who compared the land valuations of the sample neighborhoods and concluded that in the Progress neighborhood owners overvaluated their farms, possibly partially because of a strong pride in residence in an all-Negro settlement.

Neighborhood Differences in Education. As measured by the grades completed by the spouse with the highest grade attainment,

Owner neighborhoods present the widest contrast in educational achievement. The Greenscreek neighborhood has the highest average grade level (12.3) and Sandy Hook has sixteenth place or fifth from the lowest (7.3 grades). Each of these two has a narrow range for the highest and the lowest of its families, Sandy Hook from 5th to 10th grade and Greenscreek from 9th to 14th grades. No other of the 20 neighborhood samples stay within less than four intervals or eight grades. (Table 146)

Both Plantation and Plantation Transition type neighborhoods have a consistently high spread among family heads in educational attainment. This carries over to the Mixed neighborhoods, particularly in those which have just passed from the Plantation Transition status.

Neighborhoods and Land Use

The foregoing paragraphs describe the salient tenure characteristics of the several neighborhood types. Following are brief descriptions of typical individual neighborhoods representing each type.[3] While these descriptions relate primarily to land use, various other tenure related items are also brought in with the idea of presenting as nearly as possible the local setting of the interacting factors which condition tenure status. The neighborhoods cited are all in Marion County, Mississippi. The recommendations for local land use as made in 1940 by the County Agricultural Policy and Planning Committee are significantly related to the tenure patterns of these neighborhoods.

Mixed Type Neighborhoods

Pinebur. This neighborhood is in the DeSoto National Forest Area. According to the County Agricultural Policy and Planning Committee Report (7940), three of the farm major land-use areas are characterized as land not now in farms and not suited to farming. Around 1919 a lumber company, owned by a northern syndicate, finished cutting the pine lumber. Later the hardwood in the cutover ravines matured and with a rise in the price, it was cut about 1927. Finally a local partnership bought large blocks of land and in 1940-42 the last cuttings were made, stripping the land and selling the stumps. Now the cutover brush land is being sold for farm land.

---

[3] To save space only one abbreviated case statement is presented for each neighborhood type, excepting for the mixed type for which two are presented. Including the cases presented, the following neighborhood cases are available in typewritten form in the project files: Mixed type—Conerly, Edna, Pinebur, and Ras Pittman; Single racial type—Bedwell, Crawley, and Lamarion; Owner type—Sandy Hooks; Plantation type—Darbun; Plantation Transition type—Hathorn, Spring Cottage, and Stringer.

During the First World War when the virgin pine was being cut, the one-room school was partitioned with curtains and extra teachers hired to accomodate the large enrollment. This building was also used for union church services during the life of the lumber camp. The school was closed and consolidated into the Hub community in 1920.

Families remaining in the Pinebur neighborhood after 1920 lived along Little Creek in former lumber family homes and cropped patches of bottom land. In 1942 some were clearing the hill land of brush and fencing it for pasture. Tenure of the would-be owners was uncertain because of clouded deeds that resulted from tax defaults, reversions to the state, followed by tax forfeiture sales and technicalities of state granted titles in conflict with local understanding concerning ownership.

In 1942 the neighborhood had all the anxieties and uncertainties that could be expected to develop in an abandoned lumber camp with uncertain title to residences that at best are connected with meager living from hillside cutover land surrounding small patches of bottom land. In 1942 nine colored and some twenty white families lived in the neighborhood. The colored families retained ownership of the large, one-room, unpainted frame building that seated all the forty colored families in the lumber-mill heyday when only two were farmers and the others section hands, timber and sawmill workers. After the sawmill operations declined, the railroad track was taken up and the colored families scattered, only nine remaining, including the two original farming families. Their children are now transported to the Lampton Consolidated school.

Most of the lumber camp white families were Methodist and Baptist. The abandonment of the local school building led to the erection of a Baptist church building nearby. Families up on the road to the north of the lumber camp, where the farming is mostly in brush land pasturage, had organized a Tabernacle and in 1942 were reported to express pious pity for their unsaved neighbors down at the abandoned lumber camp site along the creek. This was met with some resentment on the part of the creek valley families, whose organized church congregation struggled with the vagaries of state land titles.

The vocational agriculture teacher of Hub, the high school community, conducted in 1942 a poultry study class in the Pinebur neighborhood for the white families. They at first met in the Pinebur

Baptist Church building but the families on the north hill road did not attend. The members then tried meeting in homes of the neighborhood to see if some of the families not wanting to come to the church would attend the poultry meetings in the homes. It was reported that the attendance did not improve. Consequently the meetings were transferred back to the church building, which according to local informants, "is more centrally located."

The present Pinebur neighborhood is a potential federal forest area that is within the projected Leaf River District of the DeSoto National Forest. If the forestry development is delayed for a generation, private soil tillage of the crude cutover farming methods will make the land tenure patterns unstable. It will attract families who, because of limited alternatives, choose isolation and hardship. It will produce the kind of neighborhood life that frustrated pioneers or the remnants of lumber stripping operations could hope to achieve.

Conerly. This neighborhood, in the southwest corner of the Bunker Hill community, is a relatively new settlement in an old agricultural community. The Conerly neighborhood was recently assigned its name, although Mr. Conerly, the neighborhood leader, had lived there all his life. The first settler came in 1900. Most of the present families came after 1923, buying cutover land and establishing homes. "Thirteen families of whites and six colored families compose our neighborhood," said Mr. Conerly, not having to think regarding his answer. An east-west road follows along a flat top ridge with Holiday Creek forming the north border, less than a mile north of the ridge road. The families who live along this ridge road farm the fertile bottoms of the Holiday Creek.

This ridge road is bordered on the south by Collins Creek which forms east and turns south, flanked again on the east by a gravel road running south from Bunker Hill toward Columbia, the county seat. The remainder of the Conerly families are along this north-south road that forms a T with the east-west road. The County Committee recommended that no major changes be made in the Holiday Creek Valley but recommended that the upland area be cropped less intensively. (Table 147)

The neighborhood formerly had a small graded school but in 1928 it was consolidated into the Bunker Hill community wide school that now includes 4 years of high school. A bus comes by the door of each white family, transporting the children to the community school. The Bunker Hill Baptist Church obtained a full-time resident pastor in 1931, the first open country full-time resident pastor in the county. It is the closest and only church serving the white families of Conerly, and it was reported that at least one member of each of the 13 white families is affiliated. All of the families attended, at least half of them regularly.

Of the six colored families, three attended the Harmony Church north of the county seat and three the Expose Church in the adjoining neighborhood, the Cedar Grove Community. They lived off the road and were thought by a white resident to be "possibly a little lax in their attendance." Their children attended school at Expose and are "obliged to walk the distance of five miles." These Negro families are croppers on land owned by a resident white family and a lumber company. They came in and cleared small tracts following the cut-over period of 1923-24, when the white families bought land. No colored families have yet bought any land.

Nine of the thirteen white families have electricity. A neighborhood home demonstration club is active. Neighborhood visiting is common, yet the families are not related. Six of the women in 1942 were working at the garment and parachute factory at the county seat seven miles south. The Bunker Hill vocational agriculture teacher taught a defense (wartime) class in shopwork for six weeks in the neighborhood leader's shop. Most of the thirteen family heads attended all of the lessons. This teacher also sponsored a "poet club" for the women, which was still active in 1943. Each family had a burial policy; this service brought frequent ambulance service for hospitalization calls. Of the five or six deaths in the past seven years each had professional funeral service.

This new land neighborhood has a tenure pattern that first of all is the result of favorable location for white families, even if their colored croppers fare less well in institutional services. Proximity of the new ground to an old, well-established community center enabled them to "hook on" to a going concern for school, church, electricity, county seat employment for women, and good roads.

Single Racial Type Neighborhoods

Lamarion. This Negro neighborhood is to the east of the Improve central neighborhood. It is an owner group that forms the nucleus for a Negro consolidated county line school jointly financed by Marion and Lamar counties. Most of the croppers for the white owners in the Improve central neighborhood are Negroes and they attend the Lamar Consolidated School; some also come from the Stringer and Crawley farms.

A large proportion of the families in the Lamarion school area are Negro farm owners. They have in many instances bought cutover or second growth timber land and cleared it. Only six landowning families lived in the Lamarion central neighborhood in 1927. The consolidated Negro school was formed in 1931 when a cement block building with six classrooms and an auditorium was erected. The first teacherage was erected in 1932 and another in 1934. The vocational agriculture teacher has encouraged the families to buy land as soon as possible. Two hundred dollars is considered enough to start—enough to buy eighty acres in 1942.

Many of the youth of this Negro community, as they matured, bought the nearby land and cleared it. The central neighborhood is in the rolling phase of Ruston silt loam, the leading cotton producing soil association in the Coastal Plain. Many of the youth lived with their parents the first year or longer while they were growing the crop and doing public work to pay for the land. Then as their ownership became secure, they borrowed to erect buildings, or even paid for them out of crop and timber sales. It is an area in which ownership by Negroes has been a general achievement.[4] Consequently the Negroes of this neighborhood in which the Lamarion school is located say they look down on the cropper colored families in the adjoining neighborhood of Improve because they do not own land. They associate together in their school and in the nearby Hopewell Baptist Church.

The leaders of this colored church report that at their revival meetings, half the audience are white folks who greatly aid their church efforts. A similar spirit of mutual helpfulness exists among the colored church neighborhoods. The school and church leaders say, "You can't tell the Methodists from the Baptists."

The Hopewell Church in the Lamarion central neighborhood has joint revivals with the Second Hopewell Baptist Church located two and one-half miles southeast, over in Lamar County; with the Rose Hill Methodist Church three miles west in the Improve neighbor-

[4] The Negro vocational agriculture teacher is also principal of the school. He is a native of the Delta, a graduate of Alcorn land grant college. When asked how he liked this county as compared with his home county, he said that he liked it much better. Said he, "They have a tenure setup in the Delta that isn't going to change. Here in this community a man is expected to buy a farm if he is going to get ahead in farming."

hood; and with the Blue Springs Methodist Church three miles farther to the northwest immediately west of Crawley neighborhood. The vocational agriculture teacher-principal of the Lamarion School states that "those members of the churches, either Rose Hill or Hopewell, are sooner able to do work toward the community needs of the school" than are non-members of the churches. In the last five years seven new families have moved into the Lamarion neighborhood. Now all are identified with the church which has thirty-five members from the seven families. The plan of the church leaders is to give the newcomer an opportunity to exhibit his talent. The 247 members of the Hopewell Church include seventy-five families, of which fifty are owners, one a renter, eighteen croppers, and six laborers. The officers are farm owners. They report that owners support the church better than croppers.

A building to be used for canning food was erected on the school grounds in 1936. When first built it was used certain days for white families and certain days for colored. One pressure cooker of thirty quarts capacity and another of eight quarts were used each year from 1936 to 1940. The vocational agriculture teacher was responsible for the purchase and operation of the canning equipment. Projects such as school plays and other community endeavors were used to finance the canning project.

A colored Baptist Sunday school was operated in the school building and in the one before it, since 1923. A local colored farmer served as superintendent for fifteen consecutive years. On the third Sunday of each month Sunday school is held in the Hopewell Church because that is "preaching Sunday." But on the other Sundays, Sunday school is held in the school building because of its convenience. Local informants state that the church ought to be near the school house but that it was built a mile away because of an excellent spring there.

Under Mississippi law, the Negro school program in practice is financed out of the county-wide funds, rather than by creation of special Negro districts. Leaders in the Improve special district explain that "we appropriate some of the tax money from our special district levy for the support of the Lamarion Consolidated School." Lamar County participates in the financing of this school.

The Improve-Petty consolidated school district is an area of the Ruston soil association, rated as the leading one for cotton production in the county. A long record of landownership by white families of neighborhood kinship groups has been followed in more recent years by new land settlements of white and Negro neighborhoods out farther north and west toward the county line. Hence overcrowding has not taken place in the older neighborhoods of this community, and ownership by new-comer families has been possible. Negro-white economic, educational, religious, and social relations have been cordial and cooperative. The land tenure patterns have been accompanied by long-time institutional services of a substantial order in the community.

Bedwell. This white neighborhood is located in the headwaters of Mays Creek and of a large unnamed branch on the north side of Ten Mile Creek, both of which flow eastward to Pearl River. The rolling upland soils are similar to those of the nearby Darbun neighborhood in ease of cultivation, recency of farming development from timber tracts, and in susceptibility to erosion. Here the comparison abruptly stops.

Two generations ago a group of timber worker families bought cutover land from the lumber company that stripped large blocks in this general area of the county. Many separate factors contribute to the solidarity of this neighborhood but none are stronger than the kinship ties. When enumerators returned to the neighborhood after several days of absence, they learned that a child had died the day before of diphtheria. This information was given them: "All of our men folks except one are over helping to dig the grave." This one family was continuing with farm work, and the other families didn't approve.

The families are members in the neighborhood church, the Church of God, organized in this vicinity for as long as the families could remember. The services formerly were held in the neighborhood schoolhouse, but it reverted to the former owner of the site to become a residence when school consolidation united them with the Buford district. The church considers salvation as an individual responsibility, therefore "keeps no church roll" and considers personal acknowledgement of salvation as the only requisite to membership. It was stated that families not wanting to attend this church remain in this neighborhood only a short time. No inter-neighborhood ties of church visiting draw the Bedwell families outside their own church group.

The civic leader of this neighborhood is an elderly man, a landowner, and a patriarchal family leader. But he prefers that others should lead in the church. His nephew is the designated leader, a deacon and a Sunday school teacher. The nephew is also a secular leader; he is skilled in carpentry as it is practiced in the community. He took more schooling than most of the others and measures and fits lumber with more skill. He married and after two years of other employment rented land from his father for three years and then bought a farm. The tenure pattern of the neighborhood almost invariably includes kinship to the landlord.

Incomes are low in this cotton farming neighborhood. In 1942 some were seeking wartime employment as carpenter assistants in the Gulf Coast shipyards. Cash was scarce and neighborhood activities reflected non-monetary standards. Their minister, equipped with a year of college training, commuted from his resident pastorate in an adjoining county 35 miles away to lead them in an average of three services a month. His annual salary of less than $150 was supplemented with food and other items valued at not over $50. Free will offerings and pledges of cotton lint were the main sources of cash. But when the church needs repairs, the members assemble for work and keep the cash outlay for such purposes below $5 per year.

The school was consolidated into the community grade and high school 12 years ago, and although bus transportation is furnished, the parents are far from unanimous about the desirability of the change. When four neighbors were asked how it happened that they were added to the Buford District, one of them explained: "We are about equally located to go to Buford or to Kokomo, and it is cheaper to go to Kokomo." One of the younger parents volunteered the opinion that he preferred a school "just over the hill from home, where the children could walk to school."

The notes of an interviewer add this: "Characteristic of this community are the large families and marriage at a very early age. The average age for marriage is fourteen, and it is very common for cousins to intermarry. Not only second and third cousins, but first cousins as well. The parents in most cases have more education than the children. The general impression of others is that the people of this neighborhood are afraid of strangers. They stay very much to themselves."

Although the soil productivity in this neighborhood is similar to that of the county as a whole, the average number of persons per bedroom is four, and in one case, the parents and six children share the bedroom. The entire sample of 19 white families averaged 127 in socio-economic status and ranged from 114 to 143. Timidity outside of the immediate group characterizes the members of this close-knit white Owner neighborhood. Tenure here begins and ends with social influences more powerful than rights to the use of the land. As measured by either the value of the farm business (Table 146) or the scale of operation (Table 144) this group of families has several potenital farms of the size to produce comfortable livings. The neighborhood group of farms ranks low on quality of business (index 79) with a wide range among its farms.

Owner Type Neighborhood

Sandy Hook. This neighborhood dates from plantation settlement in ante bellum days. The country mansion constructed of logs by a pioneer Methodist circuit rider still stands.[5] Plantations flourished on the west bank of the Pearl River at the turn of the century and were followed by large-scale lumber industry. Two brothers from Pennsylvania who came here in the lumber business stayed on to develop a Hereford blooded herd and fought the Texas cattle tick to a draw, only to abandon the enterprise after building up "our herd of 150 Registered Hereford cattle, raised on our cutover lands without any shelter the year round." This quotation is from the 1921 catalog of the Sandy Hook Fair, which carries a full page picture of their $50,000 Hereford bull, "to show just what can be raised on our ranges without shelter the year round." But the real difficulty was that open range neighboring cattle carried the deadly tick.

Area history verified two trends. The plantations of the first half century grew up along the water course of Pearl River. The itinerant ministry seldom became intimately related to the farming of that day, either through purchase of lands or through marriage. When they did in later life so connect themselves to agriculture, they ceased to be preachers of the gospel.

The brothers from Pennsylvania also developed potato growing in carload lots, on the sandy lands of the meandering flood plain in the Sandy Hook area. This part of Marion County is in the New Orleans milkshed. These new enterprises disturbed the traditional cotton cropper tenure patterns. The rarity of croppers and laborers on the farms of this neighborhood is an evidence of the transition to family units of farm organization.

---

[5] John Ford settled in this vicinity after years of service to the Methodist church. He acquired the ownership of a number of slaves, presumably through a marriage with the daughter of a landowner.

Plantation Type Neighborhood

Darbun. This neighborhood is in fact a central neighborhood in the high school community of the same name and represents the present day plantation conditions in the area. It is representative of the broad area lying west and back of the flood plain and gently rolling plain that has been left in trees because of the expense of drainage. This sample area in the Darbun community has a race distribution (5 white and 13 Negro) and an emphasis on cropper organization[6] (13 croppers, 1 white, 12 Negroes). (Table 146) Six miles north of Kokomo the farm families of the two counties united to create a "county-line consolidated school" that has developed a first-class open country high school. In 1922 brick buildings were erected to replace the high school building that burned the year before. Today this school serves the owner and the cropper children of the white families.

A few families in the Darbun community have large holdings of land. Interviewers' notes yield the following comments from sample families in the area: "The small landowners scattered among them know that they would soon lose their high school if the large landowners changed from white to colored croppers. The landowners must be willing to vote the tax and to keep white croppers if the school is to be maintained. One farmer in a community east of Darbun, who owns a thousand acres, prefers colored croppers. Of course the Negroes can't vote, and the white croppers are wanting the school maintained as it is. But the large landowners are pretty decent about the taxes and we have a good school. We small land owners are well pleased with it for it gives our children a good opportunity. . . . The cropper families are equally satisfied in all parts of the school district for we have 17 busses to haul the children." Another comment runs as follows: "The vocational agriculture classes enroll the children of the white croppers. They often become the best students of the school, and surprisingly so when their parents can barely read and write. See that cropper over there in the field? His son took the vocational course

[6] Meager notes sifted from many historical sources permit the construction of a plantation family-church history for the Darbun area. A plantation-owning Methodist built the China Grove Church, a famous old landmark. Some of his descendants now live in the Darbun neighborhood. The lumber boom swept eastward from McComb, Mississippi, crossing Walthal County into Marion County, where the lumber mill was built at the county seat. Times have left their changes; many whose ancestral burial plots are at the historic China Grove churchyard now attend church in Kokomo as a result of loyalties that were transferred there when lumber philanthropy furnished that booming town both a Methodist and Baptist church. Now the departed lumber industry has left behind a bit of departed glory and a struggling church situation.

here and is now earning $150 a month as an electric welder. He got his start right here in this school. It is the ignorant croppers who think they are getting cheated out of their just dues, and when they can't read and write, you have a hard time showing them the real facts. I say we need schools like this where their children have a real chance." Commenting on Negro education, a neighborhood leader stated: "The vocational agriculture teacher has night classes for the young Negro youth of the community, certain nights for them and certain nights for the white out-of-school youth. Now the government is hiring this blacksmith you see at the forge in there now. They pay him $1.25 an hour to teach the boys and men of the community, white and colored. He is an experienced blacksmith, instructing here in the shop each Monday and Tuesday. He arranges with the landlord for whom he is cropping to be absent those two days."

Plantation Transition Type Nighborhood

Hathorn. This neighborhood, with a railroad hamlet outlasting the pine lumber era, is the elementary school and church center for the farm family sample located a mile south of the hamlet, in a high ground location forming a half-mile triangle. These families farm the Pearl River bottom land lying west of them. This neighborhood sample is representative of a two to four mile band stretching along the east side of Pearl River from four miles south of Columbia to cross the county line into Jefferson Davis County. The County Land Use Committee designates it as "a bottom area with sand and sandy loam soils that are shallow in depth. The area has fair drainage. The soils are fair in natural fertility and easy to cultivate. The topography is gently rolling, accompanied by moderate sheet erosion. There are a good many swampy or marshy places within the area. There is occasional slight drainage due to overflows. . . . The major type of farming is cotton-beef cattle, with cotton as the major enterprise." Vegetable growing for the county seat cannery is a new enterprise.

The County Committee commented as follows on land use: "The major problems of this area are loss of land resources through soil erosion and excessive depletion of soil fertility. Some of the erosion may be caused by unwise cropping practices, but most of it is due to the occasional overflows which carry a great deal of soil. The excessive depletion of soil fertility is due to small farming area, prevailing system of land tenure, lack of diversification, lack of appreciation of soil resources, and lack of capital. There has been an excessive burden of local taxes but with the coming of the homestead exemption, this problem has been alleviated. Low income prevails throughout the community and is caused by poor organization and management. The type of farming needs major adjustments, lack of supplementary sources of employment, soil depletion and lack of interest which is partly caused by low income and disparity of farm prices. There are a good many ponds within the area which is conducive to mosquitoes and malaria."

Hathorn neighborhood is a periphery group, loosely attached to the railroad and state highway hamlet of Goss three miles south of it but dependent for high school upon the railroad hamlet of Oakvale four miles north. River and railroad locations have, together with the locations of county lines, made an economic and political framework that is superimposed on poor cotton soils and distance from state highways. The railroad era brought a timber development of affluence; the departed wealth has not yet been followed by a stable land tenure.

ROLLING PLAINS SAMPLE AREA IN SOUTHWESTERN OKLAHOMA

Tenure Patterns in Relation to Community Service Areas

Factors of geography are combined with modern automobile transportation in the Rolling Plains that give a distinctive type of neighborhood-community pattern. Although neighborhoods in the traditional sense are found in the Rolling Plains they are not universal and they do not as a rule add up in cluster fashion to form the community.[7]

The trade centers of the southwestern Oklahoma sample area are at junctures of railroads and highways. A few open-country high schools were established at places that later acquired daily service functions, particularly ice and convenience grocery items. But the large majority of high schools in the sample area are located at trade centers.

---

[7] For a parallel statement see Herbert Pryor and Theo L. Vaughan, *A Rural Community in Wartime: Roby, Texas,* U. S. Department of Agriculture, Bureau of Agricultural Economics, Little Rock, Ark., mimeo., June 1945, 33 pp. "The boundary of a village-centered community in the plains is not only more flexible, but is determined by factors somewhat different from those which determine the boundary of a corresponding community in the hills. In the hill country, rivers, ridges, and valleys often outline service areas and shape communities. . . . Plains communities are determined largely on the basis of service areas, maintained mostly by the extent and quality of services offered at the village center, and by a sense of belonging on the part of residents." They are "actually a series of functional service areas for trade, school, church, banking, political administration, and other activities." pp. 1-2.

Two trade area communities, Martha in the north central part of Jackson County and Eldorado in the southwest corner of the same county, are presented as cases to demonstrate how soil types and the resulting land use in combination with history of settlement have interacted with tenure patterns to determine the present community contrasts.

Martha. In 1908 when the railroad passed through this community, the townsite of Martha was platted on land that had been homesteaded in 1886 by H. C. Doughty and family, who had moved from Palo Pinto County, Texas. He re-patented this homestead with the United States government in 1898, purchasing the additional quarter section at $1.25 an acre. He was an active leader in religious undertakings of the Methodist Church and in his original platting restrictions specified, "No pool or billiard hall or saloon shall ever be conducted or maintained by the grantee, his assigns, or legal representatives on the premises hereinafter conveyed, and the limitations upon the uses of said premises shall be a covenant running with the land."

In 1926 the townsite of Martha was incorporated to permit the granting of a franchise for electricity. The corporation lines were drawn to include eight farm houses and to exclude farm land which adjoined the houses. Plans for a corporation water supply were abandoned when the wells would not meet the inspection tests. There is no city tax or levy. The streets and roads are maintained out of gasoline tax money refunded by the state. The coming of Rural Electrification Administration electric lines has removed any supposed advantage of incorporation.

Two contrasting soil types exist in the Martha community. Land to the east of the village (with the exception of the narrow strip bordering a south-flowing small creek) is "tight land," is better adapted to small grains and cotton, and is valued at $50 to $60 an acre. The risks of farming in this tight land section are high, as indicated by the year to year fluctuations of income. But when rainfall is favorable the yields of small grain and cotton are exceptionally heavy and the families pay off their accumulated debts and replace wornout farm equipment.

The land to the west and north of the village is more sandy and better withstands the dry weather. Its average value is estimated at $100 to $125 an acre, about double the "tight land" values. Alfalfa is the leading cash crop on this land. In dry years an excellent seed crop is assured, with an average income of $25 to $40 an acre.

From the AAA aerial photographs those sections of land which have been subdivided in the settlement of estates can easily be identified. In the sandy land area of high valuation the estates have been subdivided into smaller than quarter section holdings. Because this land is adapted to intensive cultivation, heirs have been desirous of maintaining their ancestral holdings, thus preventing any one heir from acquiring the farm as a unit.

Community leaders point out that the contrasts in land values and fluctuation in annual income that distinguish the eastern tight land half from the western and northern sandy land half of Martha community have not made permanent distinctions in the families of the community and that over a period of years one group seems to fare as well as the other.

Martha has two churches. In 1925 when farming looked forward to continued prosperity, the Baptist congregation replaced its wooden building with a large brick building of fourteen rooms, valued at $36,000. Much of the labor for the building was contributed by families of the church and the debt was liquidated the next year. The Methodist congregation followed with the construction of a brick building. It likewise contributed three-fourths of the labor and the building was paid for within a year.

Each of the churches was built to seat 400 and needed such provisions at the time. Now the Martha community has only about half as many people on its farms, and before 1941 the attendance had declined even more as a result of lessened participation in its services. In years past a Holiness and a Christian visiting evangelist have held revival meetings in the community but no new organization resulted. The families of the community continue to concentrate their allegiance in the two churches. Some Nazarene families live in the community, but the two pastors maintain a kindly helpful relation to all the families in the communities, and no new church group is attempted by these or the few other faiths represented in the community. The two churches during two consecutive years (1942 and 1943) collaborated in a community survey of church preference and centered their attention on reaching every family in the community.

A large gin operated by the Chickasha Cotton Oil Company is located at Martha. Just beyond it is the Farmers' Union Cooperative Gin. The farmers of the Martha community patronize their own gin, taking 4300 bales of cotton to it in 1942. The overflow of the busy season went to the other gin, adding 1100 more bales to the community's production that year. In the lean drought years of 1934 and 1936 Martha community produced only 400 bales each year, all of it going to the cooperatively owned gin.

The independent Martha telephone exchange, organized in 1909, grew to 165 subscribers in 1925 and although the service area has remained the same, the subscribers declined to 95 in 1943. The manager-operator explains the decrease as due to a proportional decrease in the number of families in the identical area, with a constant percentage served now as in 1925.

In 1940 the 77 dwelling units inside the corporation had a population of 242, a decline of 26 per cent from 1930. In 1943 citizens of the town reported that it was almost impossible to rent a house in Martha; only three were reported vacant in the 1940 census. They emphasize that grown children have moved away but that one or both parents continue to live on in the family home, thus accounting for the house shortage. The 74 occupied houses in the 1940 census were listed as 46 owner occupied and 28 tenant occupied, 62 and 38 per cent respectively.

Martha has no implement dealer although the tractor repair service is a large item of business for the local garage. Some yard goods are sold at the grocery store. Martha had an alfalfa mill and elevator about 20 years ago but lacked sufficient business to support them and now obtains such service at Blain, 7 miles northeast. In addition to the businesses listed above Martha has a hardware store-filling station and two other filling stations; a lumber yard, handling hardware, fencing, and building supplies; and a blacksmith shop.

The bank was organized in 1906, three years before the coming of the railroad and the platting of the townsite. It claims depositors in every state of the Union, a fact noted earlier that is significantly related to the inheritance of ancestral land.

During the depression of the thirties and later recovery, only three farms were foreclosed in this community, two Federal Land Bank and one National Insurance Company loan. One of these occurred each year, 1941, 1942, and 1943.

Eldorado. The coming of the Frisco Railroad westward from Altus found Eldorado already a bustling town in 1902, when the local newspaper published its first volume.[8] "By July, 1903 it was impossible to find a quarter section that hadn't been filed." Eldorado was incor-

[8] *The Eldorado Light,* Vol. 1, No. 4, August 7, 1902. Copy of this issue owned by Mrs. W. R. Summers of Eldorado.

porated in 1904. The United States Gypsum Company bought three quarter sections of land near Eldorado before 1906. At that time they began the shipment of raw dirt from a spur location three miles east of Eldorado. In 1908 their Chicago office erected a mill on the two quarter sections near town. They abandoned the former site, took up the railroad spur, and leased the quarter section for farming to the same man for the past 15 years or more. The Eldorado mill made only plaster and reached its apex of 8 carloads a day during the First World War with an average crew of 55 men. Night shifts were discontinued after 1919, the mill gradually declined in output and has been closed down since 1937. The employees had been gradually transferred to the Sweetwater, Texas, and the Midland California plants of this company.

Eldorado was a wheat country in the early days. Dry fallowing was practical in alternating years. Corn was grown for feed. Maize was grown in 1902 and reached its peak in 1908. At that time it was hauled to the Eldorado train yards and the small acreage concentrated into huge ricks. The steam threshers operated beside the ricks, pouring the threshed maize into waiting box cars. The severe drought of 1913 was followed by early fall rains and heavy seeding for wheat. People begged cattle owners to graze their rank wheat fields that winter and harvested a bumper wheat crop in 1914. Wheat did fair in this community during the First World War.

Eldorado, in keeping with its Spanish meaning of the name, had its share of farmer-speculators. One farmer about 1918 had three quarter sections of wheat that resulted in a $30,000 income tax base for him, whereas in the previous year his credit was not even good for chewing tobacco. Then after this bumper crop he bought the banker's house in Eldorado. A year or so later, he owed so much they pushed him off in his old Ford to get the motor started, and he headed for Arizona, to make a new start in the irrigated cotton country, where he again made money before he met his death in an automobile accident. "He was known as one of the hardest plungers Eldorado ever had."

Another large-scale farmer in this community, who bought land rapidly and never rented it out, was a good manager. He rode around dressed up and supervised the work of his sons and others whom he employed. He died recently, a wealthy man. Both these large-scale farmers lived east of Eldorado, in the Midway neighborhood, where farmland was as good as any in the Eldorado trade area; they moved to Eldorado afterward.

The town of Eldorado reached its largest census population in 1930, nearly 1200; the decline reduced it to 929 people in 1940, slightly less than in 1920. The town's real boom had started in 1906, the year that many of the frame business buildings were replaced with brick and native stone, and a $9,000 two-story brick school building was constructed. The Frisco Railroad that year arranged for an excursion of homeseekers to visit this and other towns nearby, and many of them stayed in this community.

Parallel with the decline of the local gypsum industry, a number of other employment opportunities disappeared from Eldorado. The establishments and professional services existing in 1936 were enumerated as 97 in a history prepared at that time. In 1943, just seven years later, 43 of these were out of existence, and only two new ones, both groceries, had been opened. Could all of this be credited to the disappearance of the one local industry? Undoubtedly not. The three local physicians and one of the two dentists departed after 1937. They may have been feeling the competition of county seat city specialization in medicine and dentistry for several years because of the automobile transportation; the actual dating of their departure was partly a wartime event and partly a result of closing the gypsum plant.

Not so readily can the agricultural processing plants be connected with either the modern highway system, the gypsum plant, or the war. The Agricultural Adjustment Program was making it easier to underwrite the risks of wheat production by relying on acreage benefit payments if drought made harvesting uneconomical. At the same time cotton reduction was being encouraged by the system of benefit payments. Wheat production could be better done with hired labor, and the reduction in cotton acreage meant a reduction in the number of tenants. Since 1936 two of the five gins have ceased operating in Eldorado; the one hatchery has closed, and one of the two produce houses has closed. In this era of good highways, the continuance of occasional drought years has caused the agricultural processing plants to concentrate in the larger cities, where the ups and downs of the weather cycle can be smoothed out somewhat among a number of soil areas.

The Eldorado high school area in 1936 was reported to be the second largest in the state, with an area of 86 square miles. This resulted from the 1929 consolidation of the Antioch, Creta, and Oklahoma Beech school districts. In 1937 the Study of Local School Units in Oklahoma, using Jackson County as an example, proposed that the county be consolidated eventually into eight administrative units. Eldorado, the nucleus of Administrative Unit No. 7, would eventually add Lincoln, Midway, and Saye, which is 1937 made a total enumeration of 1,053 and would give a total area of 151.7 square miles as compared with the current area of 86 square miles. With such large school districts and complete bus transportation, the average tenant family could move from farm to farm with little disruption of the school connections for the children.

The church groups have been less readily drawn to Eldorado. A Baptist, Methodist, and Church of Christ congregation each have a full-time resident pastor; a Christian and a Primitive Baptist Church have part-time pastoral services. In 1943 the Assembly of God congregation was newly organized and was holding services in a vacant filling station. Country neighborhoods that had continued with difficulty to maintain church meetings included Midway, Antioch, and Creta. None of these congregations were directly tied in with the Eldorado churches, either through pastoral service or denominational structure. The five churches located in Eldorado serve nearly as many farm as village families. The farm families include 64 owners, 26 renters, and 5 laborer families. All of the laborer and 20 of the 26 renter families attend the one church that attracts the most farm families, including 35 of the 64 owners. Hence the best that any one town church can claim is 25 renter and laborer families to 35 owners, whereas the 1940 census shows that the Eldorado township had 121 owner occupied and 208 tenant occupied farm dwellings. The one farm neighborhood church in the Eldorado trade area, for which data were obtained, had 7 owner, 8 renter, and 3 laborer families in its membership. It is the tenant families that in large degree are unreached by the town churches.

INSTITUTIONAL AND COMMUNITY FACTORS

The economic, social, and tenure behavior of the individual farm operator necessarily takes place within the framework provided by his sphere of free choice and his alternative opportunities for action. In this respect the tenure performance of the individual is primarily an outgrowth of the combination and function of three separate factors: (1) the individual and his family, their personal abilities, characteristics and background of experiences; (2) the farm that the individual has to work with; (3) community and institutional factors which operate from outside the individual's direct field of control but which condition his field of choice relative to tenure decisions.

The first two factors are discussed elsewhere in this report. As to the third factor, a brief discussion of these items follows: (1) local customs and the law (2) local credit, and (3) local marketing facilities.

Local Custom and the Law[9]

The economic, social, and tenure behavior of the average farmer takes place within the boundaries established by local custom and by the laws of the land. As has been pointed out in the chapter dealing with the legal aspects of farm tenure, common law provides the basis for most of the landlord-tenant laws in Arkansas, Mississippi, Oklahoma, and Texas. Louisiana uses a detailed tenancy code. Throughout its development common law has constantly relied upon customs and upon precedents in the interpretation of justice and reasonable values. In consequence the common law as interpreted by the courts has usually approximated the customs of the people. From time to time judges have by decision modified its interpretation. Other modifications have come as a result of statutory enactments. But in both cases these modifications have tended to reflect custom or widely accepted views. An illustration of the effect of custom upon statutory law may be noted in the Texas law of 1915 which limited the amount of agricultural rent to the customary "third-and-fourth."[10]

Custom, however, does not always operate inside the pattern set by law. With matters such as tenure practices and landlord-tenant relationships, custom frequently exerts a greater influence than law itself in controlling individual and group behavior. It does so because compliance with local custom usually brings group approval. The law on the other hand is often regarded as something distant, a factor that is brought into play only in extreme cases. In those cases where the farm operators settle their own differences, where the group frowns upon the idea of appealing to "outsiders" for justice, or where one of the parties to the disagreement occupies an inferior legal position, it is usually custom rather than law that determines the outcome.

The extent to which reliance upon custom or reliance upon law tends to dominate tenure practices varies with neighborhoods and

[9] Raleigh Barlowe of the United States Bureau of Agricultural Economics collaborated with the author of this chapter in writing the sections on Local Custom and the Law and Credit Facilities.

[10] This law was passed in an attempt to stop the growing practice among landlords of demanding bonus rents. It was declared unconstitutional in 1929. A somewhat similar law was passed in 1931 which gives the landlord a lien on the tenant's crops to insure the payment of debts and rents so long as the landlord charges no more than the customary third-and-fourth rent.

communities. If the people of the community rely heavily upon status (society based upon habit, custom, natural impulse and tradition), they depend less on law and more on custom than in a society of contract, organized through formal agreements or legislation.[11]

Strictly speaking, few of the families in the present survey can be described as living in either a world of status or a world of contract. Legal contracts were used and are important in all the areas studied and the law makes the recording of sales and mortgage transactions mandatory. Yet on the other extreme, many important tenure relationships involve no formal understandings and are governed largely by custom. Details of leasing and labor arrangement, for example, rarely involve written agreements and are frequently determined by customary practices.

Throughout the areas studied these pure types are mixed. With some of the poorer and more clannish neighborhoods and with some of the foreign-born farming groups the emphasis, particularly in intragroup transactions, is upon status and custom. With the larger and more commercially-minded operators emphasis is often placed upon the importance of contractual relationships, particularly when they are dealing with other businessmen. In dealing with tenants and laborers, however, these operators often follow practices based on custom and status rather than on contract. In relationships within their neighborhoods and communities those farmers who tend to look upon farming as a "way of life" rely more heavily upon custom than do those who accept farming as one of a group of business alternatives. Similarly, Negro operators, particularly in the three eastern states, usually place considerable reliance upon custom. They do so partly because of their societal arrangements and partly because most of their security stems more from custom than from appeal to the courts.

With those farmers who come closest to living in a world of contract, practice favors the use of legal advice and legal forms, if not an occasional appeal to the courts. With the *gemeinschaft* type communities, however, formal and written agreements are not only unnecessary

[11] Societal classifications based upon "status" and "contract" were used by Sir Henry Maine. (Cf. Henry S. Maine, *Village Communities in the East and West*, Henry Holt and Company, New York, 3rd ed. 1880, pp. 103-28.) A somewhat similar classification of societies as *gemeinschaft* (self-centered and governed by custom) and *gesellschaft* (more commercially minded and governed by formal arrangements) has been developed by Ferdinand von Tonnies. (Cf. Rudolf Heberle, "The Application of Fundamental Concepts in Rural Community Studies," *Rural Sociology*, VI, September 1941; 203-15; and Robert Redfield, "Rural Sociology and Folk Society," *Rural Sociology*, VIII, March 1943, pp. 68-71.)

but are sometimes even viewed with suspicion.[12] Here local custom and group opinion determine the pattern for tenure and other intragroup behavior. Issues involving serious conflicts in interest seldom arise and when they do they are usually settled within the group.

Conflicts of interest and disputes growing out of the impact of these two societal types upon each other occasionally arise. For example, the migration of numerous operators from status societies to the society of contract provided by western Oklahoma during the homesteading period resulted in a considerable number of lawsuits when the migrants found it necessary to resort to the law to defend their rights. Similarly, the settling of groups of German and Czech farmers in the Texas sample area gave rise to a dual arrangement with the farmers which often retained old world customs, attitudes, and relationships within the group but proceeded in a formal and legalistic manner with other people.

Local Customs Affecting Landlord-Tenant Relationships in the Mississippi Area. If the distinction between the cropper as a laborer and as a tenant lies in whether or not he receives half of the crop as a wage instead of paying half of *his* crop to the landlord as rent, then local custom justifies the classification of the croppers included within the Mississippi sample as tenants rather than as laborers. Not only do the croppers, in practically all classes, consider themselves as the "payers of rent" but they frequently referred to their status as being that of a "tenant." They recognized four kinds of tenants—the cash renter, the standing renter (frequently confused with the cash renter), the one-fourth (or one-third and one-fourth) share tenant, and the tenant farming on "halves."

The system of share renting on "the third and fourth" (one-third of the corn crop and one-fourth of the cotton crop are paid to the landlord as rent) is common enough in many sections of the South to be considered as a customary rental arrangement. In some parts of Jefferson Davis County and in Marion County the third and fourth system has given way to a system of renting on the fourth system. Under this customary system of renting, the tenant pays one-fourth of

[12] Robert Redfield, "Rural Sociology and Folk Society," *Rural Sociology*. VIII (March, 1943), 68-71, in describing the *gemeinschaft* or folk society observes that: "Behavior is spontaneous, traditional and uncritical. As men act with reference to one another by understandings which are tacit and traditional, there are no formal agreements. The rights and duties of individuals flow from their positions in a customary system of relationships, not from special undertakings . . . . Legislation has no place, still less jurisprudence . . . . Within the ideal folk society, its members are bound by religious and kinship ties."

his cotton and corn crops and sometimes one-fourth of certain other crops as rent. Why the customary rental system differs between these two areas is not easily explained. The farmers in all of the neighborhoods are aware of the customary sharing arrangements used in other parts of the state, but for the most part continue to permit local customs to rule their behavior in making new leasing arrangements.

In the case of the sharecroppers, well-established custom calls for an equal division of the crop or its proceeds between the cropper and his landlord. Yet, the usual cropper terms in southern Mississippi are standardized only in so far as they apply to the division of the inventories, expenses, and receipts of the two major crops, cotton and corn. A wide diversity of arrangements cover the division of certain other crops. Nearly all landlords customarily furnish their tenants and croppers with a garden and house. Also many of the share tenants are given the free use of "patches" of land for gardens including items such as Irish potatoes, sweet potatoes, cane, and sometimes a small peanut crop. Usually few if any of these crops are marketed and no occasion arises for a dispute concerning a division of receipts. However, an increase in the availability of marketing facilities has placed truck crops such as Irish and sweet potatoes and peanuts, in the commercial crop class.[13]

Although the major details of the division of responsibilities and rights between landlords and croppers are usually ruled by custom, practices regarding minor details differ. An example of diversity in minor arrangements is usually found in provisions relating to the tenant's ownership of livestock. Some croppers own only a few chickens and possibly a hog and have no facilities whereby to care for cows or other livestock. Yet in other cases, the tenants have several cows and are allowed to use the owner's pasture rent free in return for labor in keeping up the pasture fences. Still other landlords "farm" out milk cows to their tenants or even supply the tenant's family with fresh milk at no charge. These differences in details are usually related to factors such as the number of livestock owned by the tenant, the size of the tenant's family, the landlord's interest in the tenant's welfare, the size of the landlord's pasture, and the landlord's ability to supply the tenant with special perquisites.

Written leases are not in common use in southern Mississippi.

[13] A typical cropper's answer to questions concerning the division of the peanut crop was: "I don't rightly know how we're going to divide them but I think I'll get half."

Nearly all written leases involve either the 16th section school lands or the Farm Security Administration. The custom of oral leases has become so general that even the tenants and croppers accept it as the best arrangement and justify this view on the ground that they "wouldn't want to rent from a man so dishonest as to require a written lease."

Local customs do not regulate the details of the credit agreement in the same way that they govern leasing arrangements. The creditor-debtor relationship is such that emphasis is usually placed upon individual differences and capacities. The landlord's prior lien on the crops is clearly recognized and the rights of the merchant with a deed of trust are not disputed. Merchants occasionally ask a landlord to sign with his tenant in guaranteeing payment and in some cases the landlords are asked to waive all rights to a lien on advances in favor of the merchant or bank furnishing the tenant. No custom in this regard, however, has developed.

CREDIT FACILITIES

Whether or not the credit facilities supplied in any given area are satisfactory depends on the answers to such questions as: Is an adequate amount of credit available when it is most needed? Are the costs of using the credit commensurate with the values associated with its use? Does the use of credit involve obligations besides repayment with interest? Is credit available on such terms that it actually helps the farmer to make tenure progress? What risks are involved in the use of credit?

These questions suggest comparisons between the facilities provided in the different areas.[14]

For the credit secured by real estate mortgages, Federal Land Bank credit accounted for the majority of the loans in all of the sample areas except the Texas area, where the Federal Land Bank led in the number of loans outstanding but was closely followed by the insurance companies and by the SPJST (Slavonske Podporujice Jernoty Statu Texas—a benevolent lodge identified with families of Czech descent). The Farm Security Administration had a few real estate loans in all sample areas except Mississippi. The local banks had loans in all of the areas. This source of credit was particularly important in the Louisiana area. In the Mississippi area, local merchants and lumber companies provided an important source for real estate credit,

[14] See Chapter VIII, "Use and Sources of Capital," for some of these comparisons.

while in the Oklahoma sample, a considerable portion of the real estate credit used was provided by commercial mortgage companies, insurance companies and by the Oklahoma School Land Commission.

The non-real-estate credit used by the Arkansas, Mississippi, Oklahoma, and Texas sample areas was supplied by a wide variety of agencies. Some landlord credit was provided in all areas, but this source was particularly important in Arkansas and Mississippi. Merchant credit was also important in all areas, being of major importance in Mississippi. Local bank credit was extensively used in all areas and accounted for almost two-thirds of the loans made in Texas. The Farm Security Administration, the Production Credit Associations, and Feed and Seed loans also accounted for a substantial number of loans in the four sample areas, as did the loans made by private investors.

The relative cost of the farm credit used by these farmers varied from the 3 per cent interest charged on Farm Security Administration real estate loans to the 6 to 8 per cent charged by some of the banks on real estate loans; from the 4 and 5 per cent interest rates charged on the short-term credit offered by the government sponsored credit agencies to the 10 per cent interest rates charged by local merchants and bankers in Oklahoma and Texas and the 10 to 20 per cent time charges used by the local merchants in Mississippi.

Variations in the types of credit available also concern the supervision given by the credit agency. Active supervision was provided by the Farm Security Administration and by many of the landlords who made credit advances to their renters and croppers. A much less formal type of supervision or inspection was provided by a few of the merchants and bankers. In general, however, most of the credit agencies loaned capital without assuming any responsibility for the manner in which the borrower managed his farm.

As to the element of risk, there are again wide differences between the sample areas. In the Arkansas and Mississippi areas with relatively small farms and low capital requirements, the usual credit grant tends to be small. The extension of credit, however, involves a certain amount of risk to the lender. Many merchants, for instance, anticipate delinquencies on about 5 per cent of their accounts during the "average" year. In depression years, they expect even greater delinquencies. Usually, however, they carry these accounts over to the future but sometimes they find it necessary to write off their losses or foreclose on what security their borrowers have to offer.

The credit risk problem in Oklahoma and Texas is somewhat similar except for the fact that farm values are higher, more use is made of mechanized equipment, farm incomes are usually higher, and more extensive use is usually made of credit. The problem of risk is further complicated in the Oklahoma area by weather conditions and by the effect that periodic droughts have had upon crop yields. This high risk element has influenced the credit situation as well as the attitude of many operators toward "plunging" and spending. As one local credit agent observed:

> The early credit picture of the county was one largely of overuse. Owners mortgaged their lands to make improvements which were thought necessary after a good year or so. All farmers borrowed at the bank against the cotton crop and in addition had open accounts at all the stores where they did business. Each year was lived on credit and paid for at the end of the year. There is an old story that it is possible for a man to begin the year rich and end up broke but the next year to begin heavily in debt and end up with $15,000. This illustrates the risk involved in making a crop as well as the hand-to-mouth sort of living that went on in the area during the good old days. With a succession of low income years, the banks became overloaded with worthless farm paper on "good, honest farmers," and many merchants were forced into bankruptcy.

In general it may be said that local tenure patterns and credit facilities have each affected the other. The greater need for credit in the western states has brought the insurance companies and bankers into the farm credit market and the availability of additional credit has enabled many operators to advance their economic and tenure status. Similarly the relatively small credit needs of the average farmer in the eastern states has given emphasis to the importance of merchant and landlord credit and the high costs normally associated with the use of this credit have often tended to discourage rather than encourage tenure progress.

MARKETING FACILITIES

Differences in cropping systems, attitudes toward farming, and land tenure patterns are often associated with differences in marketing facilities and opportunities. But the impacts of marketing upon tenure performance are indirect and grow out of the influence of farm markets and prices upon farm incomes and the effect that farm incomes in turn have upon tenure.

The development of local marketing facilities are conditioned by local production and market demand. Throughout most of the Southwestern Region cotton has for many years been presumed to be the crop of highest comparative advantage for the farmer. It has occupied this position of importance partly because it is easily grown in the region, partly because local cotton markets have been developed, and partly because a world cotton demand has existed. The marketing facilities provided in the different areas are too standardized to provide a ready explanation for differences in individual tenure performance.

The individual farmer's opportunity to profit in the sale of his produce differs considerably under varying circumstances. Where the market is highly competitive with the various buyers bidding actively against each other, the farmer is almost sure to secure a higher price. On the other hand, if one buyer has a monopolistic position in the market, if there is collusion between the buyers, or if the farmer is bound by previous agreement or by his credit arrrangements to sell to a certain buyer, the advantages of a competitive market often disappear and the farmer takes what he can get.

These problems have led the farmers in many areas of the region and particularly the cotton farmers to organize marketing cooperatives. The organization of these cooperatives has, of course, been opposed by the middlemen who normally have handled the commodities affected. Most of the cooperatives organized have at some time or other been plagued by cut-throat competition, by problems in organization and management, and sometimes by hard times and business losses. In Oklahoma and Texas the cooperative gins and cotton marketing cooperatives have sometimes met with failures. Many of them, however, have succeeded and have helped to provide the basis for state-wide cooperative movements. In the three eastern states of the region, as typified by the Mississippi example, most of the early cotton marketing cooperatives failed because of competition, bad management, or business reverses. More recently, however, the cooperatives sponsored by the Farm Bureau and the Farm Security Administration have reported favorable progress in that state.

The growth of the cooperative movement in Oklahoma and Texas has given the farmers in those states an opportunity to sell through their cooperatives or through private gin operators and cotton buyers. In the year of the study (1942), the market was active with considerable competition existing. The cotton market in the Mississippi sample area in 1942 was more competitive than usual because of the entrance of a number of new private buyers and because of the entrance of the Farm Security Administration sponsored cooperative into the market. The addition of these new buyers made the cotton market more competitive than usual because the merchants, who normally handled the bulk of the cotton marketed in the area, found it necessary to reduce their operating margins and bid higher than normal. Under past conditions, however, the merchants have often bought the farmer's cotton pretty much at their own price. Indeed, many farmers have often found it necessary to sell their cotton through the merchants to obtain credit. Field interviews indicate that a few merchants in years past have used their power over the farmer's credit and furnish needs to force him to sell through them and to help break down local cooperative marketing associations.

The problems of marketing facilities extend beyond cotton. In 1942 the average farmer raised his full acreage allotment of cotton. His production and sale of other crops usually meant farm income over and above his income from cotton, but what he raised and sold of these crops depended upon his marketing facilities for the crops in question. The facilities provided for the sale of these other farm products differed in the several areas of the region. In the Texas area, for instance, a well-organized market existed for fat and feeder cattle and hogs and concurrent with this were good markets for wool, hides, poultry and poultry products, milk and cream, and for such surplus feed as there was in the area. In the Oklahoma area this list of marketing facilities was supplemented by markets for wheat, alfalfa, seed, and hay. The market facilities provided in the Mississippi area for products other than cotton were also extensive. The local canning plant at Columbia, the pickling plants at Columbia and Wiggins, and the early truck crop market in Copiah County provide good markets for truck crops. The large furnish stores and a few other buyers provide a market for early Irish potatoes, for cane syrup, and for miscellaneous products such as eggs, vegetables, and pecans. The large variety of timber using industries in the general area provide a market for various farm forest products such as sawlogs, veneer wood, pulpwood, ties, and stumps. All of these markets provide the farmers with opportunities for additional farm income—income that may be used in advancing their tenure status.

All three of the local survey areas discussed above had army camps or bases located nearby in 1942. This strengthened the market for such farm products as milk, butter, eggs, poultry, and fresh meat. In Oklahoma and Texas the markets for these products were organized on a somewhat more permanent basis than in Mississippi. In all three of these states, however, the demand for these products usually exceeded the supply and exceeded the ability of the local marketing facilities to make available the goods needed. This applies particularly to the demand for milk, butter, and fresh meat. Even though the opportunities existed for producing these products locally, the costs of going into the dairy or beef production business were such that very few farmers gave much consideration to it.

ATTITUDES CONCERNING LAND TENURE

The institutions that have organizational structure in the local community have been described in their relation to tenure. It is a truism that these institutional structures are accompanied by attitude patterns and that these patterns conform in known and predictable ways.

In the Coastal Plain area, as illustrated by the Mississippi Long Leaf Pine sample, tenure and family status are more nearly synonomous in the minds of the local citizens than in the Rolling Plain of Southwest Oklahoma. Yet these contrasts are only relative, and as shown in the cases described earlier, the differences among neighborhoods within the Coastal Plain country are often greater than the differences between this area and the Rolling Plain.

Broad Patterns in the Cotton Belt

An analysis was made of the attitudes of cotton belt farmers in 1936.[15] One half of the Cotton Belt Negro farmers thought they would be better off if their farms were larger. Less than one third of the white farmers, both Cotton and Corn Belt, held this opinion. Nonowners related to their landlord or employer reported much higher prospects of owning a farm within the next five years than the unrelated ones, but the excess for the related ones was much larger among Negroes than among whites. Kinship to the landlord was therefore construed to mean more to the Negro than to the white.

Local Variations in Type of Farming and Income As Related to Tenure Attitudes

Type of farming affects tenure attitudes. The Rolling Plains is in large degree a one race area and is only slightly dependent on hand labor for cotton production. Pulling the cotton bolls is the only hand operation and this is being supplanted by the cotton puller or improved type of sled for gathering the bolls.

[15] E. A. Schuler, *Social Status and Farm Tenure—Attitudes and Social Conditions of Corn Belt and Cotton Belt Farmers*, Social Research Report No. IV, Washington, U. S. Department of Agriculture, Farm Security Administration and Bureau of Agricultural Economics, April 1938. pp. iv, xi, and 253.

The large-scale farms of the Rolling Plains are more like the Corn Belt in labor organization, in ratio of capital used to labor input, and in the higher minimum level of living. The Texas Blackland Prairie is intermediate between the Rolling Plains and the Coastal Plain but much nearer the Rolling Plains. The history of settlement combines with the present type of agriculture in these three types of farming areas to produce known differences in the value systems of the three areas.

In the Rolling Plains, size of the farm operation is a clearer indicator of family status than tenure. In the Texas Blackland Prairie size is a slightly better indicator of status than tenure. In the Missis-sissippi Coastal Plains tenure status ranks with race as more important than size of the farm operation in determining family status. This is largely because tenure and race are accurate indicators of the amount of supervision, which the worker has over his farm operations. A cropper in the Coastal Plain may have a large scale of operation and produce efficiently, but his social relations are conditioned by the fact that his farm work is supervised by another. The socio-economic status of croppers in the Coastal Plain is frequently higher than that of owners, but this does not assure a family status in the community higher than that of the self-directing owner. Economic organization carries over into the family and community life, conditioning attitudes and behavior in the fundamental decisions of marriage, leadership, and status.

Will mechanization of the Cotton Belt bring changes in the status system as revealed by the attitudes here described? The status system will probably not be abandoned, but will be modified to relate, not so clearly to race and tenure, but to degree of responsibility for economic decisions. This trend has already been demonstrated in the Rolling Plains.[16]

Attitudes Toward the Farm Security Administration Home Ownership Program in the Mississippi Coastal Plain

In the Coastal Plain, the housing standards set by the Farm Security

[16] An example is the attitude toward hand labor in the cotton fields during wartime. The Rolling Plains have conventionally relied upon migratory workers for pulling the cotton bolls. During the war years this supply was less than normal. Wives of town professional families were asked to help with the emergency work. Field notes reveal how this conflict in status roles can be harmonized in a farm area of increasing mechanization. If the field labor is accompanied by the personal characteristics that distinguish the professional or white collar worker from the unskilled laborer, no conflict in status need arise. Some of these symbols are: manicured hands after the labor is completed, a nurtured suntan that avoids skin injury, modulated voice, vocal expression, and clothing style trends that indicate communication with centers of fashion.

Administration were the functional equivalent of the highest owner group. In appearance these houses were less imposing than the planter homes, but as measured by neatness of construction, labor-saving plans, and modern built-in equipment they were equal to them. Since the house as a status symbol is attached to the tenure and race status system, attitudes toward the housing feature of the farm ownership program included nonlogical aspects in large proportion. Frequently those few attitudes related directly to logical features like economy of construction, union wage rates versus use of farmer-helpers, and suitableness of design and construction to local needs were deeply buried in the avalanche of words of feeling that poured out upon the housing feature of the home ownership program.

The housing standards set by the State leaders in the Farm Security Administration program were technically sound, in the opinion of informed local people.[17] But there was severe objection to having the less experienced and underprivileged white and Negro families, who were selected as tenant-purchase cooperators, became the ones who acquired the most attractive farm houses in the community. These criticisms took the form of comment on the excessive cost of the new building construction in relation to the cost of the farm land, the poor selection of the clients, and the tendency of the clients to evade payments. A few people leveled severe criticism at the inclusion of a bath room and explained that this luxury could be added to the house after the farm debt was sufficiently amortized to be out of danger of foreclosure.

The second problem of the tenant-purchase program to receive the concerted attention of local supervisors and leaders was the part-time or off-the-farm supplementary employment issue. The Long Leaf Pine Area had only recently emerged from the timber cutting era. Few farmers had experienced a complete reliance on the farm for their cash income. It was the policy of the Farm Security Administration local supervisors to develop tenant purchase units of full-time farmers but on units small enough to meet the national objective of a family farm. This usually precluded a cropper or hired hand in the unit and meant reliance on labor of only the family members, with the exception of seasonal labor of less than a man-year of work.

This was a new pattern for the area. It involved diversification,

[17] A total of 30 special interviews were held with Farm Security Administration supervisors and committeemen, AAA committeemen, county officials, rural ministers, vocational agricultural teachers, businessmen, Farm Security Administration cooperators, and others to get additional information. These data available in the Project files.

more reliance on livestock, and the home production of the livestock feed. This new system was being developed by clients who, by national policy directive, could not obtain credit elsewhere in the community. The latter requirement severely limited the availability of clients because the local credit agencies, especially the credit merchants who also operated a bank, were ready and willing to loan at 8 per cent if the prospective farm purchaser was a good moral risk and had ready a down payment of 10 per cent. Therefore the tenant-purchase program faced not only the hazards of introducing new housing and farm building standards and practices, but its new emphasis on family-sized, full-time farms had to be developed through clients who were by the definition of availability of credit the farmers who were unable to get credit locally.

Even with these difficulties facing the tenant-purchase program, local committeemen were serving to help bring about a home-ownership advance in their farming communities. They were struggling to bring a working agreement between national policy and local resources that won for them the respect of the local leaders in the counties.

The Relation of Attitudes to Action Programs in Land Tenure

The general attitudes of the area set limits within which action of an administrative nature concerning land tenure can take place. The ways in which race relations have found expression in the institutions of the Cotton Belt are part of the limits that operate to determine what is possible in land tenure programs. Extreme differences among neighborhoods are noted in the Mississippi sample area, not only in racial composition, but in tenure composition as well. Negro farm ownership is expected and welcomed in some neighborhoods and not in others. Therefore a program of action needs to be concerned with local administration as well as with broad policy. The problems of land tenure, when rigorously stated within the existing system of values and attitudes, can then be approached with the united support of agricultural, educational, and religious leaders in the area. In the recent years of the Farm Security Administration program this has been increasingly done, but only after several transfers of antagonism have been incurred from the original problem of race and family status, to the more obvious questions of house cost and client selection. A similar transfer occured in the history of the farm credit administration, when a large number of defaults in payment were later evaluated in terms of soil type, managerial ability of borrower, and administrative policy concerning appraisal practices. Meanwhile the administrative procedures are being adjusted to the fundamental problems of race and family status. These two programs, in both policy and administrative aspects, make explicit the necessity of dealing with attitudes and value system in relation to the physical and technical requirements of the program.

ORGANIZATION ACTIVITIES AND LAND TENURE

The effectiveness with which organized activities are functioning in the local community is conditioned by the land tenure patterns and by a number of other factors, including the history of settlement. These interrelated factors have been observed for the schools, the health agencies, and the churches in selected areas.

Public Schools and Land Tenure

The high school system in the two Mississippi Coastal Plain sample counties is rapidly changing into large community consolidations. One such unit, functioning in an adjoining county, is mentioned as a highly successful demonstration of what is soon expected in this part of the state. At present the enrollment in vocational agriculture is conditioned by the location of the agricultural teacher. The tenure patterns in the communities of the county affect this in two ways. First, the race composition of the farm owner communities sets limits for the location of the white and the Negro high schools. Second, the cropper and the share tenant sons enroll in vocational agriculture only when the owner families of the high school area aid and encourage it by example and by the terms of their tenure agreements. This stage of growth in the vocational agriculture program has not yet been reached in the sample area of the Mississippi Coastal Plain, with the possible exception of one high school where Negro and white croppers are taught shop skills as a part of the out-of-school training program.

In the Rolling Plains sample area of Oklahoma, the vocational agriculture program is functioning in only a few high schools, and it has yet reached few students of any tenure. The coming of irrigation to two high school areas is expected to usher in a new need for vocational agriculture at all tenure levels, in order to hasten the adoption of suitable farming practices under the new conditions of irrigation farming.

The vocational agriculture program has developed more fully in the Texas Blackland Prairie sample area, partly as a result of early high school consolidation and partly as a result of mechanized farming. Although the majority of these high schools are town-centered, they include strong vocational agriculture departments and the father-son succession is considered a good opportunity for farm enterprises to be developed by the son. The real concern is for a plan to enable the son to acquire a farm before his father is ready to retire. The mechanized equipment has come too recently to be followed yet by sufficient increase in farm size to provide for two-family farm units.

County Health Programs and Land Tenure

The Southwestern Oklahoma sample area is served in its health program by means of specialized itinerant workers who are dispatched from the State Offices of the Oklahoma Public Health Department. The County Program is primarily a reporting, quarantining, and itinerary scheduling service to make possible the efficient services of the State Department. No significant connections or relations with land tenure were observed, except that this plan of using mobile clinic units from the State Department is well suited to the large-scale farming and town-centered institutional life of the Rolling Plains.

In the Mississippi Coastal Plain the public health program in the sample area was concerned with two major problems, pellagra and hookworm. In one county, the testing of individuals for these two specific disabling conditions was checked against the data of the tenure sample of farm families, but the sample of tested cases was too small to give conclusive tenure differences. The infection by hookworm was known to be about 40 per cent among white elementary school children in a representative community of the area. All three conditions favorable for hookworm were present—a moist soil, a soil sufficiently sandy to give air circulation in the moist upper layer, and sufficiently mild winters to prevent destruction by freezing. Health specialists were agreed that the Negro has less hookworm than whites and that any given worm burden apparently is somewhat less damaging to Negroes than to whites. Because of this the practice of examining only whites for hookworm is common throughout the hookwork region.[18]

[18] "On the other hand, hookworm infection in Negroes is important from two standpoints. First, even the light subclinical infections in the Negro segment of our population continues today to seed hookworm infection into white neighbors just as was the case originally when the hookworm was introduced into this country with the slaves. Secondly, clinical cases of hookworm disease do occur among Negroes and it has not been demonstrated that relatively light cases are harmless." — Letter from Department of Tropical Medicine, the Tulane University of Louisiana, April 11, 1946.

A number of the planters in the Long Leaf Pine Area have white croppers only and others have Negro croppers only. None of the planters specifically mentioned the hookworm problem in this connection, but it is evidently one of the factors favoring Negro population in this area.[19]

Church Programs and Land Tenure

Are there any evidences that the program of social service of the churches in the sample areas is in any significant degree related to a land tenure policy? The Rural Life Conference held in Columbia, Mississippi, in 1944 and subsequent years has appealed to ministers in large numbers. This movement to promote the discussion of some of the more urgent issues of rural life has a parallel in the Catholic Rural Life Conference, which has recently held meetings within the region.

It was ascertained that the open-country churches in the Mississippi Coastal Plain are calling full-time resident pastors. This is leading to a community program of social activities adapted to all ages and more generally adapted to all tenure types of family. Some churches, however, have taken the attitude that farming and church have nothing in common, that one is completely secular and the other sacred. But in the main, the advance toward full-time professional leadership has been accompanied by concern on the part of organized religion with the problems of economic well-being of all of the families of the community, first through expression of a richer community life, and second, through advanced educational training of the youth who are urged to complete more schooling.

The Oklahoma Rolling Plains area has rapidly moved toward town-centered churches. At present these reach mainly only landowning families. This is presumed to be a temporary stage in the evolution of the town-centered social life of the area. If it should become a permanent characteristic, the open-country families may be expected to turn to the schools for many types of social life that in the Mississippi sample area are church-centered.

In the Texas Blackland Prairie area the ethnic groups of Czech and German stock maintain open country churches or those located at farm family hamlets. These reach all tenure classes. The declining open-country churches of the native white American families are being slowly replaced by village or town-centered churches, but the

[19] Hookworm is not prevalent in the Delta area because the lack of air in the heavy soil prevents its survival.

process is accompanied by some confusion in neighborhood loyalties and some feeling on the part of young tenant families that the open-country churches have been neglected by the older owner families. There are no open-country high school and church communities in eastern Bell County composed of old American stock, comparable to those in Marion County, Mississippi. This has of course been influenced by the complex ethnic composition in the Bell County area. However, German Catholic communities in near-by Falls County have many community parallels of affiliation of high school and church area, similar to the open-country church-high school communities of Marion County, Mississippi. In these instances, the church and school working together have made the tenure differences of families seem of no hindrance in the life of the community.

CHAPTER XI

Summary and Conclusions

Basis of the Study

In concluding this report it is well to point out once more that the subject matter aim of the Regional Land Tenure Research Project was to relate farm tenure status to farm family performance. The basis of observation constituted specific areas within the Southwestern states of Arkansas, Louisiana, Mississippi, Oklahoma, and Texas. These states, although referred to as a region, vary widely in topography, climate, soils, levels of living, type of farming, farm practices, and consequently in tenure patterns.

The Eastern and Western Coastal Plains are areas of relatively great pressure of people on the land. Families are large, farms are small, and the tenancy rate is relatively high. Farm family incomes approach subsistence levels with few alternative occupational opportunities for farm people. Out-migration exceeds in-migration with a resulting economic and social loss to the area in expenditures of time and money for education, religion, health, and other group activities.

The Texas Black Land Prairie is an area of fertile soils with intermediate-sized farms. The tenancy rate is high with few croppers. Power driven equipment is prevalent. Cotton yields are high but acreages have recently been curtailed and total production has been reduced. Farm family incomes are high but operating expenses are also high. Alternative employment opportunities are available in near-by cities.

The Rolling Plain of Texas and Southwest Oklahoma is a high risk area with the bulk of the settlement dating back less than fifty years. Farms are large, becoming larger and are highly mechanized. Production is dependent on rainfall. In wet years yields are high but dry years mean crop failures and increased mobility both between farms and tenure groups. Since 1930 heavy out-migration has resulted in a net migration loss to the area.

Under these varied conditions obviously it is not possible to generalize on the detail of tenure performance for the region as a whole. In fact, one of the broad findings of the study is that the tenure arrangements of an individual are meaningful chiefly in relation to the local environment in which the arrangements occur. Consequently one of the most difficult problems faced by the study has been to separate the tenure linked factors in farm family performance from those that are incidental only. Furthermore, there is always the consideration that the factor immediately influencing the performance in question is indirectly conditioned by a tenure factor. For example, managerial skill in and of itself may not be regarded as a tenure factor, yet the acquisition of such skill is dependent in a large measure on a particular type of tenure experience. Likewise such factors as climate, soil, customs, and institutions, though not tenure factors as such, have greatly influenced types of tenure arrangements.

In general the present study has attempted to make observations on three types of questions: (1) What differences in the social and economic performance of farm families are incident to their tenure status? (2) What are the chief factors conditioning the particular tenure status of a farm family? (3) What are the underlying factors which influence tenure status and how are they related to individual farm families?

Although easy to ask, these questions are difficult to answer for the reason that the performance of the farm family is influenced by many factors other than tenure and the problem of determining the direct, not to mention the indirect, influence of tenure factors becomes complicated in the extreme. Furthermore, the tendency of a farm operator to perform in certain ways may not be related so much to his present status as to his past experience. At the beginning of the study, the proponents of each of the several disciplines included tended to regard his particular point of view as holding the key to most of the answers. Later on, these estimates were largely reversed, each one feeling that other approaches probably showed more tenure relationship to farm family performance than his own. In fact, the definite relationships were so hard to establish that in several instances the workers became skeptical at times as to whether tenure factors showed any definite relation to performance and suggested the assignment of observed performance to other indefinitely defined and general factors.

Tenure Factors Related to Farm Family Performance

Several observations are made in response to the first of the three questions, "What differences in the social and economic performance of farm families are incident to their tenure status?"

Size of Farm

For all six measures of size used—that is, labor requirements, total acres, acres in crop land, acres in some major crop, amount of livestock, and capital invested in the farm business—the average size of farms was greater among those operated by part owners than for the other tenure groups for each area and for each race, excepting for the Negroes in the Mississippi Coastal Plain. White operators in the Mississippi Coastal Plain showed a consistent pattern by all size measures from largest to smallest as follows: part owners, owners, share renters, share-cash renters. This general pattern obtained in the other areas although it was less consistent.

Crop Organization

Tenure differences in crop organzation, excepting for croppers, do not appear to be strikingly significant. Cotton, as the major crop, accounted for approximately the same percentage of crop land on the farms operated by whites and Negroes and by owners, part owners, share renters, and share-cash renters in all sample areas. As measured in terms of total acreage and crop land, the acreage of cotton tended to vary directly with size of farm irrespective of tenure classification.

Capital Investment

On the average, in all areas owners and part owners operated with a larger capital investment than renters. The relative proportions of the total farm investment which were in real estate, equipment, and livestock were not, however, significantly different. In the Oklahoma and Texas sample areas where the total farm investment was considerably greater than in Mississippi, the proportion in equipment was somewhat greater and in livestock somewhat less than in the other two areas but the differences among tenure groups within the same area were not significant.

Livestock on Farms

Owners and part owners had more livestock than renters. Although much of the difference disappeared when farms were grouped according to size, the general trend remained the same. Furthermore in none of the areas studied were there any owners with no livestock and few cases with less than one animal unit. The number of renters in these categories was much higher. Grouped by size, among the whites in the Mississippi Coastal Plain, full owners had the most livestock whereas among the colored, part owners exceeded full owners.

There are also tenure differences with respect to breeding stock; owners, for example, more often possess bulls than renters, and white operators more often possess such stock than colored operators. On small farms part owners in the Rolling Plains and Blackland samples had more livestock than owners, but on medium sized farms share-cash tenants in both the Arkansas Coastal Plain and Oklahoma Rolling Plain samples had the largest number of livestock. On large farms share-cash tenants had the largest number of livestock per 100 acres of crop land in most areas.

Farm Equipment

Most of the farm operators in the Mississippi and Arkansas Coastal Plain samples used horse drawn equipment exclusively. In the Oklahoma and Texas samples, however, many farm operators in each of the tenure categories used power equipment, some exclusively and some in combination with horses. Part owners used tractor equipment to a greater extent than other tenure groups. Share-cash renters relied on horse-drawn equipment more than owners, part owners, or share renters.

Investment in equipment and the extent of mechanization is related primarily to size of farm rather than to tenure. Certain differences appeared as between the races with respect to the ownership of cars and trucks, white operators having more than the colored of similar tenure status.

Income

Owner and part owner operators showed higher total gross incomes than renters even when size of operation was held constant. This was particularly marked in the two western areas. In the Coastal Plains areas white operators received higher incomes than Negroes of similar tenure status. Renters in the region in general received a higher proportion of total income from farm work off the farm than did owners. However, owners averaged more from nonfarm sources than renters. Gross farm income was highest for owners and part owners but elimination of the size factor reduced the difference. Part owners and share-cash renters received the highest proportion of farm income from livestock sales.

Croppers in the Farm Orzanization

Although croppers throughout most of this report are analyzed along with the other tenure groups, from the standpoint of the farm business, cropper units in many respects are only partially comparable to complete farm units. From this standpoint, a cropper tract is designed to meet a special purpose within the framework of the larger farm and as such possesses certain characteristics not common to the entire unit. As a rule, cropper tracts contained a larger percentage of cropland than the entire farm and a larger proportion of this cropland was devoted to cotton. Also more intensive methods of cotton cultivation tended to be used, resulting in larger yields. In addition, little cropland was left idle and much of it was double-cropped.

Although most of the cropper's income comes from his share of the crop on a specific tract, he also received in most cases a significant amount in the form of wages for work off his tract but on other parts of the farm. Most of the income from the crop on the home tract represented sales from cotton plus the value of products used in the home. For the crop year 1942 the gross income of cropper tracts compared very favorably with the gross income of complete farm units of corresponding size. One major factor in this situation was the unusually favorable position of the cotton enterprise that year. Good yields, particularly in the Mississippi sample area, coupled with high prices resulted in better than average incomes for those who grew cotton. Since cropper tracts tend to be devoted to cotton more exclusively than the farm as a whole, they generally benefited from this situation.

Croppers tended to be full-time croppers in the Coastal Plains to a greater extent than in the other areas. The majority of croppers in the Texas area worked for wages, whereas those in Oklahoma were about equally divided between operating croppers and wage laborers, the latter receiving a share of the production of cotton, poultry, eggs, or milk as a bonus payment. In the Coastal Plains the cropper arrangements were closely associated with the white, male, resident landlord. Although farm laborers are considered to be a part of the tenure picture, they are treated only incidentally in this report due to the limitations of the study.

Level of Living

In general, the socio-economic status of the farm families rose with increases in net family income, but at the lower end of the income scales below $300, socio-economic status remained approximately constant. Net income, however, particularly for a given year, is a less reliable indicator of socio-economic status than *scale of operation* since annual fluctuations due to weather and price affect the income but not the scale of operation.

For a given scale of farm operation, part owners rank higher in socio-economic status than renters and renters, higher than croppers. Part owners are not uniformly lower than full owners but are uniformly higher than renters. An array of all families into given groups based on status score shows no croppers in the highest status group. All tenures, however, are represented in the lowest group. The wide spread in each of the tenures demonstrates that tenure alone neither determines nor limits the status of a farm family. Because the scale of operation for all farms, owned and leased, tends to be larger in the Rolling Plains than in the other areas, it is here that one might expect the goals of economic status to tend to replace the goals of ownership.

The housing index is one of the three components of the socio-economic status measure and would be expected to reveal similar tenure contrasts. Certain reversals, however, are noted. For the Negro farmers in the Coastal Plains, full owners rank above part owners in the Arkansas and Louisiana samples but not in the Mississippi sample. For white farmers, the housing index of the part owners is much higher than that of the full owners in the combined samples of the region. There is, however, considerable fluctuation in individual cases. Considering both races and only the three broad tenure groups, the housing level of owners exceeds that of renters and renters as a whole exceeds croppers.

The index of movable possessions, also a part of the status scale, is a measure of the part of the family possessions for which the operator is himself primarily responsible, in contrast with the index of housing for which the landowner is largely in a position to determine the level of use. The broad tenure comparisons show that the combined renter group has an index considerably above that of the cropper and the combined owner group has an index slightly above that of the renter. For the index of movable possessions, renters as a whole are farther along the scale from croppers to owners than they are for the housing index. This indicates that tenants have used their consumer purchasing ability to improve their socio-economic status even though they could not do so for housing facilities.

With respect to the index of social participation, also a part of the socio-economic status measure, the combined owner group shows a higher index than the renter group. Renters in turn are followed by the croppers but the entire spread among these averages is much less than that for the housing or for the movable possessions index. Moreover, the difference is reversed as among owner and renter groups for the Negro sample in all areas. This is particularly marked in the Arkansas and Mississippi Coastal Plains. It is concluded that in the matter of social participation the differences between the owner and the renter groups are not particularly significant.

Negro croppers consistently have a higher index of social participation than white croppers. At the same time they have a lower housing index and a lower index of movable possessions. These levels likewise hold for both renter groups. The single variant in this pattern is in the housing index of Mississippi Coastal Plain share renters where whites have a lower index than Negroes.

Scale of Farm Operation and Quality of Business

Gross farm income is a measure of the size of the farm business, but among other factors it is influenced by yield and price. Therefore, for the purposes at hand a measure of the size of operation was developed which depends only on the three input factors: value of the farm business, productive man-work units of labor required, and acres in cropland. Using these three, the gross farm income expected for this combination of production factors was computed for each farm and this expected gross farm income, with average conditions of management, is called the scale of operation. The attained gross farm income, expressed as a per cent of the predicted or expected gross farm income, becomes a measure of the *quality of the farm business* for each race and tenure group.

When holding size constant by using the scale of operation within each race group in each area, the cropper group of tracts shows a higher gross quality of business than any other tenure. On the whole, the full owners make the poorest record, although in the Mississippi sample the Negro full owners rank second among their race groups, exceeded only by croppers. Share renters are below other tenures in the Arkansas white and the Mississippi Negro groups. They rank somewhat higher in other areas.

Another measure of quality of business is the operator's earnings, expressed as a percentage of the predicted or expected gross farm income. This ratio of net operator returns per hundred dollars of scale of operation is a measure of the net efficiency of production. On this measure, the croppers rank first among all the selected tenure groups for Arkansas Coastal Plain Negroes and among the Mississippi Coastal Plain whites and Negroes. In the Arkansas white sample, however, croppers are decidedly surpassed by share-cash renters. In the Oklahoma Rolling Plains the croppers drop to the bottom of the list on this measure of performance. Evidently their expenses are high for operating equipment, picking, or other labor costs. However, the variation in actual percentage was very narrow among all tenures in the Oklahoma sample.

The full and part owners rank fourth and fifth in the Arkansas Coastal Plain for both whites and Negroes and in Mississippi for the white sample. For the Mississippi Negro sample, full owners rank second, followed by share renters, part owners, and share-cash renters respectively. The 26 Arkansas white share-cash renters stand exceedingly high and the five Mississippi Negro share-cash renters stand exceedingly low on this measure of net performance in earning capacity for a given scale of operation.

The scale of operation and the gross quality of business together account for the variation in gross farm income among farms and among tenure groups. The scale of operation and the net quality of business by definition account for the variation in operator's earnings among farms and among tenure groups. There is quite general agreement between gross quality and net quality of business. This agreement would lend support to the opinion that farm profits first of all depend upon large production per unit of input. In this analysis the input is measured by the scale of operation. When the expenses of production mount at a faster rate than the gross production, the net quality will fail to keep pace with gross quality of production.

As a yardstick of how large a single farm operation can become and still contribute to the maximum good of the nation, it is proposed as a result of this analysis that so long as the operator, regardless of his tenure, continuously obtains average or above average gross and net quality of business, he continues to have a suitable size of farm, provided he continues to allot to the labor so used a wage or family level of living that is average or above for that type of farming area,

The five cropper groups have the highest gross quality of business, each exceeding 115 on this index. They are proportionally low on net quality of business although they average as high on this measure as does any other tenure group. The share-cash renter groups have the greatest amount of deviation from the line of average relation for the gross and net quality of business.

The cropper groups already have such high gross quality that they can only achieve higher net returns by getting more returns through increasing the size of their operation or through more favorable leases. They run the risk of obtaining less productive land and hence less gross quality of production if they seek more favorable leasing arrangements through change to share renter leases. For both races in the Arkansas and Mississippi Coastal Plains, the croppers exceed share renters in operator's earnings. Among Oklahoma native white families, croppers have less operator's earnings than share renters, but most of them operate considerably smaller units with highly efficient gross quality and low efficiency in net quality of business.

With these opportunities, the real problem facing the cropper families is one of going from intensive farming on high quality land, under conditions of supervision that result in high gross quality of business and average net quality of business, to a more extensive type of farming that requires a significant amount of capital, managerial ability, and risk taking. The transfer to share renting does not bring advantages, either in increased operator's earnings or in socio-economic status. Moreover, their experiences as supervised croppers do not necessarily, or even probably, equip them for managerial responsibilities that go with farming as an operating tenant who has care of livestock added to that of cash crop production. It is no small achievement for a son of a cropper to acquire the managerial experience of an operating tenant if he must do so without the benefit of parental tutelage and in competition with the landowners' sons. Nor is the problem solved by acquiring a small unproductive farm at even mortgage-free ownership.

The problem of families who are operating tenants on farms of average or larger size is somewhat more simple than the above. The only additional step they face is one of land ownership, and this can be one of part owner, preferably the purchase of the house and barns on land that can become part of the operating unit. They already have the experience of management that can be readily tested for gross quality and net quality, in relation to the stage of the business cycle and its influence on the desirability of making a purchase of land.

When these two steps on the agricultural tenure ladder are contrasted, it is apparent that the risks and the problems associated with going from supervised cropper to the status of managing or operating tenant are quite different in kind from those faced by the operating tenant who faces the choice of becoming a landowner. The comparison of croppers' achievements with those of other croppers in any one of the three sample areas, when measured by the gross and the net quality of their farm business, enables one who counsels with them, whether county agent, vocational agriculture teacher, or farm friend, to advise whether or not they are ready for the next step up the agricultural ladder. This includes the steps toward increased scale of operation in addition to, or in place of, increased equity in the farm business.

Fertility Index

A fertility index was computed for each family, based on the number of children born to the male head and divided by the number expected for his given age. The entire farm population of the United States was used as a yardstick. The white part owners show a higher fertility than the white full owners in the Arkansas and Texas samples, have a fertility index equal to that of the Louisiana sample, and are considerably lower in fertility than the part owners in the Mississippi sample. In the Arkansas and Mississippi sample areas renters of both races have significantly higher fertility rates than croppers of the respective areas. In the other three areas croppers have the higher fertility rates. This reversal demonstrates that income factors and other factors associated with tenure or method of wage payment can be more important than tenure itself. In general the high birth rates occur on low priced and low productive land. This land is found in the areas of high percentage ownership.

Leasing Arrangements

The pattern of the leasing arrangement is largely conditioned by the type of landlord who owns the land. Institutional, nonresident, nonrelated, and female landlords use the cash method of rental payment and written leases more often than other types of landlords. Other types of landlords tend to use an oral, informal arrangement.

The great bulk of farm land in the areas surveyed was owned by individual males. Women constituted around 15 per cent of the individual landlords although in some areas as high as 40 per cent were women. Estates accounted for less than 10 per cent of all landlords sampled. While the percentage in estates is not high in a given year, the importance of this type of landholding is indicated by the passage of essentially all farm land through this stage sooner or later in the transfer of ownership from one generation to another. The amount of land owned by governmental agencies and by agencies extending credit on real estate varies from year to year depending upon farm incomes. Because of the high rate of foreclosures in the thirties, the amount increased, but during the ensuing war years much of the land was sold to individual buyers.

Ethnic and Racial Relations

In leasing a farm the renter gives important consideration to both the land and the landlord. Those renting land tend to select farms owned by landlords of the same ethnic or racial group regardless of the quality or size of the farm or the proportion of the total land area owned by that particular ethnic group.

Lease Coverage

Most leases in the sample areas cover an entire farm unit. Renting of single fields was more common in the Coastal Plains than in the other areas. Renting milk cows was fairly common for croppers.

Rental Systems and Rates

The third and fourth system of renting, with its variations, was the most prevalent method of rental payment in each area sampled. The cash share variation in the Oklahoma areas represented additional cash payments for pasture or dwelling while in the Texas area it represented cash on a specified acreage of feed crop and share on the balance. In general those paying cash-share rent were making the most money.

In 1942 the value of rental per $100 valuation was highest for those paying one-half share rent. This was followed by the third and fourth rentals. Cash rentals were lowest, being near the usual interest rate. Differences in the ratios vary according to yields and prices so that conclusions based upon 1942 data should be carefully weighed.

Written Leases

The written lease showed little or no relationship to the number of years on the rent tract or to measures of soil conservation practices. It was associated with the types of landlords who had formal, contractual relationships with the lessees and with those lessees who were participating in the Farm Security Administration program. Aside from the School Land leases sampled in Oklahoma and Mississippi, the written lease apparently contributed little to the stability of the renter on a given tract of land. None of the croppers sampled had written contracts.

Kinship

The significance of kinship is largely contingent upon the characteristics of the landlord and the family to which he belongs. The fundamental consideration, therefore, is the type of landlord to which the tenant is related. If he has little to offer by way of supervision or credit standing and particularly if the land is of low productivity, the fact of kinship may have little influence on the performance of the tenant. On the other hand, a related tenant is from a landowning family so that "related tenant" becomes a partial substitute for a tenure of parent criterion. Tenants related to their landlords are involved with the economic affairs of the parental family. Under such circumstances there is a tendency for family money to be "loaned" back and forth according to relative need and supply rather than according to strict economic practices. Since distribution of wealth within the kinship group is likely to be dependent on need as well as upon input factors, a greater range of rental arrangements is to be expected for related than for nonrelated tenants.

Some of the characteristics of related tenants are: (1) they are younger than other tenants, (2) they are of landowning families, (3) they have been aided financially by their owner relatives, (4) their net worth and socio-economic status are higher, (5) they participate in the community activities more like owners than other tenants, (6) they have had schooling more comparable to owners than to other tenants. These characteristics apply to renters, croppers, and laborers related to their landlords or employers.

In addition, related tenants: (1) have leases which vary more from the traditional third and fourth or half share arrangements than the unrelated; (2) more frequently have oral leasing arrangements; (3) more often have leases of indefinite duration; (4) show a low ratio of rent to value and frequently pay no rent; (5) with landlords living near the farm receive less supervision than similar non-kinship tenants but those with landlords living more than 25 miles away receive more supervision.

Division of Management

The measure of the division of management between landlord and tenant is, among other things, a means of determining to which party the success of the farm operation should be attributed. Some overlapping occurred among the traditional tenure classes in regard to the division of management as measured by this scale. For example, some part owners performed in this regard essentially as croppers. In general, the more the landlord furnished and the nearer he was to the farm the more he supervised the operations. The management index was closely related to the method of rental payment and to the extension of credit by the landlord to the lessee. Responsibility for management increased with net worth, livestock, education, and age. As in the case of tenure change, renters usually acquired a larger share in management by moving. In the case of Farm Security Administration borrowers, supervision was transferred from the conventional type of landlord to the credit agency.

In general, the more the supervision, the higher the crop yield index within each race and tenure grouping. White renters and croppers in both Coastal Plain samples had the highest crop yield index when the management was divided more or less equally between the landlord and tenant. Supervision, therefore, appears to increase yields, or stated another way, it increases yields to add supervision to land which will respond to management. Freedom of choice on the part of the tenant is reflected in increased diversification as he increases in proportion of managment. A part of this increased diversification is accounted for by increases in the value of products used in the home.

Factors Giving Rise to Differences in Tenure Status

The second major question upon which this study has focused attention is, "What are the chief factors conditioning the farm tenure status of a given farm family?"

Institutional Environment

The tenure arrangements of an individual at any given time are meaningful chiefly in relation to the environmental setting in which the arrangements occur. Quantity of capital and acreage, use of equipment, and income distribution were quite different in the Coastal Plains from those in the other two areas sampled. In order to state the minimum requirements of land, operating capital, managerial ability, and skills needed by a farmer with specified tenure arrangements, it therefore becomes necessary to examine the pattern of such items in the area for which the recommendations are to apply.

Individuals climb the tenure ladder or achieve success in a given tenure status necessarily within the institutional framework of the environment in which they live, utilizing the farming practices and managerial opportunities available in that area. Action programs are conditioned by these limitations.

Age

Within each area studied, ownership increased with age. The percentage of ownership appeared to reach a maximum in the Coastal Plains at around 35 years of earning life—60 per cent for all Negroes and 80 per cent for whites. The settlement of the Oklahoma area was not old enough to warrant a conclusion in this regard. All racial and ethnic groups increased in ownership at essentially the same rate, the seeming differences being accounted for largely by the percentage who were owners at the beginning of earning life.

Tenure of Parents

Tenure and economic status of parents had an important bearing upon the tenure at which the children began earning life but was not related to the age at which earning life began. Although some of the children of owner parents began earning life with little more capital than those of nonowning parents, they were in an advantageous position to secure credit either directly or through the sponsorship of the parents. At any rate, the son has an heir interest in the home farm upon which he can count sometime in the future.

The sons of owners who begin farming as renters, croppers, or laborers remain in those positions a relatively short time, presumably due to parental assistance and to the ambition to equal their parents. Many sons of owners begin occupational life as owners. Over one-half of the white owner sample in the Arkansas and Mississippi Coastal Plains achieved that status prior to the age of 25. On the other hand, for the son of parents with little net worth, there is little choice within agriculture other than beginning as a farm laborer or cropper.

Parents of husband and wife appeared to have equal influence upon the tenure status of the family. Higher tenure status of the parents was positively associated with a higher educational attainment for the children, a relatively heavier out-migration of the children to nonfarm occupations and a higher beginning farm tenure status. The difference in the rate of out-migration was probably more closely related to the educational attainment than to the tenure status of the parents.

Young people tend to marry within their tenure groups and thereby concentrate the farm wealth within a relatively few families. However, most of those inheriting land receive only a part of the total inheritance and must buy the remainder from those brothers and sisters who have migrated to other farms or to nonfarm occupations. On the whole those owners who bought their farms were more efficient operators than those who inherited them.

Mobility

Three-fourths of the farm-to-farm changes involved no change in tenure status. On the other hand, four-fifths of all tenure changes were accompanied by changes in farm. A majority of all farmers sampled had never moved over 10 miles. Consequently, major community ties were unbroken by such moves. Full owners and share-cash renters in the Oklahoma sample had moved the greatest distances—a situation probably linked with the relative newness of the area.

Presumably all moves from farm to farm are made for what seem to be good reasons. From a tenure viewpoint, however, approximately two-thirds of all changes in farms in the Mississippi and Texas areas were made with no change of status. It may be that within the same general tenure status some progress was made by obtaining a higher proportion of the management function, by getting a more advantageous leasing arrangement, or a larger and more productive farm. On the positive side of the picture, three-fourths of all tenure changes are accompanied by changes in farms. Those who improved their tenure without moving were mainly tenants renting from relatives. This evidence agrees with the conclusion reached in the consideration of leasing arrangements—that the landlord largely determines the tenure under which a tract of land is operated and that the lessee must fit into the pattern as established by the landlord.

A second aspect of farm-to-farm movement concerns type of soil. Capital accumulated by nonowners on productive land is frequently invested in the ownership of poorer land. Although this is a matter of personal choice, it is obvious that less capital is required to purchase poor land than good land. The general migration picture shows that a farmer accumulates capital in a lower tenure status on good land, but as he progresses up the tenure ladder, he tends to move to land of lesser productivity. This tendency is particularly true in areas where the cropper system is followed. Obviously this relationship of poor soil and high tenure status does not apply to inheritances since inherited land is of all varieties of quality.

Capital

With a given amount of capital and available credit, a farmer has the choice of: (1) a lower tenure status, smaller proportion of income for family living and limited opportunity to invest capital in his own business, or (2) higher tenure status on a smaller farm, less productive soil, higher proportion of total farm income from the value of home-used products and possibly more income from the capital invested. As a general rule the lower the tenure status, the higher the productivity of the land available. In local areas, however, there might well be exceptions to this rule. With the higher tenure, more acres are under control of the operator, but the productivity of the soil tends to be lower and frequently the equipment and supervision which contribute to higher yields and higher incomes are lacking. As an offset, more food is raised for family living, a greater sense of security is achieved incident to the stability of location, which in turn encourages an accumulation of capital goods. Frequently, however, the income producing capacity of these owner tracts is too small to meet more than the very minimum requirements of family living.

Nonfarm Work

Although income from off-farm work appears to be equal dollar for dollar to farm income, its utility in achieving tenure advancement is of a different order. The additional income to the family can be invested in land, operating capital, savings, or family expenditures. One out of every ten farmers sampled had experienced full-time nonfarm employment during his occupational lifetime. The Czechs and Germans in the Texas Black Lands had less experience in this regard while other groups appeared to vary according to the opportunity for such work. The majority of those who had had full-time nonfarm work returned to the farm because of adverse employment opportunities. A few had managed to accumulate enough capital to start farming. In general, however, the average man who transferred from a nonfarm occupation to farming brought little capital to the farm. Off-farm work represents an opportunity to accumulate capital for the purchase of a farm but it is an opportunity difficult of utilization. Examination of individual cases showed that those who achieved ownership through other occupational routes took from five to ten years longer than those who achieved it through farming alone.

A great deal of off-farm work is carried on in addition to the current farming operation. While those with the smaller farms and with the lower tenures worked more days off-farm, the total value of such labor was lower than for those with the larger farms and the higher tenures. Small farmers and croppers in general did unskilled labor, while farmers with larger farms and higher tenures tended toward skilled labor and higher wage rates. Further examination showed that those giving the highest proportion of their time to farming were the most efficient operators. Moreover, the cash received from off-farm work was not clear profit since certain additional costs had to be met such as the expense of transportation, board, tools, and equipment. In addition, as off-farm work increased there was a tendency to increase the expenditures for commercialized recreation and store purchases of food and clothing. These expenditures add little to the comforts of farm family living as measured by the socio-economic status scale and contribute nothing to the value of farm production goods. While nonfarm work or off-farm occupation may add very little to the farm status of most individuals, it nevertheless represents an opportunity by which an individual may acquire ownership or operatorship of a farm adequate to meet his needs.

Tenure Goals

The tenure alternative which the individual farmer will choose is largely determined by his goals, abilities, resources, and opportunities. If ownership is the goal, farmers achieving it with limited capital too often are forced to accept small farms and low incomes. If income and level of living is the primary goal, with tenure merely a means to that end, a lower tenure status on productive land (with adequate equipment and livestock for efficient use of labor, sufficient assurance of stability of location to secure the maximum benefits from the better practices, and as large a farm as possible) is the alternative to be chosen. Supervision, though sometimes irksome, frequently leads to more efficient farm operation. This may be given by a landlord, an agency supplying credit, or a governmental agency. If the farmer can have a partnership arrangement with the supervisory agency on a basis of equality, it is possible to retain the dignity that is commonly associated with the ownership of land and at the same time enjoy a level of living above the minimum standards. One type of arrangement which appears to combine some of the best features of ownership and tenancy was observed in the Oklahoma Rolling Plains. In these cases the residence was not included in the farm lease. In this type of arrangement the farmer owns his dwelling and secures his income in a tenure status suited to his abilities, ambition, and capital accumulation. Mechanization and rapid transportation facilities make such an arrangement possible. Should this type of arrangement become widespread it would of course necessitate some adjustments in community organization.

Underlying Factors Related to Tenure Status

The third major question of the study is, "What are the underlying factors which influence tenure status and how are they related to individual farm families?" In a summary statement these must obviously be treated very broadly. For the purposes of the study these considerations were broken down into the following main subjects:

(1) Federal Programs and Land Tenure
(2) Land Tenure and Soil Conservation
(3) Legal Aspects of Land Tenure
(4) Uses and Sources of Capital
(5) Community and Institutional Aspects of Tenure

Federal Programs and Land Tenure

In general, each of the several government programs operated for the benefit of agriculture has evolved to meet some new and current problem. Consequently, the composite of these programs is not based on a clearly visualized set of ends or objectives. This lack of integration is due in part to the fact that it has not as yet been possible to determine a complete set of long-run ends with which the majority of the people are in substantial agreement. The present study clearly indicates that the tenure goals and the methods of their achievement vary widely over the region studied. The prosperity of those engaged in farming depends on a high level of general employment and on an active demand for agricultural products. Hence, a land tenure program needs to be undertaken as a segment of a comprehensive plan which involves the living levels of all families, both urban and rural. Farm labor efficiency has increased markedly during the past few years, which, with a fixed amount of labor available tends further to weaken its bargaining position in relation to land ownership. Industry must be the active or potential employer of the residual labor resulting from improved farm technology if a reasonably satisfactory bargaining position for the tenant and laborer is to be maintained.

It may be necessary to distinguish more sharply between programs intended to improve the economic level of the farming group as a whole and programs intended to improve the status of certain disadvantaged sub-groups if the latter programs are to be effective. In this region little progress has been made in rehabilitating those who have reached the least acceptable status. It should be observed also that those most in need of assistance are generally least fitted through education and experience for rehabilitation.

As an alternative to the present pattern of agricultural programs it is conceivable that a general program might be devised which would provide for a level of minimum conditions for those engaged in farming without undertaking specifically to influence the tenure status by which the individual operates. Such an approach is in keeping with the concept of job insurance and the social security program in general.

Several observations may be made with respect to participation in the various government programs by the families included in the sample. Participation in the Agricultural Adjustment Administration program was the most nearly universal with upwards of 95 per cent of all sample families participating excepting for the croppers of Oklahoma and Texas.

Among the many different types of services offered by the Agricultural Extension program observations were made in this study only with respect to county farm and home demonstration agents. A substantial number of all farmers were in contact with county agents. The percentage of colored farmers was lower than for white, running somewhat under 50 per cent for the Arkansas and Mississippi Coastal Plains area. In general, the higher the tenure status, the greater the number of contacts.

Roughly 45 per cent of the owners in the regional sample participated in the Farm Credit Administration program. A substantially smaller proportion of the tenants than owners, and still fewer croppers, participated. Naturally, that phase of the program which has to do with real estate credit is available only to owners. The average amount loaned for production credit was larger for owners than for tenants or croppers. However, the various tenure groups appeared to participate equally with respect to feed and seed loans.

A composite measure of participation in the several programs studied discloses that with the exception of a small number of white croppers in Oklahoma and Texas, practically all farmers in each of the several tenure groups participated in 1942 in one or more of these programs. Measured in this way, it appears that either government programs provide a relatively greater attraction to farm owners or that a higher proportion of owners were able to qualify for participation. Renters came second and croppers third.

Although any one farmer may be interested in more than one of the programs offered, they are of such nature that they are not likely to afford an inducement for the individual farmer to participate simultaneously in all of them. The programs of the Agricultural Adjustment Administration and the Agricultural Extension Service are essentially universal in their appeal; the program of the Soil Conservation Service appeals more especially to landowners. The credit facilities of the Farm Credit Administration and the Farm Security Administration are arranged to meet the needs of different types of borrowers; hence, there is little duplication of participation in these two programs.

In general, the data indicate the need for more adequate adaptation of the federal programs to meet the needs of the less favored tenure groups.

Farm Security Administration Borrowers

In connection with the work of the Project, certain special studies were made with respect to the borrowers in the Farm Security Administration.[1] The Farm Security Administration, as it functioned at the time of the study, undertook (1) to provide credit for farmers who were unable to get credit from other sources, and (2) to provide limited supervision. While the program was available to and participated in by a significant number of owners whose net worth was low, it was especially attractive to renters and to those croppers who were to become renters. Approximately 35 per cent of the white renters and 20 per cent of the colored renters participated in the Farm Security Administration program in the Mississippi and Arkansas Coastal Plains samples. The participation in the Oklahoma and Texas samples was notably less for both classes. Croppers generally did not participate in the Farm Security Administration program for two reasons: croppers who were eligible were likely to become renters as a direct result of such participation and the nature of the cropper arrangement is such that the landlord usually provides the necessary credit for the cropper to operate.

In attempting to evaluate the influence of the Farm Security Administration on the performance of its borrowers, a statistical system of matching borrowers and nonborrowers was used. The characteristics deemed important for the individual matching of cases and for which information was available are as follows: (1) tenure of parents (2) stage in family cycle (3) age of head (4) education (5) number in family at home (6) kinship to landlord (7) tenure status and (8) migration ratio. Prior to matching on the above points the cases were separated by race and sex. The above characteristics used in the matching are believed to be such as to warrant comparability between the resulting groups for the purpose of observing contrasts in certain characteristics of their 1942 status. The descriptive items thus observed for purposes of further comparison by group averages were as follows: (1) net worth (2) value of business (3) acres in farm (4) crop acres (5) yield index (6) productive man-work units and (7) credit used.

After having been matched on the basis of the above points the Farm Security Administration and non-Farm Security Administration

[1] Changed in 1946 to the Farmers Home Administration.

groups were then compared on the following items relating to rehabilitation and tenure progress: (1) degree of management index (2) index of diversification (3) labor efficiency rating (4) net income per farm (5) net income per man equivalent unit and (6) socio-economic status.

The following comparisons are noted:

Credit. Farm Security Administration rural rehabilitation borrowers operated on roughly four times as much credit as the nonborrowers. The comparison of real estate credit used for farm owner-borrowers with the real estate credit used by nonborrowers who are matched with farm owner-borrowers continued as tenants is negligible. These differences are of course to be expected since a principal function of the Farm Security Administration was to give liberal extension of credit, especially to those whose economic status was such that it was difficult for them to obtain credit elsewhere.

Degree of Management. Particularly significant in this connection is the higher degree of management exercised by borrowers than by nonborrowers. This was accomplished in part through better leasing arrangements and in part through the change in tenure status from cropper to renter and from renter to owner. This increase in responsibility marks progress up the tenure ladder, provided borrowers are capable of exercising the greater degree of management advantageously after the Farm Security Administration supervision has been withdrawn.

Diversification. Farm Security Administration clients diversify to a greater extent than comparable nonclients. This diversification involved a shift to less cotton and more livestock. There is evidence that clients under Farm Security Administration supervision have been somewhat more successful in their management of livestock than nonclients. Farm owner clients produced more cattle but fewer hogs and less poultry than comparable nonclients and also place somewhat more emphasis on minor cash crops. The effects of a diversified program of farming in stabilizing year-to-year income is not necessarily apparent in any single year and, therefore, may not be fully reflected in the report for 1942. Such effects could be better observed over a period of years.

The productive man-work days per man equivalent year is higher for nonborrowers than for borrowers except in the farm owner-loan groups. White rural rehabilitation borrowers have approximately the same number of crop acres as nonborrowers and have a slightly higher yield index. In the case of colored borrowers, there is a larger average number of crop acres per farm but a substantially lower yield index.

The larger acreages of farm owner-borrowers and the substantially higher yield index explain why the productive man-work days per man equivalent year ratios are so much higher than those of the comparable nonborrower group.

Net Income. The average net income per farm for both white and colored rural rehabilitation borrowers was less than that for comparable nonborrowers. The net income per man equivalent unit was also less for rural rehabilitation borrowers than for comparable nonborrowers. This situation is again reversed when farm owner-borrowers are compared with their respective matched groups.

With the exception of the farm owner group, the comparison of productive man-work days per man equivalent year and/or net income is disappointing from the point of view of the Farm Security Administration. On the other hand, it is possible that some of the efforts of the Farm Security Administration borrowers are not reflected in the net income figure but are translated directly into advances in level of living. However, the data indicate a need for more detailed planning of farm operations with a view to a fuller utilization of available labor. It appears obvious that the farm owner group was more rigorously selected than the rehabilitation group. The farm owner group also operates with substantially larger units.

Socio-economic Status. The socio-economic status averages slightly higher for all groups of Farm Security Administration borrowers than for the comparable non-Farm Security Administration groups. This is largely exclusive of the benefits that Farm Security Administration clients derive through membership in health groups and similar co-operative activities.

Soil Conservation Factors and Tenure

Certain special observations were also made with respect to the relation of soil conservation practices and land tenure. Among the factors which tend to affect conservation are the following: (1) Land parcels in the region are subject to frequent transfer thus making it difficult to establish long time conservation programs. Related to this is a lack of conservation philosophy incident to the recent free land era. (2) Conservation practice on the smaller tracts is relatively limited since under these circumstances it is difficult to adjust farm enterprise organization to the requirements of conservation programs. Assuming that diversification reflects a less exploitative land use, owner-operators are more conserving than tenants. Tenants unrelated to their landlords show less diversification than those who are related, and sons show greater diversification than other related tenants. (3) Where mobility is high, incentives for conservation are lacking for both the tenant and the owner, the former because he cannot reap future benefits of conservation, the latter because he feels that any investment made may be jeopardized by a rapid turnover of operators. Furthermore, installation of a comprehensive program for conservation is generally accompanied by costs, either directly in cash outlay or indirectly through temporary losses of income. Under conditions of high mobility tenants usually forego practices that promise to pay off at a distant future date. Similarly, in any given year, exploitative practices apparently pay the individual renter-operator. These factors create passiveness toward conservation programs. (4) Leasing arrangements and statutory enactments have established the owner's prior position with respect to possession and use. Consequently, the set-up of active conservation programs assumes that conservation is primarily the responsibility of the landowner. For this and other reasons, participation in conservation programs is relatively greater among owner-operators. The general experience of active public conservation agencies appears to be that in field operations the task of executing conservation plans on tenant farms depends largely on the efforts of the landowner. (5) Few written leases include statements of comprehensive conservation practices. Furthermore, those practices which are impediments to conservation are difficult to change since many of them are based on traditional procedures and attitudes. (6) The type of landowner influences the progress of conservation programs. Female landowners, estates, and those who own land primarily for anticipated mineral values show a relative lack of interest in conservation. On the other hand, a new class of landlords, of the urban occupational and residence groups, is participating to a marked degree in conservation programs. This is due partly to the fact that the land has become a place of investment for surplus nonfarm income. (7) Of great importance to conservation are the general price relationships existing at a given time. For example, high prices for beef and dairy products tend to promote conservation while the same situation for hogs, cotton, and cash grain tend to promote more exploitation.

Capital

Another underlying factor conditioning tenure performance is the matter of capital. Among the production factors in the region, capital has frequently been relatively scarce. Therefore, much of the success of farm operators in advancing their economic and tenure status has been contingent upon the skill they have shown in the acquisition and use of farm capital. Farmers in general get capital from three general sources: their own savings and capital accumulations; the use of credit; leasing or using the farm businesses belonging to others. The bulk of the owned capital used by the farmers in the region comes from farm earnings, inheritances, gifts, off-farm earnings, and miscellaneous sources such as oil royalties and pensions. Approximately two-thirds of these farmers used production or furnish credit in 1942. Production Credit Associations provided the most important sources of short term credit for the farmers in the Oklahoma and Texas sample areas, landlords, the most important source in the Arkansas Coastal Plain, and merchants, the most important source in the Mississippi Coastal Plain. Other credit sources were provided by the Farm Security Administration, equipment dealers, and private investors. In general, more renters and croppers than owners used non-real-estate credit in each of the areas. Although a large proportion of the owners reported no use of non-real-estate credit in 1942, those owners who used production or furnish credit often used larger amounts than the renter and cropper groups.

The following percentages of owners and part owners used real estate credit in 1942: Arkansas Coastal Plain, 46; Oklahoma Rolling Plain, 72; Texas Blackland Prairie, 42. Most of this real-estate credit was provided by the Federal Land Bank. The average amount per sample farm of real estate credit outstanding for each of the areas in 1942 was $1,130 for the Arkansas Coastal Plain, $792 for the Mississippi Coastal Plain, $3,950 for the Oklahoma Rolling Plain, and $5,084 for the Texas Blackland Prairie.

Those owners who had full equity in their farm real estate tended to be older than those who had real-estate mortgages, but aside from this and related factors there is little evidence to show that the mortgaged owners performed differently as farmers than the debt-free owners.

Much of the accumulated capital used by owners and tenants in the region came from farm earnings. These earnings have frequently been small. Even with the relatively good farm income conditions prevalent in 1942, 82 per cent of the owners, renters, and croppers in the Arkansas Coastal Plains area, 81 per cent of those in the Mississippi Coastal Plains, and 25 per cent of those in the Oklahoma Rolling Plains had operator's earnings of less than $570. The net family incomes were considerably higher but still 72 per cent of the farm operators in the Arkansas area, 63 per cent of those in the Mississippi area, and 10 per cent of those in the Oklahoma area were less than $1,000 in 1942. The survey data do not indicate the full extent to which the various operators have benefited through the receipt and use of inheritances, gifts, and family help. However, 22 per cent of the farm owners in the Arkansas area, 24 per cent of those in the Mississippi area, 11 per cent in the Oklahoma area, and 24 per cent of those in the Texas area acquired the first tract of their present farms in whole or in part through inheritance or through gifts. Further evidence of the importance of inheritances, gifts, and family help as a source of farming capital is suggested by the fact that a large proportion of owners, particularly in the Arkansas, Louisiana, and Mississippi areas, started as owners or acquired ownership status at a relatively early age.

Off-farm earnings have provided an important source for the capital used by the owners and tenants in their farming operations. In 1942, 70 per cent of the farmers covered in the Arkansas sample, 82 per cent of those in the Mississippi area, 53 per cent of those in the Oklahoma area, and 36 per cent of those in the Texas area reported receipts from off-farm work. Almost three-fourths of these farmers had off-farm earnings of over $50 and a fair number of operators, particularly in the Mississippi and Oklahoma area, reported off-farm earnings of over $1,000. For the regional sample more than one-half of the owners and renters and nine out of ten of the croppers reported off-farm work.

In the Arkansas and the Oklahoma Rolling Plains oil royalties and lease funds provided an important source of farming capital. Other miscellaneous sources of capital and income were supplied by pensions, soldier's bonuses, and rental payments on other property. The various sources of capital are not uniformly important in all cases. The particular source that is of strategic importance varies according to the particular needs of the individual farmer. Important as it is, the availability and use of capital is not always the bottleneck or determining factor affecting tenure status. Other significant factors such as weather conditions, market prices, farm labor, or the operator's managerial ability frequently become the strategic and limiting factors.

Legal Factors

Underlying tenure performance are many factors subject only in small measure to control by the individual farmer. One of the chief of these is legal regulations. Two legal systems have influenced the development of tenure law in the region. The Common Law of England was adopted as the basis of jurisprudence in Arkansas, Mississippi,

Oklahoma, and Texas. French and Spanish civil law has a marked effect in Louisiana, and to some extent in the other states, chiefly in that the community property system and homestead exemption laws are of Spanish origin.

The legal rights of farm people in the land they farm are important factors influencing how it will be used. The full owner has the maximum control over his land, subject of course to certain prior rights of society, and limited by the nature and scope of his title and by miscellaneous contractual restrictions in deeds, mortgages, or purchase contracts. The tenant has less control than the owner over the land he farms and the cropper less than the tenant. Tenant and cropper rights in the land are conferred by contract with the landlord, either written, oral, or implied. Obviously the landlord or employer can confer upon his tenants or croppers no greater rights in the land than he himself possesses, but, within the limitations of legality, he is free to restrict them as he desires.

Owner rights in farm lands held by various types of owners in the region are far from uniform as also are the reasons for holding title. These factors influence the use of farm land whether actual operation is by the owner, tenant, or cropper.

Landowners have been classified as public, institutional, individual, and estate. Ownership of farm land by agencies of the state usually is intended to be temporary, pending sale. This is equally true of tax-forfeited lands, school, and other trust lands. Leases of publicly-owned land, reflecting the purposes of holding, are drawn to facilitate sale and for short terms ranging from 1 to 6 years, the exception in the region being 16th section school lands in Mississippi where the lease term is 15 years. Institutional land, like much public land, frequently is temporarily held by unwilling owners who acquire title in collecting debts. Laws in all 5 states limit the maximum period of ownership. Leases, necessarily, must be for relatively brief periods or be subject to termination on sale.

Title to land by individual ownership may be held by unmarried individuals, by the husband or wife as separate property, by the spouses or others in one of several forms of joint ownership. Two schemes of marital property right are found in the region. One, developed from the common law, is found in Arkansas, Mississippi, and Oklahoma. The other, the community property system, an institution of the civil law, is established in Louisiana and Texas, and is optional in Oklahoma. In the so-called common-law states, "all the property of the spouses is owned separately by either the husband or the wife, or perhaps by both as tenants in common, joint tenants, or tenants by the entirety." In the community property states, the property of the spouses is either the separate property of the husband, the separate property of the wife, or a part of the "common fund of matrimonial gains called the community property." The exact ways in which these two systems influence tenure performance poses an interesting but largely unanswered question from the data of the present study.

Title to land is passed to others upon death of the owner by will or, in the absence of a will, by descent. The right to dispose of property by will is not a natural right but is a creature of statute and therefore subject to regulation and restriction by the state. Laws of the 5 states transmitting property by will and descent vary greatly.

A testator's right to freely devise his separate property and his interest in common property is limited by the nature and scope of the title under which he holds, by dower or curtesy rights, by homestead rights of the surviving spouse and minor children, and by other miscellaneous rights of the survivors. Title to land descends to the heirs subject to many of these same limitations. In Louisiana, children and their descendants and the decedent's parents, known as "forced heirs," cannot be disinherited, except for certain statutory reasons. Only a portion of the estate can be willed to whomsoever is deemed most deserving, and that person must be a legal heir.

The period of time land is under estate control may be relatively short, pending administration of the estate by the courts, or it may be prolonged during the minority of children and during the life of the surviving spouse holding dower, curtesy, or homestead rights.

It is common knowledge that farm estates are frequently mishandled. The degree of misuse is often related to the duration of the estate, sex of the surviving spouse, and age of heirs. Of interest in this connection is the question whether the Louisiana heritage system of devolution to "forced heirs," or the systems prevailing in the other four states of the region, which allow greater freedom to the testator, results in better operated farms, both before the parent's decease and afterwards. Also, whether the granting to the surviving spouse and minor heirs of rights to the rents and profits of the family homestead, particularly under Oklahoma and Texas laws, is more conductive to good farm operation than are arrangements under the laws of the other states, including the creation of trust estates under Louisiana law.

In legal theory, a tenant is one who pays the landlord cash or a share of the crop, or both, for the use of land, whereas a cropper is one who receives a share of the crop from his employer as payment for his labor and is merely an employee. The criterion for ascertaining whether the legal relationship between the contracting parties is landlord-tenant or employer-cropper is their intent as evidenced by the contractual agreement. A most important determinant of intent is the owner's disposition of his legal possession or "dominion" over the land to the other party. Where, by the terms of the contract, the landlord surrenders dominion over the land to the other party, the relationship of landlord-tenant is created. On the other hand, where, under the agreement, the landowner does not surrender the land but agrees to pay the occupant a share of the crop for cultivating and gathering, the cultivator is a cropper, not a lessee, and the relationship is that of employer-employee. The cropper has no estate in the land but merely a right to possession incident and dependent upon the performance of his personal engagement. The index of management for the sample farmers of the region indicates that croppers have a minimum of control over details of management.

Farm leases prevalent in the region have been grouped into 4 main types: written 1-year, written 2-years and over, oral 1-year, and oral indefinite. Rights under each type are limited by the terms of the agreement as interpreted by state laws, which vary considerably. The oral 1-year lease is the type most frequently used in the region.

Under the laws of Arkansas, Mississippi, and Texas, a tenant, unless it is otherwise agreed, takes leased premises as he finds them and makes repairs, if he desires, at his own expense. The same rule applies in Oklahoma to improvements other than dwellings. In that state, in the absence of an agreement to the contrary, the landlord must put premises leased "for occupation of human beings" in a condition fit for occupancy and thereafter keep them in repair. In Louisiana, the landlord, unless otherwise agreed, is bound to deliver premises to the tenant in good condition and also maintain them, except for certain minor repairs which the tenant must make.

A comparison of the obligation to repair leased farm dwellings under prevailing practices in the sample areas, and the legally implied incidence of that obligation when unchanged by contractual arrangements, is of considerable interest. The relationship, except for labor costs, appears generally inverse. In view of the laws in each state, one would reasonably expect prevailing practice to place all costs of repairing dwellings on the tenants in the Arkansas, Mississippi, and

Texas areas and on the landlord in Oklahoma. The reverse, however, except for labor costs in Arkansas, Mississippi, and Texas, appears to be the most common practice.

Laws relating to removal by tenants or croppers, in the absence of agreement, of their agricultural fixtures or improvements placed on leased premises are most restrictive in Oklahoma and most liberal in Louisiana. In Louisiana the landlord may compel removal or he may elect to keep the improvements, paying therefore a fair value. No state in the region except Louisiana imposes any legal duty on a landlord to pay his tenants or croppers for the unexhausted value of improvements left on leased premises, unless he has so agreed.

The extent to which reliance on custom or reliance on law tends to dominate tenure practices varies with neighborhoods and communities. Although in the case of sharecroppers well-established custom calls for an equal division of the crop or its proceeds between the cropper and his employer, the usual terms are standardized only for cotton and corn. A wide diversity of arrangement as between neighborhoods occurs with respect to other crops and livestock. The custom of oral leases in the Mississippi Coastal Plain area is so common that in many neighborhoods a written lease is regarded as a mark of distrust. Local customary practices define credit relationships in less detail than those of the lease. They are regarded as more personal and based on individual differences and capacities.

There are two principal types of credit in the region: long term, secured by real-estate mortgages; and short term, obtained without security or secured by pledge of crops or chattels. Real-estate credit is used mainly to buy farms; short term credit is used to finance current crop production, to buy livestock and farm equipment, and for family living.

Both the lien and title theories of real-estate mortgages prevail in the region. Deficiency judgments may be had in all states. Only in Arkansas is a period for redemption allowed after foreclosure sale. The predominant credit base for short term loans in the region is the debtor's crops and chattels. Liens on crop or chattels to secure a loan may be either statutory or contractual. Statutory liens are conferred on landlords only for rent owing or for advances of cash or supplies made to tenants and croppers by the landlord for purposes of crop production. A contractual lien may be conferred on anyone supplying credit, but it is usually junior to the statutory liens unless the latter have been waived. A statutory lien for advance is not conferred on landlords in Oklahoma. A landowner, landlord, tenant, or cropper can pledge, as security for a loan, only his particular interest in a crop. This interest varies by states and also varies depending on whether the rental agreement creates a tenancy, a "tenancy in common" in the crop, or a cropper relationship. Not only crops already planted but also crops to be planted within the current year may be mortgaged. In Texas mortgage on unplanted crops may extend to any number of succeeding years. Obviously, chattel mortgages on livestock, farm machinery, and equipment also may be made and, except in Arkansas, the pledge may include personal property exempt to every family from forced sale.

For croppers and tenants in the lower management score brackets, the landlords generally made the decisions relative to obtaining production and family living credit. As management scores increased, these decisions were made more frequently by the tenants.

Neighborhood and Community Institutions

Finally it may be said that individual tenure arrangements are conditioned by the institutions of the local area in which the farm family lives. In turn the system of institutions results from the interaction of many factors, including source of settlers, time of settlement, physical environment, and state of technological development. For the purpose of studying tenure characteristics in the Mississippi Coastal Plain, five types of neighborhoods were distinguished, each with more or less definite characteristics. These consist of mixed, single racial, owner, plantation, and plantation transition types. Among the single racial neighborhoods cotton farms predominated but were least common in the owner neighborhoods. Plantation neighborhoods show a much higher percentage of cotton farms than the plantation transition type. The latter approaches the mixed type, which tends more to livestock and mixed farming. The sharpest contrast exists between the single racial and the plantation transition type of neighborhoods.

Relative to socio-economic status, the single racial type, either all white or all Negro, is strikingly homogeneous, showing a strong modal group with normal distribution above and below the mode. In the plantation neighborhoods the croppers cluster in the three lower intervals of the socio-economic status scale. Owners are in much higher intervals, with broad gaps separating them from the cropper families. Farm operations are largest in the plantation neighborhoods. Owner neighborhoods have the narrowest range in scale of operation and all neighborhood types, except the plantation transition, include one or more neighborhoods with farms falling within the smaller scale groups. Although all of the neighborhoods under consideration are agricultural, some of them, on the basis of farm operators' earnings operate at a net loss. Most of the deficit is made up by nonfarm work. Owner neighborhoods present the widest range of educational achievement.

In the Rolling Plains factors of geography are combined with modern automobile transportation in such a way as to give a distinctive type of neighborhood-community pattern. Although traditional type neighborhoods are found in the Rolling Plains, they are not universal and they do not as a rule add up in cluster fashion to form the community. Neighborhood and community institutions have been greatly influenced in the Rolling Plain by the increasing size of farms and the consequent decreasing number of families. Size of farm operation in this area tends to be a better index of status than tenure. Also there is a tendency for status to be increasingly accounted for in terms of responsibility for management rather than in terms of race and tenure.

In the Rolling Plains area the trend is toward the town centered church and schools. These churches at present, however, reach mainly the landholding families. On the other hand, the open country churches of the Czech and German groups in the Texas Blackland area reach all tenure groups. Land tenure patterns in these areas tend to set the limits for the location of schools and to some extent they influence the type of agricultural subjects taught. In looking forward to future planning it cannot be too strongly emphasized that the differing tenure attitudes found in the several neighborhoods and communities set a practical foundation upon which any and all action programs must be carried forward.

Appendix A

DEFINITION AND EXPLANATION OF TERMS[1]

ACRES

On many farms it was difficult to decide how many acres should be included in the cropland figure. In Texas, for example, Johnson grass had taken over nearly all of some farms. Sometimes it was harvested for hay, sometimes grazed and sometimes entirely abandoned. In other instances it was on land usually used for crops. Frequently it was cultivated to varying extents with the intention of getting a better hay crop. On some farms it over-ran a crop which had been planted.

In Arkansas, Lespedeza, although usually sowed for hay or pasture, offered a wide variety of situations. In both states, however, the enumerators entered a total cropland figure which was, in their best judgment, a correct figure. In editing the schedules, it was assumed that the total cropland figure was correct so that the parts were adjusted to fit that total. An exception to this procedure was made in Mississippi where the total cropland figure was built up from the parts since the total cropland was not entered on the printed schedule. In the other states, in some cases, garden and idle cropland had been omitted by the enumerator from the

[1] The definitions presented herewith were worked out in a general way during the formulation of the schedules but were extensively revised and added to during the tabulation and analysis of the data. This work was coordinated through the Regional Office by means of a 5 x 8 card system. Each tenure worker in the region was a cooperator in this work and was furnished a complete file of the definitions together with the various changes as the work progressed. Necessary changes in old definitions and additions of new ones were accomplished by adjusting the card files accordingly. The definitions were not officially adopted for project use until passed on by all workers concerned. During the course of the study it was discovered that there existed within the region a considerable diversity in the use of terms. Regional clearance in the use of these terms is considered to have been one of the important advantages of the regional research approach. In the past, valid comparison of area data has been greatly handicapped. In many instances comparisons have not been attempted in the face of variations in definitions; in other instances researchers have made spurious comparisons due to differences of which they were unaware in the usage of terms.

total cropland. In such instances these figures were edited into the total acreage. In cases where the land was not included in total cropland but a hay crop was harvested, the physical acreage was shown as pasture (improved pasture in Texas, open pasture in Arkansas) but the harvested acreage was included in the acres in hay crop and was also counted as double cropped so that the acres would not be included in the physical acres in cropland.

Cotton was listed separately for all states, truck and garden acreage was combined because it was difficult to separate the acreages in Mississippi and Arkansas. In those states, and to some extent in Texas, a large acreage of truck and garden represented a cash crop. The acreage of one additional cash crop was handled on an individual crop basis. This crop varied by states: Oklahoma, wheat; Arkansas and Mississippi, peanuts; Texas had no other single important cash crop, so a measure of cropland grass pasture in rotation was tabulated. The other crops were grouped into grain, feed crops (corn, grain sorghum headed or combined, velvet beans, oats, and occasionally other grains harvested for feed grains), hay and forage crops (hay, silage, sorghum bundle feed), annual rotation pastures (sudan, small grain, idle cropland, including summer fallow), and other acres in cropland. Other acres included cash crops not specified and crops planted for government payment. Most of the crops offered little difficulty in classification since they were harvested according to the intent at time of planting. Crops with two types of yields, such as alfalfa seed and hay, and those with several possible types of yields depending upon the method of harvest, raised questions of classification.

The latter type problem was very difficult in cases of crop failure. If alfalfa seed was produced the crop was classed as a cash crop. All peanuts in Oklahoma were also classed as cash crops. The primary purpose of raising these crops was for sale of the seed and not for the hay. If part of the production were sold and part fed, as in the case of corn and oats in some cases, the usual or chief disposal was employed. Annual rotation pasture included those crops stated as pastured in 1942. It is very likely that all crops in Mississippi and Arkansas, including cotton, were pastured to some extent. Some sudan in Oklahoma in 1942 was a complete failure and no pasturage was realized. In such cases the acreage was classed Other. Sudan harvested as hay was included in hay and forage crop acreages. In Texas, hubam and sweet clover harvested for seed were included in other cash crops, but if they were harvested for hay, were included in hay and forage crop acreages. Acreages of crops destroyed by greenbugs or which failed for any reason were classified according to the usual disposal of such crops.

Annual rotation pasture. Crops pastured but not harvested by mechanical means.

Commercial truck. Truck crops, orchard and small fruit planted primarily for sale. Does not include home garden.

Cotton. Cotton *planted.*

Cropland. Total cropland acreage in the sum of acres in crops, truck garden, orchard, idle cropland, rotation pasture and open pasture.

Cropland pasture. Includes meadow and Johnson grass grazed. Acreages tabulated in this category are included by the AAA in total cropland. Similar land not included by the AAA in total cropland is tabulated as non-crop open pasture.

Double cropped. The term "double cropped" usually refers to two plantings of different crops on the same physical acreage. Soybeans or peas planted between the rows of 12 acres of corn or in the rows at laying-by time were counted as 12 acres of each crop, with 12 acres being shown as double cropped. A summer crop followed by a winter crop such as vetch or oats was counted as double cropped land. Likewise, land left idle during the summer but planted to a winter cover crop was counted as double cropped. Neither the cutting of two crops of alfalfa nor the planting of two crops in alternate rows was considered as double cropping. In the latter case, half of the acreage was shown for each crop. The complication arising from reported harvest of hay from non-crop open pasture was handled by classifying the land as pasture, counting the acreage as hay, and counting the same acres as double cropped, since two uses were made. This procedure makes it possible to check the total acres in cropland against the sum of parts making up the whole. When double cropped acres are subtracted out, the difference between "total acres in cropland" and the sum of all tabulated parts is comprised of acres in other cash crops, acres planted for AAA benefit payments, acres left on the ground and acres turned as green manure crops, none of which were tabulated.

Farm. All land used (owned and/or rented) by the farmer and his family, laborers hired by him, or sub-tenants directly under his supervision, was considered as constituting the farm. Land rented out to managing tenants was deducted though it might have been a part of the ownership unit. Land used for pasture in common by two or more farmers was allocated to those sharing in its use in proportion to the number of livestock each person grazed on it. Some difficulty was experienced in determining the acreage in cropper tracts. They were unsually built up by adding acres of specific crops to the cropper's share of pasture and woods used exclusively by him.

Farmstead and waste. All land not included as cropland, pasture, or woods is classified in this category. It includes farmsteads (exclusive of garden), roads, ponds, sinks, ditches, etc. On a few schedules idle cropland was entered as waste, but such entries were edited accordingly.

Feed grain. Corn and oats not clearly indicated as cash crops, and grain sorghums were the more common crops included.

Hay and forage crops. The usual hay crops included alfalfa, other legumes, sudan, millet, sweet sorghum, meadow, Johnson grass, and wild hay.

Idle cropland. Included summer fallow as well as cropland strictly idle.

Interplanted. Land planted in alternate (or ratio of two to one) rows of different crops on the same land. It also included cases of two crops planted in the same row, in which case the the total acreage is counted for each crop, as well as being classed as double cropped and interplanted.

Intertilled. Land planted with row crops and subject to cultivation. In general, all land in crops other than hay (clovers including hubam, alfalfa, lespedeza, meadow and Johnson grass), small grains (wheat, oats, barley, rye and rice), and flax were classed as intertilled. Usually in Oklahoma, and in Texas to a somewhat lesser extent, Sudan is planted in rows and is probably cultivated even though sometimes pastured. For ease in coding, all sudan in Texas and Oklahoma was considered a row crop; in the other states the classification varied.

Legumes. All legumes were included whether planted as a summer crop or as a winter cover crop.

Non-crop open pasture. All open pasture not included with cropland acres was classified in this category. In Texas and Oklahoma open pasture was classified as "improved" or "unimproved" and tabulated separately. In other states only the total acreage was tabulated.

Peanuts. Acres of all peanuts planted regardless of disposal. Most of the peanuts were planted for market, but yields were so low in 1942 that only a small part of the crop was sold. Most of the hay was used on the farm. In Oklahoma and Texas the acres in peanuts were included with other crops, while in other states they were tabulated separately.

Rented out. This item differentiates those who rent out land and therefore exercise landlord functions in addition to their farm operations as described in detail by the schedule data. Rented-out acres were not considered as part of the home farm. Therefore, no inventory data, crop and livestock organization data, labor data, etc., were enumerated on such acreages. Net income received from such acreages was included in non-farm income. The leasing of mineral rights was tabulated independently as a separate landlord function.

Rent tract. The total of acres in the tract of land rented from a specific landlord. It is a measure of physical size of farm for each type of lease.

Truck and garden. All land planted in orchard, truck crops, and garden. No attempt was made to separate commercial truck from that planted solely for home use. In many cases it was impossible to determine the intent at planting time. Actual disposition varies from year to year with volume produced and price. The size of acreage is an indication of the extent to which the orchard or truck is commercial.

Wheat. Wheat was tabulated separately for Oklahoma, where it is an important cash crop. It included wheat planted with intention of harvest, in contrast to that planted for grazing, which was coded as annual rotation pasture. Some volunteer wheat was included in both categories. In other states the small amount of wheat grown was classified as a feed grain crop if used on the farm and as other cash crop if sold.

Woods. No tabulation between pastured and unpastured woods was made in Texas and Oklahoma because of the small acreages involved but in other states these categories were tabulated separately.

Acquisition

Acres acquired in first tract of farm. This relates to both full and part owners and concerns acquisition by inheritance, purchase, gift or homestead.

Source of cash in acquiring first tract of farm. Frequently, notes or the tenure history were used as additional sources of data to those listed under source of funds. Since Arkansas schedules did not incude the source of cash used as down payment, but did show the way the farm was paid out during the years, they had to be edited to determine the source of cash in acquiring first tract. In most cases the facts were on the schedule in the form of notes, but a few cases had nothing entered and were, therefore, coded not ascertainable.

Source of credit in acquiring first tract of farm. If the tract was inherited but the present owner assumed mortgage on tract, the mortgage was treated as credit. If equity in tract was inherited but remainder was purchased by assuming mortgage or by other means, the assumed mortgage was treated as credit.

Method of acquiring first tract of farm. Nine methods were listed. Other includes a gift plus purchase and/or mortgage, or other combinations of two or more of the methods listed. For example, if an owner had acquired his first tract of land partly through inheritance and partly through trade, it was tabulated as "Other."

Tracts of land acquired. Number of separate tracts acquired in making up this farm.

Years since first tract this farm acquired. Date of acquisition as reported on schedule was subtracted from 1942 to get the number of years since acquisition of the first tract of farm.

AGE

Age at marriage. Age at first marriage.

Age entered school of household/family members. The code of not ascertainable was given if no entry on the schedule was made for this question, yet other entries show the child had completed one or more grades. If, for a child of six or seven, no entry was made for "age entered school" or for "grade completed," it was assumed that the child had not entered school. A few older children and adults were reported as having never entered school and were so coded.

Age left home of household/family members. For the family head this was enumerated and edited as of starting earning life. This was edited to agree with the tenure history data table entries.

The history was on the person named as operator, and in the case of widows, their tenure during the time they were living with their husbands was considered to be that of their husbands. A few cases left home more than once. For these cases the tenure history will show "unpaid family laborer," then the occupation away from home, followed by "unpaid family laborer," and then a definite occupation in a subsequent year. The "number of years since first tenure reported" for these cases will be the number of years "on own" rather than the total number of years since first leaving home (going on own.) A few cases were described as orphans at an early age and an arbitrary age of twelve was taken for them to begin work even though the history showed ages of seven or even earlier. Cases of Negroes becoming croppers at seven or eight were accepted as stated if there was sufficient evidence to show that they were making a crop at that time. In one case, an estate was settled (to the satisfaction of the interested parties) when the person interviewed was six years old and he became owner of a tract of land. The note stated that when he became six the family considered that he was capable of making a crop and the land was divided. The age of six was used as stated.

"Age left home" was not changed if it checked within two years of the first tenure status reported. This allows for the differences in accuracy of reporting age (age on last birthday) and crop year (March to October). In cases where the status previous to first tenure reported was that of unpaid family laborer, the "age left home" was calculated by subtracting the year of first tenure reported from 1942 and the difference subtracted from present age. This computed figure was entered as age left home without regard to "age at marriage." This will mean that some farmers leave home before marriage, others a considerable number of years after marriage, and still others at time of marriage. The difference in "age at marriage" and "age left home" will partially represent the transition period of a boy's life from that stage where his father pays all expenses and gives him spending money, through the period of acquiring the ownership of livestock or possibly getting wages from father for certain jobs, to the status of relative economic independence. Economic independence will never become complete, but it does get to the point where income and expense data can be secured on the individual. Many boys in this transition period work from a few days to several months a year off the farm, pocketing all the money received for such work. They may or may not contribute any part of the money to the family living. Since this period is so variable in its details, the period is included in the category of "unpaid family laborer." It is apparent to even the most casual observer that the term "unpaid family laborer" is a misnomer and the status needs more detailed study. Unless more detailed data were available as to who was operating the land, "partnerships with father" or partnerships with two or more other members of the family were not counted as a tenure status. The entries on the schedules for these partnerships were: "farming at home," "farming with father," etc. A partnership with one brother was counted as being "on own."

In cases where it was clear that the person interviewed had been "on his own" previous to the first reported tenure status, a new column was set up to account for the period. The tenure during this period was edited to be as specific as the notes indicated.

Age of household/family members. Age at last birthday was tabulated for single years of life. Children not yet one year of age were coded zero. Age was entered by enumerators on most schedules as of date of last interview, which approximated the end of 1942. When Oklahoma schedules were transcribed to the regional forms, year of birth was subtracted from 1942, hence the regional schedule entry was age at last birthday for the close of 1942. For deceased members the age is age at death.

ANIMAL UNITS

All tenure groups except full owners were edited to include all livestock used. The method of entering livestock used but not owned varied from state to state, and it was necessary to make the summations as uniform as possible.

The average of beginning and ending inventory was used for determining the animal units for each class of livestock, in all states except Texas. For the Texas schedules the data were refined by adding a fraction of the purchases made during the year. The standards used were those suggested at the First Workers' Conference as follows:

	Animal Units
1 work animal	1
1 milk or beef cow or bull	1
2 heifers or steers	1
4 calves (dairy or beef)	1
7 ewes or rams	1
5 sows or fat hogs	1
10 pigs (or 1000 lbs. wt.)	1
100 hens	1
50 turkeys	1

The refinement used for the Texas schedules added to the average inventory the following fractions of livestock purchased as suggested at the First Workers' Conference:

½ of animal units of work stock purchased
½ of animal units of cattle purchased
⅓ of animal units of swine purchased
¼ of animal units of sheep purchased

Values were shown for beginning and ending inventory of used and owned livestock where such detail was available. There was little difficulty except for croppers. Arkansas showed the value of each class of livestock by ownership; the other states usually gave the number of animals without the value. This means that for croppers in all states except Arkansas, the value of farm business will not include livestock and equipment owned by landlords. Some of this is rather difficult to determine at best, with the landlord owning two tractors or perhaps 50 mules. The croppers will likely show one or two mules owned by landlord. However, there is little difference in the two situations. The landlord has several mules available and the cropper uses one or two depending upon the particular operation which he is doing. Some of the notes specified one mule, some two mules, where one mule and occasionally two mules were needed; others were not specific, but the equipment table showed one or two sets of harness; others stated that landlord furnished team and wagon for hauling cotton and the cropper furnished the labor. The most definite figure was edited onto the schedule for these cases. The edited data are as accurate as more specific entries of the enumerators, when the actual operation of a cropper tract of land is considered.

CHURCH

Church denomination of male and female heads. Membership was limited to whether or not the person officially belonged to the organization in question, without reference to participation, attendance, etc.

COLOR AND SEX

Color and national origin. This item brings together into workable groups and various cultural types of people sampled. In Arkansas, Louisiana, and Mississippi, the two types were white and Negro. While there were a few cases of cooperators born in England or other countries, such individuals had lost their former cultural identities so that such a breakdown would be meaningless. Then, too, only a few such cases were involved. All persons of some Negro blood were classified as Negro with no finer distinctions of degrees.

In Oklahoma, two categories were used in the code. The classification of "other" includes one owner born in Sweden, one owner born in Russia, one renter born in Germany, one Mexican cropper, one Negro cropper, and four Negro laborers. The cultural identity of these individuals was strong even though they had been in Oklahoma for some time.

In Texas the Negroes and Mexicans were combined in one group for most sorts although a breakdown of each group by sex of operator and a more detailed breakdown of national origin was made for certain comparisons.

Color and sex of head. The head is understood to be the operator.

COMMUNICATION

Communication index. A worksheet was made for this index, using the following weights:

						Yes	No
Automobile						2	0
All-weather roads						1	0
Visits to trade center by head							
per month:	0	1	2	3	4		
score:	0	¼	½	¾	1		
Electricity in home						1	0
Radio						1	0
Daily newspaper						1	0
Magazines						1	0
Farm paper						½	0

The index range is from 0 to 8.5

Roads listed on the state highway department's current county map as grade and drain are scored as all-weather.

Lighting from a windcharger was scored zero for electricity.

Possession of a radio out of service condition and not in use during previous twelve months was scored zero.

Daily newspaper does not include weekly or semi-weekly papers.

Magazines exclude farm papers or farm journals.

Farm paper includes any farm paper or farm journal.

CREDIT

Amount of real estate credit granted. This is the original amount of real estate mortgage still in effect during at least a part of 1942.

Credit was divided into real estate and other credit. An attempt was made to refine the other credit into production and consumption uses, but the purposes indicated on the schedule were not in sufficient detail to warrant such refinement. Then, too, it is quite likely that the other credit was used for a number of purposes which included both production and consumption.

Several factors were used to represent a realistic indication of credit for the purpose of financing the ownership of land. No minimum was set up for each factor, but rather a combination of all of the factors was used. For example, the length of term was usually ten years or longer, but if other factors were present which usually went with a real estate loan, and the length of term were only three years, such a case might well be classified as real estate credit. These factors are described as follows: Length of term: usually over ten years; purpose: to buy land, or to refinance a loan on land; security: mortgage on land; interest rate: low, (usually six per cent or less); source: Federal Land Bank, other bank, former owner, FSA; amount: the original loan of over one-third the valuation at the time.

Federal Land Bank credit used, 1942. This is the amount outstanding at the end of 1942 plus principal paid in 1942 to the Farm Credit Administration as a real estate loan and which is wholly secured by farm land mortgage as collateral. Also included are joint stock land bank loans and a few purchase contracts from the Federal Land Bank. In Oklahoma these data were secured from FCA records.

Farm Security Administration debt outstanding. This is the total amount owed to the Farm Security Administration at the end of 1942 on all types of loans. Grants are not included.

Farm Security Administration Rural Rehabilitation credit used, 1942. The largest amount of principal owed on a Rural Rehabilitation loan during 1942. It includes the amount outstanding at the beginning of the year plus any amount granted during the year. In Arkansas and Oklahoma these data were secured from the FSA records.

Farm Security Administration Rural Rehabilitation debt at beginning of 1942 (credit). The sum of rehabilitation loans carried over from 1941 or previous years. Some of this credit runs for as much as three years.

Farm Security Administration real estate credit used, 1942. The largest amount owed by the cooperator to the FSA during 1942 for the purchase of a farm and for which the farm is security. It is the amount of credit outstanding at the end of the year plus principal paid during the year.

Length of term of real estate credit. The number of years real estate credit is to extend from date originally obtained.

Other-than-real-estate credit outstanding. The amount still owed at the end of 1942. The amount owed on real estate credit, though not coded, can be derived by subtracting this figure from outstanding credit.

Outstanding credit. The total debt owed at the end of the year, including real estate credit, production credit, and credit for family living. Interest left unpaid was added to the principal to become the new principal owed at the beginning of 1943. Debts owed on land not considered a part of the operating unit are not included.

Payments on debts in 1942. The amount paid on principal of real estate and other credit during the year. It does not include current interest. The principal includes interest due in former years and unpaid at beginning of current year.

Production Credit Association or Feed and Seed credit used, 1942. These two types of loans, (1) Production Credit Association Credit, (2) Feed and Seed Loan, are identified separately. In either instance the amount specified in the new credit plus any indebtedness that may have been carried over from previous years. In Oklahoma these data were secured from FCA records; in the other states from the Farm and Family Schedules.

Purpose of real estate credit. Ordinarily real estate credit should be for the purpose of purchasing land or refinancing original loans on such purchases. However, some real estate loans are made for various other purposes. A few purely production and family living loans are classified as real estate credit because lenders required land mortgages for security.

Purpose of other-than-real-estate credit. Entries of "Furnish" on the schedules were coded as a combination of "To finance current crop production" and "Family living." Also, entries of "Rehabilitation" were coded as a combination of three purposes: (1) to buy livestock and farm equipment, (2) to finance current crop production, and (3) family living.

Security for other-than-real-estate credit. Ordinarily the security for such credit is a crop lien or chattel mortgage. However, some farmers obtain their credit without execution of written mortgages.

Source of furnish credit used. Furnish credit was defined as credit used for family living. Since the usual FSA and PCA financial budgets by months include both operating costs and family living costs, credit from these sources was coded as both production and furnish credit unless there was definite statement that the full amount of the credit was used for production purposes.

Source of production credit used. Production credit was defined as credit used to purchase livestock, equipment, fertilizer, materials of various kinds, to make repairs, to pay labor, and to take care of other cash costs of the farm's operation.

Source of real estate credit. This covers all real estate credit, even though final payment was made during the year of the survey.

Source of production and furnish credit. This item is a combination of the two items: source of production credit used and source of furnish credit used. The emphasis is placed on the function of the landlord in the mortgagor-mortgagee relationship rather than the specific type of person or agency extending credit.

EDUCATION

Grade retardation of children. The average retardation of all children in the family. Dividing children into those in school and those completed schooling roughly divides them into age groups. Children under 5 years were not considered. Deceased children 5 years of age and over at time of death were classified as having completed school. Children 16 years of age and over who had never gone to school were classified in the completed school group.

Education of head. In Louisiana and Texas, where there were (1942) only seven years of grade school, the 8th grade was interpreted as the first year of high school; the 11th grade as the senior year of high school; the 12th grade as the first year of college and the 15th grade as the fourth year of college.

"Other" included all education above the fourth year of college, business training, vocational training, nurses' training, etc.

Head or spouse completing highest grade. The highest grade completed by either the male or the female head—whichever had the highest.

Household/family members education. The education was expressed on the schedule as highest grade completed.

Equipment

Equity in livestock and equipment owned (per cent). Value of livestock and equipment owned minus all credit used which did not have real estate as security, divided by the sum of value of livestock and equipment owned. Average inventory of livestock is used and the value of equipment includes the total value of car and truck regardless of the extent of non-farm use.

Rent tract value of livestock and equipment rented. As a general rule these data were not secured on the schedule for croppers in Mississippi. Entries were used, however, where shown.

Rent tract value of unpaid labor on improvements and equipment. A dollar value was placed on all labor applied by the tenant to the landlord's property. Quite a few tenants "keep up" the place as their sole payment of rent.

Types of equipment used. Items of costly equipment not generally owned by all farmers are listed if used (owned or rented) by the cooperator.

Type of power and size of equipment. The classification was based on an over-all examination of the equipment table and the presence or absence of workstock during the crop year, 1942. Some farmers changed type of power during the year. In such cases the month of change was the determining factor. Those farmers without cropland and those hiring all of their machine work done were coded as having no equipment.

Since the data on the schedule were for possession and not use, problems arose in regard to interpretation. Many tractor farmers had kept their horse-drawn equipment and some work stock for a few years after the purchase of the tractor. Most of these cases were coded as combinations, although it is fairly certain that the horse-drawn equipment was used to only a slight extent. The number of days of tractor use together with the number of acres in row crops aided in making a decision in such cases.

Certain items were considered as key items in classifying, cultivating equipment being a chief one. The presence of two row planters aided in deciding between one row and two row sizes in marginal cases. Georgia stocks, scratchers, crickets, Kellys, Averys, single stocks, Sutton harrows, and all turning plows up to 9 inches in size were counted as one-half row equipment. All two horse cultivators, riding cultivators and 12 or 14 inch turning plows were counted as one row equipment. "One-way" or two bottom plows were considered as two row equipment.

Value of equipment. All equipment located on the farm was included in estimating this figure, which was designated as the sale value at the end of the year. Usually equipment depreciates annually in value, but for many items the sale values actually increased in 1942 because of wartime shortages. Therefore, market values of some equipment, e.g. tractors in Oklahoma, were scaled down by the enumerators to approximately normal sale values.

Equipment purchased in 1942 was included. That used in 1942 but sold before the end of the year was not included in the ending inventory, money received from sale of such equipment being included as an item of income. The per cent farm use of cars and trucks was applied to the total value of cars and trucks to get that portion of their value to be included with farm equipment. The total value of equipment owned in partnership was included. Equipment borrowed for special jobs was not included in computing values. No values were obtained for Mississippi and Texas croppers except for equipment owned.

Value of equipment owned. The value at the end of 1942 of equipment owned entirely by the cooperator (including farm share of owned car and truck) plus his share of jointly-owned equipment, make up this figure. Because of inflated prices in 1942, the enumerators made downward revisions in the value of some items which actually would command a market price higher than the original cost. The figure actually recorded on the schedule was an approximation of normal market value.

Value of livestock and equipment owned. The sum of value of livestock owned and value of equipment owned as explained for the item "Value of farm business." For this item average inventory value of livestock is used and the value of equipment includes the total value of car and truck regardless of the extent of non-farm use.

Building depreciation. This includes the estimated amount of annual depreciation and/or expenditures actually made on building upkeep.

Cash rent paid. The amount of cash rent or cash value of standing rent paid to a landlord by the tenant operator.

Cost of cropper labor. The estimated value of crops and livestock products accruing to the cropper or tenant whose production is shown in the gross income for the farm unit.

Equipment repairs in 1942. The total cash expense on repairs and maintenance of the equipment used, representing expenditures of both landlord and tenant. It has the same limitation for Mississippi and Texas croppers as does value of equipment. The percentage used in determining the farm use inventory of cars and trucks was applied to repairs on these items and the dollar share was included in the total expenses. New purchases or differences paid in trades were not counted as repairs. The cost of all new parts and hired labor, including blacksmithing, was included. Expenditures for operating fuel were not included in this figure.

Fertilizer purchased. Copied from a list furnished the Regional Project by state workers. Commercial fertilizer was used mainly on cotton but also to some extent on corn and other crops. No fertilizer was used in Oklahoma or Texas.

Hired labor. Includes the estimated value of board as well as cash wages given hired workers in connection with the operation of the farm.

Interest charge on investment. A flat rate of 5 per cent was applied to value of farm business owned. For the Arkansas farms interest paid on real estate credit was deducted from this charge.

Interest on production credit. Interest and service charges paid or to be paid on short-term credit.

Livestock expenses. Includes such items as serums and veterinary services.

Machinery operation and repairs. Includes cost of fuel, lubricants, parts, and all blacksmith, garage work and machine hire. Cost of new equipment is not included.

Operator's labor. An estimate of the wage the operator would have had to pay someone else to do his work on the farm.

Real estate improvements. Cash expenditures for labor and/or materials by landlord or tenant are included. Major additions to the dwelling or outbuildings were not counted as repairs but were included in the ending inventory value of real estate improvements.

Share rental payment. Includes crop and livestock share rent paid. In cases where values of calves given in payment of rent were not shown on the schedule an estimate of $15.00 was applied.

Taxes paid. Includes personal, as well as real estate, taxes.

Unpaid family labor. This was copied from a list furnished the Regional Project by Oklahoma workers. For Arkansas a rate of $1.25 per day was applied to the days of unpaid family labor listed on the schedule. For Mississippi the same procedure was followed in the use of $1.50 as the daily rate.

FAMILY

Amount of support member gives family and family gives member. Coded in actual dollars, for each individual family member who had been away from the parental home one year or more.

At-home. Family is construed to mean the head, wife (or husband), children of head, stepchildren of head and adopted children of head. Any person who lived in the household during the past twelve months was listed as another member of the household. The non-family members of the household are divided into two groups: (1) persons related by blood or marriage to the head; and (2) persons not related to the head in any way.

"At home" is not a measure of labor supply but rather of residence, since it includes those who worked or attended school and returned home over the week end.

Members of the family include head, wife (or husband) children of head, stepchildren of head, and adopted children of head. Members of family were divided into two groups: (1) those living at home; and (2) those living away from home. The number of family members at home includes every member of the family who lived in the home any part of the past twelve months, unless notes or other information indicated that the person was visiting or was at home only temporarily. Thus, a member who died during the past twelve months and is shown to have lived in the home a part of the year is included in the total number of members in the family at home.

Members of household include persons in household related to family or any person other than a member of the family who is living in the household and is related by blood or marriage to the head of the family. Persons in household not related to family include any person living in household who is not related by blood or marriage to head of family.

Away-from-home members. Included are related individuals as nieces, nephews, grandchildren, etc.—not adopted but considered as adopted children—who have been a part of this economic unit but have been away twelve months during the past year. While these individuals lived in this home they were considered members of the household but not as members of the family.

Very few individuals were involved in this category. Included also in family away from home are "separated" and "divorced" living spouses of the head.

If a son has succeeded his father as head in the parental household, his younger brothers and sisters away from home were tabulated as away-from-home. These same brothers and sisters, however, when living in the house were considered not as members of the family but as members of the household, after the son became the head. In other words, these children would cease to be members of this family when neither parent is any longer head of the family. This does not affect in any way the cycle status of the family.

Birth order of living children of male head. This measure, when standardized in comparable age groups, provides for the study of participation and other factors for children in relation to order of birth. Because only the living children are tabulated, this measure is not a direct measure of fertility.

Cycle status of head. "Single person" signifies one who has never been married. Oldest child refers to living children only and includes stepchildren or adopted children. The tabulations for this item are set up in such a way so that normal families may readily be separated from broken families.

Marital status of head. All marriages beyond the second were coded as "Other" regardless of whether the person is now divorced, widowed, or married.

If data were lacking to classify a spouse as either widowed or divorced, the item was coded as widowed. "Single" indicates that head has never been married.

Stage in family cycle. Although broken families can be classified according to stage in the cycle of generations, they may not have direct comparability with single union matings for adaption to economic factors of production; hence they are separately coded. Single head may not be directly compared with married couples for factors such as unpaid family labor. Oldest child refers to living children only, but includes stepchildren and adopted children. The classification used is that developed by Charles P. Loomis in: "The Growth of the Farm Family in Relation to Its Activities," North Carolina A.E.S. Bul. No. 298, June, 1934; "The Study of the Life Cycle of Families," *Rural Sociology,* June, 1936, pp. 180-99. The distinction between stages 4 and 5 of this code is that developed by Gordon W. Blackwell, "Correlates of Stage of Family Development Among Farm Families on Relief," *Rural Sociology,* VII, pp. 161-74, June, 1942.

FAMILY LABOR

Man-equivalent days of family labor on farm. Family labor is the total of operator's labor and unpaid family/household labor on the farm. Hours, weeks, months, "all year," and cwt. of cotton picked were reduced to man-equivalent days as follows:

10 hours equal 1 day
1 week equals 5 days
1 month equals 20 days
1½ cwt. equals 1 day

Off-farm days of family labor. All entries of off-farm days of family labor were included excepting occupations of army and relief programs.

Receipts from off-farm work, family labor. All entries of family labor receipts from work off farm were included excepting occupations of army and relief programs.

FARM BUSINESS

Credit used as per cent of farm business owned. This is a measure of credit in 1942 expressed as a ratio to the farm business owned. The range extends to infinity since a few farms (laborers or croppers) owned nothing and had borrowed a considerable amount against the crop or against expected wage earnings.

Dollar equity in farm business. The owner's share of dollar equity in farm business was computed on the basis of farm business owned as follows: Real estate owned plus equipment owned plus livestock owned minus total outstanding credit equals farm investment owned.

Equity in farm business (per cent). This comprises value of farm business owned minus total debt as of July, 1942, divided by the value of farm business used.

Livestock value. This was not a tabulated item but was computed as the difference between value of farm business and the sum of values of real estate and equipment. No change in inventory value of workstock was made due to flunctuation in market value. Colts increasing in size were allowed to increase in value, and purchases and sales of workstock were shown as changes in inventory. In any event, the ending inventory for all livestock was taken. Nonoperating croppers in Mississippi and Oklahoma have incomplete data for livestock, no estimate being made of value of workstock used by this class of tenant.

Net worth. This measure of economic status is calculated by subtracting outstanding credit from value of farm business owned.

Per cent equity in farm business. The owner's share of per cent equity in farm business is the equity in total farm business, both owned and rented.

Quality of farm business. The quality of farm business is a measure of the earning capacity of the farm when compared with the average earning capacity of farms of its size. (See Appendix B, Scale of Operation and Farm Tenure, for further explanation.)

Rent tract value of farm business. This is dollar value of the amount of farm business for each lease. This item was tabulated by type of lease which indicates the ratio of rent to value of property leased.

Size of farm business. This measure is the composite of three measures of size: Value of farm business, Production Man-Work Units, and Acres in cropland. (See Appendix B, Scale of Operation and Farm Tenure, for further explanation.)

Value of farm business owned. The portion of the farm business owned and operated by the cooperator, including real estate, equipment (with farm share of car and truck) and livestock.

Value of farm business. The value of real estate used (owned and/or rented), plus closing inventory of livestock and equipment used (including farm share of car and truck). If the schedule did not indicate the percentage farm use of cars and trucks, it was edited thus: car or truck only, either was estimated as 90 per cent farm use in Oklahoma and Texas, 80 per cent farm use in Arkansas, and the usual per cent found on similar farms in Mississippi; car and truck, car estimated as 50 per cent farm use and truck 100 per cent farm use. Trucks used extensively for off-farm work, such as logging, were scaled down in proportion to the extent of such use. The full value of machinery owned in partnership was included. Value of livestock was not punched but was determined by subtracting the sum of value of real estate and value of equipment from value of farm business.

FEED

Alfalfa hay available for feed. The cooperator's portion, less sales, is tabulated separately for Oklahoma farms. For Texas farms it is tabulated with "other hay," while in the other states it is tabulated with "legume hay." For converting bales to tons where not shown, it was assumed that a bale of alfalfa hay weighs 67 pounds.

Corn available for feed. The amount remaining of production accruing to the cooperator after deductions of sales and home use. It may or may not have been used wholly for feed, since most farmers used a small amount for seed. It is simply the amount available for feeding livestock if the farmer needed it.

Grain sorghum available for feed. This item includes the cooperator's portion of harvested grain less that sold or to be sold. For Mississippi any entry of grain sorghum was converted to corn equivalents and tabulated with other grain, while for other states it was tabulated separately.

Johnson grass hay available for feed. The cooperator's portion, less sales, was tabulated as a separate item for Texas farms, while it was included with other hay for other states.

Legume hay available for feed. The cooperator's portion, less sales, of all legumes harvested for hay was tabulated as a separate item for Arkansas and Mississippi farms. For Oklahoma farms it includes all legume hay except alfalfa (which is tabulated as a separate item). Legume hay is included with other hay in Texas. For converting bales to tons where not shown, it was assumed that a bale of peanut hay weighs 60 pounds, soybean hay 57 pounds, and other legume hay 67 pounds.

Meadow hay available for feed. The cooperator's portion, less sales, is tabulated separately for Texas farms but included with other hay in other states. For converting bales to tons where not shown it was assumed that a bale of meadow hay weighs 67 pounds in Oklahoma and Texas and 65 in Arkansas.

Oats hay available for feed. The cooperator's portion, less sales, was tabulated with other hay in Oklahoma and Texas, while in other states it was tabulated separately. For converting bales to tons where not shown, it was assumed that a bale of oats hay weighs 67 pounds.

Oats available for feed. Only the cooperator's portion of oats harvested for grain, less those sold or to be sold, was included. As in the case of corn a part of the amount shown for this item is actually used for seeding purposes.

Other grain available for feed (corn equivalents). The cooperator's portion of miscellaneous grain crops harvested, less sales, home use, and those specifically indicated on the schedule as being for seed, were converted to corn equivalent units and tabulated as other grain. Conversion factors based on Henry and Morrison, *Feeds and Feeding,* are as follows:

	corn equivalent
One bushel threshed grain sorghum equals	.95
100 pounds grain sorghum heads equals	1.41
One bushel barley equals	.81
One bushel wheat equals	1.02
One bushel cowpeas equals	.97
One bushel soybeans equals	1.20
One bushel mixed grains equals	.92
One bushel sweet potatoes equals	.33
One bushel velvet beans equals	1.10
100 pounds velvet beans equals	1.50

Other hay available for feed. The cooperator's portion, less sales, of all hay not tabulated elsewhere is included in this miscellaneous category. Some of the types found include sudan, millet, wild hay, oats in Oklahoma and Texas, other small grains, legumes in Texas, and Johnson grass and meadow hay for all states except Texas. For converting bales to tons where not shown, the following conversion factors were used:

Peanuts	60 pounds
Soybeans	57 pounds
Sudan and millet	60 pounds
Meadow	65 pounds (Arkansas) and 67 pounds (Oklahoma)
All other	67 pounds

Sorghum hay and forage available for feed. The cooperator's portion, less sales, of both sweet and grain sorghum harvested for hay or forage was tabulated for farms in all states. For converting bundles and bales to tons where not shown, it was assumed that a bundle weighs 10 pounds and a bale 67 pounds. Grain sorghum cut for forage was converted on the basis of 65 pounds per bale.

Velvet beans available for feed. This includes the cooperator's portion of harvested beans less those sold or to be sold. For Mississippi, where a considerable number of farmers feed velvet beans to livestock, this item was tabulated separately, while for other states it was converted to corn equivalents and included with other grain. It is likely that a high percentage of velvet beans were harvested primarily for seed, but if the enumerator did not specify that purpose on the schedule, it was assumed that they were available for feed.

FERTILITY

Children born to male head. This includes all children of the male, born to this or any precious union. It does not include his step children, adopted children or, foster children. Stillbirths were not counted as children born.

Children born to male was the measure adopted (rather than children born to female) because the farm production and tenure data are characteristics associated with the age, earning life, and marital status of the male head. This procedure of relating fertility of the male to his occupational history is more completely logical in a tenure study than to relate the fertility of the present female head to his occupation history. The schedules provide a more complete record of his offspring by former matings than for the female head's former matings.

Fertility index. Specific rates for five year age groups of rural-farm women in the U. S., 1940, (multiplied by 5) were cumulated into an ogive, giving total children born to specified five year age groups of women 10 to 49 years (at the end of each five year age period). It was assumed that husbands of this sample were on the average 2½ years older than their wives and that the women of this sample were to be compared with the 90 per cent of the rural-farm women of U. S. who marry during their lifetime. The female cumulated rate was divided by .90 and used for the next older five year age group of males. This is the expected number of children for families of the sample classified by age of husband. The actual number of children born to the male head divided by the expected number gave the fertility ratio for a family. The code for this item gives the specified ranges in the fertility ratio as punched on the card. (For further explanation see Appendix B, The Fertility Index.)

HEALTH

Days unable to work during past year. The field workers recorded days unable to work during the past year; and for those not of working age, the days of comparable illness were recorded. This measure ignores illness of less serious nature that partially reduces efficiency.

Telephone calls. Only the calls made for medical advice were tabulated. Those made for business purposes or to make an appointment were not included.

HIRED LABOR

Man-equivalent days of hired labor on farm. Where days of labor were not available the following cash equivalents were used: Oklahoma cottonsnapping cash wage totals were divided by $6.50 to give number of days worked; Texas cotton picking cash wage totals were divided by $3.25; other wage rates were considered to average $2 per day in Oklahoma and Texas, $1.50 per day in the other states.

HOUSEHOLD

Months at home of household/family members. A member of the family who died during the past year and who is shown to have lived some months in the home is treated as a member of the family living at home the specified months during the year. For all nonfamily members of the household in the home at date of interview, the number of months in this home during past year was the entry. The family residence of the individual is the basis for months at home. Thus a husband who is supporting his family by working away from home any part of, or even all of the year is designated as in the home twelve months. Similarly, a son or daughter attending college, and economically a member of the family, is considered at home.

Persons in household. This, in addition to any person other than head, mate, children, stepchildren, or adopted children of head, includes any person who lived in the household during the past twelve months. There are some instances where it is known from other information on the schedule that two related but distinctly separate family groups lived in one household. On such schedules these related individuals are included in the number in the household, but not in the family.

Relation to head of household/family members. In order to make the data on the punch card internally consistent, if a female is designated as operator of the farm, then she is also designated as head of the household/family, even though her husband is a member of the family. A few wives were so designated as operator of the farm because the husband worked away from home or was physically incapacitated for operation of the farm. To the extent that the data were available, all enumerated living or deceased former spouses of the designated head are included.

INCOME

AAA adjustment payment (1942). This is the amount of adjustment payment computed by the AAA to have been earned by the cooperator. It does not include adjustments for increases for small payments or deductions for administrative expense. Practice and parity payments were handled in the same way.

Crop sales gross income. The cash equivalent of all items sold, to be sold, or traded from the 1942 crop production was included in this tabulation. For each state, income from each of the three major crops was tabulated individually, with income from miscellaneous crops being a residual obtained by subtracting the sum of the three tabulated items from total crop sales. Individual crops were tabulated as follows: (1) Cotton sales. This represents returns from both lint and seed. Cotton stored in connection with a CCC loan is considered sold at the amount of the loan. In cases of cotton having to be hauled to a distant warehouse, involving considerable expense, such expense has been deducted from the gross returns. (2) Wheat sales. Wheat loan prices have been used where applicable, with transportation charges to a storage elevator deducted from the gross returns. (3) Corn sales. Corn traded for meal was excluded, being considered as home use, whereas corn traded for feed was considered as sold.

Farm's 1942 AAA adjustment payment. The amount computed by AAA to have been earned in 1942 for crop acreage adjustment on the farm (AAA definition) of which the cooperator's operations were all or part. This does not include adjustments for increases in small payments or deductions for administrative expense.

Farm's 1942 AAA allowable adjustment payment. The maximum amount available to the farm for acreage adjustment in 1942 if the farm were in full performance. This relates to the farm as defined by AAA of which the cooperator's operation was all or a part.

Farm's 1942 allowable practice payment. The maximum amount available to be earned by the adoption of conservation practices on the farm as defined by AAA of which the cooperator's operation was all or a part.

Farm's 1942 AAA parity payment. The amount of parity payment computed by AAA to have been earned in 1942, for the farm of which the cooperator's operation was all or a part. Parity payments were made in 1942 on wheat only. The data were secured from AAA records.

Farm income, percentage of gross income. This percentage was computed by dividing the sum of crop sales, livestock product sales, livestock sales (corrected for purchase and changes in inventory) home use of crops, livestock, and livestock products by the gross income. As computed it is a measure of dependency upon the farm for income.

Family earnings. This was computed by deducting operating expenses and interest charge on investment (exclusive of value of unpaid family labor and operator's labor) from gross farm income. It is the compensation, including the value of family living from the farm, for operator's labor and management, and for labor of unpaid members of the operator's family.

Farm's 1942 AAA practice payment. The amount of conservation (practice) payments computed by AAA to have been earned (not to exceed the maximum allowable) on the farm (AAA definition) of which the cooperator's operations were all or a part. This does not include adjustments for increases for small payments or deductions for administrative expense.

FSA cumulative grants exclusive of 1942. The sum of all amounts listed as direct grants to the cooperator, by FSA or its predecessor agencies, during the period 1933 to 1941, inclusive.

FSA grants, 1942. The number of dollars which the cooperator received in direct grant from FSA in 1942. Data were secured from FSA records.

Gross income. All income of the cooperator and his family was included. Sales include "sold, to be sold, and traded." Income from the following sources, with further breakdowns of each, was coded and tabulated: (1) Crop sales. (2) Livestock sales. (3) Livestock product sales.

(4) Home use of farm products. (5) Miscellaneous farm income. (6) Nonfarm income.

Gross farm income. Gross income includes items from crop sales plus gross from livestock sales plus gross income from sales of livestock products plus value of home use of farm products plus value of crop and livestock productions accruing to the operator's croppers or tenants plus value of share rent paid to landlord. It does not include those items classified under miscellaneous farm income and nonfarm income.

Home use of farm products. All products were valued at market price at the farm. Products given away were included as home use at the same unit value. Prices of some products, milk for example, varied widely from farm to farm in all states other than Mississippi, since the farmer was usually asked to place a "right" value on the product.

Home used products were classified as follows: (1) Home use of beef. (2) Home use of pork. (3) Home use of dairy products. (4) Home use of poultry and eggs. (5) Home use of vegetables, fruits, and other edible crops. (6) Home use of wood products. This item is not tabulated separately but was dervived by considering it a residual to account for the difference between the sum of values of tabulated items and the total of all home used products.

Livestock products sales, gross income.

(1) Dairy products sales included butter, cream, and milk sold. Sales of milk varied from bulk milk sold for cheese to bottled milk involving considerable labor expenditures on the raw product. Marketing costs were not deducted from the sale price, but if the farmer shipped cream or bulk milk the money received by him as reported to the enumerator likely had transportation charge deducted.

(2) Eggs sales. Since comparatively few farms kept records, this item was difficult to estimate. The farmer was requested to estimate his daily production at four different dates; corrections were made for changes in the number of layers. This was checked against the farmer's estimate of eggs used in the home plus hatching, plus sales. In case of variation an average of the two results was entered on the schedule.

(3) Other income included that received from sales of wool and hides and receipts from breeding fees. These were not tabulated separately but were computed as residuals.

Livestock sales. Sales were adjusted for changes in inventory and purchases during the year. Gifts received were included as purchases and livestock given away were included as sales at estimated values, since most gifts over a period of years were considered as trades, rather than as true gifts.

The sales of livestock were classified as follows: (1) Cattle sales. (2) Hog sales. (3) Poultry sales. (4) Other livestock sales. This was not a tabulated item but was obtained by subtracting the sum of the preceding three tabulated items from the total income from livestock sales.

Miscellaneous farm income. Miscellaneous farm income was classified as follows:

(1) AAA payments.

(2) Wood products sold. Items included in this category are timber, pulp wood, posts, fuel wood, naval stores, and stumps.

(3) Off-farm work. Remuneration to any member of the family considered as part of the cooperator's economic unit for work performed off the family's immediate farm unit is included in this item. It is a gross value without deduction for travel expenses, room, board, union fees, etc., required of some types of off-farm employment.

(4) Other miscellaneous farm income consists of sale of machinery, buildings, and old equities in cotton and wheat in the CCC loan, crop insurance payments received by the farmer during 1942, and rentals received for machinery and livestock included in his operating unit.

Net family income. This is the net income available to the family for investment and family living. It includes: (1) Family earnings. (2) Other income. (3) Interest charge on investment. This gives the same total that would be obtained by subtracting all cash farm expenses from gross income. The figure used for Arkansas and Mississippi was computed in the Regional Office, using expense data sent in by the states. Included in Mississippi cash farm expenses were depreciation charge for work stock and buildings. The figure used for Oklahoma was computed from listings on a worksheet prepared in the state and sent the Regional Office. It consisted of: (1) Returns to capital and family labor (labor and management wage if no capital was employed). (2) Value of farm products used in the home. (3) Other non-farm income not included in farm summary.

Nonfarm income. This category included gifts, inheritances, pensions, rent from property not included in the operating unit, oil royalties and payments for leases.

Operator's earnings. Computed by subtracting the value of unpaid family labor from family earnings. It represents the compensation for the operator's labor and management.

Rent tract value of crops produced. The total value of all crops produced on each rent tract or lease. Cash crops were computed at sale price and feed crops at the average price if none were sold. Where only crop rent was paid it was possible to compare cash method of rental payment with the various share methods of rental payment which were prevalent in the area, as to economic advantage in 1942.

Wages from landlord, percentage of gross income. This constitutes total amount of wages received by the entire family for working for the landlord at farming or other occupation, divided by the gross income of the family. Wages were interpreted to include only cash wages and did not include perquisites or other non-cash considerations. This item is a measure of the cropper-laborer tendency and is particularly applicable to croppers.

LABOR

Acreage cropped out. Acres on which some share of the total production was given to croppers under the supervision of the operator.

Cotton chopping, days hired labor. Where cost data are shown on the schedules, hired labor has been reduced to man-equivalent days by the following conversion factors: Cash wages of $2.00 in Oklahoma and Texas equals one day. Cash wages of $1.50 in other states equals one day.

Cotton harvesting, days hired labor. Where cost or volume data are shown on the schedules, hired labor has been reduced to man-equivalent days by the following conversion factors: 150 pounds seed cotton picked equals one day. Cash wages of $6.50 for cotton snapping in Oklahoma equals one day.

Family days of labor on farm. This corresponds to the term "unpaid family labor." A few farmers reported the payment of wages to their children for work done on the farm, especially for cotton picking. However, if these children were considered a part of the family unit, the labor was converted to unpaid family labor, since the money was retained in the family unit. For converting other units of work done to days, the following factors were used: 10 hours equal 1 day; 1 week equals 5 days; 1 month equals 20 days.

Family labor on farm as percent of total family labor. The total number of man equivalent days the family reported working on the farm as described on the crop table and real estate inventory table, divided by the sum of the number of days of farm and nonfarm work reported for all members of the family. For this measure, labor has been divided into farm and nonfarm. Farm labor is that expended on the acreage designated as the farm of the cooperator and on the livestock designated as livestock used. All other labor is classified as nonfarm even though some of it may have been in agriculture on other farms. This is a measure of the distribution of the family labor. It ignores the quality and the wages received for such work, either on or off the farm.

Family labor on farm as percentage of total farm labor. The base for this percentage is the total number of man-equivalent days of labor reported as expended on the acreage and livestock included in the farm business used for each cooperator. The total number of days is divided into hired labor and family labor (including that of the operator). Work done by croppers for which the croppers got a share of the crop and custom work paid by cash or by a share of the crop did not enter into the computation. In a few cases the operator paid his family to pick cotton. Such entries were edited to be family labor rather than hired labor, since the money involved stayed in the family unit.

Hired labor days worked. Where only cost or volume data were shown on the schedules, hired labor was reduced to man-equivalent days as follows:

> 150 pounds seed cotton picked equals one day.
> Cash wages of $6.50 for cotton snapping in Oklahoma equals one day.
> Wages for other work in Oklahoma and Texas considered as $2.00 per day.
> Wages for other work in other states considered as $1.50 per day.

This item does not include the hiring of man and machine such as combining, threshing, or plowing with both man and tractor.

Man-equivalent units of family labor available. In all states other than Arkansas, those members of the family at home less than six months were omitted, while those at home six months or more were given full credit. Enumerators in Arkansas obtained from the farmers their estimate of the amount of work each member of the family could do. For other states the following man-equivalent units were used:

Age	*Male*	*Females*
	MISSISSIPPI	
8-15	0.3 unit	0.2 unit
16-59	1.0 unit	.3 unit
60-69	.6 unit	.0 unit
	OKLAHOMA	
10-13	0.5 unit	0.3 unit
14-17	.7 unit	.5 unit
18-37	1.0 unit	.7 unit
38-44	1.0 unit	.6 unit
45-64	.8 unit	.4 unit
65-up	.5 unit	.2 unit

Age	*Male*	*Females*
	TEXAS	
8-15	0.5 unit	
16-65	1.0 unit	
Wife of operator	(if under 50)	0.6 unit
8-12		.2 unit
13-17		.5 unit
18-50		.8 unit

Man-equivalent days of family labor on farm. Family labor is the total of the operator's labor and unpaid family/household labor on the farm. Hours, weeks, months, "all year" and cwt. (cotton picking) were reduced to man-equivalent days as follows:

> 10 hours equal 1 work day
> 1 week equals 5 days
> 1 month equals 20 days
> 1½ cwt. equals 1 day

Operator, days of labor on farm. In computing the number of days the following conversion factors were used:

> 10 hours equal 1 day
> 1 week equals 5 days
> 1 month equals 20 days

Productive man-work units. A productive man-work unit (PMWU) is the amount of directly productive work accomplished by one man working under average conditions during a 10-hour day. Workers in Arkansas and Oklahoma calculated PMWU for individual schedules. Other state workers furnished the Regional Office a list of labor requirements for most of the enterprises. The summary item used for each farm in these tabulations was the total of labor requirements for all its crop and livestock enterprises as indicated below.

ARKANSAS

Crop	*PMWU per acre*
Cotton	11.0
Corn, grain	3.0
Corn, interplanted	3.5
Corn, fodder	4.0
Sorghum, syrup	13.8
Irish potatoes	7.5
Sweet potatoes	12.0
Watermelons	6.5
Canning tomatoes	13.0
Beans, dry	4.0
Peanuts, hay or nuts	6.0
Peanuts pastured	2.4
Lespedeza	.3
Other hay	1.2
Apples or peaches	13.0
Grapes	15.0
Nonbearing trees	2.0
Unkept orchard	3.0
Strawberries	30.0
Strawberries, 1st year	16.0
Small grain	2.0
Cowpeas or soybeans	3.0
Garden	9.0
Red clover hay	1.5
Cowpea or soybean hay	2.0
Lespedeza hay	1.3
Millet or sorghum hay	2.0
Alfalfa hay	3.2
Timothy or prairie hay	1.0
Wild hay	1.2
Sorghum pastured	1.5

Livestock	*PMWU per head*
Dairy cows	13.0
Beef cattle 2 yrs. & up	3.0
Other cattle	2.0
Colts	2.0
Sows	3.0
Other hogs	.5
Sheep	.5
Goats	.3
Poultry	.22

MISSISSIPPI

Crop	PMWU Per Acre *Harvested*	*Left or pastured*
Cotton	11.8	–
Corn	3.8	2.5
Peanuts	6.6	3.0
Small grain	.6	–
Small grain, hay	2.3	–
Small grain, turned	–	1.2
Cowpeas, seed	2.9	1.2
Cowpeas, beans	1.5	1.2
Velvet beans	2.9	1.2
Cowpea or soybean hay	2.0	1.2
Sudan or Johnson grass hay	3.0	1.0
Lespedeza hay	1.4	1.2
Sorghum, seed or hay	2.0	–
Sorghum silage	1.5	–
Wild hay	1.2	–

Cane, syrup	11.7	1.5
Beans, green	12.8	–
Irish potatoes	7.8	–
Sweet potatoes	9.3	6.2

MISSISSIPPI

Crop	PMWU Per Acre Harvested	Left or pastured	Livestock (average inventory)	PMWU per head
Melons	6.5	4.3	Workstock	8.0
Cucumbers	15.0	10.0	Dairy cows	14.0
Peppers	12.0	–	Beef cows	2.5
Butter beans	15.0	–	Sow or gilt	7.2
Other truck-garden	10.0	6.7	Poultry	.42
Rice	3.0	1.0	All heifers	2.5
Crotalaria	–	2.0	Bull	2.5
Winter cover crop	–	1.5	Other hogs	1.0
			Sheep	1.0
			Goats	1.0
			Bees, hive	.5

OKLAHOMA

Crop	PMWU Per Acre Harvested	Left or pastured	Livestock	PMWU	
Wheat	0.32	0.20	Workstock	3.7	per A.U.
Oats	.41	.20	Milk cows	8.6	per head
Barley	.36	–	Other cattle	.8	per head
Rye	.35	–	Sheep and lambs	.5	per head
Mixed grain	.36	–	Sows and pigs	7.0	per A.U.
Flax	.38	–	Hens	.13	per head
Corn	1.14	.25	Chickens raised	.06	per head
Peanuts, hay or nuts	3.30	–	Turkeys raised	.15	per head
Cotton	2.37	–			
Grain sorghum	.67	.25			
Sorghum forage	.88	.25			
Alfalfa	1.17	.137			
Other tame hay	.58	–			
Wild hay	.49	–			
Sudan pasture	–	.20			

TEXAS

Enterprise	Owners and Part Owners: Horse equipment	Owners and Part Owners: Tractor equipment	Tenants and Croppers: Horse equipment	Tenants and Croppers: Tractor equipment
Crops				
Cotton, harvested	4.97	4.02	4.54	3.78
Cotton, left	2.37	1.63	2.41	1.53
Corn, harvested	2.07	1.35	2.10	1.20
Corn, left	.93	.45	.93	.39

Corn, turned	1.26	.61	1.26	.53
Cane, harvested	1.93	1.94	1.92	1.93
Cane, left	.31	.34	.32	.33
Cane, turned	.64	.50	.65	.47
Cowpeas, soybeans and castor beans (same as for cane).				
Gr. sorg., headed	2.44	1.55	2.44	1.56
Gr. sorg., combined	1.74	.85	1.74	.86
Gr. sorg., bundled	2.07	1.14	2.07	1.15
Gr. sorg., left	1.42	.53	1.42	.54
Gr. sorg., turned	1.75	.69	1.75	.68
Millet, maize and hegari (same as for grain sorghum).				
Sudan, harvested feed	2.09	1.45	2.09	1.46
Sudan, pastured	1.00	.42	1.00	.43
Sudan, turned	1.33	.58	1.33	.57

TEXAS

	Owners and Part Owners		Tenants and Croppers	
Enterprise	*Horse equipment*	*Tractor equipment*	*Horse equipment*	*Tractor equipment*
Crops				
Oats, cut, threshed	1.21	.91	1.22	.91
Oats, combined	.63	.33	.64	.33
Oats, left	.54	.24	.55	.24
Oats, turned	.87	.40	.88	.38
Oat hay (small grain)	1.63	1.27	1.64	1.27
Barley and wheat (same as for oats).				
Johnson grass hay	1.09	1.03	1.09	1.03
Sweet clover	1.09	1.03	1.09	1.03
Alfalfa	1.09	1.03	1.09	1.03
Sweet clover not harvested	.54	.24	.55	.24
Meadow hay	.79	.74	.79	.74
Hubam, harv. seed	.82	.42	.82	.42
Onions, harvested	7.75	6.95	7.75	6.95
Onions, not harvested	3.88	3.48	3.88	3.48
Garden	9.00	9.00	9.00	9.00
Orchard, producing	1.3	1.3	1.3	1.3
Orchard, young trees	.2	.2	.2	.2

Enterprise	Owners and Part Owners	Tenants and Croppers
Livestock (average inventory)		
Workstock	7.0	6.6
Dairy cows	12.0	11.2
Hogs, sows	14.7	15.9
100 hens	18.8	20.8

Ratio of labor used to PMWU. This figure was computed in days from the regional schedule according to the following formula:

> (Operator's labor on farm plus family's labor on farm plus hired labor) divided by (PMWU minus PMWU of cropper or tenant)

LANDLORD

Distance to farm from landlord's residence. Distances not reported were ascertained by map if the location of the residence was given.

Families supervised by landlord. Cropper and laborer families directly under the supervision of the landlord as well as renter families with little or no supervision are included.

Frequency of supervision. Visits to and from the landlord make up this item. Considered as separate items they measure who initiates the contacts and who is responsible for the number of them that take place. An exchange of letters was counted as one visit.

Number of landlords. In numerous instances a given tenant had more than one landlord, in which case it was necessary to make a selection between them. Other things equal, this judgment was made on an acreage basis.

Occupation of landlord. Occupation was determined from the schedule either from (1) direct statement as to occupation, or (2) major source of income. For those cases of female landlords whose husbands were employed, the occupation of the husband was tabulated rather than the occupation of the wife which usually was "housewife."

Type of landlord. This constituted a rough classification indicating the occupation or main source of income of the landlord. Approximately 40 different occupations were coded.

LEASE

Arrangements for present lease; exchange of labor and equipment. An attempt to determine to what extent and under what conditions the landlord and tenant trade farm work and machinery.

Length of lease. All oral agreements were coded as one-year leases. If notes or other data indicated that they were indefinite or automatic, they were so tabulated; otherwise they were considered one-year leases.

Number of lease. Each lease was arbitrarily identified by number. The number one lease was not necessarily the most important lease for a particular tenant or part owner. A separate card was punched for each lease thus making it possible in some of the tabulations to make the lease the unit of measure rather than the number of farms or farmers as was used for most of the tabulations.

Property covered by lease. This is a classification of the lease in terms of the nature of the resources rented. A farm unit is considered to be a marketable tract of land together with the improvements. A farmstead is defined as the dwelling, barn, and other outbuildings together with the houselot and barnlot. Field rent is the renting of one or two small fields for a specific crop or crops. An example would be the renting of ½ acre of land for cane. The renting of corn land only or cotton land only from one landlord with a farm unit acquired by other means would constitute field rent for the corn land. Equipment and workstock are considered as one item because of the possibility of tractor power. The inclusion of any equipment or livestock in the lease is considered enough to affect the classification.

Type of lease; form and length. All oral leases were assumed to be one year in length, even though some schedules reported otherwise. Written leases of lengths other than specified were coded as other types. Most of these were two-year leases.

MANAGEMENT

Degree of management index. A dittoed form was developed for use in computing the index for degree of management. A scale of 16 items was developed to compute the index. The index measures division of management between lessor and lessee, not between mortgager and mortgagee nor between farm operator and governmental action agency. (For further information see, Appendix B, Division of Management Score.)

Division of responsibility for management. This item is the sum of the scores for the 14 specific managerial functions used in computing index of management. Distance from farm to landlord's residence and frequency of supervision were deleted from the index in computing this item.

The items used in determining the division of responsibility as between landlord and tenant were as follows: kinds of acres and crops; amount and kinds of livestock; planting and cultivating; harvesting and securing fertilizer; securing production and furnish credit; crop rotation and marketing; record keeping and AAA responsibility.

Rent tract index of management. The same measure as degree of management index but applied to a specific rent tract relation between landlord and tenant.

MOVES

Increase in total acres of present farm over previous farm. This applies to the situation immediately preceding and following the last move and not to changes in size of farm apart from moving.

Last move of family. The code is based on a logarithmic series of mile intervals, on the assumption that distance is thus related to factors that induce migration.

Migration index. The average number of moves previously made by each "five year of earning life" group of farm family heads was used to produce a generalized smooth curve. (For further explanation see Appendix B, The Migration Index.)

Miles from home. The distance of the child's residence from its parents' present residence measured in miles. The intervals of miles distance are a logarithmic series. This has been termed the radius of migration from the parental home.

Moves with no change in school, church, or trade center. A change in church, school and trade center is deemed to represent a change in neighborhood. For the Arkansas sample these data were obtained for the years 1932 to 1942 only. From these measures and total number of moves the number of moves within the neighborhood area and between such areas was measured.

Number of moves. This constituted a simple count of all entries other than zero for miles moved. Unless there were schedule notes to the contrary an entry of zero from miles moved, nonfarm occupations were considered as one move to a new location and an additional move to the next farm.

Place of birth and first tenure/occupational experience. Since the sample areas in Arkansas and Mississippi were adjacent to the state of Louisiana, an additional category was set up for Louisiana as a place of birth for those cases sampled in Arkansas and Mississippi. Southern states included all the states in the Regional Project and extended north to the Ohio River and east to the Atlantic. West Virginia was not classified as a southern state but Virginia was. Midwestern states began with Ohio and included all states to the west as far as the Kansas, Nebraska, Dakota tier of states including Missouri. "Other states" were New Mexico, Colorado, Washington, and Oregon. The foreign countries represented in place of birth were Czechoslovakia—15, Germany and Mexico—3 each; and one case each from England, Russia, Sweden and Austria-Hungary.

Range of child's residence. The present residence of the child away from the parental home was measured by categories of political boundaries —county and state. (Note that only the present residence of parents and of child is considered.)

Residence by census classification. The present residence of the child away from home was classified as farm, rural-nonfarm, urban or other. Other includes rural when not designated as farm or nonfarm. It also includes urban area, when not designated as whether inside or outside the corporate limits.

Type of moves and distance. Each case was classified as belonging to one of three types of moves or combinations of these types. The points selected for breaking the class intervals were the same points as used for other measures of distance moved and were the troughs of the frequency distribution curve for distance moved. The three distances approximate intraneighborhood moves, intracounty moves and intercounty moves. Classification is based on reported changes. If the distance of all moves was not reported, consideration was given to place of birth and visiting with neighbors who were related to determine the classification.

Years on this farm. This refers to consecutive years the cooperator operated or worked for wages on this farm. If the cooperator rented out the entire farm, such renting out would break the continuity of "years on this farm."

Years on this farm is a measure of stability on the present operating unit as either owner, part owner, renter, cropper, or wage hand. It coincides with the term as used by the census excepting that wage laborer has been added. Unless there was information to the contrary, schedule entries other than zero for miles moved was taken to indicate a change in farm.

Years on rent tract. The number of consecutive years the operator operated all or part of the rent tract under consideration is measured by this item. The crop year 1942 was included in the number of years on present tract.

NEIGHBORHOOD

Name of county. The name of the county in which the farm was listed by AAA was coded for this item. While the farm was usually listed in the county in which it was located geographically, such was not always the case. The item as coded represents the AAA administrative unit rather than the political unit.

Name in neighborhood. A list of the neighborhoods entered on schedules was compiled for Arkansas and Mississippi. Any neighborhood being in two counties was given different codes for the part in each county. In Louisiana, the neighborhood data were not clear, so trade centers were used. In Oklahoma, the trade centers and counties were used. For Texas, few entries were found in the blank for neighborhood name. Since the entries were more complete in the blank for community name, these were tabulated. Many of these entries however were a mixture of neighborhood and community names.

OPERATING UNIT

Families in operating unit. Number of families in operating unit was tabulated for Mississippi schedules as reported by the interviewed farmer; his croppers were included or not, as he considered them. For Oklahoma schedules, this entry was edited in after study of other sections of the schedule. For Arkansas schedules, the families on those portions of land rented out or cropped out were included in the operating unit, provided the operator exercised relatively close supervision over the rented out or cropped out land.

Families working for head. This comprises the total number of cropper and resident laborer families (including single individuals) reported working for the cooperator on the farm under consideration. The cooperator's own family was not included, nor was seasonal hired labor.

PARTICIPATION

AAA participation (years). The number of years in which the cooperator received payment for participation in the AAA program.

Active FSA clients, 1942. The cases were classified as those having an active Rehabilitation, Tenant Purchase, or Water Facilities loan in 1942. A loan calling for repayment according to plan in 1942 was considered to be active. These cases were under the supervision of the local FSA supervisor.

4-H Club attendance by family. A summation of attendances by all members of the family including adult sponsors at 4-H Club meetings.

County farm agent, contacts with. The total number of visits to the farm of the cooperator by county farm agent or calls upon the county farm agent off the farm.

Distance to church. The number of miles to church was adjusted to the nearest whole number before tabulating. The general rule for exactly five-tenths was followed: Drop the half if the remainder becomes an even whole number, add a half if the resulting whole number is even.

Farm Security Administration status. This item was used to classify the cooperator by the kind and number of programs sponsored by FSA which he had at various times used.

FSA, AAA, SCS, FCA, Agricultural Extension. The number of programs (AAA, FSA, FCA, SCS, and Agr. Ext.) in which the cooperator participated in 1942.

Farm Security Administration, contacts with in 1942. The total number of visits to the farm of the cooperator by a farm or home supervisor or calls upon the farm or home supervisor off the farm by any member of cooperator's household.

Farm Security Administration, participation in supplementary programs. This relates only to 1942 and includes:

(1) Cooperative and community service loan
(2) Participation in a medical cooperative sponsored by FSA
(3) Participation in neighborhood discussion groups sponsored by FSA
(4) Water facilities loan, active during 1942.

Participation in items (2) and (3) is not confined in all instances to active clients of the FSA.

Farm Security Administration, years of participation in. The total number of years in which the cooperator is classified as an active client by reason of having used some form of credit made available through FSA or its predecessor agencies.

Home Demonstration Club attendance. A summation of attendance by all members of the family.

Participation. This includes a listing of the various organizations, measuring degrees of participation in local meetings. This group does not include the federal action agencies such as AAA, SCS, FSA, and FCA. Examination of the field schedules showed that annual total of meetings fell in the following ranges: 12-14, 24-26, 48 and over.

Degree of participation	ANNUAL NUMBER OF MEETINGS *48 and over*	*24 to 26*	*12 to 14*
less than ¼	under 12	under 6	under 3
¼ to ¾	12 to 35	6 to 17	3 to 8
¾ or more	36 and over	18 to 26	9 to 14

Other social participation. Type of participation was tabulated as well as the kind of organization in which the participation occurred. Player and teacher are considered as types of participation in contrast with spectator or member.

Public work relief programs. The code used here is a combination of "Yes or No" answers to the question of any member of the family participating in any year in one of the work relief programs. WPA, NYA, and CCC include the various agencies which preceded them under other titles. Participation in public assistance programs are included in a separate category.

Soil Conservation Service, years of participation in. The number of years in which the cooperator reported any participation. Participation may consist of visits to or from the SCS representative, the maintenance of demonstrations sponsored by SCS, or the receipt of aid by SCS in conservation practices.

Soil Conservation Service, contacts with. The total number of visits to the farm of the cooperator by a representative of SCS or calls upon the representative of the SCS off the farm by any member of cooperator's household.

REAL ESTATE

Acres of land owned. Acres now owned is considered here as acres now owned and operated.

Barns, value of. The value of all barns as recorded by the enumerator. This is the amount added by their presence to the market value of the farm.

Dwelling, value of. The dwelling is defined as the house occupied by the cooperator. Its value is the amount it adds to the market value of the farm.

Equity in real estate used (percentage). The value of real estate owned minus the debt against it as of July, 1942, divided by the value of real estate used.

Equity in real estate owned, percentage. The value of real estate owned minus the amount of debt against the real estate as of July, 1942, divided by the value of real estate owned. This is a measure of net worth in a going concern rather than a closing inventory net worth. If no income results over and above the current operating and living expenses, the debt on land will not be reduced. If an income does result, it does not necessarily follow that the debt will be reduced. Net income may be used for family living or to increase the size of farm operations by purchasing livestock, equipment, or real estate.

Fences, value of. The figure obtained by the enumerator for this item is an estimate of the value of all fences used, including those around gardens. Fencing practices varied by localities. Some farmers fenced in the cropland, others the pasture land, while still others completely fenced and cross fenced their farms. The value listed on any particular schedule represents a figure somewhere between the cost of construction minus depreciation and the value added to bare land.

Improvements owned, value of. The market value of all additions made to the bare land owned by the cooperator. It also included buildings and other improvements owned and used by tenants or laborers and placed on land belonging to the others.

Improvements, value of. This represents the amount the improvements contribute to the market value of the real estate. In some cases it was necessary to scale down initial cost less depreciation in order to conform to this definition of value. The parts making up the total real estate value were adjusted by the enumerators to equal the market value of the whole.

Leased real estate, value of. This refers to all real estate leased from all landlords concerned.

Owned real estate, percentage of real estate used. The value of real estate owned, divided by the value of all real estate included in the cooperator's farm. Real estate includes land and improvements. Following this definition, many cooperators classified as nonowners reported owning a chicken house, some fencing, possibly the dwelling, and a few owned the farmstead site. The latter item constituted the ownership of land in addition to improvements. On the other hand a few full owners reported using land or improvements which they did not own. This item measures the extent of the characteristic even though the case has been classified in one of the usual tenure categories.

Value of real estate. Cooperators were asked for an estimate of the market value of all real estate operated (owned and/or rented) in 1942. In some cases it was extremely difficult to estimate the value of cropper tracts or of farms with parts of the land rented out, because such tracts are seldom, if ever, on the market. The figure used is the best possible estimate of the cooperator and the enumerator of the value of the land operated, plus improvements on such acreages.

Water systems, value of. The value figure for water systems tends to be the cost of man-made improvements minus depreciation rather than value added to real estate. Wells were listed as the cost of digging or drilling plus cost of casing and other equipment, minus depreciation. Artificial ponds were valued somewhere between cost of construction and value added to the farm. Cisterns and pipe were estimated somewhat like dwellings on value added to the farm. Windmills were given at market value of the windmill and tower since they are often sold in the same manner as livestock would be sold. This value is for systems used rather than for those owned. Many renters own a considerable portion of the water systems used. They have little significance in Arkansas, Louisiana, and Mississippi, with springs and shallow wells the rule, but are important in Texas and Oklahoma. Values of zero do not mean that there is no water available, but that little or no improvements have been made by man.

RENTAL PAYMENT

Crop method of rental payment. No differentiation was made in this classification between ⅓ and ¼ share rent. Such differences properly belong to specific crops and are handled in that manner. Standing rent is the payment of a fixed amount of produce. Bonus cash rent is interpreted to be the payment of cash in addition to the share rent on crops produced. The cash is not paid at a rate per acre for specified types of land use but on the basis of a flat sum per year.

Livestock method of rental payment. The "calf rent" type of proposition with the tenant getting all the milk and paying for all feed is the typical cropper perquisite type situation. Similar arrangements frequently obtained for poultry. These are not true production leases but arrangements to improve the real income of the cropper with but little expense on the part of the landlord. In some areas, livestock men used the "calf rent" proposition in a cow and calf enterprise to raise calves in order to avoid feed and upkeep costs on the cow. Some livestock men farmed out as many as twenty or more cows each year in this manner.

A sharing of livestock and/or livestock products (other than poultry) was considered as a complete livestock share lease. If the poultry share leases had been of sufficient size, they would have been classified as livestock share lease but in the main they were only small flocks for home use.

Ratio of rental payment to farm business rented. The total value of rental payment for each rent tract was divided by the value of property leased. Rent included crop share or standing rent at the sale price or at the usual price per unit, cash rent, taxes, additional AAA money accruing to the landlord, and repair costs on improvements including unpaid labor by the tenant. No value was placed on the calf in case of "calf rent" leases and none on "keep of the landlord." The value of property leased was computed for each rent tract as was the rent. However, for Mississippi the value of equipment and livestock rented was not ascertained on the schedule and could not be included in the totals. This accounts to some extent for the unusually high ratios for Mississippi.

Rent tract cash rental payment for real estate, equipment, and power. Cash rent for equipment and power places the tenant in this respect in an intermediate position between renter and cropper.

Rent tract value of livestock and products as rental payment. This item applies to livestock leases. For most of the cases of "calf rent" the value of the calf is unknown.

Rent tract value of rental payment. The total value of rental payment computed for each rent tract or lease. Together with value of farm business rented, it shows the ratio of rent to value for groups of leases by type.

Rent tract additional cash rental payment. A classification of cash rentals which are in addition to the customary share rental arrangement.

Value of rental payment. For cases having more than one landlord it was impossible to separate rental data. This category therefore constitutes value of total rental payment. The value of the crop paid as rent is based on the price receieved for the same product when sold. If cane syrup toll was paid and no syrup sold, the value of that used in the home was divided by the amount used in the home to get the price used in computing the value of the landlord's share. Figures for Oklahoma were furnished on value of crop productions paid as rent. To these were added cash rents and value of days of labor.

Conversion amounts or values used in all states for computing rental payments are as follows: 60 pounds of peanut hay equals one bale; 60 pounds of beans equals one bushel; 30 bales of lespedeza equals one ton; (66.7 lbs. equals one bale) $15 a ton equals $.0075 per pound; 30 pounds of peanuts equals one bushel; 35 bales of soybeans equals one ton; (57.14 lbs. equals one bale).

Days of Unpaid Family Labor for Landlord were included in Value of Rental Payment with the following rates per day:

Arkansas and Mississippi, $1.00; Oklahoma and Texas, $2.00

Where average prices on farm products were omitted from the schedules, the following average prices were used for computing value of rental payment:

Arkansas:		
Corn and corn meal	$ 1.00	per bushel
Sweet and Irish potatoes	1.20	per bushel
Peanuts	1.20	per bushel
Peanut hay	20.00	per ton
All peas	1.50	per bushel
Beans	1.50	per bushel
Bean hay	20.00	per ton
Melons	.01	per pound
Molasses—sorghum	.75	per gallon
Syrup	1.00	per gallon
Fruit	1.00	per bushel
Wood	1.35	per rick
Peanuts (nuts)	80.00	per ton
Cotton lint (½ and ½)	.18	per pound
Cotton lint (all other kinds)	.19	per pound
Chickens	.75	each
Young chickens	.50	each

Legume hay	15.00 per ton	
Non-legume hay	10.00 per ton	

MISSISSIPPI:

All legume hay	$12.00 per ton	
Oat hay	12.00 per ton	
Native hay	3.00 per ton	
Sorghum feed	10.00 per ton	
Velvet beans	2.00 per bushel	
Green peas	2.00 per bushel	
Oats	.50 per bushel	
Peanuts	1.50 per bushel	
Corn for meal	.85 per bushel	
All corn	.75 per bushel	
All sweet potatoes	.50 per bushel	
Eggs	.30 per dozen	
Milk	.20 per gallon	
Poultry, hens	.75 each	
Friers	.50 each	
Wood for fuel (some areas)	3.00 per cord	

TEXAS:

Onions	.85 per bushel	
Millet	.35 per bushel	
Barley	.55 per bushel	
Wheat	.90 per bushel	
Maize	.70 per bushel	50 lbs., 1 bu.
Oats	.50 per bushel	
Sweet sorghum	.50 per bushel	
Grain sorghum	.50 per bushel	
Kafir	.50 per bushel	
Hegari	.05 per bushel	
Johnson grass hay	.25 per 50 lb. bale	
Sudan and Millet hay	.25 per 50 lb. bale	
Dorso, combined; Sweet sorghum (10-lb. bundles); Sweet sorghum hay; Milo	.007 per pound	

SOCIO-ECONOMIC STATUS

(See Appendix B, The Farm Family Socio-Economic Status Scale)

SOIL

Soil classification. Arkansas: The predominant soil type for cropland was selected from a soils map embracing the farm unit, checked to some extent by field observations. Since no soils map was available for Columbia County this classification could not be made for sample farms in that county. The major soil types were coded for tabulation, while those types occurring infrequently in the sample were coded (R) for rejection in card sorting.

Mississippi: Soil types were grouped into three classes: (1) good soils

(2) soils capable of response to good management, and (3) poor soils. In addition, the enumerators classified the cropland of each farm as to degree of erosion, and seriousness of drainage problems. Four classes of erosion damage were recognized, also three slope classes and three drainage situations.

Oklahoma: Farms were classified according to size of soil particles determined by physical analysis. Fine, medium, and coarse soil classes were recognized. A farm with more than one of the three classes or some soil not usually found in the area was classed as having "mixed soil."

Texas: No soil classes were set up. Instead, the five-year average cotton yield was used as a measure of productivity.

TENURE CHANGE

Farm laborer, years as. The number of years the cooperator has been employed as a farm laborer, not including years spent as unpaid family laborer. If both a cropper and laborer in any year, cooperator is classified as a cropper in that year. If a farm laborer at least half the year and otherwise employed the remainder of the year, the cooperator is counted as a farm laborer in such year.

Mobility of head. Changes of tenure after the operator entered the farming occupation independent of his parents in his earning life.

Moves with no tenure change. The tenure steps in descending order are assumed to be as follows: owner, renter, cropper, and laborer. Part owners are included with owners and indeterminate tenures are included with renters.

Owner, years as. This is the number of years cooperator farmed as an owner-operator or part-owner-operator. This item does not include the number of years in which cooperator was not a farm operator.

Renter, years as. This is the number of years cooperator farmed as a share or cash tenant but not as a cropper, owner, or part owner.

Tenure status prior to FSA participation. The tenure status of the cooperator in the year prior to the year in which he first received loans or grants from the FSA.

Type of tenure change. This item is a classification of types of tenure change based on the first reported farm tenure status and the following tenure history of the individual.

Years of earning life before marriage. This is a measure of the experience of the individual during the period of preparation for farming before marriage.

Years of earning life. From 1942 is subtracted the first year of earning life, and from the remainder is subtracted any intervening years entered as at home.

For those cases who began on their own, subsequently returned home and left a second time, the total number of years on their own was tabulated.

TENURE STATUS

Farm tenure and nonfarm occupational status of child and child's spouse. The tenure classification as entered by the field enumerator is the only available schedule information. The occupational classification for these codes was obtained from the two publications: U. S. *Classified Index of Occupations,* U. S. Dept. of Commerce, Bureau of the Census, Sixteenth Census of the U. S.: 1940. Washington, D. C.: Gov't Printing Office, 1940. 199 pages. U. S. *Alphabetical Index of Occupations and Industries,* U. S. Dept. of Commerce, Bureau of the Census, Sixteenth Census of the U. S.: 1940. Washington, D. C.: Gov't Printing Office, 1940. 607 pages. A skeleton outline of this classification of occupations is used in the 1940 Census publications. See series of bulletins titled *Population,* Third Series: THE LABOR FORCE—Occupation, Industry, Employment and Income, Table 11.

First farm tenure status of head. This classification describes the tenure of the head upon first entering farming.

Mate's parents, tenure status/occupation of. The item refers to the present mate. If the mate was reared by other than blood parents, the tenure status/occupation of the foster parents was coded. If the entry on the schedule indicates that the parents of the mate were deceased or retired at the time of the mate's marriage, then the tenure status/occupation previous to death or retirement was used.

Parents, tenure status of. This item measures the combination of tenure status of parent of male head and tenure status of parent of female head. Cases of unmarried heads, one parent with tenure status unknown or nonfarm were coded as if both parents had the tenure status of the one which was known.

Present tenure status of head. Present tenure status conforms rather closely to the census classification of tenure. The major groups are: full owner, part owner, indeterminate tenure, renter, cropper, laborer, and other. Although the basis for classifying each case follows the census definitions to a great extent some differences may be noted. If an owner rented a few acres of land rent free and used it for some relatively unimportant crop (not a cash crop), he was classed as a full owner. On the other hand, a few farmers classed as renters, croppers, and laborers owned their farmstead, or some of the buildings on the land which they used but to which they had no title. The renters owned all the improvements on nearly all tracts owned by the Oklahoma School Land Commission and the County Boards of Education in Mississippi. The value of such improvements or of farmsteads was shown as real estate owned but the ownership of that type of real estate was ignored in determining the tenure classification. This procedure follows the thinking expressed at the First Workers' Conference of using a common sense method on marginal cases. The use of free range and the renting out of additional tracts owned but not covered in the schedule were ignored in determining tenure status.

Another type of marginal case necessitated the new tenure category of "indeterminate tenure." This term was used for those cases which were neither owner nor tenant due to a tacit but not a legal transfer of title. A son was "given" a tract of land by his father, but there had been no transfer of title. Other examples occurred when the son operated the farm after the death of the father and expected to inherit the farm after taking care of the mother until her death. One case in Oklahoma involved an expected inheritance from an uncle. However, the uncle died in late 1942 and the nephew did not inherit. This was known because the schedule was taken in the summer of 1943. Since during the crop year 1942, the nephew operated the farm with the expectation of ownership, he was classed as an indeterminate. This was the "one case in one hundred" that did not turn out as expected. In another case in Texas the cooperator had "purchased" the farm from other heirs, but was to pay his mother share rent as long as she lived and the title was still in his deceased father's name. The reason for the category of "indeterminate" was not entirely philosophical but was mainly practical because it was impossible to apply either the ownership questions or the leasing arrangement questions to cases of this sort.

Ownership of power was taken as the key item in differentiating between renters and croppers. Any cooperator hired primarily for wages but receiving all or a share of the crops (other than garden) from specified acreages as a perquisite was classed as a cropper. Sharing of livestock or livestock products did not in itself constitute a cropper situation.

At the First Workers' Conference a tenure of cropper-laborer was suggested to conform somewhat to the definition used in Barton and McNeely's study. The nature of the sample by states permitted the omission of the cropper-laborer category. In Texas the operating cropper was not sampled. Those cases designated as croppers are actually cropper-laborers. In Arkansas no laborers were sampled, and in the Coastal Plains area there are few of the cropper-laborer type of individuals. All croppers are classed as croppers, and the extent of working for the landlord for wages can be measured for each individual. In Oklahoma all three types were sampled (croppers, croppers-laborers, and laborers). Because of the small number of cases, the croppers and the cropper-laborers were grouped together as croppers. In Mississippi there were no strictly cropper-laborers, although in one case a laborer received the free use of seven acres of cropland as a perquisite on which he had some cotton. The income from the crops raised on such acreages was only a small proportion of the total income.

Mississippi, Louisiana, and Oklahoma sampled the rural population and included some cases of nonoperating owners, laborers with nonfarm occupations, and various persons just "living in rural areas." These are classed as other. A considerable number in Jackson Parish, Louisiana, lived on tracts of land up to five acres in size with a garden, a cow, chickens, hogs, and possibly a little cotton. These cases were classed as "other" because the cooperators were occupied full time in the paper mill and were incidentally living on farms and receiving some income from their farming operations. Although classified as other than farming occupation, the schedules were processed in the same way as the other schedules in the sample.

TITLE STATUS

Title status to land. This item measures the extent to which the cooperator is an owner of the land under consideration. The code of "owner, but title not passed" was used for those who are in the process of buying or otherwise acquiring title to land but for the year 1942, the title was not registered in their name. The code "life estate" was used for those cases with either the husband or wife dead and the remaining spouse operating the farm. This type of situation varied with the state law in respect to inheritance and must be interpreted accordingly. The code of "retired, son operating" is used for those cases of owner-operators who are nominal operators but in reality are retired while the son is in the process of taking over both the operation of the farm and of inheriting the farm. The code "owner in prospect" represents the same situation with the schedule taken on the son. The code "heir interest" was used when the cooperator rented from the estate in which he or his wife had an undivided interest. In many of these cases the cooperator was acting as administrator for the estate. The code "owner in prospect" was used when the cooperator rented from an individual to whom he was closely related (e.g. father, father-in-law, or grandparents) and upon whose death the cooperator would normally inherit all or part of the property. Such death (intestate) would create an estate ownership and the cooperator was then coded as "heir interest." There are a few cases of partnerships in which the real estate was divided about equally for operational purposes. Such situations are coded as "partnership, one-half interest in twice the real estate shown." The most frequently used codes were "full title" and "no ownership title in farm."

TYPE OF FARMING

Diversification index. Man labor requirements for each crop and livestock enterprise were computed, workstock being omitted by all states except Oklahoma. Classes of enterprises set up by workers in the various states were:

Oklahoma	*Texas*	*Other States*
Workstock	All cattle	All cattle
Milk cows	Swine	Swine
Other cattle	Poultry	Poultry
Hens	Sheep and lambs	Cotton
Chickens raised	Cotton	Other cash crops
Turkeys raised	Small grain	Feed crops
Swine	Other cash crops	All other enterprises
Sheep and lambs	Feed crops	
Cotton and peanuts	Pasture	
Small grain	All other enterprises	
Row crops for feed grain		
Hay and forage crops		
Rotation pasture		
All other enterprises		

The fraction of total labor requirements devoted to each class of enterprise was squared. Then the sum of these squares was divided into one (1) to give the index. For example, a farm having .5 of its labor devoted to cotton, .25 devoted to cattle, and .25 devoted to feed crops would have its index computed as follows:

$$\frac{1}{[(.5)^2 + (.25)^2 + (.25)^2]} = 2.67$$

Type of farming. Workers in Mississippi and Oklahoma classified individual farms into the various categories listed below; Texas workers set up criteria for classifying, while Regional Office personnel adapted the Mississippi system to Arkansas farms.

Texas

Based on the ratio of cotton sales to sales of livestock and livestock products, the following classes were set up:

1. Cotton farms	—100 cotton: 0-50 livestock & livestock products
2. Cotton-livestock farms	—100 cotton: 51-100 livestock & livestock products
3. Livestock-cotton farms	—100 cotton: 101 and over & livestock products
4. None	—No sales of either type

Oklahoma

Based largely on the proportion of total labor requirements for various enterprises, with some other measures considered to meet certain situations, the following types of farms were recognized:

1. Crop farms—farms were classed as crop farms whenever there was only sufficient livestock for home use and the sale of some surplus livestock products. Although there are in this group farms with only cotton and some farms with both cotton and small grains, it was felt that in order to obtain a sufficient number of cases only one type of crop farm would be identified.

2. Cotton-general farms—these farms have more livestock than is needed for home use, less than 51 per cent of the labor is used on livestock and less than 5 per cent of the labor is used on small grain.
3. Cotton-wheat-general farms—these farms vary from No. 2 only in that more than 5 per cent of the labor is spent on small grains.
4. Livestock-general farms—these are farms on which more than 51 per cent of the labor is spent on livestock. In addition, a few farms which ordinarily would not be included in this group were classed as livestock-general farms because more than 60 per cent of their receipts came from livestock and livestock products.
5. None—no crops or livestock.

Mississippi

1. Cotton—farms having at least 3 acres of cotton and a minimum of 20 per cent of their cropland in cotton and having no other important cash enterprise.
2. Cotton-livestock—farms having the minimum cotton acreage under "1" above and having 5 or more animal units of mature livestock, omitting workstock, with at least 1 animal unit to each 7 acres of cropland. On multiple family farms having 5 or more animal units of mature livestock, livestock is compared to the operator's share of total cropland.
3. Cotton-truck—farms having the minimum cotton acreage under "1" above and having 1 acre or more of commercial truck crops with at least 1 acre or more of commercial truck crops and at least 1 acre to each 5 acres of cotton, and not having enough livestock to qualify under "2" above.
4. General—farms having 3 acres or more of cotton and meeting one of the following conditions:
   a. Having *less than* 20 per cent of their cropland in cotton and having 1 acre or more of commercial truck with at least 1 acre to each 5 acres of cotton or having 4 or more animal units of mature livestock with at least one animal unit to each 7 acres of cropland.
   b. Having *less than* 20 per cent of their cropland in cotton and having both livestock and truck as supplemental enterprises to the extent of 4 or more animal units of mature livestock with at least 1 animal unit to each 12 acres of cropland, and 1 acre or more of commercial truck with at least 1 acre to each 10 acres in cotton.
   c. Having *more than* 20 per cent of their cropland in cotton and meeting both requirements under 4a above.
5. Incidental or subsistence—farms having less than 3 acres of cotton and not having enough livestock to qualify elsewhere.
6. None—no crops or livestock.

Arkansas

1. Cotton—farms having at least six acres of cotton and a minimum of 20 per cent of their cropland in cotton and having no other important cash enterprises. Idle land and land cropped out was excluded in computing the percentage of cropland in cotton.
2. Cotton-truck—(a) farms meeting the cotton requirements of cotton type farms and having at least one acre of commercial truck with at least one acre of truck for each six acres of cotton and having no other important cash enterprises. A few farms with no cotton (truck farms) were included in this type.

   (b) Cotton-peanut farms were included in this type as being those with at least six acres of cotton and with at least one acre of peanuts for oil for every two acres of cotton and having no other important cash enterprises.
3. Cotton-livestock—farms meeting the cotton requirements of cotton type farms and having at least five animal units of productive livestock with at least one ainmal unit to each seven acres of crops (idle land and cropland cropped out are excluded). One livestock-truck farm and a few strictly livestock farms (no cotton) are included in this class.
4. General—farms having at least six acres of cotton and either:
   (a) *less* than 20 per cent of the acres in crops planted to cotton and meeting one of the following requirements:
      (1) at least one acre of commercial truck with at least one acre of truck to each six acres of cotton;
      (2) at least one acre of peanuts for oil with at least one acre of peanuts for each two acres of cotton;
      (3) at least five animal units of productive livestock and at least one animal unit for each seven acres of crops;
      (4) combinations of any two of the above but with the following minimum ratios: one acre of truck to ten acres of cotton, one acre of peanuts to three acres of cotton, one animal unit of productive livestock to twelve acres of crops;
   (b) *more* than 20 per cent of the acres in crops planted to cotton and meeting two or more of the qualifications stated in (a) 1, 2, or 3.
5. Incidental or subsistence—farms having less than six acres of cotton and not over ten acres of cotton, truck, and peanuts combined and not having enough livestock to qualify elsewhere.
6. None—no crops or livestock.

YIELD

Cotton, five-year average yield of. For Mississippi, Oklahoma, and Texas schedules, the data on five-year average cotton yield were obtained direct from AAA office records. On some schedules there are entries for subtenants. Whenever two or more entries were given for average yields, the yield on the larger tract was used. If the yield on the larger tract was not ascertainable, the yield for the tract next in size was used. In coding the item, the actual number of pounds was divided by ten and rounded off to the nearest whole number.

Cotton, 1942 production. This is the actual production on the farm and was used in calculating acreage yields for groups of farms.

Crop yield index. This is a measure of the relationship of yields per acre of the major crops on one farm to those of the state area sample. Workers in the several states suggested crops which were used in computing this index.

Oklahoma	*Texas*	*Other states*
Cotton	Cotton	Cotton
Wheat	Corn	Corn
Sorghum for grain	Oats	
Sorghum for forage	Sorghum for grain	
Alfalfa seed	Sorghum for forage	
	Meadow hay	

The first step in deriving the index involved a calculation of average yield of individual crops for the state area sample. For a farm using only cotton and corn as bases, further steps may be illustrated as follows:

1. Acres in cotton + acres in corn = Acres base crops

2. $$\frac{\text{Cotton production}}{\text{Average yield}} + \frac{\text{Corn production}}{\text{Average yield}} = \text{Acres required with average yields}$$

3. $$\frac{\text{Acres required with average yields}}{\text{Acres base crops}} \times 100 = \text{Crop yield index}$$

Appendix B

GENERAL PROCEDURE FOR EDITING SCHEDULES

A great amount of effort was expended in an attempt to get uniform data from all schedules. This in part was achieved by field editing, by editing at the time of transcription from field schedules to the printed regional form, and finally by intensive editing in the Regional Office. Editing in the Regional Office was particularly necessary since a total of fifty different enumerators secured the schedules in the five states. In most instances these enumerators had at least Master's degrees in one or the other of the subject matter disciplines. Nevertheless, differences of background and experience and particularly differences in handling the schedule work in the several states necessitated careful editing to secure uniformity. Likewise the states sometimes used slightly different definitions in an attempt to fit the schedules to local conditions, and in many instances the same definition was given varying interpretations.

As stated in the Definition of Terms (Appendix A) these discrepancies were ironed out, so far as possible, in editing. All editing in the Regional Office was done by staff members or under the close supervision of staff members. The schedules were edited to fit conceptual definitions. If the item in question conformed to the definition it was accepted. If not, it was edited to conform. Many schedules had to be edited to fit the 1942 calendar year as to age, education of those still in school, deaths, births, and members away from home.

Simple editing was done directly on the schedule, also some coding of combinations of items. The more complicated indices and summary measures were computed on work sheets before transfer to master sheets for punching. All of this editing was done, it should be pointed out, before the tabulated data were returned to the states for use by the individual state tenure workers.

DIVISION OF MANAGEMENT SCORE[1]

The measure developed and used in this study expresses as a continuum the classification of farmers into "operators" and "laborers receiving a

[1] Statement developed by R. J. Ramsey.

portion of the crop in lieu of wages." The score represents a position on a scale of the division of management between landlord and tenant or between employer and employee. The influence of credit agencies, governmental programs or any other third party was not considered in the determination of the score.

Former studies in Louisiana and the comparison of tenure status in the Corn Belt with that in the Cotton Belt served as pilot studies for the determination of the measure.[2] A total of 16 items were finally selected as valid for inclusion in the score. Other items were tested but either lacked sufficient percentage of replies for usage or were not reliable in their relationship to the balance of the items. *Distance from farm to residence of landlord* was used as a measure of availability for supervision. *Frequency of supervision* was used as a measure of the number of contacts between landlord and lessee. The other fourteen items were definite items of management for crop and livestock production. Arbitrary scores were assigned each reply in the determination of tentative scores. Each lease was considered as a unit for observation.

Some editing, or at least verification with other tables, was necessary. Distance from farm to landlord's residence was checked at times by a map, by data in the table of family visiting, and by miles moved in a few cases. Notes on frequency of supervision often had to be translated into numbers. The number used for scoring represents the total number of contacts between landlord and tenant during which the farm business was discussed. Answers of "weekly" or "monthly" were translated assuming a nine-month crop year. Letters were included as contacts where such cases were mentioned. An exchange of letters was considered to be one contact. In a few cases the lessee was acting as agent for the estate from which he was renting. The frequency of supervision in these cases and in others where the landlord and tenant lived in the same house was interpreted to be "daily" unless a definite statement to the contrary was made.

Notes of "landlord specified cotton acreage" or "must be in AAA program" and other details of crop organization being left to tenant were interpreted as "divided" for kind and acreages of crops. This means that "divided" represents that either the responsibility for kind and acreage of all crops was divided or that some crops were the landlord's responsibility and others were those of the tenant. Divided responsibility as checked probably ranged from 1 per cent to 99 per cent and the validity of the category will be determined by further experimentation. In cases where the landlord furnished the tenant workstock, cows, or other kinds of

[2] Ralph J. Ramsey and Harold Hoffsommer, *Procedure in Delineating Types of Tenancy Areas in Louisiana*, mimeo. pub. of USDA and Louisiana AES, Washington, 1941 and E. A. Schuler, *Social Status and Farm Tenure—Attitudes and Social Conditions of Corn Belt and Cotton Belt Farmers*, Social Report No. IV, USDA Washington, 1938, pp. 153-61.

livestock as shown by "livestock ownership arrangement" in the table on "Operator's Livestock: Inventory, Production and Disposal," the division of management for kinds and amount of livestock was accepted if checked either "landlord" or "divided." If checked "tenant," it was edited to be "divided." It was thought that if the source of the livestock was the landlord, the landlord would have some control over how many and what kinds were used on the tract.

Production credit and furnish credit were handled in somewhat the same fashion as kind of livestock in that if the source of supply were the landlord, it was assumed that the landlord had some control over the items. In a few cases of related tenants and credit-agency landlords, descriptive notes explained that the tenant had relatively complete control over credit even though it was secured from the landlord. Such specific notes were accepted as validating a check of "Tenant" for control over credit. Production credit was interpreted as credit to buy seed, fertilizer, livestock or equipment. Furnish credit was credit for family living. In many cases it was impossible to distinguish between the two so that the two items were described identically. If no credit were used, the reasoning was that the tenant furnished his own credit and the tenant column was checked.

Record keeping was left blank on some schedules or a note was made that no records were kept. However, there are always AAA forms, including records of yields, productions and acreages, and gin tickets. For those eligible farmers, income tax forms would be included as records. With this interpretation of farm records, in general the keeping records was edited to follow the marketing of the crop and the signing of the AAA blanks as operator unless a more specific note or check mark indicates something different. The matter of furnish and production credit is involved in record keeping. If the source is the landlord, it is likely that the landlord keeps records on those items which are definitely a part of the farm business. In addition to the landlord's keeping gin tickets, AAA forms, and records of credit operation, the tenant also kept records of the same things. Such cases were edited to be "divided."

After editing as indicated above, there were some schedules with unknown for one or more items. These schedules were not used for validation purposes nor for the derivation of scores. After the items were validated and the score was determined by the procedure described later, the expected score for the item left blank was entered. That assumed, if the pattern is the same for two cases in respect to fifteen items, it is likely to be the same for the sixteenth item. Or it assumed that the sixteenth item follows the same pattern as that indicated by the other fifteen items. This technique was used to *classify* schedules and such cases were not included in determination of relationships or descriptions of groups of cases in terms of specific tenure.

After assigning arbitrary scores to all characteristics, the items were tested for internal consistency using the critical ratio test for differences between successive and extreme quartiles of the total score.[3]

The critical ratios for the leases in the Mississippi sample are typical of all the leases sampled and represent a more nearly normal distribution of replies. (Table 65) Since all but one of the items were graduated the differences appear somewhat erratic in some cases. In regard to "distance," there were very few replies of "same house" and this reply was combined with that of "less than one-half mile." For the Mississippi area there were few replies of "over 5 miles." More detailed examination of distance in respect to other items indicated that for Mississippi, distances greater than 5 miles could be put into one interval and receive the same score. The critical distance varied slightly for the other areas. The two extremes of the graduated replies for all items showed fairly high critical ratios for most of the successive quartiles (2 or greater) and were consistent in direction. As between extreme quartiles, the lowest and highest graduated replies were higher than 5 for all items except "but divided between landlord and tenant." The middle position of "divided" (and average distances and frequencies of supervision) changed direction about the middle of the scale and the critical ratio of the extreme quartiles for such replies was not consistent in direction for all items. The low critical ratios between particular successive quartiles indicate that some items differentiate to a greater extent at one end of the scale than the other. Again, the presence of a middle position reply necessitated the use of judgment in selecting items with the greatest significance and differentiating power. The matter of a landlord employing an agent tended to minimize the influence of distance as a reply and required individual study. The use of an agent had little influence in the Arkansas and Mississippi samples but in Oklahoma and Texas, agents supervised (as measured by the other items in the total score) more than those landlords living at the maximum distance and not using agents. The conclusion based on the data agrees with the logical conclusion and observations in the field.

The items selected were finally weighted by class intervals according to their sigma values. Scores were computed for the sigma values of the percentage distribution of responses for each state and for the total of the four states. As stated elsewhere, scores were computed for each lease and an average score for all leases for those lessees with multiple leases. Scores were computed using both state and regional sigma values

[3] The formulae used were taken from Arkin and Colton, *An Outline of Statistical Methods,* Fourth Edition, pp. 114-22. The term "critical ratio" is used rather than "number of standard errors" or t-value for convenience and follows the terminology used by Sewell in the *Construction and Standardization of a Scale for the Manual of the Socio-economic Status of Oklahoma Farm Families,* Oklahoma AES Tech. Bul. 9, Stillwater, 1940, pp. 32-39.

but little differences was noted except for the shifted scale. The use of the scale in the present study is primarily to classify lessees into broad groups and the actual score was not used. In order to facilitate coding into a two-digit figure, a constant was subtracted from each total score. This process shifted the scale and had no effect upon the classification into class intervals. The actual scores for each response for both the state scoring and the regional scoring indicate the differences by states for each single item and the close similarity between the two methods.

In order for the reader to understand the score more fully the percentage distribution of response for each item was computed for each of five class intervals using all leases in the four-state sample as a population for study. (Tables 80 and 81) These computations reveal the close association of the total score with each of its component parts.

THE FARM FAMILY SOCIO-ECONOMIC STATUS SCALE[4]

The socio-economic status scale was separated into three indexes, the first two of which are slightly different than those used by Sewell in his preliminary form of the scale, therefore different titles are used for the first two indexes. The three are as follows:

Number of Items	NAME OF INDEX	*Possible Range in Score* *Maximum*	*Minimum*
12	Housing	78	23
16	Movable Possessions	104	45
8	Social Participation	48	23
36	The Scale	230	91

I. *Housing*
Scale Items

	SCORE Yes	No
1. Construction of house: Brick, stucco, etc. or painted frame — Score: 5; Unpainted frame or other — Score: 3		
2. Room-person ratio: Number of rooms? . . divided by Number of Persons? . . equals . . Ratio: Below 1.00 — 3; 1.00-1.99 — 5; 2.00-2.99 — 7; 3.00 and up — 9		
3. Separate dining room?	6	3
4. Separate kitchen?	6	3
5. Separate living room?	6	3
6. Living room floors finished?	7	4
7. Living room woodwork finished?	5	2
8. Living room wall construction: Plaster — Score: 6; Wall board — 5; Ceiling — 4; Building paper or no inside wall — 2		

[4] Statement developed by Merton D. Oyler.

	Score Yes	Score No
9. Living room walls decorated?	5	2
13. Lighting facilities:		

	Electric or Gas	*Mantle or Pressure*	*Oil lamps, others or none*
Score:	8	6	3

	Yes	No
14. Water piped into the house?	8	4
15. Kitchen sink?	7	4

II. *Movable Possessions*

10. Living room floor covering:

	Rugs or carpets	*Linoleum or bare floors*
Score:	6	3

	Yes	No
11. Shades and curtains or drapes on living room windows?	5	2

12. Living room lounge:

	Divan, davenport, or studio couch	*Day bed or couch*	*Bed, cot, or none*
Score:	6	5	3

	Yes	No
16. Linoleum on kitchen floor?	5	2
17. Power washer?	6	3

18. Refrigerator:

	Mechanical	*Ice*	*Other or none*
Score:	8	6	3

	Yes	No
19. Radio?	6	3
20. Telephone?	6	3
21. Automobile? (other than truck)	5	2
22. Furniture insured?	7	4
23. Family takes a daily newspaper?	6	3

24. Number of magazines regularly taken? ....

Number:	0-1	2-3	4-5	6 and up
Score:	3	5	7	8

25. Approximate number of books in the home? ....

Number:	0-7	8-49	50-99	100 and up
Score:	3	5	7	8

26. Wife's education? (grades completed) ....

Number:	0-7	8	9-11	12	13 and up
Score:	2	4	6	7	8

27. Husband's education? (grades completed) ....

Number:	0-7	8	9-11	12	13 and up
Score:	3	5	6	7	8

	Yes	No
28. Husband's life insured?	6	3

III. *Social Participation*

	Yes	No
29. Husband a church member?	5	3
30. Husband attends church? (¼ of meetings)	6	3
31. Husband attends Sunday School? (¼ of meetings)	6	3
32. Husband a member of a farm cooperative?	8	4
33. Wife a church member?	5	2
34. Wife attends church? (¼ of meetings)	5	2
35. Wife attends Sunday School? (¼ of meetings)	6	3
36. Wife a member of an extension or P. T. A. group?	8	4

General and Specific Directions for Use of the Socio-economic Status Scale

(The general directions and the introductory specific directions are quoted from Oklahoma Agricultural Experiment Station Technical Bulletin No. 9, "The Construction and Standardization of a Scale for the Measurement of the Socio-economic Status of Oklahoma Farm Families," by William H. Sewell. Stillwater, Oklahoma, April 1940, pp. 86-88. The additional specific directions are decisions that were made at the time of scaling the score items.)

"General Directions to Enumerator—The answers to the questions listed in the scale provide a quantitative descripition of farm family socio-economic status. These questions were adopted after analysis of a large number of items designed to measure socio-economic status. They were chosen according to a statistical technique for item selection. Therefore, do not let your opinion concerning the merit of any question influence your enumeration of it. It is essential that every question be answered as carefully as possible. Many of the questions can be answered by observation; where they cannot be, you must ask. If possible, take the schedule in the living room of the family being rated, and try to see the kitchen.

After having ascertained the answer to a question, check or circle the the correct description. "Y" is the abbreviation for "Yes." "N" is the abbreviation for "No." Some questions have a choice of several answers. In such cases you must check the reply that is the most accurate description. *Check only one answer to each question.*"

I. *Housing*

1. "Construction of House. If paint is badly checked, in poor repair, or indistinct, rate as unpainted frame."[5]
   Printed Schedule item C-1-2 and 3
   Score of 5:
      brick, stucco
      native stone
      all types of weather boards having condition of paint 1, 2, 3 (La. 5, 4, 3).
   Score of 3:
      log
      all types of weather board having condition of paint 4, 5 (La. 2, 1).
   N.A. assigned the mean score, which for all states equals 4.
2. "Room-person ratio. Number of rooms refers to the number of rooms in the house used for living purposes. Persons means the total number of persons living in the house, regardless of their relationship, age, or sex."
   Printed Schedule C-2-1; B-col. D.
   Number of rooms used for kitchen, dining, living, and bedrooms. Liv-

[5] See n. 6.

ing rooms include music, library, solarium; but not dogtrot, hall, bath, storage, junkroom, pantry, laundry, basement room for workshop, or storm cellar.

3. "Separate dining room. This means that the room is used only as a dining room. If it is used as a combination dining room and kitchen or any other combination, do not give credit for separate dining room."
Printed Schedule item C-2-2.
If no entry was made for dining room and if it was unbracketed with kitchen, it was edited as joint with kitchen.
4. "Separate kitchen. If used as dining room, living, or bedroom as well as a kitchen, do not give credit for separate kitchen."
Printed Schedule item C-2-2.
5. "Separate living room. For the purposes of this scale, every house has a living room. If there is only one room in the house, it must be considered as the living room. If the interviewer is not sure which room this is, he may ask the interviewee what room the family considers as its living room. As a further explanation it may be said that the living room is the one in which the family entertains visitors and guests or uses for its chief gathering place during leisure hours. If the room is used as a bedroom, dining room, or kitchen, or any combination of these, it may not be considered as a separate living room."
Printed Schedule item C-2-2.
6. "Living room floors finished. This means floors that have been varnished, stained, or painted. If badly checked, in poor repair, or indistinct, rate as unfinished."[6]

Printed Schedule item C-2-4g.
Floor finish:

	Louisiana						*All Other States*				
Unfinished	1	2	3	4	5	Unfinished	1	2	3	4	5
Painted	1	2	3	4	5	Painted	1	2	3	4	5
Varnished	1	2	3	4	5	Varnished	1	2	3	4	5
Score:		4		7		Score:		7		4	

N.A. equals 5.

7. "Living room woodwork finished. Same as 6."
Printed Schedule item C-2-4i.
(i) Woodwork

	Louisiana						*All Other States*				
Unfinished	–	–	–	–	–	Unfinished	–	–	–	–	–
Painted	1	2	3	4	5	Painted	1	2	3	4	5
Varnished	1	2	3	4	5	Varnished	1	2	3	4	5
Score:		4		7		Score:		7		4	

N.A. equals 3.

[6] Scale items 1, 6, and 7 require a rating on condition of paint to complete the scoring if the surface is painted. Hence absence of this rating (1, 2, 3, 4, 5) may require that the mean score be assigned for such item. Field enumerators in Louisiana were instructed to consider 5 a high rating and 1 a low rating. The other four states used the opposite direction of value, with 1 as a high rating.

8. "Living room wall construction. This refers to the inside wall. Plaster board, wall board, masonite, etc., are to be considered wall board. Ceiling refers to beaded ceiling, shiplap, weather-board, etc. Newspapers, tar-paper, etc., tacked over the frame are to be considered as building paper."
   Printed Schedule item C-2-4a.
   N.A. equals 5.
   Entries of "ceiling is weather board" or "ceiling is studding" were scored as no inside wall.
9. "Living room walls decorated. Wall paper, fancy plaster, painted walls, etc., constitute decorated walls. This has no reference to pictures or other adornments on the walls."
   Printed Schedule item C-2-4b.
   N.A. equals 3.
13. "Lighting facilities. Under mantel lights include Aladdin, Coleman, acetylene, pressure lamps, etc. Others self-explanatory."
   Printed Schedule item C-2-4k.
   N.A. equals 5.
   If a gas, mantel or pressure, is used to supplement a windcharger, the score is 6. If kerosene is used to supplement windcharger, the score is
   N.A. equals 5.
14. "Water piped into house. Self-explanatory."
   Printed Schedule item C-2-7.
   N.A. equals 4.
   A pump inside the house is full score.
15. "Kitchen sink. Check this carefully, since many homes have kitchen sinks even though they do not have water piped into house."
   Printed Schedule item C-2-5c.
   N.A. equals 4.

II. *Movable Possessions*

10. "Living room floor covering. Consider large or small cloth rugs and carpets as rugs. Do not give credit for congoleum, linoleum, etc."
   Printed Schedule item C-2-4h.
   N.A. equals 4.
11. "Shades and curtains or drapes on living room windows. Give credit only when there are both blinds and curtains or drapes. Any one alone should be considered 'n.'"
   Printed Schedule item C-2-4e.
   N.A. equals 3.
12. "Living room lounge. If there is a bed or cot in the room, give credit for this only, regardless of the presence of the other items."
   Printed Schedule item C-2-41.
   N.A. equals 4.

16. "Linoleum on kitchen floor. Give credit for congoleum or linoleum rugs that cover the major portion of the floor space. Do not give credit for small pieces on an otherwise bare floor."
    Printed Schedule item C-2-5e.
    N.A. equals *3*.
17. "Power washer. Give credit for electric, gasoline, or water power washer. If family sends washing out, give credit. Do not give credit for any type of hand-operated washer."
    Printed Schedule item C-2-8a.
    "Help-yourself" service was assigned the full score.
    N.A. for Oklahoma equals *4*, for other States N.A. equals *3*.
18. "Refrigerator. Mechanical refers to all refrigerators operated by electricity, gas, gasoline, etc. Ice refers to ice boxes and ice chests. Do not give credit for summer cellar, etc."
    Printed Schedule item C-2-5d.
    N.A. equals *5*.
19. "Radio. Self-explanatory." Possession of a radio out of service condition and not in use during previous twelve months is considered as not having a radio.
    Printed Schedule item C-2-13.
    N.A. equals *5*.
20. "Telephone. Self-explanatory."
    Note: Enter in pencil the item numbers "21. Auto, 26. Wife's education, and 27. Husband's education" directly under the items 11 to 23 in the last column on page 1, lower right hand corner.
    Printed Schedule item C-2-15.
    N.A. equals *3*.
21. "Automobile. Give credit for all pleasure motor cars regardless of year, model, or make. Do not give credit for pickup, truck, or tractor." Verify auto use (or possession for use) under both C-3, column 1 on page 1 and E-2, line 1 on page 2 of the Printed Schedule. Possession of a car that has not been in working order any time during the previous twelve months is considered as not having an automobile.
22. "Insurance on furniture. Give credit where household goods are covered by either a blanket or a separate policy."
    Printed Schedule item C-2-22.
    N.A. equals *4*.
23. "Daily newspaper. Do not give credit for weekly or semi-weekly papers."
    Printed Schedule item C-2-16.
    N.A. equals *5*.

24. "Magazines. Include all publications, other than newspapers, regularly bought or subscribed to, regardless of their subject matter."
Printed Schedule item C-2-18.
N.A. equals 5.

25. "Books. Estimate the number of bound books in the living rooms. If none can be seen, you may ask."
Printed Schedule item C-2-19.
N.A. equals 4.

26. "Wife's education.[7] Give credit for the highest grade completed. Count high school graduation and one or more year of college or two years of technical training (business college, draftsman training, etc.) as 13 and up. In other cases give credit for technical training on the basis of one grade for each two years."

Grades La. and Texas	0-6	7	8-10	11	12 and up
Grades Ark., Miss. and Okla.	0-7	8	9-11	12	13 and up
Score:	2	4	6	7	8

Louisiana and Texas have only in very recent years increased the common school grades from 7 to 8.

Printed Schedule item B-1, line 1, Column I.
N.A. equals 5.

27. "Husband's education.[8] Same as for wife."
Grades for the five states were grouped as for the wife.
Printed Schedule item B-1, line 2, Column I.
N.A. equals 5.

28. "Husband's life insured.[9] Credit is to be given for any regular life insurance policy regardless of its amount or type. Burial policies, etc., are not to be counted as life insurance."

III. *Social Participation*[10]

29. "Husband a church member. Membership depends only on whether or not a person belongs to the organization. Do not confuse membership with participation, attendance, etc. One may be a member even though he no longer attends, contributes, or otherwise participates."
Printed Schedule item B-3-lower (a).
N.A. equals 5.

30. "Husband attends church. One-fourth or more of the regular meetings must be attended for credit to be given on this question. Be sure to learn how often the group meets before answering this and similar questions."

---

[7] "If a broken or irregular family, count Male household head as Husband or Female head as Wife."

[8] See n. 7.

[9] See n. 7.

[10] See n. 7.

Printed Schedule item Q-1, line 1, Column H.
N.A. equals 5.

31. "Husband attends Sunday school. Same as above."
Printed Schedule item Q-1, line 2, Column H.
N.A. equals 4.

32. "Husband member of a farm cooperative. Include in this question (membership on a basis of 29 above) all farm cooperatives regardless of type."
Printed Schedule item Q-1, Occupational and Economic, lines 6 to 12, Columns H and preceding.
N.A. equals 5.
When an economic cooperative is checked in either of the first two columns, membership is assumed.
These organizations in Texas were considered as farm cooperatives:
SPJST
KTZT
Cotton cooperatives
Lodge fire insurance cooperatives
Church fire insurance cooperatives
RVOS, Catholic economic society
German Mutual Aid Insurance Cooperative
St. Michael's Society (Insurance and sick benefit)
Texas organizations not considered as farmer cooperatives include:
Beef Cattle clubs
Bell County Jersey Cattle Club
Son of Herman ODHS
PJCMT
ODHS
In Oklahoma the Lawton Cattle Association and the Oklahoma Cotton Grower's Association were edited as farmer cooperatives when they were listed by the enumerator.
In all states: A C&CS loan (cooperative and community service of the FSA) was considered as a farmer cooperative membership. Typical projects were "peanut picker" and "mower and rake." All Mississippi FSA schedules were considered as full score for this item because the operator was a member of the State Marketing and Purchasing Cooperative. If only one head is scored, double that score.

33. "Wife a church member. Same as for husband."
Printed Schedule item B-3, lower (b).
N.A. equals 5.

34. "Wife attends church. Same as for husband."
Printed Schedule item Q-1, line 1, Column W.
N.A. equals 5.

35. "Wife attends Sunday school. Same as for husband."
Printed Schedule item Q-1, line 2, Column W.
N.A. equals 4.

36. "Wife member of extension or P.T.A. group. Include here Home Demonstration and all other extension or P.T.A. clubs. (Membership on basis of 29 above)."
Printed Schedule item Q-1, lines Educational 1 and 8, Column W.

Scoring Instructions. The scores were placed directly on the printed schedules to the left of the appropriate items. Orange crayon was used for Housing items, blue crayon for Movable Possessions items, and red crayon for Social Participation items. The totals for these three indexes were entered in appropriate colors of crayon at the lower margin of page 1, preferably under the next to the last column. If footnotes on this page of the schedule prevented, the scores were moved left, to column 12 of item 3, "Changes in Levels of Living." The sum of these three indexes entered in pencil is the socio-economic status score.

Scoring Omissions. When N.A. was the entry on the schedule for the particular scale item, the mean was computed from standardization data reported by Sewell in "The Restandardization of a Sociometric Scale," *Social Forces,* March, 1943, pp. 302-11. The data are given in Table 5, p. 308 of that article. An example for scale item 2 is presented as a more complex computation:

Oklahoma had 51.4 "per cent possessing the item."

As this is a graduated item, a footnote reference cites pp. 62-66 of Okla. A.R.S. Technical Bul. 9, where it is reported that credit is given for only those descriptions in bold type. i.e., rooms per person ratios of 1.0 or above. Hence 51.4 of Oklahoma farm families scored 5 or more, and the mean is estimated as 5. Use of data in the first four columns of the table in Appendix c, ibid, permits more exact computation of a mean score, which is 4.4 for Oklahoma. Louisiana whites had 70 per cent possessing the item. Hence the mean of 5 is a better estimate. Actually items 2, 3, 4 and 5 were never edited as N.A. in this study. A very close approximation could always be edited from the given data. Where a value for the mean score is given in the specific directions above, it was used for edited entries of N.A.

This procedure for scoring omissions is different from that given by Sewell in his original instructions, (Okla. Tech. Bul. 9, p. 88) which accompanied the scale. His method assumed that the total of N.A. items in a given schedule would have the same proportionate weight as the reported items. The method herein used assumed that if the scale were shortened to include only the reported items for any given schedule, that the score thus obtained could be made comparable with all computed scores by adding in the mean scores for missing items. Each method has objections, but the number of N.A. items in any schedule was very seldom more than 2, hence the problem is a minor one.

THE MIGRATION INDEX[11]

When comparisons are made concerning the amount of migration by various tenure groups, races, and other classifications of farm families, a technique is needed for holding constant the effect of age. Earlier studies of farm family migration have developed approximations of age standardization to remove the effect of age when studying the relation of tenure and migration. McMillan has reviewed these earlier studies and has used the technique of age classification to group the more than 1,000 Oklahoma open country families of his study into four quartiles of increasing degrees of migration, first holding age of the male head constant by sorting into five-year age groups.[12]

Using McMillan's raw data to construct a generalized age curve of migration, it was discovered that the cumulative increase in the number of moves was sufficiently regular that a smoothed age curve could be constructed by the free hand method. The number of moves (changes of residence) previously made by each family head were averaged for each "five-years of earning life group." These averages (with one whole number added to each) are plotted as X-marks in Figure 1.

The one whole number is added to these averages in order to provide for a corresponding increase in the vertical scale, thus avoiding zero in the scale and the ratio for number of moves. The smoothed curve constructed by the free hand method is shown in heavy outline in Figure 1. From this curve are read the expected number of moves for each five-year group based on the number of years of earning life. These expected values are entered as the "Total" line at the bottom of Work Table A1. The body of this table is then filled in by computing the ratio of moves to expected moves. The number of moves (actual plus one) is divided by the appropriate "expected number of moves" to obtain the entry for each column in the given line of Table A1.

Returning to Figure 1, the migration ratio is set up as a series of logarithmic intervals to convert the highly skewed distribution of ratios to a normal distribution. For the thousand Oklahoma families the average number of moves is the expected number of moves and the migration ratio is therefore 1.00. This becomes the lower limit of interval 5 in the Migration code (right hand margin of Figure 1). The logarithmic intervals selected for the migration ratio are the ones which determine the location of the auxiliary curves that are shown in Figure 1. For example,

---

[11] Statement developed by Merton D. Oyler.

[12] Robert T. McMillan, "Migration and Status of Open Country Families in Oklahoma," *Oklahoma Agricultural Experiment Station* Techincal Bulletin No. T-19, Stillwater, September, 1943, pp. 17-19.

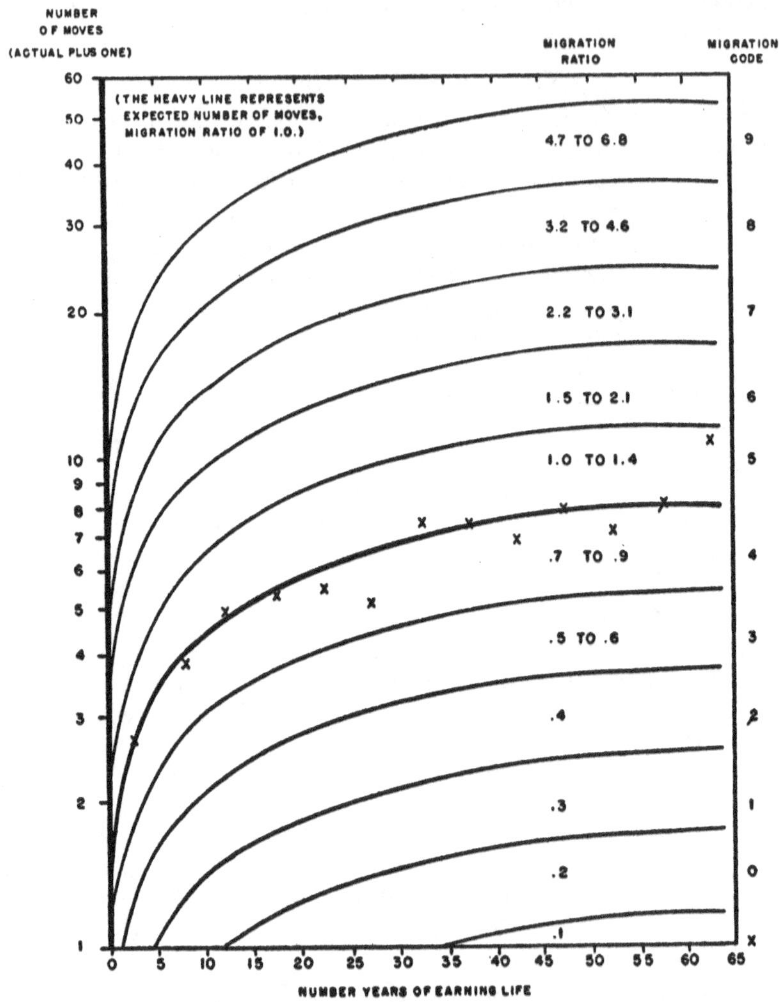

FIGURE I

Migration Ratio and Migration Code, Based on Number of Moves in Relation to Years of Earning Life

if the ratio of number of moves (actual plus one) to expected number of moves is at least 1 and less than 1.5, then its value will be located for any "year of earning life" group, somewhere between the heavy line and the next auxiliary curve immediately above it, and will be assigned a migration code of 5 (Work Tables A1, A2, A3, A4 and A5).

WORK TABLE A1

Ratio of Moves (coded number of moves made plus 1) to expected number of Moves, by five-year intervals of earning life

Moves made†	YEARS OF EARNING LIFE*												
	0-4	5-9	10-14	15-19	20-24	25-29	30-34	35-39	40-44	45-49	50-54	55-59	60-64
0..........	.4	.2	.2	.2	.2	.2	.1	.1	.1	.1	.1	.1	.1
1..........	.7	.5	.4	.4	.3	.3	.3	.3	.3	.3	.3	.3	.2
2..........	1.1	.8	.6	.5	.5	.5	.4	.4	.4	.4	.4	.4	.4
3..........	1.5	1.0	.8	.7	.7	.6	.6	.5	.5	.5	.5	.5	.5
4..........	1.9	1.2	1.0	.9	.8	.8	.7	.7	.7	.7	.6	.6	.6
5..........	2.2	1.5	1.2	1.1	1.0	.9	.9	.8	.8	.8	.8	.8	.8
6..........	2.6	1.8	1.5	1.3	1.1	1.1	1.0	1.0	.9	.9	.9	.9	.9
7..........	3.0	2.0	1.7	1.5	1.3	1.2	1.1	1.1	1.1	1.1	1.0	1.0	1.0
8..........	3.3	2.2	1.9	1.6	1.5	1.4	1.3	1.2	1.2	1.2	1.2	1.2	1.1
9..........	3.7	2.5	2.1	1.8	1.6	1.5	1.4	1.4	1.3	1.3	1.3	1.3	1.2
10..........	......	2.8	2.3	2.0	1.8	1.7	1.6	1.5	1.5	1.4	1.4	1.4	1.4
11..........	......	3.0	2.5	2.2	2.0	1.8	1.7	1.6	1.6	1.6	1.6	1.5	1.5
12..........	......	......	2.7	2.4	2.1	2.0	1.9	1.8	1.7	1.7	1.7	1.7	1.6
13..........	......	......	3.0	2.5	2.3	2.1	2.0	1.9	1.9	1.8	1.8	1.8	1.8
14..........	......	......	......	2.7	2.5	2.3	2.1	2.1	2.0	2.0	1.9	1.9	1.9
15..........	......	......	......	2.9	2.6	2.4	2.3	2.2	2.1	2.1	2.1	2.1	2.0
16..........	......	......	......	3.1	2.8	2.6	2.4	2.3	2.3	2.2	2.2	2.2	2.1
17..........	......	......	......	3.3	3.0	2.7	2.6	2.5	2.4	2.4	2.3	2.3	2.3
18..........	......	......	......	3.5	3.1	2.9	2.7	2.6	2.5	2.5	2.5	2.4	2.4
TOTAL‡.......	2.7	4.0	4.8	5.5	6.1	6.6	7.0	7.3	7.5	7.6	7.7	7.8	8.0

*Years of earning life as coded in actual years, in green crayon on the printed regional schedule, Section K, to the left and above line 1.

†Moves made as coded on the printed regional schedule in green crayon, Section K, to the left of line 9. (One whole number was added to this series before computing the above table).

‡Expected number of moves for given number years of earning life.

THE FERTILITY INDEX[13]

A generalized age curve of fertility was developed in order to express the observed number of children in a family as a ratio in relation to the expected number of children to be born for a given age of parent. (Figures II and III.) For this purpose Work Table A6 was prepared, using births per thousand rural-farm women in the United States, 1940. The specific annual births per 5-year age group of women are multiplied by five to cumulate births for 5-year age groups. These products are cumulated into a continuously increasing amount of expected births to each 1,000 women (column 3) and to each 1,000 women of the 90 per cent who marry during their lifetime (column 7).

Children born to the male head are standardized for age of male head. This procedure permits each family to be classified into an appropriate fertility index group. Hence all families can then be grouped regardless of age, into appropriate fertility index levels to compare the fertility of tenure

[13] Statement developed by Merton D. Oyler.

Work Table A2
Code for Migration Index

Moves made†	Years of Earning life*												
	0-4	5-9	10-14	15-19	20-24	25-29	30-34	35-39	40-44	45-49	50-54	55-59	60-69
0...........	2	0	0	0	0	0	X	X	X	X	X	X	X
1...........	4	3	2	2	1	1	1	1	1	1	1	1	0
2...........	5	4	3	3	3	3	2	2	2	2	2	2	2
3...........	6	5	4	4	4	3	3	3	3	3	3	3	3
4...........	6	5	5	4	4	4	4	4	4	4	3	3	3
5...........	7	6	5	5	5	4	4	4	4	4	4	4	4
6...........	7	6	6	5	5	5	5	5	4	4	4	4	4
7...........	7	6	6	6	5	5	5	5	5	5	5	5	5
8...........	8	7	6	6	6	5	5	5	5	5	5	5	5
9...........	8	7	6	6	6	6	5	5	5	5	5	5	5
10...........	..	7	7	6	6	6	6	6	6	5	5	5	5
11...........	..	7	7	7	6	6	6	6	6	6	6	6	6
12...........	..	..	7	7	6	6	6	6	6	6	6	6	6
13...........	..	..	7	7	7	6	6	6	6	6	6	6	6
14...........	..	..	..	7	7	7	6	6	6	6	6	6	6
15...........	..	..	..	7	7	7	7	7	6	6	6	6	6
16...........	..	..	..	7	7	7	7	7	7	7	7	7	7
17...........	..	..	..	8	7	7	7	7	7	7	7	7	7
18...........	..	..	..	8	7	7	7	7	7	7	7	7	7
Total‡.......	5	5	5	5	5	5	5	5	5	5	5	5	5

*Years of earning life as coded in actual years, in green crayon on the printed regional schedule, Section K, to the left and above line 1.

†Moves made as coded on the printed regional schedule in green crayon, Section K, to the left of line 9. (One whole number was added to this series before computing the above table).

‡The total is the expected average. Hence it is a code of 5, although it is at the lower limit of code 5, the heavy X- line in Figure 1.

classes in relation to their income, size of business, socio-economic status, etc.

The male head is selected in preference to the female head because the fertility rate is to be related to farm management and other occupational factors of the male head, that are more directly dependent on the age of the male head.

The cumulated totals of expected births (column 7 of Work Table A6) are transformed through three adjustments before transferring them to the "Total" line at the bottom of Work Table A7. The cumulative total of column 7 from Work Table A6 is plotted as an ogive in Figure 1. Each 5-year group "cumulated total" in column 7 represents the total number of children expected at the end of the 5-year period and includes all children yet born to the mothers at the end of the given 5-year interval. For example 1,000 women at the end of their 29th year would have 1,851.7 children. This cumulated total for women at their 30th birthday is now applied to the 5-year group of women centering at age 30, or the ages 27½ to 32½ years of age. It is assumed, from general information on ages of

WORK TABLE A3

Migration Index. Frequency distribution converted to arithmetic values, to contrast with the geometric mean*

Code (1)	Arithmetic midpoint of interval (2)	OKLAHOMA NATIVE WHITE FAMILIES				
				Computations of geometric mean and standard deviation		
		Frequency (3)	Arithmetic mean (col. 2 x col. 3) (4)	d† (5)	fd‡ (6)	fd^2 (7)
X.......	.12115	2	.24230	−5	− 10	50
0.......	.17783	9	1.60047	−4	− 36	144
1.......	.26103	16	4.17648	−3	− 48	144
2.......	.38313	27	10.34451	−2	− 54	108
3.......	.56234	35	19.68190	−1	− 35	35
4.......	.82541	88	72.63608	0	0	0
5.......	1.2115	64	77.53600	1	64	64
6.......	1.7783	53	94.24990	2	106	222
7.......	2.6103	15	39.15450	3	45	135
8.......	3.8313	1	3.83130	4	4	16
9.......	5.6234	3	16.87020	5	15	75
Y.......	N.A.	(1)	....			
		314	340.32364		−183 234	993

$\frac{340.32364}{313}$ = 1.0873, arithmetic mean in terms of the ratio.

Sum of fd = +51

Midpoint of the logarithmic intervals (see Table A5).

Code interval	Logarithmic midpoint	Deviation from assumed mean
4	.91667−1	0
5	.08333	1

$\frac{\text{Sum of } fd^2}{N} = \frac{993}{313} = 3.1725 = S^2$

$C = \frac{51}{313} = .163;\ C^2 = .026569$

$s^2 = Sa^2 - C^2 = 3.1459$

Difference, .16666 = one interval

C = .163 intervals

.163 x .16666 = .027167

int. 4 midpt. = .91667−1

mean in logs. = .94383−1

s = 1.7736 in interval units

interval = .16667 in logarithms

s = .2956 in logarithms

Reading the antilog, Geometric mean = .87868

Arithmetic mean = 1.0873

*For a discussion of the geometric mean as an average of ratios, see F. C. Mills, *Statistical Methods* applied to Economics and Business, 1938 Edition, pp. 125-32; 134-36. Also see pp. 588-96.

†Column 5: Deviation from assumed mean.

‡Column 6: Assumed deviations multiplied by frequencies (Column 3 x column 5).

TABLE A4

Logarithmic series of intervals for a scale of 6 intervals to a cycle*

Fertility Code	Migration Code	Lower Limit of Interval		Midpoint of Interval	
		Log	Number	Log	Number
	X	.00000−1	.10000	.08333−1	.12115
	0	.16667−1	.14678	.25000−1	.17783
	1	.33333−1	.21544	.41667−1	.26103
X	2	.50000−1	.31623	.58333−1	.38313
1	3	.66667−1	.46416	.75000−1	.56234
2	4	.83333−1	.68129	.91667−1	.82541
3	5	.00000	1.0000	.08333	1.2115
4	6	.16667	1.4678	.25000	1.7783
5	7	.33333	2.1544	.41666	2.6103
6	8	.50000	3.1623	.58333	3.8313
7	9	.66667	4.6416	.7500	5.6234
8	..	.83333	6.8129	.91666	8.2541
9	..	1.00000	10.000	1.08333	12.115
..	..	1.66667	14.678		

*This scale was used in the migration and fertility ratios. A cycle is a multiple of ten, e.g., from 1 to 10 or 10 to 100, etc.

TABLE A5

Logarithmic series of intervals for a scale of two and one-half intervals to a cycle*

Miles moved, Code	Lower Limit of Interval		Midpoint of Interval	
	Log	Number	Log	Number
0	.0000−1	.1000	.20−1	.15849
1	.40 −1	.25119	.60−1	.3984
2	.80 −1	.63096	.00	1.0000
3	.20	1.5849	.40	2.5119
4	.60	3.9811	.80	6.3096
5	1.0	10.000	1.20	15.849
6	1.4	25.119	1.60	39.811
7	1.8	63.096	2.00	100.0
8	2.2	158.49	2.40	251.19
9	2.6	398.11	2.80	630.96
X	3.0	1000.	3.20	1584.9
...	3.4	2500.	3.60	3981.1

*This scale was used in the code for "miles moved on last move". A cycle is a multiple of ten, e.g., from 1 to 10 or 10 to 100, etc.

farm family spouses, that farm women on the average marry husbands 2 to 3 years their senior. Hence for the children ever born to women, the equivalent ages of the male heads would average 2½ years older. So the births to women 25 to 29 are cumulated to age 30 and centered on ages 27½ to 32½ for women, or ages 30 to 34 for male heads. These two

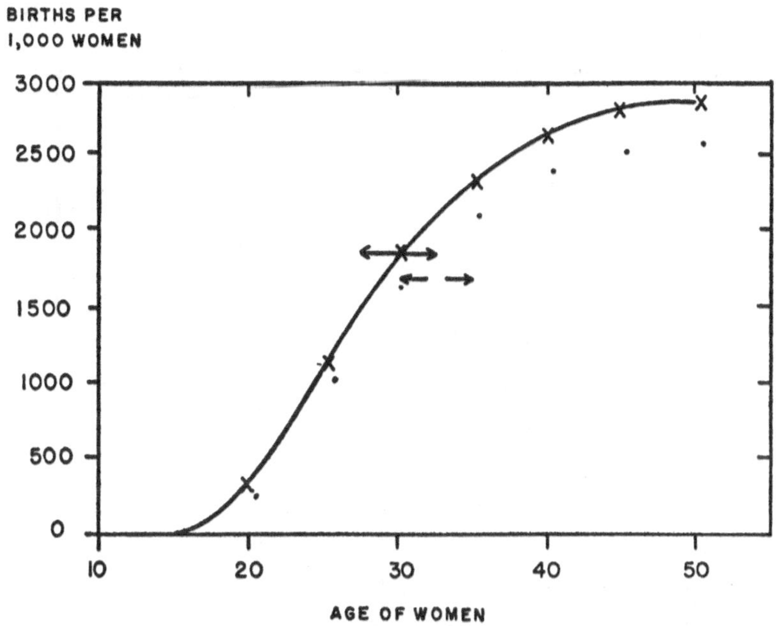

FIGURE II

Cumulated births per 5-year age period of women, for child-bearing ages of women, for child-bearing ages of women in the rural-farm population of the United States

(Rates for the curve are based on the 90 per cent who marry; the dotted points are for rates based on all women, unadjusted for percentage married. Logarithmic intervals were used in the construction of the punch card code for the fertility index. The lower limit of each interval is listed in the middle pair of columns in Table A4, for the corresponding "Fertility Code" as given in the left stub of that table. Work Table A8 gives the code for the appropriate combinations of children in relation to specified ages of male head. This table is used when coding the fertility ratio of the male head. Given the age of the male head and the number of children born to him, the code is read at the juncture of the appropriate column and line.)

transformations are accomplished by assigning fertility rates accumulated for women 25 to 29, to male heads 30 to 34 years and likewise lifting the age 5 years for all age groups when transforming from female to male head in rate expectancies. The rates per 1,000 males are converted to rates per male, by dividing by 1,000. Thus the 1,851.7 in the above example becomes 1.852 and this in turn is increased by 1 to become 2.852, the latter step being a shift in the entire vertical scale of Table A7, in order to avoid infinity in the fertility ratio.

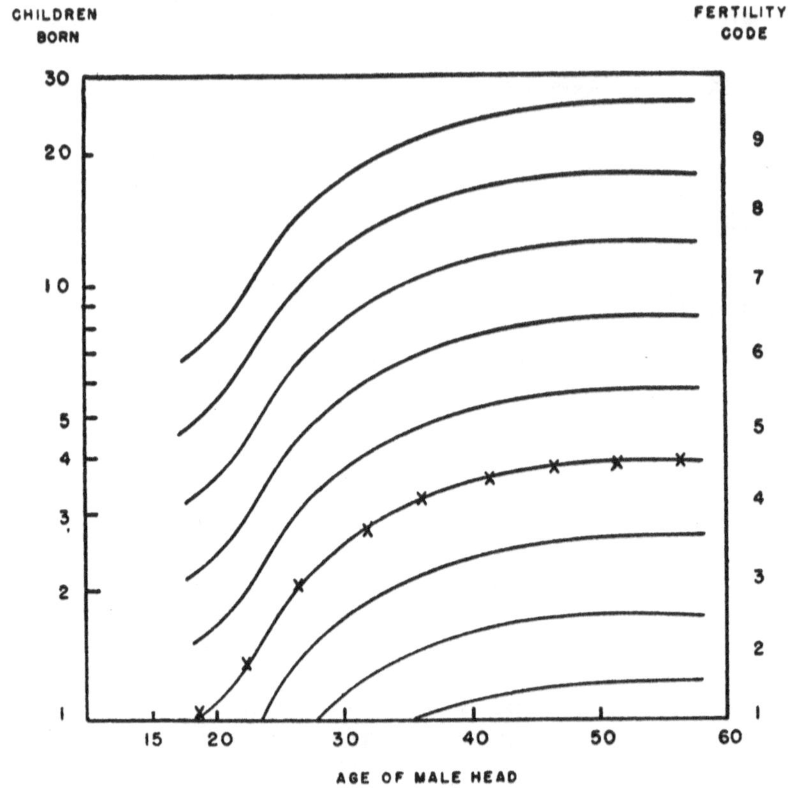

FIGURE III

Fertility ratio and fertility code of male head, based on number of children born as related to expected number born to male parents of each age.*

* This scale was shifted one whole number to avoid zero in the ratio of actual to expected births.

Table A7 is completed by filling in the body of the table the appropriate ratios for specified numbers of children (plus one as accomplished by an increase of one in the vertical scale to avoid infinity), divided by the expected number per male head of the indicated age.

The expected number of children for rural-farm male heads is plotted as a series of X-marks on the bold outline curve of Figure 2, the third curve from the bottom of the graph. Thus the observed children for the rural-farm specific age groups of women become the expected number for specific age groups of male heads who are 5 years older.

BIRTHS PER THOUSAND RURAL FARM WOMEN IN THE UNITED STATES, 1940

Explanation of columns, their source or method of computation:

2. Data from *Vital Statistics of U. S.*, Supplement for 1939-1940, Part III.

Rates for all ages, 59.8; this, multiplied by 45, the number of years in child-bearing span, gives the expected number of children as 2691. The 2526 is obtained by multiplying 505.2, (the summation of column 2) by 5, the number of years in each five-year interval. The excess of 165 is partly due to rounding to one decimal, but mostly to smaller numbers in the older and less fertile age groups, to deaths of women during the child-bearing period, and to migration from rural-farm to other residential groups of population.

3. Obtained by multiplying column (2) by 5 and cumulating products.
4. Date from U. S. Census, 1940, Population, Vol. IV, Part I, Table 6, Page 20.

Percentage of women married in the rural-farm population for specified ages by five-year intervals.

From the data of column (4) it is estimated that at least 90 per cent of the women have married during their lifetime. This includes some who are reported as widows in the table cited above.

5. Obtained by dividing corresponding entry in column (2) by .90.
6. Obtained by multiplying column (5) by 5.
7. Cumulation of column (6).

SCALE OF OPERATION AND FARM TENURE[14]

A major problem in dealing with farm tenure is that of devising a method whereby the efficiency of tenure arrangements can be measured as apart from the various other factors upon which they are superimposed. The size or scale of operation is one of the most fundamental of these

TABLE A6

Births per thousand rural farm women in the United States, 1940

Age of women	Births per 1000 Women, 1940		Percentage married 1940	Expected Births to 1000 Women Who Marry During Lifetime		
	Annual rate	Cumulated total		Annual rate	Total births	Cumulated total
1	2	3	4	5	6	7
10-14	.7	3.5	.1	.777	3.9	3.9
15-19	57.1	289.0	14.6	63.44	317.2	321.1
20-24	147.3	1025.5	59.2	163.67	818.4	1139.5
25-29	128.2	1666.5	81.0	142.44	712.2	1851.7
30-34	90.8	2120.5	86.6	100.89	504.5	2356.2
35-39	56.9	2405.0	88.5	63.22	316.1	2672.3
40-44	21.8	2514.0	88.4	24.22	121.1	2793.4
45-49	2.3	2525.5	87.2	2.56	12.8	2806.2
summation	505.2	......	....	561.32	2806.2	

[14] Statement developed by Merton D. Oyler.

TABLE A7

Ratio of births to expected number of births for 5-year age intervals of male heads

Children born†	Age of Male Head*								
	15-19	20-24	25-29	30-34	35-39	40-44	45-49	50-54	55 and over
0	.996	.76	.47	.35	.30	.27	.26	.26	.26
1	1.99	1.51	.93	.70	.60	.54	.53	.53	.53
2	2.99	2.27	1.40	1.05	.89	.82	.79	.79	.79
3	3.98	3.03	1.87	1.40	1.19	1.09	1.05	1.05	1.05
4	4.98	3.78	2.34	1.75	1.49	1.36	1.32	1.31	1.31
5	....	4.54	2.80	2.10	1.79	1.63	1.58	1.58	1.58
6	....	5.30	3.27	2.45	2.09	1.91	1.85	1.84	1.84
7	....	6.06	3.74	2.80	2.38	2.18	2.11	2.10	2.10
8	....	6.81	4.20	3.15	2.68	2.45	2.37	2.36	2.36
9	....	7.57	4.67	3.50	2.98	2.72	2.64	2.63	2.63
10	....	....	5.14	3.86	3.28	3.00	2.90	2.89	2.89
11	....	....	5.61	4.21	3.58	3.27	3.16	3.15	3.15
12	....	....	6.07	4.56	3.87	3.54	3.42	3.42	3.42
13	....	....	6.54	4.91	4.17	3.81	3.69	3.68	3.68
14	....	....	7.01	5.26	4.47	4.08	3.95	3.94	3.94
15	....	....	7.48	5.61	4.77	4.36	4.22	4.20	4.20
16	....	....	7.95	5.96	5.07	4.63	4.48	4.47	4.47
17	....	....	8.41	6.31	5.36	4.90	4.74	4.73	4.73
18	....	....	8.88	6.66	5.66	5.17	5.01	4.99	4.99
19	....	....	9.35	7.01	5.96	5.45	5.27	5.25	5.25
Total‡	1.0039	1.321	2.140	2.852	3.356	3.672	3.793	3.806	3.806

*Age of male head as entered on the printed regional schedule, Section B-1, column B, line 1.

†Children born to male head as coded in green crayon on the printed regional schedule, Section B-1, column A. in the box heading.

‡Expected number of children born to male head of specified age, as computed in work table A7, column 7, with one whole number added, to avoid infinity in the ratio. Thus for male heads age 15 to 19, the 3.9 births per thousand (for female heads) becomes 1,003.9 per thousand or 1.0039 per male head.

factors and at the same time, one of the most difficult to disentangle. It is fundamental in the sense that little real comparison can be made between the functioning of tenure factors between a series of farms unless the factor of size is controlled through measurement. No tenure arrangement will work satisfactorily if the scale of operation is too small to provide income for an adequate level of living. In other words, on small farms, family living may be unsatisfactory—but not because of the tenure arrangements. It thus becomes necessary in tenure analysis to measure the effect of size or scale of operation so as to isolate the pure tenure factors as nearly as possible. The presence of large numbers of small scale units in the Southwestern Region renders this type of analysis particularly important.

It has been difficult, however, to isolate the effect of size from that of the other tenure factors since no measure of size has been at hand which would apply satisfactorily to all parts of the region. Type of soil, intensity of farming, mechanization, and in general the varying quantities

WORK TABLE A8

Code for fertility ratio of male heads

Children born†	Age of Male Head*								
	15-19	20-24	25-29	30-34	35-39	40-44	45-49	50-54	55 and over
0.....	4	4	3	2	1	1	1	1	1
1.....	6	6	4	4	3	3	3	3	3
2.....	7	7	5	5	4	4	4	4	4
3.....	8	7	6	5	5	5	5	5	5
4.....	9	8	7	6	6	5	5	5	5
5.....	..	8	7	6	6	6	6	6	6
6.....	..	9	8	7	6	6	6	6	6
7.....	..	..	8	7	7	7	6	6	6
8.....	..	..	8	7	7	7	7	7	7
9.....	..	..	9	8	7	7	7	7	7
10.....	..	..	9	8	8	7	7	7	7
11.....	..	..	9	8	8	8	7	7	7
12.....	..	..	9	8	8	8	8	8	8
13.....	..	..	..	9	8	8	8	8	8
14.....	..	..	..	9	8	8	8	8	8
15.....	..	..	..	9	9	8	8	8	8
16.....	..	..	..	9	9	8	8	8	8
17.....	..	..	..	9	9	9	9	9	9
18.....	..	..	..	9	9	9	9	9	9
19.....	..	..	..	..	9	9	9	9	9
TOTAL‡.	5	5	5	5	5	5	5	5	5

*Age of male head as entered on the printed regional schedule, Section B-1, column B, line 1.

†Children born to male head as coded in green crayon on the printed regional schedule, Section B-1, column A, in the box heading.

‡The total is the expected average. Hence it is a code of 5, although it is at the lower limit of code 5, the heavy X- line in Figure 2.

of land, labor, and capital that go into the farming enterprise in the different type of farming areas has made a size comparison most difficult.

This problem is not acute where it is desired only to make an interval analysis of farm management factors and particularly if such analysis is confined to a single type of farming area. In the present study, however, where several types of farming areas are included and it is desirable also to view the farm as a whole in order to arrive at tenure generalizations, it becomes necessary to have an over-all measure which will satisfy the conditions for all areas in the region. The general aim of such a method is to measure tenure performance while the factor of size of operation is also measured separately and in combination with other performance factors. In this way it becomes possible to compare the tenure efficiency of all farms in the region regardless of their size. In other words, the influence of the factor of size is eliminated by comparing the results of each tenure group with the average performance of the given size group of farms in the given area. In order to isolate the influence of size, it becomes necessary to first arrive at a suitable method of measuring it.

As has already been indicated, the conventional existing measures are unsuited to the purpose at hand. The productive man-work unit probably comes as near to the need as any single measure but in the Southwestern Region it is deficient as an over-all measure due to the differences over the Region in mechanization and other factors. Variation in intensity of farming also renders this measure of unequal application in the several parts of the Region. Likewise the other conventional measures, value of business, acres of cropland and gross farm income, do not fill the requirements of an over-all measure. In order to solve these difficulties, the above mentioned measures, value of farm business, productive man-work units, and acres in cropland, were combined and the validity of the combination tested against gross farm income in each area. It was found that the combined measure accounts for 64 to 76 per cent of the variation in the gross income.

That part of the variation in gross farm income not explained by the variation in scale of operation is assumed to be "quality of the farm business." Before accepting this unexplained variation as a valid measure of quality or efficiency of the farm operation as a going concern, it is possible to test this assumption. Four factors, that are known from previous studies to be indicators of superior efficiency in farm operation include: Ratio of labor used to productive man-work units, five-year average yield of cotton, crop yield index, and price index. It is assumed that the higher a farm ranks on the range of each of these factors, the higher will be the quality of the farm business. If the rank on all four of these efficiency factors is averaged, the result would be expected to correlate highly with the "quality of farm business."

Any farms that deviate widely from this expected line of relationship are worthy of careful examination to see if other explanations are in evidence. Among those suggested are, an exceptionally efficient leasing arrangement and an exceptionally favorable combination of enterprises on the given farm. These and other influence not classified as scale of operation, nor yet as one of the four efficiency factors that were collectively termed quality of farm business, will no doubt be found. Some of them can logically be added to the list of factors comprising quality of farm business, but some will no doubt be considered random or chance factors not associated with management control.

Another way to measure the quality of business is to express the family earnings as a per cent of the scale of operation. The latter is a logarithmic distribution but the family earnings distribution tends to be much more nearly a normal arithmetic distribution. Therefore, it would probably be necessary to use the numerical value for each distribution, and to express the dollar value of family earnings as a percentage of the dollar value of scale of operation (the expected or predicted gross farm income for the given farm operational unit). The percentages so obtained for a group of farms would probably form a skewed distribution and would need to be rectified to become a normal distribution of quality of farm business, to be comparable with the results obtained by the first described method.

The "quality of business" is an indication of the managerial success of the enterprise for any given scale of operation. For farms of a given scale of operation, certain tenure arrangements are in themselves identified with risk-taking and the insurable returns to such risk. For example, when crop insurance is purchased, this outlay becomes a part of the cost of production. If no crop insurance is carried, then any savings so obtained are lumped in with returns to management, because risk-taking is a fundamental part of management. Similarly, the renter who pays cash rent is assuming a bigger risk than is the share-renter and with equal managerial ability should achieve a larger return on his management and labor.

How Scale of Operation Is Measured.

It is known from many studies of farm organization and management that with equally applied management, the larger the farm business inputs, the larger the gross farm income will be.[15] The zero order correlations obtained by relating each size input factor in turn with gross farm income show that in the Arkansas and Mississippi Coastal Plain samples the number of productive man-work units is the best single indicator of size of business, using gross farm income as the criterion of size (Table A). But it is not consistently the best. It is evidently far superior in the Arkansas and Mississippi Coastal Plain samples, but in the Oklahoma Rolling Plain and in the Texas Blackland Prairie samples, the value of business becomes a slightly better indicator of gross farm income. When the four areas are combined into one distribution the productive man-work units measure falls to a low third place as an indicator of size of the gross farm income.

TABLE A

Amount of superiority of the multiple coefficient of determination over zero order coefficients of determination for estimating amount of gross farm income, for four sample areas in the Southwestern Region

AREA	Coefficient of determination, predicting gross farm income from: Three factors $(R_{1.234})^2$	*Value of business* $(r_{12})^2$	*PMWU* $(r_{13})^2$	*Acres in cropland* $(r_{14})^2$	*Superiority of multiple over simple correlation*
All four areas	.72	.65	.39	.62	.07
Arkansas Coastal Plain	.64	.36	.61	.31	.03
Miss. Coastal Plain	.72	.45	.69	.53	.03
Okla. Rolling Plain	.65	.54	.50	.43	.11
Texas Blackland Prairie	.76	.69	.66	.55	.07

[15] For a statement of the influence of the size of business, in no matter what form it is measured, based on a review of farm management studies in the cotton section of the United States, see D. Gray Miley, *Farm Management Research in the South*, University of Virginia, 1941, Unpublished dissertation.

What is the result when all three measures of input are combined into a multiple indicator of gross farm income? Using each area sample as an independent problem, let us see how much more of the gross farm income variation is estimated by using all three measures of size as compared with the highest single indicator of size.

Using the coefficients of determination and comparing the highest zero order coefficient with the multiple coefficient, the explained variation in gross farm income is increased by 3 per cent in the Arkansas, 3 per cent in the Mississippi, 7 per cent in the Texas, and 11 per cent in the Oklahoma sample, when the multiple regression is used. (Table A). But when all four areas are considered as one sample, then the value of business becomes the best single predictor and the explained variation is increased by 7 per cent, when the multiple regression is used.

What suggestions can be offered to account for this superiority of the value of business measure when all areas are considered together? The productive man-work unit measure has been computed on the basis of specific requirements for the local area, or at least the method varied sharply as among state procedures for determining the normal requirement to be used for the sample in the respective state. Hence a specific state sample would not be directly comparable with samples of farms in other states.

Acres in cropland, as a measure of size, do show wide variations among sample areas, but yields per acre also vary among sample areas and may vary in the opposite direction. Hence value of farm business, which is a composite measure of total productive capacity, including acres and yield, would be expected to be a better predictor of gross farm income in the region as a whole than would acres in cropland.

The Regression Equation.

The three measures of size, as used in this analysis are highly intercorrelated. These correlation coefficients in the four area samples range from .66 (Value of business with PMWU in the Mississippi sample) to a high extreme of .89 (Acres in cropland with PMWU in the same State sample), and all the correlations for pairs of these factors in the other sample areas range somewhere in between these extremes. With such high intercorrelations, it is unsatisfactory to use partial correlation to measure the separate influence of the respective input measures of size to explain the size of the gross farm income.

The zero order correlations of each of these input measures of size separately with gross farm income are also consistently high, ranging from .56 to .83. It was noted earlier (Table A) that the multiple coefficient of correlation accounts for from 3 to 11 per cent more of the variation in gross farm income than does any one of the three input measures used in this analysis. Therefore it is worth while to use the combination of the three measures (X_2 Value of farm business, X_3 Productive man-work units, X_4 Acres in cropland) to estimate the expected amount of gross farm income, X_1.

The relative importance of each three measures in the equation for measuring size is based on the Beta coefficients obtained in the regression analysis. By definition, the sum of these three weights of relative importance equals the coefficient of determination, the square of the multiple R. coefficient. These relative importance values do not appear directly or obviously to have any relation to the coefficients that are used as constants in the multiple regression equation, because the Beta coefficients are pure relatives, based on the raw or original farm measures divided by the standard deviation of such original measures. The coefficients in the regression equation are not standard score relatives, they are raw or original measure relatives.

The variables used in this problem are found to have skewed distributions, as was to be expected from experience in previous studies. The logarithms of the data result in approximately normal distributions. The predictions are then made on linear relationships of logarithmic values.[16] It should be emphasized that, for the raw data, this results in a curvilinear relationship for any two of these factors and curved surface relationships when a three- or four-factor solution is established. Rectifying the data by use of logarithms to establish linear relationships does not change the nature of the relationships for the original raw data. This process merely simplifies the multiple factor solution, and permits the application of normal curve theory for standard deviation and standard error of estimate, both of which are then expressed in logarithms, or percentages, of the original data.[17]

The regression equations for the four area samples and the total sample as developed by this method are:

Arkansas	$\text{Log}\,{}_cX_1 = .167\,\text{Log}\,X_2 + 1.067\,\text{Log}\,X_3 - .254\,\text{Log}\,X_4 + .177$
Mississippi	$\text{Log}\,{}_cX_1 = .202\,\text{Log}\,X_2 + 1.034\,\text{Log}\,X_3 - .218\,\text{Log}\,X_4 + .181$
Oklahoma	$\text{Log}\,{}_cX_1 = .453\,\text{Log}\,X_2 + .538\,\text{Log}\,X_3 + .086\,\text{Log}\,X_4 + .261$
Texas	$\text{Log}\,{}_cX_1 = .435\,\text{Log}\,X_2 + .216\,\text{Log}\,X_3 + .180\,\text{Log}\,X_4 + .736$
All 4 areas	$\text{Log}\,cX_1 = .406\,\text{Log}\,X_2 + .351\,\text{Log}\,X_3 + .255\,\text{Log}\,X_4 + .403$

In these equations:

X_1 is Gross farm income	X_3 Productive man-work units
X_2 is Value of farm business	X_4 Acres in cropland

In the Arkansas and Mississppi samples, the productive man-work unit measure receives a factor weight in excess of 1. This is more than six times

[16] "The regression systems of a normal correlation surface are linear." See John F. Kenney, *Mathematics of Statistics*, Part II, p. 71, Theorem 11. (1945).

[17] For an application of this method to farm management data, see Gerhard Tintner and O. H. Brownlee, "Production Functions Derived from Farm Managment Records," *Journal of Farm Economics*, August, 1944.

the comparable weighting of this variable in the Texas sample and approximately twice its weighting in the Oklahoma sample. Parallel with this contrast, the Arkansas and Mississippi factor weights for acres in cropland are both minus values, while these weightings for Oklahoma and Texas are positive. These combinations of factor weights suggest that any increase in crop acres in the Arkansas and Mississippi sample areas, without a corresponding increase in productive man-work units, would result in lowered gross income because it would mean shifting from cotton to a less intensive crop, or from double cropping to only one crop a year on the same land.

If a general equation is wanted that will be applicable to all four areas, it can be used effectively, but of course will not be quite as accurate as would one for the specific type of farming area. The one for all four areas in combination is given above, along with the four specific ones for the type-of-farming areas.

TABLE B

Geometric mean,* standard deviation and standard error of estimate of the gross farm income for farms in four sample areas of the Southwestern Region

Area	*Geometric mean*	*Standard deviation* (σ)	STANDARD ERROR OF ESTIMATE *Amount* ($S_{1.234}$)	*Per cent of S. D.* ($S_{1.234} \div \sigma$)
The four areas	3.1394	.3844	.20362	52.97%
Ark. Coastal Plain	2.9301	.2930	.17649	60.24%
Miss. Coastal Plain	2.9849	.3090	.16199	52.43%
Okla. Rolling Plain	3.5659	.3119	.18542	59.45%
Tex. Blackland Prairie	3.2961	.2652	.13046	49.23%

* The geometric mean is expressed as a logarithm in this table in order to appraise the two measures of dispersion in the same units of measure as are used for the central tendency.

The amount of increase in error that accompanies the use of the more general equation can be seen by comparisons of the standard error of estimate for the five equations (Table B, column 3). The equation for the four areas in combination gives a standard error of estimate (.20362) almost .02 higher than for the highest single sample, that of the Oklahoma Rolling Plain area. This is a better indicator of the accuracy of prediction than is the coefficient of multiple determination because the latter is influenced by the length of the range, and of course the range is longer for the combined sample than for any one area sample.

The predicted gross farm income ($_cX_1$) is calculated for each specific farm, using its specific dollars of value of business, its specific productive man-work units, and its specific acres in cropland. The predicted gross farm income is a measure of size, based on the three input factors. For the given sample of farms in each local area, the normal distribution of farms is selected for predictive purposes. The "normal" is defined as a range of plus three to minus three standard deviation units, measured first in terms of the productive man-work units, the most reliable input measure of size; and measured secondly in terms of the gross farm income, which is the output measure of size. Farms either smaller or larger than this selected range are quite abnormal in size and are not considered reliable in this prediction problem for measuring size. These farms are retained in most phases of the analysis but are so coded that they do not disturb the accuracy of the predictions for the normal farms.

The predicted gross farm income (${}_{c}X_1$) necessarily lies on the regression line of the multiple regression equation for size of business. It is the amount of gross farm income expected under average conditions of management for the specified amounts of input of value of business, productive man-work units, and cropland acres. It becomes the composite measure of size.

The observed gross farm income (X_1) minus the predicted gross farm income (${}_{c}X_1$)is the deviation from expected amount, and is expressed as a plus or minus value. The logarithm of each is used for the subtraction, hence the difference represents a percentage. If it is plus, then the production as measured in dollars is above the average for the given size of business; if minus, the production is below the average for the given size of business. Because only one year of production is measured, this deviation may represent an annual fluctuation. A three- or a five-year average would be a much more stable measure of production but a single year of production is quite useful for this problem.

How can these regression equations be modified to respond to changes in average or expected gross farm income that result from changes in the business cycle, and other annual farm income factors, such as weather effects upon yields and acreage control adjustments? An example will be given, based on the Texas Blackland sample. All of these annual fluctuations in expected gross income are grouped together. The annual estimates for gross farm income are reported in a recent release of the U. S. Bureau of Agricultural Economics.[18]

The gross farm incomes for the years 1930 to 1944 are considered to be the base. The 1942 gross farm income of Blackland Prairie farms is given as 143 in relation to the 14-year base period. For the sample of 312 farms in 1942, the geometric mean of the gross farm income was determined

[18] Wylie D. Goodsell, Ronald W. Jones and Russell W. Bierman, *Typical Family-Operated Farms, 1930-45, Adjustments, Costs, and Returns,* F. M. 55, Processed, 91 pp., April, 1946. Data from the Regional Land Tenure Research Project were used in the construction of the data for the cotton-grain sorghum, Southern Plains farms, pp. 74-77 and for the Black Prairie Area, Texas, pp. 78-81. It is the latter series from which the gross farm income estimates are quoted for this example.

from the farm and family survey to be 3.2981 in logarithms or $1,987. Setting this at 143, the base of 100 would be $1,390. Although the relatives for the 14-year period were for arithmetic averages of the gross farm income, they are here used as relatives for geometric or logarithmic averages. This is presumed to introduce no significant error.

The Texas Blackland equations:

$cX_1 = .435 \text{ Log } X_2 + .216 \text{ Log } X_3 + .180 \text{ Log } X_4 + .736$

for 1942:

$3.2981 - .435\ (3.8712) - .216\ (2.4562) - .180\ (1.9367) - .736$

> Substituting the base period mean of $1,390, reading its logarithm as 3.1430, and using this to replace 3.2981, the only change to be made on the right hand side of the equation is to subtract from A-value of .736, the difference between the 3.2981 and 3.1430, or .1551; .736 minus .1551 = .581, the new *A* constant.

Tenure and size of business. Tenure differences accounted for only a small amount of the difference in the equations for estimating the amount of gross farm income by predicting from the three input measures of size. This conclusion was reached by comparing the Negro cropper group with owners and renters of both races, using the Arkansas Coastal Plain sample.

For both groups, the number of productive man-work units is the best single measure for the size of business, because it correlates highest with gross farm income (Table C). For the owner and renter group, the value of business is the second best predictor of gross farm income, but for the croppers, the acres in cropland become the second best predictor when used alone as a single measure of size.

TABLE C

Amount of superiority of the multiple coefficient of determination over zero order coefficients of determination for estimating amount of gross farm income, for contrasting tenure groups in the Arkansas Coastal Plain sample

TENURE	Coefficient of determination, predicting gross farm income from: *Three factors* $(R_{1.234})^2$	*Value of business* $(r_{12})^2$	*PMWU* $(r_{13})^2$	*Acres in cropland* $(r_{14})^2$	*Superiority of multiple over simple correlation*
All tenures	.64	.36	.62	.31	.02
Owners and renters	.65	.44	.61	.33	.04
Croppers (Negro)	.68	.30	.66	.39	.02

When all three measures of input are combined in order to estimate the expected amount of gross farm income, the combined measure increases the explained variation by 4 per cent for the owner-renter group and by 2 per cent for the cropper group, when contrasted with the best single measure of size, the productive man-work units (Table C, right-hand column). It is therefore concluded that one equation is suitable for use in measuring the scale of operation, rather than to have a different equation for each tenure group. Because the multiple correlation gives the significantly higher (4 per cent) determination for the owner-renter group it is concluded that the multiple regression equation should be used. It is demonstrated to be especially useful for the owner and renter farms, and it somewhat improves the estimate for the cropper farms, which of course already were well measured in size by use of the productive man-work units.[19]

It is significant that for the Arkansas Negro croppers, the value of farm business becomes a less useful predictor of gross farm income, while the other two measures become better predictors of gross farm income, when compared with all owners and tenants in the Arkansas Coastal Plains. This is also demonstrated by comparison of the Beta Coefficients of the two multiple regression equations.

The scale of operation in a simplified form. Once the scale of operation has been developed by use of the rigorous techniques already described, it is possible to present the results in more familiar terms for its practical use in the analysis of the farm business. We begin by stating the average size and the range in size for those farms considered to be within normal range of size, for the four areas and for the combined sample from the four areas that are included in this analysis (Table D).

TABLE D

Average gross income and range of normal variation from average, for 1498 farms in four sample areas of the Southwestern Region

AREA	*Average* gross income in dollars*	*Range of normal† variation from average, in dollars*		
Four areas	$1,379	$ 97	to	$19,610
Arkansas Coastal Plain	851	112	to	6,444
Mississippi Coastal Plain	966	114	to	8,162
Oklahoma Rolling Plain	3,682	427	to	31,750
Texas Blackland Prairie	1,987	318	to	12,417
Arkansas Coastal Plain				
Owners and renters	853	104	to	7,006
Negro croppers	786	169	to	3,648

* This is the geometric mean.

† The normal variation is defined as -3σ, $+3\sigma$, thereby excluding 59 farms: 3 of Arkansas sample, 6 of Mississippi sample, 23 of Oklahoma sample, and 27 of Texas sample. The samples are treated as logarithmic distributions, hence the sigma values and the mean are logarithmic values, expressed in this table as anti-logarithms.

---

[19] If the scale of operation is being measured for croppers only or for owners and tenants only, in the Arkansas Coastal Plain, these specific equations may be useful. They were developed from the above described treatment of the data:

Owners & Renters........ $\text{Log}\ {}_{C}X_1 = .307\ \text{Log}\ X_2 + .975\ \text{Log}\ X_3 - .227\ \text{Log}\ X_4 - .070$

Croppers .... $\text{Log}\ {}_{C}X_1 = .016\ \text{Log}\ X_2 + 1.143\ \text{Log}\ X_3 - .242\ \text{Log}\ X_4 + .578$

The range in expected gross income for normal farms was determined for each area separately, and these farms were then considered as one distribution to define the normal range for the combined four-area sample.

Hence this range begins at a lower amount ($97) than does any single area sample (Arkansas, $112). But it extends upward to an amount ($19,610) not nearly so high as that for the highest single area sample (Oklahoma, $31,750). This tendency of the combined four-area sample to extend lower than the lowest range for any single area and to extend not near as high as the highest range for any one area sample is explained as the result of combining two very dissimilar types of distribution. The Oklahoma and Texas area samples have high modal groups, the Oklahoma area having an especially high central tendency. The Arkansas and Mississippi area samples have low modal groups, the Arkansas having a somewhat lower central tendency than the Mississippi area sample.

Tenure comparisons. The Arkansas owners and renters had an average gross income essentially the same as that for the entire sample, including croppers. The normal range in gross income is greater with the croppers excluded, because the croppers tend to group around the average for all farms, thus making their standard deviation smaller than for all tenures. Removal of these average size farms (croppers) from the total group of farms gives a remainder (owners and renters) that has a larger standard deviation and larger range than has the entire Arkansas sample.

Appendix C

STATISTICAL TABLES

Table 1

Original* classification of farm and family schedules tabulated by Regional Land Tenure Research Project by sample area tenure and race

	Number of Cases Classified By Tenure										
	Total	Full owner	Part owner	Indeterminate	Cash renter	Share renter	Share-cash	Cropper	Other tenant	Laborer	Other
Regional Total†	1841	616	228	62	59	406	100	264	17	66	23
White	1182	476	168	34	39	266	50	83	8	36	22
Negro	512	96	43	25	20	109	10	176	8	24	1
Czech	104	31	10	2	..	27	30	2	1	1	..
German	32	11	7	1	..	3	10	..	..	..	..
Mexican	2	..	..	..	..	..	..	1	..	1	..
Other‡	9	2	..	..	..	1	..	2	..	4	..
Arkansas Coastal Plain	562	137	59	32	35	170	18	98	10	..	3
Standard Sample											
White	226	79	34	12	18	49	8	20	3	..	3
Negro	248	47	21	16	15	61	6	77	5	..	..
FSA Sample											
White	47	9	3	..	1	31	2	..	1	..	..
Negro	41	2	1	4	1	29	2	1	1	..	..
Louisiana Coastal Plain	290	163	20	13	6	30	..	48	3	4	3
White	224	152	18	12	5	20	..	13	2	..	2
Negro	66	11	2	1	1	10	..	35	1	4	1
Mississippi Coastal Plain	327	152	34	9	11	24	2	87	2	6	..
White	189	116	15	5	8	15	..	29	1	..	..
Negro	138	36	19	4	3	9	2	58	1	6	..
Oklahoma Rolling Plain	323	85	64	4	7	89	11	16	1	29	17
White	314	83	64	4	7	88	11	14	1	25	17
Other‡	9	2	..	..	..	1	..	2	..	4	..
Texas Blackland	339	79	51	4	..	93	69	15	1	27	..
Native white	182	37	34	1	..	63	29	7	..	11	..
Negro	19	..	..	..	..	..	..	5	..	14	..
Czech	104	31	10	2	..	27	30	2	1	1	..
German	32	11	7	1	..	3	10	..	..	..	..
Mexican	2	..	..	..	..	..	..	1	...	1	..

*This classification was revised and consolidated as shown in Table 2.

†Does not include: (1) Follow-up study in Arkansas, (2) Additional FSA cases sampled in Mississippi and Texas.

‡This classification is for Oklahoma only and consists of two owners, one born in Sweden and one in Russia, one renter born in Germany, one Mexican cropper, one Negro cropper, and four Negro laborers.

TABLE 2

Basic classification of farm and family schedules tabulated by Regional Land Tenure Research Project by sample area and race

State and Race	Total	Owner			Renter			Cropper
		Total	Full owner	Part owner	Total	Share-cash	Share	
REGIONAL TOTAL	1662	842	614	228	564	159	405	256
White	1213	703	518	185	425	129	296	85
Negro	449	139	96	43	139	30	109	171
ARKANSAS	517	196	137	59	223	53	170	98
White	254	125	88	37	109	29	80	20
Negro	263	71	49	22	114	24	90	78
LOUISIANA	267	183	163	20	36	6	30	48
White	208	170	152	18	25	5	20	13
Negro	59	13	11	2	11	1	10	35
MISSISSIPPI	310	186	152	34	37	13	24	87
White	183	131	116	15	23	8	15	29
Negro	127	55	36	19	14	5	9	58
OKLAHOMA								
White	267	147	83	64	106	18	88	14
TEXAS								
White	301	130	79	51	162	69	93	9
Native	170	71	37	34	92	29	63	7
Czech	100	41	31	10	57	30	27	2
German	31	18	11	7	13	10	3	..

Table 2 represents the basic race and tenure classification to be used in the regional analysis. It is a revision of Table 1 as follows: (1) eliminates Other in Oklahoma leaving remaining cases all native white (2) eliminates Negro and Mexican in Texas leaving remaining cases all white (3) eliminates the following tenure classes: Indeterminate, Other tenant, Laborer and Other (4) combines Cash renter and Share-cash renter. Elimination of certain schedules does not mean that they are discarded from the general study but rather that such cases fall within tenure and race groups too small and heterogeneous to be carried along on this basis in the general analysis.

TABLE 3

Comparison of various measures of size of farms, classified by race and tenure of operator, in four sample areas of the Southwestern Region

Area, race, and tenure status	Number of cases	Productive man work units	Acres in farm	Acres in cropland	Acres in cotton	Animal units, productive livestock	Value of farms business (hundred dollars)
ARKANSAS COASTAL PLAIN							
White							
Owners	78	297	127	57	13	5.9	41
Part owners	33	398	163	71	20	6.4	44
Share-cash renters	26	285	122	44	12	5.3	27
Share renters	49	291	124	53	14	3.9	30
Croppers	20	284	69	42	16	3.1	22
Negro							
Owners	47	259	103	49	12	3.4	27
Part owners	19	350	123	67	18	3.9	32
Share-cash renters	21	203	92	34	10	2.5	17
Share renters	60	235	106	42	13	2.3	19
Croppers	77	217	40	31	14	1.6	12
MISSISSIPPI COASTAL PLAIN							
White							
Owners	109	349	108	44	11	6.8	33
Part owners	14	394	201	52	14	7.5	36
Share-cash renters	7	160	61	20	5	2.3	13
Share renters	15	232	63	32	9	2.7	17
Croppers	27	227	44	26	9	1.8	12
Negro							
Owners	34	307	82	40	11	3.0	25
Part owners	19	259	56	32	9	3.0	17
Share-cash renters	5	206	38	25	11	0.6	11
Share renters	9	207	51	25	7	2.3	11
Croppers	55	211	31	25	9	1.2	8
OKLAHOMA ROLLING PLAIN							
White							
Owners	80	253	207	149	40	14.8	140
Part owners	63	332	437	254	61	22.7	189
Share-cash renters	18	268	272	167	48	15.7	130
Share renters	88	256	244	170	50	10.4	113
Croppers	8	189	166	121	47	16.5	67
TEXAS BLACKLAND PRAIRIE							
White							
Owners	73	308	115	96	30	8.8	99
Part owners	51	511	219	185	56	14.1	159
Share-cash renters	67	289	109	89	30	7.6	77
Share renters	90	293	116	96	31	7.2	74
Croppers	9	121	33	31	19	2.2	22

TABLE 4

Percentage distribution of farms according to productive man-work units, by race and tenure of operator, in four sample areas of the Southwestern Region

Area, race, and tenure status	Number of cases	PERCENTAGE OF FARMS WITH PRODUCTIVE MAN WORK UNITS OF					
		Less than 100	100 to 200	200 to 300	300 to 400	400 to 600	600 and over
ARKANSAS COASTAL PLAIN							
White							
Owners	79	5	22	34	20	13	6
Part owners	34	3	12	29	21	23	12
Share-cash renters	26	4	27	34	12	19	4
Share renters	49	4	12	47	21	16	..
Croppers	20	..	20	45	25	5	5
Negro							
Owners	47	6	30	34	17	11	2
Part owners	21	5	14	28	19	24	10
Share-cash renters	21	10	43	34	10	5	..
Share renters	61	7	42	28	11	10	2
Croppers	77	5	50	27	12	6	..
MISSISSIPPI COASTAL PLAIN							
White							
Owners	116	4	22	28	16	18	12
Part owners	15	..	7	46	20	20	7
Share-cash renters	8	..	75	12	13	..	..
Share renters	15	7	27	46	20	..	..
Croppers	29	3	45	35	14	3	..
Negro							
Owners	36	6	30	14	16	28	6
Part owners	19	11	21	26	37	5	..
Share-cash renters	5	..	60	20	20	..	..
Share renters	9	..	56	33	11	..	..
Croppers	58	2	53	28	14	3	..
OKLAHOMA ROLLING PLAIN							
White							
Owners	83	7	28	41	12	8	4
Part owners	63	2	16	24	36	17	5
Share-cash renters	18	6	16	39	33	6	..
Share renters	88	5	25	44	16	10	..
Croppers	12	33	34	33	..	..	..
TEXAS BLACKLAND PRAIRIE							
White							
Owners	79	1	22	28	28	15	6
Part owners	51	..	2	12	25	39	22
Share-cash renters	69	..	10	61	23	3	3
Share renters	93	1	11	46	30	10	2
Croppers	9	33	56	11	..	..	..

TABLE 5

Land use on farms, classified by race and tenure of operator, in four sample areas of the Southwestern Region

Area, race, and tenure status	Number of cases	Acres in farm	Per Cent of Farm in					
			Cropland	Woods			Non-cropland open pasture	Other
				Not pastured	Pastured	Total		
ARKANSAS COASTAL PLAIN								
White								
Owners	79	126	44	28	14	42	11	3
Part owners	34	160	44	33	10	43	10	3
Share-cash renters	26	122	36	41	10	51	11	2
Share renters	49	124	42	35	12	47	9	2
Croppers	20	69	61	20	10	30	8	1
Negro								
Owners	47	103	47	33	10	43	7	3
Part owners	21	124	56	28	8	36	6	2
Share-cash renters	21	92	37	49	8	57	5	1
Share renters	61	106	40	43	9	52	6	2
Croppers	77	40	79	5	5	10	9	2
MISSISSIPPI COASTAL PLAIN								
White								
Owners	116	115	39	20	34	54	5	2
Part owners	15	192	27	27	41	68	4	1
Share-cash renters	8	64	35	37	22	59	3	3
Share renters	15	63	52	14	23	37	9	2
Croppers	28	44	59	1	34	35	4	2
Negro								
Owners	36	83	48	23	21	44	4	4
Part owners	19	56	57	21	15	36	3	4
Share-cash renters	5	38	64	10	18	28	4	4
Share renters	9	51	51	11	35	46	*	3
Croppers	58	31	83	5	8	13	2	2
OKLAHOMA ROLLING PLAIN								
White								
Owners	82	208	72	..	..	0	24	4
Part owners	63	437	58	..	..	1	37	4
Share-cash renters	18	272	62	..	..	0	33	5
Share renters	88	244	70	..	..	0	24	6
Croppers	11	127	73	..	..	0	22	5
TEXAS BLACKLAND PRAIRIE								
White								
Owners	79	118	84	..	..	2	11	3
Part owners	51	219	85	..	..	0	13	2
Share-cash renters	69	107	83	..	..	1	15	1
Share renters	93	117	83	..	..	*	14	3
Croppers	9	33	98	..	..	0	2	0

*Less than 0.5 per cent.

TABLE 6

Cropland use on farms, classified by race and tenure of operator, in four sample areas of the Southwestern Region

Area, race and tenure status	Number of cases	Acres in cropland	PER CENT OF ACRES IN CROPLAND			Crop acres in per cent of acres in cropland
			Cropped	Idle	Double cropped	
ARKANSAS COASTAL PLAIN						
White						
Owners	79	56	78	22	13	90
Part owners	34	70	87	13	16	103
Share-cash renters	26	44	90	10	10	100
Share renters	49	53	81	19	15	96
Croppers	20	42	93	7	16	109
Negro						
Owners	47	49	84	16	8	93
Part owners	21	69	87	13	9	96
Share-cash renters	21	34	95	5	6	101
Share renters	61	43	87	13	8	95
Croppers	77	31	98	2	11	110
MISSISSIPPI COASTAL PLAIN						
White						
Owners	116	45	94	6	24	118
Part owners	15	51	94	6	37	131
Share-cash renters	8	23	89	11	11	100
Share renters	15	32	91	9	16	107
Croppers	28	26	99	1	16	115
Negro						
Owners	36	40	95	5	19	114
Part owners	19	32	91	9	27	118
Share-cash renters	5	25	94	6	5	99
Share renters	9	25	98	2	21	119
Croppers	58	25	100	*	15	114
OKLAHOMA ROLLING PLAIN						
White						
Owners	82	150	93	7	4	97
Part owners	63	254	91	9	7	98
Share-cash renters	18	167	93	7	4	97
Share renters	88	170	92	8	9	99
Croppers	11	94	82	18	2	84
TEXAS BLACKLAND PRAIRIE						
White						
Owners	79	100	94	6	4	98
Part owners	51	185	95	5	5	100
Share-cash renters	69	88	94	6	5	99
Share renters	93	97	93	7	6	99
Croppers	9	31	100	0	0	100

*Less than 0.5 per cent

TABLE 7

Crop organization on farms, classified by race and tenure of operator, in four sample areas of the Southwestern Region

Area, race, and tenure status	Number of cases	Crop acres	PER CENT OF CROP ACRES IN						
			Cotton	Feed grain	Wheat	Hay and forage	Crop-land pasture	Truck and garden	Other
ARKANSAS COASTAL PLAIN									
White									
Owners	79	51	26	31	..	10	20	9	4
Part owners	34	72	27	31	..	11	19	6	6
Share-cash renters	26	44	28	31	..	6	23	7	5
Share renters	49	51	28	30	..	7	18	9	8
Croppers	20	46	34	33	..	3	18	4	8
Negro									
Owners	47	45	27	32	..	7	6	13	15
Part owners	21	66	30	32	..	3	16	7	12
Share-cash renters	21	34	28	30	..	7	18	10	7
Share renters	61	40	32	33	..	3	15	8	9
Croppers	77	34	40	30	..	*	18	7	5
MISSISSIPPI COASTAL PLAIN									
White									
Owners	116	53	21	37	..	8	11	6	17
Part owners	15	67	20	35	..	8	11	8	18
Share-cash renters	8	23	24	43	..	4	13	8	8
Share renters	15	35	25	40	..	7	8	5	15
Croppers	28	30	29	46	..	*	8	6	11
Negro									
Owners	36	46	23	42	..	7	9	6	13
Part owners	19	38	24	38	..	5	12	7	14
Share-cash renters	5	25	42	39	..	2	2	8	7
Share renters	9	30	24	34	..	12	6	7	17
Croppers	58	29	31	45	..	*	8	6	10
OKLAHOMA ROLLING PLAIN									
White									
Owners	82	146	28	24	14	7	16	1	10
Part owners	63	249	24	29	24	6	11	1	5
Share-cash renters	18	162	29	31	15	5	8	1	11
Share renters	88	167	30	26	16	7	12	1	8
Croppers	11	79	45	21	16	7	10	1	0
TEXAS BLACKLAND PRAIRIE									
White									
Owners	79	98	32	44	..	6	9	2	7
Part owners	51	185	30	40	..	7	13	1	9
Share-cash renters	69	88	34	41	..	8	9	1	7
Share renters	93	96	33	42	..	7	7	2	9
Croppers	9	31	61	33	..	3	1	1	1

*Less than 0.5 per cent.

TABLE 8

Index of diversification for race and tenure groups for 1662 farm families in five sample areas of the Southwestern Region (Regional average of diversification index is 3.37 and equals base of 100)

Area and race	Owner			Renter			Cropper
	Total	Full owner	Part owner	Total	Share-cash	Share	
ALL AREAS	108	109	104	104	107	103	76
White	108	110	104	105	108	103	80
Negro	107	107	106	103	102	103	74
ARKANSAS COASTAL PLAIN	109	111	104	105	109	104	75
White	108	110	102	105	108	104	77
Negro	111	112	107	105	109	104	75
LOUISIANA COASTAL PLAIN	100	101	94	93	98	92	68
White	100	102	91	92	92	92	77
Negro	96	94	111*	95	126*	92	64
MISSISSIPPI COASTAL PLAIN	110	111	104	98	95	100	82
White	112	113	103	103	117	96	91
Negro	104	104	105	90	61	106	77
OKLAHOMA ROLLING PLAIN	116	120	110	105	103	106	74
TEXAS BLACKLAND PRAIRIE	106	108	102	106	110	104	64
Native	98	102	93	103	104	102	64
Czech	117	114	125	108	109	107	63*
German	111	112	109	122	124	116*	..

*Less than five cases. See Table 2 for number of cases in each category.

TABLE 9

Acres in cropland and per cent in cotton on farms of three sizes in terms of labor requirements, classified by race and tenure of operator, in four sample areas of the Southwestern Region

Area, race, and tenure status	LESS THAN 200 PRODUCTIVE MAN-WORK UNITS			200 TO 300 PRODUCTIVE MAN-WORK UNITS			300 PRODUCTIVE MAN-WORK UNITS AND OVER		
	Number of cases	Acres in crop-land	Per cent in cotton	Number of cases	Acres in crop-land	Per cent in cotton	Number of cases	Acres in crop-land	Per cent in cotton
ARKANSAS COASTAL PLAIN									
White									
Owners	21	34	13	27	46	21	31	80	27
Part owners	5	24	21	10	41	30	19	97	28
Share-cash renters	8	30	23	9	36	28	9	64	31
Share renters	8	32	25	23	46	26	18	71	28
Croppers	4	29	35	10	35	40	6	63	37
Negro									
Owners	17	30	18	16	52	24	14	68	28
Part owners	4	27	28	6	42	29	11	99	29
Share-cash renters	11	26	29	7	40	27	3	48	29
Share renters	30	29	28	17	48	30	14	65	33
Croppers	42	23	43	20	31	45	15	54	44
MISSISSIPPI COASTAL PLAIN									
White									
Owners	31	18	23	32	31	24	53	68	26
Part owners	1	26	31	7	31	30	7	75	25
Share-cash renters	6	18	26	1	38	16	1	38	26
Share renters	5	24	27	7	35	24	3	41	31
Croppers	13	18	37	10	29	31	5	39	34
Negro									
Owners	13	16	24	5	34	24	18	59	28
Part owners	6	17	17	5	29	33	8	45	30
Share-cash renters	3	19	41	1	24	33	1	46	48
Share renters	5	21	30	3	28	25	1	37	32
Croppers	32	17	37	16	28	33	10	46	35
OKLAHOMA ROLLING PLAIN									
White									
Owners	29	91	20	33	136	26	20	259	33
Part owners	11	134	20	15	178	25	37	320	24
Share-cash renters	4	69	35	7	170	22	7	221	33
Share renters	26	106	30	39	156	28	23	267	30
TEXAS BLACKLAND PRAIRIE									
White									
Owners	18	52	27	22	69	32	39	140	31
Part owners	1	71	28	6	79	31	44	202	30
Share-cash renters	7	47	34	42	71	34	20	140	32
Share renters	11	53	29	43	74	34	39	134	32

TABLE 10

Cotton acreage, yield, and contribution to income on farms, classified by race and tenure of operator, in four sample areas of the Southwestern Region

Area, race, and tenure status	Number of cases	Acres in cotton	Per cent of farm in cotton	Per cent of cropland in cotton	Cotton yield (pounds per acre)	Cotton Sales in Per Cent of: Crop sales	Gross income from farm	Gross income
Arkansas Coastal Plain								
White								
Owners	79	13	10	23	205	84	35	28
Part owners	34	19	12	28	194	87	45	32
Share-cash renters	26	12	12	28	213	90	42	34
Share renters	49	14	11	27	183	88	46	39
Croppers	20	16	23	38	245	92	54	45
Negro								
Owners	47	12	12	25	159	89	45	37
Part owners	21	20	20	29	187	98	57	52
Share-cash renters	21	10	10	28	188	92	56	46
Share renters	61	13	12	30	162	94	63	44
Croppers	77	14	35	44	200	95	55	49
Mississippi Coastal Plain								
White								
Owners	116	11	10	25	382	89	51	37
Part owners	15	13	7	26	451	89	61	44
Share-cash renters	8	5	8	24	244	92	34	19
Share renters	15	9	13	26	314	92	57	46
Croppers	28	9	20	34	378	90	54	39
Negro								
Owners	36	11	13	27	296	89	58	49
Part owners	19	9	16	28	255	86	52	36
Share-cash renters	5	11	28	42	249	96	77	52
Share renters	9	7	14	29	218	94	50	39
Croppers	58	9	29	35	415	94	63	55
Oklahoma Rolling Plain								
White								
Owners	82	42	20	28	297	85	51	47
Part owners	63	61	14	24	268	84	49	47
Share-cash renters	18	48	18	29	247	91	48	46
Share renters	88	50	20	29	271	88	54	51
Croppers	11	35	28	38	241	91	53	46
Texas Blackland Prairie								
White								
Owners	79	31	26	31	179	92	47	45
Part owners	51	56	26	30	159	90	45	44
Share-cash renters	69	30	28	34	169	95	43	43
Share renters	93	32	27	33	166	96	46	43
Croppers	9	19	57	61	166	96	46	36

TABLE 11

Cotton acreage and yield on farms of three sizes in terms of labor requirements, classified by race and tenure of operator, in four sample areas of the Southwestern Region

Area, race, and tenure status	Less Than 200 Productive Man-work Units			200 to 300 Productive Man-work Units			300 Productive Man-work Units and Over		
	Number of cases	Acres in cotton	Yield (pounds per acre)	Number of cases	Acres in cotton	Yield (pounds per acre)	Number of cases	Acres in cotton	Yield (pounds per acre)
ARKANSAS COASTAL PLAIN									
White									
Owners	21	5	182	27	10	191	31	22	214
Part owners	5	5	232	10	12	210	19	27	189
Share-cash renters	8	7	157	9	10	221	9	20	226
Share renters	8	8	102	23	12	187	18	20	194
Croppers	4	10	210	10	14	232	6	23	267
Negro									
Owners	17	6	133	16	13	157	14	19	169
Part owners	4	8	120	6	12	176	11	28	196
Share-cash renters	11	7	141	7	11	201	3	14	255
Share renters	30	8	121	17	14	163	14	22	192
Croppers	42	10	174	20	14	216	15	24	217
MISSISSIPPI COASTAL PLAIN									
White									
Owners	31	4	273	32	7	373	53	18	399
Part owners	1	8	275	7	9	336	7	18	520
Share-cash renters	6	4	230	1	6	183	1	10	320
Share renters	5	6	294	7	8	297	3	13	358
Croppers	13	7	390	10	9	399	5	13	335
Negro									
Owners	13	4	308	5	8	261	18	16	299
Part owners	6	3	176	5	10	262	8	13	264
Share-cash renters	3	8	222	1	8	325	1	22	250
Share renters	5	6	278	3	7	205	1	12	83
Croppers	32	6	393	16	9	434	10	16	425
OKLAHOMA ROLLING PLAIN									
White									
Owners	29	18	306	33	35	247	20	86	328
Part owners	11	27	116	15	44	250	37	78	270
Share-cash renters	4	24	225	7	37	164	7	72	294
Share renters	26	30	226	39	45	251	23	81	309
TEXAS BLACKLAND PRAIRIE									
White									
Owners	18	14	196	22	22	192	39	44	269
Part owners	1	20	150	6	24	159	44	62	159
Share-cash renters	7	16	178	42	24	182	20	45	154
Share renters	11	16	140	43	25	161	39	43	70

TABLE 12

Value of farm business for operators, classified by race and tenure, in four sample areas of the Southwestern Region

Area, race, and tenure status	Number of cases	Value of Farm Business (dollars)				Per Cent of Total Value		
		Total farm business	Real estate	Equipment	Livestock	Real estate	Equipment	Livestock
Arkansas Coastal Plain								
White								
Owners	79	4082	3191	300	591	78	7	15
Part owners	34	4376	3438	313	625	79	7	14
Share-cash renters	26	2692	1981	230	481	74	8	18
Share renters	49	2996	2331	198	467	78	7	15
Croppers	20	2205	1575	197	433	71	9	20
Negro								
Owners	47	2666	2181	126	359	82	5	13
Part owners	21	3281	2443	187	651	74	6	20
Share-cash renters	21	1686	1333	109	243	79	7	14
Share renters	61	1875	1507	87	282	80	5	15
Croppers	77	1209	790	144	276	65	12	23
Mississippi Coastal Plain								
White								
Owners	115	3362	2458	241	663	73	7	20
Part owners	15	3467	2393	450	623	69	13	18
Share-cash renters	8	1400	1000	90	310	72	6	22
Share renters	15	1707	1340	57	310	79	3	18
Croppers	29	1166	1034	23	108	89	2	9
Negro								
Owners	36	2508	1925	158	426	77	6	17
Part owners	19	1653	1221	113	318	74	7	19
Share-cash renters	5	1060	840	80	140	79	8	13
Share renters	9	1111	744	64	302	67	6	27
Croppers	58	819	752	4	64	92	0	8
Oklahoma Rolling Plain								
White								
Owners	82	13995	11426	1318	1251	82	9	9
Part owners	63	18887	14500	2058	2329	77	11	12
Share-cash renters	18	12950	10094	1223	1632	78	9	13
Share renters	88	11267	8749	1262	1256	78	11	11
Croppers	8	6725	4475	1034	1216	67	16	27
Texas Blackland Prairie								
White								
Owners	79	10119	8158	1141	820	81	11	8
Part owners	51	15937	13125	1518	1294	82	10	8
Share-cash renters	69	7701	6120	852	729	79	11	10
Share renters	93	7439	5896	853	690	79	11	10
Croppers	9	2244	2011	49	184	90	2	8

TABLE 13

Value of farm real estate for operators, classified by race and tenure, in four sample areas of the Southwestern Region

Area race, and tenure status	Number of cases	VALUE OF FARM REAL ESTATE (dollars)				PER CENT OF TOTAL VALUE		
		Total real estate	Land	Improvements other than dwelling	Dwelling	Land	Improvements other than dwelling	Dwelling
ARKANSAS COASTAL PLAIN								
White								
Owners	79	3191	1725	649	816	54	20	26
Part owners	34	3438	1891	841	706	55	25	20
Share-cash renters	26	1981	1192	308	481	60	16	24
Share renters	49	2331	1512	331	488	65	14	21
Croppers	20	1575	995	235	345	63	15	22
Negro								
Owners	47	2181	1287	313	581	59	14	27
Part owners	21	2443	1638	395	410	67	16	17
Share-cash renters	21	1333	929	148	257	70	11	19
Share renters	61	1507	1156	149	202	77	10	13
Croppers	77	790	492	129	169	63	16	21
MISSISSIPPI COASTAL PLAIN								
White								
Owners	115	2458	1338	521	599	54	21	25
Part owners	15	2393	1527	400	467	64	17	19
Share-cash renters	8	1000	425	238	338	42	24	34
Share renters	15	1340	813	213	313	61	16	23
Croppers	29	1034	621	121	293	60	12	28
Negro								
Owners	36	1925	1361	275	289	71	14	15
Part owners	19	1221	874	116	232	72	9	19
Share-cash renters	5	840	500	120	220	60	14	26
Share renters	9	744	489	89	167	66	12	22
Croppers	58	752	509	64	179	68	8	24
OKLAHOMA ROLLING PLAIN								
White								
Owners	82	11426	8894	1055	1477	78	9	13
Part owners	63	14500	11829	1630	1041	82	11	7
Share-cash renters	18	10094	8878	661	556	88	6	6
Share renters	88	8749	7406	742	601	85	8	7
Croppers	8	4475	3475	638	362	78	14	8
TEXAS BLACKLAND PRAIRIE								
White								
Owners	79	8158	5299	1370	1490	65	17	18
Part owners	51	13125	10190	1771	1165	78	13	9
Share-cash renters	69	6120	4765	694	661	78	11	11
Share renters	93	5896	4465	717	714	76	12	12
Croppers	9	2011	1444	122	444	72	6	22

TABLE 14

Value of farm business for farms of three sizes in terms of labor requirements, classified by race and tenure of operator, in four sample areas of the Southwestern Region

Area, race, and tenure status	Less Than 200 Productive Man-work Units			200 to 300 Productive Man-work Units			300 Productive Man-work Units and Over		
	Number of cases	Value of farm business: Average (hundred dollars)	Value of farm business: Dollars per acre of crop-land	Number of cases	Value of farm business: Average (hundred dollars)	Value of farm business: Dollars per acre of crop-land	Number of cases	Value of farm business: Average (hundred dollars)	Value of farm business: Dollars per acre of crop-land
Arkansas Coastal Plain									
White									
Owners	21	23	68	27	37	80	31	56	70
Part owners	5	22	92	10	23	56	19	60	62
Share-cash renters	8	14	49	9	23	63	9	42	66
Share renters	8	18	56	23	27	59	18	39	55
Croppers	4	12	43	10	19	55	6	34	54
Negro									
Owners	17	19	64	16	24	46	14	39	57
Part owners	4	13	47	5	21	49	11	47	47
Share-cash renters	11	10	39	7	23	57	3	28	57
Share renters	30	12	43	17	23	49	14	27	41
Croppers	42	9	37	20	11	36	15	23	42
Mississippi Coastal Plain									
White									
Owners	31	16	88	32	25	82	52	49	72
Part owners	1	7	27	7	15	49	7	58	78
Share-cash renters	6	11	62	1	27	71	1	20	53
Share renters	5	6	25	7	23	66	3	22	54
Croppers	14	9	48	10	11	38	5	21	53
Negro									
Owners	13	11	70	5	14	41	18	38	65
Part owners	6	6	38	5	18	60	8	23	52
Share-cash renters	3	9	50	1	9	38	1	16	35
Share renters	5	8	39	3	12	43	1	23	62
Croppers	32	6	36	16	9	32	10	13	29
Oklahoma Rolling Plain									
White									
Owners	29	83	90	33	111	82	20	270	104
Part owners	11	135	101	15	129	72	37	229	72
Share-cash renters	4	44	65	7	77	45	7	231	105
Share renters	26	66	62	39	102	65	23	183	69
Texas Blackland Prairie									
White									
Owners	18	52	102	22	70	102	39	141	101
Part owners	1	62	87	6	77	97	44	173	85
Share-cash renters	7	44	94	42	65	91	20	114	82
Share renters	11	41	77	43	62	84	39	97	72

TABLE 15

Productive livestock and workstock on farms, classified by race and tenure of operator, in four sample areas of the Southwestern Region

Area, race, and tenure status	Number of cases	Animal Units Per Farm			Animal Units Per Hundred Acres of Cropland		
		Productive livestock	Workstock	Total livestock	Productive livestock	Workstock	Total livestock
ARKANSAS COASTAL PLAIN							
White							
Owners	79	5.8	2.2	8.0	10.3	3.9	14.2
Part owners	34	6.3	3.5	9.8	9.0	5.0	14.0
Share-cash renters	26	5.3	2.0	7.3	12.2	4.7	16.9
Share renters	49	3.9	2.5	6.4	7.3	4.8	12.1
Croppers	20	3.1	2.4	5.5	7.4	5.7	13.1
Negro							
Owners	47	3.4	2.0	5.4	7.0	4.1	11.1
Part owners	21	3.8	2.4	6.2	5.5	3.5	9.0
Share-cash renters	21	2.5	1.5	4.0	7.3	4.4	11.7
Share renters	61	2.3	1.7	4.0	5.4	3.9	9.3
Croppers	77	1.6	1.7	3.3	5.2	5.5	10.7
MISSISSIPPI COASTAL PLAIN							
White							
Owners	116	7.2	2.2	9.4	16.2	4.9	21.1
Part owners	15	7.1	1.9	9.0	13.9	3.7	17.6
Share-cash renters	8	2.9	1.1	4.0	12.7	4.9	17.6
Share renters	15	2.7	1.3	4.0	8.5	4.0	12.5
Croppers	28	1.8	1.7	3.5	6.9	6.4	13.4
Negro							
Owners	36	3.2	1.9	5.1	7.9	4.7	12.6
Part owners	19	3.0	1.7	4.7	9.4	5.4	14.8
Share-cash renters	5	0.6	1.1	1.7	2.4	4.4	6.7
Share renters	9	2.3	1.2	3.5	9.3	5.0	14.2
Croppers	58	1.2	1.6	2.8	4.6	6.5	11.1
OKLAHOMA ROLLING PLAIN							
White							
Owners	82	14.6	1.9	16.5	9.7	1.2	10.9
Part owners	63	22.7	1.3	24.0	8.9	0.5	9.4
Share-cash renters	18	15.7	1.8	17.5	9.4	1.1	10.5
Share renters	88	10.4	1.4	11.8	6.1	0.8	6.9
Croppers	11	12.3	0.9	13.2	13.1	0.9	14.0
TEXAS BLACKLAND PRAIRIE							
White							
Owners	79	8.9	2.3	11.2	8.9	2.3	11.2
Part owners	51	14.1	2.7	16.8	7.6	1.4	9.0
Share-cash renters	69	7.5	2.2	9.8	8.5	2.5	11.0
Share renters	93	7.3	2.3	9.5	7.5	2.3	9.8
Croppers	9	2.2	0.3	2.5	7.1	0.9	8.0

TABLE 16

Percentage distribution of farms according to animal units of productive livestock, by race and tenure of operator, in four sample areas of the Southwestern Region

Area, race, and tenure status	Number of cases	Per Cent of Farms With Animal Units of Productive Livestock of									
		None	Less than 1	1 to 2	2 to 3	3 to 5	5 to 7	7 to 11	11 to 15	15 to 31	31 and over
ARKANSAS COASTAL PLAIN											
White											
Owners	79	..	2	4	22	26	19	14	8	5	..
Part owners	34	..	..	6	20	20	24	21	6	3	..
Share-cash renters	26	..	..	15	23	27	19	12	..	..	4
Share renters	49	2	4	15	25	28	18	4	..	4	..
Croppers	20	..	15	40	10	25	5	..	..	5	..
Negro											
Owners	47	..	6	21	23	28	17	5	..	..	..
Part owners	21	..	..	14	29	33	24	..	..	..	..
Share-cash renters	21	..	19	33	19	14	15	..	..	..	..
Share renters	61	..	20	32	21	18	5	2	2	..	..
Croppers	77	1	30	39	10	16	2	2	..	..	..
MISSISSIPPI COASTAL PLAIN											
White											
Owners	116	..	3	9	16	27	19	10	7	5	4
Part owners	15	..	13	27	13	13	..	14	..	20	..
Share-cash renters	8	..	12	38	12	13	25	..	..	..	..
Share renters	15	7	13	27	13	33	7	..	..	..	..
Croppers	28	4	18	50	14	7	7	..	..	..	..
Negro											
Owners	36	3	14	11	25	33	6	8	..	..	..
Part owners	19	..	21	21	16	21	16	5	..	..	..
Share-cash renters	5	20	20	60	..	..	..	..	..	..	..
Share renters	9	..	..	56	22	22	..	..	..	..	..
Croppers	58	3	40	38	15	2	..	2	..	..	..
OKLAHOMA ROLLING PLAIN											
White											
Owners	83	..	..	2	2	8	11	24	19	23	11
Part owners	64	..	..	..	3	6	2	12	9	47	21
Share-cash renters	18	..	..	..	6	6	22	22	11	22	11
Share renters	88	1	..	3	9	11	15	22	14	22	3
Croppers	13	..	..	23	15	8	15	15	16	..	8
TEXAS BLACKLAND PRAIRIE											
White											
Owners	79	..	..	1	5	14	23	32	11	13	1
Part owners	51	..	..	..	..	6	8	29	16	35	6
Share-cash renters	69	..	..	..	3	12	32	40	9	3	1
Share renters	93	..	1	1	9	26	22	27	7	7	..
Croppers	9	..	..	22	56	22	..	..	..	..	..

TABLE 17

Percentage of farmers possessing specified farm animals by color and tenure for 1290 cases in four sample areas of the Southwestern Region

Area and tenure*	Native White			Other†		
	Bull	Sow	Boar	Bull	Sow	Boar
ARKANSAS COASTAL PLAIN	*Per cent*	*Per cent*	*Per cent*	*Per cent*	*Per cent*	*Per cent*
Full owner	23	47	6	17	70	11
Part owner	38	62	3	5	71	19
Share-cash renter	27	50	..	5	52	..
Share renter	14	39	6	7	56	2
Cropper	..	40	10	..	34	3
MISSISSIPPI COASTAL PLAIN						
Full owner	29	63	15	14	69	11
Part owner	20	60	13	5	74	10
Share-cash renter	..	38	..	..	..	..
Share renter	7	60	7	..	56	11
Cropper	..	34	3	..	36	3
OKLAHOMA ROLLING PLAIN						
Full owner	37	41	..	..	..	..
Part owner	64	53	..	..	..	..
Share-cash renter	28	56	6	..	..	..
Share renter	19	53	..	..	..	..
TEXAS BLACKLAND PRAIRIE						
Full owner	43	40	14	33	55	7
Part owner	47	65	12	24	76	6
Share-cash renter	28	62	7	10	60	5
Share renter	29	51	6	7	57	3

*Croppers were omitted for Oklahoma and Texas because of numerical unimportance.
†Other is a combination of Czech and German for Texas and is Negro for Arkansas and Mississippi.

Table 18

Type of power equipment used on farms, classified by race and tenure of operator, in four sample areas of the Southwestern Region

Area, race, and tenure status	Number of cases	Number of Farms Reporting Use of			Per Cent of Farms Reporting Use of		
		Horse-drawn equipment	Tractor equipment	Horse-drawn and tractor equipment	Horse-drawn equipment	Tractor equipment	Horse-drawn and tractor equipment
Arkansas Coastal Plain							
White							
Owners	75	74	..	1	97	..	3
Part owners	34	34	..	..	100	..	..
Share-cash renters	26	26	..	..	100	..	..
Share renters	49	48	..	1	98	..	2
Croppers	20	20	..	..	100	..	..
Negro							
Owners	45	45	..	..	100	..	..
Part owners	21	21	..	..	100	..	..
Share-cash renters	21	21	..	..	100	..	..
Share renters	61	61	..	..	100	..	..
Croppers	77	76	..	1	99	..	1
Mississippi Coastal Plain							
White							
Owners	113	110	..	3	97	..	3
Part owners	14	13	..	1	93	..	7
Share-cash renters	8	8	..	..	100	..	..
Share renters	14	14	..	..	100	..	..
Croppers	26	25	..	1	96	..	4
Negro							
Owners	35	35	..	..	100	..	..
Part owners	17	17	..	..	100	..	..
Share-cash renters	5	5	..	..	100	..	..
Share renters	9	9	..	..	100	..	..
Croppers	12	12	..	..	100	..	..
Oklahoma Rolling Plain							
White							
Owners	79	25	51	3	32	64	4
Part owners	64	5	59	..	8	92	..
Share-cash renters	17	6	11	..	35	65	..
Share renters	85	22	62	1	26	73	1
Croppers	9	1	8	..	11	89	..
Texas Blackland Prairie							
White							
Owners	78	29	33	16	37	42	21
Part owners	51	10	30	11	20	59	21
Share-cash renters	68	33	30	5	49	44	7
Share renters	93	36	51	6	39	55	6
Croppers	8	2	2	4	25	25	50

Table 19

Percentage of farmers possessing specified farm equipment by race and tenure for 1290 cases in four sample areas of the Southwestern Region

Area and tenure*	Native White					Other†				
	Car	Truck	Cane mill, com-bine‡	Grain binder	Haying equip.	Car	Truck	Cane mill, com-bine‡	Grain binder	Haying equip.
	Per cent	*Per cent*	*Per cent*	*Per cent*	*Per cent*	*Per cent*	*Per cent*	*Per cent*	*Per cent*	*Per cent*
Arkansas Coastal Plain										
Full owner	29	24	1	..	20	6	6	2	..	8
Part owner	44	24	..	..	26	19	14	5	..	10
Share-cash renter	27	8	..	..	8	14	10	..	..	10
Share renter	18	10	4	..	14	8	..	2	..	..
Cropper	25	10	..	..	..	12	4	1	..	3
Mississippi Coastal Plain										
Full owner	26	18	4	..	28	19	8	11	..	8
Part owner	7	40	..	..	27	21	16	5	..	5
Share-cash renter	25	..	12	..	12	20	..	20	..	..
Share renter	..	7	..	..	..	22	..	..	..	11
Cropper	17	7	..	..	7	9	..	2	..	..
Oklahoma Rolling Plain										
Full owner	83	20	8	24	43					
Part owner	89	38	44	44	28					
Share-cash renter	89	28	6	39	28					
Share renter	81	18	13	18	20					
Texas Blackland Prairie										
Full owner	92	19	8	16	76	93	36	2	12	76
Part owner	94	26	9	18	71	94	29	..	..	76
Share-cash renter	90	10	3	3	62	100	10	..	..	55
Share renter	87	14	3	10	46	100	7	..	..	60

*Croppers were omitted for Oklahoma and Texas because of numerical unimportance.
†Other is a combination of Czech and German for Texas and is Negro for Arkansas and Mississippi.
‡Cane mill applies to Arkansas and Mississippi; combine applies to Oklahoma and Texas.

TABLE 20

Labor use on farms without croppers, classified by race and tenure of operator, and by acres in cropland, in two sample areas of the Southwestern Region

Area, race, tenure status and acres in cropland	Number of cases	Days of labor used	PER CENT OF LABOR USED			Productive man work units	Index of labor efficiency*
			Operator	Family	Hired		
ARKANSAS COASTAL PLAIN							
White owners							
Less than 20 acres in cropland	2	280	43	46	11	190	68
20 to 40 acres in cropland	23	290	72	23	5	192	66
40 to 80 acres in cropland	21	362	57	23	20	286	79
80 acres and over	6	397	43	24	33	388	98
White renters							
Less than 20 acres in cropland	3	203	79	18	3	87	43
20 to 40 acres in cropland	24	304	70	23	7	207	68
40 to 80 acres in cropland	39	395	55	35	10	304	77
80 acres and over	7	460	47	26	27	477	104
Negro owners							
Less than 20 acres in cropland	2	185	81	16	3	75	41
20 to 40 acres in cropland	15	342	61	34	5	171	50
40 to 80 acres in cropland	20	425	48	41	11	297	70
80 acres and over	2	530	34	66	0	390	74
Negro renters							
Less than 20 acres in cropland	7	216	81	16	3	91	42
20 to 40 acres in cropland	43	364	60	38	2	177	49
40 to 80 acres in cropland	26	438	48	50	2	291	66
80 acres and over	5	728	33	64	3	472	65
MISSISSIPPI COASTAL PLAIN							
White owners							
Less than 20 acres in cropland	23	202	50	44	6	146	72
20 to 40 acres in cropland	29	271	60	31	9	252	93
40 to 80 acres in cropland	19	354	41	44	15	383	108
80 acres and over	1	670	27	69	4	810	121
White renters							
Less than 20 acres in cropland	3	100	57	40	3	120	120
20 to 40 acres in cropland	16	259	61	29	10	213	82
40 to 80 acres in cropland	3	443	26	72	2	313	71
Negro owners							
Less than 20 acres in cropland	9	148	76	17	7	108	73
20 to 40 acres in cropland	8	296	50	48	2	225	76
40 to 80 acres in cropland	7	536	28	68	4	401	75
Negro renters							
Less than 20 acres in cropland	3	157	83	13	4	140	89
20 to 40 acres in cropland	11	245	55	44	1	216	88
40 to 80 acres in cropland	1	460	35	43	22	370	80

*Ratio of productive man-work units to days of labor used.

TABLE 21

Gross income of farm operators, classified by race and tenure, in four sample areas of the Southwestern Region

Area, race, and tenure status	Number of cases	Gross income (dollars)	PER CENT OF GROSS INCOME		
			Gross income from farm	Off-farm work	Other non-farm income
ARKANSAS COASTAL PLAIN					
White					
Owners	76	1545	80	8	12
Part owners	34	1910	70	12	18
Share-cash renters	26	1553	80	16	4
Share renters	48	1107	84	13	3
Croppers	18	1028	82	17	1
Negro					
Owners	46	958	86	9	5
Part owners	20	1321	90	8	2
Share-cash renters	21	758	83	16	1
Share renters	60	827	83	15	2
Croppers	73	645	88	10	2
MISSISSIPPI COASTAL PLAIN					
White					
Owners	112	1766	73	22	5
Part owners	15	2144	73	27	*
Share-cash renters	8	1156	56	44	0
Share renters	15	923	80	20	0
Croppers	28	901	74	24	2
Negro					
Owners	35	1137	84	12	4
Part owners	19	993	68	28	4
Share-cash renters	5	930	68	30	2
Share renters	9	624	79	21	0
Croppers	57	705	88	11	1
OKLAHOMA ROLLING PLAIN					
White					
Owners	82	4836	92	3	5
Part owners	62	5887	95	3	2
Share-cash renters	17	3758	96	3	1
Share renters	87	3738	94	6	*
Croppers	11	1881	86	14	0
TEXAS BLACKLAND PRAIRIE					
White					
Owners	78	2468	94	3	3
Part owners	49	3522	98	1	1
Share-cash renters	68	1796	99	1	0
Share renters	92	1853	93	7	*
Croppers	9	900	78	20	2

*Less than 0.5 per cent.

Table 22

Gross income of farm operators for farms of three sizes in terms of productive man-work units, classified by race and tenure, in four sample areas of the Southwestern Region

Area, race, and tenure status	Less Than 200 Productive Man-work Units			200 to 300 Productive Man-work Units			300 Productive Man-work Units and Over		
	Number of cases	Gross income: Average (dollars)	Gross income: Per cent from farm	Number of cases	Gross income: Average (dollars)	Gross income: Per cent from farm	Number of cases	Gross income: Average (dollars)	Gross income: Per cent from farm
Arkansas Coastal Plain									
White									
Owners	21	785	84	25	1400	77	30	2196	80
Part owners	5	756	92	10	1576	64	19	2391	70
Share-cash renters	8	885	63	9	1194	85	9	2501	84
Share renters	8	545	77	22	1054	78	18	1422	90
Croppers	3	387	91	9	981	78	6	1417	86
Negro									
Owners	16	672	72	16	913	90	14	1332	90
Part owners	4	605	88	6	917	85	10	1849	92
Share-cash renters	11	553	75	7	876	85	3	1233	92
Share renters	29	566	70	17	805	86	14	1396	93
Croppers	39	494	82	19	624	92	15	1061	92
Mississippi Coastal Plain									
White									
Owners	31	1264	47	31	1433	74	50	2285	81
Part owners	1	620	100	7	1383	56	7	3124	79
Share-cash renters	6	948	52	1	1180	100	1	2380	41
Share renters	5	588	69	7	966	82	3	1377	83
Croppers	13	747	68	10	1023	72	5	1056	87
Negro									
Owners	13	642	74	5	858	88	17	1596	87
Part owners	6	562	55	5	1306	54	8	1119	83
Share-cash renters	3	803	54	1	790	100	1	1450	72
Share renters	5	546	89	3	680	70	1	850	65
Croppers	31	528	80	16	749	91	10	1175	95
Oklahoma Rolling Plain									
White									
Owners	29	3273	78	33	3802	96	20	8808	97
Part owners	11	3823	92	15	4406	92	36	7134	96
Share-cash renters	4	1995	97	6	3197	92	7	5246	98
Share renters	26	2156	94	39	3319	94	22	6351	93
Texas Blackland Prairie									
White									
Owners	17	1501	91	22	2040	94	39	3131	94
Part owners	1	1270	92	5	1584	92	43	3800	98
Share-cash renters	7	1136	100	42	1612	99	19	2448	99
Share renters	11	978	85	43	1706	90	38	2273	96

TABLE 23

Gross farm income of farms, classified by race and tenure of operator and by size in terms of labor requirements, in three sample areas of the Southwestern Region

Area, race, and tenure status	All Farms		Less Than 200 Productive Man-work Units		200 to 300 Productive Man-work Units		300 Productive Man-work units and Over	
	Number of cases	Gross farm income (dollars)	Number of cases	Gross farm income (dollars)	Number of cases	Gross farm income (dollars)	Number of cases	Gross farm income (dollars)
Arkansas Coastal Plain								
White								
Owners	79	1220	21	628	27	982	31	1827
Part owners	34	1601	5	690	10	1178	19	2064
Share-cash renters	26	1274	8	522	9	1026	9	2191
Share renters	49	1105	8	484	23	954	18	1575
Negro								
Owners	47	765	17	445	16	782	14	1135
Part owners	21	1251	4	506	6	796	11	1769
Share-cash renters	21	652	11	420	7	754	3	1269
Share renters	61	791	30	423	17	819	14	1543
Mississippi Coastal Plain								
White								
Owners	114	1503	31	552	32	1083	51	2345
Part owners	15	1838	1	578	7	998	7	2857
Share-cash renters	8	697	6	515	1	1143	1	1345
Share renters	15	927	5	523	7	1000	3	1430
Negro								
Owners	36	1056	13	463	5	732	18	1575
Part owners	19	798	6	330	5	871	8	1103
Share-cash renters	5	653	3	466	1	791	1	1078
Share renters	9	580	5	572	3	573	1	640
Oklahoma Rolling Plain								
White								
Owners	82	4313	29	2430	33	3636	20	8162
Part owners	62	5746	11	3577	15	4001	36	7135
Share-cash renters	17	4013	4	1868	6	3072	7	6044
Share renters	88	4271	26	2376	39	3734	23	7326

TABLE 24

Gross income from farm of farm operators, classified by race and tenure, in four sample areas of the Southwestern Region

Area, race, and tenure status	Number of cases	Gross income from farm (dollars)	PER CENT OF GROSS INCOME FROM FARM				
			Crop sales	Livestock sales	Livestock product sales	Value of home-used products	Other income from farm
ARKANSAS COASTAL PLAIN							
White							
Owners	76	1231	42	11	10	24	13
Part owners	34	1343	52	11	8	24	5
Share-cash renters	26	1252	47	15	5	28	5
Share renters	48	928	52	8	5	30	5
Croppers	18	849	59	7	2	28	4
Negro							
Owners	46	818	51	6	3	32	8
Part owners	20	1190	58	8	2	26	6
Share-cash renters	21	629	60	4	2	30	4
Share renters	60	689	56	4	1	33	6
Croppers	73	566	58	5	1	30	6
MISSISSIPPI COASTAL PLAIN							
White							
Owners	112	1291	58	9	4	23	6
Part owners	15	1551	69	6	1	17	7
Share-cash renters	8	644	37	11	14	33	4
Share renters	15	735	63	3	1	30	3
Croppers	28	661	60	3	1	33	3
Negroes							
Owners	35	962	65	4	1	25	5
Part owners	19	676	61	4	1	29	5
Share-cash renters	5	630	80	−3	0	22	1
Share renters	9	491	53	*	*	43	4
Croppers	57	616	67	2	1	25	5
OKLAHOMA ROLLING PLAIN							
White							
Owners	82	4461	60	17	12	6	5
Part owners	62	5609	58	23	7	5	7
Share-cash renters	17	3622	53	20	11	9	7
Share renters	87	3504	61	16	9	8	6
Croppers	11	1626	59	10	9	18	4
TEXAS BLACKLAND PRAIRIE							
White							
Owners	78	2318	52	15	17	11	5
Part owners	49	3430	50	18	18	9	5
Share-cash renters	68	1785	46	17	17	16	4
Share renters	92	1722	48	16	16	15	5
Croppers	9	700	49	7	18	26	*

*Less than 0.5 per cent

TABLE 25

Comparison of selected characteristics of farms of Negro owners with and without croppers in two sample areas of the Southwestern Region

Item	Arkansas Coastal Plain		Mississippi Coastal Plain	
	Negro owners with croppers	Negro owners without croppers	Negro owners with croppers	Negro owners without croppers
Number of cases	8	39	14	25
Productive man-work units	341	242	389	229
Acres in farm	168	90	107	62
Acres in cropland	67	45	50	31
Acres in cotton	17	11	14	8
Cotton yield (pounds)	164	157	322	269
Animal units, productive livestock	3.9	3.3	3.9	2.5
Animal units, workstock	2.2	2.0	2.5	1.4
Value of farm business	3588	2477	3357	1732
Value of real estate	3062	2000	2607	1312
Value of equipment	136	124	224	102
Value of livestock	389	353	526	318

TABLE 26

Land use on cropper tracts, classified by race of cropper, in two sample areas of the Southwestern Region

Item	ARKANSAS COASTAL PLAIN		MISSISSIPPI COASTAL PLAIN	
	White croppers	Negro croppers	White croppers	Negro croppers
Number of cases	20	77	28	58
Acres in tract	69	40	44	31
Per cent of tract in cropland	61	79	59	83
Per cent of tract in woods not pastured	20	5	1	5
Per cent of tract in woods pastured	10	5	34	8
Per cent of tract in non-cropland open pasture	8	9	4	2
Per cent of tract in other use	1	2	2	2
Acres in cropland	42	31	26	25
Per cent of cropland cropped	93	98	99	100
Per cent of cropland idle	7	2	1	*
Per cent of cropland double-cropped	16	11	16	15
Crop acres	46	34	30	29
Crop acres in per cent of acres in cropland	109	110	115	114
Per cent of crop acres in cotton	34	40	29	31
Per cent of crop acres in feed grain	33	30	46	45
Per cent of crop acres in hay and forage	3	*	*	*
Per cent of crop acres in cropland pasture	18	18	8	8
Per cent of crop acres in truck and garden	4	7	6	6
Per cent of crop acres in other crops	8	5	11	10
Acres in cotton	16	14	9	9
Per cent of tract in cotton	23	35	20	29
Per cent of cropland in cotton	38	44	34	35
Cotton yield (pounds per acre)	245	200	378	415

*Less than 0.5 per cent.

TABLE 27

Percentage distributions of cropper tracts according to total acres, acres in cropland, and acres in cotton, by race of cropper, in two sample areas of the Southwestern Region

Item	Arkansas Coastal Plain		Mississippi Coastal Plain	
	White croppers	Negro croppers	White croppers	Negro croppers
Number of cases	20	77	29	58
Per cent of tracts with total acres of:				
Less than 30	15	38	38	60
30 to 50	40	47	41	31
50 to 70	10	8	10	5
70 to 100	10	4	7	2
100 to 140	15	1	..	2
140 and over	10	2	4	..
Per cent of tracts with acres in cropland of:				
Less than 10	..	..	3	2
10 to 20	..	18	31	41
20 to 30	30	39	42	33
30 to 40	25	21	14	12
40 to 50	20	10	7	5
50 and over	25	12	3	7
Per cent of tracts with acres in cotton of:				
Less than 3	..	1	..	..
3 to 7	..	5	35	34
7 to 11	20	29	45	43
11 to 15	35	29	17	12
15 to 23	35	22	3	9
23 and over	10	14	..	2

TABLE 28

Percentage distribution of cropper tracts according to productive man-work units, by race of cropper, in two sample areas of the Southwestern Region

Item	Arkansas Coastal Plain		Mississippi Coastal Plain	
	White Croppers	Negro Croppers	White Croppers	Negro Croppers
Number of cases	20	77	29	58
Per cent of tracts with productive man-work units of:				
Less than 100	..	5	3	2
100 to 200	20	50	45	53
200 to 300	45	27	35	28
300 to 400	25	12	14	14
400 to 600	5	6	3	3
600 and over	5	..	..	..

TABLE 29

Gross income of croppers, classified by race, in two sample areas of the Southwestern Region

Item	Arkansas Coastal Plain		Mississippi Coastal Plain	
	White croppers	Negro croppers	White croppers	Negro croppers
Number of cases	18	73	28	57
Total gross income (dollars)	1028	645	901	705
Gross income from tract (dollars)	849	566	661	616
Gross income from work off tract (dollars)	172	66	218	79
Gross income from other sources (dollars)	7	13	22	10
Per cent of gross income from tract	82	88	74	88
Per cent of gross income from work off tract	17	10	24	11
Per cent of gross income from other sources	1	2	2	1
Gross income from crop sales	499	329	396	416
Gross income from livestock sales	56	30	18	11
Gross income from livestock product sales	20	6	9	5
Gross income from use of home-grown products	240	169	220	153
Gross income from other tract sources	34	32	18	31
Crop sales in per cent of gross income from tract	59	58	60	67
Livestock sales in per cent of gross income from tract	7	5	3	2
Livestock product sales in per cent of gross income from tract	2	1	1	1
Use of home-grown products in per cent of gross income from tract	28	30	33	25
Income from other tract sources in per cent of gross income from tract	4	6	3	5
Gross income from cotton sales (dollars)	459	314	355	389
Cotton sales in per cent of crop sales	92	95	90	94
Cotton sales in per cent of gross income from tract	54	55	54	63
Cotton sales in per cent of total gross income	45	49	39	55

TABLE 30

Index of socio-economic status for race and tenure groups for 1580 farm families in five sample areas of the Southwestern Region (Regional scale value is 151 and equals base of 100)

Area and race	Owner			Renter			Cropper
	Total	Full owner	Part owner	Total	Share-cash	Share	
ALL AREAS	106	104	110	99	99	100	87
White	108	106	114	102	101	103	91
Negro	92	92	92	88	88	87	85
ARKANSAS COASTAL PLAIN	99	98	99	89	91	88	85
White	103	102	104	92	95	90	87
Negro	91	91	90	86	87	86	84
LOUISIANA COASTAL PLAIN	101	101	103	91	92	91	86
White	101	101	104	91	89	91	88
Negro	99	99	99*	92	105*	91	85
MISSISSIPPI COASTAL PLAIN	97	97	95	92	92	91	86
White	100	100	99	91	94	89	87
Negro	91	91	92	92	89	94	86
OKLAHOMA ROLLING PLAIN	118	116	120	109	103	111	104
TEXAS BLACKLAND	120	120	122	106	104	108	95
Native	124	123	124	108	107	109	96
Czech	117	117	118	103	102	105	92*
German	113	117	108	106	105	108*	..

*Less than five cases. See Table 2 for number of cases in each category.

TABLE 31

Per cent of families in each of five socio-economic status* groups, by race and tenure of operator, for five sample areas of the Southwestern Region

Area, race, and tenure status	Number of families	PER CENT OF FAMILIES IN EACH STATUS GROUP: Low 104 to 123	Below average 124 to 143	Average 144 to 163	Above average 164 to 183	High 184 to 213
ARKANSAS COASTAL PLAIN						
White						
Full owner	79	2	27	37	29	5
Part owner	34	3	27	27	38	5
Renter	75	16	52	25	6	1
Cropper	20	35	45	15	5	..
Negro						
Owner	47	7	68	21	4	..
Part owner	21	14	52	34	..	..
Renter	82	26	70	4	..	..
Cropper	77	42	54	4	..	..
LOUISIANA COASTAL PLAIN						
White						
Full owner	152	5	32	34	24	5
Part owner	18	6	22	33	28	11
Renter	25	20	48	32	..	..
Cropper	13	15	70	15	..	..
Negro						
Owner	11	..	46	36	18	..
Part owner	2	..	..	100	..	..
Renter	11	..	73	18	9	..
Cropper	35	29	71	..	..	..
MISSISSIPPI COASTAL PLAIN						
White						
Full owner	116	6	39	31	16	8
Part owner	15	..	33	47	20	..
Renter	23	9	65	22	4	..
Cropper	29	31	48	17	4	..
Negro						
Owner	36	14	61	22	3	..
Part owner	19	11	58	26	5	..
Renter	14	..	86	14	..	..
Cropper	58	36	59	5	..	..
OKLAHOMA ROLLING PLAIN						
Native white						
Full owner	83	3	7	14	40	36
Part owner	64	..	2	17	34	47
Renter	106	1	14	27	41	17
Cropper	14	7	7	50	36	..
TEXAS BLACKLAND PRAIRIE						
White						
Full owner	79	..	6	5	46	43
Part owner	51	..	6	6	37	51
Renter	162	3	15	38	32	12
Cropper	9	..	56	33	11	..

*The mean index for all sampled families in the region is 151, the standard deviation, 19.9.

TABLE 32

Index of housing for race and tenure groups for 1580 farm families in five sample areas of the Southwestern Region (Regional average of 50 equals base of 100)

Area and race	Owner			Renter			Cropper
	Total	Full owner	Part owner	Total	Share-cash	Share	
ALL AREAS	108	106	111	98	96	98	83
White	111	109	116	101	98	103	88
Negro	91	92	89	84	88	83	81
ARKANSAS COASTAL PLAIN	100	100	100	86	90	84	82
White	104	104	105	89	92	88	87
Negro	93	94	91	83	88	82	81
LOUISIANA COASTAL PLAIN	101	102	98	88	87	88	81
White	102	102	99	88	85	89	87
Negro	97	99	90*	86	95*	85	79
MISSISSIPPI COASTAL PLAIN	95	96	92	88	92	86	82
White	99	99	98	86	93	82	83
Negro	87	86	88	90	90	91	81
OKLAHOMA ROLLING PLAIN	120	121	119	107	98	109	98
TEXAS BLACKLAND	130	131	130	107	102	111	97
Native	136	136	135	111	106	114	98
Czech	123	123	124	101	97	105	95*
German	126	132	117	105	104	108*	..

*Less than five cases. See Table 2 for number of cases in each category.

TABLE 33

Index of movable possessions for race and tenure groups for 1580 farm families in five sample areas of the Southwestern Region (Regional average of 65 equals base of 100)

Area and race	Owner			Renter			Cropper
	Total	Full owner	Part owner	Total	Share-cash	Share	
ALL AREAS	106	104	112	101	100	101	83
White	110	107	118	107	105	108	92
Negro	85	85	85	79	78	79	78
ARKANSAS COASTAL PLAIN	96	95	97	85	88	83	79
White	103	102	105	92	96	89	87
Negro	84	84	84	78	78	78	78
LOUISIANA COASTAL PLAIN	101	101	101	89	88	89	79
White	102	101	104	91	90	91	83
Negro	90	92	81*	84	81*	84	78
MISSISSIPPI COASTAL PLAIN	96	97	93	84	86	82	82
White	100	100	100	87	92	85	87
Negro	86	85	87	78	78	79	80
OKLAHOMA ROLLING PLAIN	125	123	128	118	110	120	111
TEXAS BLACKLAND	122	120	126	111	109	113	99
Native	127	124	130	114	112	115	99
Czech	116	114	123	107	106	108	100
German	116	118	112	111	111	111*	..*

*Less than five cases. See Table 2 for number of cases in each category.

TABLE 34

Index of social participation for race and tenure groups for 1580 farm families in five sample areas of the Southwestern Region

(Regional average of 36 equals base of 100)

Area and race	Owner			Renter			Cropper
	Total	Full owner	Part owner	Total	Share-cash	Share	
ALL AREAS	102	101	105	100	100	99	98
White	101	100	104	98	98	97	93
Negro	105	105	107	106	106	107	100
ARKANSAS COASTAL PLAIN	99	98	102	101	100	101	94
White	99	98	102	98	98	97	86
Negro	99	98	102	104	103	104	97
LOUISIANA COASTAL PLAIN	102	101	110	100	102	100	101
White	101	100	109	94	98	93	99
Negro	117	116	124*	114	124*	112	102
MISSISSIPPI COASTAL PLAIN	103	102	108	107	104	109	100
White	100	100	104	102	99	104	95
Negro	110	110	110	116	113	118	103
OKLAHOMA ROLLING PLAIN	101	98	106	98	96	98	99
TEXAS BLACKLAND	103	103	102	97	99	96	87
Native	101	100	102	95	97	94	90
Czech	110	110	108	102	102	103	75*
German	93	93	94	94	94	97*	...

*Less than five cases. See Table 2 for number of cases in each category.

TABLE 35

Average socio-economic status score value for 1204 farm families classified by scale of operation, race and tenure, in four sample areas of the Southwestern Region

Area and race	Number of cases	AVERAGE SOCIO-ECONOMIC STATUS SCORE FOR FAMILIES WITH SCALE OF OPERATION* OF						
		Less than $214	$214 to 463	$464 to 999	$1,000 to 2,153	$2,154 to 4,641	$4,642 to 9,999	$10,000 and over
	Families	*Score*	*Score*	*Score*	*Score*	*Score*	*Score*	*Score*
ARKANSAS COASTAL PLAIN								
White								
Full owner	79	119	143	149	159	179	...	...
Renter	78	...	121	135	147	149	...	...
Cropper	20	...	119	131	137	139	...	...
Negro								
Full owner	47	...	167	135	144	149	...	...
Renter	86	...	127	130	133	...	...	...
Cropper	77	...	120	127	132	...	...	...
MISSISSIPPI COASTAL PLAIN								
White								
Full owner	114	...	139	139	149	169	169	...
Renter	24	...	134	134	149	...	...	...
Cropper	28	...	139	131	129	...	...	...
Negro								
Full owner	36	119	132	134	144	134	...	...
Renter	15	...	139	141	132	...	...	...
Cropper	58	129	124	129	131	...	...	...
OKLAHOMA ROLLING PLAIN								
White								
Full owner	82	...	...	132†	168	173	188	199
Part owner	61	...	...	...	156	177	187	184
Renter	106	...	...	142†	154	165	174	189
TEXAS BLACKLAND PRAIRIE								
White								
Full owner	37	...	...	169†	176	189	206	...
Part owner	34	...	...	...	177	187	193	199
Renter	92	...	...	144	158	173	179	...
Czech and German								
Full owner	42	...	...	189	171	184	...	...
Part owner	17	...	...	...	167	175	...	...
Renter	71	...	...	...	156	158	...	...

*The scale of operation is expressed as dollars of expected gross farm income.

TABLE 36

Average socio-economic status scale in relation to size of business, for 1363 farm families* in four sample areas of the Southwestern Region

Size of business†	Average of Socio-economic Status Scale				
	All areas	Arkansas Coastal Plain	Mississippi Coastal Plain	Oklahoma Rolling Plain	Texas Blackland Prairie
All families	153	139	141	172	169
215- 315	130	127	133	...	137
316- 463	130	129	132	...	136
464- 680	133	132	135	124	139
681- 999	136	136	135	143	151
1,000- 1,467	148	146	144	151	157
1,468- 2,153	160	153	150	162	165
2,154- 3,161	168	160	155	165	175
3,162- 4,641	177	171	172	174	184
4,642- 6,812	182	...	169‡	180	194
6,813- 9,999	188	...	...	187	199‡
10,000-14,677	196	...	...	196	199‡

*Farms having an expected or predicted gross farm income of less than $215, and a few farms for whom size was not ascertained, were omitted from the selected range. The omitted cases total 100 in the four states. Only one of these had an expected gross income exceeding $14, 677; it was an Oklahoma farm of over $22,000 expected gross income.

†Expressed in dollars of expected gross income. (For method of calculation see *Editing Procedure*).

‡Less than five cases.

TABLE 37

Average socio-economic status scale in relation to net family income for 1078 farm families* in three sample areas of the Southwestern Region

Net family income	All three areas	Average of Socio-economic Status Scale		
		Arkansas Coastal Plain	Mississippi Coastal Plain	Oklahoma Rolling Plain
All families†	148	139	141	172
147 to 214	128	127	136‡	...
215 to 315	133	130	137	129‡
316 to 463	132	130	133	142
464 to 680	135	134	134	152
681 to 999	142	142	137	153
1,000 to 1,467	148	146	143	159
1,468 to 2,153	160	153	155	168
2,154 to 3,162	171	150	166	174
3,163 to 4,641	174	157	189‡	175
4,642 to 6,812	186	159‡	...	188
6,813 to 9,999	194	...	...	194
10,000 to 14,677	189‡	...	...	189‡

*Fourteen families having net family income of less than $147 and 32 families for whom net family income was not ascertained, were omitted from the selected range.
†Based on 1078 families: 452 in the Arkansas, 313 in the Mississippi, 313 in the Oklahoma sample.
‡Less than five cases.

TABLE 38

Comparison of various indexes of farm family status for families classified by race and tenure of operator in four sample areas in the Southwestern Region

Area, race, and tenure	Number of cases	Socio-economic status	Scale of operations $1379=100	Median operator's earnings $380=100	Median net family income $978=100	Farm median net worth $1,181=100	Average education (of higher spouse) 8.58=100
		Index	*Index*	*Index*	*Index*	*Index*	*Index*
ARKANSAS COASTAL PLAIN							
White							
Owner	79	102	70	88	86	305	97
Part owner	34	104	91	112	207	215	104
Share-cash renter	26	95	67	130	88	40	98
Share renter	49	90	67	110	82	31	92
Cropper	20	87	62	110	67	15	97
Negro							
Owner	47	91	60	47	56	202	80
Part owner	21	90	75	54	70	148	77
Share-cash renter	21	87	49	50	53	25	69
Share renter	61	86	51	39	59	22	73
Cropper	77	84	49	65	50	6	71
MISSISSIPPI COASTAL PLAIN							
White							
Owner	116	100	91	98	121	208	110
Part owner	15	99	95	116	132	144	120
Share-cash renter	8	94	51	52	86	37	117
Share renter	15	89	58	84	64	13	92
Cropper	29	87	57	86	78	17	102
Negro							
Owner	36	91	67	50	81	161	89
Part owner	19	92	62	42	72	99	87
Share-cash renter	5	89	51	17	75	21	93
Share renter	9	94	56	48	45	28	98
Cropper	58	86	48	89	65	2	82
OKLAHOMA ROLLING PLAIN							
White							
Owner	83	116	239	367	270	662	106
Part owner	64	120	351	530	356	712	120
Share-cash renter	18	103	258	386	241	195	104
Share renter	88	111	239	377	155	155	116
Cropper	14	104	183	209	144	33	115
TEXAS BLACKLAND PRAIRIE							
White							
Owner	79	120	156	..	..	650	97
Part owner	51	122	229	..	..	624	120
Share-cash renter	69	104	134	..	..	117	108
Share renter	93	108	129	..	..	113	118
Cropper	9	95	51	..	..	23	109

TABLE 39

Average age of head for race and tenure groups for 1580 farm families in five sample areas of the Southwestern Region

Area and race	Owner			Renter			Crop-per
	Total	Full owner	Part owner	Total	Share-cash	Share	
	Years	*Years*	*Years*	*Years*	*Years*	*Years*	*Years*
ALL AREAS	52	54	48	44	44	44	41
White	52	53	48	44	43	44	40
Negro	56	58	49	47	48	46	42
ARKANSAS COASTAL PLAIN	55	57	49	47	47	46	41
White	54	55	49	47	45	47	39
Negro	57	60	49	47	50	46	41
LOUISIANA COASTAL PLAIN	52	52	54	48	50	48	43
White	52	52	54	48	50	48	47
Negro	52	52	50*	50	52*	50	41
MISSISSIPPI COASTAL PLAIN	51	51	48	42	42	42	40
White	49	49	46	41	45	39	36
Negro	55	58	49	43	37	46	42
OKLAHOMA ROLLING PLAIN	51	56	45	43	49	42	39
Native white	51	56	45	43	49	42	39
TEXAS BLACKLAND PRAIRIE	53	55	49	42	41	44	41
Native white	55	59	50	44	40	45	42
Czech	51	52	45	41	41	40	40*
German	51	51	50	41	40	44*	..

*Less than five cases. See Table 2 for number of cases in each category.

TABLE 40

Socio-economic status scale by race, tenure and age of head for 1404 farm families in four sample areas of the Southwestern Region

Area and age of family head	White				Negro			
	Full owner	Part owner	Renter	Cropper	Full owner	Part owner	Renter	Cropper
ARKANSAS COASTAL PLAIN								
Under 30 years	...	139*	138	137*	...	139*	131	128
30-39 years	158	161	141	129	...	131*	136	125
40-49 years	153	161	137	132	140	135	129	129
50-59 years	161	159	140	131*	147	139	131	124
60 years and over	153	158	135	...	133	141*	132	126
MISSISSIPPI COASTAL PLAIN								
Under 30 years	140	129*	132	134	...	...	144*	133
30-39 years	145	151	139*	127	136*	141*	141	132
40-49 years	150	154*	136	129	142	140	132*	127
50-59 years	155	155	152*	149*	136	141*	139*	130
60 years and over	154	144*	141	119*	135	134*	139*	125
OKLAHOMA ROLLING PLAIN								
Under 30 years	174*	179*	171	159*				
30-39 years	182	179	168	155				
40-49 years	178	185	164	167*				
50-59 years	176	179	164	...				
60 years and over	173	171	159	119*				
TEXAS BLACKLAND PRAIRIE								
Under 30 years	149*	169*	159	159*				
30-39 years	177*	185	163	146*				
40-49 years	188	182	161	149*				
50-59 years	180	183	158	132*				
60 years and over	181	183*	158	...				

*Based on less than 5 cases.

TABLE 41

Place of birth of 1551 family heads by race for four sample areas in the Southwestern Region

Area and race	All family heads	Place of Birth of Family Head*: County of present residence	State of present residence	State adjoining sample area†	Other southern state	Mid-western state	Other state	Foreign country	Un-known
	Number	*Number*	*Number*	*Number*	*Number*	*Number*	*Number*	*Number*	*Number*
ARKANSAS COASTAL PLAIN	562	369	90	62	33	2	2	1	3
White	273	171	48	20	30	2	1	1	..
Negro	289	198	42	42	3	..	1	..	3
MISSISSIPPI COASTAL PLAIN	327	200	106	4	14	2	..	..	1
White	189	113	64	2	8	2	..	..	..
Negro	138	87	42	2	6	..	..	..	1
OKLAHOMA ROLLING PLAIN‡	323	..	100§	130	59	21	4	4	5
TEXAS BLACKLAND PRAIRIE	339	144	128	..	37	3	..	18	9
Native white	182	81	62	..	37	1	..	..	1
Czech	104	46	40	..	..	1	..	16	1
German	32	8	21	..	..	1	..	2	..
Negro, Mexican	21	9	5	..	..	..	..	..	7

*Male head was used for all cases except unmarried females.

†For the Arkansas Coastal Plain, the state adjoining the sample area is Louisiana; for Mississippi, the state is Louisiana; and for Oklahoma, the state is Texas.

‡No division by race for Oklahoma.

§Includes "county of residence" due to the fact that county of birth was not ascertained.

TABLE 42

Division of management between leasor (s) and leasee by race and tenure of leasee for 950 cases in four sample areas of the Southwestern Region

Area and division of management score*	RACE AND TENURE OF LEASEE					
	White			Negro		
	Part owner	Renter	Cropper	Part owner	Renter	Cropper
	Number	*Number*	*Number*	*Number*	*Number*	*Number*
ARKANSAS COASTAL PLAIN						
2-19	..	..	2	..	1	41
20-39	..	..	6	..	1	24
40-59	..	1	6	..	21	11
60-79	4	17	5	6	23	2
80-95	32	93	1	16	74	..
MISSISSIPPI COASTAL PLAIN						
2-19	..	..	7	5	..	30
20-39	2	..	12	..	2	21
40-59	2	6	6	3	4	6
60-79	3	5	4	2	5	1
80-95	8	13	..	9	4	..
OKLAHOMA ROLLING PLAIN						
2-19	..	..	2			
20-39	1	..	4			
40-59	2	5	4			
60-79	8	11	1			
80-95	51	92	1			
TEXAS BLACKLAND PRAIRIE						
2-19	..	..	..			
20-39	..	1	2			
40-59	..	1	3			
60-79	8	36	3			
80-95	43	125	..			

*A high score indicates a high proportion of the managing done by the leasee.

TABLE 43

Distribution of leases classified by residence of individual landlord for 985 leases in four sample areas in the Southwestern Region

Distance from farm to residence of landlord	Arkansas Coastal Plain		Mississippi Coastal Plain		Oklahoma Rolling Plain		Texas Black-land Prairie	
	Number	*Per cent*	*Number*	*Per cent*	*Number*	*Per cent*	*Number*	*Per cent*
Same house	10	2.6	6	3.4	13	6.7	3	1.3
Less than .5 mile	89	22.8	97	54.5	16	8.3	47	20.9
.5- .9 mile	19	4.9	16	9.0	5	2.6	3	1.3
1.0- 1.9 mile	38	9.8	20	11.2	11	5.7	15	6.7
2.0- 4.9 mile	50	12.8	18	10.1	21	10.9	2	23.1
5.0- 9.9 mile	63	16.2	8	4.5	34	17.6	31	13.8
10.0-24.9 mile	66	17.0	5	2.8	25	12.9	28	12.4
25.0-49.9 mile	15	3.9	..	...	5	2.6	7	3.1
50.0-99.9 mile	16	4.1	2	1.1	9	4.7	2	0.9
100 mile and over	23	5.9	6	3.4	54	28.0	37	16.5
Total reported	389	100.0	178	100.0	193	100.0	225	100.0

TABLE 44

National origin of selected foreign-born elements in population of Bell County, Texas 1870-1940*

Census year	Total foreign born	NATIONAL ORIGIN†				
		Germans	Czechs			
			Total	Czecho-slovakia	Austria	Bohemia
1940	978	154	352	341	11	..
1930	991	265	517	493	24	..
1920	1933	280	608	581	27	..
1910	2013	577	854	...	854	..
1900	1230	517	284	...	74	210
1890	1079	519	122	...	62	60
1880	327	121	...	...	...	...
1870	84	...	...	...	...	...

*Data compiled from U. S. Census of Population, 1870-1940. Table on Country of Birth of foreign born population.

†Two cultural groups constitute the major portion of the foreign-born population in Bell County, Germans and Czechs. The Czechs were not enumerated separately in each census year but were included under the Austrian Empire in 1900 and under Austria and Bohemia in 1890 and 1880.

Table 45

Index of fertility of male family heads for race and tenure groups for 1580 farm families in five sample areas of the Southwestern Region (Regional ratio for 1841 male family heads is 1.193 and equals base of 100)

Area and race	Owner			Renter			Crop-per
	Total	Full owner	Part owner	Total	Share-cash	Share	
All Areas	101	104	93	101	103	101	97
White	99	103	89	96	103	94	104
Negro	109	106	117	121	107	126	95
Arkansas Coastal Plain	106	106	105	123	107	132	97
White	99	104	88	117	103	125	92
Negro	117	108	139	130	113	137	98
Louisiana Coastal Plain	103	103	100	89	84	90	93
White	104	104	104	97	87	100	107
Negro	83	85	69*	72	69*	72	88
Mississippi Coastal Plain	111	111	111	128	117	136	102
White	114	113	124	137	136	138	121
Negro	106	108	101	116	92	132	94
Oklahoma Rolling Plain	90	98	80	93	116	89	95
Texas Blackland Prairie	89	91	86	86	98	79	90
Native	84	93	75	85	104	78	86
Czech	94	91	101	85	88	83	101*
German	98	82	132	96	110	61*	...

*Less than five cases. See Table 2 for number of cases in each category.

TABLE 46

Farm tenure status of children* of present operators for race and tenure groups for 1572 farm families in four sample areas in the Southwestern Region

Area and tenure of children	Race and Tenure of Present Operator					
	White			Negro		
	Owner	Renter	Cropper	Owner	Renter	Cropper
	Per cent	*Per cent*	*Per cent*	*Per cent*	*Per cent*	*Per cent*
ARKANSAS COASTAL PLAIN	100	100	100	100	100	100
Owner	15	6	..	11	6	2
Renter	8	16	14	11	15	6
Cropper	†	8	14	16	27	38
Laborer	†	2	19	2	5	6
Nonfarm	76	68	53	60	47	48
MISSISSIPPI COASTAL PLAIN	100	100	100	100	100	100
Owner	25	8	11	13	..	6
Renter	6	5	..	5	7	2
Cropper	4	11	18	17	53	40
Laborer	1	..	..	2	..	10
Nonfarm	64	76	71	63	40	42
OKLAHOMA ROLLING PLAIN	100	100	100‡			
Owner	12	6	..			
Renter	14	22	20			
Cropper	†	1	20			
Laborer	2	8	..			
Nonfarm	71	63	60			
TEXAS BLACKLAND PRAIRIE	100	100	100‡			
Owner	7	3	..			
Renter	20	22	26			
Cropper	1	2	..			
Laborer	1	1	12			
Nonfarm	71	72	62			

*Children as used in this table are those children living away from home. Tenure status of husband is used for married daughters.

†Less than 0.5 per cent.

‡Distribution based on less than 10 cases.

TABLE 47

Nonfarm occupation* of children† of present operator for race and tenure groups for 1572 farm families in four sample areas of the Southwestern Region

Area and occupation of children	Race and Tenure of Present Operator					
	White			Negro		
	Owner	Renter	Cropper	Owner	Renter	Cropper
	Per cent	*Per cent*	*Per cent*	*Per cent*	*Per cent*	*Per cent*
ARKANSAS COASTAL PLAIN	100	100	100	100	100	100
Professional	9	..	..	6	1	..
Proprietor	8	..	5	1	..	..
Clerical	10	8	..	..	1	..
Craftsmen	8	10	10	1	1	..
Operatives	18	26	28	15	4	8
Service	12	17	10	13	9	14
Nonfarm laborer	11	7	..	24	31	26
Farm	24	32	47	40	53	52
MISSISSIPPI COASTAL PLAIN	100	100	100	100	100	100
Professional	7	..	3	2	..	..
Proprietor	3	..	..	1	..	..
Clerical	6	3	14	1	..	4
Craftsmen	7	14	11	1	..	..
Operatives	23	24	11	7	13	4
Service	12	30	18	18	7	20
Nonfarm laborer	6	5	14	33	20	14
Farm	36	24	29	37	60	58
OKLAHOMA ROLLING PLAIN	100	100	100‡			
Professional	11	7	..			
Proprietor	6	6	..			
Clerical	8	4	..			
Craftsmen	10	15	20			
Operatives	15	11	..			
Service	19	17	40			
Nonfarm laborer	2	3	..			
Farm	29	37	40			
TEXAS BLACKLAND PRAIRIE	100	100	100‡			
Professional	9	5	..			
Proprietor	6	3	..			
Clerical	12	9	..			
Craftsmen	7	6	..			
Operatives	11	25	38			
Service	22	19	12			
Nonfarm laborer	4	5	12			
Farm	29	28	38			

*See U. S. Census of Population, 1940, Third Series, Table 13 for details of classification used. Service includes domestic service.

†Children as used in this table are those children living away from home. The occupation of husband is used for married daughters.

‡Distribution based on less than 10 cases.

TABLE 48

Grade attainment of 2252 children 20-39 years of age by sex and age of children and by race and tenure of parental family in four sample areas of the Southwestern Region

Area, race and tenure of parental family	Age and Sex of Children			
	20-29 years of age		30-39 years of age	
	Male	Female	Male	Female
ARKANSAS COASTAL PLAIN	*Grade*	*Grade*	*Grade*	*Grade*
White				
Owner	9.7	10.5	9.9	10.3
Renter	7.9	9.1	8.1	8.9
Cropper	7.5	7.7	...	...
Negro				
Owner	8.1	8.7	7.1	8.1
Renter	6.7	7.3	5.9	6.5
Cropper	5.1	5.5	5.5	4.9
MISSISSIPPI COASTAL PLAIN				
White				
Owner	9.5	9.9	10.1	9.5
Renter	8.1	9.7	9.5*	10.3
Cropper	12.5*	9.1	7.9	7.5*
Negro				
Owner	7.1	8.3	6.3	7.5
Renter	3.5	5.5*	7.5*	5.1
Cropper	5.1	6.1	3.9*	5.7
OKLAHOMA ROLLING PLAIN				
Native white				
Owner	12.1	11.5	11.1	12.3
Renter	10.1	10.9	9.7	11.1
TEXAS BLACKLAND PRAIRIE				
Native white				
Owner	12.1	11.9	12.7	11.7
Renter	10.1	11.1	10.3	11.1
Czech and German				
Owner	10.3	10.3	9.3	9.3
Renter	10.3	9.7	5.5*	6.3

*Based on less than 5 cases.

Table 49

First tenure status of present operator by race and tenure of parents* for 1841 farm families in five sample areas of the Southwestern Region

Area and first tenure of operator	Race and Tenure of Parents									
	White					Negro				
	Owner-owner	Owner-renter	Owner-other	Renter-renter	Other	Owner-owner	Owner-renter	Owner-other	Renter-renter	Other
	Per cent	*Per cent*	*Per cent*	*Per cent*	*Per cent*	*Per cent*	*Per cent*	*Per cent*	*Per cent*	*Per cent*
Arkansas Coastal Plain	100	100	100†	100	100†	100	100	100	100	100
Owner	29	12	14	..	17	20	10	3	6	..
Renter	36	35	..	55	17	26	17	16	40	13
Cropper	15	37	57	15	66	36	37	55	37	57
Laborer	8	8	29	10	..	8	19	23	9	23
Nonfarm	12	8	..	20	..	10	17	3	9	2
Louisiana Coastal Plain	100	100	100†	100†	..	100†	100†	100	100†	100
Owner	37	9	14	..	..	66	14	33	25	..
Renter	27	36	43	..	..	..	43	67	50	74
Cropper	15	14	29	33	..	..	43	..	25	13
Laborer	11	18	..	33	..	17	..	..	..	..
Nonfarm	9	23	14	33	..	17	..	..	..	13
Mississippi Coastal Plain	100	100	100†	100†	100	100	100†	100	100†	100
Owner	42	25	..	20	..	8	..	..	..	14
Renter	14	25	33	20	14	19	..	5	50	3
Cropper	18	25	58	..	57	40	33	62	50	62
Laborer	1	..	..	..	..	6	33	10	..	10
Nonfarm	25	25	8	60	29	26	33	24	..	10
Oklahoma Rolling Plain	100	100	100†	100	100†					
Owner	7	6	..	4	17					
Renter	47	48	..	43	33					
Cropper	14	11	..	16	17					
Laborer	17	21	50	26	33					
Nonfarm	15	14	50	10	..					
Texas Blackland Prairie	100	100	100†	100	100†					
Owner	6	3	..	2	..					
Renter	57	64	100	49	29					
Cropper	8	11	..	16	29					
Laborer	17	12	..	26	29					
Nonfarm	11	11	..	7	13					

*Tenure of parents refers to parents of both husband and wife, giving equal weight to each. Owner-other is made up of owner-cropper and owner-laborer. Other is made up of renter-cropper, renter-laborer, cropper-cropper, cropper-laborer, and laborer-laborer. The category of other is numerically unimportant except for Negroes.

†Distribution based on less than 10 cases.

TABLE 50

Percentage ownership by years of earning life, tenure of parents* and race for 1401 farm families in four sample areas of the Southwestern Region

Area and years of earning life	Race and Tenure of Parents							
	White			Negro				
	Owner-owner	Owner-renter	Renter-renter	Owner-owner	Owner-renter	Owner-other	Renter-renter	Other
	Per cent	*Per cent*	*Per cent*	*Per cent*	*Per cent*	*Per cent*	*Per cent*	*Per cent*
ARKANSAS COASTAL PLAIN								
Under 20 years	50	17	21	17	8	7	10	0
20-39 years	54	44	10	51	25	7	20	11
40 years and over	82	50†	100†	75	47	33	50†	20
MISSISSIPPI COASTAL PLAIN								
Under 20 years	64	50	100†	29	0†	14	0†	6
20-39 years	88	67†	100†	77	25†	46	..	0
40 years and over	87	100†	100†	93	0†	33†	..	38
OKLAHOMA ROLLING PLAIN								
Under 20 years	45	42	14					
20-39 years	64	42	25					
40 years and over	82	75	80					
TEXAS BLACKLAND PRAIRIE								
Under 20 years	18	14	11					
20-39 years	67	57	33					
40 years and over	74	50†	60					

*Tenure of parents refers to parents of both husband and wife, giving equal weight to each. Owner-other is made up of owner-cropper and owner-laborer. Other is made up of renter-cropper, renter-laborer, cropper-cropper, cropper-laborer, and laborer-laborer. The category of other is numerically unimportant except for Negroes.

†Less than 5 cases.

TABLE 51

Index of highest education of head or spouse for race and tenure groups for 1580 farm families in five sample areas of the Southwestern Region (The regional average of highest grade completed is 8.58 grades and equals base of 100)

Area and race	Owner			Renter			Cropper
	Total	Full owner	Part owner	Total	Share-cash	Share	
ALL AREAS	106	104	111	102	101	102	83
White	110	108	118	109	107	110	102
Negro	84	85	83	76	75	77	73
ARKANSAS COASTAL PLAIN	92	92	94	83	85	82	77
White	100	98	104	95	98	93	97
Negro	80	81	77	73	69	74	71
LOUISIANA COASTAL PLAIN	116	116	123	96	126	90	71
White	118	118	125	105	128	99	93
Negro	90	87	105*	76	117*	72	63
MISSISSIPPI COASTAL PLAIN	104	105	102	99	108	95	89
White	111	110	120	101	117	92	102
Negro	88	89	87	97	93	99	82
OKLAHOMA ROLLING PLAIN	112	107	120	114	104	115	115
TEXAS BLACK LAND	106	97	120	112	108	118	109
Native	124	112	136	123	119	125	113
Czech	84	82	89	99	97	102	93*
German	85	84	87	108	107	109*	...

*Less than five cases. See Table 2 for number of cases in each category.

TABLE 52

Labor use on farms without croppers, classified by race and tenure of operator and by acres in cropland, in two sample areas of the Southwestern Region

Area, race, tenure status and acres in cropland	Number of cases	Days of labor used	Per Cent of Labor Used			Productive man-work units	Index of labor efficiency*
			Operator	Family	Hired		
ARKANSAS COASTAL PLAIN							
White owners							
Less than 20 acres in cropland	2	280	43	46	11	190	68
20 to 40 acres in cropland	23	290	72	23	5	192	66
40 to 80 acres in cropland	21	362	57	23	20	286	79
80 acres and over	6	397	43	24	33	388	98
White renters							
Less than 20 acres in cropland	3	203	79	18	3	87	43
20 to 40 acres in cropland	24	304	70	23	7	207	68
40 to 80 acres in cropland	39	395	55	35	10	304	77
80 acres and over	7	460	47	26	27	477	104
Negro owners							
Less than 20 acres in cropland	2	185	81	16	3	75	41
20 to 40 acres in cropland	15	342	61	34	5	171	50
40 to 80 acres in cropland	20	425	48	41	11	297	70
80 acres and over	2	530	34	66	0	390	74
Negro renters							
Less than 20 acres in cropland	7	216	81	16	3	91	42
20 to 40 acres in cropland	43	364	60	38	2	177	49
40 to 80 acres in cropland	26	438	48	50	2	291	66
80 acres and over	5	728	33	64	3	472	65
MISSISSIPPI COASTAL PLAIN							
White owners							
Less than 20 acres in cropland	23	202	50	44	6	146	72
20 to 40 acres in cropland	29	271	60	31	9	252	93
40 to 80 acres in cropland	19	354	41	44	15	383	108
80 acres and over	1	670	27	69	4	810	121
White renters							
Less than 20 acres in cropland	3	100	57	40	3	120	120
20 to 40 acres in cropland	16	259	61	29	10	213	82
40 to 80 acres in cropland	3	443	26	72	2	313	71
Negro owners							
Less than 20 acres in cropland	9	148	76	17	7	108	73
20 to 40 acres in cropland	8	296	50	48	2	225	76
40 to 80 acres in cropland	7	536	28	68	4	401	75
Negro renters							
Less than 20 acres in cropland	3	157	83	13	4	140	89
20 to 40 acres in cropland	11	245	55	44	1	216	88
40 to 80 acres in cropland	1	460	35	43	22	370	80

*Ratio of productive man-work units to days of labor used.

TABLE 53

Age left school for children 20-29 years of age by race and sex of children and by tenure of parental family in four sample areas of the Southwestern Region

Area and tenure of parental family	Race and Sex of Children			
	Native white		Other*	
	Male	Female	Male	Female
	Years	*Years*	*Years*	*Years*
ARKANSAS COASTAL PLAIN				
Owner	18.2	17.9	18.9	18.5
Renter	16.6	17.4	17.8	17.5
Cropper	17.4†	17.2†	17.4	16.8
MISSISSIPPI COASTAL PLAIN				
Owner	18.0	17.6	17.7	18.0
Renter	16.4	16.7	16.3†	16.5†
Cropper	21.0†	17.9	17.1	16.8
OKLAHOMA ROLLING PLAIN				
Owner	19.7	18.6		
Renter	18.5	18.1		
TEXAS BLACKLAND PRAIRIE				
Owner	18.4	18.1	17.2	17.5
Renter	17.2	17.3	17.2	16.4

*Negro in Arkansas and Mississippi; Czech and German in Texas.
†Based on less than ten cases.

TABLE 54

Grade retardation* of children completed school by race and tenure for 1580 farm families in five sample areas of the Southwestern Region

Area and race	Owner			Renter			Cropper
	Total	Full owner	Part owner	Total	Share-cash	Share	
	Grades	*Grades*	*Grades*	*Grades*	*Grades*	*Grades*	*Grades*
ALL AREAS	1.13	1.18	1.01	1.52	1.54	1.52	2.90
White	.69	.77	.48	.86	1.01	.79	1.34
Negro	3.36	3.37	3.33	3.95	3.99	3.93	3.68
ARKANSAS COASTAL PLAIN	2.05	2.18	1.75	2.77	2.52	2.88	3.64
White	1.27	1.43	.91	1.50	1.11	1.70	1.61
Negro	3.34	3.44	3.11	3.94	4.27	3.82	4.17
LOUISIANA COASTAL PLAIN	.77	.72	1.16	2.17	1.33	2.33	2.37
White	.57	.51	1.12	1.22	1.50†	1.15	.90
Negro	3.34	3.67	1.50†	4.32	.50†	4.70	2.92
MISSISSIPPI COASTAL PLAIN	1.59	1.45	2.23	2.59	1.63	3.11	2.72
White	.84	.91	.28	1.91	.46	2.68	1.17
Negro	3.38	3.18	3.77	3.71	3.50†	3.83†	3.50
OKLAHOMA ROLLING PLAIN	.35	.54	.11	.36	.74	.28	1.50
Native white	.35	.54	.11	.36	.74	.28	1.50
TEXAS BLACKLAND PRAIRIE	.60	.67	.49	.69	1.08	.41	1.69
Native white	.35	.41	.29	.45	.57	.40	2.17†
Czech	1.04	.96	1.30	1.07	1.35	.75	....
German	.57	.76	.28	.77	1.75†	2.50†	....

*The average retardation was computed for the children of each family. Normal was assumed to be one grade attained for each year of age beginning at age six.

†Based on less than 5 cases.

TABLE 55

Percentage of farmers reporting various tenures and average number of years spent in each tenure by race and present tenure for 1482 farmers in four areas of the Southwestern Region

Area, race, and present tenure	Number of cases	Owner		Renter		Cropper		Laborer		Nonfarm	
	Number	*Per cent*	*Years*	*Per cent*	*Years*	*Per cent*	*Years*	*Per cent*	*Years*	*Per cent*	*Years*
ARKANSAS COASTAL PLAIN											
White											
Full owner	88	100	27	47	7	24	4	10	2	23	6
Part owner	37	100	21	59	8	24	4	8	4	19	5
Renter	113	24	13	100	13	52	8	13	5	39	7
Cropper	20	10	10	45	9	100	8	35	7	30	5
Negro											
Full owner	49	100	32	45	8	31	5	16	2	16	14
Part owner	22	100	16	77	12	50	4	9	15	14	5
Renter	120	12	15	100	13	76	10	33	3	21	7
Cropper	78	5	12	36	9	100	12	57	4	26	6
MISSISSIPPI COASTAL PLAIN											
White											
Full owner	116	100	19	34	6	26	5	2	1	33	11
Part owner	15	100	16	27	5	27	12	13	6	33	10
Renter	24	21	7	100	8	50	7	17	2	54	11
Cropper	29	21	17	21	4	100	8	7	2	41	4
Negro											
Full owner	36	100	22	36	3	47	10	8	13	33	11
Part owner	19	100	16	32	7	58	6	11	2	58	8
Renter	15	0	..	100	9	47	7	20	16	20	4
Cropper	58	5	16	16	3	100	15	28	3	26	10
OKLAHOMA ROLLING PLAIN											
Native white											
Full owner	85	100	22	72	10	21	4	27	4	38	10
Part owner	64	100	14	75	10	9	7	12	4	16	10
Renter	108	15	12	100	16	31	4	30	5	41	6
Cropper	16	0	..	44	6	100	6	62	15	50	4
Laborer	29	3	1	69	12	45	4	100	9	59	5
TEXAS BLACKLAND PRAIRIE											
Native white											
Full owner	37	100	22	78	12	14	5	16	3	30	12
Part owner	34	100	14	85	14	18	2	15	3	18	9
Renter	92	11	11	100	16	23	4	24	6	18	9
Cropper	7	0	..	43	14	100	8	43	5	14	10
Laborer	11	0	..	36	3	45	7	100	8	0	..
Czech and German											
Full owner	42	100	18	76	11	14	7	26	3	19	3
Part owner	17	100	12	76	13	6	2	29	2	12	16
Renter	71	4	5	100	16	15	2	18	5	13	4

TABLE 56

Assortative marriage by members of tenure group by race in four sample areas of the Southwestern Region

Race and tenure of parents of female head	Tenure of Parents of Male Head							
	Owner		Renter		Cropper*		Non-farm	
	Number	*Per cent*	*Number*	*Per cent*	*Number*	*Per cent*	*Number*	*Per cent*
ARKANSAS COASTAL PLAIN								
White		100		100		100		100
Owner	132	76	24	53	3	33	7	88
Renter	28	16	13	29	2	22	1	12
Cropper*	4	2	1	2	4	45	0	..
Non-farm	11	6	7	16	0	..	0	..
Negro		100		100		100		100
Owner	66	54	29	45	21	33	2	40
Renter	29	24	26	40	6	9	2	40
Cropper*	22	18	8	12	34	53	0	..
Non-farm	5	4	2	3	3	5	1	20
MISSISSIPPI COASTAL PLAIN								
White		100		100		100		100
Owner	117	85	4	68	7	54	3	38
Renter	8	6	1	16	1	8	1	12
Cropper*	7	5	0	..	3	23	0	..
Non-farm	5	4	1	16	2	15	4	50
Negro		100		100		100		100
Owner	45	69	0	..	12	27	4	50
Renter	6	9	0	..	2	4	0	..
Cropper*	11	17	1	100	29	68	2	25
Non-farm	3	5	0	..	2	4	2	25
OKLAHOMA ROLLING PLAIN†		100		100		100		100
Owner	112	62	33	45	1	14	7	51
Renter	43	24	29	40	2	29	3	21
Cropper*	3	2	3	4	3	43	1	7
Non-farm	22	12	8	11	1	14	3	21
TEXAS BLACKLAND PRAIRIE								
Native white		100		100		100		100
Owner	61	68	24	37	0	..	4	67
Renter	25	28	36	55	0	...	0	..
Cropper*	0	..	3	5	2	100	0	..
Non-farm	4	4	2	3	0	...	2	33
Czech		100		100		...		100
Owner	51	81	16	57	0	...	2	67
Renter	9	14	10	35	0	...	0	..
Cropper*	1	2	1	4	0	...	0	..
Non-farm	2	3	1	4	0	...	1	33
German		100		100		100		100
Owner	25	87	2	100	0	...	0	...
Renter	1	3	0	...	0	...	0	...
Cropper*	1	3	0	...	0	...	0	...
Non-farm	2	7	0	...	0	...	0	...

*Laborer included with cropper: Arkansas, 3 cases; Mississippi, 2 cases; Oklahoma, 8 cases; and Texas, 8 cases.
†No breakdown by color due to small numbers of "other than native white."

TABLE 57

Participation in the Agricultural Extension Program by race and tenure for 1313 farm families in four sample areas of the Southwestern Region, 1942

Area, race, and tenure	Number of families	Contacts With Farm and Home Agents		Participation In 4-H Club Work	
		Per cent contacted	Average number of contacts	Per cent participation	Average attendance
Arkansas Coastal Plain					
White					
Owner	113	40	4.1	11	21.1
Renter	75	32	2.9	14	12.2
Cropper	20	25	2.6	10	21.5
Negro					
Owner	68	50	3.6	24	15.4
Renter	82	33	2.7	9	22.6
Cropper	77	31	3.0	5	35.2
Mississippi Coastal Plain					
White					
Owner	131	37	3.6	22	18.6
Renter	23	17	3.6	17	14.0
Cropper	29	17	2.6	10	13.3
Negro					
Owner	55	45	3.1	33	23.2
Renter	14	36	3.6	33	18.6
Cropper	58	14	1.9	3	7.5
Oklahoma Rolling Plain					
Native white					
Owner	147	38	4.6	14	24.5
Renter	106	32	5.2	17	14.4
Cropper	14	21	3.7	0	0.0
Texas Blackland Prairie					
Native white					
Owner	71	24	2.7	6	15.5
Renter	92	17	2.4	9	14.1
Cropper	7	0	0.0	0	0.0
Czech and German					
Owner	59	12	2.7	22	9.2
Renter	70	6	1.8	8	14.2
Cropper	2	0	0.0	0	0.0

TABLE 58

Percentage single (marital status) by color and tenure for 1739 farm family heads in five sample areas of the Southwestern Region

Area and race	Full owner	Part owner	Indeterminate	Renter	Cropper	Laborer
ALL AREAS	*Per cent*	*Per cent*	*Per cent*	*Per cent*	*Per cent*	*Per cent*
White	1.2	.6	54.1	2.5	3.4	0.0
Negro	1.1	2.4	0.0	.9	1.2	0.0
ARKANSAS COASTAL PLAIN						
White	2.5	0.0	41.7	1.3	0.0	...
Negro	2.1	4.8	0.0	0.0	1.3	...
LOUISIANA COASTAL PLAIN						
White	1.3	0.0	91.7	3.7	0.0	...
Negro	0.0	0.0*	0.0*	0.0	5.7	0.0*
MISSISSIPPI COASTAL PLAIN						
White	0.0	0.0	0.0	4.2	6.9	...
Negro	0.0	0.0	0.0*	6.7	1.7	0.0
OKLAHOMA ROLLING PLAIN						
Native white†	2.4	1.6	25.0*	3.7	6.2	0.0
TEXAS BLACKLAND PRAIRIE						
Native white	0.0	0.0	100.0*	3.3	0.0	0.0
Czech	0.0	0.0	100.0*	0.0	0.0*	0.0*
German	0.0	0.0	0.0*	0.0	...	...

*Less than five cases.

†Includes two foreign born full owners, one foreign born renter, one Mexican cropper, one Negro cropper and four Negro laborers.

TABLE 59

Farm net worth by years of earning life, tenure of parents* and race for 1401 farm families in four sample areas of the Southwestern Region

Area and years of earning life	Race and Tenure of Parents							
	White			Negro				
	Owner-owner	Owner-renter	Renter-renter	Owner-owner	Owner-renter	Owner-other	Renter-renter	Other
	Dollars	*Dollars*	*Dollars*	*Dollars*	*Dollars*	*Dollars*	*Dollars*	*Dollars*
ARKANSAS COASTAL PLAIN								
Under 20 years	178	38	70	45	30	33	32	11
20-39 years	222	184	32	116	77	36	44	37
40 years and over	346	230†	231†	164	143	72	246†	53
MISSISSIPPI COASTAL PLAIN								
Under 20 years	165	116	87†	89	10†	19	20†	8
20-39 years	311	144†	164†	164	59†	85	..	6
40 years and over	330	99†	250†	194	100†	100†	..	41
OKLAHOMA ROLLING PLAIN								
Under 20 years	439	329	187					
20-39 years	717	528	258					
40 years and over	1202	652	1145					
TEXAS BLACKLAND PRAIRIE								
Under 20 years	249	213	176					
20-39 years	594	553	411					
40 years and over	661	480†	678					

*Tenure of parents refers to parents of both husband and wife, giving equal weight to each. Owner-other is made up of owner-cropper and owner-laborer. Other is made up of renter-cropper, renter-laborer, cropper-cropper, ropper-laborer, and laborer-laborer. The category of other is numerically unimportant except for Negroes.
†Less than 5 cases.

TABLE 60

Age at ownership acquisition by method of acquisition and race for 664 owners in four sample areas of the Southwestern Region

Area and race	Method of Ownership Acquisition							
	Inheritance		Gift		Purchase		Homestead*	
	Number	*Age*	*Number*	*Age*	*Number*	*Age*	*Number*	*Age*
ARKANSAS COASTAL PLAIN								
White	22	30	7	28	97	29	..	..
Negro	13	33	1	22	55	31	..	..
MISSISSIPPI COASTAL PLAIN								
White	23	30	5	26	99	32	2	25
Negro	13	34	2	32	38	36	..	..
OKLAHOMA COASTAL PLAIN								
Native white	17	33	1	38	125	33	15	28
TEXAS BLACKLAND PRAIRIE								
Native white	14	36	..	..	56	38	..	..
Czech	12	32	..	..	29	35	..	..
German	5	30	..	..	13	39	..	..

*Includes one owner born in Sweden and one in Russia.

TABLE 61

Age at which operator acquired farm ownership by race for 771 owners in four sample areas of the Southwestern Region

Area and race	All cases	Age at Acquiring Ownership					
		Less than 25	25 to 29	30 to 34	35 to 39	40 to 44	45 and over
	Number	*Number*	*Number*	*Number*	*Number*	*Number*	*Number*
All areas	771	199	176	136	102	78	80
Per cent total	100	25.8	22.8	17.7	13.2	10.1	10.4
Cumulative percentage	..	25.8	48.6	66.3	79.5	89.6	100.0
ARKANSAS COASTAL PLAIN							
White	152	63	37	22	11	11	8
Negro	95	25	25	14	12	5	14
MISSISSIPPI COASTAL PLAIN							
White	144	54	29	21	17	12	11
Negro	59	10	13	3	15	8	10
OKLAHOMA ROLLING PLAIN*	179	34	45	45	24	19	12
TEXAS BLACKLAND PRAIRIE							
Native White	79	5	12	21	13	10	18
Czech	43	7	11	5	8	8	4
German	20	1	4	5	2	5	3

*No breakdown by national origin.

TABLE 62

Median operator's earnings for race and tenure groups for 1094 farm families in three sample areas of the Southwestern Region

Area and race	Owner		Renter		Cropper
	Full	Part	Share-cash	Share	
ARKANSAS COASTAL PLAIN	*Dollars*	*Dollars*	*Dollars*	*Dollars*	*Dollars*
White	336	426	492	416	416
Negro	177	204	191	149	248
MISSISSIPPI COASTAL PLAIN					
White	374	441	196	320	328
Negro	189	160	66	183	339
OKLAHOMA ROLLING PLAIN					
White	1,393	2,013	1,466	1,432	793

TABLE 63

Percentage of farm families with varying degrees of off-farm work by tenure status for 1470 farm families in four sample areas of the Southwestern Region

Area and tenure	Number of cases	Days Worked on Farm as a Per Cent of Total Days Family Worked					
		0 to 9.9	10 to 29.9	30 to 49.9	50 to 69.9	70 to 89.9	90 to 100
	Per cent	*Per cent*	*Per cent*	*Per cent*	*Per cent*	*Per cent*	*Per cent*
ARKANSAS COASTAL PLAIN							
Full owner	135	....	1.5	.7	4.4	11.9	81.5
Part owner	59	....	....	6.8	8.5	18.6	66.1
Renter	232	.4	....	1.3	6.5	25.9	65.9
Cropper	98	....	....	2.0	3.1	34.7	60.2
MISSISSIPPI COASTAL PLAIN							
Full owner	151	2.0	6.0	8.6	12.6	29.8	41.1
Part owner	34	2.9	5.9	14.7	14.7	26.5	35.3
Renter	39	....	5.1	7.7	15.4	41.0	30.8
Cropper	87	....	....	3.4	12.6	36.8	47.1
Laborer	6	83.3	16.7	....	....	....	....
OKLAHOMA ROLLING PLAIN							
Full owner	85	1.2	2.4	3.5	1.2	9.4	82.4
Part owner	64	....	1.6	1.6	3.1	17.2	76.5
Renter	108	1.0	....	1.9	10.2	11.1	75.9
Cropper	15	13.3	6.7	13.3	....	6.7	60.0
Laborer	29	96.6	3.4	....	....	....	....
TEXAS BLACKLAND PRAIRIE							
Full owner	76	2.6	....	5.3	1.3	5.3	85.5
Part owner	51	....	....	....	3.9	9.8	86.3
Renter	161	....	....	1.9	4.3	13.0	80.7
Cropper	13	7.7	30.8	38.5	7.7	7.7	7.7
Laborer	27	100.0	....	....	....	....	....

TABLE 64
Percentage of families with varying degrees of off-farm work by size of farm (PMWU) for 1536 families in four sample areas of the Southwestern Region

Area and productive man-work units	Number of cases	Days Worked on Farm as a Per Cent of Total Days Family Worked					
		0 to 9.9	10 to 29.9	30 to 49.9	50 to 69.9	70 to 89.9	90 to 100
	Per cent	*Per cent*	*Per cent*	*Per cent*	*Per cent*	*Per cent*	*Per cent*
ARKANSAS COASTAL PLAIN							
Under 100	26	....	3.8	3.8	7.7	26.9	57.7
100 to 199.9	160	....	.6	1.9	6.9	27.5	63.1
200 to 299.9	198	....	....	1.5	4.5	24.2	69.7
300 to 599.9	156	.6	.6	2.6	5.8	19.2	71.2
600 and over	18	....	....	....	11.1	5.6	83.3
MISSISSIPPI COASTAL PLAIN							
Under 100	19	31.6	15.8	15.8	5.3	15.8	15.8
100 to 199.9	106	0	4.7	10.4	15.1	34.9	34.9
200 to 299.9	92	2.2	2.2	4.3	13.0	35.9	42.4
300 to 599.9	91	0	2.2	5.5	12.1	33.0	47.3
600 and over	18	5.6	11.1	11.1	5.6	11.1	55.6
OKLAHOMA ROLLING PLAIN							
Under 100	60	68.3	5.0	0.0	3.3	6.7	16.7
100 to 199.9	66	3.0	3.0	7.6	4.5	7.6	74.2
200 to 299.9	103	1.0	....	1.9	4.9	13.6	78.6
300 to 599.9	84	0	1.2	1.2	4.8	9.5	83.3
600 and over	6	....	....	....	....	16.7	83.3
TEXAS BLACKLAND PRAIRIE							
Under 100	37	75.7	10.8	5.4	5.4	2.7	0.0
100 to 199.9	40	....	2.5	5.0	7.5	7.5	77.5
200 to 299.9	112	....	....	2.7	2.7	13.4	81.2
300 to 599.9	123	1.6	....	4.1	1.6	9.8	82.9
600 and over	21	....	....	....	4.8	....	95.2

TABLE 65

Relationship between farm-to-farm migration and change in farm tenure status for Mississippi Coastal Plain and Texas Blackland Prairie samples by race

Area and race	PERCENTAGE OF MOVES WITH			Percentage of tenure changes accompanied by change in farm
	No tenure change	Tenure change		
		Up	Down	
	Per cent	*Per cent*	*Per cent*	*Per cent*
Texas				
Native white	68.1	25.8	6.1	79.3
Czech and German	68.6	27.6	3.8	79.8
Mississippi				
White	56.4	30.8	12.8	86.9
Negro	71.0	21.6	7.4	78.2

TABLE 66

Percentage distribution of leases reported for each type, classified by landlord and FSA status for 1037 leases in four sample areas in the Southwestern Region

Type of Lease	CLASS OF LANDLORD						FSA clients
	Individual				Estate	Institutional	
	Male	Female	Related	Not related			
	Per cent	*Per cent*	*Per cent*	*Per cent*	*Per cent*	*Per cent*	*Per cent*
ARKANSAS COASTAL PLAIN							
Oral, indefinite	17	15	37	13	41	15	4
Oral, 1 year	58	53	40	60	33	54	26
Written, 1 year	18	30	15	21	13	31	49
Written, 2 years and over	7	2	8	6	13	0	21
Total leases reported	100	100	100	100	100	100	100
MISSISSIPPI COASTAL PLAIN							
Oral, indefinite	15	14	37	7	*	*	7
Oral, 1 year	77	71	61	83	*	*	29
Written, 1 year	4	10	0	6	*	*	21
Written, 2 years and over	4	5	2	4	*	*	43
Total leases reported	100	100	100	100	*	*	100
OKLAHOMA ROLLING PLAIN							
Oral, indefinite	33	43	55	25	20	0	17
Oral, 1 year	45	32	30	46	60	6	26
Written, 1 year	13	16	4	20	0	63	17
Written, 2 years and over	9	9	11	9	20	31	40
Total leases reported	100	100	100	100	100	100	100
TEXAS BLACKLAND PRAIRIE							
Oral, indefinite	20	23	38	12	29	0	13
Oral, 1 year	72	70	59	75	67	3	20
Written, 1 year	4	7	2	8	0	97	40
Written, 2 years and over	4	0	1	5	4	0	27
Total leases reported	100	100	100	100	100	100	100

*Inadequate sample: base less than 10 cases.

TABLE 67

Class of landlord holding 1221 leases in four sample areas in the Southwestern Region for all leasees and for FSA borrowers only

Area and class of landlord	Total leases reported		Leases reported by FSA borrowers	
	Number	*Per cent*	*Number*	*Per cent*
ARKANSAS COASTAL PLAIN	498	100.0	147	100.0
Male	355	71.3	102	69.4
Female	71	14.3	22	15.0
Estate*	58	11.6	19	12.9
Institution	14	2.8	4	2.7
MISSISSIPPI COASTAL PLAIN	199	100.0	17	100.0
Male	158	79.4	15	88.2
Female	27	13.6	1	5.9
Estate*	6	3.0	..	....
Institution	8	4.0	1	5.9
OKLAHOMA ROLLING PLAIN	239	100.0	39	100.0
Male	141	59.0	27	69.2
Female	60	25.1	5	12.8
Estate*	18	7.5	1	2.6
Institution	20	8.4	6	15.4
TEXAS BLACKLAND PRAIRIE	285	100.0	15	100.0
Male	151	53.0	8	53.3
Female	81	28.4	6	40.0
Estate	24	8.4	..	....
Institution	29	10.2	1	6.7

*Includes land owned in partnership: Arkansas—1 case, Oklahoma—6 cases.

TABLE 68

Average total acreage per ownership tract by type of owner for seven selected parishes of Louisiana, 1939*

Type of owner	Allen	Bien-ville	Cal-casieu	Con-cordia	Red River	St. Mary	West Feli-ciana
WHITE	*Acres*	*Acres*	*Acres*	*Acres*	*Acres*	*Acres*	*Acres*
Male	97	105	56	401	128	151	256
Female	54	87	44	351	111	121	270
Estate†	325	141	134	782	149	168	371
NEGRO							
Male	...	69	14	35	58	11	101
Female	41	41	14	27	42	18	55
Estate†	...	80	23	50	...	13	126
INSTITUTIONS							
Banks, Ins. Co.	360	158	242	2540	384	597	1425
Lumber Industry	2800	2724	2263	8466	2812	205	1646
Government	40	41	102	....	15	126	....
Other	1373	264	467	1180	508	3061	1925

*Unpublished data of cooperative project between Louisiana Agricultural Experiment Station and Bureau of Agricultural Economics taken from complete coverage of the 1939 Tax Rolls for all rural lands.

†Includes tracts owned jointly by two or more individuals.

TABLE 69

Distribution of 1165 landlords according to crop method of rental payment for four sample areas of the Southwestern Region

Area and crop method of rental payment	Type of Landlord							
	Male		Female		Estate		Institution	
	Number	*Per cent*	*Number*	*Per cent*	*Number*	*Per cent*	*Number*	*Per cent*
ARKANSAS COASTAL PLAIN	337	100	70	100	57	100	14	100
Cash	44	13	12	17	4	7	5	36
⅓ - ¼ Share	171	51	43	61	29	51	6	43
½ Share	91	27	4	6	3	5	2	14
Other	31	9	11	16	21	37	1	7
MISSISSIPPI COASTAL PLAIN	154	100	27	100	6	100	6	100
Cash	12	8	3	11	2	33	2	33
⅓ - ¼ Share	31	20	8	30	..	..	..	..
½ Share	89	58	7	26	..	..	..	..
Other	22	14	9	33	4	67	4	67
OKLAHOMA ROLLING PLAIN	133	100	53	100	15	100	18	100
Cash	15	11	3	6	..	..	4	22
⅓ - ¼ Share	90	68	47	89	12	80	4	22
Share-cash	9	7	2	4	1	7	7	39
Other	19	14	1	2	2	13	3	17
TEXAS BLACKLAND PRAIRIE	143	100	79	100	24	100	29	100
⅓ - ¼ Share	78	54	58	73	16	67	13	45
Share-cash	42	29	19	24	6	25	14	48
½ Share	13	9	1	1	..	..	..	..
Other	10	7	1	1	2	8	2	7

TABLE 70

Percentage distribution of ownership tracts classified by type of owner for seven selected parishes of Louisiana, 1939*

Type of owner	Allen	Bienville	Calcasieu	Concordia	Red River	St. Mary	West Feliciana
	Per cent	*Per cent*	*Per cent*	*Per cent*	*Per cent*	*Per cent*	*Per cent*
WHITE	91.8	78.2	88.5	83.4	86.7	90.4	84.9
Male	67.9	53.9	50.0	59.3	59.4	47.3	38.6
Female	15.5	13.1	22.7	11.9	17.7	14.2	22.8
Estate†	8.4	11.2	15.8	12.2	9.6	28.9	23.5
NEGRO	...	15.8	2.6	9.4	8.1	1.6	12.7
Male	...	9.9	1.5	6.4	5.4	0.6	5.2
Female	...	2.9	0.8	1.2	2.7	0.3	2.6
Estate†	...	3.0	0.3	1.8	...	0.7	4.9
INSTITUTIONS	8.2	6.0	8.9	7.2	5.2	8.0	2.4
Banks, Ins. Co.	2.5	1.9	2.4	2.0	0.7	1.2	0.4
Lumber Industry	2.9	1.3	0.9	1.5	0.6	0.8	1.2
Government	0.8	1.4	1.1	...	0.1	0.2	...
Other	2.0	1.4	4.5	3.7	3.8	5.8	0.8
TOTAL	100.0	100.0	100.0	100.0	100.0	100.0	100.0

*Unpublished data of cooperative project between Louisiana Agricultural Experiment Station and Bureau of Agricultural Economics. Source: 1939 Tax Rolls.

†Includes tracts owned jointly by two or more individuals.

TABLE 71

Percentage of total acreage in farm land* by type of owner for five selected parishes of Louisiana, 1939†

Type of owner	Bienville	Calcasieu	Concordia	St. Mary	West Feliciana
WHITE	*Per cent*	*Per cent*	*Per cent*	*Per cent*	*Per cent*
Male	41.8	48.1	17.4	39.7	46.1
Female	37.8	40.4	22.6	26.5	49.7
Estate‡	32.2	31.5	19.5	2.1	4.3
NEGRO					
Male	54.0	35.5	44.0	96.5	59.4
Female	47.2	15.3	39.0	96.1	49.7
Estate‡	50.2	27.2	26.1	96.0	40.2
INSTITUTIONS					
Banks, Ins. Co.	43.8	65.2	10.6	50.0	22.8
Lumber Industry	.1	1.1	.4	5.0	2.1
Government	25.9	15.8	....	0.0	....
Other	8.5	50.0	28.9	14.7	28.8

*Farm land is defined as cropland and pasture as classified for tax purposes.

†Unpublished data of cooperative project between Louisiana Agricultural Experiment Station and Bureau of Agricultural Economics taken from complete coverage of the 1939 Tax Rolls for all rural lands.

‡Includes tracts owned jointly by two or more individuals.

TABLE 72

Labor organization of 1453 farm operators* by size of farm (PMWU) for four sample areas of the Southwestern Region

Area and labor organization	Productive Man-work Units									
	Under 100		100-199		200-299		300-399		400 and over	
	Number	*Per cent*	*Number*	*Per cent*	*Number*	*Per cent*	*Number*	*Per cent*	*Number*	*Per cent*
ARKANSAS COASTAL PLAIN	26	100	158	100	199	100	91	100	84	100
Under 10% hired labor	23	88	140	89	142	71	53	58	28	33
10-49% hired labor	..	..	14	9	36	18	18	20	18	22
50% and over hired labor	..	..	..	..	1	1	2	2	6	7
Used croppers†	3	12	4	2	20	10	18	20	32	38
MISSISSIPPI COASTAL PLAIN	13	100	106	100	92	100	52	100	57	100
Under 10% hired labor	12	93	81	76	65	71	36	69	8	14
10-49% hired labor	..	..	20	19	15	16	7	14	7	12
50% and over hired labor	..	..	2	2	..	..	..	..	1	2
Used croppers†	1	8	3	3	12	13	9	17	41	72
OKLAHOMA ROLLING PLAIN	13	100	63	100	103	100	55	100	35	100
Under 10% hired labor	9	69	28	44	25	24	6	11	3	9
10-49% hired labor	4	31	30	48	65	63	31	56	17	48
50% and over hired labor	..	..	5	8	9	9	18	33	14	40
Used croppers†	..	..	..	..	4	4	..	..	1	3
TEXAS BLACKLAND PRAIRIE	9	100	41	100	113	100	79	100	65	100
Under 10% hired labor	8	89	29	71	57	50	26	33	5	8
10-49% hired labor	1	11	8	20	52	46	39	49	22	34
50% and over hired labor	..	..	3	7	4	4	11	14	28	43
Used croppers†	..	..	1	2	..	..	3	4	10	15

*Croppers are not included in farm operators.

†No breakdown by extent to which croppers were used or by percentage that hired labor is of total farm labor used for those farm operators using croppers.

TABLE 73

Percentage distribution for type of leases classified by distance from farm to landlord's residence for 1037 leases in four sample areas in the Southwestern Region

Area and type of lease	Distance to Landlord's Residence		
	Less than 1 mile	1-9.9 miles	10 miles and over
	Per cent	*Per cent*	*Per cent*
ARKANSAS COASTAL PLAIN	100	100	100
Oral, indefinite	17	14	20
Oral, 1 year	68	55	48
Written, 1 year	11	25	22
Written, 2 years and over	4	6	10
MISSISSIPPI COASTAL PLAIN	100	100	100
Oral, indefinite	18	15	7
Oral, 1 year	79	67	50
Written, 1 year	3	8	7
Written, 2 years and over	0	10	36
OKLAHOMA ROLLING PLAIN	100	100	100
Oral, indefinite	42	34	28
Oral, 1 year	46	40	34
Written, 1 year	6	16	25
Written, 2 years and over	6	10	13
TEXAS BLACKLAND PRAIRIE	100	100	100
Oral, indefinite	17	18	18
Oral, 1 year	83	69	48
Written, 1 year	0	10	30
Written, 2 years and over	0	3	4

TABLE 74

Percentage distribution of leases classified by type of property leased and tenure groups for 1149 leases in four sample areas in the Southwestern Region

Tenure of leasee	Type of Property Leased (per cent)				
	Farm units	Additional land*	Cropland farmstead equipment and power	Misc. types†	Number of leases per 100 farmers
ARKANSAS COASTAL PLAIN					
Part owner	13.4	56.7	0.0	29.9	117
Renter	71.1	15.3	0.7	12.6	133
Cropper	1.0‡	1.0‡	95.0	3.0‡	103
MISSISSIPPI COASTAL PLAIN					
Part owner	11.6	65.1	0.0	23.3	126
Renter	64.6	20.8	2.1‡	12.5	126
Cropper	1.1‡	5.3	85.1	8.5	108
OKLAHOMA ROLLING PLAIN					
Part owner	47.2	38.9	0.0	13.9	130
Renter	70.4	26.4	0.0	3.2‡	131
Cropper	18.7‡	0.0	25.0‡	56.3	100
TEXAS BLACKLAND PRAIRIE					
Part owner	44.8	43.3	0.0	11.9	131
Renter	83.5	10.0	0.0	6.5	125
Cropper	0.0	0.0	100.0	0.0	100

*Consists mainly of cropland although the field rent lease is predominate for Arkansas share renters and Mississippi part owners. A few part owners in all states except Texas had pasture land.

†Consists of farmstead, equipment and power, and livestock leases with little or no cropland involved.

‡Less than 5 cases.

TABLE 75

Comparison of size, value and rental payment for different types of property rented for 1227 cases in four sample areas of the Southwestern Region

Area and type of property covered by lease	Number of cases	Total acres in rent tract (average)	Cropland acres in rent tract (average)	Value of rent tract* (average)	Ratio of rent to value†	Ratio of rent to gross income‡
	Number	*Acres*	*Acres*	*Dollars*	*Per cent*	*Per cent*
ARKANSAS COASTAL PLAIN						
Farm unit	251	109	44	1,820	7.7	19.5
Additional land	97	25	18	449	17.4	24.8
Cropland, farmstead, power and equipment	98	47	34	1,322	31.1	46.9
Other	68	50	20	797	6.1	16.9
MISSISSIPPI COASTAL PLAIN						
Farm unit	47	65	29	1,095	11.9	19.9
Additional land	48	10	8	246	28.5	31.2
Cropland, farmstead, power and equipment	81	36	26	848§	55.7§	46.9
Other	28	43	17	600	27.5	35.6
OKLAHOMA ROLLING PLAIN						
Farm unit	129	234	141	7,345	9.2	27.4
Additional land	64	116	75	4,808	9.5	25.3
Cropland, farmstead, power and equipment	4	149	136	6,350	16.5	51.2
Other	22	90	67	3,533	12.3	30.2
TEXAS BLACKLAND PRAIRIE						
Farm unit	203	109	90	5,749	7.1	27.8
Additional land	51	55	52	2,482	10.2	30.3
Cropland, farmstead, power and equipment	15	24	23	1,493	21.0	49.3
Other	21	22	20	9,840	1.8	30.0

*Value of real estate, livestock, equipment and power.
†Value of rental payment divided by value of all property leased.
‡Value of rental payment divided by gross farm income for the rent tract.
§No data were collected on value of equipment and workstock and by cropper. Therefore the ratio is slightly higher due to the omission.

TABLE 76

Median ratio of rent to value of property rented* by different methods of crop rental payment for 1007 cases in four sample areas of the Southwestern Region

Area and race of leasee	Crop Method of Rental Payment				
	Cash standing	⅓-¼ share	½ share	Share-cash	Other†
	Per cent	*Per cent*	*Per cent*	*Per cent*	*Per cent*
ARKANSAS COASTAL PLAIN	7.9	10.1	39.5	8.9‡	3.7
White	7.1	9.7	34.7	52.8‡	4.4
Negro	10.4	10.7	40.7	7.8‡	1.4
MISSISSIPPI COASTAL PLAIN	12.3	23.9	62.9	24.7‡	12.0
White	8.5	16.5	55.0	...	6.7
Negro	16.5	26.4	66.0	24.7‡	16.5
OKLAHOMA ROLLING PLAIN	8.3	11.3	34.1	7.2	7.8
Native white	8.3	11.3	34.1	7.2	7.8
TEXAS BLACKLAND PRAIRIE	6.6‡	7.9	20.8	8.0	5.2
Native white	6.6‡	8.0	22.4	7.1	5.0
Czech	...	8.1	33.2‡	9.0	6.6‡
German	...	6.7	....	7.6	...

*Ratio of rent to value was computed for each lease as the percentage that the total value of the rental payment was of the value of the property rented. The value of workstock and equipment was not included in value of property rented for Mississippi.

†Includes days of labor, upkeep of rent tract, no rent, and combinations not specified.

‡Based on less than 5 cases.

TABLE 77

Percentage of leases concentrated at modal arrangement* for selected details of 1043 leases classified by method of rental payment in four sample areas of the Southwestern Region

Item	Arkansas Coastal Plains			Mississippi Coastal Plains			Oklahoma Rolling Plains			Texas Blackland Prairie		
	Cash renter	Share renter	Share cropper	Cash renter	Share renter	Share cropper	Cash renter	Share renter	Share cropper	Cash renter	Share renter	Share cropper
Crop Expenses												
Cotton seed	100T	92T	74L	100T	94T	98L	100T	99T	100T	100T	100T	83L
Fertilizer	97T	93L¼	100L½	100T	97L¼	92L⅓	†	†	†	†	†	†
Spray materials	98T	74L¼	92L½	100T	100T	100L⅓	100T	94T	100T	52L¼	65T	50L½
Harvesting	100T	99T	92T	100T	100T	91T	100T	86T	94T	100T	100T	100T
Ginning	98T	96L¼	100L½	100T	100L¼	97L⅓	100T	95L¼	95L¼	99L¼	98L¼	91L½
Machine hire	100T	83T	†	100T	100T	‡	100T	95T	94T	55T	85T	40L
Hauling cotton	100T	92T	81L	100T	76T	35L	100T	97T	100T	96T	97T	25T
Maintenance												
Repair dwelling	74L	79L	94L	‡	90L½	99L⅓	100T	58T	70T	91L	83L	100L
Repair other imp.	60L	78L	94L	56T	87L	96L	80T	72T	100T	79L	72L	91L
Labor on improvements	95T	90T	93T	73T	60T	42L	100T	100T	67T	92T	86T	‡
Productions												
Cotton, lint	100T	98L¼	100L½	100T	97L¼	98L⅓	100T	98L¼	100L¼	98L¼	100L¼	92L½
Cotton, seed	100T	95L¼	99L½	100T	97L¼	98L⅓	100T	98L¼	100L¼	99L¼	100L¼	77L½
Feed grain§	98T	92L⅓	96L½	100T	71L¼	99L⅓	100T	97L⅓	73L½	99L¼	46L⅓	90L½
Peanuts	100T	34L¼	74L½	92T	58L¼	74L⅓	100T	100L¼	†	†	†	†
Alfalfa, seed	†	†	†	†	†	†	†	62L⅓	100L¼	†	†	†
Alfalfa, hay	†	†	†	†	†	†	†	62L⅓	100L¼	†	†	†
AAA payments‡	95	93	95	80	89	96	84	81	68	98	99	62

*The letters T and L are used in the table to indicate tenant and landlord respectively. The fraction to the right of the letter indicates the fraction the tenant and landlord pays, furnishes, or receives. A letter without a fraction indicates all. Figures to the left of the letters represent the percentage of leases having that particular division (the modal arrangement).

†Item does not apply because of no crop planted or no expense reported.

‡No modal arrangement.

§Texas share-cash modal division of feed grain is ⅓ share for part of acreage and cash per acre for balance.

‡Modal arrangement for division of AAA payment is "according to AAA regulation" for all columns.

TABLE 78

Years on rent tract by form and length of lease and method of crop rental payment for 911 leasees renting cropland in four sample areas of the Southwestern Region

Area and years on rent tract by leasee	METHOD OF CROP RENTAL PAYMENT											
	Cash, standing, ⅓-¼ share, share-cash								½ share*			
	Oral, indefinite		Oral, 1 year		Written, 1 year		Written, 2 years and over		Oral, indefinite		Oral, 1 year	
	Number	*Per cent*	*Number*	*Per cent*	*Number*	*Per cent*	*Number*	*Per cent*	*Number*	*Per cent*	*Number*	*Per cent*
ARKANSAS COASTAL PLAIN		100		100		100		100		100		100
1-2 years	10	24	63	47	48	58	10	36	4	27	51	62
3-4 years	9	22	23	17	15	18	9	32	4	27	12	15
5-9 years	10	24	26	19	13	16	6	21	1	6	12	15
10 years and over	12	30	23	17	7	8	3	11	6	40	7	8
MISSISSIPPI COASTAL PLAIN		100		100		100		100		100		100
1-2 years	0	..	25	65	5	62	3	60	9	69	50	62
3-4 years	3	60	4	11	0	0	1	20	1	8	9	11
5-9 years	1	20	4	11	2	25	0	..	2	15	13	16
10 years and over	1	20	5	13	1	13	1	20	1	8	9	11
OKLAHOMA ROLLING PLAIN		100		100		100		100		100		100
1-2 years	8	13	28	44	15	44	8	47	0	..	2	25
3-4 years	9	15	11	17	4	12	1	6	0	..	3	38
5-9 years	11	19	11	17	6	18	1	6	1	100	2	25
10 years and over	31	53	14	22	9	26	7	41	0	..	1	12
TEXAS BLACKLAND PRAIRIE		100		100		100		100		..		100
1-2 years	8	20	38	37	10	31	4	58	0	..	12	86
3-4 years	3	8	15	15	10	31	1	14	0	..	1	7
5-9 years	13	32	26	26	7	22	1	14	0	..	0	..
10 years and over	16	40	22	22	5	16	1	14	0	..	1	7

*No cases of ½ share written leases sampled.

TABLE 79

Case count* of leases classified by method of rental payment on cropland and race of leasee for four sample areas of the Southwestern Region

Area and race of leasee	All leases	Method of Rental Payment on Cropland: Cash standing†	⅓ or ¼ Crop-share	Crop-share plus cash‡	½ Crop-share	No rent	Other methods	Method of payment unknown	No cropland rented
	Number	*Number*	*Number*	*Number*	*Number*	*Number*	*Number*	*Number*	*Number*
ARKANSAS COASTAL PLAIN									
White	223	39	122	2	22	8	21	3	6
Negro	302	34	137	1	78	14	18	5	15
MISSISSIPPI COASTAL PLAIN									
White	89	9	21	0	36	4	14	1	4
Negro	116	12	21	1	61	9	10	1	1
OKLAHOMA ROLLING PLAIN§	246	24	153	20	10	5	8	15	11
TEXAS BLACKLAND PRAIRIE									
Native white	176	3	113	33	6	1	7	4	10
Negro, Mexican	6	0	0	0	6	0	0	0	0
Czech	87	0	45	34	2	1	5	0	1
German	23	0	8	14	0	0	0	0	1

*Includes regular sample Arkansas, Mississippi, Oklahoma, and Texas and Special FSA Arkansas.

†Includes 7 leases of standing rent: Arkansas, 1 white and 4 Negro; Mississippi, 1 Negro; Oklahoma, 1 case.

‡Share rent on specified acres and cash rent per acre on other acres: Arkansas, 1 white and 1 Negro; Oklahoma, 3 cases; Texas, all cases. Share rent plus cash rent for pasture, house or not identified: Arkansas, 1 white; Mississippi, 1 Negro; Oklahoma, 17 cases.

§No color breakdown is given for Oklahoma due to small sample of "other than native white."

TABLE 80

Percentage of selected management items decided by landlord, tenant, or divided for each total division of management score interval for all leases in total of four sample areas of the Southwestern Region

Management item	Division of Management Score				
	Under 20	20 to 39	40 to 59	60 to 79	80 and over
	Per cent	*Per cent*	*Per cent*	*Per cent*	*Per cent*
Kind of crops decided by:					
Landlord	92	71	45	20	2
Divided	5	12	21	26	3
Tenant	3	17	34	54	95
Acres of each crop decided by:					
Landlord	93	83	51	21	1
Divided	5	10	23	25	3
Tenant	2	7	26	54	96
Kind of livestock decided by:					
Landlord	83	39	21	7	0
Divided	10	17	15	10	*
Tenant	7	44	64	83	100
Amount of livestock decided by:					
Landlord	77	41	22	10	*
Divided	10	18	13	9	1
Tenant	13	41	65	81	99
Planting of crops decided by:					
Landlord	64	28	4	*	0
Divided	31	56	34	4	1
Tenant	5	16	62	96	99
Cultivating of crops decided by:					
Landlord	62	14	0	0	0
Divided	30	54	25	2	*
Tenant	8	32	75	98	100
Harvesting of crops decided by:					
Landlord	52	13	4	0	0
Divided	39	46	15	2	*
Tenant	9	41	81	98	100
Securing fertilizer decided by:					
Landlord	96	80	38	7	0
Divided	4	19	38	16	2
Tenant	0	1	24	77	98
Securing production credit decided by:					
Landlord	93	73	31	4	*
Divided	2	16	22	4	3
Tenant	6	11	47	92	97
Securing furnish credit decided by:					
Landlord	82	53	38	10	1
Divided	5	19	13	8	*
Tenant	13	28	49	82	99
Crop rotation program decided by:					
Landlord	98	59	28	6	*
Divided	2	37	44	15	1
Tenant	0	4	28	79	99
Marketing decided by:					
Landlord	88	54	28	4	0
Divided	9	39	44	24	3
Tenant	3	7	28	72	97
Record keeping done by:					
Landlord	88	64	33	11	1
Divided	10	31	33	25	3
Tenant	2	5	33	64	96
AAA forms signed as operator by:					
Landlord	100	88	79	54	4
Tenant	0	12	21	46	96

*Less than 0.5 per cent.

TABLE 81

Distribution of landlords by distance from residence to rent tract and frequency of supervision for each total division of management score interval for all leases in total of four sample areas of the Southwestern Region

Item	DIVISION OF MANAGEMENT SCORE				
	Under 20	20 to 39	40 to 59	60 to 79	80 and over
Distance from rent tract to residence of owner	*Per cent*	*Per cent*	*Per cent*	*Per cent*	*Per cent*
Same house	3	6	1	2	0
Under .5 mile	25	15	5	1	0
.5- .9	5	3	3	0	0
1.0- 1.9	5	2	0	1	0
2.0- 4.9	20	23	7	5	0
5 - 9.9	17	19	16	3	9
10 -24.9	14	20	19	12	6
25 -49.9	8	9	11	13	4
50 -99.9	3	6	9	9	3
100 miles and over	*	7	29	54	78
Frequency of supervision by landlord					
Daily	67	35	10	3	1
100 miles and over	11	18	4	3	0
50-99	8	13	13	4	*
25-49	8	16	18	5	1
10-24	6	11	21	19	6
5- 9	0	5	12	22	10
2- 4	0	1	19	28	28
Less than 2	0	1	3	16	54

*Less than 0.5 per cent.

TABLE 82

Division of management score by race of leasee and method of crop rental payment for 1104 cases in four sample areas of the Southwestern Region

Area and race of leasee	AVERAGE DIVISION OF MANAGEMENT SCORE*				
	Cash standing	1/3-1/4 share	1/2 share	Share-cash	Other†
ARKANSAS COASTAL PLAIN					
White	90	85	51	90‡	85
Negro	85	79	28	65‡	75
MISSISSIPPI COASTAL PLAIN					
White	81	71	38	..	81
Negro	80	61	23	85‡	70
OKLAHOMA ROLLING PLAIN					
Native white§	86	79	36	83	69
TEXAS BLACKLAND PRAIRIE					
Native white	91‡	83	51	77	65
Czech	..	76	35‡	81	81‡
German	..	83	..	84	..

*A high score indicates a high proportion of the managing done by the leasee.
†Includes rental payment by labor, upkeep of rent tract, no rent, and combinations not specified.
‡Based on less than 5 cases.
§Includes one 1/3 - 1/4 share lease by a native of Germany and two 1/2 share leases, one by a Negro and the other by a Mexican.

TABLE 83
Median productive man-work units by race, tenure, and division of management score for 929 farms in the four sample areas of the Southwestern Region

Area, race, and tenure	Division of Management Score				
	10 to 19	20 to 39	40 to 59	60 to 79	80 to 94
ARKANSAS COASTAL PLAIN	*Units*	*Units*	*Units*	*Units*	*Units*
White					
Part owner	.....	.....	.....	450.0*	328.6
Renter	.....	.....	450.0*	245.0	254.7
Cropper	275.0*	200.0	300.0	275.0	350.0*
Negro					
Part owner	.....	.....	.....	450.0	287.5
Renter	350.0*	500.0*	196.4	185.4	219.0
Cropper	185.9	200.0	212.5	250.0*	.....
MISSISSIPPI COASTAL PLAIN					
White					
Part owner	.....	225.0*	200.0*	275.0*	450.0
Renter	.....	.....	200.0	175.0	225.0
Cropper	225.0	190.0	225.0	275.0*	.....
Negro					
Part owner	262.5	.....	275.0*	250.0*	287.5
Renter	.....	300.0*	150.0*	208.3	153.3*
Cropper	200.0	187.5	200.0	125.0*	.....
OKLAHOMA ROLLING PLAIN					
White					
Part owner	.....	175.0*	325.0*	333.3	331.6
Renter	.....	.....	287.5	275.0	242.4
TEXAS BLACKLAND PRAIRIE					
White					
Part owner	.....	.....	.....	450.0	461.1
Renter	.....	275.0*	175.0*	268.8	263.0

*Less than 5 cases.

TABLE 84

Average value of livestock and equipment owned by race, tenure, and division of management score for 929 farms of the Southwestern Region

Area, race, and tenure	Division of Management Score				
	10 to 19	20 to 39	40 to 59	60 to 79	80 to 94
Arkansas Coastal Plain	*Dollars*	*Dollars*	*Dollars*	*Dollars*	*Dollars*
White					
Part owner	...	...	...	775*	1,069
Renter	...	...	1,300*	571	615
Cropper	50*	33	333	260	1,000*
Negro					
Part owner	...	...	...	533	806
Renter	500*	500*	314	335	386
Cropper	85	112	127	250*	...
Mississippi Coastal Plain					
White					
Part owner	...	350*	200*	567*	1,875
Renter	...	...	283	240	469
Cropper	67	100	250	100*	...
Negro					
Part owner	300	0	633*	250*	733
Renter	...	700*	225*	260	250*
Cropper	67	48	100	100*	...
Oklahoma Rolling Plain					
White					
Part owner	...	3,000*	5,700*	3,050	3,876
Renter	...	...	3,560	2,036	2,356
Texas Blackland Prairie					
White					
Part owner	...	...	...	2,662	2,723
Renter	...	1,600*	1,900*	1,458	1,505

*Less than five cases.

TABLE 85

Average crop yield index by race, tenure, and division of management score for 930 farms in four sample areas of the Southwestern Region

Area, race, and tenure	Division of Management Score				
	10 to 19	20 to 39	40 to 59	60 to 79	80 to 94
ARKANSAS COASTAL PLAIN					
White					
Part owner	...	...	...	120*	108
Renter	...	...	80*	94	106
Cropper	100*	126	144	108	80*
Negro					
Part owner	...	...	...	154	84
Renter	80*	160*	76	78	70
Cropper	98	114	106	90*	...
MISSISSIPPI COASTAL PLAIN					
White					
Part owner	...	120*	100*	94*	130
Renter	...	...	100	72	104
Cropper	118	116	136	104*	...
Negro					
Part owner	72	...	120*	50*	80
Renter	...	70*	120*	64	44*
Cropper	116	110	86	60*	...
OKLAHOMA ROLLING PLAIN					
Native white					
Part owner	...	160*	130*	120	100
Renter	...	...	120	106	88
TEXAS BLACKLAND PRAIRIE					
White					
Part owner	...	...	...	122	102
Renter	...	80*	120*	102	100

*Less than five cases.

TABLE 86

Average diversification index by race, tenure, and division of management score for 929 farmers in four sample areas of the Southwestern Region

Area, race, and tenure	Division of Management Score				
	10 to 19	20 to 39	40 to 59	60 to 79	80 to 94
ARKANSAS COASTAL PLAIN					
White					
Part owner	....	....	....	3.15*	3.45
Renter	....	....	2.75*	3.35	3.55
Cropper	2.50*	2.25	2.50	3.35	2.25*
Negro					
Part owner	....	....	....	3.50	3.65
Renter	2.25*	2.25*	3.30	3.50	3.65
Cropper	2.40	2.50	3.10	3.50*	....
MISSISSIPPI COASTAL PLAIN					
White					
Part owner	....	3.75*	3.00*	3.75*	3.45
Renter	....	....	3.00	2.85	4.05
Cropper	2.80	3.25	3.10	3.15*	....
Negro					
Part owner	3.35	....	3.40*	3.50*	3.70
Renter	....	3.75*	3.15*	3.15	2.65*
Cropper	2.60	2.70	2.65	2.75*	....
OKLAHOMA ROLLING PLAIN					
Native white					
Part owner	....	4.75*	4.75*	3.55	3.60
Renter	....	....	3.25	3.15	3.65
TEXAS BLACKLAND PRAIRIE					
White					
Part owner	....	....	....	2.95	3.50
Renter	....	2.75*	3.75*	3.45	3.60

*Less than five cases.

TABLE 87

Value of home use by race, tenure, and division of management score for 929 farms in the four sample areas of the Southwestern Region

Area, race, and tenure	Division of Management Score				
	10 to 19	20 to 39	40 to 59	60 to 79	80 to 94
ARKANSAS COASTAL PLAIN	*Dollars*	*Dollars*	*Dollars*	*Dollars*	*Dollars*
White					
Part owner	...	...	...	388*	322
Renter	...	...	210*	295	333
Cropper	240*	165	297	220	320*
Negro					
Part owner	...	...	...	268	329
Renter	180*	560*	199	258	235
Cropper	156	183	195	185*	...
MISSISSIPPI COASTAL PLAIN					
White					
Part owner	...	225*	145*	273*	289
Renter	...	...	218	136	247
Cropper	167	234	277	158*	...
Negro					
Part owner	160	...	197	170*	228
Renter	...	345*	140*	158	170*
Cropper	145	168	117*	210*	...
OKLAHOMA ROLLING PLAIN					
White					
Part owner	...	90*	235*	272	319
Renter	...	...	220	248	314
TEXAS BLACKLAND PRAIRIE					
White					
Part owner	...	...	...	286	208
Renter	...	160*	160*	266	270

*Less than five cases.

TABLE 88

Per cent of all families with specified division of management scores who were FSA borrowers by race and tenure for 930 farm families in four sample areas of the Southwestern Region

Area, race, and tenure	Division of Management Score				
	10 to 19	20 to 39	40 to 59	60 to 79	80 to 94
ARKANSAS COASTAL PLAIN	*Per cent*	*Per cent*	*Per cent*	*Per cent*	*Per cent*
White					
Part owner	..	..	..	25*	12
Renter	..	..	0*	41	54
Cropper	0*	0	0	20	0*
Negro					
Part owner	..	..	..	33	12
Renter	0*	0*	14	39	50
Cropper	0	0	0	50*	..
MISSISSIPPI COASTAL PLAIN					
White					
Part owner	..	0*	0*	33*	0
Renter	..	..	50	40	23
Cropper	0	0	0	0*	..
Negro					
Part owner	20	..	0*	50*	22
Renter	..	50*	0*	0	25*
Cropper	0	0	0	0*	..
OKLAHOMA ROLLING PLAIN					
Native white					
Part owner	..	0*	0*	12	20
Renter	..	..	20	27	20
TEXAS BLACKLAND PRAIRIE					
White					
Part owner	..	..	..	0	0
Renter	..	0*	0*	6	10

*Less than five cases.

TABLE 89

Percentage of operators related to landlord by race, tenure, and division of management score for 924 farm families in four sample areas of the Southwestern Region

Area, race, and tenure	Division of Management Score				
	10 to 19	20 to 39	40 to 59	60 to 79	80 to 94
ARKANSAS COASTAL PLAIN	*Per cent*	*Per cent*	*Per cent*	*Per cent*	*Per cent*
White					
Part owner	..	..	..	50*	38
Renter	..	..	0*	35	19
Cropper	50*	0	17	20	0*
Negro					
Part owner	..	..	..	0	38
Renter	0*	0*	19	17	11
Cropper	0	4	27	50*	..
MISSISSIPPI COASTAL PLAIN					
White					
Part owner	..	100*	0*	33*	50
Renter	..	..	33	40	15
Cropper	29	67	33	75*	..
Negro					
Part owner	0	..	0*	50*	56
Renter	..	50*	50*	40	75*
Cropper	7	10	17	0*	..
OKLAHOMA ROLLING PLAIN					
Native white					
Part owner	..	100*	50*	25	35
Renter	..	..	40	45	31
TEXAS BLACKLAND PRAIRIE					
White					
Part owner	..	..	..	57	46
Renter	..	0*	0*	36	31

*Less than five cases.

TABLE 90

Average age of head by race, tenure, and division of management score for 930 farm families in the four sample areas of the Southwestern Region

Area, race, and tenure	Division of Management Score				
	10 to 19	20 to 39	40 to 59	60 to 79	80 to 94
ARKANSAS COASTAL PLAIN	*Years*	*Years*	*Years*	*Years*	*Years*
White					
Part owner	....	....	....	47.5*	48.5
Renter	....	....	32.5*	44.3	47.5
Cropper	43.5*	38.9	38.5	37.5	32.5*
Negro					
Part owner	....	....	....	53.9	47.9
Renter	32.5*	42.5*	42.5	48.7	47.5
Cropper	38.9	38.7	43.7	37.5*	....
MISSISSIPPI COASTAL PLAIN					
White					
Part owner	....	43.5*	27.5*	43.9*	49.1
Renter	....	....	37.5	29.1	48.3
Cropper	28.9	32.7	44.1	42.9*	....
Negro					
Part owner	47.5	....	38.9*	47.5*	52.9
Renter	....	37.5*	47.9*	47.5	32.5*
Cropper	42.9	42.5	42.9	37.5*	....
OKLAHOMA ROLLING PLAIN					
White					
Part owner	....	22.5*	37.5*	34.3	44.3
Renter	....	....	43.7	39.3	43.1
TEXAS BLACKLAND PRAIRIE					
White					
Part owner	....	....	....	47.7	48.5
Renter	....	32.5*	37.5*	38.3	42.9

*Less than five cases.

TABLE 91

Productive livestock on farms of three sizes in terms of acres in cropland, classified by race and tenure of operator, in four sample areas of the Southwestern Region

Area, race, and tenure status	Less Than 40 Acres in Cropland			40 to 60 Acres in Cropland			60 Acres and Over in Cropland		
	Number of cases	Animal units of productive livestock per		Number of cases	Animal units of productive livestock per		Number of cases	Animal units of productive livestock per	
		Farm	Hundred acres of cropland		Farm	Hundred acres of cropland		Farm	Hundred acres of cropland
ARKANSAS COASTAL PLAIN									
White									
Owners	30	4.7	15.4	24	6.1	12.3	25	6.9	7.4
Part owners	11	4.5	16.0	8	4.5	9.1	15	8.6	8.2
Share-cash renters	12	3.1	11.4	10	7.9	16.2	4	5.8	7.1
Share renters	14	3.6	12.4	19	3.2	6.7	16	4.8	6.1
Negro									
Owners	19	3.1	10.7	17	3.1	6.2	11	4.5	5.5
Part owners	7	3.1	10.4	4	3.2	6.8	10	4.5	4.3
Share-cash renters	15	2.3	7.9	6	3.0	6.4	....	....	....
Share renters	34	1.7	6.3	15	2.2	4.4	12	4.0	5.1
MISSISSIPPI COASTAL PLAIN									
White									
Owners	66	4.1	17.2	26	9.4	19.5	24	13.5	13.9
Part owners	9	2.7	8.6	1	5.0	11.9	5	15.4	17.4
Share-cash renters	8	2.9	12.7	..	....	....	..	....	....
Share renters	12	2.5	8.5	3	3.7	8.3	..	....	....
Negro									
Owners	18	1.9	7.4	..	....	....	7	5.1	6.7
Part owners	13	3.3	13.6	11	4.0	8.1	..	....	....
Share-cash renters	4	0.8	3.8	6	2.3	4.8	..	....	....
Share renters	9	2.3	5.0	1	0.0	0.0	..	....	....
	Less Than 80 Acres in Cropland			80 to 160 Acres in Cropland			160 Acres and Over in Cropland		
OKLAHOMA ROLLING PLAIN									
White									
Owners	19	10.4	17.1	41	11.9	9.5	22	23.1	8.4
Part owners	1	35.0	50.0	15	16.9	12.8	47	24.3	8.2
Share-cash renters	4	9.8	15.8	7	17.6	13.4	7	17.1	6.5
Share renters	9	2.4	4.2	50	9.6	7.3	29	14.1	5.2
TEXAS BLACKLAND PRAIRIE									
White									
Owners	40	6.8	12.5	26	10.3	9.6	13	12.8	5.9
Part owners	5	8.0	13.5	26	11.3	9.8	20	19.2	6.3
Share-cash renters	40	6.6	11.5	25	7.5	7.2	4	16.8	5.4
Share renters	40	5.1	8.9	45	9.1	8.0	8	8.0	4.0

TABLE 92

Percentage of cropland acres in intertilled crops by size of farm and tenure for 885 white farm operators in four sample areas of the Southwestern Region

Area and tenure	Size of Farm		
	Small*	Medium†	Large‡
ARKANSAS COASTAL PLAIN	*Per cent*	*Per cent*	*Per cent*
Owners	84.2	75.9	67.9
Part owners	94.5	98.2	75.4
Share-cash renters	98.5	79.9	86.4§
Share renters	90.2	83.3	71.5
MISSISSIPPI COASTAL PLAIN			
Owners	93.2	87.1	90.7
Part owners	97.1	95.2§	86.0
Share-cash renters	93.9	....	....
Share renters	88.3	8.3§	....
OKLAHOMA ROLLING PLAIN			
Owners	72.4	65.9	52.8
Part owners	28.6§	83.2	48.7
Share-cash renters	93.1§	64.4	52.5
Share renters	79.2	66.3	55.2
TEXAS BLACKLAND PRAIRIE			
Owners	101.4	77.4	74.0
Part owners	77.7	83.4	72.9
Share-cash renters	89.2	82.0	54.3§
Share renters	91.3	82.7	80.5

*Small farms for Arkansas and Mississippi are under 40 acres of cropland, for Oklahoma and Texas are under 80 acres of cropland.

†Medium sized farms for Arkansas and Mississippi are 40.0 to 59.9 acres of cropland, for Oklahoma and Texas are 80.0 to 159.9 acres of cropland.

‡Large farms for Arkansas and Mississippi are 60.0 acres and over of cropland, for Oklahoma and Texas are 160.0 acres and over of cropland.

§Based on less than 5 cases.

TABLE 93

Participation in the Soil Conservation Service Program by race and tenure for 1313 farm families in four sample areas of the Southwestern Region, 1942

Area, race, and tenure	Total cases	1942 Participation	Average visits
ARKANSAS COASTAL PLAIN	*Number*	*Per cent*	*Number*
White			
Owner	113	9.7	2.3
Renter	75	4.0	0.3
Cropper	20	5.0	0
Negro			
Owner	68	6.0	0.7
Renter	82	4.0	0
Cropper	77	0	0
MISSISSIPPI COASTAL PLAIN			
White			
Owner	131	0	0
Renter	23	0	0
Cropper	29	0	0
Negro			
Owner	55	0	0
Renter	14	0	0
Cropper	58	0	0
OKLAHOMA ROLLING PLAIN			
White			
Owner	147	7.0	3.9
Renter	106	2.0	0
Cropper	14	0	0
TEXAS BLACKLAND PRAIRIE			
White			
Owner	130	10.0	2.7
Renter	162	4.0	2.3
Cropper	9	0	0

TABLE 94

Participation in the Agricultural Adjustment Administration Program by race and tenure for 1313 farm families in four sample areas of the Southwestern Region, 1942

Area, race, and tenure	Total cases	1942 participation	Average 1942 Payments	
			Adjustment*	Practice*
ARKANSAS COASTAL PLAIN	*Number*	*Per cent*	*Dollars*	*Dollars*
White				
Owner	113	96	24.67	18.02
Renter	75	96	20.58	14.62
Cropper	20	95	20.00	10.00
Negro				
Owner	68	97	15.48	12.20
Renter	82	99	15.62	12.09
Cropper	77	99	15.52	4.83
MISSISSIPPI COASTAL PLAIN				
White				
Owner	131	99	33.42	18.80
Renter	23	100	18.89	8.00
Cropper	29	100	14.35	3.33
Negro				
Owner	55	100	20.23	12.22
Renter	14	100	10.00	2.00
Cropper	58	98	14.34	7.77
OKLAHOMA ROLLING PLAIN				
White				
Owner	147	99	121.68	41.09
Renter	106	97	90.00	37.89
Cropper	14	43	50.00	37.50
TEXAS BLACKLAND PRAIRIE				
White				
Owner	130	99	84.00	38.80
Renter	162	100	45.49	26.67
Cropper	9	90	22.00	0

*The average payment is computed on the basis of those who participated.

TABLE 95

Characteristics of leasee by length and type of leasing arrangement for 1037 leases in four sample areas of the Southwestern Region

Area and type of lease	Number of leases	AVERAGE VALUE FOR SPECIFIED ITEMS			
		Migration index*	Years of earning life	Division of manage-ment†	Diversi-fication index‡
ARKANSAS COASTAL PLAIN					
Oral, indefinite	82	94	28	75	2.98
Oral, 1 year	251	112	23	65	3.21
Written, 1 year	90	124	25	84	3.32
Written, 2 years and over	30	113	26	87	3.36
MISSISSIPPI COASTAL PLAIN					
Oral, indefinite	27	89	17	52	3.14
Oral, 1 year	131	121	21	42	2.96
Written, 1 year	9	126	23	78	3.03
Written, 2 years and over	10	93	29	85	3.48
OKLAHOMA ROLLING PLAIN					
Oral, indefinite	68	80	21	82	3.28
Oral, 1 year	84	118	24	75	3.20
Written, 1 year	38	108	22	79	3.18
Written, 2 years and over	24	142	25	79	3.54
TEXAS BLACKLAND PRAIRIE					
Oral, indefinite	52	68	20	82	3.28
Oral, 1 year	174	83	20	77	3.20
Written, 1 year	42	79	23	78	3.13
Written, 2 years and over	8	81	21	79	3.38

*Regional migration ratio is .6709 and equals base of 100.
†High score indicates a high proportion of the managing done by the leasee.
‡Increase in numerical value indicates more diversification.

TABLE 96

Method of crop rental payment by type of lease (form and length) for 1108 leases in four sample areas of the Southwestern Region

Area and type of lease	METHOD OF CROP RENTAL PAYMENT									
	Cash, standing		⅓ - ¼ share		½ share		Share-cash		Other*	
	Number	*Per cent*	*Number*	*Per cent*	*Number*	*Per cent*	*Number*	*Per cent*	*Number*	*Per cent*
ARKANSAS COASTAL PLAIN........	68	100	242	100	97	100	3	100	40	100
Oral, indefinite................	8	12	37	15	15	15	0	..	20	50
Oral, 1 year..................	33	48	118	49	82	85	1	33	17	43
Written, 1 year..............	23	34	63	26	0	..	2	67	1	2
Written, 2 years and over......	4	6	24	10	0	..	0	..	2	5
MISSISSIPPI COASTAL PLAIN.......	16	100	40	100	94	100	1	100	26	100
Oral, indefinite................	0	..	5	12	13	14	..	..	9	35
Oral, 1 year..................	8	50	30	75	81	86	1	100	11	42
Written, 1 year..............	6	38	2	5	0	..	..	..	1	4
Written, 2 years and over......	2	12	3	8	0	..	..	..	5	19
OKLAHOMA ROLLING PLAIN........	23	100	145	100	9	100	20	100	10	100
Oral, indefinite................	2	9	57	39	1	11	1	5	6	60
Oral, 1 year..................	10	43	60	42	8	89	2	10	1	10
Written, 1 year..............	8	35	15	10	0	..	13	65	1	10
Written, 2 years and over......	3	13	13	9	0	..	4	20	2	20
TEXAS BLACKLAND PRAIRIE.......	3	100	166	100	14	100	81	100	10	100
Oral, indefinite................	0	..	31	19	0	..	16	20	3	30
Oral, 1 year..................	3	100	106	64	14	100	46	57	5	50
Written, 1 year..............	0	..	22	13	0	..	19	23	1	10
Written, 2 years and over......	0	..	7	4	0	..	0	..	1	10

*Includes rental payment by labor, upkeep of rent tract, no rent, and combinations not specified.

TABLE 97

Percentage of operators who have resided on present farm less than five years for race and tenure groups for 1580 farm families in five sample areas of the Southwestern Region

Area and race	Owner		Renter		Cropper
	Full	Part	Share-cash	Share	
ALL AREAS	15	21	60	54	71
White	16	19	60	54	80
Negro	6	33	63	52	67
ARKANSAS COASTAL PLAIN	4	22	64	66	74
White	5	15	69	80	75
Negro	2*	33	57	56	74
LOUISIANA COASTAL PLAIN	10	5*	67	63	50
White	10	5	80	75	69
Negro	9*	..	..	40*	42
MISSISSIPPI COASTAL PLAIN	20	41	77	62	79
White	23	47	62	80	93
Negro	11	37	100	44*	72
OKLAHOMA ROLLING PLAIN	29	17	56	47*	64
TEXAS BLACKLAND	16	20	55	40	78
Native	19	24	59	41	86
Czech	16	20*	60	37	100*
German	9*	..	30	33*	..

*Less than five cases. See Table 2 for number of cases in each category.

TABLE 98

Land ownership in the Southwestern Region

State	Total land area**	Public Ownership: Federal 1940†		Public Ownership: Federal 1945‡		Public Ownership: State§		Proportion of land area in farms‡	
	Acreage	*Acreage*	*Per cent**	*Acreage*	*Per cent**	*Acreage*	*Per cent**	*Acreage*	*Per cent**
Arkansas......	33,744,000	2,536,600	7.5	2,949,736	8.7	642,493	1.9	18,044,542	53.5
Louisiana......	28,913,280	665,540	2.3	1,223,655	4.2	530,152	1.8	9,996,108	34.6
Mississippi....	30,348,800	1,103,360	3.6	1,515,236	5.0	141,446	0.5	19,156,058	63.1
Oklahoma.....	44,341,120	3,249,840	7.3	3,619,976	8.2	1,093,280	2.5	34,803,317	78.5
Texas.........	168,732,160	870,620	0.5	2,446,010	1.4	3,660,418	2.2	137,683,372	81.6
Total......	306,079,360	8,425,960	2.8	11,754,613	3.8	6,067,789	2.0	219,683,397	71.8

**1940 Census.
†S.C.S. unpublished data, table 1, April 1941.
‡L. A. Reuss and O. O. McCracken, *Federal Rural Lands*, USDA, BAE, June 1947.
§Partial and preliminary unpublished reports, USDA, BAE, 1947; Arkansas data as of 1941; Louisiana, 1941; Mississippi, 1945; Oklahoma, 1944; and Texas, 1946. Data on land ownership by counties, municipalities and other local units of government are not available. In Oklahoma, tax-delinquent land reverts to the counties. One source estimated tax-forfeited lands held by Oklahoma counties in 1935 at 600,000 acres.
‡1940 Census.
*Per cent of total land area.

TABLE 99

Race and sex of landlord by method of crop rental payment and race of leasee for 979 landlords in four sample areas of the Southwestern Region

Area, race and sex of landlord	Method of Crop Rental Payment and Race of Leasee						
	½ share crop rental			Other methods of rental payment			
	Native white	Negro*	Czech	Native white	Negro	Czech	German
	Number	*Number*	*Number*	*Number*	*Number*	*Number*	*Number*
ARKANSAS COASTAL PLAIN							
White							
Male	22	59	..	105	90	..	..
Female	..	3	..	33	17	..	..
Negro							
Male	..	7	..	1	24	..	..
Female	..	..	..	..	12	..	..
MISSISSIPPI COASTAL PLAIN							
White							
Male	31	45	..	31	17	..	..
Female	3	1	..	7	5	..	..
Negro							
Male	..	10	..	..	15	..	..
Female	..	1	..	..	8	..	..
OKLAHOMA ROLLING PLAIN							
White							
Male	8	2	..	116	..	..	..
Female	..	..	..	48	..	..	..
TEXAS BLACKLAND PRAIRIE							
Native white							
Male	4	6	..	50	..	5	1
Female	1	..	..	38	..	3	2
Czech							
Male	..	..	2	6	..	48	2
Female	..	..	..	3	..	14	..
German							
Male	1	..	..	3	..	3	8
Female	..	..	..	3	..	1	6

*Includes Mexican in Oklahoma and Texas.

TABLE 100

Age of landlord by method of crop rental payment and race of leasee for 814 landlords in four sample areas of the Southwestern Region

Area and race of leasee	All methods of rental payment	METHOD OF CROP RENTAL PAYMENT				
		Cash	¾-¼ share	½ share	Share-cash	Other
ARKANSAS COASTAL PLAIN		*Years*	*Years*	*Years*	*Years*	*Years*
White................	57	55	58	51	35*	57
Negro................	60	81	60	58	55*	68
MISSISSIPPI COASTAL PLAIN						
White................	54	45*	56	51	..	60
Negro................	54	51*	61	53	55*	52
OKLAHOMA ROLLING PLAIN						
Native white†.........	61	58	62	66	60	54*
TEXAS BLACKLAND PRAIRIE						
Native white..........	60	50*	62	48	52	49
Czech................	62	..	63	60*	61	53*
German..............	69	..	75	..	66	..

*Less than 5 cases.

†Includes one ¾ - ¼ share lease by a native of Germany and two ½ share leases, one by a Negro and the other by a Mexican.

TABLE 101

Percentage of lease with varying division of management scores by years on rent tract and method of rental payment for 882 leases in four sample areas of the Southwestern Region

Area, method of rental payment, and division of management score	YEARS ON RENT TRACT			
	1 to 2	3 to 4	5 to 9	10 and over
ARKANSAS COASTAL PLAIN	*Per cent*	*Per cent*	*Per cent*	*Per cent*
Cash and ⅓ - ¼ share...	100.0	100.0	100.0	100.0
Under 30............	.8	0.0	0.0	2.3
30 to 69.............	10.9	11.1	11.5	11.4
70 and over..........	88.3	88.9	88.5	86.3
½ Share...............	100.0	100.0	100.0	100.0
Under 30............	51.8	43.7	46.2	53.8
30 to 69.............	46.4	50.0	46.2	38.5
70 and over..........	1.8	6.3	7.6	7.7
MISSISSIPPI COASTAL PLAIN				
Cash and ⅓ - ¼ share...	100.0	100.0*	100.0*	100.0*
Under 30............	6.5	12.5	0.0	0.0
30 to 69.............	25.8	62.5	28.6	50.0
70 and over..........	67.7	25.0	71.4	50.0
½ Share...............	100.0	100.0	100.0	100.0
Under 30............	63.2	50.0	86.7	50.0
30 to 69.............	36.8	40.0	13.3	40.0
70 and over..........	0.0	10.0	0.0	10.0
OKLAHOMA ROLLING PLAIN				
Cash ⅓ - ¼ share.......	100.0	100.0	100.0	100.0
Under 30............	9.3	8.3	0.0	1.8
30 to 69.............	33.3	29.2	24.0	16.4
70 and over..........	57.4	62.5	76.0	81.8
½ Share...............	100.0*	100.0*	100.0*	100.0*
Under 30............	33.3	100.0	66.7	0.0
30 to 69.............	66.7	0.0	0.0	100.0
70 and over..........	0.0	0.0	33.3	0.0
TEXAS BLACKLAND PRAIRIE				
Cash and ⅓ - ¼ share...	100.0	100.0	100.0	100.0
Under 30............	0.0	0.0	2.1	0.0
30 to 69.............	37.3	37.9	29.8	23.3
70 and over..........	62.7	62.1	68.1	76.7
½ Share...............	100.0	100.0*	0.0	100.0*
Under 30............	58.3	0.0	0.0	100.0
30 to 69.............	41.7	100.0	0.0	0.0
70 and over..........	0.0	0.0	0.0	0.0

*Based on less than ten cases.

TABLE 102

Value of all improvements and of dwellings, cash repair cost on all improvements, and ratio of cash repair costs to value of all improvements by race and tenure for 1006 farmers in three sample areas of the Southwestern Region

Area, race and tenure	Number of cases	Value of all improvements	Value of dwelling	Cash repair costs on all improvements	Ratio of repair costs to value of all improvements
ARKANSAS COASTAL PLAIN		*Dollars*	*Dollars*	*Dollars*	*Per cent*
White					
Owner	79	1466	816	34	2.3
Part owner	34	1547	706	42	2.7
Renter	78	823	600	24	2.9
Cropper	20	580	345	12	2.1
Negro					
Owner	47	894	581	15	1.7
Part owner	21	805	433	41	5.1
Renter	87	371	221	7	1.9
Cropper	77	297	169	6	2.0
OKLAHOMA ROLLING PLAIN					
Native white					
Owner	82	2532	1477	112	4.4
Part owner	64	2644	1028	135	5.1
Renter	107	1323	593	68	5.1
Cropper	8	933	367	4	.4
TEXAS BLACKLAND PRAIRIE					
Native white					
Owner	37	3486	1673	72	2.1
Part owner	34	3224	1141	40	1.2
Renter	92	1549	740	37	2.4
Cropper	7	686	543	10	1.5
Czech and German					
Owner	42	2307	1329	46	2.0
Part owner	17	2359	1212	61	2.6
Renter	71	1201	630	23	1.9
Cropper	2	150*	100*	10*	6.7*

*Less than five cases.

TABLE 103

Volume of other-than-real-estate credit used in 1942 by tenure groups for 1463 families in four sample areas of the Southwestern Region

Tenure	Total Cases	No credit reported	Less than $100	$100 to $499	$500 to $999	$1000 to $1999	$2000 to $2999	$3000 and over	Volume unknown
	Number	*Number*	*Number*	*Number*	*Number*	*Number*	*Number*	*Number*	*Number*
ALL AREAS	1463	511	200	490	147	76	11	3	25
Owner	442	213	26	141	38	15	..	..	9
Part owner	204	94	15	56	17	17	5	..	..
Indeterminate	45	9	7	22	4	2	..	1	..
Cash tenant	51	9	14	18	6	1	1	1	1
Share tenant	316	63	28	124	63	28	3	1	6
Share-cash	96	30	4	37	12	11	2	..	..
Cropper	215	29	94	80	4	1	..	..	7
Other tenant	12	1	3	6	1	1	..	..	..
Laborer	62	47	7	6	1	..	..	..	1
Other	20	16	2	..	1	..	..	..	1

TABLE 104

Percentage of farmers using credit for farm production or farm family living by race and tenure for 1358 farmers in four sample areas of the Southwestern Region

Area and race	Full owner	Part owner	Indeterminate	Share-cash renter	Share renter	Cropper
	Per cent	*Per cent*	*Per cent*	*Per cent*	*Per cent*	*Per cent*
ARKANSAS COASTAL PLAIN						
White	34	59	58	77	86	75
Negro	79	86	94	90	93	82
MISSISSIPPI COASTAL PLAIN						
White	62	53	80*	62*	100	90
Negro	83	79	75*	80*	89*	100
OKLAHOMA ROLLING PLAIN						
Native white	34	42	75*	72	70	50
TEXAS BLACKLAND PRAIRIE						
Native white	40	53	100*	76	81	43*
Czech	45	10	100*	70	56	50*
German	55	43*	0*	40	67*	..

*Based on less than 10 cases. See Table 2 for number of cases in each category.

TABLE 105

Case distribution by race and by principal tenure groups for value of operator's earnings in 1942 for 1177 cases in three sample areas of the Southwestern Region

Area, race and tenure	-$420 or more	-$1 to -$419	$0 to $261	$262 to $568	$569 to $926	$927 to $1,343	$1,344 to $1,829	$1,830 to $3,056	$3,057 to $4,724	$4,725 or more	Amount unknown
	Number	*Number*	*Number*	*Number*	*Number*	*Number*	*Number*	*Number*	*Number*	*Number*	*Number*
ARKANSAS COASTAL PLAIN*											
White†	2	19	67	102	52	27	1	2	1	..	..
Owner	1	10	37	43	17	15	1	1	..	..	..
Renter	1	7	24	43	28	8	..	1	1	..	..
Cropper	..	..	4	12	2	2	..	..	..	..	..
Negro†	2	49	124	92	17	2	2	1	..	..	..
Owner	1	14	29	20	5	1	..	1	..	..	..
Renter	1	29	50	31	6	1	2	..	..	..	..
Cropper	..	4	37	33	4	..	..	..	..	..	..
MISSISSIPPI COASTAL PLAIN											
White†	2	19	50	66	34	12	3	..	..	..	3
Owner	2	17	30	39	26	12	3	..	..	..	2
Renter	..	2	9	10	3	..	..	..	..	..	..
Cropper	..	..	11	14	3	..	..	..	..	..	1
Negro†	..	17	53	48	9	5	..	..	..	..	..
Owner	..	9	27	14	3	2	..	..	..	..	..
Renter	..	3	7	5	..	..	..	..	..	..	..
Cropper	..	5	17	28	5	3	..	..	..	..	..
OKLAHOMA ROLLING PLAIN											
White†	9	11	22	18	32	44	49	69	27	8	5
Owner	5	6	7	6	15	22	17	46	16	7	2
Renter	3	4	5	5	11	20	28	22	10	..	..
Cropper	1	..	1	3	4	..	3	1	..	..	3

*Includes Arkansas Special FSA sample of 88 cases.
†Includes indeterminants and others but not laborers.

Table 106

Purpose for which real estate credit was reported used in 1942 by 282 farm owners in four sample areas of the Southwestern Region

Area and race	All areas	Arkansas Coastal Plain		Mississippi Coastal Plain		Oklahoma Rolling Plain	Texas Blackland Prairie		
		White	Negro	White	Negro	White*	Native white	Czech	German
	Number	*Number*	*Number*	*Number*	*Number*	*Number*	*Number*	*Number*	*Number*
All purpose	282	24	10	69	17	107	25	19	11
To buy this farm	213	13	4	45	12	89	23	17	10
Refinance old morgtage	21	1	1	7	1	10	..	..	1
Finance farm inprovements	13	2	..	6	2	1	1	1	..
Financc livestock and equipment purchases	4	1	1	1	1	..	..	..	..
Farm expenses (production and family expenses)	8	..	2	4	..	1	..	1	..
Refinance old debts other than mortgage	10	2	..	5	1	2	..	..	..
Other	3	..	..	..	..	3	..	..	..
Purpose unknown	10	5	2	1	..	1	1	..	..

*Includes one born in Sweden and one born in Russia.

Table 107

Percentage distribution of methods reported used by owners in acquiring first tract of present farm for 662 owners by race in four sample areas of the Southwestern Region

Area and race	All methods	Inheritance	Gift	Inheritance plus cash or credit	Cash purchase	Cash plus credit	Credit	Trade	Trade plus cash or credit	Homestead	Other method
	Per cent	*Per cent*	*Per cent*	*Per cent*	*Per cent*	*Per cent*	*Per cent*	*Per cent*	*Per cent*	*Per cent*	*Per cent*
All Areas	100	15	2	3	15	44	16	0	1	3	1
Arkansas Coastal Plain	100	17	4	1	19	28	27	2	1	..	1
White	100	17	5	1	23	25	24	2	2	..	1
Negro	100	19	2	..	13	33	33	..	..	..	..
Mississippi Coastal Plain	100	15	4	5	20	38	16	..	1	1	..
White	100	14	4	4	23	38	15	..	..	2	..
Negro	100	17	4	7	11	40	19	..	2	..	..
Oklahoma Rolling Plain	100	9	1	2	9	56	10	..	2	10	1
Native white	100	9	1	2	9	56	10	..	2	10	1
Texas Blackland Prairie	100	21	..	3	11	59	4	..	1	..	1
Native white	100	20	..	..	13	61	6	..	..	..	..
Czech	100	22	..	8	12	54	..	..	2	..	2
German	100	22	..	6	..	66	6	..	..	..	..

TABLE 108

Method of acquisition used by 670 farm owners in acquiring first tract of their present farms by race in four sample areas of the Southwestern Region

Area and race	All methods	Inheritance	Gift	Inheritance plus cash or credit	Cash purchase	Cash plus credit	Credit	Trade	Trade plus cash or credit	Homestead	Other method	Method of acquisition unknown
	Number	*Number*	*Number*	*Number*	*Number*	*Number*	*Number*	*Number*	*Number*	*Number*	*Number*	*Number*
ALL AREAS	672	102	16	17	102	291	105	3	7	17	4	8
ARKANSAS COASTAL												
PLAIN	198	34	8	1	38	55	53	3	2	..	1	3
White	127	21	7	1	29	32	30	3	2	..	1	1
Negro	71	13	1	..	9	23	23	..	..	..	..	2
MISSISSIPPI COASTAL												
PLAIN	186	27	7	9	36	70	30	..	1	2	..	4
White	131	18	5	5	30	49	20	..	..	2	..	2
Negro	55	9	2	4	6	21	10	..	1	..	..	2
OKLAHOMA ROLLING												
PLAIN	159	14	1	3	14	89	17	..	3	15	2	1
Native white	157	14	1	3	14	88	16	..	3	15	2	1
TEXAS BLACKLAND												
PRAIRIE	129	27	..	4	14	77	5	..	1	..	1	..
Native white	70	14	..	..	9	43	4	..	..	..	..	..
Czech	41	9	..	3	5	22	..	..	1	..	1	..
German	18	4	..	1	..	12	1	..	..	..	..	..

TABLE 109

Average amount of real estate and other-than-real-estate credit used in 1942 and average amount of other-than-real-estate credit due at the end of 1942 for those farm families using credit in four sample areas of the Southwestern Region

Area and race	Cases of R E credit	Average amount of R E credit used	Cases using non R E credit	Average amount of non R E credit used	Average amount of non R E outstanding at end of year
	Number	*Dollars*	*Number*	*Dollars*	*Dollars*
ARKANSAS COASTAL PLAIN....	34	1130	348	259	92
White..................	24	1143	134	330	137
Negro..................	10	1098	221	259	64
MISSISSIPPI COASTAL PLAIN...	86	792	249	221	44
White..................	69	792	130	254	56
Negro..................	17	794	119	185	32
OKLAHOMA ROLLING PLAIN*...	107	3950	141	905	345
TEXAS BLACKLAND PRAIRIE...	55	5084	184	499	185
Native white............	25	6492	110	549	145
Negro, Mexican.........	..	....	4	47	...
Czech..................	19	4189	55	439	256
German.................	11	3427	15	444	258

*No breakdown by race due to small number of "other than native white."

TABLE 110

Source of real estate credit used in 1942 by 829 farm owners in five sample areas of the Southwestern Region

Credit source	All cases	Arkansas Coastal Plain	Louisiana Coastal Plain	Mississippi Coastal Plain	Oklahoma Rolling Plain	Texas Blackland Prairie
	Number	*Number*	*Number*	*Number*	*Number*	*Number*
All sources	829	181	183	186	149	130
No real estate credit used	466	147	102	100	42	75
Total credit cases	363	34	81	86	107	55
Federal Land Bank	195	18	55	52	55	15
Farm Security Administration	15	4	2	..	6	3
Local bank	27	3	16	5	1	2
Insurance company	27	..	1	..	12	14
Commercial mortgage Company	15	..	..	..	15	..
Lumber company	6	..	..	6	..	..
SPJST or RVOS*	10	..	..	..	..	10
Oklahoma School Land Commission	11	..	..	..	11	..
Local merchant	14	..	..	14	..	..
Related individual	13	..	5	3	..	5
Unrelated individual	22	9	2	4	3	4
Other	8	..	..	2	4	2

*SPJST and RVOS are Czechoslovakian benevolent and insurance societies.

TABLE III

Participation in the Farm Security Administration Program by race and tenure for 1313 farm families in four sample areas of the Southwestern Region, 1942

Area, race, and tenure	Total cases	FSA borrowers		Contacts per borrower	Rural Rehabilitation Credit		Farm Ownership Credit	
					Loans	Average amount	Loans	Average amount
	Number	*Number*	*Per cent*	*Number*	*Number*	*Dollars*	*Number*	*Dollars*
ARKANSAS COASTAL PLAIN								
White								
Owner	113	9	12	3.7	9	471	2	3,350
Renter	75	22	34	4.0	4	252	..	.....
Cropper	20	1	5	0.0	..	...	..	.....
Negro								
Owner	68	7	10	5.0	6	488	1	2,800
Renter	82	16	20	5.9	16	551	..	.....
Cropper	77	..	0	...	0	...	..	.....
MISSISSIPPI COASTAL PLAIN								
White								
Owner	131	12	9	2.6	10	530	..	.....
Renter	23	8	35	4.8	6	506	..	.....
Cropper	29	..	0	...	..	...	..	.....
Negro								
Owner	55	14	25	4.6	12	455	0	.....
Renter	14	2	14	9.0	0	...	..	.....
Cropper	58	..	0	...	..	...	..	.....
OKLAHOMA ROLLING PLAIN								
White								
Owner	147	22	15	5.0	18	458	6	8,083
Renter	106	22	21	5.3	25*	538	..	.....
Cropper	14	0	0	...	1†	380	..	.....
TEXAS BLACKLAND PRAIRIE								
White								
Owner	130	3	2	8.0	0	...	1	7,900
Renter	162	14	9	3.0	14	762	..	.....
Cropper	9	..	..	...	..	...	..	.....

*Excluding one unusually large loan.
†Collection only; Case inactive.

TABLE 112

Source of other-than-real-estate credit used in 1942 by 1463 families in four sample areas of the Southwestern Region

Credit source	All areas	Arkansas Coastal Plain	Mississippi Coastal Plain	Oklahoma Rolling Plain	Texas Blackland Prairie
	Number	*Number*	*Number*	*Number*	*Number*
All cases	1463	474	327	323	339
No use of credit reported	511	119	77	169	146
Total credit cases	952	355	250	154	193
Landlord	152	93	49	2	8
Merchant	142	25	93	10	14
Local Bank	263	61	25	57	120
Emergency Feed and Seed Loan	67	55	11	..	1
Farm Security Administration	162	61	39	46	16
Production Credit Association	71	20	23	17	11
Merchant and landlord	14	7	6	1	..
Related individual	27	8	1	8	10
Unrelated individual	22	16	1	4	1
Other source	24	9	..	6	9
Source unknown	8	..	2	3	3

TABLE 113

Purpose for which other-than-real-estate credit was used in 1942 by 952 families in four sample areas of the Southwestern Region

Purpose of credit	All areas	Arkansas Coastal Plain		Mississippi Coastal Plain		Oklahoma Rolling Plain	Texas Blackland Prairie
		White	Negro	White	Negro	*	*
	Number	*Number*	*Number*	*Number*	*Number*	*Number*	*Number*
All purposes	952	134	221	130	120	154	193
To buy livestock and farm equipment	78	5	2	6	1	29	35
To finance current crop production	306	62	74	60	27	31	52
For family living	59	7	5	5	26	5	11
To buy livestock and farm equipment and to finance current crop production	60	2	1	3	2	19	33
To buy livestock and farm equipment and for family living	253	37	106	34	46	9	21
To finance current crop production and for family living	101	4	18	18	10	37	14
To buy livestock and farm equipment, to finance current crop production, and for family living	4	..	..	..	..	2	2
Refinance old debts	19	2	2	2	4	3	6
Other	10	..	..	..	..	2	8
Unknown	62	15	13	2	4	17	11

*No breakdown by race.

TABLE 114

Security offered for other-than-real-estate credit used in 1942 by 945 families in four sample areas of the Southwestern Region

Area and race	Number of cases	No security	Personal note	Crop lien	Chattel mortgage	Chattel mortgage and crop lien	Other security	Security not reported
	Number	*Number*	*Number*	*Number*	*Number*	*Number*	*Number*	*Number*
ALL AREAS	952	77	38	279	240	198	6	114
ARKANSAS COASTAL PLAIN								
White	134	14	..	32	32	36	..	20
Negro	221	12	2	98	29	43	..	37
MISSISSIPPI COASTAL PLAIN								
White	130	8	4	48	20	37	2	11
Negro	120	12	..	60	8	26	..	14
OKLAHOMA ROLLING PLAIN*	154	13	10	1	93	15	..	22
TEXAS BLACKLAND PRAIRIE*	193	18	22	40	58	41	4	10

*No breakdown by race.

TABLE 115

Median net worth of farm business for race and tenure groups for 1580 farm families in five sample areas of the Southwestern Region

Area and race	OWNER		RENTER		Cropper
	Full	Part	Share-cash	Share	
ARKANSAS COASTAL PLAIN	*dollars*	*dollars*	*dollars*	*dollars*	*dollars*
White	3,607	2,544	467	371	173
Negro	2,382	1,744	300	266	74
LOUISIANA COASTAL PLAIN					
White	2,524	2,885	247	378	147
Negro	2,055	1,389*	247*	439	67
MISSISSIPPI COASTAL PLAIN					
White	2,457	1,700	433	150	200
Negro	1,900	1,167	250	333	27
OKLAHOMA ROLLING PLAIN					
White	7,814	8,404	2,300	1,833	386
TEXAS BLACKLAND PRAIRIE					
Native	9,567	7,700	1,269	1,470	207
Czech	5,300	7,700	1,243	1,026	300*
German	8,020	5,300	1,033	1,100*	...

*Less than five cases. See Table 2 for number of cases in each category.

TABLE 116

Median per cent equity in farm business for race and tenure groups for 1662 farm families in five sample areas of the Southwestern Region

Area and race	OWNER		RENTER		Cropper
	Full	Part	Share-cash	Share	
ARKANSAS COASTAL PLAIN					
White	92.67	78.12	16.88	.09	4.27
Negro	91.90	68.00	11.88	2.32	1.05
LOUISIANA COASTAL PLAIN					
White	92.70	55.00	15.00	20.00	11.25
Negro	87.50	15.00*	45.00*	30.00	2.10
MISSISSIPPI COASTAL PLAIN					
White	88.25	71.00	31.67	.09	3.89
Negro	87.00	71.00	5.10	18.75	.07
OKLAHOMA ROLLING PLAIN					
Native white	76.00	53.08	16.67	16.11	7.78
TEXAS BLACKLAND PRAIRIE					
Native white	92.88	50.00	14.06	16.30	7.00
Czech	77.00	60.00	16.11	16.18	10.00*
German	82.50	55.00	20.00	27.50*	.....

*Less than five cases. See Table 2 for number of cases in each category.

TABLE 117

Distribution by race and tenure of net family incomes reported in 1942 for 1027 cases in three sample areas of the Southwestern Region

Area, race, and tenure	$0 to 315	$316 to 463	$464 to 680	$681 to 999	$1,000 to 1,467	$1,468 to 2,171	$2,172 to 3,162	$3,163 to 4,641	$4,642 to 6,812	$6,813 or more
	Number	*Number*	*Number*	*Number*	*Number*	*Number*	*Number*	*Number*	*Number*	*Number*
ARKANSAS COASTAL PLAIN										
White										
Owners	3	14	20	19	22	19	5	4	2	..
Renters	4	6	20	20	14	11	1	1	..	..
Croppers	..	5	5	4	3	2	..	..	..	..
Negro										
Owners	6	12	18	15	8	5	..	1	..	..
Renters	15	13	30	12	11	3	1	..	..	..
Croppers	10	24	24	9	6	..	..	..	..	..
MISSISSIPPI COASTAL PLAIN										
White										
Owners	3	7	16	25	29	31	11	3	..	..
Renters	2	3	6	7	5	1	..	..	..	..
Croppers	1	5	7	8	6	1	..	..	..	..
Negro										
Owners	6	6	14	13	10	4	1	..	..	..
Renters	3	3	4	2	2	..	..	..	..	..
Croppers	8	13	13	15	8	..	..	..	..	..
Laborers	1	2	2	..	..	..	..	..	..	..
OKLAHOMA ROLLING PLAIN										
All cases										
Owners	1	2	..	2	15	25	33	37	20	11
Renters	1	3	1	11	14	31	22	16	8	..
Croppers	..	..	1	4	4	3	3	..	..	..
Laborers	2	..	11	10	5	2	..	..	..	..

TABLE 118

Volume of other-than-real-estate credit used in 1942 by 1463 families by race in four sample areas of the Southwestern Region

Area and race	Total cases	No credit reported	Less than $100	$100 to $499	$500 to $999	$1000 to $1999	$2000 to $2999	$3000 and over	Volume unknown
	Number	*Number*	*Number*	*Number*	*Number*	*Number*	*Number*	*Number*	*Number*
ALL AREAS	1463	511	200	490	147	76	11	3	25
ARKANSAS COASTAL PLAIN	474	119	92	213	41	7	..	..	2
White	226	92	19	85	24	5	..	..	1
Negro	248	27	73	128	17	2	..	..	1
MISSISSIPPI COASTAL PLAIN	327	77	77	130	22	4	..	..	17
White	189	59	28	75	15	2	..	..	10
Negro	138	18	49	55	7	2	..	..	7
OKLAHOMA ROLLING PLAIN*	323	169	11	45	44	40	8	3	3
TEXAS BLACKLAND PRAIRIE	339	146	20	102	40	25	3	..	3
Native white	182	69	8	57	28	16	3	..	1
Negro, Mexican	21	11	4	4	..	..	..	..	2
Czech	104	49	6	33	9	7	..	..	..
German	32	17	2	8	3	2	..	..	..

*No breakdown by race due to small number of "other than native white."

TABLE 119

Security offered for other-than-real-estate credit used in 1942 by race and tenure of borrowers in four sample areas of the Southwestern Region

Area, race, and tenure	Total cases		No security		Personal note		Crop lien		Chattel mortgage		Chattel mortgage and crop lien		Other security		Security unknown	
	No.	*Per cent*	*No.*	*Per cent*	*No.*	*Per cent*	*No.*	*Per cent*	*No.*	*Per cent*	*No.*	*Per cent*	*No.*	*Per cent*	*No.*	*Per cent*
ALL AREAS	874	100	67	8	38	4	261	30	232	27	188	21	6	..	2	9
ARKANSAS COASTAL PLAIN																
Total credit cases	318	100	23	7	3	1	116	37	57	18	73	23	..	..	6	14
White: Owner	27	100	4	15	..	..	6	22	7	26	6	22	..	..	4	15
Part owner	20	100	..	..	..	..	4	20	4	20	8	40	..	..	4	20
Share-cash renter	20	100	..	..	..	..	8	40	5	25	4	20	..	..	3	15
Share renter	42	100	5	12	..	..	5	12	14	33	15	36	..	..	3	7
Cropper	15	100	3	20	..	..	5	33	..	..	2	13	..	..	5	33
Negro: Owner	37	100	..	..	1	3	17	46	6	16	11	30	..	..	2	5
Part owner	18	100	1	6	..	..	9	49	1	6	6	33	..	..	1	6
Share-cash renter	19	100	..	..	..	..	9	47	6	32	4	21	..	..	..	..
Share renter	57	100	3	5	2	4	17	30	12	21	16	28	..	..	7	12
Cropper	63	100	7	11	..	..	36	57	2	3	1	2	..	..	17	27
MISSISSIPPI COASTAL PLAIN																
Total credit cases	241	100	17	7	4	2	106	44	28	12	60	25	2	1	24	10
White: Owner	72	100	4	6	3	4	19	26	16	22	23	32	1	1	6	8
Part owner	8	100	..	..	1	12	2	25	1	12	2	25	1	12	1	12
Share-cash renter	5	100	..	..	..	..	1	20	..	..	3	60	..	..	1	20
Share renter	15	100	..	..	..	..	4	27	3	20	8	53	..	..	..	..
Cropper	26	100	3	12	..	..	20	76	..	..	..	..	..	..	3	12
Negro: Owner	30	100	2	7	..	..	8	27	5	16	13	43	..	..	2	7
Part owner	15	100	..	..	..	..	5	33	2	13	5	33	..	..	3	20
Share-cash renter	4	100	2	50	..	..	1	25	..	..	1	25	..	..	..	..
Share renter	8	100	..	..	..	..	3	38	..	..	5	62	..	..	..	..
Cropper	58	100	6	10	..	..	43	74	1	2	..	..	..	..	8	14
OKLAHOMA ROLLING PLAIN*																
Total credit cases	139	100	13	9	10	7	1	1	89	64	15	11	..	..	11	8
Owner	28	100	3	11	3	11	1	4	18	64	2	7	..	..	1	4
Part owner	27	100	1	4	4	15	..	..	19	70	..	..	..	..	3	11
Share-cash renter	13	100	2	15	..	..	..	..	8	62	3	23	..	..	..	..
Share renter	63	100	7	11	2	3	..	..	42	67	7	11	..	..	5	8
Cropper	8	100	..	..	1	12	..	..	2	25	3	38	..	..	2	25
TEXAS BLACKLAND PRAIRIE																
Total credit cases	176	100	14	8	21	12	38	21	58	33	40	23	4	2	1	1
Native white: Owner	15	100	3	20	2	13	3	20	6	40	1	7	..	..	..	..
Part owner	18	100	2	11	3	17	4	22	2	11	6	33	..	..	1	6
Share-cash renter	22	100	1	5	2	9	5	23	9	40	5	23	..	..	..	..
Share renter	51	100	2	4	4	8	11	22	18	35	16	31	..	..	..	..
Cropper	3	100	..	..	..	..	1	33	..	..	2	67	..	..	..	..
Czech and German																
Owner	20	100	3	15	6	30	2	10	5	25	1	5	4	20	..	..
Part owner	4	100	1	25	2	50	..	..	1	25	..	..	..	..	..	..
Share-cash renter	25	100	1	4	1	4	9	36	10	40	4	16	..	..	..	..
Share renter	17	100	..	..	1	6	3	18	7	41	5	29	1	6	..	..
Cropper	1	100	1	100	..	..	..	..	..	..	..	..	..	..	..	..

*No breakdown by race.

TABLE 120

Security offered for other-than-real-estate credit used in 1942 by source of credit for farm families of both races in four sample areas in the Southwestern Region

Source of credit	Total cases		No security		Personal note		Crop lien		Chattel mortgage		Chattel mortgage and crop lien		Other security		Security unknown	
	No.	*Per cent*	*No.*	*Per cent*	*No.*	*Per cent*	*No.*	*Per cent*	*No.*	*Per cent*	*No.*	*Per cent*	*No.*	*Per cent*	*No.*	*Per cent*
ALL AREAS	874	100	67	8	38	4	261	30	232	27	188	21	6	1	82	9
ARKANSAS COASTAL PLAIN																
Total credit cases	318	100	23	7	3	1	116	37	57	18	73	23	..	..	46	14
Landlord	91	100	11	12	1	1	49	54	1	1	6	7	..	..	23	25
Merchant	22	100	4	18	..	..	7	32	2	9	5	23	..	..	4	18
Local Bank	57	100	2	4	2	4	7	12	13	23	29	50	..	..	4	7
Federal Agencies	119	100	2	2	..	..	48	40	36	30	24	20	..	..	9	8
Individual	22	100	4	18	..	..	2	9	4	18	6	27	..	..	6	27
Other	7	100	..	..	..	..	3	43	1	14	3	43	..	..	..	..
MISSISSIPPI COASTAL PLAIN																
Total credit cases	241	100	17	7	4	2	106	44	28	12	60	25	2	1	24	9
Landlord	54	100	4	7	..	..	44	82	..	..	..	..	..	..	6	11
Merchant	88	100	9	10	2	2	36	41	6	7	24	27	1	1	10	12
Local Bank	24	100	..	..	2	8	7	29	5	21	6	25	1	4	3	13
Federal Agencies	72	100	3	4	..	..	18	25	17	24	30	42	..	..	4	5
Individual	2	100	1	..	..	..	1	100	..	..	..	..	..	..	..	..
Other	...	...	..	..	..	..	..	..	..	..	..	..	..	..	..	..
Unknown	1	100	..	..	..	..	..	..	..	..	..	..	..	..	1	100
OKLAHOMA ROLLING PLAIN																
Total credit cases	139	100	13	9	10	7	1	1	89	64	15	11	..	..	11	8
Landlord	2	100	1	50	..	..	..	..	1	50	..	..	..	..	..	..
Merchant	8	100	..	..	..	..	..	..	3	38	4	50	..	..	1	12
Local Bank	53	100	4	8	8	15	1	2	31	58	4	8	..	..	5	9
Federal Agencies	57	100	..	..	..	..	..	..	49	86	5	9	..	..	3	5
Individual	12	100	6	50	2	17	..	..	3	25	1	8	..	..	..	..
Other	4	100	2	50	..	..	..	..	1	25	1	25	..	..	..	..
Unknown	3	100	..	..	..	..	..	..	1	33	..	..	..	..	2	67
TEXAS BLACKLAND PRAIRIE																
Total credit cases	176	100	14	8	21	12	38	21	58	33	40	23	4	2	1	1
Landlord	3	100	1	33	..	..	..	..	2	67	..	..	..	..	..	..
Merchant	12	100	2	17	..	..	2	17	7	58	1	8	..	..	..	..
Local Bank	117	100	7	6	12	10	30	26	35	29	30	26	2	2	1	1
Federal Agencies	27	100	..	..	2	7	5	19	13	48	7	26	..	..	..	..
Individual	11	100	3	27	7	64	1	9	..	..	..	..	..	..	..	..
Other	6	100	1	17	..	..	..	..	1	17	2	33	2	33	..	..

TABLE 121

Volume of other-than-real-estate credit used in 1942 by source for 1463 families in four sample areas of the Southwestern Region

Source of credit	Credit cases	Less than $100	$100 to $499	$500 to $999	$1000 to $1999	$2000 to $2999	$3000 and over	Amount unknown
	Number	*Dollars*	*Dollars*	*Dollars*	*Dollars*	*Dollars*	*Dollars*	*Number*
All sources	952	200	490	147	76	11	3	25
Landlord	152	80	65	4	1	1	..	1
Merchant	142	42	79	10	4	..	..	7
Landlord and merchant	14	4	9	..	..	..	..	1
Local bank	263	29	161	48	22	2	..	1
Emergency Feed and Seed Loan	67	22	42	3	..	..	..	..
Farm Security Administration	162	2	48	60	35	5	1	11
Production Credit Association	71	4	44	9	10	2	2	..
Related individual	27	4	14	6	2	1	..	..
Unrelated individual	22	3	15	2	2	..	..	..
Other source	25	6	13	4	..	..	..	2
Source not reported	7	4	..	1	..	..	..	2

TABLE 122

Source of production and family living credit by race and tenure for 1029 farmers using such credit in four sample areas of the Southwestern Region

Area and race	All sources	Source of Credit						
		Land-lord	Mer-chant	Local Bank	FSA	PCA	Other credit agency	Indi-vidual
	Per cent	*Per cent*	*Per cent*	*Per cent*	*Per cent*	*Per cent*	*Per cent*	*Per cent*
ARKANSAS COASTAL PLAIN								
White								
Full owner	100	..	15	29	22	15	4	15
Part owner	100	..	5	55	15	10	5	10
Share-cash renter	100	..	..	20	30	5	35	10
Share renter	100	10	2	26	43	5	7	7
Cropper	100	59	7	13	7	..	7	7
Negro								
Full owner	100	..	8	24	11	19	24	14
Part owner	100	11	11	6	17	11	11	33
Share-cash renter	100	16	6	21	10	10	32	5
Share renter	100	25	10	12	25	..	19	9
Cropper	100	84	5	..	..	..	2	9
MISSISSIPPI COASTAL PLAIN								
White								
Full owner	100	..	31	21	18	20	10	..
Part owner	100	..	76	12	12	..	..	..
Share-cash renter	100	..	80	..	20	..	..	..
Share renter	100	..	20	20	53	7	..	..
Cropper	100	27	53	8	..	8	4	..
Negro								
Full owner	100	..	47	7	33	10	3	..
Part owner	100	20	40	..	26	7	7	..
Share-cash renter	100	..	25	25	..	..	25	25
Share renter	100	25	38	..	25	12	..	..
Cropper	100	72	26	..	..	..	..	2
OKLAHOMA ROLLING PLAIN								
Native white								
Full owner	100	..	4	36	25	18	4	14
Part owner	100	4	..	48	33	15	..	..
Share-cash renter	100	7	8	23	31	15	8	8
Share renter	100	..	7	39	33	8	3	10
Cropper	100	..	33	50	17	..	..	..
TEXAS BLACKLAND PRAIRIE								
Native white								
Full owner	100	..	6	60	7	20	..	7
Part owner	100	..	..	88	..	6	..	6
Share-cash renter	100	5	..	73	14	4	4	..
Share renter	100	2	2	65	21	2	2	6
Cropper	100	..	33	67	..	..	..	..
Czech and German								
Full owner	100	..	10	60	..	..	5	25
Part owner	100	..	..	50	..	..	..	50
Share-cash renter	100	4	24	60	4	4	..	4
Share renter	100	..	6	71	..	17	6	..
Cropper	100	..	..	..	..	..	..	100

TABLE 123

Participation in the Farm Credit Administration Program by race and tenure for 1313 farm families in four sample areas of the Southwestern Region, 1942

Area, race, and tenure	Total cases	PARTICIPATION 1942						
		In combined program	Federal Land Bank Credit		Production Credit		Feed and Seed Credit	
			Loans	Average Amount	Loans	Average Amount	Loans	Average Amount
	Number	*Number*	*Number*	*Dollars*	*Number*	*Dollars*	*Number*	*Dollars*
ARKANSAS COASTAL PLAIN								
White								
Owner	113	17.7	13	668	7	203	0	0
Renter	75	17.3	..	...	3	333	9	126
Cropper	20	5.0	..	...	0	0	1	350
Negro								
Owner	68	40.0	2	550	15	191	12	196
Renter	82	16.0	..	...	3	70	14	96
Cropper	77	1.0	..	...	0	...	1	80
MISSISSIPPI COASTAL PLAIN								
White								
Owner	131	42.7	40	597	15	341	7	133
Renter	23	4.0	..	...	1	250	0	0
Cropper	29	10.0	..	...	2	120	1	100
Negro								
Owner	55	28.0	9	644	4	225	2	135
Renter	14	11.0	..	...	1	120	0	...
Cropper	58	0	..	...	0	...	0	...
OKLAHOMA ROLLING PLAIN								
White								
Owner	147	43.0	57	2877	10	668	1	150
Renter	106	7.0	..	...	6	1337	1	160
Cropper	14	0	..	...	0	...	0	...
TEXAS BLACKLAND PRAIRIE								
White								
Owner	130	4.0	15	3167	3	1417	0	...
Renter	162	2.5	1*	1000	6	518	1	100
Cropper	9	0	..	...	0	...	0	...

*This renter has a Federal Land Bank loan on land other than that operated by him.

TABLE 124

Comparison by various measures of average value of farm and average worth, earnings, and income of farmers and farm families for four sample areas of the Southwestern Region

Area, race, and tenure	Net worth	Value of farm business used	Gross income	Gross farm income	Operator's earnings	Family earnings	Family net income
	Dollars	*Dollars*	*Dollars*	*Dollars*	*Dollars*	*Dollars*	*Dollars*
ARKANSAS COASTAL PLAIN							
White							
Owner	3868	4082	1545	1065	382	463	1156
Part owner	3454	4376	1910	1271	448	536	1351
Share-cash	733	2688	1553	1189	693	770	1168
Share renter	417	2996	1107	883	418	588	837
Cropper	142	2205	1028	815	445	588	804
Negro							
Owner	2517	2666	859	753	201	389	719
Part owner	2174	3281	1321	1127	327	387	931
Share-cash	324	1686	758	606	224	386	606
Share renter	257	1875	827	647	242	479	680
Cropper	115	1209	645	534	265	424	539
MISSISSIPPI COASTAL PLAIN							
White							
Owner	3087	3362	1766	1208	411	541	1237
Part owner	2820	3467	2144	1436	423	583	1304
Share-cash	459	1400	1156	617	238	314	747
Share renter	198	1707	923	714	315	497	1125
Cropper	117	1166	901	643	354	503	767
Negro							
Owner	2232	2508	1137	916	271	483	824
Part owner	1207	1653	993	648	186	350	767
Share-cash	206	1060	930	620	79	225	540
Share renter	329	1111	624	470	196	329	...
Cropper	64	819	705	585	342	487	615
OKLAHOMA ROLLING PLAIN							
White							
Owner	11954	14139	4821	4295	1615	1854	2984
Part owner	10029	18725	5849	5188	2091	2258	3483
Share-cash	2569	12950	3758	3384	1548	1648	2366
Share renter	2203	11267	3737	3322	1469	1850	2197
Cropper	553	6725	1866	1514	866	1082	1345
TEXAS BLACKLAND PRAIRIE							
Native white							
Owner	11095	12314	2802	2533			
Part owner	8533	18459	3889	3573			
Share-cash	1664	9590	2015	1896			
Share renter	1542	8067	2018	1773			
Cropper	226	2129	877	658			
Czech-German							
Owner	6468	8185	2181	1947			
Part owner	6617	10877	2766	2571			
Share-cash	1269	6332	1644	1576			
Share renter	1095	6120	1511	1350			
Cropper	245	2650	980	840			

TABLE 125

Median value of farm business for race and tenure groups for 1580 farm families in five sample areas of the Southwestern Region

Area and race	Owner		Renter		Cropper
	Full	Part	Share-cash	Share	
ARKANSAS COASTAL PLAIN	*dollars*	*dollars*	*dollars*	*dollars*	*dollars*
White	3,375	3,278	2,643	2,975	1,625
Negro	2,505	2,583	1,306	1,460	924
LOUISIANA COASTAL PLAIN					
White	2,517	2,250	1,750	2,438	1,333
Negro	2,667	2,500*	750*	1,333	958
MISSISSIPPI COASTAL PLAIN					
White	2,828	2,250	1,500	1,812	865
Negro	2,000	1,750	917	850	778
OKLAHOMA ROLLING PLAIN					
White	9,900	16,543	7,500	9,808	6,500
TEXAS BLACK LAND					
Native	10,500	17,682	7,389	7,343	2,250
Czech	6,875	10,700	5,900	6,250	2,750*
German	9,000	12,000	6,000	4,500*	.....

*Less than five cases. See Table 2 for number of cases in each category.

TABLE 126

Distribution of farmers by farm net worth for race and tenure groups for 1366 farmers in four sample areas of the Southwestern Region

Area, race and tenure*	All cases	FARM NET WORTH							
		Less than $100	$100 to $499	$500 to $1,299	$1,300 to $2,899	$2,900 to $6,099	$6,100 to $12,499	$12,500 to $25,299	$25,300 and over
	Number	*Number*	*Number*	*Number*	*Number*	*Number*	*Number*	*Number*	*Number*
ARKANSAS COASTAL PLAIN									
White									
Owner	113	..	..	7	44	53	7	2	..
Renter	78	15	31	24	8	..	..	..	..
Cropper	20	8	11	1	..	..	..	..	..
Negro									
Owner	68	..	3	17	26	20	2	..	..
Renter	87	21	53	12	1	..	..	..	..
Cropper	77	44	31	2	..	..	..	..	..
MISSISSIPPI COASTAL PLAIN									
White									
Owner	124	2	4	22	50	35	9	2	..
Renter	21	7	7	7	..	..	..	..	..
Cropper	28	14	14	..	..	..	..	..	..
Negro									
Owner	52	1	11	10	20	9	1	..	..
Renter	13	1	11	1	..	..	..	..	..
Cropper	56	44	12	..	..	..	..	..	..
Laborer	6	5	1	..	..	..	..	..	..
OKLAHOMA ROLLING PLAIN									
Native white									
Owner	147	..	..	2	9	46	53	26	11
Renter	105	4	8	25	38	28	2	..	..
Cropper	14	2	7	4	1	..	..	..	..
Laborer	25	12	12	1	..	..	..	..	..
TEXAS BLACKLAND PRAIRIE									
Native white									
Owner	71	..	..	1	5	20	24	18	3
Renter	92	1	6	36	44	3	2	..	..
Cropper	7	1	6	..	..	..	..	..	..
Laborer	11	4	7	..	..	..	..	..	..
Czech and German									
Owner	59	..	..	1	7	24	24	3	..
Renter	71	..	5	41	25	..	..	..	..
Negro and Mexican									
Cropper	6	6	..	..	..	..	..	..	..
Laborer	15	15	..	..	..	..	..	..	..

*No laborers were sampled in the Arkansas Coastal Plain; all laborers in the Mississippi sample were Negro. Two Czech croppers and one Czech laborer are not included in this table. The Negroes and Mexicans sampled in Texas were either croppers or laborers.

TABLE 127

Percentage distribution of farms according to value of farm business, by race and tenure of operator, in four sample areas of the Southwestern Region

Area, race, and tenure status	Number of cases	PER CENT OF FARMS WITH VALUE OF BUSINESS OF					
		Less than $1500	$1500 to $3500	$3500 to $5500	$5500 to $7500	$7500 to $15500	$15500 and over
ARKANSAS COASTAL PLAIN							
White							
Owners	79	5	48	31	9	6	1
Part owners	34	6	50	26	3	15	..
Share-cash renters	26	19	54	23	..	4	..
Share renters	49	10	62	22	6	..	..
Croppers	20	45	40	10	5	..	..
Negro							
Owners	47	28	42	26	4	..	..
Part owners	21	24	52	14	5	..	5
Share-cash renters	21	66	24	10	..	..	..
Share renters	61	52	36	10	2	..	..
Croppers	77	79	17	4	..	..	..
MISSISSIPPI COASTAL PLAIN							
White							
Owners	115	21	46	21	5	7	..
Part owners	15	33	33	27	..	..	7
Share-cash renters	8	50	50	..	..	..	..
Share renters	15	33	67	..	..	..	..
Croppers	29	83	11	3	3	..	..
Negro							
Owners	36	33	42	14	8	3	..
Part owners	19	42	58	..	..	..	..
Share-cash renters	5	60	40	..	..	..	..
Share renters	9	78	22	..	..	..	..
Croppers	58	95	15	..	..	..	..
OKLAHOMA ROLLING PLAIN							
White							
Owners	82	1	1	9	21	44	24
Part owners	64	..	..	2	3	40	55
Share-cash renters	18	..	6	28	16	22	28
Share renters	88	..	6	11	16	42	25
Croppers	8	..	25	12	25	38	..
TEXAS BLACKLAND PRAIRIE							
White							
Owners	79	..	4	19	20	41	16
Part owners	51	..	2	..	14	45	39
Share-cash renters	69	..	6	29	26	36	3
Share renters	93	..	10	18	33	36	3
Croppers	9	33	45	22	..	..	..

Table 128

Average gross farm incomes and average operator's earnings for 1004 operators of farms of four different sizes measured in terms of value of farm business used, classified by race and tenure for three sample areas of the Southwestern Region

Area, race, and tenure	Value of Farm Business											
	Under $1,500			$1,500 - 5,499			$5,500 - 11,499			$11,500 and over		
	Number of cases	Average gross farm income	Average operator's earnings	Number of cases	Average gross farm income	Average operator's earnings	Number of cases	Average gross farm income	Average operator's earnings	Number of cases	Average gross farm income	Average operator's earnings
	No.	*Dollars*	*Dollars*	*No.*	*Dollars*	*Dollars*	*No.*	*Dollars*	*Dollars*	*No.*	*Dollars*	*Dollars*
Arkansas Coastal Plain												
White: Owner	3	591	297	61	1,063	379	11	1,903	446	2	2,156	262
Part owner	2	412	200	26	1,479	508	3	1,972	470	3	3,086	66
Renter	11	534	246	62	1,191	544	5	2,397	820	..	.....	.....
Cropper	9	1,030	389	10	1,245	428	1	4,320	1,119	..	.....	.....
Negro: Owner	12	476	151	32	831	203	2	1,732	468	..	.....	.....
Part owner	5	548	142	14	1,160	340	1	5,363	2,392	1	1,918	−1,004
Renter	46	513	164	39	1,059	322	1	903	154	..	.....	.....
Cropper	61	749	224	16	1,458	418	..	.....	.....	..	.....	.....
Mississippi Coastal Plain												
White: Owner	23	607	244	76	1,403	463	12	3,623	325	2	7,718	860
Part owner	6	1,096	226	8	1,638	440	..	.....	.....	1	7,879	1,468
Renter	10	459	143	14	1,147	420	..	.....	.....	..	.....	.....
Cropper	23	1,034	349	4	1,239	348	1	2,263	499	..	.....	.....
Negro: Owner	12	455	185	20	1,181	282	4	2,238	472	..	.....	.....
Part owner	8	400	112	11	1,087	240	..	.....	.....	..	.....	.....
Renter	11	594	204	4	798	79	..	.....	.....	..	.....	.....
Cropper	54	996	312	3	2,264	874	..	.....	.....	..	.....	.....
Oklahoma Rolling Plain												
White: Owner	1	447	185	8	1,927	834	42	2,760	1,024	31	7,159	2,664
Part owner	..	.....	.....	1	1,374	14	12	3,370	1,348	49	6,417	2,316
Renter	..	...	...	21	1,835	777	44	3,281	1,186	41	6,563	2,166
Cropper	..	...	...	3	2,913	1,307	4	3,180	1,171	1	4,653	581

TABLE 129

Correlations between pairs of measures of size of business for four sample areas in the Southwestern Region*

Area and measure	Productive man work units X_3	Acres in cropland X_4	Gross farm income $X_1=X_5$
ALL AREAS			
Value of business X_2..........	.5344	.8336	.8064
Productive MWU X_3..........	.....	.6238	.6266
Acres in cropland X_4	.....	.....	.7848
ARKANSAS COASTAL PLAIN			
Value of business X_2..........	.6754	.6796	.6032
Productive MWU X_3..........	.....	.7825	.7821
Acres in cropland X_4..........	.....	.....	.5606
MISSISSIPPI COASTAL PLAIN			
Value of business X_2..........	.6596	.6871	.6674
Productive MWU X_3..........	.....	.8917	.8326
Acres in cropland X_4..........	.....	.....	.7266
OKLAHOMA ROLLING PLAIN			
Value of business X_2..........	.6816	.7206	.7338
Productive MWU X_3..........	.....	.7504	.7101
Acres in cropland X_4..........	.....	.....	.6564
TEXAS BLACKLAND PRAIRIE			
Value of business X_2..........	.8384	.6978	.8278
Productive MWU X_3..........	.....	.8633	.8109
Acres in cropland X_4..........	.....	.....	.7398

*Based on all tenures except laborer and other. The case count was 557 for Arkansas, 303 for Mississippi, 267 for Oklahoma, 312 for Texas, and 1439 for the four areas.

TABLE 130

Coefficients of multiple determination based on correlation of gross farm income with three measures of size of business and relative importance of these measures for four sample areas in the Southwestern Region*

Area	Coefficient of determination $(R_{1.234})$†	RELATIVE IMPORTANCE OF†		
		X_2	X_3	X_4
All areas.................	.720	.372	.162	.186
Arkansas Coastal Plain.....	.637	.102	.426	.109
Mississippi Coastal Plain...	.725	.138	.477	.110
Oklahoma Rolling Plain....	.647	.326	.266	.054
Texas Blackland Prairie....	.758	.424	.162	.172

*X_1 Gross farm income; X_2 Value of farm business; X_3 Productive man-work units; X_4 Acres in cropland

†Relative importance in the equation for measuring size.

TABLE 131

Volume of other-than-real-estate credit used by principal tenure groups in 1942 by state areas for 1336 farm families in four sample areas of the Southwestern Region

Area and tenure	Total cases	No credit reported	Less than $100	$100 to $499	$500 to $999	$1000 to $1999	$2000 to $2999	$3000 and over	Volume unknown
	Number	*Number*	*Number*	*Number*	*Number*	*Number*	*Number*	*Number*	*Number*
ALL AREAS	1336	439	184	462	141	74	11	2	23
ARKANSAS COASTAL PLAIN									
Owner	181	79	12	79	9	2	..	..	..
Renter	165	19	34	81	27	4	..	..	..
Cropper	97	12	42	39	1	1	..	..	2
MISSISSIPPI COASTAL PLAIN									
Owner	186	61	24	71	18	3	..	..	9
Renter	39	6	6	17	4	1	..	..	5
Cropper	87	3	45	36	..	..	..	..	3
OKLAHOMA ROLLING PLAIN									
Owner	149	94	1	19	14	18	3	..	..
Renter	108	31	2	20	25	22	5	2	1
Cropper	16	7	3	2	3	..	..	..	1
TEXAS BLACKLAND PRAIRIE									
Owner	130	73	4	28	14	9	2	..	..
Renter	163	47	7	67	26	14	1	..	1
Cropper	15	7	4	3	..	..	..	..	1

TABLE 132

Percentage distribution of volume of other-than-real-estate credit used by principal tenure groups in 1942 by state areas for 1336 farm families in four sample areas of the Southwestern Region

Area and race	Total cases	No credit reported	Less than $100	$100 to 499	$500 to 999	$1000 to 1999	$2000 to 2999	$3000 and over
	Per cent	*Per cent*	*Per cent*	*Per cent*	*Per cent*	*Per cent*	*Per cent*	*Per cent*
ALL AREAS	100	33	14	35	11	6	.8	.2
ARKANSAS COASTAL PLAIN								
Owner	100	44	6	44	5	1	..	..
Renter	100	12	21	49	16	2	..	..
Cropper	100	13	44	41	1	1	..	..
MISSISSIPPI COASTAL PLAIN								
Owner	100	34	14	40	10	2	..	..
Renter	100	18	18	50	11	3	..	..
Cropper	100	4	54	42	..	..	..	..
OKLAHOMA ROLLING PLAIN								
Owner	100	63	1	13	9	12	2	..
Renter	100	29	2	18	23	21	5	2
Cropper	100	47	20	13	20	..	..	..
TEXAS BLACKLAND PRAIRIE								
Owner	100	56	3	21	11	7	2	..
Renter	100	29	4	41	16	9	1	..
Cropper	100	50	20	21	..	..	..	..

TABLE 133

Comparison of farm owners with varying equities in real estate owned by median age, net worth, gross income in 1942, socio-economic status, crop yield, and diversification indices for 680 owners, part owners and others in four sample areas of the Southwestern Region

Area and owner equity groups	Number of cases	Median age	Median net worth*	Median gross income*	Median socio-economic status score	Median crop yield index	Median diversi-fication index
	Number	*Years*	*Dollars*	*Dollars*			
ARKANSAS COASTAL PLAIN							
All owners	199	55.0	24.7	14.6	147.9	102.1	3.63
100% equity	152	56.8	26.6	13.8	145.7	97.1	3.59
70– 99% equity	20	58.3	27.2	15.0	145.7	103.3	3.58
40– 69% equity	9	43.0	19.0	15.0	151.5	85.0	3.75
0– 39% equity	18	50.0	8.0	20.0	156.5	130.0	4.00
MISSISSIPPI COASTAL PLAIN							
All owners	185	51.7	20.4	16.3	143.0	98.7	3.69
100% equity	97	54.4	23.7	15.8	143.0	98.5	3.81
70– 99% equity	48	48.2	22.1	19.5	147.8	106.0	3.72
40– 69% equity	31	51.5	12.6	14.7	140.4	98.3	3.66
0– 39% equity	9	42.5	17.0	10.9	134.0	60.0	4.10
OKLAHOMA ROLLING PLAIN							
All owners	166	51.5	59.8	45.9	177.1	95.9	3.78
100% equity	48	60.0	107.9	53.5	182.6	96.7	3.50
70– 99% equity	31	46.7	109.6	50.9	174.8	110.6	3.56
40– 69% equity	52	49.1	50.3	41.7	171.8	72.0	4.12
0– 39% equity	35	41.6	25.6	37.4	175.5	80.0	3.38
TEXAS BLACKLAND PRAIRIE							
All owners	130	54.1	68.8	28.7	182.2	106.4	3.56
100% equity	73	55.9	84.0	27.7	185.7	107.2	3.58
70– 99% equity	16	53.0	73.8	29.9	184.0	130.0	3.38
40– 69% equity	20	51.2	72.6	33.4	182.0	110.0	3.50
0– 39% equity	21	51.2	21.6	26.8	173.3	96.0	3.62

*Value computed to nearest hundred dollars.

TABLE 134

Percentage of present owners who acquired ownership before they were 25 years old and before they were 30 years old by race and by tenure of one or both sets of patents for four sample areas of the Southwestern Region

Area and race	OWNERSHIP ACQUIRED BEFORE OPERATOR WAS 25 YEARS OLD			OWNERSHIP ACQUIRED BEFORE OPERATOR WAS 30 YEARS OLD		
	Total cases	Both sets of parents owners	Either set of parents owners	Total cases	Both sets of parents owners	Either set of parents owners
	Number	*Per cent*	*Per cent*	*Number*	*Per cent*	*Per cent*
ALL AREAS	190	80.5	94.7	357	75.9	91.0
ARKANSAS COASTAL PLAIN						
White	56	87.5	96.4	92	85.9	96.7
Negro	24	50.0	91.7	48	54.2	81.3
MISSISSIPPI COASTAL PLAIN						
White	54	88.9	98.1	82	86.6	95.1
Negro	10	70.0	80.0	23	69.6	82.6
OKLAHOMA ROLLING PLAIN*	30	83.3	96.7	69	68.1	89.9
TEXAS BLACKLAND PRAIRIE						
Native white	5	60.0	80.0	17	64.7	76.5
Czech	6	66.7	83.3	16	75.0	93.8
German	5	100.0	100.0	10	90.0	100.0

*No breakdown on national origin.

TABLE 135

Percentage distribution method of farm ownership acquisition for owners acquiring farms at different ages for 664 cases in four sample areas of the Southwestern Region

Age at which ownership was acquired	Total cases		Inheritance or gift	Inheritance plus cash or credit	Cash purchase	Cash plus credit	Credit	Other method*
	Number	*Per cent*	*Per cent*	*Per cent*	*Per cent*	*Per cent*	*Per cent*	*Per cent*
All ages	664	100.0	17.8	2.6	15.4	43.8	15.8	4.6
Less than 25	164	100.0	23.2	3.1	21.3	34.1	10.4	7.9
25-29	152	100.0	14.5	1.3	15.8	44.1	18.4	5.9
30-34	115	100.0	16.5	.9	11.3	50.4	14.8	6.1
35-39	91	100.0	15.4	3.3	18.7	46.1	14.3	2.2
40-44	75	100.0	18.7	6.7	4.0	45.3	25.3	...
45 and over	67	100.0	16.4	1.5	14.9	50.8	16.4	...

*Includes homesteading, trades, and trades plus cash or credit.

TABLE 136

Distribution by volume of off-farm earnings reported for 1942 for 1331 cases by race and tenure for four sample areas of the Southwestern Region

Area, race, and tenure	Number of cases	Receipts From Off-farm Work								
		None	Less than $50	$50 to $149	$150 to $249	$250 to $449	$450 to $949	$950 to $1,949	$1,950 and over	Amount unknown
	Number	*Number*	*Number*	*Number*	*Number*	*Number*	*Number*	*Number*	*Number*	*Number*
ARKANSAS COASTAL PLAIN										
White										
Owner	113	55	16	15	7	4	11	3	..	2
Renter	78	19	16	21	5	9	4	4	..	..
Cropper	20	5	3	6	1	2	3	..	..	..
Negro										
Owner	68	30	18	10	2	4	3	1	..	..
Renter	87	15	28	18	7	15	3	1	..	..
Cropper	77	5	40	26	4	..	1	1	..	..
MISSISSIPPI COASTAL PLAIN										
White										
Owner	131	29	17	20	9	14	22	10	8	2
Renter	24	3	4	6	1	5	4	1	..	..
Cropper	29	5	4	10	1	3	4	1	..	1
Negro										
Owner	55	11	15	8	10	6	3	1	1	..
Renter	15	3	4	4	..	2	1	1	..	..
Cropper	58	3	26	15	12	2	..	..	..	..
OKLAHOMA ROLLING PLAIN										
Native white										
Owner	147	79	14	18	7	8	15	4	2	..
Renter	107	46	17	13	8	6	10	6	1	..
Cropper	14	4	1	4	..	1	2	2	..	..
TEXAS BLACKLAND PRAIRIE										
Native white										
Owner	71	57	1	7	1	2	2	1	..	..
Renter	92	57	7	8	7	8	3	2	..	..
Cropper	7	1	..	1	2	3	..	..	..	..
Czech and German										
Owner	59	41	9	3	1	3	1	..	1	..
Renter	71	57	4	4	2	2	2	..	..	..
Cropper	2	1	..	1	..	..	..	..	..	..
Negro and Mexican										
Cropper	6	..	..	1	1	3	1	..	..	..

TABLE 137

Percentage of farm owners by race and by method of farm acquisition who reported one or more years of nonfarm occupation experience for four sample areas in the Southwestern Region

Area and race	Owners with non-farm occupation experience	METHOD USED IN OWNERSHIP ACQUISITION				
		All methods	Inheritance or gift	Cash purchase	Cash plus credit	Credit
	Number	*Per cent*	*Per cent*	*Per cent*	*Per cent*	*Per cent*
ALL AREAS	171	25.8	16.3	30.4	26.8	25.7
ARKANSAS COASTAL PLAIN						
White	31	24.6	13.8	27.6	34.4	20.0
Negro	13	18.8	7.1	22.2*	21.7	17.4
MISSISSIPPI COASTAL PLAIN						
White	34	26.4	10.7	26.7	36.7	25.0
Negro	23	43.4	33.3	83.3*	28.6	60.0
OKLAHOMA ROLLING PLAIN						
White†	48	30.4	22.2	21.4	30.3	29.4
TEXAS BLACKLAND PRAIRIE						
Native white	14	20.0	14.3	55.5*	14.0	25.0*
Czech and German	8	13.6	17.6	0.0*	14.7	0.0*

*Less than ten cases.
†Includes two cases of foreign born whites.

TABLE 138

Participation in the Agricultural Extension Program by race and tenure for 1313 farm families in four sample areas of the Southwestern Region, 1942

Area, race, and tenure	Total number of cases	Per cent contacted*	Average number of contacts*
ARKANSAS COASTAL PLAIN			
White			
Owner	113	40	4.07
Renter	75	32	2.87
Cropper	20	25	2.60
Negro			
Owner	68	50	3.60
Renter	82	33	2.70
Cropper	77	31	3.00
MISSISSIPPI COASTAL PLAIN			
White			
Owner	131	37	3.63
Renter	23	17	3.64
Cropper	29	17	2.60
Negro			
Owner	55	45	3.10
Renter	14	36	3.60
Cropper	58	14	1.90
OKLAHOMA ROLLING PLAIN			
White			
Owner	147	38	4.64
Renter	106	32	5.15
Cropper	14	21	3.67
TEXAS BLACKLAND PRAIRIE			
White			
Owner	130	18	2.70
Renter	162	12	1.90
Cropper	9	0	0

*Visits to or from farm and home demonstration agents.

TABLE 139

Participation in all government agricultural programs by race and tenure for 1313 farm families in four sample areas of the Southwestern Region, 1942

Area, race, and tenure	Total cases	1942 Participation	Average programs
	Number	*Per cent*	*Number*
ARKANSAS COASTAL PLAIN			
White			
Owner	113	98	1.8
Renter	75	100	1.7
Cropper	20	95	1.3
Negro			
Owner	68	100	1.8
Renter	82	100	1.6
Cropper	77	99	1.1
MISSISSIPPI COASTAL PLAIN			
White			
Owner	131	98	1.8
Renter	23	100	1.6
Cropper	29	96	1.3
Negro			
Owner	55	98	1.9
Renter	14	100	1.5
Cropper	58	98	1.1
OKLAHOMA ROLLING PLAIN			
White			
Owner	147	99	2.0
Renter	106	100	1.7
Cropper	14	64	1.2
TEXAS BLACKLAND PRAIRIE			
White			
Owner	130	100	1.5
Renter	162	100	1.3
Cropper	9	33	1.0

TABLE 140

Average status for various characteristics of Farm Security Administration borrowers compared with nonborrowers for 89 matched pairs of families by race for a sample area in the Arkansas Coastal Plain, 1942

Characteristic compared	WHITE		NEGRO		FARM OWNER LOANS	
	RR borrowers	Non-borrowers	RR borrowers	Non-borrowers	FSA	Non-FSA
PAIRING FACTORS						
Total families	30	30	44	44	15	15
Age of head	43.3	45.0	46.9	46.8	44.3	43.9
Highest grade either spouse	7.7	7.4	5.9	5.9	7.7	7.5
Family members at home	4.6	4.0	5.6	5.6	4.9	4.8
Migration ratio	1.02	.95	1.11	1.07	1.09	1.05
DESCRIPTIVE FACTORS						
Net worth (dollars)	306	978	59	269	2413	1414
Value of business (dollars)	2857	2654	1923	1814	5397	3194
Acres in farm	122	112	116	93	143	126
Acres in crops	46	47	48	42	64	56
Yield index	1.11	1.07	.78	.92	1.43	1.16
PMWU	223	197	216	220	320	274
Credit used (dollars)	615	150	541	155	345	164
					3,219*	130*
REHABILITATION FACTORS						
Index of management	84.5	87.8	83.6	56.6	..	..
Index of diversification	3.96	3.32	3.87	3.3	3.95	3.62
PMWU per MEU	92	102	65	73	107	105
Net income per farm (dollars)	960	974	640	668	1677	1084
Net income per MEU (dollars)	360	460	183	211	537	396
Socio-economic status	140	136	133	127	160	143

*Real estate credit.

Abbreviations used: RR, Rural Rehabilitation; PMWU, Production man-work units; MEU, Man equivalent units.

TABLE 141

Average status for various characteristics of Farm Security borrowers compared with nonborrowers for 36 matched pairs of families by race for a sample area in the Mississippi Coastal Plain, 1942

Characteristic compared	WHITE		NEGRO	
	RR borrowers	Non-borrowers	RR borrowers	Non-borrowers
PAIRING FACTORS				
Total families	20	20	16	16
Age of head	45.3	45.3	50	49
Highest grade either spouse	7.9	8.7	7.8	7.4
Family members at home	5.0	4.8	5.2	4.8
Migration ratio	1.08	1.06	.67	.62
DESCRIPTIVE FACTORS				
Net worth (dollars)	1301	1672	1614	1607
Value of business (dollars)	2313	2220	2347	2055
Acres in farm	86	70	76	69
Acres in crops	35	33	39	40
Yield index	.98	1.1	.61	.99
PMWU	226	212	262	257
Credit used (dollars)	1004	220	445	420
REHABILITATION FACTORS				
Index of management	70	56	61	41
Index of diversification	3.66	3.70	3.58	3.30
PMWU per MEU	127	130	152	131
Net income per farm (dollars)	889	1077	707	927
Net income per MEU (dollars)	533	752	395	451
Socio-economic status	140	138	141	137

Abbreviations used: RR, Rural Rehabilitation; PMWU, Productive man-work units; MEU, Man equivalent units.

TABLE 142

Average status for various characteristics of Farm Security borrowers compared with nonborrowers for 36 matched pairs of white families for a sample area in the Oklahoma Rolling Plains, 1942

Characteristic compared	Rural Rehabilitation borrowers	Non-FSA borrowers
PAIRING FACTORS		
Total families	36	36
Age of head	45	45
Highest grade either spouse	9.3	9.5
Family members at home	4.2	4.3
Migration ratio	1.32	1.23
DESCRIPTIVE FACTORS		
Net worth (dollars)	2835	3480
Value of business (dollars)	9892	12187
Acres in farm	207	260
Acres in crops	142	153
Yield index	.83	1.07
PMWU	151	124
Credit used (dollars)	2026	716
REHABILITATION FACTORS		
Index of management	75	66
Index of diversification	4.0	3.6
PMWU per MEU	75	69
Net income per farm (dollars)	2329	2519
Net income per MEU (dollars)	1183	1549
Socio-economic status	170	169

Abbreviations used: PMWU, Productive man-work units; MEU, Man equivalent units.

TABLE 143

Number of households, by race and tenure, in the neighborhood samples of the Mississippi Coastal Plain area

Type of neighborhood	Number of schedules	Total white	WHITE HOUSEHOLDS					Total Negro	NEGRO HOUSEHOLDS					
			Owner	Part owner	Indeterminate	Renter	Cropper		Owner	Part owner	Indeterminate	Renter	Cropper	Laborer
AREA TOTAL	327	189	116	15	5	24	29	138	36	19	4	15	58	6
Mixed	119	74	43	4	4	14	9	45	13	6	2	6	16	2
Clem	15	8	4	..	2	2	..	7	1	..	..	2	3	1
Prentiss	16	4	2	..	1	..	1	12	1	1	..	..	9	1
Carson	17	13	9	1	1	..	2	4	..	..	..	1	1	..
Conerly	13	10	6	2	..	..	2	3	..	1	..	..	2	..
Ras Pittman	16	7	4	..	..	3	..	9	7	..	..	2	..	..
Edna	18	13	7	..	..	4	2	5	1	3	..	..	1	..
Pinebur	24	19	11	1	..	5	2	5	1	1	2	1	..	..
Single Racial														
White	54	51	30	4	1	4	12	3	1	..	..	..	2	..
Good Hope	15	14	11	..	..	..	3	1	..	..	..	..	1	..
Crawley	20	18	8	2	1	..	7	2*	1	..	..	..	1	..
Bedwell	19	19	11	2	..	4	2	..	..	..	..	..	..	..
Negro	34	..	..	..	..	..	..	34	19	5	1	4	5	..
Spring Hill	17	..	..	..	..	..	..	17	8	2	1	3	3	..
Progress	17	..	..	..	..	..	..	17	11	3	..	1	2	..
Owner	23	15	12	1	..	1	1	8	1	5	..	..	1	1
Greenscreek	10	10	8	1	..	1	..	..	..	..	..	..	..	..
Sandy Hook	13	5	4	..	..	..	1	8	1	5	..	..	1	1
Plantation	33	10	8	..	..	..	2	23	..	..	..	..	20	3
New Hebron	15	5	4	..	..	..	1	10	..	..	..	..	8	2
Darbun	18	5	4	..	..	..	1	13	..	..	..	..	12	1
Plantation Transition	64	41	26	9	2	5	5	25	2	3	1	5	14	..
Spring Cottage	18	9	7	..	..	2	..	9	1	1	1	3	3	..
Oakvale	15	5	3	2	..	..	..	10	1	2	..	2	5	..
Hathorn	21	17	8	2	..	2	5	4	..	..	..	..	4	..
Stringer	10	10	8	5	2	1	..	2	..	..	..	..	2	..

*These two Negro families are on the edge of the Crawley neighborhood. They probably are a part of an adjoining Negro neighborhood.

TABLE 144

Socio-economic status, scale of operation, and type of farming in twenty selected neighborhoods in two counties of the Mississippi Coastal Plain area

Type of neighborhood	Number of schedules	Average socio-economic status score	NUMBER OF FAMILIES HAVING SOCIO-ECONOMIC STATUS OF											NUMBER OF FARMS HAVING SCALE OF OPERATION OF												NUMBER OF FARMS HAVING TYPE OF FARMING OF					
			104-113	114-123	124-133	134-143	144-153	154-163	164-173	174-183	184-193	194-203	204-213	Under $ 147	$147- 214	215- 315	316- 463	464- 680	681- 999	1000-1467	1468-2153	2154-3161	3162-4641	4642 & over	Unknown	Cotton	Cotton-livestock	Cotton-truck	General	Incidental	None
AREA TOTAL	327	...	2	42	90	83	39	31	20	10	7	2	1	6	3	8	20	66	80	79	32	20	7	3	3	237	38	116	19	11	6
Mixed	119	...	1	15	33	25	20	13	8	2	1	..	1	3	2	2	7	31	27	28	9	8	1	..	1	91	11	4	6	5	2
Clem	15	139	..	3	2	6	2	..	2	..	..	..	..	1	..	..	1	3	3	3	3	..	1	..	..	11	3	..	..	..	1
Prentiss	16	138	..	5	4	3	1	1	1	..	..	..	1	1	..	..	2	4	4	3	..	2	..	..	..	12	1	2	..	..	1
Carson	17	144	1	..	3	5	4	2	2	..	..	..	..	..	..	..	..	3	2	6	2	4	..	..	..	16	..	1	..	..	..
Conerly	13	144	..	1	4	3	1	2	1	1	..	..	..	..	..	..	..	3	4	4	1	1	..	..	..	12	1	..	..	..	..
Ras Pittman	16	141	..	3	4	3	3	1	1	..	1	..	..	1	1	..	2	6	5	1	..	..	..	..	..	13	..	..	1	2	..
Edna	18	146	..	..	5	2	5	5	1	..	..	..	..	..	..	1	..	4	1	7	3	1	..	..	1	10	4	1	2	1	..
Pinebur	24	137	..	3	11	3	4	2	..	1	..	..	..	..	1	1	2	8	8	4	..	..	..	..	..	17	2	..	3	2	..
Single Racial																															
White	54	...	..	8	22	11	8	3	2	..	..	..	..	..	..	3	..	11	17	12	6	3	1	..	1	47	6	..	1	..	..
Good Hope	15	144	..	1	3	4	3	2	2	..	..	..	..	..	..	1	..	..	6	4	2	1	1	..	..	10	5	..	..	..	..
Crawley	20	137	..	2	7	5	5	1	..	..	..	..	..	..	..	1	..	4	6	6	1	2	..	..	..	18	1	..	1	..	..
Bedwell	19	127	..	5	12	2	..	..	..	..	..	..	..	..	..	1	..	7	5	2	3	..	..	..	1	19	..	..	..	..	..
Negro	34	...	..	4	7	12	5	5	1	..	..	..	..	..	1	..	2	5	9	10	5	2	..	..	..	30	1	1	2	..	..
Spring Hill	17	140	..	2	5	3	4	3	..	..	..	..	..	..	1	..	2	4	4	5	1	..	..	..	..	16	..	..	1	..	..
Progress	17	140	..	2	2	9	1	2	1	..	..	..	..	..	..	..	..	1	5	5	4	2	..	..	..	14	1	1	1	..	..
Owner	23	...	..	4	5	7	2	3	..	2	..	..	..	..	..	2	2	2	7	6	4	..	..	..	..	10	2	4	3	3	1
Greenscreek	10	145	..	1	1	4	1	2	..	1	..	..	..	..	..	..	..	..	3	4	3	..	..	..	..	3	..	4	3	..	..
Sandy Hook	13	137	..	3	4	3	1	1	..	1	..	..	..	..	..	2	2	2	4	2	1	..	..	..	..	7	2	..	..	3	1
Plantation	33	...	..	7	8	9	..	2	2	1	2	2	..	3	..	3	3	5	8	8	..	1	4	..	..	24	5	1	..	..	3
New Hebron	15	146	..	4	2	4	..	1	2	..	..	2	..	2	..	1	2	3	1	5	..	1	..	..	..	11	2	..	..	..	2
Darbun	18	137	..	3	6	5	..	1	..	1	2	..	..	1	..	..	1	2	7	3	..	..	4	..	..	13	3	1	..	..	1
Plantation																															
Transition	64	...	1	4	15	19	4	5	7	5	4	..	..	..	..	..	6	12	12	15	8	6	1	3	1	35	13	6	7	3	..
Spring Cottage	18	148	1	1	4	5	..	1	3	..	3	..	..	..	..	..	..	5	4	4	1	3	..	..	1	9	4	3	2	..	..
Oakvale	15	145	..	1	2	7	1	2	..	2	..	..	..	..	..	..	3	1	4	3	3	..	..	1	..	11	2	..	1	1	..
Hathorn	21	139	..	1	6	4	2	1	4	2	1	..	..	..	..	..	3	5	3	4	3	1	1	1	..	11	3	2	3	2	..
Stringer	10	141	..	1	3	3	1	1	..	1	..	..	..	..	..	..	..	1	1	4	1	2	..	1	..	4	4	1	1	..	..

TABLE 145

Quality of farm business, operator's earnings, and net family income in twenty selected neighborhoods in two counties of the Mississippi Coastal Plain area

Type of neighborhood	No. of families in samples	Quality of farm business	No. of Farms Having Quality of Farm Business of: Under 31.6	.6- 39.7	.8- 50.0	.1- 63.0	.1- 79.3	.4- 99.9	100.0-125.8	125.9-158.4	158.5-199.4	199.5-251.1	251.2-	Unknown
		Index												
AREA TOTAL	327	98	3	2	10	21	39	67	94	48	30	7	3	3
Mixed	119	95	1	..	4	11	17	23	36	14	8	2	2	1
Clem	15	96	1	..	..	2	1	3	5	1	1	..	1	..
Prentiss	16	122	..	..	..	1	2	1	1	4	4	2	1	..
Carson	17	79	..	..	2	2	2	4	6	1	..	..	..	..
Conerly	13	115	..	..	..	..	..	1	6	4	2	..	..	..
Ras Pittman	16	90	..	..	2	1	..	6	3	3	1	..	..	..
Edna	18	81	..	..	..	1	3	4	9	..	..	..	..	1
Pinebur	24	76	..	..	..	4	9	4	6	1	..	..	..	..
Single Racial														
White	54	97	1	1	2	1	4	11	20	8	5	..	..	1
Good Hope	15	131	..	..	1	..	..	..	8	3	3	..	..	..
Crawley	20	98	..	..	..	..	3	4	8	4	1	..	..	..
Bedwell	19	79	1	1	1	1	1	7	4	1	1	..	..	1
Negro	34	85	..	1	2	2	6	11	7	3	1	1	..	..
Spring Hill	17	88	..	..	2	1	3	5	3	1	1	1	..	..
Progress	17	82	..	1	..	1	3	6	4	2	..	..	..	..
Owner	23	88	..	..	..	3	5	5	6	2	2	..	..	..
Greenscreek	10	102	..	..	..	1	2	..	4	1	2	..	..	..
Sandy Hook	13	78	..	..	..	2	3	5	2	1	..	..	..	..
Plantation	33	124	..	..	..	..	..	6	9	8	7	3	..	..
New Hebron	15	131	..	..	..	..	..	2	4	3	4	2	..	..
Darbun	18	118	..	..	..	..	..	4	5	5	3	1	..	..
Plantation Transition	64	102	1	..	2	4	7	11	16	13	7	1	1	1
Spring Cottage	18	75	..	..	1	4	4	2	6	1	..	..	..	1
Oakvale	15	119	..	..	..	..	2	2	3	5	2	..	1	..
Hathorn	21	103	..	..	1	..	4	4	6	5	2	1	..	..
Stringer	10	116	..	..	..	..	..	3	2	2	3	..	..	..

Type of neighborhood	Average of operator's earnings	No. of Farms Having Operator's Earnings: −585 to $ 420	−419 to 227	−226 to 1	0 to 261	262 to 568	569 to 926	927 to 1343	1344 to 1829	Unknown
	Dollars									
AREA TOTAL	205	1	3	31	103	109	42	17	3	18
Mixed	148	..	..	14	44	38	12	3	..	8
Clem	142	..	..	1	5	9	..	..	..	..
Prentiss	253	..	..	..	4	7	3	..	..	2
Carson	245	..	..	2	2	6	2	1	..	4
Conerly	413	..	..	1	1	4	4	2	..	1
Ras Pittman	30	..	..	5	6	4	1	..	..	..
Edna	131	..	..	1	9	5	2	..	..	1
Pinebur	49	..	..	4	17	3	..	..	..	..
Single Racial										
White	314	..	..	3	9	22	13	2	1	4
Good Hope	508	..	..	..	1	6	5	2	1	..
Crawley	289	..	..	..	5	9	6	..	..	..
Bedwell	153	..	..	3	3	7	2	..	..	4
Negro	173	..	1	2	12	13	2	2	..	2
Spring Hill	149	..	..	1	8	7	..	1	..	..
Progress	199	..	1	1	4	6	2	1	..	2
Owner	296	..	..	3	9	3	2	6	..	..
Greenscreek	630	..	..	..	1	2	2	5	..	..
Sandy Hook	39	..	..	3	8	1	..	1	..	..
Plantation	160	1	..	2	12	14	3	1	..	..
New Hebron	110	..	..	1	8	5	1	..	..	..
Darbun	201	1	..	1	4	9	2	1	..	..
Plantation Transition	229	..	2	7	17	19	10	3	2	4
Spring Cottage	51	..	..	4	7	2	2	..	..	3
Oakvale	361	..	1	1	3	6	1	1	1	1
Hathorn	252	..	1	2	7	4	5	1	1	..
Stringer	390	..	..	..	..	7	2	1	..	..

Type of neighborhood	Average net family income	No. of Families Having Net Income of: $ 46-$ 67	68- 99	100- 146	147- 216	217- 315	316- 463	464- 680	681- 999	1000-1467	1468-2171	2172-3162	3163-4641	Unknown
	Dollars													
AREA TOTAL	780	1	2	3	4	17	41	64	73	63	37	12	2	8
Mixed	779	1	..	2	1	6	16	23	27	23	11	6	1	2
Clem	663	..	..	1	..	..	3	3	3	4	1	..	..	..
Prentiss	712	..	..	..	..	..	6	2	5	2	..	..	1	..
Carson	787	..	..	1	..	1	..	2	5	5	2	..	..	1
Conerly	1171	..	..	..	..	..	..	4	1	1	5	2	..	..
Ras Pittman	690	1	..	..	..	2	2	4	4	1	..	2	..	..
Edna	681	..	..	..	1	1	1	4	3	7	..	..	..	1
Pinebur	808	..	..	..	..	2	4	4	6	3	3	2	..	..
Single Racial														
White	817	..	..	..	1	1	5	11	13	12	9	1	..	1
Good Hope	1109	..	..	..	1	..	..	1	3	3	6	1	..	..
Crawley	830	..	..	..	..	..	..	6	5	6	3	..	..	..
Bedwell	559	..	..	..	..	..	5	4	5	3	..	..	..	1
Negro	691	..	1	..	..	2	4	8	9	6	4	..	..	..
Spring Hill	601	..	1	..	..	1	2	6	3	3	1	..	..	..
Progress	780	..	..	..	..	1	2	2	6	3	3	..	..	..
Owner	781	..	..	..	..	1	4	5	3	4	5	..	..	1
Greenscreek	1013	..	..	..	..	..	1	2	..	2	4	..	..	1
Sandy Hook	621	..	..	..	..	1	3	3	3	2	1	..	..	..
Plantation	592	..	..	..	2	2	5	8	8	6	1	..	..	1
New Hebron	636	..	..	..	1	1	2	3	3	3	1	..	..	1
Darbun	558	..	..	..	1	1	3	5	5	3	..	..	..	..
Plantation Transition	865	..	1	1	..	5	7	9	13	12	7	5	1	3
Spring Cottage	685	..	1	..	..	3	2	2	3	3	1	1	..	2
Oakvale	972	..	..	..	..	1	3	2	1	5	1	1	1	..
Hathorn	882	..	..	1	..	1	2	3	6	1	4	2	..	1
Stringer	961	..	..	..	..	..	..	2	3	3	1	1	..	..

TABLE 146

Average education (of higher spouse) and value of farm business, for total sample of families in twenty selected neighborhoods in two counties of the Mississippi Coastal Plain area

Type of neighborhood	Schedule number	Average grade	Average Education: None	Grade 1 & 2	Grade 3 & 4	Grade 5 & 6	Grade 7 & 8	Highschool 1 & 2	Highschool 3 & 4	College 1 & 2	College 3 & 4 or more	Unknown	Average dollars	Value of Farm Business: 0.01	500.00	1,000.00	1,500.00	2,000.00	2,500.00	3,500.00	5,500.00	7,500.00	15,000.00	Unknown
AREA TOTAL	327	...	3	4	28	46	116	60	54	12	1	3	....	37	67	55	38	24	48	34	10	10	1	3
Mixed	119	...	1	2	7	17	44	20	22	5	1	..	....	14	18	22	14	13	18	10	4	1	..	1
Clem	15	7.5	1	..	3	2	3	..	4	2	..	..	1800	2	3	3	1	..	3	2	..	1	..	..
Prentiss	16	7.1	..	1	1	5	5	2	1	1	..	..	1350	4	5	2	1	1	..	2	1	..	..	..
Carson	17	9.1	..	..	..	..	9	4	3	1	..	..	2150	1	4	..	2	3	2	3	2	..	..	..
Conerly	13	9.1	..	..	..	2	3	6	1	..	1	..	1850	..	3	2	1	5	1	1	..	..	..	..
Ras Pittman	16	8.7	..	1	1	..	7	1	5	1	..	..	1650	4	..	2	4	1	5	..	..	..	..	..
Edna	18	8.3	..	..	1	1	10	2	4	..	..	..	2150	1	1	4	1	1	6	2	1	..	..	1
Pinebur	24	7.9	..	..	1	7	7	5	4	..	..	..	1250	2	6	9	4	2	1	..	..	..	..	..
Single Racial																								
White	54	...	1	..	4	8	20	13	7	1	..	..	....	3	10	11	8	6	8	5	..	2	..	1
Good Hope	15	8.9	..	..	..	1	5	7	2	..	..	..	2200	1	..	2	4	3	2	2	..	1	..	..
Crawley	20	8.9	..	..	..	..	12	3	4	1	..	..	1800	..	3	7	2	3	3	2	..	..	..	..
Bedwell	19	6.1	1	..	4	7	3	3	1	..	..	..	1550	2	7	2	2	..	3	1	..	1	..	1
Negro	34	...	..	1	4	5	17	4	3	..	..	..	....	2	4	7	8	..	7	3	3	..	..	..
Spring Hill	17	6.9	..	1	2	4	6	2	2	..	..	..	1550	2	3	2	7	..	2	1	..	..	..	..
Progress	17	7.5	..	..	2	1	11	2	1	..	..	..	2400	..	1	5	1	..	5	2	3	..	..	..
Owner	23	...	..	..	..	4	5	4	4	5	..	1	....	6	3	2	3	1	5	3	..	..	..	..
Greenscreek	10	12.3	..	..	..	..	..	1	4	5	..	..	2400	..	..	2	2	..	4	2	..	..	..	..
Sandy Hook	13	7.3	..	..	..	4	5	3	..	..	..	1	1050	6	3	..	1	1	1	1	..	..	..	..
Plantation	33	...	..	1	8	5	8	2	7	1	..	1	....	6	8	8	2	..	1	3	2	3	..	..
New Hebron	15	7.5	..	1	3	2	2	2	2	1	..	1	1500	5	3	2	..	..	1	3	..	1	..	..
Darbun	18	6.9	..	..	5	3	6	..	4	..	..	..	1700	1	5	6	2	..	..	..	2	2	..	..
Plantation Transition	64	...	1	..	5	7	22	17	11	..	..	1	....	6	20	5	3	4	9	10	1	4	1	1
Spring Cottage	18	8.3	..	..	1	1	9	4	3	..	..	..	2000	1	6	..	1	..	6	2	..	1	..	1
Oakvale	15	7.5	..	..	3	2	4	4	2	..	..	..	1700	2	3	4	1	2	..	2	..	..	1	..
Hathorn	21	8.3	1	..	..	3	5	6	5	..	..	1	2000	2	9	1	..	2	..	5	..	2	..	..
Stringer	10	7.9	..	..	1	1	4	3	1	..	..	..	2325	1	2	..	1	..	3	1	1	1	..	..

TABLE 147

Local land use data and recommendations for land classes that include the eleven sampled neighborhoods in Marion County Mississippi

Neighborhoods, arranged by land use types	Land Use Areas		Per cent white	Per Cent Having Tenure of				Owned by farmers	Per Cent of Land				
	Major no. class	Additional no. class		Full owner	Part owner	Tenant	Cropper		Cultivated	Open pasture	Timber	Cutover	Open range
Pinebur	...	20 B	..	..	..	..	..	..	2	0	..	..	..
	...	19 B	..	..	..	..	..	..	2	0	5	92	..
	...	21 B	..	..	..	..	..	..	2	0	5	92	..
Edna	8 E2	..	25	30	10	10	50	50	15	10	74	..	2
	25 D	..	No houses	..	..	..	..	0	4	1	94	..	..
	18 B	..	No houses	..	..	..	..	..	3	0	5	91	2
	19 B	..	No houses	..	..	..	..	..	2	0	4	93	..
	10 A	..	15	95	0	4	1	90	50	10	2	36	2
Spring Cottage	10 A	..	15	95	0	4	1	90	50	10	2	36	2
Crawley	16 E2	..	95	50	0	5	45	75	50	5	40	..	..
	...	26 B	..	..	..	..	..	50	5	0	93	..	..
Stringer	17 E2	..	20	35	0	5	60	95	40	4	10	40	..
	...	18 B	No houses	..	..	..	..	..	3	0	5	91	2
Conerly	14 E2	..	No houses	..	..	..	..	..	15	10	74	..	..
	12 E1	..	50	30	0	3	67	90	40	10	43	..	..
Hathorn	8 E2	..	25	30	10	10	50	50	15	10	74	..	2
Ras Pittman	11 E1	..	65	25	0	3	72	85	60	5	25	..	..
	8 E2	..	25	30	10	10	50	50	15	10	74	..	2
	8 E2	..	25	30	10	10	50	50	15	10	74	..	2
Sandy Hook	6 E2	..	50	40	0	10	50	80	40	6	42	..	..
	...	7 B	No houses	..	..	..	..	90	1	..	85	14	99
Darbun	1 E2	..	40	30	0	5	65	95	50	2	2	39	..
	2 E2	..	90	75	0	0	25	95	40	3	52	..	..
Bedwell	2 E2	..	90	75	0	0	25	95	40	3	52	..	..

Appendix D

OTHER STUDIES IN THE SOUTHWESTERN REGION

ARKANSAS:

(Series of four bulletins).

Baker, J. A. and McNeely, J. G. *Land Tenure in Arkansas, I. The Farm Tenancy Situation.* Arkansas Agricultural Experiment Station Bulletin No. 384, Fayetteville, 1940.

McNeely, J. G. and Barton, Glen T. *Land Tenure in Arkansas, II. Change in Labor Organization on Cotton Farms.* Arkansas Agricultural Experiment Station Bulletin No. 397, Fayetteville, 1940.

McNeely, J. G., Barton, Glen T., and Hedges, Trimble R. *Land Tenure in Arkansas, III. Income and Changes in Tenure Status of Share Renters, Share Croppers, and Wage Laborers on Cotton Farms.* Arkansas Agricultural Experiment Station Bulletin 438, Fayetteville, 1943.

Osgood, Otis T. and White, John W. *Land Tenure in Arkansas, IV. Further Changes in Labor Used on Cotton Farms, 1939-44.* Arkansas Agricultural Experiment Station Bulletin No. 459, Fayetteville, 1945.

Blalock, H. W. *Plantation Operations of Landlords and Tenants in Arkansas.* Arkansas Agricultural Experimental Station Bulletin No. 339, Fayetteville, 1937.

Brannen, C. O. *Land Tenure and Plantation Organization.* U. S. Department of Agriculture Bulletin 269, Washington, 1924.

Charlton, J. L. *Social Aspects of Farm Ownership and Tenancy in the Arkansas Ozarks.* Arkansas Agricultural Experiment Station Bulletin 471, Fayetteville, 1947.

Gile, B. M. *Organization and Management of Agricultural Credit Corporations in Arkansas.* Arkansas Agricultural Experiment Station Bulletin No. 259, Fayetteville, 1931.

Gile, B. M. and Moore, A. N. *Farm Credit Situation in Southwestern Arkansas.* Arkansas Agricultural Experiment Station Bulletin No. 237, Fayetteville, 1929.

McCormick, T. C. *Farm Standards of Living in Faulkner County, Arkan-*

sas. Arkansas Agricultural Experiment Station Bulletin No. 279, Fayetteville, 1932.

Metzler, W. H. *Relationship of Tenure to Farming Practices, Family Life, and Community Participation of Farmers in Upland Areas of Arkansas.* Typewritten preliminary report.

Moore, Arthur N. and Brannen, C. O. *Facts and Problems of Farm Credit in Craighead County, Arkansas.* Arkansas Agricultural Experiment Station Bulletin No. 233, Fayetteville, 1929.

Nourse, E. G. *A Preliminary Survey of Land Tenure in Arkansas.* University of Arkansas Bulletin, Vol. 13, No. 11, Fayetteville, 1919.

Solberg, Erling D. *The Legal Aspects of Farm Tenancy in Arkansas.* Arkansas Agricultural Experiment Station Bulletin No. 468, Fayetteville, 1947.

Sparlin, Estal E. *Farm Credit in Hempstead County.* Arkansas Agricultural Experiment Station Bulletin No. 399, Fayetteville, 1940.

LOUISIANA:

Grigsby, S. Earl and Hoffsommer, Harold. *Cotton Plantation Laborers, A Socio-economic Study of Laborers on Cotton Plantations in Concordia Parish, Louisiana.* Louisiana Agricultural Experiment Station Bulletin No. 328, Baton Rouge, 1941.

Hoffsommer, Harold and Ramsey, Ralph J. *Louisiana Farm Laborers and Total War.* Louisiana State University and Agricultural and Mechanical College Bulletin No. 346, Baton Rouge, 1942.

Hoffsommer, Harold. *The Resident Laborer on the Sugar Cane Farm.* Louisiana Agricultural Experiment Station Bulletin No. 334, Baton Rouge, 1941.

Hoffsommer, Harold. *The Sugar Cane Farm, A Social Study of Labor and Tenancy.* Louisiana Agricultural Experiment Station Bulletin No. 230, Baton Rouge, 1940.

NeNoir, Ellen and Smith, T. L. *Rural Housing in Louisiana.* Louisiana Agricultural Experiment Station Bulletin No. 290, Baton Rouge, 1937.

Ramsey, R. J. *Criteria for Classifying Louisiana Tenants.* Master's Thesis, Louisiana State University, 1940.

Ramsey, Ralph J. and Hoffsommer, Harold. *Farm Tenancy in Louisiana.* U. S. Department of Agriculture in cooperation with Louisiana Agricultural Experiment Station, Washington, D. C., 1941. (mimeo.)

Ramsey, Ralph J. and Hoffsommer, Harold. *Procedure in Delineating Type of Tenancy Areas in Louisiana.* U. S. Department of Agriculture in cooperation with Louisiana Agricultural Experiment Station, Washington, D. C., 1941. (mimeo.)

Tatum, Julien R. *Landlord-Tenant Rental Agreements in Louisiana.* Thesis, University of Louisiana, 1939.

Vasey, Tom and Folsom, Josiah C. *Survey of Agricultural Labor Con-*

ditions in Concordia Parish, Louisiana. U. S. Department of Agriculture, Washington, D. C., 1937.

MISSISSIPPI:

Boeger, E. A. and Goldenweiser, E. A. *A Study of the Tenant Systems of Farming in the Yazoo-Mississippi Delta.* U. S. Department of Agriculture Bulletin No. 337, Washington, D. C., 1916.

Dickins, Dorothy. *A Nutrition Investigation of Negro Tenants in the Yazoo-Mississippi Delta.* Mississippi Agricultural Experiment Station Bulletin No. 254, State College, 1928.

Dickens, Dorothy. *Improving Levels of Living of Tenant Families.* Mississippi Agricultural Experiment Station Bulletin 365, State College, 1942.

Dickins, Dorothy. *Occupations of Sons and Daughters of Mississippi Cotton Farmers.* Mississippi Agricultural Experiment Station Bulletin No. 318, State College, 1937.

Dickins, Dorothy. *Owner Farm Families in Poor Agricultural Areas and Cropper Farm Families in Rich Agricultural Areas.* Mississippi Agricultural Experiment Station Bulletin No. 359, State College, 1941.

Langsford, E. L. and Thibodeaux, B. H. *Plantation Organization and Operation in the Yazoo-Mississippi Delta Area.* U. S. Department of Agriculture Bulletin No. 692, Washington, D. C., 1939.

Welch, Frank J., *The Plantation Land Tenure System in Mississippi.* Mississippi Agricultural Experiment Station Bulletin 385, State College, 1943.

OKLAHOMA:

Coleman, William J. and Hockley, H. Alfred. *Legal Aspects of Landlord-Tenant Relationships in Oklahoma.* Oklahoma Experiment Station Bulletin No. 241, Stillwater, 1940.

Duncan, O. D. and Sanders, J. T. *A Study of Certain Economic Factors in Relation to Social Life Among Oklahoma Cotton Farmers.* Oklahoma Agricultural Experiment Station Bulletin No. 211, Stillwater, 1933.

Lynch, Russell Wilford. *Czech Farmers in Oklahoma: A Comparative Study of the Stability of a Czech Farm Group in Lincoln County, Oklahoma, and the Factors Relating to Its Stability.* Oklahoma A & M College Bulletin No. 13, Stillwater, 1942.

MacMillan, Robert T. *Migration and Status of Open Country Families.* Oklahoma Agricultural Experiment Station Bulletin No. T-19, Stillwater, 1943.

McMillan, Robert T. *Farm Housing in Southern Oklahoma,* Oklahoma Agricultural Experiment Station Bulletin No. 290, Stillwater, 1945.

McMillan, Robert T. *Social Factors Related to Farm Housing in Southern Oklahoma.* Oklahoma Agricultural Experiment Station Bulletin No. T-22, Stillwater, 1945.

McMillan, Robert T. and Duncan, O. D. *Social Factors of Farm Ownership in Oklahoma.* Oklahoma Agricultural Experiment Station Bulletin No. B-289, Stillwater, 1945.

Southern, John Hoyle. *Farm Tenancy Areas in Oklahoma.* Unpublished.

Southern, John Hoyle. *Farm Tenancy in Oklahoma.* Oklahoma Agricultural Experiment Station Bulletin No. 239, Stillwater, 1939.

TEXAS:

Lee, V. P. *Short-Term Farm Credit in Texas.* Texas Agricultural Experiment Station Bulletin No. 351, Austin, 1927.

Motheral, Joseph. *Recent Trends in Land Tenure in Texas.* Texas Agricultural Experiment Station Bulletin No. 641, Austin, 1944.

Motheral, Joe R. *Type of Farm Tenancy in Texas.* U. S. Department of Agriculture in cooperation with Texas Agricultural Experiment Station, Austin, 1941.

Sanders, J. T. *Farm Ownership and Tenancy in the Black Prairie of Texas.* U. S. Department of Agriculture Bulletin No. 1068, Austin, 1922.

Solberg, Erling D. *Legal Aspects of Landlord Tenant Relations in Texas.* Unpublished manuscript.

Vasey, Tom and Folsom, Josiah C. *Survey of Agricultural Labor Conditions in Karnes County, Texas.* U. S. Department of Agriculture, Washington, D. C., 1937.

Index of Subjects

Index of Authors

www.ingramcontent.com/pod-product-compliance
Lightning Source LLC
LaVergne TN
LVHW090253210926
848480LV00001B/12
9780807879979